THE INTERNATIONAL ECONOMY

Second Edition

Peter B. Kenen

PRINCETON UNIVERSITY

Prentice-Hall International, Inc.

ISBN 0-13-472580-8

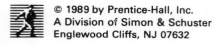
© 1989 by Prentice-Hall, Inc.
A Division of Simon & Schuster
Englewood Cliffs, NJ 07632

Printed in the Republic of Singapore

10 9 8 9 6 5 4

ISBN 0-13-472580-8

Prentice-Hall International (UK) Limited, *London*
Prentice-Hall of Australia Pty. Limited, *Sydney*
Prentice-Hall Canada Inc., *Toronto*
Prentice-Hall Hispanoamericana, S.A., *Mexico*
Prentice-Hall of India Private Limited, *New Delhi*
Prentice-Hall of Japan, Inc., *Tokyo*
Simon & Schuster Asia Pte. Ltd., *Singapore*
Editora Prentice-Hall do Brasil, Ltda., *Rio de Janeiro*
Prentice-Hall, Inc., *Englewood Cliffs, New Jersey*

CONTENTS

iii

TWO

COMPARATIVE ADVANTAGE
AND THE GAINS FROM TRADE, *13*

THREE

ECONOMIC EFFICIENCY
AND COMPARATIVE ADVANTAGE, *34*

FOUR

FACTOR ENDOWMENTS
AND COMPARATIVE ADVANTAGE, *51*

FIVE

FACTOR SUBSTITUTION
AND A MODIFIED RICARDIAN MODEL,   69

SIX

FACTOR SUBSTITUTION
AND THE HECKSCHER-OHLIN MODEL,   88

SEVEN

IMPERFECT COMPETITION
AND INTERNATIONAL TRADE,   111

ELEVEN

THE POLITICAL ECONOMY OF INTERNATIONAL TRADE, *210*

TWELVE

THE BALANCE OF PAYMENTS
AND FOREIGN-EXCHANGE MARKET, *247*

THIRTEEN

INCOMES AND THE CURRENT ACCOUNT, *270*

FOURTEEN

FIFTEEN

SIXTEEN

SEVENTEEN

STOCKS, FLOWS, AND MONETARY EQUILIBRIUM, *353*

EIGHTEEN

ASSET MARKETS, EXCHANGE RATES, AND ECONOMIC POLICY, *373*

NINETEEN

THE POLITICAL ECONOMY OF INTERNATIONAL MONEY, *404*

PREFACE

This book grew out of another. The earlier book, *International Economics,* was published by Prentice Hall in 1964 and went through three editions (the last one coauthored by Raymond Lubitz). It was widely used but sometimes criticized because it was too difficult for elementary courses and too brief for intermediate courses. I began work on the new book expecting to fill gaps but to keep it shorter than most other texts. Each chapter turned into three, however, as I filled more gaps and carried the analysis further. I can only hope that quality has kept pace with quantity.

The book is designed for undergraduates. Those who have taken intermediate courses in micro and macro theory (or are taking them concurrently) will not find it difficult. Those who have less preparation will have to work harder, but they will find that new concepts and tools are explained as they are introduced. Mathematical sophistication is not needed. There is not much algebra in the text. I rely mainly on diagrams. When algebra is used to prove a point, moveover, it is put in notes that accompany the text but do not interrupt it. (Algebra is used extensively in the presentation of national-income analysis, but it is the sort that students usually encounter in the principles course.) Some of the diagrams are complicated, because trade problems are intrinsically complicated; they involve two countries and commodities, and sometimes involve two factors of production. But I have tried to lead the reader through them carefully, even a bit tediously. Furthermore, I have tried to follow the advice of my own students, who urged me not to introduce a diagram unless I will use it more than once.

Empirical evidence has been combined with theory: examples are found in Chapters 3 and 4, on the Ricardian and Heckscher–Ohlin models, and in Chapters 16 and 17, on the efficiency of foreign-exchange markets and the validity of purchasing-power parity. Three chapters deal with history and institutions: Chapter 11 reviews the history of trade policy, describes the General Agreement on Tariffs and Trade (GATT), and discusses current issues. Chapter 19 reviews the history of the monetary system, describes the International Monetary Fund (IMF), and examines alternative exchange-rate arrangements in light of recent experience. Finally, Chapter 20 deals with the management of the international economy; it reexamines the roles of the GATT and the IMF, explores the problems of coordinating national policies, and touches on other current concerns, including the prudential regulation of multinational banking and third-world debt.

Some things are left out. I have not dealt thoroughly with North-South relations and have dropped the brief discussion of East-West trade that appeared in the first edition, to make room for other trade-policy problems, including the liberalization of trade in services. I have not given much attention to current work on rational expectations and exchange-rate behavior. But I have filled one gap in the first edition by adding a chapter on imperfect competition and international trade.

Those who want to use this book in a one-term course may have to omit some chapters, but I have tried to make that easier by rearranging the presentation of trade theory. In the first edition, two trade models featuring factor substitution were presented in a single chapter, and the materials on trade and growth were presented in another chapter. In this edition, each model is presented in a separate chapter, and its use is illustrated by analyzing trade and growth. It is therefore possible to introduce the modified Ricardian (specific-factor) model, which is used extensively in later chapters, and to illustrate the links between trade and growth, without going through the general Heckscher–Ohlin model.

If I were giving a short course, I would omit Chapters 6, 7, and 8, on the general Heckscher–Ohlin model, imperfect competition, and factor movements, and Chapters 16, 17, and 18, on expectations and capital movements, the monetary model, and the portfolio-balance model. Instructors should decide from the start whether to assign the algebraic notes. They are interdependent, because the notation developed in one is used again in others without repeating definitions.

I am grateful to students and colleagues at Princeton University who used the first edition of this text and made a great many helpful suggestions. I am also grateful to colleagues who read parts of the original and revised manuscripts and helped me to improve the book, especially to Polly Allen, Robert Baldwin, Patrick Conway, Richard Cooper, Alan

Deardorff, Avinash Dixit, Gene Grossman, Anne Krueger, Harvey Lapan, and Robert Solomon. Two graduate students at Princeton deserve special thanks: Judith McDonald for working carefully through the algebraic notes and fixing some of my mistakes, and John Leahy for hunting down the numbers needed to update the book and suggesting a number of improvements. Readers should thank my daughter, Judy, for the typographical errors they do not find, but should blame me for those that remain.

1

THE NATION AS AN ECONOMIC UNIT

ORIGINS AND ISSUES

The study of international trade and finance is among the oldest specialties in economics. It was conceived in the sixteenth century, a lusty child of Europe's passion for Spanish gold, and grew to maturity in the turbulent years that witnessed the emergence of modern nation-states. It attracted the leading economists of the eighteenth and nineteenth centuries, including David Hume, Adam Smith, David Ricardo, and John Stuart Mill, whose work supplied a legacy of insight and concepts that continue to guide economists today. In fact, their work on international economic problems produced some of the most important tools of analysis used by modern economics. An early version of the "quantity theory of money" was developed by Hume to show how foreign trade affects the level of domestic prices. The first full formulation of the "law of supply and demand" was developed by Mill to explain price determination in international markets. Many recipients of the Nobel Prize in economics have studied international problems, including Paul Samuelson, Wassily Leontief, Bertil Ohlin, and James Meade.

International economics flourishes today because the facts and issues that brought it into being continue to demand attention. By participating in international trade, each national economy is able to use its resources most efficiently—to concentrate on those activities it is best suited to conduct—and to reap significant economies of scale. In consequence, trade raises real income in each country. These are the same sorts of gains that we reap as individuals by specializing in a single occupation rather than meeting all our needs by producing our own food, clothing, and so on. Trade is beneficial in other ways. Improvements in

1

technology originating in one country are shared automatically with other countries. They are shared directly when they are embodied in new capital equipment that is sold on world markets. They are shared indirectly when they raise efficiency or product quality in the export industries of the country in which they originate.

By participating in international capital markets, countries can grow faster. By borrowing on those markets to supplement domestic savings, they are able to raise their rates of capital formation. The United States borrowed abroad in the nineteenth century, and many less-developed countries do so now. By lending on those markets, countries can put their savings to work more productively than they can at home. International trade in claims and liabilities raises the efficiency with which an economy can allocate resources across time, just as trade in goods and services raises the efficiency with which it can allocate resources at each point in time.

Foreign trade and finance pose hard problems as well as opportunities. They raise complex economic problems, because they affect the internal behavior of each national economy. They raise delicate political problems, because they affect relations among governments.

By affecting the allocation of domestic resources, trade affects the distribution of domestic income. Changes in the level or composition of a country's trade can call for large shifts in resources and thus redistribute incomes. The astonishing growth of the Japanese economy has forced the older industrial economies of the United States and Western Europe to make adaptations affecting major industries and whole regions. This process is far from complete. The rapid growth of manufacturing in Korea, Taiwan, and other less-developed countries has required additional adaptations, not only in the older industrial countries but in Japan as well.

Events in international markets can affect levels of domestic employment, growth rates, and inflation rates. The unprecedented increase in the world price of oil that began in 1973 was an important cause of *stagflation* in oil-importing countries— the painful combination of high unemployment, slow growth, and rapid inflation. Changes in the prices of other raw materials affect the export earnings of the less-developed countries, which determine their ability to import machinery and other capital goods. Therefore, they influence the pace of development.

Commercial and financial arrangements among countries affect the functioning of domestic policies. The effectiveness of monetary policy, for example, is influenced strongly by exchange-rate arrangements. A government that tries to peg its exchange rate—to fix the price of its currency in terms of some other currency—may not be able to pursue an independent monetary policy. Changes in its money supply will spill out through its balance of payments with the outside world, and this will happen rapidly when, as now, national financial markets are closely linked. A government that allows its exchange rate to float—to be determined by supply and demand in the foreign-exchange markets— will be able to pursue an independent monetary policy. It will discover, however, that a change in its monetary policy alters its exchange rate in ways that magnify and modify the domestic impact of the policy change.

DIMENSIONS OF POLICY INTERDEPENDENCE

The links between national economies created by trade and other international transactions produce an interdependence between national policies, even between policies designed primarily to achieve domestic goals. Policies that stimulate aggregate demand in one country will increase its demand for imports, and the imports of one country are the exports of another. Therefore, those policies will stimulate demand in other countries, and their governments must then modify their policies to stabilize their economies. The money flows that take place with pegged exchange rates offer another illustration. An increase in one country's money supply that spills out through its balance of payments tends to increase other countries' money supplies, and they must then make compensatory changes in their policies to combat "imported" inflation.

These money flows do not take place when exchange rates float, but the policy interdependence crops up in another form. Exchange rates are *shared* variables. The price of the Deutsche mark in terms of the U.S. dollar defines the price of the dollar in terms of the mark. When one mark costs 50 cents, one dollar costs 2 marks. A change in one country's exchange rate translates automatically into changes in other countries' rates.

The domestic effects of a change in the exchange rate are less obvious in a large economy like that of the United States than in smaller, more open economies like those of Western Europe. Indeed, they went almost unnoticed a few years ago. When asked to rank three key prices in order of their influence on domestic production, employment, and the general price level, an American would have put the wage rate first, the price of oil next, and the exchange rate last. A German would probably have put the exchange rate first, the price of oil next, and the wage rate last.[1] But the foreign trade of the United States has grown

more rapidly than has its gross national product, raising the ratio of trade to output. The ratio remains much lower than in other major countries, but the U.S. economy has become more open in this and other ways, and that trend has started to influence it policies. The United States is able to pursue an independent monetary policy, because it allows its currency to float, but it cannot exercise its independence without allowing for the impact of exchange-rate changes on its own economy, the economies of other countries, and the policies of other countries. The character of policy interdependence is affected by exchange-rate arrangements and other ways in which economies are linked. The fact of interdependence is inescapable.

No government can be totally indifferent to the economic policies of other governments, and the growth of economic openness, illustrated in Table 1-1, has raised sensitivities. Governments pay close attention to each others' policies and pay attention to a wide range of policies. They watch each others' agricultural policies, which can affect world prices and supplies of food. They watch each others' energy policies, which can affect the outlook for the world price of oil. They watch each oth-

---

[1] The German might have pointed out, moreover, that the price of oil in Germany depends on the exchange rate. World oil prices are quoted in dollars. Therefore, the price expressed in Deutsche marks is determined in part by the price of the dollar in terms of the mark.

TABLE 1-1 Trends in Economic Openness: Averages of Exports and Imports of Goods and Services as Percentages of Gross National Product in the Seven Economic Summit Countries

Country	1965	1975	1985
Canada	19.5	24.2	28.0
France	12.1	18.1	23.7
Germany	19.0	24.9	33.1
Italy	13.4	21.7	26.8
Japan	10.3	13.7	14.5
United Kingdom	18.8	26.3	28.3
United States	4.7	8.0	8.5

Source: International Monetary Fund, *International Financial Statistics.*

ers' subsidies to domestic industries, which can affect the fortunes of their own export industries. As in the past, however, they pay closest attention to the policies that have the most direct effects on trade flows and exchange rates. For this reason, changes in tariffs and other trade controls are regulated by a formal code of conduct, the General Agreement on Tariffs and Trade (GATT), and policies affecting exchange rates are subject to looser but regular review in the International Monetary Fund (IMF) and other international organizations.

Policy interdependence has an extra dimension in the case of the United States. Although it does not dominate the world economy as it did in the decades following World War II, it is still the largest national economy, and the U.S. dollar is by far the world's most important currency. American monetary and fiscal policies have worldwide effects by way of their influence on economic activity in the United States and thus the U.S. demand for other countries' goods, their influence on world prices, and their influence on interest rates, financial flows, and exchange rates. Thus, the tightening of U.S. monetary policy that brought on the deep recession of 1981–82 helped to trigger the international debt crisis that began in 1982; by raising world interest rates, it raised the debtor countries' interest payments, and by reducing the debtors' exports and their export prices too, it reduced their ability to make those payments. American trade, agricultural, and energy policies are no less important for the health of the world economy. As a consequence, the policies of the United States are subject to close scrutiny by other governments and to frequent criticism.

The criticism is not always justified. It is sometimes used to cloak the deficiencies of other countries' policies and frequently reflects dissatisfaction with the state of the world rather than U.S. policy. It can be ex-

asperating. Some years ago, the United States was accused of following a lax monetary policy and "exporting" inflation to the rest of the world. The charge had some validity. But when the United States tightened its monetary policy to combat inflation, it was accused of raising world interest rates and depressing economic activity in other countries. One European economist, sympathetic to the plight of U.S. officials obliged to respond to incessant criticism, put the matter nicely. According to the critics, he said, "the American economy is unsafe at any speed."

Nevertheless, the United States must pay attention to its special role in the international economy and to the concerns of other countries. Controversies about economic policies migrate quickly into the political domain, affecting the quality of cooperation in diplomatic and strategic matters. Allies dissatisfied with U.S. economic policies soon start to express dissatisfaction with U.S. leadership in political affairs. The importance of economic issues is underscored by the practice adopted several years ago. The leaders of the seven main industrial countries, listed in Table 1-1, attend an annual Economic Summit to review economic problems and policies.

SOVEREIGNTY AND TRADE

Economists are fond of abstract formulations. We build elaborate models, with n countries, m commodities, and so on. But the questions to which we apply ourselves and the examples we choose to illustrate our findings are frequently inspired by practical concerns. In his famous demonstration of the gains from foreign trade, David Ricardo dealt with two countries, England and Portugal, trading two commodities, cloth and wine. He chose this example because it would be meaningful to his British audience. It evoked the oldest international agreement to reduce trade barriers, the Methuen Treaty of 1703, which cut British tariffs on Portuguese wines in exchange for free entry of British textiles into Portugal.

The Mercantilist View

Early writers on international trade, the Mercantilists of the seventeenth century, were also concerned with a practical problem—establishing and consolidating royal authority at home and abroad. Royal authority was challenged at home by the old nobility, whose powers derived from their feudal rights to raise both revenues and armies from the countryside. It was challenged abroad by rivalry for empire in the New World. To establish royal authority at home, the crown had to raise and pay armies. To compete for empire abroad, it had to build ships. Its power, then, depended on its ability to cultivate new sources of revenue—to foster and tax domestic and foreign commerce.

The most famous French Mercantilist, Jean Baptiste Colbert, minister to Louis XIV, dismantled internal trade barriers and subsidized new industries. In one decree, he offered bounties to companies that brought Flemish weavers to France and trained new craftsmen. It was also necessary, however, to provide an adequate supply of money, gold and silver in those days. Money was required to carry out trade and to pay the taxes levied on that trade. The crown had also to accumulate "treasure" to pay for its armies and navies. Critics of the Mercantilists, including Adam Smith, accused them of confusing gold and silver with national wealth. Some of them did, but others were quite clear about their policy objectives. They paid close attention to the gathering of "treasure" because they identified the nation with the crown and therefore identified the wealth of the nation with the gold and silver that the crown could accumulate—with the means of payment for military power.

Spain extracted gold and silver from the Aztecs and the Incas. Britain, France, and other countries had then to extract them from Spain through foreign trade. For the Mercantilists, gold and silver were the gains from trade, to be earned by encouraging exports and discouraging imports. These are the words of Thomas Mun, a British merchant, published in 1664:

The ordinary means . . . to increase our wealth and treasure is by *Forraign Trade,* wherein wee must ever observe this rule; to sell more to strangers yearly than wee consume of theirs in value. For suppose that when this Kingdom is plentifully served with the Cloth, Lead, Tinn, Iron, Fish and other native commodities, we doe yearly export the overplus to forraign Countries to the value of twenty two hundred thousand pounds; by which means were are enabled beyond the Seas to buy and bring in forraign wares for our use and Consumptions, to the value of twenty hundred thousand pounds; By this order duly kept in our trading, we may rest assured that the Kingdom shall be enriched yearly two hundred thousand pounds, which must be brought to us in so much Treasure; because that part of our stock which is not returned to us in wares must necessarily be brought home in treasure.[2]

One can find many flaws in Mercantilist logic, the chief flaw being one that David Hume attacked. A country that increases its money supply by exporting more than it imports will find that its prices start to rise. This will undermine its competitive position in world markets. Its exports will fall, its imports will rise, and it will start to export money. It was, indeed, the main aim of the Classical economists, including David Hume and Adam Smith, to prove that the crown and its ministers cannot defy the "natural laws" that govern social processes—that intervention by the state is self-defeating in the long run and apt to reduce national prosperity.

---

[2]Thomas Mun, *Englands Treasure by Forraign Trade,* 1664, ch. ii.

The Classical View

The Mercantilists of the seventeenth century believed in a world of conflict, the world of Thomas Hobbes in which the state of nature was a state of war. They took for granted the need for regulation to maintain order in human affairs, including economic affairs. The Classical economists of the eighteenth century believed in a world of harmony, the world of John Locke in which the state of nature was a state of peace. They rejected regulation as unnecessary. When Hume explained that prices and trade flows would regulate the quantity of money automatically, and Smith explained that an "invisible hand" would harness competition in the marketplace to benefit society at large, both were expressing their belief in a benign natural order.

Most important for our purposes, the Classical economists defined national prosperity in quite different terms from those used by the Mercantilists. They were concerned with the welfare of the crown's subjects, not that of the crown itself. Therefore, they measured the gains from trade quite differently. Exports were the means of acquiring imports, rather than gold and silver, and thus using the nation's resources most efficiently. Restrictions on imports were illogical. These are the words of Adam Smith, published in 1776, a bit more than a century after those of Thomas Mun:

To give the monopoly of the home-market to the produce of domestic industry, in any particular art or manufacture, is in some measure to direct private people in what manner they ought to employ their capitals, and must, in almost all cases, be either a useless or a hurtful regulation. . . . It is the maxim of every prudent master of a family, never to attempt to make at home what it will cost him more to make than to buy. The taylor does not attempt to make his own shoes, but buys them of the shoemaker. The shoemaker does not attempt to make his own clothes, but employs a taylor. . . .

What is prudence in the conduct of every private family, can scarce be folly in that of a great kingdom. If a foreign country can supply us with a commodity cheaper than we ourselves can make it, better buy it of them with some part of the produce of our own industry, employed in a way in which we have some advantage. The general industry of the country, being always in proportion to the capital which employs it, will not thereby be diminished, no more than that of the above-mentioned artificers; but only left to find out the way in which it can be employed to the greatest advantage. It is not employed to the greatest advantage when it is thus directed toward an object which it can buy cheaper than it can make.[3]

Smith's reasoning is not rigorous. What is "prudence" for a family *can* be "folly" for a kingdom. Furthermore, "advantage" must be defined quite carefully. That task was left to David Ricardo. Smith's argument, however, illustrates effectively the approach adopted by the Classical economists.

As Smith and his successors believed that the role of government should be sharply limited, they did not pay much attention to the ways in which national sovereignty affects foreign trade and causes it to differ intrinsically from domestic trade. When we come to Ricardo's demonstration of the gains from trade, we will see that the countries in his model could be towns or regions instead of sovereign states. They are places with endowments of labor and capital that move freely between economic activities but cannot move at all between places. In much of Classical trade theory and much modern theory too, international trade is differentiated from domestic trade by the international mobility of goods and the *im*mobility of labor and capital.

We will use this same device to simplify the presentation of trade theory but should not be misled by it. There have been times,

---

[3] Adam Smith, *The Wealth of Nations*, 1776, bk. iv, ch. ii.

especially in the nineteenth century, when international movements of labor were larger than internal movements. Furthermore, distances within a country can be greater than distances between them, affecting the costs of moving goods and people. New York is farther from California than is France from Germany. In any case, trade theory is not interested primarily in flows of goods from place to place; it is interested in flows from country to country. Countries are distinguished from places or regions by the forms and functions of their governments. The separate study of international economics must take as its starting point the existence and variety of sovereign states.

How Governments Affect International Transactions

Trade and other international transactions frequently receive special treatment. Most governments use taxes, subsidies, and direct controls to discriminate between residents and foreigners even when they undertake identical activities. But there are many other ways in which the exercise of sovereignty can influence the conduct of foreign trade. All governments supply *public goods,* including the legal and monetary systems that furnish the framework for economic activity. They may not discriminate deliberately between domestic and foreign transactions when they discharge these basic functions. Each government, however, discharges them differently, which means that transactions between countries are affected differentially.

The various activities of governments have three effects on international transactions: (1) They give rise to differences in the ways that the residents of a single country perceive and respond to domestic and foreign opportunities. (2) They give rise to differences in the ways that the residents of

different countries perceive and respond to identical opportunities. (3) They add to the risks and costs of all transactions, but more to those of foreign than domestic transactions, because changes in one country's national policies affect that country's residents without necessarily affecting other countries' residents.

In most countries, laws and customs are fairly uniform. It is therefore quite easy to move goods, labor, and capital from place to place. The tax system is also homogeneous within a country, but tax systems differ markedly from country to country. True, the tax laws of the 50 U.S. states differ in important ways. But the federal tax system tends to neutralize differences among the states' tax systems, because state taxes are deductible from federal income taxes. Furthermore, federal grants and spending tend to diminish local differences in the quantity and quality of public services that might otherwise influence decisions about the location of economic activity.

Internal monetary differences are smallest of all. Nationwide markets connect financial institutions within the United States. Funds flow freely from region to region, and borrowers can raise cash where it is cheapest, whittling down regional differences in credit conditions. Finally, and most important, a single currency is used throughout the country. A five-dollar bill issued by the Federal Reserve Bank of Richmond circulates freely in the United States; it must be accepted everywhere. How much more complicated life would be if merchants refused to accept currency coming from another Federal Reserve District! You would have to look at every dollar bill, weed out those from other Districts, and take them to a bank to swap them for local currency. You would have to trade one kind of dollar for another when you crossed state lines.

Goods flow freely among the 50 states. In fact, the U.S. Constitution expressly forbids local interference with interstate commerce. The authors of the Constitution believed that free trade among the states would help to cement their fragile political union. The countries of Western Europe created the Common Market for similar reasons, as a first step toward political confederation. They allow goods to move freely within Western Europe and impose a common tariff on goods from outside. But trade between countries is usually burdened by tariffs and is often limited by other devices—quotas that restrict quantities imported and controls on purchases of foreign currencies.

These trade barriers are doubly restrictive. First, they raise the domestic prices of foreign goods, which handicaps those goods in competition with domestic products. Second, they impose a costly workload on the would-be importer. Figure 1-1 reproduces a fragment from the U.S. tariff schedule. Use it to compute the duty on a $50 watch, 0.8 inch wide with 16 jewels, having a self-winding mechanism and one adjustment.

International transactions usually involve two or more moneys. An American wholesaler importing French champagne has first to determine its price in French francs, then the price of the franc in terms of the dollar, to calculate the price that must be charged in the United States. After ordering the champagne, the wholesaler must buy francs with dollars and pay them over to the French supplier. There are thus extra costs and risks involved in the transaction. The costs are the commissions charged by the dealers in foreign currencies. The risks arise because exchange rates can change.

Under present international monetary arrangements, the exchange rates for most major currencies float. They move up and down from day to day, responding to changes in supply and demand, and the short-term fluctuations can be very large. In December 1984, the U.S. dollar bought 9.59 French francs; in December 1985, just one year later, it bought only 7.56 francs; and in February 1988, it bought only 5.73 francs, as shown in Figure 1-2. Similar risks existed, however, when exchange rates were pegged, as most of them were before 1973. Rates did not fluctuate significantly from one day to the next, but they could be altered abruptly and by large amounts. In 1956, the French government devalued the franc from 3.50 per dollar to 4.20 per dollar; in 1957, the franc was devalued again to 4.90 per dollar; and in 1969, there was a third devaluation to 5.55 per dollar.[4] Each large change took place suddenly.

Day-to-day changes in exchange rates can cut into traders' profits, and large changes can turn profits into losses. An American wholesaler importing French champagne could lose heavily if the price of the franc rose on the foreign-exchange market after the firm had signed its contract with its French supplier but before it had purchased its francs.[5]

---

[4] As indicated earlier, exchange rates can be quoted in another way. One can deal with the dollar price of the French franc. Using this approach, the franc fell from 28.6 cents to 23.8 cents in 1956, to 20.4 cents in 1959, and 18.0 cents in 1969. These computations made it easy to see why the changes are described as devaluations; they reduced the dollar value of the franc. Hereafter, exchange rates will be defined as the prices of foreign currency in units of domestic currency. From the French standpoint, then, the franc-dollar rate in Figure 1–2 was 5.73 francs per dollar on February 9, 1988; from the American standpoint, it was 17.46 cents per franc.

[5] Traders and investors can sometimes protect themselves against exchange-rate changes by buying or selling foreign currency on the *forward* market. There, they can arrange to swap dollars for French francs in 30, 60, or 90 days at a price (exchange rate) agreed on today. Forward rates for certain currencies are shown in Figure 1-2. They will be discussed again in Chapter 16.

Watch movements, assembled, without dials or hands, or with
dials or hands whether or not assembled thereon:

   Having over 17 jewels:

      Valued not over $15 each .... $5.37 each

      Valued over $15 each .... $4.37 each

   Having no jewels or not over 17 jewels:

      Not adjusted, or self-winding (or if a self-winding device
      cannot be incorportated therein), and not constructed or
      designed to operate for a period in excess of 47 hours
      without rewinding:

         Having no jewels or only 1 jewel:

            Not over 0.6 inch in width ....   79¢ each

            Over 0.6 but not over 1.77 inches in width ....   67¢ each

         Having over 1 jewel but not over 7 jewels:

            Not over 0.6 inch in width .... $1.58 each

            Over 0.6 but not over 0.9 inch in width .... $1.22 each

         . . .

         Having over 7 but not over 17 jewels:

            Valued not over $15 each:

               Not over 0.6 inch in width .... $1.80 each + 9¢ for
                                                                        each jewel over 7

               Over 0.6 but not over 0.9 inch in width .... $1.35 each + 9¢ for
                                                                       each jewel over 7

            . . .

            Valued over $15 each:

               Not over 0.6 inch in width .... $1.58 each + 8¢ for
                                                                          each jewel over 7

               Over 0.6 but not over 0.9 inch in width .... $1.22 each + 8¢ for
                                                                          each jewel over 7

        . . .

Adjusted or self-winding, whether or not adjusted (or if a self-
winding device can be incorporated therein), or constructed or
designed to operate for a period in excess of 47 hours without

rewinding ....   base rate + 47¢ each
                                                                         if self-winding + 47¢
                                                                     for each adjustment

FIGURE 1-1 A Fragment of the U.S. Tariff Schedule
The tariff on a single watch has sometimes to be calculated by adding
up a base rate determined by the value, width, and number of jewels,
the duty on each extra jewel, the duty on the self-winding mechanism,
and the duty on each adjustment.

Perspectives and Criteria

International economists view the world as a community of separate states, each with its own constellation of natural resources, capital, labor, and knowledge, its own social and economic institutions, and its own economic policies. We usually assume that transport costs are negligible and that markets are perfectly competitive. We frequently adopt the Classical assumption that labor and capital are perfectly mobile within a country but not free to move from one country to another.

Foreign Exchange
TUESDAY, FEB. 9, 1988

	Fgn. currency in dollars		Dollar in fgn. currency	
	Tue.	Mon.	Tue.	Mon.
f-Argent (Austral)	.1835	.1835	5.4500	5.4500
Australia (Dollar)	.7115	.7110	1.4050	1.4065
Austria (Schilling)	.0833	.0838	12.00	11.93
c-Belgum (Franc)	.0280	.0281	35.67	35.53
f-Belgum (Franc)	.0278	.0280	35.91	35.77
Brazil (Cruzado)	.0121	.0119	82.00	83.50
Britain (Pound)	1.7500	1.7500	.5714	.5714
30-day fut	1.7470	1.7468	.5724	.5725
60-day fut	1.7430	1.7423	.5737	.5740
90-day fut	1.7390	1.7388	.5750	.5751
Canada (Dollar)	.7899	.7899	1.2660	1.2605
30-day fut	.7886	.7886	1.2680	1.2680
60-day fut	.7874	.7874	1.2700	1.2700
90-day fut	.7868	.7868	1.2710	1.2710
y-Chile (Peso)	.0041	.0041	244.00	244.00
Colombia (Peso)	.0035	.0036	279.40	277.10
Denmark (Krone)	.1540	.1539	6.4975	6.4960
c-Egypt (Pound)	.4545	.4545	2.2000	2.2000
f-Ecudr (Sucre)	.003173	.003181	315.15	314.35
Finland (Mark)	.2429	.2430	4.1160	4.1150
France (Franc)	.1746	.1743	5.7270	5.7385
Greece (Drachma)	.0074	.0073	135.25	135.50
Hong Kong (Dollar)	.1281	.1281	7.8040	1.8040
y-India (Rupee)	.0763	.0768	13.1100	13.0200
Indnsia (Rupiah)	.000602	.000602	1660.00	1660.00
Ireland (Punt)	1.5685	1.5672	.6376	.6381
Israel (Shekel)	.6293	.6293	1.5890	1.5890
Italy (Lira)	.000800	.000800	1249.00	1250.00
Japan (Yen)	.007752	.007752	129.00	129.00
30-day ft	.007770	.007770	128.70	128.70
60-day ft	.007785	.007809	128.45	128.05
90-day ft	.007803	.007813	128.15	128.00
Jordan (Dinar)	2.9940	2.9940	.33400	.33400
Kuwait (Dinar)	3.6100	3.6100	.27645	.27700
Lebanon (Pound)	.00247	.00247	404.00	404.00
z-Mexico (Peso)	.000438	.000438	2280.00	2280.00
Nethrlnds(Guilder)	.5227	.5234	1.9130	1.9105
N. Zealand (Dollar)	.6565	.6630	1.5230	1.5080
Norway (Krone)	.1552	.1560	6.4425	6.4090
Pakistan (Rupee)	.0571	.0571	17.50	17.50
y-Peru (Inti)	.0303	.0303	33.00	33.00
z-Philpns (Peso)	.0479	.0478	20.8700	20.9000
Portugal (Escudo)	.007143	.007168	140.00	139.50
Saudi Arab (Riyal)	.2666	.2667	3.7509	3.7500
Singapore (Dollar)	.4952	.4953	2.0195	2.0190
So. Korea (Won)	.001289	.001290	775.30	775.30
So. Africa (Rand)	.4945	.4945	2.0220	2.0220
Spain (Peseta)	.008772	.008803	114.00	113.60
Sweden (Krona)	.1644	.1649	6.0840	6.0640
Switzerlnd (Franc)	.7194	.7189	1.3900	1.3910
30-day fut	.7225	.7222	1.3840	1.3846
60-day fut	.7260	.7255	1.3775	1.3782
90-day fut	.7286	.7284	1.3725	1.3728
Taiwan (NT $)	.0349	.0349	28.62	28.62
Turkey (Lira)	.000882	.000882	1133.00	1133.00
U.A.E. (Dirham)	.2723	.2723	3.6725	3.6730
z-Uruguay (Peso)	.0036	.0036	273.25	273.25
z-Venzuel (Bolivar)	.0301	.0331	30.3000	30.2000
W. Grmny (Mark)	.5893	.5882	1.6970	1.7000
30-day fut	.5908	.5898	1.6925	1.6955
60-day fut	.5924	.5916	1.6880	1.6903
90-day fut	.5942	.5931	1.6830	1.6860
Yugslvia (Dinar)	.000791	.000791	1264.00	1264.00

The Federal Reserve Board's index measuring the value of the dollar against 10 other currencies weighted on the basis of trade was 91.01 Tuesday, off 0.11 points or off 0.12 percent from Monday's 91.24. A year ago the index was 99.24.

Late closing prices as of 3:00 p.m. Eastern Time as gathered by First American Bank of New York.

c-commercial rate, f-financial rate, v-official rate, z-floating rate, r-revised.

FIGURE 1-2   Foreign Exchange Rates
Exchange rates are quoted in two ways: in dollars per unit of foreign currency and units of foreign currency per dollar. The French franc, for example, was quoted on February 9, 1988, at $0.1746 per franc (i.e., at 17.46 cents). It was therefore quoted at 5.727 francs per dollar. For most currencies, rates are for spot (immediate) delivery. For some important currencies, there are quotations for future delivery, in 30, 60, or 90 days. Copyright © 1988 by The New York Times Company; reprinted by permission.

Using these assumptions, we seek to explain international flows of goods, services, and assets; assess their impact on domestic economic welfare; and forecast their responses to changes in national policies. We concentrate on policies designed expressly to regulate foreign trade and payments—those involving tariffs, exchange rates, and the tax treatment of foreign-source income. But we must also look at general economic policies, at tax rates, public spending, monetary management, labor legislation, and the rest, because they define the economic environment in which international transactions take place.

International economists sometimes study trade and payments from the standpoint of a single country, but we are just as likely to adopt a cosmopolitan perspective, viewing matters from the standpoint of the whole world. When taking the national viewpoint, we usually begin by pretending that the country under study has been isolated from the outside world, then begins to trade with others. When taking the cosmopolitan viewpoint, we sometimes begin by pretending that there have been no differences in economic policies and no barriers to trade among regions, then turn the regions into nations, each with its own institutions and policies. The perspectives and assumptions we adopt can color our conclusions dramatically, especially those that pertain to assessments of policies. You must be sure to ascertain what perspective we are taking.

In almost all circumstances, however, international economists are concerned with individuals. We are the intellectual descendants of Adam Smith and of the nineteenth-century Utilitarians, and though we treat the nation as an economic unit for analytical purposes, we do not usually regard it as the end in view. We appraise a change in economic policy by the criteria employed in other branches of economics. Such a change is good potentially if the individuals who benefit from it can compensate the individuals who lose.[6] Furthermore, we use the same tests of economic performance that guide economists in other fields.

First, we are concerned with efficiency: How do international trade and payments affect the allocation of resources within a country? How do they redistribute economic tasks among the participating countries?

Second, we are concerned with equity: How does trade redistribute income and wealth within a country? How does it redistribute them among countries?

Third, we are concerned with stability: How do trade and payments affect an economy's responses to disturbances, its vulnerability to unemployment and inflation, and the uses of monetary and fiscal policies to achieve stability?

Fourth, we are concerned with growth: How does foreign trade affect a country's growth rate? How does growth affect its trade? Should the less-developed countries gear their economies to international markets or should they protect their infant industries from international competition?

Efficiency and equity will be the main issues in Chapters 2 through 11, where standard tools of microeconomic analysis will be used to show how trade affects domestic resource allocation and the distribution of the national income. Stability will be the chief concern in Chapters 12 through 19, where standard tools of macroeconomic analysis will be used to show how trade and other international transactions affect the level of economic activity, unemployment, and inflation, and the conduct of monetary and fiscal policies. Growth will be one main concern in Chapter 20, which will look at the international economic system as a whole, the problems of developed and less-developed countries, and issues that are likely to dominate international economic relations in the years ahead.

---

[6] We do not agree among ourselves, however, on the need to carry out this sort of compensation. Some of us believe that we have done our work when we have shown that compensation is possible—that the gains of those who come out ahead are large enough to offset the losses of those who fall behind. Others say that compensation must actually be undertaken before we can endorse a policy change. Some take an intermediate position, saying that compensation should be undertaken if the losers have smaller incomes than the gainers, a view that embodies a personal judgment about inequality. These issues will crop up again in Chapter 11.

SUMMARY

The earliest writers on international economics, the Mercantilists of the seventeenth century, gave great weight to the role of the state. They measured the gains from trade by the "treasure" that a country could accumulate through trade, and they urged the state to maximize this sort of gain by encouraging exports and discouraging imports. The Classical economists of the eighteenth century took a different view. They measured the gains from trade by the increase in efficiency that can be achieved by concentrating on those activities in which an economy has a competitive advantage, and they urged the state to abstain from regulating foreign trade.

Modern economists measure the gains from trade in much the same way as the Classical economists, but they pay more attention to the role of government. Trade and other international transactions are influenced by many economic policies, including those adopted for domestic reasons. Conversely, a country's international transactions impinge on the conduct of domestic policies. The exchange-rate regime can influence heavily the effectiveness of monetary policy. Furthermore, the tasks of domestic policies are complicated by international disturbances—by changes in incomes, prices, and interest rates in other countries.

The problems of economic interdependence have long been familiar to policymakers in most countries; their national economies are very open compared to the American economy. But the problems are becoming familiar to Americans, too. The American economy has become more open. Furthermore, U.S. economic policies affect the health of the world economy, and controversies about economic policies tend to migrate into the political arena, affecting the quality of cooperation in diplomatic and strategic matters.

RECOMMENDED READINGS

Many topics covered briefly in this chapter will be studied more thoroughly in later chapters, and longer lists of readings are appended to those chapters. Here are three references that do not fit in elsewhere:

On the views and contributions of the Mercantilists and Classical economists, see Joseph Schumpeter, *History of Economic Analysis* (New York: Oxford University Press, 1954), pt. II, chs. 3, 7.

The opening of the U.S. economy and its implications are examined in Richard N. Cooper, "The United States as an Open Economy," in R. W. Hafer, ed., *How Open Is the U.S. Economy?* (Lexington, Mass: Lexington Books, D.C. Heath, 1986), ch. 1.

On trends in openness and related issues, see Sven Grassman, "Long-Term Trends in Openness of National Economies," *Oxford Economic Papers*, 32 (March 1980).

CHAPTER

2

COMPARATIVE ADVANTAGE AND THE GAINS FROM TRADE

PRICES AND TRADE PATTERNS

Differences in prices from country to country are the basic cause of trade. They reflect differences in costs of production. Trade serves in turn to minimize the real resource costs of worldwide production, which is a way of saying that trade serves to maximize the real value of production from worldwide resources. It does so by permitting and encouraging producers in each country to specialize in those economic activities that make the best uses of their country's resources.

Why should costs differ from country to country? How can Japan produce cars, cameras, and calculators more cheaply than the United States? Many people would reply that Japan has lower costs because it has lower wage rates, and wages are important

costs. This explanation sounds plausible enough and is based in fact. But it is inadequate. If wage rates were decisive for cost differences and trade, Japan would undersell the United States in every product line and market. Yet Japan imports large numbers of products from the United States, from aircraft to grain, and other countries with much lower wage rates than Japan buy American products in great variety and quantity. Differences in wage rates by themselves cannot explain trade patterns. We must look further for the basis of trade.

An enduring two-way flow of goods must be traced to systematic international differences in *structures* of costs and prices. Some things must be cheaper to produce at home and will be exported to other countries. Some things must be cheaper to produce abroad and will be imported from other countries. This generalization is known as the *law of comparative advantage* and can be put this way:

> **In a world of competitive markets, trade will occur and be beneficial whenever there are international differences in relative costs of production.**

Japan can export cars and cameras because its endowment of land, labor, capital, and technology allow it to expand its outputs of those goods with the smallest sacrifice of other domestic outputs. The United States can export aircraft and grain because it can expand its outputs of those goods with the smallest sacrifice. Cars may be less costly than aircraft in both countries, grain less costly than cameras, but the cost differences are not uniform, and the cross-country variation in those differences leads to beneficial trade.

It is the main task of this chapter to prove the law of comparative advantage. Reasons for differences in relative costs are explored in Chapters 3 and 4.

PRODUCTION, CONSUMPTION, AND TRADE IN A SINGLE COMMODITY

The effects of differences in relative costs cannot be examined by looking at one market at a time. It is necessary to look at an entire national economy, and compare it with another. Therefore, international trade theory cannot make much use of partial-equilibrium price theory—of ordinary demand and supply curves. It must use general-equilibrium theory most of the time. Demand and supply curves can be used, however, to show how trade in a single commodity affects production and consumption in the domestic market and to quantify the gains from trade.

Equilibrium Before Trade Is Opened

In Figure 2-1, the domestic demand curve for cameras is D_H, and the domestic supply curve is S_H. When there is no international trade in cameras, equilibrium will be established at E. The domestic price of a camera will be OP, production will be OQ, and production will necessarily equal consumption. The diagram, however, says much more.

When domestic markets are perfectly competitive, the supply curve is the sum of the marginal cost curves of domestic firms. Accordingly, the area under the supply curve measures the total cost of camera production. (Strictly speaking, it measures the total variable cost, but fixed cost plays no role in this analysis.) If OQ cameras are produced, total cost is given by the area of the triangle OQE. But total payments to producers (revenues) are given by the area of the rectangle $OQEP$. Therefore, the area of the triangle OEP measures profit or *producer surplus*.

The area under the demand curve is meaningful, too. Under somewhat restrictive assumptions that need not detain us here, it measures the cash equivalent of the utility that consumers derive from their purchases of cameras.[1] If OQ cameras are consumed, that cash equivalent is the area $OQET$. But consumers pay $OQEP$ for their cameras. Therefore, the area of the triangle PET measures net benefit or *consumer surplus*.

---

[1] There are three such assumptions: (1) Utility can be measured in *cardinal* numbers, allowing us to know the *size* of the increase in utility conferred by an increase in consumption, not merely that there is an increase. (2) The utilities of individuals are measured in comparable units, allowing us to give them *common* cash equivalents. (3) The marginal utility of income is constant, allowing us to use an income or cash measure that does not grow or shrink when price changes alter incomes.

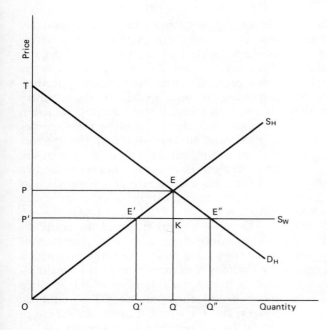

FIGURE 2-1 Effects of Opening Trade in a Single Good
Before trade is opened, the domestic price is *OP*, and the quantity *OQ* is produced to satisfy domestic demand. When trade is opened at the world price *OP'*, production falls to *OQ'*, consumption rises to *OQ"*, and *Q'Q"* is imported to close the gap. The production effect is *Q'Q*, and the corresponding welfare gain is *E'KE*. The consumption effect is *QQ"*, and the corresponding welfare gain is *KE"E*.

Equilibrium After Trade Is Opened

Suppose now that trade in cameras is opened and that the world's supply curve is S_W. The world price of cameras is *OP'*, lower than the old domestic price, *OP*, and the world price must come to prevail in the domestic market if there are no transport costs or tariffs. Domestic firms will cut back production to *OQ'*. Domestic consumers will step up their purchases to *OQ"*. The gap between domestic demand and supply, *Q'Q"*, will be filled by imports.

What are the effects on economic welfare? Producer surplus will be *OE'P'*. It will fall by *P'E'EP*. Consumer surplus will be *P'E"T*. It will rise by *P'E"EP*. As the increase in consumer surplus exceeds the decrease in producer surplus by *E'E"E*, consumers can compensate producers and come out ahead. The area *E'E"E* measures the gain from trade in cameras. Note that it can be divided into two parts. The decrease in domestic output, *Q'Q*, contributes *E'KE*.

This is the *production effect*. The increase in domestic purchases, *QQ"*, contributes *KE"E*. This is the *consumption effect*.

This simple diagram, however, is deficient in a number of respects. It relies on restrictive assumptions needed to measure consumer surplus. It does not describe the economic costs and benefits of exporting other goods to pay for imported cameras. It says nothing about the reasons for the difference in pretrade prices—why the world price of cameras is lower than the pretrade domestic price. These matters can be investigated one at a time, using a general-equilibrium model.

PRODUCTION AND CONSUMPTION IN GENERAL EQUILIBRIUM

Much of international trade theory can be developed using a very simple general-equilibrium model. It contains two countries that produce two commodities requiring two factors of production. The model cannot be made to yield testable hypotheses about the commodity composition of international trade. A more complicated model with many countries and commodities is needed for that purpose. Nevertheless, the simple model can be used to illustrate the law of comparative advantage and the nature of the gains from trade. It also furnishes testable hypotheses about the general character of trade.

The model is developed in three steps. First, we will show how production, consumption, and prices are determined when there is no trade. Second, we will show how trade affects a single country. Third, we will look at two countries together to show how world prices are determined and how the gains from trade are distributed.

Supply Conditions

Supply conditions in a country producing two commodities can be described by a *production transformation curve* (sometimes called a production possibilities curve). It shows the combinations of commodities that the country can produce, given its resources, technology, and economic organization. The curve TT' in Figure 2-2 is the transformation curve for a country producing cameras and grain. If the country devoted all its resources to the production of cameras, output would be OT cameras. If it devoted all its resources to the production of grain, output would be OT' grain. If it divided its resources between the two activities, it would arrive at a point such as D, where camera output is OX_1 and grain output is OX_2.

The position and shape of the transformation curve depend on the quantities of land, labor, and other resources with which the country is endowed and on its technology. If it had more land, it could produce more grain; the distance OT' would be longer, and the whole transformation curve would be steeper. If it had a better way of making cameras, it could produce more cameras; the distance OT would be longer, and the whole transformation curve would be flatter. These possibilities are explored

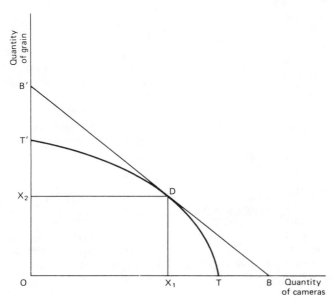

FIGURE 2-2   The Production Transformation Curve
The position and shape of the curve TT' are determined by the country's supplies of the factors of production and its technology. When the relative price of a camera is given by the slope of the line BB', the country will produce at D. Its camera output will be OX_1, and its grain output will be OX_2. Its real national product will be OB measured in cameras or OB' measured in grain.

more thoroughly in the next two chapters, which deal with sources of comparative advantage.

Note that the curve TT' gets steeper as camera output rises. The country must sacrifice increasingly large quantities of grain output to raise camera output. This property has many names—convexity, increasing opportunity cost, and so on. It can have many causes. There may be decreasing returns to scale in one or both sectors. There may be a fixed factor of production in each sector, which means that the other (variable) factors will have diminishing marginal products. (If the number of camera factories is fixed, for example, the hiring of additional workers will raise camera output by smaller and smaller amounts.) The same result will obtain, however, when all factors of production are freely transferable from one sector to the other but must be combined in different proportions—when camera production typically requires more labor per unit of land than grain production. Whatever the cause, moreover, the property appears to be pervasive.

Prices, Outputs, and National Product

When domestic markets are perfectly competitive, prices are flexible, and firms maximize profits, the economy will maximize its national product measured in real terms, and production will be determined uniquely by relative prices.[2]

Let the relative price of a camera be equal to the *slope* of the line BB' and thus equal to the slope of the curve TT' at D. A competitive economy will produce at D and will thereby maximize its national product.

---

[2] This list of conditions is not complete. Two others receive attention in advanced trade theory: (1) there can be no tax or subsidy on the output of one good or use of one factor; taxes and subsidies must be uniform. (2) Uncertainty about future prices must not affect firms' responses to current prices.

An algebraic demonstration is given in Note 2-1, which also introduces the basic mathematical notation used in this book. A geometric demonstration can be furnished in two steps: (1) by showing that the distances OB and OB' measure the national product in real terms and (2) by showing that production at D maximizes the distances OB and OB' and thus maximizes the national product.

The relative price of a camera is its ordinary (dollar) price divided by the price of grain:

$$\text{Relative camera price} = \frac{\text{price of a camera}}{\text{price of grain}}$$

It measures the amount of grain that must be given up to purchase a camera. Let that price be equal to the slope of the line BB':

$$\text{Relative camera price} = \frac{OB'}{OB}$$

Note that OB'/OB equals X_2B'/X_2D, because the triangles OBB' and X_2DB' are similar. Furthermore, X_2D equals OX_1. Therefore, the relative price of a camera can be redefined as X_2B'/OX_1. This definition will be useful shortly.

The value of the national product is the sum of the values of the country's outputs measured at their market prices:

Value of national product
= grain output × price of grain
+ camera output × price of a camera

Dividing both sides by the price of grain,

$\dfrac{\text{Value of national product}}{\text{Price of grain}}$
= grain output
+ camera output × $\dfrac{\text{price of a camera}}{\text{price of grain}}$

Or

National product measured in grain
= grain output + camera output
× relative camera price

Note 2-1

Let the economy produce x_1 cameras at price p_1 and x_2 grain at price p_2. The value of national output, y, is

$$y = p_1x_1 + p_2x_2$$

Keeping prices constant, let firms move along the transformation curve, changing camera output to x_1' and grain output to x_2'. The value of output will change to

$$y' = p_1x_1' + p_2x_2'$$

Subtracting y from y',

$$y' - y = p_1(x_1' - x_1) + p_2(x_2' - x_2)$$

Throughout this book, the symbol d denotes a change in any variable, so $dy = (y' - y)$, and so on. Therefore,

$$dy = p_1dx_1 + p_2dx_2$$

Competitive firms that maximize profits will increase camera output ($dx_1 > 0$) and decrease grain output ($dx_2 < 0$) whenever this raises the value of national output ($dy > 0$). But they cannot do so indefinitely, because the transformation curve is *convex*. Each increase in camera output causes a larger decrease in grain output, reducing the net addition to the value of national output. Eventually, the changes in camera and grain outputs neutralize each other so that $dy = 0$, and

$$p_1dx_1 = -p_2dx_2$$

or

$$\frac{p_1}{p_2} = -\frac{dx_2}{dx_1}$$

The left side of this expression is the relative price of a camera; it measures the amount of grain that must be paid to purchase one camera. The right side is the slope of the transformation curve at the point that maximizes the value of national output; it measures the amount of grain that must be sacrificed to produce an additional camera.

When production is at D, however, grain output is OX_2, camera output is OX_1, and the relative price of a camera is X_2B'/OX_1. Therefore,

National product measured in grain

$$= OX_2 + OX_1 \times \frac{X_2B'}{OX_1}$$
$$= OX_2 + X_2B' = OB'$$

National product measured in grain is actual grain output *plus* the grain equivalent at market prices of actual camera output. National product measured in cameras can be obtained in a similar way or more directly. Divide the national product measured in grain by the relative price of a camera:[3]

National product measured in cameras

$$= \frac{\text{national product measured in grain}}{\text{relative camera price}}$$
$$= OB' \div \frac{OB'}{OB} = OB' \times \frac{OB}{OB'} = OB$$

_____

[3] This equation follows from the fact that

National product measured in cameras
 × price of a camera
= national product measured in grain
 × price of grain

so that

National product measured in cameras
= national product measured in grain
 × $\dfrac{\text{price of grain}}{\text{price of a camera}}$

It is actual camera output *plus* the camera equivalent at market prices of actual grain output.

The proof is completed in Figure 2-3, which shows that production at D maximizes real national product, whether it is measured in cameras or grain. As before, the transformation curve is TT', and the relative price of a camera is given by the slope of the line BB'. Suppose that production starts at H, where camera output is OX_1' and grain output is OX_2'. Draw the line AA' passing through H and parallel to BB'. It marks off the distances OA and OA', which measure real national product in cameras and grain, respectively, when H is the output point. Clearly, these are smaller than OB and OB', which measure real national product when D is the output point.

Competitive firms will not stay at H. They will produce more cameras and less grain, moving the economy along the transformation curve in the direction of D. They will do this because it will increase their profits. (The line AA' is steeper than the transformation curve at H. Therefore, the value of an increase in camera output will exceed the value of the corresponding decrease in grain output.) By moving in this direction, moreover, firms raise the real national product, and when they arrive at D, they maximize it. The gaps AB and $A'B'$ disappear. If firms went beyond D, they would reduce real national product. If they moved to H', for example, it would fall again to OA and OA'. But profits would fall, too.

In brief, a competitive economy will arrive and stay at D, where the relative price of a camera is equal to the slope of the transformation curve, also known as the *marginal rate of transformation.*

Demand Conditions

Demand conditions in a country consuming two commodities can be described by a *community indifference map*. It is built from individuals' indifference maps, which

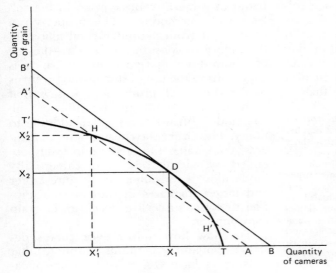

FIGURE 2-3 Efficiency in Domestic Production

When the relative price of a camera is given by the slope of the line BB', production at D is efficient and production at H is not. Both points lie on the transformation curve TT', so the factors of production are fully employed. With production at D, however, real national product is OB measured in cameras. With production at H, it is only OA.

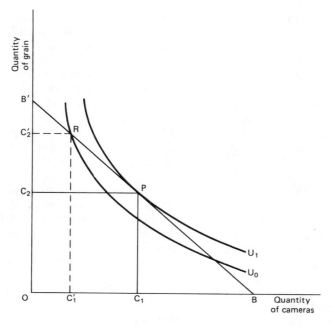

FIGURE 2-4   The Indifference Map
All collections of commodities that lie
on one indifference curve yield the
same level of utility (satisfaction), but
any collection on U_1 is superior to any
collection on U_0. When income is OB
measured in cameras, and the relative
price of a camera is given by the slope
of the line BB', the consumer will
choose the collection given at P, purchasing OC_1 cameras and OC_2 grain.
That collection is superior to any other
on or below BB', such as the collection at R.

show how those individuals rank various
collections of commodities.[4]

An indifference map is made up of *indifference curves*. Two are shown in Figure 2-4.
The point P defines a collection of commodities, OC_1 cameras and OC_2 grain. The
indifference curve U_1 divides all such collections into three groups. Those that lie
below U_1 are inferior to the collection at
P; they furnish lower levels of utility
(satisfaction). Those that lie above it are superior to the collection at P; they furnish
higher levels of utility. And those that lie

right on U_1 are equivalent to the collection
at P; they furnish the same level of utility,
which is why the consumer is said to be indifferent when asked to choose among
them.

Note that the indifference curves get
flatter as cameras replace grain in the collection of commodities. This property can
be derived from a fundamental axiom in
the theory of consumer behavior—the law
of diminishing marginal utility—which is
analogous to the law of diminishing returns
in the theory of production. It says that
each increase in the consumption of one
commodity furnishes a smaller addition to
utility. The larger the consumption of cameras, the smaller the increase in utility obtained by adding one more camera. By
implication, a consumer will require larger
and larger increases in camera consumption to offset successive decreases in grain
consumption.

To show how indifference curves describe demand conditions, suppose that
consumers have OB of real income mea-

[4]To build a community indifference map from individual indifference maps, one must make a number
of assumptions, but these are less restrictive than those
that must be made to measure consumer surplus. It is
not necessary to adopt a cardinal measure of utility, to
measure the utilities of individuals in comparable
units, or to keep the marginal utility of income constant. It is sufficient to assume that all individuals have
the same indifference maps and that income elasticities of demand are unity (that a 1 percent increase in
real income causes a 1 percent increase in the demand
for each commodity). Alternatively it is sufficient to assume that all individuals have the same sources of income.

sured in cameras and that the relative price of a camera is given by the slope of the line BB'. Consumers can buy any combination of cameras and grain lying on BB'. They can have OC'_1 cameras and OC'_2 grain and will then wind up at R on the indifference curve U_0. They can also have OC_1 cameras and OC_2 grain and will then wind up at P on the indifference curve U_1. Consumers will choose P, of course, and they can do no better. It lies on the highest indifference curve attainable when real incomes and the relative price of a camera are given by the line BB'.

Because of the role that it plays in Figure 2-4, the line BB' is often called a *budget line*. It depicts the two constraints that confront consumers: the sizes of the incomes they can spend and the prices at which they

can spend them. Therefore, the outcome at P can be described by saying that the composition of demand is given by the point on the budget line at which its slope is equal to the slope of an indifference curve, also known as the *marginal rate of substitution*.

Equilibrium in the Closed Economy

When we looked for equilibrium in a single market and there was no trade, we sought the price at which the market cleared—at which domestic demand was equal to domestic supply. It was given by the point E in Figure 2-1. When we look for equilibrium in two markets together, we must seek the point at which both markets clear. It is the point E in Figure 2-5. Let us see what happens there.

FIGURE 2-5 Equilibrium in the Closed Economy
Under competitive conditions, equilibrium will be established at E. Camera output will be OQ_1 and will equal the demand for cameras. Grain output will be OQ_2 and will equal the demand for grain. The relative price of a camera will equal the slope of the line BB', and the value of national output will be OB measured in cameras.

When production takes place at E, the supply of cameras is OQ_1 and the supply of grain is OQ_2. In a competitive economy, however, production will remain at E only when the relative price of a camera is equal to the slope of the transformation curve at E and thus equal to the slope of the line BB'. When this condition is satisfied, moreover, the national product measured in cameras is OB, and it must equal the national income in this simple economy (where there are no adjustments for depreciation, indirect taxes, etc.). The values of the goods produced at E must equal the wages, rents, and profits paid to the factors of production. Therefore, the line BB' must be the budget line, and consumers will wind up at E, because U_1 is the highest indifference curve they can reach when they face that budget line. The demand for cameras will be OQ_1 and will equal the supply. The demand for grain will be OQ_2 and will also equal the supply.

Two features of this equilibrium deserve special attention. (1) We can locate E without knowing the relative price of a camera. When firms maximize profits and consumers maximize utility, equilibrium in a closed economy is established at the point of *tangency* between the transformation curve and an indifference curve, just as equilibrium in a single market is established at the point of intersection between the supply and demand curves. The marginal rate of transformation is equated to the marginal rate of substitution, and each of them must equal the relative price of a camera. Hence, we can infer that price from the slopes of the two curves at their tangency; we can draw the line BB' after we have found the point E. (2) When one market clears, the other must clear, too. Once we have found the relative price that clears the camera market, we have found the relative price that clears the grain market. In other words, there is only one independent market in a two-commodity

model. This point is proved algebraically in Note 2-2.

What would happen if, by chance, the relative price of a camera were different from the equilibrium price? Suppose the price were lower than the price given by the slopes of the curves at E. Firms would move to the northwest along the transformation curve, reducing the supply of cameras below OQ_1. Consumers would move to the southeast through the indifference map, raising the demand for cameras above OQ_1. There would be an *excess demand* for cameras, which would raise the relative price of a camera, moving the economy back to E. This is the only equilibrium point for the closed economy.

TRADE IN GENERAL EQUILIBRIUM

When analyzing trade in a single commodity, using Figure 2-1, we asked what would happen when the world price of a camera was lower than the domestic price prevailing before trade. Let us address the same question to the two-commodity economy. How does trade affect production, consumption, and economic welfare when the relative price of a camera is lower in the world market than it was in the domestic market before trade was opened?

Equilibrium in the Open Economy

The effects of trade are shown in Figure 2-6. Before the opening of trade, the economy is in equilibrium at E, as in Figure 2-5. The relative price of a camera is given by the slopes of the transformation curve TT' and the indifference curve U_1. (In this and later diagrams, the budget line BB' is omitted, because it would clutter the diagram unnecessarily.)

Suppose that the relative price of a camera is lower in the outside world. Represent it by the slope of the line FF'. When trade is opened (and there are no transport costs or tariffs), the world price replaces the ear-

Note 2-2

Recall the definition of the value of national output given in Note 2-1:

$$y = p_1 x_1 + p_2 x_2$$

In this simple model, national output must equal national income. In a closed economy, moreover, national income must equal total spending (consumption) on cameras and grain. Therefore,

$$y = p_1 c_1 + p_2 c_2$$

where c_1 and c_2 are the quantities of cameras and grain demanded by consumers. Accordingly,

$$p_1 c_1 + p_2 c_2 = p_1 x_1 + p_2 x_2$$

and

$$p_1(c_1 - x_1) = p_2(x_2 - c_2)$$

If there is an *excess demand* for cameras $(c_1 > x_1)$, there must be an *excess supply* of grain $(x_2 > c_2)$. If the market for cameras clears $(x_1 = c_1)$, the market for grain must clear, too $(x_2 = c_2)$.

In an open economy, total domestic spending need not always equal national income, because there can be foreign borrowing or lending. Even in the absence of borrowing or lending, however, the equations in this note make an important point. An excess demand for cameras shows up as a demand for imports, and the corresponding excess supply of grain shows up as a supply of exports. Therefore, a country's demand for imports will equal its supply of exports at every set of prices. We invoke this point later, when interpreting *trade triangles* (Figure 2-6) and constructing an *offer curve* (Figure 2-9).

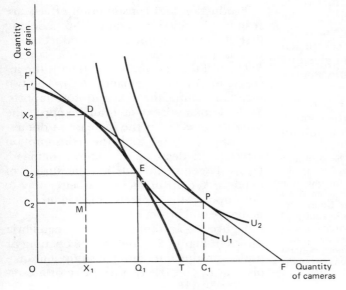

FIGURE 2-6 Equilibrium in the Open Economy

Before trade is opened, production and consumption take place at *E,* and the relative price of a camera is given by the slope of the transformation curve at that point. When trade is opened at a lower world price, given by the slope of the line *FF'*, production moves to *D* and consumption moves to *P*. Camera output falls to OX_1, domestic consumption rises to OC_1, and $X_1 C_1$ of camera imports fill the gap. Grain output rises to OX_2, domestic consumption falls to OC_2 and $C_2 X_2$ of grain exports remove the surplus. The trade triangle is *MPD*. Grain exports pay for camera imports.

lier domestic price. Guided by the world price, profit-maximizing firms will move the output point to D, where the slope of the transformation curve is equal to the slope of FF'. Camera output will fall to OX_1, and grain output will rise to OX_2. The national product measured in cameras will be OF, it will equal the national income, and FF' will be the budget line. Accordingly, consumers will maximize utility by moving to the point P, where the slope of the budget line is equal to the slope of the indifference curve U_2. The demand for cameras will rise to OC_1, and the demand for grain will fall to OC_2.

If the economy were closed, there would be an excess demand for cameras (equal to $X_1 C_1$) and an excess supply of grain (equal to $C_2 X_2$). The new situation would not be sustainable. When the economy can trade with the outside world, it can satisfy its excess demand for cameras by importing $X_1 C_1$ and sell off its excess supply of grain by exporting $C_2 X_2$. Production at D can be reconciled with consumption at P, because domestic markets can be cleared by trading grain for cameras. Trade is beneficial, moreover, because consumers can choose any collection of commodities lying on the budget line FF' and thus reach the indifference curve U_2. They are not compelled to choose the particular collection given by the tangency of the transformation curve with the indifference curve U_1.[5]

The grain exports shown in Figure 2-6 are just large enough to pay for the camera imports. This was proved algebraically in

[5] Note that the gains from trade can be illustrated easily without drawing indifference curves. As the budget line FF' lies to the northeast of the old equilibrium point E, it includes collections of commodities containing more cameras and more grain. Unless consumers' demands can be *satiated* by finite quantities of commodities, these collections are necessarily superior to the collection defined by E. (Consumers may prefer the collection defined by P, containing more cameras and less grain, but could have a collection containing more of *both* commodities.)

Note 2-2, and it can be illustrated geometrically by looking at two triangles, OFF' and MPD. The legs of the triangle OFF' measure the relative price of a camera in the world market:

$$\text{Relative camera price} = \frac{\text{price of a camera}}{\text{price of grain}} = \frac{OF'}{OF}$$

But the triangle OFF' is similar to the triangle MPD, identified hereafter as the *trade triangle*. Therefore, $OF'/OF = MD/MP$. Furthermore, MD measures the quantity of grain exports (MD equals $C_2 X_2$), and MP measures the quantity of camera imports (MP equals $X_1 C_1$). As a consequence,

$$\frac{\text{Price of a camera}}{\text{Price of grain}}$$
$$= \frac{MD}{MP} = \frac{\text{quantity of grain exports}}{\text{quantity of camera imports}}$$

and

Quantity of camera imports × price of a camera
$$= \text{quantity of grain exports}$$
$$\times \text{ price of grain}$$

The country's foreign trade is balanced.

Sources of the Gains from Trade

Production and consumption effects are readily identified in Figure 2-6. Looking first at camera imports, the production effect is the decrease in domestic supply, $X_1 Q_1$, and the consumption effect is the increase in domestic demand, $Q_1 C_1$. The two together define the demand for imports, $X_1 C_1$. Looking next at grain exports, the production effect is the increase in domestic supply, $Q_2 X_2$, and the consumption effect is the decrease in domestic demand, $Q_2 C_2$. Together they define the supply of exports, $X_2 C_2$. But there is a better way to decompose the effects of trade in a general-equilibrium model.

Figure 2-7 replicates the equilibria shown in Figure 2-6. Before the opening of trade, production and consumption take place at E, and the relative price of a cam-

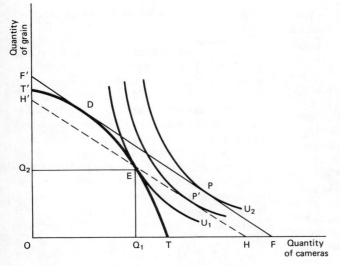

FIGURE 2-7 Decomposition
of the Gains from Trade
The gain from international exchange
is defined by the shift of consumption
from *E* to *P'*, which lies on an indifference curve higher than U_1 but
lower than U_2. The gain from international specialization is defined by the
shift of production from *E* to *D*, permitting the additional shift of consumption from *P'* to *P*, which lies
on U_2.

era is given by the slope of the indifference curve U_1 where it passes through *E*. After the opening of trade, production takes place at *D*, consumption takes place at *P*, and the relative price of a camera is given by the slope of *FF'* (which equals the slope of the transformation curve at *D* and the slope of the indifference curve at *P*). The increase in economic welfare (utility) is represented by the movement from U_1 to U_2, which can be divided into two parts.

One part is the *gain from international exchange*. It can be measured by supposing momentarily that production is fixed at *E* even after trade is opened. Draw the line *HH'* through *E* and parallel to *FF'* so that the slope of *HH'* measures the relative price of a camera in the world market. The distance *OH* measures real national product in cameras; it is the fixed output of cameras, OQ_1, *plus* the camera equivalent of the fixed output of grain, OQ_2. As *OH* also measures real income, *HH'* is the budget line, and consumers move to *P'*. They reach an indifference curve higher than U_1 but lower than U_2. The movement of consumption from *E* to *P'* is the gain from international exchange.

The other part of the increase in welfare is the *gain from international specialization*. It can be measured by relaxing the assumption that production is fixed at *E*, and allowing the output point to move from *E* to *D*. National product and national income rise from *OH* to *OF*. Consumers move from *P'* to *P* and reach the higher indifference curve U_2. The movement of consumption from *P'* to *P* is the gain from international specialization, made possible by the shift in the composition of production.[6]

DETERMINATION OF INTERNATIONAL PRICES

We have completed two of the three steps required to prove the law of comparative advantage. We have shown how demand and supply conditions determine

[6] The term *specialization* is often used in trade theory to describe a limiting case in which a country devotes all its resources to the production of the export commodity and does not produce any of the import-competing commodity. We will encounter such a case in the next chapter. In this book, specialization is used more broadly to describe the movement of production away from the pretrade point. The limiting case will be described as *complete* specialization.

domestic prices in a closed economy producing two commodities. We have shown
how that economy responds when confronted by worl prices different from domestic prices, a process summarized by the
appearance of the trade triangle defining
the demand for imports and supply of exports. We are now ready to take the third
step: to show how world prices are determined and that they reflect international
differences in cost and price structures.

The trade triangle was *MPD* in Figure 2-
6. When the relative price of a camera was
equal to the slope of *FF'*, the quantity of
grain exports was *MD*, and the quantity of
camera imports was *MP*. Furthermore,
trade was balanced. Grain exports were just
large enough to pay for camera imports
when they were exchanged at world prices.

When an economy is very small, its trade
does not affect world prices. It is like an individual producer or consumer in a domestic market. It can exchange any quantity of
grain for the corresponding quantity of
cameras without affecting the relative price
of a camera in the world market. When an
economy is not that small, however, its attempt to sell *MD* of grain and buy *MP* of
cameras may affect world prices. When this
happens, the shape of the trade triangle is
altered, changing the supply of grain exports and demand for camera imports.

When can we be sure that a trade triangle depicts an international equilibrium?
The conditions can be identified easily by
looking at an international economy consisting of two countries. (World markets
can be competitive even when the international economy has only two countries. The
number of countries does not matter if
each country's markets are competitive and
governments do not try to monopolize
their countries' foreign trade. Trade unites
the countries' competitive markets, and the
sums of competitive markets are also competitive.)

Equilibrium with Trade Between Two Countries

The two countries are described by Figure 2-8. The domestic transformation
curve is *TT'*. The foreign transformation
curve is $T_f T_f'$. As *OT'* is larger than OT_f'
and *OT* is smaller than OT_f, there is an obvious sense in which the domestic economy
is better suited to produce grain than cameras, compared to the foreign economy.

To emphasize the influence of cost conditions on international trade, the two
countries are assumed to have identical
demand conditions, represented by the
common indifference curves U_0, U_1, and
U_2.

Look first at the internal equilibria before trade is opened. In the domestic economy, production and consumption take
place at *E*, where the transformation curve
TT' is tangent to the indifference curve U_0.
In the foreign economy, they take place at
E*, where the transformation curve $T_f T_f'$ is
tangent to that same indifference curve.[7]
Clearly, the relative price of a camera is
higher in the domestic economy than in the
foreign economy, which is what we would
expect, because the domestic economy is
better suited to producing grain than cameras.

Look next at the effects of opening
trade. When the two countries' markets are
unified, common prices must prevail, and
they must clear the unified markets. There
are two ways to state this last condition:

[7] The two countries do not have to start on the
same indifference curve. This special case is chosen to
simplify the diagram, and the conclusions drawn from
it are quite general. But the common *set* of indifference curves has a special property that could be important if the countries started on different curves.
The income elasticities of demand are unity. Geometrically, points of common slope such as *P* and *P** lie
on a straight line from the origin. In technical terms,
the indifference curves are *homothetic*. This property
prevents country size from influencing demand conditions and relative prices.

FIGURE 2-8 Equilibrium in a Two-Country World
Before trade is opened, domestic production and consumption take place at E on the domestic transformation curve TT'; foreign production and consumption take place at E^* on the foreign transformation curve $T_f T_f'$. The relative price of a camera is higher at E than at E^*. When trade is opened, a common price is established, equal to the slopes of the (parallel) lines PD and P^*D^*. Domestic production moves to D, domestic consumption moves to P, and domestic consumers move from U_0 to the higher indifference curve U_1. Foreign production moves to D^*, foreign consumption moves to P^*, and foreign consumers move from U_0 to the higher indifference curve U_2. The common price must be one at which trade triangles are equal. Domestic grain exports, DM, must equal foreign grain imports, P^*M^*. Domestic camera imports, PM, must equal foreign camera exports, M^*D^*.

(1) Global camera output, defined as the sum of the two countries' outputs, must equal the global demand for cameras, and global grain output must equal the global demand for grain. (2) The quantity of camera imports demanded by one country must equal the quantity of camera exports supplied by the other, and the same equality must hold for trade in grain.[8] Geometrically, the two countries must have identical (congruent) trade triangles. These conditions can be fulfilled only when the relative price of a camera in the world camera market lies between the prices that prevailed internally before trade was opened.

This common price is represented by the slopes of the parallel lines PD and P^*D^* in Figure 2-8. They are flatter than the slope of the indifference curve U_0 at E (the world price is lower than the old internal price in the domestic economy). They are steeper than the slope of that indifference curve at E^* (the world price is higher than the old internal price in the foreign economy). The

---

[8] The algebra of Note 2-2 can be used to prove that these are indeed two ways to state the same condition. Working with camera production and consumption, the first statement can be written as $x_1 + x_1^* = c_1 + c_1^*$, where x_1 and c_1 are domestic production and consumption, and x_1^* and c_1^* are foreign production and consumption. Rearranging this equation, $x_1^* - c_1^* = c_1 - x_1$, which is the second statement, because $x_1^* - c_1^*$ is the foreign supply of camera exports and $c_1 - x_1$ is the domestic demand for camera imports.

common price is the equilibrium price, because the unified market clears.

As the opening of trade reduces the relative price of a camera in the domestic economy, production moves from E to D and consumption moves from E to P, just as they did in Figure 2-6. The trade triangle is MPD. The domestic economy demands MP of camera imports in exchange for MD of grain exports. As the opening of trade raises the relative price of a camera in the foreign economy, production moves from $E*$ to $D*$, and consumption moves from $E*$ to $P*$. The trade triangle is $M*D*P*$. The foreign economy demands $M*P*$ of grain imports in exchange for $M*D*$ of camera exports.

Furthermore, the common price is the price at which the two trade triangles are identical. Therefore, the domestic demand for camera imports is equal to the foreign supply of camera exports (MP equals $M*D*$), and the foreign demand for grain imports equals the domestic supply of grain exports ($M*P*$ equals MD). When one of these conditions is satisfied, moreover, the other must also be satisfied. This follows from the fact that both world markets have to clear whenever one of them clears (a fact that follows in turn from the algebra of Note 2-2). It follows also from the fact that each country's trade is balanced: its demand for imports is equal in value to its supply of exports.

To prove that the relative price of a camera has to lie between the old internal prices, suppose momentarily that this were not so. Let the common price be equal to the old internal price in the foreign economy (i.e., to the slope of U_0 at $E*$). Outputs and consumption would not change in the foreign economy, and it would not offer exports or demand imports. But outputs and consumption would change significantly in the domestic economy. The change in output, indeed, would be larger than the change shown in Figure 2-8 (the

movement from E to D), because the relative price of a camera would fall farther. Therefore, the domestic economy would demand camera imports and offer grain exports, and world markets would not clear. There would be an excess demand for cameras and an excess supply of grain, and these would raise the relative price of a camera until it came to lie between the old internal prices in the two economies.

The Terms of Trade and Gains from Trade

The common price given by the lines PD and $P*D*$ defines the *terms of trade* between the two economies. These are the terms on which each economy can acquire imports from the other. A reduction in the relative price of its import improves a country's terms of trade. In this particular illustration, a reduction in the relative price of a camera, making PD and $P*D*$ flatter, would improve the terms of trade of the domestic economy and worsen the terms of trade of the foreign economy. The terms of trade determine the distribution of the gains from trade. If PD and $P*D*$ were flatter, improving the domestic terms of trade but worsening the foreign terms of trade, domestic consumers could reach an indifference curve higher than U_1 but foreign consumers could not reach U_2. Consumers in both countries would still gain from trade, but domestic consumers would gain more and foreign consumers would gain less.

Comparative Advantage Once Again

Figure 2-8 has several uses. It shows how world prices are established. They must clear the unified national markets of the trading countries by equating one country's demand for imports to the other's supply of exports. It shows that each country gains from trade and the distribution of the gains. Domestic consumers move from E

on the indifference curve U_0 to P on the higher indifference curve U_1. Foreign consumers move from E^* on the curve U_0 to P^* on the higher curve U_2. Finally, it illustrates the law of comparative advantage.

If the two countries shown in Figure 2-8 had identical transformation curves, there could be no trade between them. The points E and E^* would coincide, and the two countries' prices would be the same without any trade. The unification of national markets would be without consequence, as it would not alter relative prices. Each country's firms would stay at E, and each country's consumers would stay there, too. Internal supplies would satisfy internal demands in each country separately. There would be no gain from international specialization and no gain from international exchange.

When the countries' transformation curves are different, the unification of national markets changes relative prices, affecting production and consumption in each country. Both countries gain from specialization and exchange. Note in particular the nature of the gain from international specialization. The domestic economy is better suited to produce grain than cameras, compared to the foreign economy. With the opening of trade, it exploits its comparative advantage. Reacting to the fall in the relative price of a camera, domestic firms produce more grain and fewer cameras, and the economy thus tends to specialize in grain production. The foreign economy has a comparative advantage in camera production—the mirror image of the domestic economy's advantage in grain production—and also exploits its advantage. Reacting to the rise in the relative price of a camera, foreign firms produce more cameras and less grain, and the economy thus tends to specialize in camera production.

Looking at these same reactions from another standpoint, we can say that trade offsets the difference in relative scarcities. Before trade is opened, cameras are relatively scarce in the domestic economy, because it is not well suited to produce them. Trade diminishes that scarcity. Similarly, grain is relatively scarce in the foreign economy, but trade diminishes that scarcity.

In the circumstances describes by Figure 2-8, where the countries' demand conditions are identical, a difference in relative scarcities is necessarily due to a difference in supply conditions. It could be due, however, to a difference in demand conditions. If two countries have identical transformation curves but different indifference maps, their relative prices will differ before trade, but the opening of trade will equalize their prices and be beneficial.

To take account of this last possibility, the law of comparative advantage can be restated in terms of price differences rather than cost differences:

In a world of competitive markets, trade will occur and be beneficial whenever countries' relative prices would be different without trade.

The difference in pretrade prices can be due to a difference in supply (cost) conditions, a difference in demand conditions, or a combination of the two.

OFFER CURVES AND INTERNATIONAL EQUILIBRIUM

Figure 2-8 describes equilibrium with trade between two countries. The trade triangles are identical. It does not show, however, how market processes establish equilibrium. This can be done most easily by deriving an *offer curve* to summarize the relevant conditions in each country, and by putting the two countries' offer curves together.

Deriving an Offer Curve

An offer curve for the domestic economy is shown in the upper part of Figure 2-9. The horizontal axis records its trade in cameras. The vertical axis records its trade in grain. The offer curve *JOJ* uses information about relative prices to connect the two trade flows. When the relative price of a camera is equal to the slope of the line *FF'* drawn through the origin of the diagram, the domestic economy demands *OV* of camera imports and supplies *VW* of grain exports.

The offer curve is derived from the transformation curve and the indifference map. Look back at Figure 2-8. When the relative price of a camera is equal to the slope of U_0 at *E*, the domestic economy does not make any export offer whatsoever. This point corresponds to the origin of the offer curve in Figure 2-9. The slope of the offer curve at its origin, given by the dashed line tangent to that curve, corresponds to the slope of U_0 at *E*. When the relative price of a camera is lower than the price at *E* in Figure 2-8, the domestic economy offers grain exports in exchange for camera imports. When that price is equal to the slope of *PD*, for instance, it offers *MD* of grain exports and demands *MP* of camera imports. These quantities are repro-

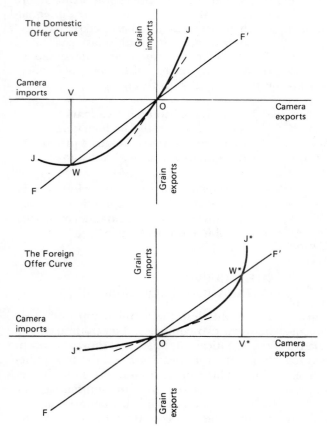

FIGURE 2-9   Offer Curves
The curve *JOJ* shows export supply and import demand at each set of prices. When the relative price of a camera is given by the slope of the line *FF'*, the domestic economy will supply *VW* of grain exports and demand *OV* of camera imports. The triangle *OWV* corresponds to the trade triangle *MPD* in Figure 2-8. The slope of *JOJ* at its origin, shown by the dashed line, corresponds to the slope of the domestic transformation curve at *E* in Figure 2-8. The domestic economy will not offer or demand either good when world and domestic prices are the same.

duced in Figure 2-9. The line *FF'* has the same slope as the line *PD* in Figure 2-8. The offer of grain exports is *VW* (equal to *MD*), and the demand for camera imports is *OV* (equal to *MP*). The trade triangle *OVW* generated by the line *FF'* is identical to the trade triangle *MPD* in Figure 2-8.

Each point on the offer curve *JOJ* produces one such triangle. Those in the southwest quadrant of Figure 2-9 are generated when the relative price of a camera is lower than the price given by the slope of U_0 at *E* in Figure 2-8. The domestic economy offers grain exports in exchange for camera imports. Those in the northeast quadrant are generated when the relative price of a camera is higher than the price at *E*. The domestic economy offers camera exports in exchange for grain imports. (The offer curve cannot pass through the northwest quadrant when trade is balanced; the economy cannot demand camera and grain imports simultaneously. The curve cannot pass through the southeast quadrant either; the economy cannot offer camera and grain exports simultaneously.)

Each point on the offer curve corresponds uniquely to a production point on the transformation curve and to a consumption point on an indifference curve. Offer curves, said one economist, resemble the hands of a clock. They convey much information in a simple fashion but are driven by a complex mechanism hidden behind them.

The offer curve for the foreign economy is shown in the lower part of Figure 2-9. It is flatter at its origin than the domestic offer curve, because U_0 is flatter at E^* than at *E*. Furthermore, the line *FF'* intersects the foreign offer curve in the northeast quadrant. The foreign economy supplies OV^* of camera exports and demands V^*W^* of grain imports. The trade triangle OV^*W^* is identical to the trade triangle $M^*D^*P^*$ in Figure 2-8.

Combining Offer Curves

Figure 2-9 could be used to locate equilibrium. We could rotate the line *FF'* through each origin, generating pairs of triangles, until we located the matching pair *OVW* and OV^*W^*. One country's trade triangle would have to lie in the southwest quadrant, the other in the northeast quadrant, and they would have to be identical. By putting the two offer curves in one diagram, however, we can locate equilibrium more easily.

This is done in Figure 2-10. The domestic offer curve *JOJ* is drawn as before. The foreign offer curve J^*OJ^* has been flipped over. The part appearing in the southwest quadrant now shows the foreign supply of camera exports and the foreign demand for grain imports. This is done so that the horizontal axis of the diagram can measure the foreign supply of camera exports along with the domestic demand for camera imports, and the vertical axis can measure foreign demand for grain imports along with the domestic supply of grain exports.

If the two offer curves had the same slopes at the origin, they would be tangent to each other and would not intersect at any other point in Figure 2-10, not in the northeast quadrant nor the southwest quadrant. This repeats a statement made before. If two countries' internal prices are identical when there is no trade between them, they will not engage in trade when markets are unified. If the curves have different slopes at the origin, however, they will always intersect at some other point in the northeast quadrant or the southwest quadrant. This repeats the law of comparative advantage stated in terms of price differences. If two countries' prices differ when there is no trade between them, they will engage in trade when markets are unified.

In Figure 2-10, the domestic offer curve

FIGURE 2-10   Locating Equilibrium with Offer Curves
The domestic offer curve, *JOJ*, is drawn as in Figure 2-9. The foreign offer curve, *J*OJ**, is redrawn with axes reversed. The intersection of the curves at *W* defines equilibrium with trade. World prices (the terms of trade) are given by the slope of *FF'*, drawn from *O* to *W*. Domestic exports of grain, *VW*, equal foreign imports, and domestic imports of cameras, *OV*, equal foreign exports.

is steeper at the origin than the foreign offer curve, so the two curves intersect at *W* in the southwest quadrant. World prices (the terms of trade) are given by the slope of the line drawn from the origin to the intersection. It is labeled *FF'* as usual. The domestic economy demands *OV* of camera imports, and the foreign economy supplies them. The foreign economy demands *VW* of grain imports, and the domestic economy supplies them.

Figure 2-10 can be used to repeat an earlier exercise. Let the relative price of a camera be equal to the slope of the line *HH'*, steeper than *FF'*. How will world markets respond? The domestic economy will move to *Z*, and the foreign economy will move to *Z**. The domestic offer of grain exports will be smaller than the foreign demand, and there will thus be an excess demand for grain on the world market. The domestic demand for camera imports will be smaller than the foreign supply, and there will be an excess supply of cameras. The relative price of a camera

will fall, making *HH'* flatter and narrowing the gap between *Z* and *Z** on the two countries' offer curves. It will continue to fall until *HH'* coincides with *FF'*, and equilibrium is established at *W*.

Offer curves are used in subsequent chapters to show how demand conditions, economic growth, and other phenomena affect the distribution of the gains from trade and to study the effects of tariffs and other trade barriers.

SUMMARY

Ordinary demand and supply curves can be used to illustrate the main effects of trade. When the world price of a commodity is lower than its domestic price, trade raises the quantity demanded by domestic consumers (the consumption effect) and reduces the quantity supplied by domestic producers (the production effect). The increase in consumer surplus is larger than the decrease in producer surplus, and the difference measures the gain from trade.

But trade involves a two-way flow of commodities and can be analyzed completely only by using a general-equilibrium model. The simplest model of this sort contains two commodities. Supply conditions are represented by a transformation curve. Demand conditions are represented by an indifference map. In a closed economy, the markets for the two commodities can clear when production and consumption take place at a common point; it is the tangency between an indifference curve and the transformation curve. In an open economy, they can clear when production and consumption take place at different points defining a trade triangle. The gains from trade are represented by the movement to a higher indifference curve. They can be decomposed into gains from international exchange and gains from international specialization.

A two-country model is required to show how the terms of trade are established. The quantity of exports offered by one country must equal the quantity of imports demanded by the other. (The two countries' trade triangles must be identical.) The terms of trade determine how the gains from trade are distributed. Offer curves are helpful in showing how market forces establish the terms of trade, and they can

be used to illustrate the law of comparative advantage. Trade will take place and be beneficial whenever two countries' relative prices would be different without trade.

RECOMMENDED READINGS

On transformation curves, indifference curves, and trade patterns, see Wassily W. Leontief, "The Use of Indifference Curves in the Analysis of Foreign Trade," *Quarterly Journal of Economics,* 24 (May 1933); reprinted in American Economic Association, *Readings in the Theory of International Trade* (Philadelphia: Blakiston, 1949), ch. 10.

For another derivation of the offer curve and extensive applications, see James E. Meade, *A Geometry of International Trade* (London: Allen & Unwin, 1952), chs. i–v.

For a way to illustrate the gains from trade without using community indifference curves, see Peter B. Kenen, "On the Geometry of Welfare Economics," *Quarterly Journal of Economics,* 71 (August 1957); reprinted in P. B. Kenen, *Essays in International Economics* (Princeton, N.J.: Princeton University Press, 1980).

The most general restatement of the gains from trade, going beyond the two-commodity model, is given by Paul A. Samuelson, "The Gains from International Trade Once Again," *Economic Journal,* 72 (December 1962); reprinted in J. N. Bhagwati, ed., *International Trade: Selected Readings* (Cambridge, Mass.: MIT Press, 1981), ch. 10.

3

ECONOMIC EFFICIENCY AND COMPARATIVE ADVANTAGE

SOURCES OF COMPARATIVE ADVANTAGE

Opportunities for international trade arise because of differences in supply and demand conditions. That was the main point made in Chapter 2. In that chapter, however, we focused on supply conditions and will continue to do so. This chapter and the next will show how they affect transformation curves, influencing patterns of production and trade.

The shape and position of a country's transformation curve are determined by its factor supplies and the efficiency with which it uses them. They depend on its endowment of land, labor, and capital and on the state of technology. Differences between endowments and technologies lead to predictable differences between transformation curves.

There are large differences in national endowments, reflecting the gifts of nature and the fruits of human effort. The gifts of nature are not distributed evenly. Some countries are rich in petroleum, coal, and iron ore. Some have huge waterfalls that can generate cheap power. Some have fertile plains that can grow large grain crops. Some have the rainfall needed to grow rice or cotton. Others have too much or next to none. Most important, some countries have the combinations of resources required for certain activities. One may have the plains *and* rainfall needed to grow grain. Another may have a rich deposit of iron ore close to a river that can carry iron to coal. Finally, some countries have supplies of labor adequate to operate large factories, but others have too little labor to work their land efficiently.

In one sense, a country's labor force is a

natural resource. In another, it reflects human ingenuity. Mere numbers are the gift of nature. But the skills and attitudes of workers reflect schooling and training, and they have large effects on comparative advantage. A country rich in people but poor in skills may be well suited to certain activities but not to producing manufactured goods. Going a step farther, it is important to distinguish among types of skills. Some countries have large numbers of factory workers adept at assembling cars, cameras, and calculators. Others have abundant supplies of scientists and engineers, and they can specialize in new, research-laden products. It has been argued, for example, that the United States enjoys a comparative advantage in research and innovation but loses out to other countries as each new product ages, the market for it grows, and the knowledge needed to produce it spreads to other countries. There is a *product cycle*, it is said, that forces the United States to race ahead in research and innovation merely to stand still in world markets.

One part of a country's capital stock is embodied in its labor force. Scientific, industrial, and other skills represent investments in human capital. Another part of the capital stock is embodied in physical equipment: roads, harbors, and dams; trucks, aircraft, ships, and turbines; factories and office buildings; tractors, lathes, and computers. These represent the portion of past output that was saved and invested, rather than being consumed.

Natural resources and knowledge can interact powerfully. Bauxite was not valued as a natural resource until the development of the electrolytic process for extracting aluminum and of the cheap power required by that process. Aluminum itself was not very valuable until the metal-working industries found ways to use it instead of steel. Pitchblende was a geological cu-

riosity until human ingenuity and malevolence found a use for uranium and ways to separate its isotopes.

Population and technology interact, too. Modern mass-production methods need large markets and are apt to take root first in regions of dense settlement that can consume large lots of standardized products. As a consequence, such regions are likely to enjoy a comparative advantage in mass-produced goods and may be able to retain it vis-à-vis regions that start later or start on a smaller scale. Notice that comparative advantage has a time dimension. It depends on the state of technology at a given moment and on the subsequent diffusion of technology. It also depends on the history of capital accumulation and the composition of the capital stock resulting from it.

The models presented in this chapter and the next cannot capture all these important phenomena. In fact, they make drastic simplifications. The quantity of labor is uniform within each country. Workers can move from industry to industry without retraining. Capital can be transferred, too, without the need to extract it from one embodiment and lodge it in another—without running down the stock of tractors and building up the stock of computers. In this initial presentation, moreover, labor and capital requirements are fixed in each industry and country, although they differ among industries and may differ among countries. Labor and capital are complements rather than substitutes. This assumption is not relaxed until Chapter 5.

The model developed in this chapter shows how differences in technology create opportunities for trade. It is based on the example that David Ricardo used to prove the law of comparative advantage. The model developed in the next chapter concentrates on differences in factor supplies. It is an outgrowth of the model used by Eli

Heckscher and Bertil Ohlin, two Swedish economists, to demonstrate the influence of factor endowments on international specialization.

PRODUCTION AND TRADE IN THE RICARDIAN MODEL

Consider two countries, Britain and Portugal, producing two commodities, cloth and wine. Each country has a fixed supply of labor. Each industry requires a fixed number of workers to produce one unit of output.[1] These requirements describe the state of technology in each country, and they are not the same in Britain and Portugal.

The British Economy

Britain has 180 workers. Three are needed to produce 1 yard of cloth per day. Six are needed to produce 1 gallon of wine. This is all we need to know to derive the British transformation curve. If all of Britain's workers were employed in cloth production, the country could produce 60 yards per day; this quantity is represented by the distance OB in Figure 3-1. If all those workers were employed in wine pro-

duction, Britain could produce 30 gallons per day; this quantity is represented by the distance OB'. The line BB' is Britain's transformation curve.

Unlike the transformation curves in Chapter 2, this curve is a straight line. Its slope is given by the ratio of labor requirements in the cloth and wine industries, and labor requirements are constant. They do not depend on the levels of output. The relative price of cloth is given by the slope of the transformation curve and is thus equal to the ratio of labor requirements. When Britain produces both commodities, then, the relative price of cloth is fixed. It does not depend on demand conditions.

An algebraic demonstration of these propositions is supplied by Note 3-1. Here is a numerical illustration of the relationship between the relative price of cloth and the ratio of labor requirements. Under competitive conditions, prices equal total unit costs in long-run equilibrium. When labor is the only input, moreover, total unit costs must equal unit labor costs. Therefore,

Price = wage rate
$\qquad\qquad$ × labor required per unit of output

and

$$\frac{\text{Price of cloth}}{\text{Price of wine}} = \frac{\text{labor required per yard of cloth}}{\text{labor required per gallon of wine}}$$
$$= \frac{3}{6} = \frac{1}{2}$$

which corresponds to the slope of BB' in Figure 3-1, where OB' is half as long as OB.

Although demand conditions do not affect the relative price of cloth, they do affect the output mix. In the absence of foreign trade, equilibrium will be established at E, where the indifference curve U_1 is tangent to the British transformation curve. Cloth output will be OX_1 and will equal cloth consumption. Wine output will be OX_2 and will equal wine consumption.

---

[1] The Ricardian model is thus based on a labor theory of value, but Ricardo and other Classical economists used that theory only as an analytical convenience. It was not the centerpiece of Classical economics in the way that it became the centerpiece of Marxian economics. There is a role for capital in Classical economics, but it is complementary to the role of labor. Capital is used to hire labor (and buy raw materials) during the "period of production" before output emerges and can be sold. Capital constitutes a "wages fund" rather than a stock of machinery. When wage rates are the same in each industry, however, the wages fund is proportional to employment in each industry. Therefore, total costs, including the costs of capital, are proportional to labor costs. When working with the Ricardian model, then, we can focus exclusively on labor requirements. When working with the factor-endowments model, where capital plays a separate role in production, we have to take account of capital requirements, too.

Note 3-1

There are $\bar{L}$ workers, and all are employed in cloth or wine production,

$$\bar{L} = L_1 + L_2$$

where L_1 is employment in cloth production and L_2 is employment in wine production. A fixed number of workers, a_1, is required to produce 1 yard of cloth and another fixed number, a_2, to produce 1 gallon of wine. Therefore,

$$L_1 = a_1 x_1 \quad \text{and} \quad L_2 = a_2 x_2$$

where x_1 is cloth output and x_2 is wine output.

Substituting into the labor equation,

$$\bar{L} = a_1 x_1 + a_2 x_2$$

Solving for x_2,

$$x_2 = \frac{\bar{L}}{a_2} - \left(\frac{a_1}{a_2}\right) x_1$$

That is the equation for the transformation curve. Its vertical intercept is $\bar{L}/a_2$, measuring wine output when there is no cloth output. Its slope, the marginal rate of transformation, is a_1/a_2, the ratio of labor requirements, and it is constant.

When labor is the only factor of production, wages are the only costs. When labor requirements are constant, average and marginal costs are equal. As prices must equal marginal costs under competitive conditions,

$$p_1 = wa_1 \quad \text{and} \quad p_2 = wa_2$$

where p_1 is the price of cloth, p_2 is the price of wine, and w is the wage rate. (There is only one wage rate, because workers can move freely between sectors.) Therefore,

$$\frac{p_1}{p_2} = \frac{wa_1}{wa_2} = \frac{a_1}{a_2}$$

The relative price of cloth, p_1/p_2, is equal to the ratio of labor requirements and thus equal to the slope of the transformation curve.

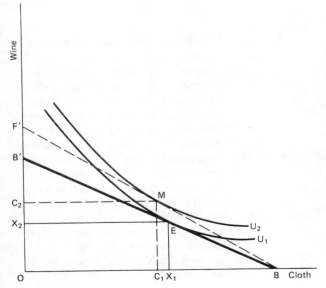

FIGURE 3-1 The British Economy
With a fixed supply of labor and fixed labor requirements in each sector, Britain's transformation curve is BB'. Before trade is opened, the relative price of cloth is given by the slope of the transformation curve, and equilibrium is established at E, where an indifference curve is tangent to the transformation curve. Britain produces and consumes OX_1 cloth and OX_2 wine. When trade is opened and the relative price of cloth is given by the slope of the line BF', Britain specializes completely in cloth production, producing OB. Consumers move to M, demanding OC_1 cloth and OC_2 wine. The trade triangle is $C_1 BM$.

Trade and the Offer Curve

If Britain confronts foreign prices different from domestic prices, it will specialize completely in one commodity and import the other. Let the slope of the line BF' be the relative price of cloth in the world market. Britain will abandon the production of wine, and all of Britain's workers will be hired to make cloth. Cloth output will rise to OB. When cloth is the only output, moreover, OB also measures real income in terms of cloth, and BF' is the budget line. British consumers will move to M, where BF' is tangent to the indifference curve U_2. They will demand OC_1 cloth and OC_2 wine. Therefore, Britain's export offer will be BC_1 cloth (domestic output *less* domestic demand), and Britain's import demand will be OC_2 wine. The trade triangle will be C_1BM.

The same outcome is depicted in Figure 3-2, which shows the British offer curve. The linear segment AA' corresponds to the transformation curve BB' in Figure 3-1,

having the same length and slope. The distance OA' is equal to the distance EB in Figure 3-1. It shows that British firms will increase cloth output from OX_1 to OB whenever the relative price of cloth exceeds by the slightest amount the slope of the transformation curve. The extension $A'J'$ reflects the behavior of British consumers as the relative price of cloth rises farther, moving consumers to points such as M in Figure 3-1. The distance OA is equal to the distance EB' in Figure 3-1, showing that British firms will increase wine output from OX_2 to OB' whenever the relative price of cloth falls below the slope of the transformation curve. The extension AJ reflects the behavior of British consumers as the relative price of cloth continues to fall. When the relative price of cloth is equal to the slope of FF' (which equals the slope of BF' in Figure 3-1), Britain's export offer is OV cloth, its import demand is VW wine, and the trade triangle is OVW, which is identical to the triangle C_1BM in Figure 3-1.

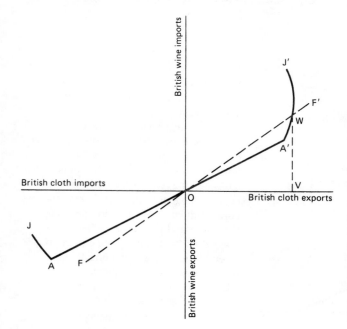

FIGURE 3-2 The British Offer Curve The offer curve $JAOA'J'$ is derived from the transformation curve and indifference map shown in Figure 3-1. The segment AA' corresponds to the transformation curve BB'. The distance OA' equals EB in Figure 3-1, and the distance OA equals EB'. When the relative price of cloth is higher than that given by the slope of the segment AA', Britain will offer cloth exports and demand wine imports. When it equals the slope of FF' (the slope of BF' in Figure 3-1), Britain will offer OV cloth exports (equal to C_1B in Figure 3-1) in exchange for VW wine imports (equal to C_1M in Figure 3-1).

The Portuguese Economy

Portugal is smaller than Britain. It has only 120 workers. But Portuguese technology is more advanced. Two workers are required to produce 1 yard of cloth, compared with three in Britain. Three workers are required to produce 1 gallon of wine, compared with six in Britain. If Portugal employs all its workers in cloth production, its output will be 60 yards per day; this is the distance OP in Figure 3-3. If it employs all of them in wine production, its output will be 40 gallons per day; this is the distance OP'. The Portuguese transformation curve is PP' and is steeper than the British curve. Portugal has an *absolute* advantage in both wine and cloth production, because it has smaller labor requirements in both industries. It has a *comparative* advantage in wine production, however, because its absolute advantage is bigger in that industry.

In the absence of foreign trade, the Portuguese economy will be at E^*, producing OX_1^* of cloth and OX_2^* of wine. If trade is opened with the outside world and the relative price of cloth is given by the slope of FP' (equal to that of BF' in Figure 3-1), Portugal will specialize completely in wine,

producing OP' gallons. Its export offer will be C_2^*P' wine, and its import demand will be OC_1^* cloth.[2] The trade triangle is $C_2^*M^*P'$. The linear segment of Portugal's offer curve will be steeper than that of Britain's offer curve, because its transformation curve is steeper.

Equilibrium in International Trade

In Chapter 1, you read a famous passage in which Adam Smith argued for free trade, but were warned that Smith's argument was not precise enough. Recall one sentence:

---

[2] Figures 3-1 and 3-3 have been drawn to illustrate two possibilities mentioned in Chapter 2. In Figure 3-1, OC_1 is smaller than OX_1. The opening of trade reduces British cloth consumption. Accordingly, the British export offer, C_1B, is larger than the increase in cloth production, X_1B. In Figure 3-3, OC_2^* is larger than OX_2^*. The opening of trade raises Portuguese wine consumption, and the Portuguese export offer, C_2^*P', is smaller than the increase in wine production, X_2^*P'. British consumers demand more wine and less cloth as wine becomes cheaper in Britain, but Portuguese consumers demand more wine and more cloth as cloth becomes cheaper in Portugal. In both countries, however, consumers gain from trade by moving to higher indifference curves.

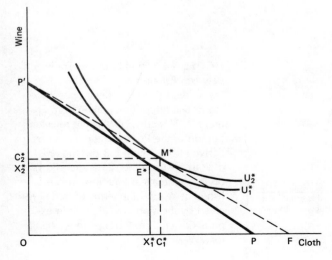

FIGURE 3-3 The Portuguese Economy
Portugal's transformation curve is PP'. Before trade is opened, the relative price of cloth is given by the slope of the transformation curve, and equilibrium is established at E^*. Portugal produces and consumes OX_1^* cloth and OX_2^* wine. When trade is opened and the relative price of cloth is given by the slope of the line FP' (equal to the slope of BF' in Figure 3-1), Portugal specializes completely in wine, producing OP'. Consumers move to M^*, demanding OC_1^* cloth and OC_2^* wine. The trade triangle is $C_2^*M^*P'$.

If a foreign country can supply us with a commodity cheaper than we ourselves can make it, better buy it of them with some part of the produce of our own industry, employed in a way in which we have some advantage.

If the words "cheaper" and "advantage' are not qualified carefully, this sentence cannot forecast trade between Britain and Portugal. Wine is "cheaper" in Portugal than in Britain, because labor requirements are lower, but cloth is cheaper, too. Britain does not have an outright "advantage" in wine or cloth production. If "cheaper" is used in the relative sense and "advantage" in the comparative sense, however, the passage tells us what we need to know. As wine is relatively cheap in Portugal and cloth relatively cheap in Britain, there can be gainful trade. Portugal can export wine, and Britain can export cloth.

In the Ricardian model, demand conditions do not affect internal prices before trade is opened. Prices are determined by labor requirements. Therefore, demand conditions cannot affect the trade pattern. But they do affect the terms of trade and, therefore, the distribution of the gains from trade.

The British offer curve is flatter at its origin than the Portuguese offer curve. In consequence, the two curves must intersect in the northeast quadrant when they are put together in a single diagram. That quadrant is shown in Figure 3-4. The relevant portion of the British offer curve is *OJ*. (It is the portion shown as *OA'J'* in Figure 3-2.) The relevant portion of the Portuguese offer curve is *OJ**. (It is the one that would lie in the southwest quadrant when drawn by itself, but it has been flipped over as in Chapter 2 to measure matching trade flows on the same axes.) Equilibrium in trade between Britain and Portugal is established at *W*. Britain exports *OV* cloth and imports *VW* wine. Portugal exports *VW* wine and imports *OV* cloth. The terms of trade are given by the slope of *OF*. Because each country lies on the curved portion of its offer curve, both countries gain from trade. Consumers reach indifference curves higher than those tangent to their countries' transformation curves.

There are at least two instances, however, in which one country's consumers can appropriate all the gains from trade. Re-

FIGURE 3-4 Equilibrium in Trade Between Britain and Portugal
The curve *OJ* is the relevant portion of the British offer curve, taken from Figure 3-2. The curve *OJ** is the relevant portion of the Portuguese offer curve, derived from Figure 3-3 but flipped over to measure the same trade flows on the same axes. Equilibrium is established at *W*, and the terms of trade are given by the slope of *OF*. Britain exports *OV* cloth to Portugal in exchange for *VW* wine.

turn momentarily to Figure 3-1. If British tastes are biased strongly in favor of cloth consumption, E will be closer to B, and the segment EB will be shorter. Therefore, the segment OA' of the British offer curve will be shorter, too, causing the curve to look like OJ' in Figure 3-4. Equilibrium in trade between Britain and Portugal will be established at W', and the terms of trade will be given by the slope of the Portuguese offer curve. Portugal will export wine and import cloth but will not specialize completely in wine production; it will continue to produce some cloth. More important, trade will not reduce the relative price of cloth in Portugal, and Portuguese consumers will remain on the same indifference curve they reached before trade was opened (the curve U_1^* in Figure 3-3). Market forces will still cause trade, but Portuguese consumers will not gain or lose. British consumers will appropriate all the gains from trade.

The same thing can happen if the British economy is much smaller than the Portuguese economy. Britain's transformation curve will be shorter, which means that its offer curve will have a shorter linear segment. Once again, the offer curve will look like OJ' in Figure 3-4, and equilibrium will be established at W'. Britain will specialize completely in cloth production, but it will not produce enough to satisfy British and Portuguese demands. Portugal will produce some cloth, and the relative price of cloth in the world market will be what it was in Portugal before trade was opened. Once again, British consumers will appropriate all the gains from trade.

This last result may puzzle you. A small country, you may say, will be relatively weak. Why should its consumers be able to appropriate all the gains from trade? The puzzlement derives from a common mistake—associating economic size with market power. No one is exercising market power in this illustration. Both countries' markets are perfectly competitive, and so

are the sums of those markets. Governments do not attempt to influence quantities or prices. Therefore, a small country can appropriate large gains from trade. The merging of its markets with those of another country will not have much effect on the other country's prices, and it will have no effect at all if the small country is very small indeed. That is the case described by equilibrium at W' in Figure 3-4.

Output Patterns in the Ricardian Model

Demand and supply conditions can generate three sets of outcomes in this simple Ricardian model. They are summarized by Figure 3-5, using a *global* transformation curve, PQB', built up from the national transformation curves. (The British curve is shown here as $P'QB'$. The Portuguese is shown as BPQ.) These are the three outcomes:

1. When the terms of trade are given by the slope of FF', which is steeper than the British transformation curve but flatter than the Portuguese, global output will be at Q. Britain will specialize completely in cloth, producing $P'Q$, and Portugal will specialize completely in wine, producing BQ. This will be the equilibrium point if the two countries' consumers, taken together, demand OB cloth (equal to $P'Q$ produced by Britain) and demand OP' wine (equal to BQ produced by Portugal). Both countries' consumers will gain from trade.

2. When the terms of trade are given by the slope of PQ, which is the Portuguese segment of the global transformation curve, global output will be at some such point as Q'. Britain will specialize completely in cloth, producing $P'Q$, and Portugal will specialize partially in wine, producing OX_2^* wine and BX_1^* cloth. This will be the equilibrium point if the two countries' consumers demand OX_1^* cloth (equal to $P'Q$ produced by Britain *plus* BX_1^* produced by Portugal) and demand OX_2^* wine (equal to OX_2^* produced by Portugal). British consumers will appropriate all the gains from trade. Portuguese consumers will not gain or lose.

3. When the terms of trade are given by the slope of QB', which is the British segment of the

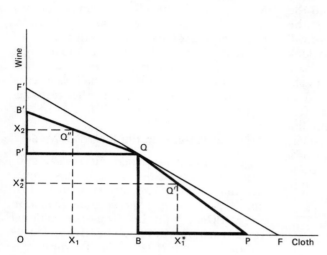

FIGURE 3-5 Demand Conditions and Specialization
When the relative price of cloth is equal to the slope of *FF'* and thus lies between the prices that prevailed in Britain and Portugal before trade was opened, equilibrium will lie at *Q*. Britain will specialize completely in cloth, producing *OB*. Portugal will specialize completely in wine, producing *OP'*. When the relative price of cloth is equal to the price that prevailed in Portugal before trade was opened, equilibrium will lie at some such point as *Q'*. Britain will specialize completely in cloth, producing *OB*. Portugal will produce OX_2^* wine and BX_1^* cloth. Portugal will export enough wine to satisfy British demand and pay for its own imports of cloth.

global transformation curve, global output will be at some such point as *Q"*. Britain will specialize partially in cloth, producing OX_1 cloth and $P'X_2$ wine, and Portugal will specialize completely in wine, producing *BQ*. This will be the equilibrium point if the two countries' consumers demand OX_1 cloth (equal to OX_1 produced by Britain) and demand OX_2 wine (equal to *BQ* produced by Portugal *plus* $P'X_2$ produced by Britain). Portuguese consumers will appropriate all the gains from trade. British consumers will not gain or lose.

In all three cases, of course, Britain will export cloth and Portugal will export wine. The pattern of trade is determined completely by comparative costs, represented by the slopes of the countries' transformation curves. The pattern of production, however, is determined by demand and supply conditions jointly, because they determine the terms of trade. The distribution of the gains from trade is likewise affected by demand conditions, because of their influence on the terms of trade.

WAGES, PRICES, AND COMPARATIVE ADVANTAGE

British consumers do not examine comparative costs when deciding whether to buy British or Portuguese cloth. They look at the prices charged for the two countries' products. It is therefore important to show how market forces translate comparative costs into market prices. This is done algebraically in Note 3-2 and is illustrated here by a numerical example.

Recall the statement made before, that prices have to equal unit labor costs in the Ricardian model. When we know the wage rate in each country, then, and labor requirements per unit of output, we know the country's prices. Exchange rates must be used, however, to compare two countries' prices.

Suppose that the British wage rage is £1.50 per day and that the exchange rate between the pound and dollar is $2.00 per pound. The British wage rate works out at

Note 3-2

When Britain specializes completely in cloth production, the world price of cloth, p_1, is given by its labor cost in Britain:

$$p_1 = wa_1$$

where w and a_1 have the definitions given in Note 3-1. When Portugal specializes completely in wine production, the world price of wine, p_2, is given by its labor cost in Portugal:

$$p_2 = w^*a_2^*$$

where w^* is the Portuguese wage rate, expressed in the same currency as the British wage rate, and a_2^* is the labor requirement in Portuguese wine production.

The relative price of cloth is thus given by

$$\frac{p_1}{p_2} = \left(\frac{w}{w^*}\right)\left(\frac{a_1}{a_2^*}\right)$$

When the relative price of cloth must change to reach equilibrium in world markets, the change must be brought about by altering the wage-rate ratio w/w^*, because a_1 and a_2^* are constants.

The first equation in this note can also be used to obtain the real wage in Britain measured in cloth:

$$\frac{w}{p_1} = \frac{1}{a_1}$$

The higher the labor requirement in cloth production, the lower the productivity of labor and the lower the real wage measured in cloth.

The real wage in Britain measured in wine can then be defined by

$$\frac{w}{p_2} = \left(\frac{w}{p_1}\right)\left(\frac{p_1}{p_2}\right) = \left(\frac{1}{a_1}\right)\left(\frac{p_1}{p_2}\right)$$

The higher the relative price of cloth, the higher the real wage measured in wine, given the labor requirement in cloth production. In other words, the real wage measured in wine, the import good, rises as Britain's terms of trade improve.

$3.00 per day. As three workers are required to produce 1 yard of cloth in Britain and six are required to produce 1 gallon of wine, these will be the dollar prices of British goods:

Price of British cloth	$ 9.00 per yard
Price of British wine	18.00 per gallon

Suppose that the Portuguese wage rate is £150 per day and that the exchange rate between the escudo and dollar is $0.02 per escudo. The Portuguese wage rate also works out at $3.00 per day. As two workers are required to produce 1 yard of cloth in Portugal and three are required to produce 1 gallon of wine, these will be the dollar prices of Portuguese goods:

Price of Portuguese cloth	$6.00 per yard
Price of Portuguese wine	9.00 per gallon

If trade were opened at these wage rates and exchange rates, both products would be cheaper in Portugal than in Britain. Portugal's absolute advantage in cloth and wine would mask Britain's comparative advantage in cloth.

Under these circumstances, however, both countries' consumers would try to buy both cloth and wine in Portugal, increasing the demand for labor in Portugal and decreasing the demand for labor in Britain. The wage rate would rise in Portugal and fall in Britain. Suppose that the Portuguese wage rate rose to $3.75 per day when expressed in dollars while the British wage rate fell to $2.25 per day. The price of cloth in Portugal would rise to $7.50 per yard, the price in Britain would fall to $6.75, and both countries' consumers would start to buy British cloth. The price of wine in Portugal would rise to $11.25 per gallon, the price in Britain would fall to $13.50, and both countries' consumers would continue to buy Portuguese wine. The changes in the two countries' wage rates would allow market prices to reflect Britain's comparative advantage in cloth. They would offset Portugal's absolute advantage by charging a higher wage for more efficient Portuguese labor.[3]

---

[3] The same adjustment could be made by changing exchange rates. Suppose that wage rates are absolutely rigid in Britain and Portugal while exchange rates are free to fluctuate in response to changes in supply and demand. With the opening of trade at the initial exchange rates, the increase in demand for Portuguese goods will raise the demand for escudos, which are needed to pay for Portuguese goods, and will thus raise the dollar price of the escudo. The decrease in demand for British goods will reduce the demand for pounds, and will thus reduce the dollar price of the pound. If the escudo rises to $0.025 per escudo, the Portuguese wage rate will work out at $3.75 per day. If the pound falls to $1.50 per pound, the British wage rate will work out at $2.25 per day. These are the numbers used in the text. Changes in exchange rates, then, can substitute for changes in wage rates. This conclusion has an important implication. Any judgment one might make about wage-rate relationships is an implicit judgment about the exchange rates used to express the wage rates in a common currency. Judgments about exchange rates, however, must be made in a broad macroeconomic framework, which is therefore the *only* legitimate framework for making broad judgments about wage-rate relations.

We cannot know where wage rates will settle without the information conveyed by the offer curves in Figure 3-4. The terms of trade between Britain and Portugal are determined by supply and demand conditions, and we need to know the terms of trade before we can know where wage rates will come to rest. When Britain produces cloth and Portugal produces wine, the terms of trade, wage rates, and labor requirements must satisfy this equation:

$$\frac{\text{Price of British cloth}}{\text{Price of Portuguese wine}}$$
$$= \frac{\text{British labor requirement per yard}}{\text{Portuguese labor requirement per gallon}}$$
$$\times \frac{\text{British wage rate}}{\text{Portuguese wage rate}}$$

We cannot know the wage-rate ratio without knowing the terms of trade and labor requirements per unit of output.

One general conclusion can be drawn without knowing more, and it is one of the most important points made by trade theory. Differences in wage rates usually reflect differences in productivity. Countries with low wage rates do not necessarily have an "unfair" advantage over their competitors. Their low wage rates compensate for low productivity and are needed to translate comparative advantage into market prices. This point will crop up again when we look at a famous statistical test of the Ricardian model and at the "cheap foreign labor" argument for tariffs.

The algebra of Note 3-2 makes one other point. In the Ricardian trade model, there is a neat relationship between the consumers' gains from trade and the real wage rate expressed in terms of the imported good. Consider the relationship from the British standpoint. When prices equal unit labor costs, the real wage expressed in cloth is given by

$$\frac{\text{British wage rate}}{\text{Price of cloth}}$$
$$= \frac{1}{\text{labor requirement per yard in Britain}}$$

Therefore, this real wage is one-third of a yard of cloth per day. Furthermore, it is not affected by the opening of trade, because cloth production continues in Britain, and labor requirements do not change. But the real wage expressed in wine is given by

British wage rate
Price of wine

$$= \frac{\text{British wage rate}}{\text{price of cloth}} \times \frac{\text{price of cloth}}{\text{price of wine}}$$

Therefore, this real wage will rise whenever the opening of trade raises the relative price of cloth in Britain, permitting British consumers to gain from trade. Coming at this proposition from the opposite direction, the real wage in wine will be unaffected by the opening of trade when Britain does not specialize completely in cloth production and British consumers do not gain from trade.

When there is more than one factor of production, as in the factor-endowments model studied in the next chapter, the relationship between the gains from trade and the real wage is more complicated. It will require careful examination.

EXTENDING THE RICARDIAN MODEL

The Ricardian model is easily extended to cover many countries and commodities if it is extended one way at a time.

Trade with Many Countries

In Figure 3-6, the model is extended to cover four countries producing wine and cloth. The four countries' transformation curves are identified by Roman numerals, and they are used to build a global transformation curve much like the one in Figure 3-5.

Suppose that the terms of trade are equal to the slope of FF'. Global output will be at Q, and all four countries will specialize completely. Countries I and II will specialize in cloth, producing OX_1 between them. They will export cloth in exchange for wine. Countries III and IV will specialize in wine, producing OX_2 between them. They will export wine in exchange for cloth. World markets will be in equilibrium if the four countries' consumers demand

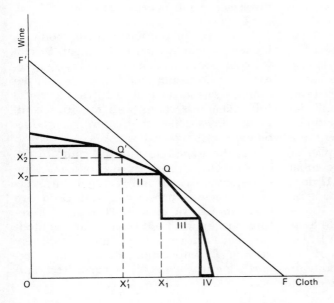

FIGURE 3-6 Trade with Two Commodities and Many Countries
When the relative price of cloth is equal to the slope of FF', countries I and II specialize completely in cloth, and countries III and IV specialize completely in wine. Total cloth output is OX_1, and total wine output is OX_2. When the relative price of cloth is equal to the slope of country II's transformation curve, country I specializes completely in cloth, country II produces some cloth and some wine, and countries III and IV specialize completely in wine. Total cloth output is OX_1', and total wine output is OX_2'.

OX_1 cloth and OX_2 wine. All four countries' consumers will gain from trade. The situation is perfectly analogous to the situation at Q in Figure 3-5.

Suppose that the terms of trade are equal instead to the slope of country II's transformation curve. Global output will be at a point such as Q', and three countries will specialize completely. Country I will specialize in cloth and will therefore export cloth in exchange for wine. Countries III and IV will specialize in wine and will export wine in exchange for cloth. Country II, however, will produce both cloth and wine, and we cannot say anything about its trade. World markets will be in equilibrium if the four countries' consumers demand OX_1' cloth and OX_2' wine. Consumers in countries I, III, and IV will gain from trade, but those in country II will not gain or lose. The situation is closely analogous to the one at Q' in Figure 3-5, apart from the uncertainty about trade by country II.

Why is there uncertainty in one case and not the other? In Figure 3-5, which dealt with the two-country case, one country had to export wine when the other imported it. But Britain imported wine at Q', because it specialized completely in cloth, and we could therefore be sure that Portugal exported wine, even when it did not specialize completely. In Figure 3-6, which deals with the four-country case, some country has to export wine when others import it, but this does not tell us what country II will do. Country I must import wine, and countries III and IV must export wine. Hence, there are three possibilities at Q': (1) Supplies of wine from countries III and IV are equal to country I's demand, and country II does not trade at all. (2) Supplies from countries III and IV are smaller than country I's demand, so country II exports wine. (3) Supplies from countries III and IV are larger than country I's demand, so country II imports wine. Demand and supply conditions

in the world as a whole, including those in country II, dictate the trade pattern for country II.

Trade with Many Commodities

Figure 3-7 extends the Ricardian model to cover four commodities produced by two countries, Britain and Portugal. It uses information about labor requirements to show how the costs of producing each commodity depend on relative wage rates. When labor is the only input, this statement must be true:

$$\frac{\text{British production cost}}{\text{Portuguese production cost}}$$
$$= \frac{\text{labor requirement in Britain}}{\text{labor requirement in Portugal}}$$
$$\times \frac{\text{British wage rate}}{\text{Portuguese wage rate}}$$

The slope of the cloth line in Figure 3-7 is $(3/2)$, because three workers are needed to produce 1 yard of cloth in Britain and two workers are needed to produce 1 yard in Portugal. The slope of the wine line is $(6/3)$ or $(2/1)$, because six workers are needed to produce 1 gallon of wine in Britain and three workers are needed to produce 1 gallon in Portugal.

If the cost of producing a commodity is higher in Britain than in Portugal, Britain will not produce that commodity. Therefore, the horizontal line in Figure 3-7, denoting cost ratios equal to 1, plays a crucial role. Its intersections with the four commodity lines define the pattern of production at each wage-rate ratio.

Let the wage-rate ratio be equal to the distance OW'. The costs of producing wine are equal in Britain and Portugal. The costs of producing corn, steel, and cloth are lower in Britain than in Portugal. Therefore, Britain will produce all four commodities, but Portugal will specialize completely in wine. By implication, Portugal must export wine in exchange for corn, steel, and

FIGURE 3-7 Trade with Two Countries and Many Commodities
In equilibrium, the wage-rate ratio can be no lower than *OW'* and no higher than *OW"*. If it were lower than *OW'*, the costs of producing all four commodities would be lower in Britain than in Portugal; if it were higher than *OW"*, the costs of producing all four commodities would be higher in Britain than in Portugal. When the wage-rate ratio is OW_1, Britain produces cloth and steel, and Portugal produces corn and wine. When the ratio is OW_2, Britain produces cloth, Portugal produces corn and wine, and both countries produce steel.

cloth, and Britain must import wine although it produces some wine of its own. (Note that the wage-rate ratio cannot be lower than *OW'*, because Portugal must produce something.)

Let the wage-rate ratio be equal to the distance *OW"*. The costs of producing cloth are equal in Britain and Portugal. The costs of producing steel, corn, and wine are higher in Britain than in Portugal. Therefore, Britain will specialize completely in cloth, and Portugal will produce all four commodities. By implication, Britain must export cloth in exchange for steel, corn, and wine, and Portugal must import cloth although it produces some cloth of its own. (The wage-rate ratio cannot be higher than *OW"*, because Britain must produce something.)

When equilibrium occurs at one of these extremes, there are no ambiguities. The pattern of production is clear. So is the trade pattern. Outcomes are equally clear at certain other points. If the wage-rate ra-

tio equals the distance OW_1, the costs of producing cloth and steel are lower in Britain than in Portugal, and those of producing corn and wine are lower in Portugal. Therefore, Britain will specialize completely in cloth and steel, and Portugal will specialize completely in corn and wine. Britain will export cloth and steel in exchange for corn and wine.

At certain other points, however, the trade pattern is ambiguous. If the wage-rate ratio equals the distance OW_2, the cost of producing cloth is lower in Britain, the costs of producing corn and wine are lower in Portugal, and the costs of producing steel are the same in the two countries. The pattern of production is clear. Britain will produce cloth and steel; Portugal will produce steel, corn, and wine. Some trade flows are equally clear. Britain will export cloth; Portugal will export corn and wine. But we cannot know which country will export steel. If Britain is large compared to Portugal, it may be able to satisfy the world's demand for cloth and its own demand for steel, yet have enough labor to export steel to Portugal. If Portugal is large compared to Britain, it may be able to satisfy the world's demands for wine and cloth and its own demand for steel, yet have enough labor to export steel to Britain.

When there are more commodities than countries, there can be uncertainty about the trade pattern, even when the pattern of production is clear. The problem is similar to that encountered when there are more countries than commodities. When the output point is Q' in Figure 3-6, we do not know what product country II will export. When the wage-rate ratio is OW_2 in Figure 3-7, we do not know what country will export steel. When there are many countries or commodities, it is always possible to forecast some trade flows, but others cannot be predicted without comprehensive information on supply and demand conditions.

AN EMPIRICAL TEST
OF THE RICARDIAN MODEL

Economic models can never be completely realistic. If they were not simpler than the real world, they could not help us to cut through complexities and organize our thinking. The Ricardian model is far too simple to describe precisely the causes and

effects of international trade. The main statements made by that model, however, highlight important relationships, and some of them are verifiable. They can be used to forecast actual trade flows, despite the existence of tariffs and other trade barriers.

One test of the Ricardian model was conducted by Robert M. Stern, and his work is summarized in Table 3-1. It looks at the exports of Great Britain and the United States in 1950, a year for which we have detailed data on productivity (labor requirements) in those countries' industries. It concentrates on British and American exports to third countries, to avoid distortions introduced by differences in British and American trade barriers.[4]

---

[4] British exports to the United States are affected by American trade barriers, and American exports to Britain are affected by British barriers. Therefore, the two countries' *bilateral* trade is distorted by the differences between their trade barriers. British and American exports to France are both affected by French trade barriers, but the effects on the two countries' exports are more or less uniform. (This was not completely true in 1950, when some European countries discriminated against goods from the United States to conserve scarce dollars, and members of the British Commonwealth gave preferential treatment to British exports. It would not be true today, because Britain and France are members of the European Community, whose members accept each others' exports freely.)

TABLE 3-1 Output per Worker and Comparative Export Performance, Great Britain and The United States, 1950

		NUMBER OF INDUSTRIES	
Difference in Output per Worker	*Total*	*U.S. Exports Smaller than British*	*U.S. Exports Larger than British*
U.S. output per worker less than 3.4 times British	26	22	4
U.S. output per worker at least 3.4 times British	13	3	10
Total	39	25	14

Source: Robert M. Stern, "British and American Productivity and Comparative Costs in International Trade," *Oxford Economic Papers*, 14 (October 1962).

In 1950, output per worker was much higher in the United States than in Great Britain. In other words, labor requirements were much lower. This was true in almost every industry, conferring an absolute advantage on the United States. But wage rates in the United States were about 3.4 times as high as those in Great Britain, washing out that absolute advantage and allowing each country to exploit its comparative advantage.

To show that this was true, we can use the wage differences between the two countries to classify the 39 industries included in Stern's study. In 26 industries, output per worker in the United States was less than 3.4 times as high as in Great Britain. In light of what we have learned from Figure 3-7, we should expect Great Britain to have its comparative advantage in those industries. In 13 other industries, output per worker in the United States was at least 3.4 times as high as in Great Britain, and we should expect the United States to have its comparative advantage in them. These predictions are borne out in Table 3-1. In 22 of the first 26 cases, British exports were larger than American exports. In 10 of the other 13 cases, American exports were larger.

These uniformities are striking. The number of exceptions, seven in all, is smaller than we might anticipate, knowing that tariffs and other trade barriers distort trade flows, that each of the 39 industries contains many firms producing distinct commodities, and that differences in productivity are not the only cause of trade.

SUMMARY

In the Ricardian trade model, cross-country differences in relative prices are due to differences in labor requirements. One country may use less labor in all its industries. Its absolute advantage in efficiency, however, does not prevent it from trading beneficially with other, less efficient countries. It will have a comparative advantage in those activities where its absolute advantage is largest.

As labor requirements are constant in the Ricardian model, labor costs are constant too. Therefore, demand conditions do not determine the trade pattern in the two-country, two-commodity case. They do help to determine the terms of trade, however, and thus influence the distribution of the gains from trade. If one country is much larger than the other (or has tastes biased heavily toward the other's export good), the other country may appropriate all the gains from trade. In this same case, the large country will not specialize completely.

When there are many countries or commodities, demand and supply conditions determine jointly the set of commodities that each country produces and, therefore, the pattern of commodity trade.

Real wage rates are determined by labor requirements and the terms of trade. Money wage rates are determined in the process of transforming absolute into comparative advantage. A country with low labor requirements in all its industries will have a higher money wage than a country with high labor requirements, given the exchange rate between their currencies. Therefore, wage comparisons may be misleading. A country with low wages does not necessarily enjoy an "unfair" advantage in trade; low wages usually reflect low productivity.

This fact shows up clearly in empirical work based on the Ricardian model. Wage rates were higher in the United States than in Great Britain, but productivity was higher, too. The United States had a comparative advantage in those activities where U.S. productivity exceeded British productivity by more than the difference in wage rates.

RECOMMENDED READINGS

The model developed in this chapter is based on the example in David Ricardo, *On the Principles of Political Economy and Taxation*, 1821, ch. vii; the definitive version is in P. Sraffa, ed., *The Works and Correspondence of David Ricardo* (New York: Cambridge University Press, 1953), Vol. I. The contributions of Ricardo and other Classical economists are reviewed in Jacob Viner, *Studies in the Theory of International Trade* (New York: Harper & Row, 1937), ch. viii.

For an early attempt to extend the Ricardian model to many countries and commodities, see Frank D. Graham, "The Theory of International Values Re-examined," *Quarterly Journal of Economics*, 28 (November 1928); reprinted in American Economic Association, *Readings in the Theory of International Trade* (Philadelphia: Blakiston, 1949), ch. 14. Another way of extending the model to many commodities is given in Rudiger Dornbusch, Stanley Fischer, and Paul A. Samuelson, "Comparative Advantage, Trade, and Payments in a Ricardian Model with a Continuum of Goods," *American Economic Review*, 67 (December 1977).

For empirical work on the Ricardian model, see Robert M. Stern, "British and American Productivity and Comparative Costs in International Trade," *Oxford Economic Papers*, 14 (October 1962). Also, G. D. A. MacDougall, "British and American Exports: A Study Suggested by the Theory of Comparative Costs," *Economic Journal*, 61 (December 1951); reprinted in American Economic Association, *Readings in International Economics* (Homewood, Ill.: Richard D. Irwin, 1968), ch. 32.

The "product cycle" approach to comparative advantage mentioned at the start of this chapter is set out in Raymond Vernon, "International Investment and International Trade in the Product Cycle," *Quarterly Journal of Economics*, 80 (May 1966).

CHAPTER

4

FACTOR ENDOWMENTS AND COMPARATIVE ADVANTAGE

THE NEED FOR ANOTHER MODEL

The Ricardian model in Chapter 3 served several important purposes. It furnished an explanation for differences in supply conditions, traced the roles of supply and demand conditions in determining trade patterns and distributing the gains from trade, and directed our attention to the wage-price adjustments needed to achieve equilibrium in international markets. It was extended easily to study trade by many countries and trade in many commodities.

But it shed less light on other important issues: the influence of differences in factor supplies on international specialization and the influence of trade on the income distribution. Another model is needed to study them.

This model was developed by Eli Heckscher and Bertil Ohlin in the 1920s

and was refined thereafter by many economists, including Paul Samuelson. It suppresses deliberately the main cause of trade in the Ricardian model, the differences between countries' labor requirements, by assuming that all countries have the same technologies, and rules out some other causes, too. The versions we will study, for example, rule out the influence of country size by assuming that there are no economies of scale, and they rule out the influence of demand conditions by assuming that consumers have identical tastes.

The Heckscher–Ohlin approach to trade theory, also known as the factor-endowments approach, is based on two suppositions:

1. Commodities differ in their factor requirements. Cars require more capital per

worker than, say, furniture or cloth, and aircraft require more than cars. In other words, commodities can be ranked by *factor intensity*.

2. Countries differ in their factor endowments. Some have much capital per worker and some have very little. In other words, countries can be ranked by *factor abundance*.

These suppositions lead to the fundamental theorem of the Heckscher–Ohlin model. A capital-abundant country will tend to specialize in capital-intensive commodities and will therefore export those commodities in exchange for labor-intensive commodities, relieving its relative scarcity of labor. Putting the theorem in general terms:

Trade is based on differences in factor abundance and reduces the principal effects of those differences.

There are two ways to prove the Heckscher–Ohlin theorem. We can show that differences in factor endowments give rise to differences in transformation curves. This strategy produces the *factor-proportions version* of the Heckscher–Ohlin theorem. Alternatively, we can show that differences in factor prices give rise to differences in commodity prices. This strategy produces the *relative-price version* of the theorem. Under certain strong assumptions, moreover, it leads to another proposition, that trade eliminates differences in factor prices. Both strategies are illustrated in this chapter.

There are several variants of the Heckscher–Ohlin model. The version studied in this chapter borrows an assumption used by the Ricardian model. It works with fixed factor requirements per unit of output. The version studied in Chapter 6 relaxes that assumption. Factor requirements will depend on factor prices.

FACTOR ENDOWMENTS, PRODUCTION, AND TRADE IN THE HECKSCHER–OHLIN MODEL

In the Ricardian model, the shape of the transformation curve depended on labor requirements and on the supply of labor. In the Heckscher–Ohlin model, its shape depends on labor and capital requirements, taken together, and on supplies of labor and capital.

Factor Endowments and the Transformation Curve

If an economy had an unlimited supply of capital, its outputs would depend on labor requirements and on the supply of labor, just as in the Ricardian model. The economy would operate on the line LL' in Figure 4-1, the *labor constraint,* which looks like a Ricardian transformation curve. By using all its labor to grow corn, the economy could produce OL bushels. By using all its labor to make steel, it could produce OL' tons. By dividing its supply of labor between the two activities, the economy could produce combinations of corn and steel lying on LL'. At each point on LL', moreover, the relative price of corn would be given by the slope of the labor constraint, which equals the ratio of labor requirements in the two activities.

If the economy had an unlimited supply of labor, its outputs would depend on capital requirements and on the supply of capital. This situation is described by the line KK', the *capital constraint* for the economy. By using all its capital to grow corn, the economy could produce OK bushels. By using all its capital to make steel, it could produce OK' tons. By dividing its supply of capital between the two activities, the economy could produce combinations of corn and steel lying on KK'. At each point on KK', the relative price of corn would be

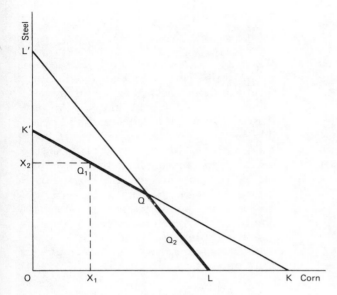

FIGURE 4-1 Fixed Factor Supplies, Factor Requirements, and the Output Mix
The supply of labor and labor requirements determine the position and slope of the labor constraint *LL'*. The supply of capital and capital requirements determine the position and slope of the capital constraint *KK'*. The transformation curve is *LQK'*, and the full-employment output point is Q.

given by the slope of the capital constraint, which equals the ratio of capital requirements.

When supplies of labor and capital are not unlimited, the labor and capital constraints operate together to define an economy's transformation curve. It is *LQK'* in Figure 4-1, and is obtained by asking what the economy can produce with limited supplies of labor and capital. Suppose that it produces OX_1 bushels of corn. Because its supply of capital is limited, its steel output is limited to OX_2 tons.

Three output points are shown in Figure 4-1. At the point just mentioned, Q_1, outputs are determined by the capital constraint, and the relative price of corn is given by the slope of that constraint. The economy is using all its capital, but some of its labor is unemployed. At the point Q_2, by contrast, outputs are determined by the labor constraint, and the relative price of corn is given by the slope of that constraint. The economy is using all its labor, but some of its capital is unemployed. Finally, there is the point Q, where *LL'* and *KK'* inter-

sect, and outputs are determined by both constraints together. The economy is using all its labor and all its capital, and Q can therefore be described as the *full-employment output point*. The relative price of corn at Q is given by demand conditions. When the economy produces and consumes at Q, an indifference curve passes through that point, and the relative price of corn is equal to the slope of that indifference curve.

Note that the labor constraint is steeper than the capital constraint. This says that steel is the capital-intensive commodity and corn the labor-intensive commodity. Proof is provided by Note 4-1, but a simple experiment can make the point clearly. Let the economy start at Q, where both factors of production are fully employed. Suppose that it raises its corn output. It will move to some such point as Q_2, lying on the labor constraint, where labor is fully employed, but some capital is idle. The increase in corn output has absorbed all the labor released by the decrease in steel output, but it has not absorbed all the capital. By implica-

Note 4-1

In the x_1 industry, one unit of output requires a_1 and labor and b_1 capital, so the amounts employed are

$$L_1 = a_1x_1 \quad \text{and} \quad K_1 = b_1x_1$$

In the x_2 industry, one unit of output requires a_2 labor and b_2 capital, so the amounts employed are

$$L_2 = a_2x_2 \quad \text{and} \quad K_2 = b_2x_2$$

When a country's fixed supplies of labor and capital, $\overline{L}$ and $\overline{K}$, are fully employed,

$$\overline{L} = L_1 + L_2 = a_1x_1 + a_2x_2$$
$$\overline{K} = K_1 + K_2 = b_1x_1 + b_2x_2$$

Solving these equations for x_2, we obtain the labor and capital constraint shown in Figure 4-1:

$$x_2 = \frac{\overline{L}}{a_2} - \left(\frac{a_1}{a_2}\right)x_1 \quad \text{and} \quad x_2 = \frac{\overline{K}}{b_2} - \left(\frac{b_1}{b_2}\right)x_1$$

When $(a_1/a_2) > (b_1/b_2)$, the labor constraint is steeper, as in Figure 4-1. But this condition can be written as $(b_2/a_2) > (b_1/a_1)$. Furthermore, b_2/a_2 is the ratio of capital to labor required by a unit of x_2 output, known as the capital-labor ratio, k_2, in the x_2 industry. Similarly, b_1/a_1 is the capital-labor ratio, k_1, in the x_1 industry. When the labor constraint is steeper, then, it is because $k_2 > k_1$ (the x_2 industry is more capital intensive than the x_1 industry).

Solving the labor and capital constraints for x_1 and x_2, the full-employment outputs,

$$x_1 = \frac{b_2\overline{L} - a_2\overline{K}}{a_1b_2 - a_2b_1} \quad \text{and} \quad x_2 = \frac{a_1\overline{K} - b_1\overline{L}}{a_1b_2 - a_2b_1}$$

But $(a_1b_2) > (a_2b_1)$ when $(b_2/a_2) > (b_1/a_1)$, so the denominator is positive. Therefore, an increase in $\overline{K}$ raises x_2 output and reduces x_1 output, proving the Rybczynski theorem.

tion, steel uses more capital per worker than corn, and steel is the capital-intensive commodity.

The Rybczynski Theorem

What happens with an increase in the supply of capital? The answer is given by Figure 4-2. The capital constraint shifts outward from KK' to $K^*K^{*'}$, and the transformation curve becomes $LQ^*K^{*'}$. The full-employment output point is displaced from Q to Q^*, so steel output rises and corn output falls.

This outcome is known as the Rybczynski theorem, after the economist who discovered it, and can be stated in this form:

When factor supplies are fully employed and factor requirements are given, an increase in the supply of one factor of production raises the output of the commodity which uses that factor intensively and reduces the output of the other commodity.

This theorem is basic to the functioning of the Heckscher–Ohlin model. It is used shortly to show how international differences in factor endowments determine the trade pattern. It is used again in Chapter 6 to show how changes in factor endowments affect the terms of trade.

A formal proof of the Rybczynski theorem is given in Note 4-1. Another illustra-

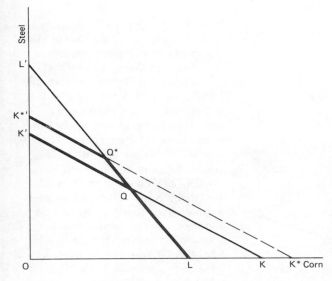

FIGURE 4-2 The Rybczynski Theorem
An increase in the supply of capital
shifts the transformation curve from
LQK' to $LQ*K*'$ and shifts the
full-employment point from Q to $Q*$.
As steel is more capital intensive than
corn, the full-employment output of
steel rises and the full-employment
output of corn falls.

tion is given in Figure 4-3, which shows explicitly how factor intensities and factor supplies determine the location of the full-employment output point. The slope of the line OC measures the *capital-labor ratio* in corn production, and distances along the line measure corn output. When output is OC_1 bushels, then, $O\overline{L}$ labor and $\overline{L}C_1$ capital are used to grow corn. The slope of the line OS measures the capital-labor ratio in steel production, and distances along the line measure steel output. When output is OS_1 tons, then, $O\overline{K}$ capital and $\overline{K}S_1$ labor are used to make steel. As steel is the capital-intensive commodity, OS is steeper than OC.

Suppose that the economy has $O\overline{L}$ labor and $O\overline{K}$ capital. Its factor endowment is defined by the point N. If it produces nothing but corn, the labor-intensive commodity, it can grow OC_1 bushels; it uses all its labor, but C_1N of its capital is idle. If it produces nothing but steel, the capital-intensive commodity, it can make OS_1 tons. It uses all its capital, but S_1N of its labor is idle. There is just one way that it can use its entire factor endowment. Draw a line NT parallel to OS until it intersects OC at T. As

NT is parallel to OS, it can be used to measure steel output, along with the quantities of labor and capital used in making steel. At T, then, the economy produces NT steel and OT corn. These are the amounts that were shown at Q, the full-employment output point in Figures 4-1 and 4-2.

Increase the supply of capital to $O\overline{K}'$, holding the supply of labor constant at $O\overline{L}$. The new factor endowment is given by N' and the full-employment outputs of steel and corn are given by T'. The economy can produce $N'T'$ steel and OT' corn. But $N'T'$ is longer than NT, and OT' is shorter than OT. Therefore, the increase in the supply of capital raises the full-employment output of steel, the capital-intensive commodity, and reduces the full-employment output of corn, the labor-intensive commodity.

The Factor-Proportions Version of the Heckscher–Ohlin Theorem

To see how a difference in factor endowments leads to international trade, consider two countries, Manymen and Fewmen, described by Figure 4-4. They have

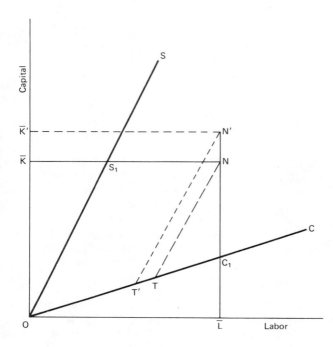

FIGURE 4-3 Fixed Factor Supplies, Factor Intensities, and the Output Mix Distances along OC measure corn output, and its slope measures the capital-labor ratio in corn production. Distances along OS measure steel output, and its slope measures the capital-labor ratio in steel production. A country with $O\overline{L}$ labor and $O\overline{K}$ capital can produce as much as OC_1 corn (but C_1N of its capital will be idle). It can produce as much as OS_1 steel (but S_1N of its labor will be idle). It can produce combinations of corn and steel, however, and one such combination employs both factors fully. It is OT corn and NT steel. An increase in the supply of capital to $O\overline{K}'$ raises the full-employment output of steel to $N'T'$ and reduces the full-employment output of corn to OT'.

FIGURE 4-4 Equilibrium in Trade Between Manymen and Fewmen Before trade is opened, Manymen is at the full-employment point Q on its transformation curve LQK. The relative price of corn is given by the slope of the indifference curve U_0 where it intersects Q. Fewmen is at the labor-constrained point E^* on its transformation curve $L^*Q^*K^*$. The relative price of corn is given by the slope of the indifference curve U_0 where it intersects E^*. When trade is opened, the relative price of corn is given by the slopes of the lines QP and P^*Q^*. In Manymen, producers stay at Q, and consumers move to P on the indifference curve U_1. The trade triangle is MQP. In Fewmen, producers move to the full-employment point Q^*, increasing steel output and reducing corn output, and consumers move to P^* on the indifference curve U_2. The trade triangle is $M^*P^*Q^*$.

identical demand conditions, represented by the indifference curves U_0, U_1, and U_2. They have the same technologies, which means that the slopes of the labor and capital constraints will be the same in the two countries. They differ only in their factor endowments. Manymen has a large labor force and small stock of capital. Fewmen has a small labor force and large stock of capital.

The Rybczynski theorem tells us how their transformation curves will differ. The curve for Manymen is LQK. The curve for Fewmen is $L^*Q^*K^*$. When labor and capital are fully employed in each country, at Q and Q^*, Manymen produces more corn than Fewmen, because corn is the labor-intensive commodity, and Fewmen produces more steel than Manymen, because steel is the capital-intensive commodity.[1]

Before trade is opened between the two countries, Manymen produces at its full-employment point Q, putting its consumers on U_0, the highest indifference curve they can reach. The relative price of corn in Manymen is equal to the slope of U_0 at Q. Fewmen produces at E^*, on its labor constraint, putting its consumers on that same indifference curve, and the relative price of corn in Fewmen is equal to the slope of U_0 at E^* (and equal to the slope of the transformation curve.)[2] The relative price of

corn, the labor-intensive commodity, is lower in Manymen, the labor-abundant country, because U_0 is flatter at Q than at E^*. Therefore, there is an opportunity for trade.

After trade is opened, the relative price of corn must be the same in Manymen and Fewmen. It is given by the slopes of the (parallel) lines QP and P^*Q^* connecting the countries' production and consumption points and forming their trade triangles. The relative price of corn must rise in Manymen and fall in Fewmen. In Manymen, production remains at Q, but consumers move to P on the indifference curve U_1. Its trade triangle is MQP. In Fewmen, production move to Q^*, and consumers move to P^* on the indifference curve U_2. Its trade triangle is $M^*P^*Q^*$. Manymen exports MQ corn, the labor-intensive commodity. Fewmen exports M^*Q^* steel, the capital-intensive commodity.

Note that both countries wind up at their full-employment output points. This diagram, then, illustrates two possibilities. Outputs do not change in Manymen, which started and remains at its full-employment point. In other words, its gains from trade are gains from international exchange. But outputs change in Fewmen as it moves from E^* to Q^*, increasing its steel production and decreasing its corn production. Its gains from trade include gains from international specialization.

We have thus proved the factor-proportions version of the Heckscher–Ohlin theorem, linking the trade pattern to factor endowments. The labor-abundant country always exports the labor-intensive commodity, and increases its production of that commodity if it did not start at its full-

---

[1] The two countries' transformation curves can be derived by supposing that they start with the same factor supplies, then increasing the supply of labor in Manymen and the supply of capital in Fewmen. Suppose that they start with factor supplies that give them the transformation curve L^*ZK in Figure 4-4. An increase in the supply of labor shifts the labor constraint from L^*Z to LQ, giving the transformation curve for Manymen. An increase in the supply of capital shifts the capital constraint from KZ to K^*Q^*, giving the transformation curve for Fewmen.

[2] It is possible to draw U_0 in a way that would put Fewmen at its full-employment point and is likewise possible to draw it in a way that would put Manymen on its capital constraint. The case shown in Figure 4-4 was chosen to cover two possibilities at once. It also rules out one possibility. When countries have identi-

cal demand conditions, the relative price of corn cannot be higher in Manymen than Fewmen. (The two countries need not start on the same indifference curve; this solution was chosen for convenience, as in Chapter 2.)

employment point. The capital-abundant country always exports the capital-intensive commodity, and increases its production of that commodity if it did start at its full-employment point.[3]

FACTOR PRICES, COMMODITY PRICES, AND TRADE IN THE HECKSCHER–OHLIN MODEL

There is a strong relationship between commodity and factor prices in the Heckscher–Ohlin model. An increase in the relative price of the labor-intensive commodity raises the relative price of labor, defined as the wage of labor divided by the return to capital.

Factor Use and Factor Prices

Look back at Figure 4-1, where labor and capital constraints were used to derive the transformation curve. At a point such as Q_1 on the capital constraint, some of the country's labor is unemployed. In the absence of institutional arrangements that keep wage rates from falling (union contracts, for example, and minimum-wage laws), the wage rate must be zero. Therefore, the relative price of labor must be zero. At a point such as Q_2 on the labor constraint, some of the country's capital is unemployed, and the return to capital must be zero. Therefore, the relative price of labor must be infinite. At Q, both factors are fully employed, the wage rate and return to capital are both positive, and the relative price of labor must be positive, too.

At points such as Q_1, moreover, the relative price of corn is given by the slope of the capital constraint, and it is not lower at

any other point on the transformation curve. At points such as Q_2, that price is given by the slope of the labor constraint, and it is not higher at any other point. At Q, the price must lie between these two extremes.

These results are summarized in Figure 4-5. The horizontal axis shows the relative price of corn, and the vertical axis shows the relative price of labor. The distance OP' is the relative price of corn when Q_1 is the output point, and that price can go no lower. The curve in the diagram says that the relative price of labor is zero at that point, because some of the country's labor is unemployed and the wage rate must be zero. The distance OP'' is the relative price of corn when Q_2 is the output point, and that price can go no higher. The curve says that the relative price of labor tends to infinity at that point, because some of the country's capital is unemployed and the return to capital must be zero. The curve itself makes an additional statement. The relative price of labor rises with the relative price of corn, because corn is the labor-intensive commodity. When the relative price of corn is OP_1, the relative price of labor is OW_1; when the relative price of corn rises to OP_2, the relative price of labor rises to OW_2.

A proof of this last proposition is given by Note 4-2, which also shows that the relationship in Figure 4-5 holds in both countries, Manymen and Fewmen, because they have identical technologies. They have different transformation curves, because they have different factor endowments. But both of them will have idle workers (and wage rates will be zero) when the relative price of corn is equal to the slope of the capital constraint and thus equal to OP' in Figure 4-5. Both of them will have idle capital (and the return to capital will be zero) when the relative price of corn is equal to the slope of the labor constraint and thus equal to OP''. And the curves connecting

---

[3] In the more general version of the model presented in Chapter 6, the labor-abundant country will always increase its production of the labor-intensive commodity, and the capital-abundant country will always increase its production of the capital-intensive commodity.

FIGURE 4-5 Factor and Commodity Prices
When the relative price of corn is given by the slope of the capital constraint, shown here by the distance OP', some labor is unemployed, the wage rate is zero, and the relative price of labor is zero. When the relative price of corn is given by the slope of the labor constraint, shown here by the distance OP'', some capital is unemployed, the return to capital is zero, and the relative price of labor is infinite. When the relative price of corn lies between these extremes, the relative price of labor is positive and rises with the relative price of corn. When the relative price of corn rises from OP_1 to OP_2, the relative price of labor rises from OW_1 to OW_2.

Note 4-2

In long-run competitive equilibrium, prices equal total unit costs, which are equal in turn to factor payments per unit of output. Therefore,

$$p_1 = wa_1 + rb_1 \quad \text{and} \quad p_2 = wa_2 + rb_2$$

where p_1 and p_2 are the prices of x_1 and x_2, w is the wage rate, and r is the return to capital. Solving these equations simultaneously,

$$w = \frac{b_2 p_1 - b_1 p_2}{a_1 b_2 - a_2 b_1} \quad \text{and} \quad r = \frac{a_1 p_2 - a_2 p_1}{a_1 b_2 - a_2 b_1}$$

Note 4-1 showed that the denominators are positive when the x_2 industry is more capital intensive than the x_1 industry. Denote them hereafter by D. Furthermore, the numerators are positive at the full-employment point. Rewrite the equations:

$$w = \frac{b_2 p_2}{D}\left(\frac{p_1}{p_2} - \frac{b_1}{b_2}\right) \quad \text{and}$$

$$r = \frac{a_2 p_2}{D}\left(\frac{a_1}{a_2} - \frac{p_1}{p_2}\right)$$

We know that $(p_1/p_2) > (b_1/b_2)$. Otherwise, the economy would be on its capital constraint. Therefore, w is positive. We know that $(p_1/p_2) < (a_1/a_2)$. Otherwise, the economy would be on its labor constraint. Therefore, r is positive.

To derive the relationship shown in Figure 4-5, divide one equation by the other:

$$\frac{w}{r} = \frac{b_2}{a_2}\left[\frac{(p_1/p_2) - (b_1/b_2)}{(a_1/a_2) - (p_1/p_2)}\right]$$

Therefore, an increase in p_1/p_2 raises w/r; it increases the numerator and decreases the denominator.

those two points will be the same in both countries, because they have the same factor requirements.

Figure 4-5 has three uses. It can be used to prove the relative-price version of the Heckscher–Ohlin theorem, to show how trade affects the income distribution in each country, and to show when trade will equalize their factor prices.

The Relative-Price Version of the Heckscher–Ohlin Theorem

Before the opening of trade, the relative price of corn must be lower in Manymen than in Fewmen. That was true in Figure 4-4, where Manymen began at Q and Fewmen began at E^*. It is also true when both countries start at their full-employment points. Therefore, the curve in Figure 4-5 tells us that the relative price of labor had to be lower in Manymen before trade was opened, which leads us directly to the relative-price version of the Heckscher–Ohlin theorem. If the relative price of labor is lower in one country before trade is opened, the relative price of the labor-intensive commodity must likewise be lower, and the country will export the labor-intensive commodity.

The Stolper–Samuelson Theorem

The effects of trade on factor prices and the income distribution are described by the Stolper–Samuelson theorem, named after the two economists who proved it. It can be put this way:

> **The opening of trade raises the relative price of labor in the labor-abundant country and reduces it in the capital-abundant country.**

By implication, trade will raise the *share* of labor in the real income of the labor-abundant country and reduce the share of capital. It will have the opposite effect on the income distribution in the capital-abundant country.

The proof of the theorem is simple. We have already seen that trade raises the relative price of corn in the labor-abundant country. An increase in the relative price of corn, however, raises the relative price of labor, the factor used intensively in growing corn.

The Stolper–Samuelson theorem can be put in stronger form. The increase in the relative price of corn that occurs in the labor-abundant country must raise the real wage and reduce the real return to capital. The decrease that occurs in the capital-abundant country must reduce the real wage and raise the real return to capital. These assertions hold, moreover, for both definitions of the real wage, in terms of steel or corn, and for both definitions of the real return to capital. This strong form of the Stolper–Samuelson theorem is proved in Note 4-3.

The Stolper–Samuelson theorem can be put differently. The opening of trade reduces the effects of differences in factor endowments. Labor is abundant in Manymen and scarce in Fewmen, a fact reflected by the countries' factor prices before trade is opened. The relative price of labor is lower in Manymen than in Fewmen. By raising the relative price of labor in Manymen and reducing it in Fewmen, trade reduces the effect of the difference in factor endowments.

The Factor-Price-Equalization Theorem

The factor-price-equalization theorem carries this conclusion to its logical limit. If there were no trade barriers or transport costs, trade would *equalize* the two countries' factor prices, not merely reduce the difference between them. It would therefore eliminate completely the effect of the difference in factor endowments.

Note 4-3

The equations for w and r in Note 4-2 can be used to show how a change in relative prices affects the real wage rate and real return to capital.

Beginning with the real wage and the real return measured in units of x_2, divide both sides of both equations by p_2:

$$\frac{w}{p_2} = \frac{b_2}{D}\left(\frac{p_1}{p_2} - \frac{b_1}{b_2}\right) \quad \text{and} \quad \frac{r}{p_2} = \frac{a_2}{D}\left(\frac{a_1}{a_2} - \frac{p_1}{p_2}\right)$$

Therefore, an increase in p_1/p_2, the relative price of the labor-intensive good, raises the real wage of labor and reduces the real return to capital when both are measured in x_2.

Turning to the real wage and real return measured in units of x_1, divide both sides of both equations by p_1:

$$\frac{w}{p_1} = \left(\frac{b_2}{D}\right)\left(\frac{p_2}{p_1}\right)\left(\frac{p_1}{p_2} - \frac{b_1}{b_2}\right)$$

$$= \frac{b_2}{D}\left[1 - \left(\frac{b_1}{b_2}\right)\left(\frac{p_2}{p_1}\right)\right]$$

$$\frac{r}{p_1} = \left(\frac{a_2}{D}\right)\left(\frac{p_2}{p_1}\right)\left(\frac{a_1}{a_2} - \frac{p_1}{p_2}\right)$$

$$= \frac{a_2}{D}\left[\left(\frac{a_1}{a_2}\right)\left(\frac{p_2}{p_1}\right) - 1\right]$$

But p_2/p_1 falls when p_1/p_2 rises, raising the numerator of the first equation and reducing the numerator of the second. Therefore, an increase in the relative price of the labor-intensive good raises the real wage of labor and reduces the real return to capital when both are measured in x_1.

Notice, finally the implications of these equations for the factor-price-equalization theorem. When p_1/p_2 is the same in both countries, real wage rates and real returns to capital are the same in both countries.

If there were no trade barriers or transport costs, trade would equalize completely the relative prices of corn in Manymen and Fewmen. That is what it did in Figure 4-4. When those countries have the same technologies, moreover, they will share the relationship described by Figure 4-5, connecting the relative prices of labor and corn. Therefore, trade would equalize completely the relative prices of labor in Manymen and Fewmen. If the relative prices of corn were equalized at OP_1 in Figure 4-5, the relative prices of labor would be equalized at OW_1.

This theorem can be extended in the same way as the Stolper–Samuelson theorem. If there were no trade barriers or transport costs, trade would equalize the two countries' real wage rates and would also equalize their real returns to capital. This strong form of the theorem is proved in Note 4-3, and is taken up again in Chapter 6.

EXTENDING THE HECKSCHER–OHLIN MODEL

The Heckscher–Ohlin model can be extended by adding more countries, more commodities, and more factors of production. When we move in one direction at a time, however, we run into difficulties.

Adding Countries

When we add a third country by itself, the pattern of trade becomes ambiguous, much as it was in Figure 3-6, which extended the Ricardian model. The country with the largest stock of capital per worker will export the capital-intensive commodity, and the country with the smallest stock per worker will export the labor-intensive commodity. But we cannot predict the trade of the third country without detailed information about supply and demand conditions. All three countries will produce at their full-employment points; the pattern of production is unambiguous. The third country's trade, however, can go either way.

Adding Commodities

When we add a third commodity by itself, the pattern of production becomes ambiguous. Consider again a country that has $O\bar{L}$ labor and $O\bar{K}$ capital. When there are two commodities, corn and steel, the country can employ its factors fully by producing at T in Figure 4-6, where it grows

OT corn and makes NT steel. When it can manufacture blankets, too, and the capital intensity of that activity is given by the slope of the line OB, it has other ways to use its factors fully. It can produce at T', where it manufactures OT' blankets and makes NT' steel. It can also produce more complicated combinations. Draw a line HH' parallel to OB. The country can produce OH corn, HH' blankets, and NH' steel. When the number of commodities exceeds the number of factors, we cannot predict production in each country. And when we do not know the pattern of production, we cannot predict the pattern of trade.

It is still possible, however, to make useful statements about the factor content of a country's trade. It can be shown, for example, that Manymen's exports are more labor intensive, on average, than Fewmen's exports. It can likewise be shown that trade has the usual effects on factor prices. The relative price of labor rises in Manymen and falls in Fewmen, and trade can still equalize the two countries' factor prices.

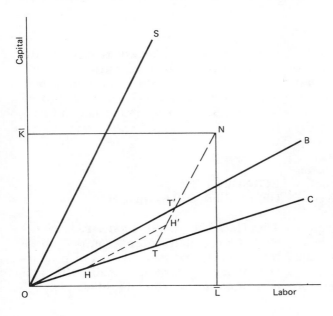

FIGURE 4-6 Fixed Factor Supplies, Factor Intensities, and the Output Mix When the Number of Commodities Exceeds the Number of Factors A country with $O\bar{L}$ labor and $O\bar{K}$ capital can employ both factors fully by producing OT corn and NT steel. It can also do so by producing OT' blankets and NT' steel. And it can do so by producing OH corn, HH' blankets, and NH' steel.

Adding Factors

When we add a third factor by itself, the Heckscher–Ohlin model tends to break down. The number of commodities is too small to determine the prices of the factors of production. It is therefore impossible to identify an abundant factor in each country, to forecast the trade pattern, or to forecast the effects of trade on factor prices and the income distribution.

Another Approach

The Heckscher–Ohlin model can be extended neatly to more complicated cases by adding countries, commodities, and factors of production at the same time, but only in a way that satisfies a special condition. The number of countries must equal the number of commodities, which must equal the number of factors. (The two-country, two-commodity, two-factor model is, of course, the smallest that can satisfy this special condition.) In models that are "even" in this sense, each country will have a full-employment point at which it produces a collection of commodities that is uniquely linked to its factor endowment. Factor prices will differ from country to country before trade is opened, and trade will have predictable effects on factor prices.

But it is hard to make simple statements about these large models. When there are many factors of production, it is hard to say that one factor is "the" abundant factor in a particular country. It is also hard to say that a particular commodity is intensive in one factor. The detailed study of these models may be more interesting to mathematicians than to economists.

EMPIRICAL WORK ON THE HECKSCHER–OHLIN MODEL

The first and most famous quantitative study of the Heckscher–Ohlin model was conducted by Wassily Leontief, using trade data and factor requirements for the United States. Some of his results are shown in Table 4-1, along with results obtained by Robert Baldwin, who worked with later data.

The Leontief Paradox

Leontief computed the amounts of capital and labor required to produce $1 million of U.S. exports in 1951 and those required to produce $1 million of import-competing commodities. Believing that the United States is a capital-abundant country and invoking the Heckscher–Ohlin theorem, Leontief expected to show that U.S. export production is more capital intensive than U.S. import-competing production. That is not what he found. The capital-labor ratio was about $13,000 per worker year in export production and about $13,700 per worker year in import-competing production. Looking at his numbers in another way, they say that a $1 million increase in U.S. exports balanced by an increase in U.S. imports and, therefore, a cutback in import-competing production, would reduce the demand for capital by about $46,000 and raise the demand for labor by about 6 worker years. Baldwin's calculations lead to similar results.[4]

Many efforts have been made to resolve this paradox and have helped us to understand the strengths and weaknesses of the Heckscher–Ohlin model. Some concentrated on the underlying logic of the model, with particular attention to the possibility of *demand reversals* and *factor reversals* that can upset the principal predictions of the model. Others concentrated on the lim-

---

[4] Using data for 1972, however, another study comes up with rather different findings. The capital-labor ratio is higher in export production, and a balanced increase in U.S. trade raises the demands for capital *and* labor. See Robert M. Stern and Keith E. Maskus, "Determinants of the Structure of U.S. Foreign Trade, 1958–76," *Journal of International Economics,* 11 (May 1981).

TABLE 4-1   Domestic Capital and Labor Requirements of Export and Import-Competing Production in the United States, 1951 and 1962

| | REQUIREMENTS PER MILLION DOLLARS OF PRODUCTION | | |
Computation	Capital ($ thousands)	Labor (worker years)	Capital per Worker ($ thousands)
Trade in 1951 and input requirements for 1947 (Leontief):			
Export production	2,257	174	12.97
Import-competing production	2,303	168	13.71
Effect on factor use of balanced increase in trade	−46	+6	—
Trade in 1962 and input requirements for 1958 (Baldwin):			
Export production	1,876	131	14.32
Import-competing production	2,132	119	17.92
Effect on factor use of balanced increase in trade	−256	+12	—

Sources: Wassily W. Leontief, "Factor Proportions and the Structure of American Trade: Further Theoretical and Empirical Analysis," *Review of Economics and Statistics*, 38 (November 1956), and Robert E. Baldwin, "Determinants of the Commodity Structure of U.S. Trade," *American Economic Review*, 61 (March 1971).

itations of the two-factor framework and ways of introducing additional factors of production into empirical and theoretical work.

Demand Reversals and Factor Reversals

What is a demand reversal and how might it explain the Leontief paradox? Suppose that the United States had more capital per worker than its trading partners, the supposition with which Leontief began, but that tastes in the United States were more strongly biased in favor of capital-intensive commodities. In the absence of international trade, the relative price of labor might be lower, not higher, than in other countries, and the United States would export labor-intensive commodities with the opening of trade. It was this possibility that led economists to distinguish carefully between definitions of factor abundance in terms of factor supplies and

in terms of relative factor prices, the distinction that produced the two versions of the Heckscher–Ohlin theorem. (Those versions coincided earlier in this chapter, where Manymen exported the labor-intensive commodity, because demand conditions were identical in Manymen and Fewmen.)

Demand reversals, however, are not likely to explain the Leontief paradox. Evidence about demand conditions suggests that they are similar in the major industrial countries that account for the largest part of world trade. If there were important differences, moreover, they would probably reflect differences in income levels, which cannot explain the paradox. Consumers with high incomes tend to demand large quantities of services, and services tend to be labor intensive. We would therefore expect demand conditions in the United States, a high-income country, to raise the relative price of labor rather than reduce it.

A factor reversal is a difference between countries' rankings of commodities according to factor intensities. There would be a factor reversal if steel were more capital intensive than corn in the United States, but corn were more capital intensive than steel in other countries. If the United States exported corn and other countries exported steel, and we looked at the factor requirements of U.S. foreign trade, we would find that its export production was less capital intensive than its import-competing production. When we looked at the factor requirements of other countries' trade, however, we would find that their export production was also less capital intensive than their import-competing production. These findings would not resolve the Leontief paradox, but they would warn us against drawing general conclusions from calculations based on one country's data, which is what Leontief tried to do.

Factor reversals do occur, although their frequency is subject to dispute, and they need not be due to differences in technology. When we come to the general version of the Heckscher–Ohlin model, where factor intensities depend on factor prices, we will see that factor reversals can occur even when countries have access to the same technologies. As a practical matter, however, factor reversals do not appear to account for the Leontief paradox. In fact, the one reversal that has been well documented makes the paradox more paradoxical. The United States does export corn, along with other agricultural commodities, but agriculture is capital intensive in the United States and labor intensive in other countries.[5] By removing agricultural commodities from the trade calculations, then, we would reduce even further the capital intensity of U.S. export production.

[5] See Seiji Naya, "Natural Resources, Factor Mix, and Factor Reversal in International Trade," *American Economic Review*, 57 (May 1967).

Natural Resources, Skills, and Human Capital

Soon after the publication of Leontief's work, two economists suggested explanations of his paradox that have one theme in common. The two-factor form of the Heckscher–Ohlin model, using only capital and labor, is not sufficiently realistic.

Jaroslav Vanek called attention to the role of nonagricultural land, represented by the roles of raw materials in U.S. foreign trade.[6] As minerals bulk large on the import side, import-competing production may be regarded as being more intensive in *non*agricultural land than is export production. Vanek went on to argue that capital and land are complementary in the production of raw materials, especially in the United States, so that the apparent capital intensity of import-competing production shown by Leontief's calculations may actually reflect the land intensity of that production.

Donald Keesing pointed out that it may be misleading to treat labor as a single factor of production. When we subdivide the U.S. labor force by skill, we find that export production is more skill intensive in the United States than import-competing production.[7] It may therefore be best to think

[6] Jaroslav Vanek, "The Natural Resource Content of Foreign Trade, 1870–1955, and the Relative Abundance of Natural Resources in the United States," *Review of Economics and Statistics*, 41 (May 1959).

[7] Donald B. Keesing, "Labor Skills and Comparative Advantage," *American Economic Review*, 56 (May 1966). Keesing's explanation was anticipated by Leontief, who suggested that American labor is more efficient than foreign labor. Keesing also drew attention to the great intensity with which U.S. export industries employ scientific skills, thus linking the notion of skill intensity to a notion mentioned in Chapter 3, that the United States enjoys a comparative advantage in research-intensive products. See Donald B. Keesing, "The Impact of Research and Development on United States Trade," in P. B. Kenen and R. Lawrence, eds., *The Open Economy* (New York: Columbia University Press, 1968).

TABLE 4-2   Factor Intensities and the Structure of U.S. Trade

Factor Requirement	Effect on Export Measure
Physical capital in dollars	Negative
Human capital in dollars	Positive
Labor in worker years	Negative

Source: William H. Branson and Nikolaos Monoyios, "Factor Inputs in U.S. Trade," *Journal of International Economics,* 7 (May, 1977). Export measure is difference between exports and imports.

of the United States as a skill-abundant country. Alternatively, we may treat skills as investments in human capital, estimate the amounts of human capital employed in export production and import-competing production, and add these estimates of human capital to Leontief's estimates of physical capital. This procedure reverses the paradox. Export production in the United States turns out to be more capital intensive than import-competing production.[8]

Both points have been pursued in more recent investigations. Table 4-2 summarizes one such study, which looks at the ability of factor requirements to explain an *export measure* for each class of commodities. (The export measure is the difference between exports and imports in that class.) Physical capital and raw labor are shown to have negative effects on the export measure; industries intensive in these factors appear mainly on the import side rather than the export side. Human capital is shown to have a positive effect; industries intensive in that factor appear mainly on the export side. This particular study, then, does not resolve the Leontief paradox. It tends in-

stead to ratify Keesing's suggestion that the United States is abundantly endowed with skills or human capital.

Table 4-3 summarizes another study covering some 60 countries, which looks at the ability of factor endowments to explain cross-country differences in the same sort of export measure. Instead of asking how factor requirements affect the roles of various commodities in U.S. foreign trade, it asks how various countries' factor endowments affect those countries' roles in various types of trade.

This study does not show so clearly the influence of skills. Large endowments of professional and technical workers appear to contribute positively to a country's comparative advantage in temperate-zone agricultural commodities but negatively to its comparative advantage in three types of manufactured goods. Large supplies of literate workers appear to contribute negatively to comparative advantage in raw materials and temperate-zone agricultural commodities, positively to comparative advantage in labor-intensive and capital-intensive manufactures, but negatively to comparative advantage in chemicals (which, like machinery, are not especially capital or labor intensive). But the results are strongly consistent with Vanek's emphasis on the importance of natural resources. Comparative advantage in raw materials is positively associated with minerals production (standing for a country's raw-materials endowment) and negatively associated with capital and labor endowments. Comparative advantage in agricultural commodities is positively associated with large endowments of tropical and temperate-zone land, and the latter, in turn, are negatively associated with comparative advantage in most sorts of manufacturing (because countries well endowed with land will tend to export agricultural goods and import manufactures).

[8] Peter B. Kenen, "Nature, Capital and Trade," *Journal of Political Economy,* 73 (October 1965); reprinted in P. B. Kenen, *Essays in International Economics* (Princeton, N.J.: Princeton University Press, 1980).

TABLE 4-3 Factor Endowments and the Structure of World Trade

| | EFFECT ON EXPORT MEASURE | | | | | | |
| | AGRICULTURAL PRODUCTS | | | MANUFACTURED PRODUCTS | | | |
National Endowment	Raw Materials	Tropical	Temperate Zone	Labor Intensive	Capital Intensive	Machinery	Chemicals
Capital	Negative	Negative	Negative	None	Positive	Positive	Positive
Labor							
Professional and technical	None	None	Positive	Negative	Negative	Negative	None
Nonprofessional							
Literate	Negative	None	Negative	Positive	Positive	None	Negative
Illiterate	None	None	None	None	Positive	None	None
Land							
Tropical	None	Positive	Positive	None	None	None	Negative
Temperate zone	None	Positive	Positive	None	Negative	Negative	Negative
Minerals production	Positive	None	None	None	None	None	None

Source: Edward E. Leamer, *Sources of International Comparative Advantage* (Cambridge, Mass.: MIT Press, 1986), Table 6.6 (1975 data). List of factors omits coal and oil production (which are not included in minerals production) and dry land; list of commodities omits oil (which is not included in raw materials trade), forest products, and animal products, and it combines two categories of temperate-zone land (which is shown as having a significant effect when either category has one); export measure is difference between exports and imports. Effects are shown as "none" when t-statistics are lower than 2.0.

The last word is not in. There is need for more work on trade theory itself and for new approaches to verification.

SUMMARY

In the Heckscher–Ohlin model, cross-country differences in relative prices are due to differences in factor endowments, which are therefore the basic cause of trade. The factor-proportions version of the Heckscher–Ohlin theorem says that a country with much capital per worker will export capital-intensive commodities, while a country with little capital per worker will export labor-intensive commodities. The relative-price version of the theorem says that a country where the wage rate is high relative to the return on capital will export capital-intensive commodities, while a country where the wage rate is relatively low will export labor-intensive commodities.

Three other theorems can be extracted from the Heckscher–Ohlin model. The Rybczynski theorem describes the relationship between a country's factor endowment and its outputs at its full-employment point. An increase in the supply of one factor raises the country's output of the commodity intensive in that factor and reduces its output of the other commodity. The Stolper–Samuelson theorem describes the effect of trade on a country's factor prices. Trade raises the relative price of labor in the labor-abundant country and reduces the relative price of labor in the capital-abundant country. (It also raises the real wage in the labor-abundant country and reduces the real return to capital and has the opposite effects in the capital-abundant country.) The factor-price-equalization theorem carries this result to its logical limit. When there are no trade barriers or transport costs, trade will equalize completely the real earnings of the factors of production.

The Heckscher–Ohlin model can be extended to cover many countries, commodities, and factors. When this is done in one direction at a time, however, it is hard to make clear statements about outputs and trade flows or the influence of trade on factor prices. When we add a third country, the trade pattern is ambiguous. When we add a third commodity, production and trade patterns are both ambiguous. When we add a third factor, the model tends to break down completely, because there are too few commodities to determine factor prices. These difficulties do not arise when we increase the numbers of countries, commodities, and factors simultaneously, but maintain "evenness" among the numbers. It is not easy to interpret the conclusions, however, because the notions of factor abundance and factor intensity lose their simplicity.

Empirical work on the Heckscher–Ohlin model has produced surprises. Early work by Leontief suggested that the United States is a labor-abundant country rather than a capital-abundant country; its export production is more labor intensive than its import-competing production. This paradox is not adequately explained by demand reversals or factor reversals. It is perhaps explained by the omission of natural resources and of skills or human capital from Leontief's calculations.

RECOMMENDED READINGS

Many important contributions to the literature on the Heckscher–Ohlin model relate to the general version developed in Chapter 6, and some of them are listed at the end of that chapter. Here are readings that do not relate specifically to that version and some that deal with quantitative work on the model:

Most of the basic results in this chapter were stated or anticipated in the classic paper by Eli Heckscher, "The Effect of Foreign Trade on the Distribution of Income," *Economisk Tidskrift*, 21 (1919), reprinted in American Economic Association, *Readings in the Theory of International Trade* (Philadelphia: Blakiston, 1949), ch. 13. The model is developed more thoroughly by Bertil Ohlin, *Interregional and International Trade* (Cambridge, Mass.: Harvard University Press, 1933), chs. i–vii.

The Leontief paradox was first reported in Wassily Leontief, "Domestic Production and Foreign Trade: The American Capital Position Reexamined," *Economia Internazionale*, 7 (February 1954), reprinted in American Economic Association, *Readings in International Economics* (Homewood, Ill.: Richard D. Irwin, 1968), ch. 30. (See also the paper cited in the source note to Table 4-1, which contains revised calculations.)

Attempts to explain the Leontief paradox are surveyed in two papers by Robert Baldwin, which also present important empirical work. See Robert E. Baldwin, "Determinants of the Commodity Structure of U.S. Trade," *American Economic Review*, 61 (March 1971), and his "Determinants of Trade and Foreign Investment: Further Evidence," *Review of Economics and Statistics*, 61 (February 1979).

Recent empirical work on U.S. foreign trade is reported in Robert M. Stern and Keith E. Maskus, "Determinants of the Structure of U.S. Foreign Trade, 1958–76," *Journal of International Economics*, 11 (May 1981).

5

FACTOR SUBSTITUTION AND A MODIFIED RICARDIAN MODEL

INTRODUCTION

Chapter 2 showed that consumers gain from trade whenever supply conditions differ systematically from country to country. Chapters 3 and 4 introduced two trade models designed to account for differences in supply conditions. In the Ricardian model, they arise because technologies differ across countries in ways that are not uniform across commodities. In the Heckscher–Ohlin model, they arise because factor endowments differ across countries and factor intensities differ across commodities. Empirical research suggests that these models are too simple to explain trade patterns accurately but that they are useful ways to organize our thinking. The main hypotheses drawn from the models are verified partially by quantitative work.

In both models, the opening of foreign trade has profound effects on the national

economy. It alters the composition of domestic output, the ways that factors of production are distributed across activities, and the real earnings of those factors. The effects on real earnings and the income distribution call for close attention, because they will influence domestic politics and thus help us to understand why governments adopt trade policies that appear to ignore or reject the basic teachings of trade theory.

This chapter and the next study those effects more closely by relaxing an assumption used in Chapters 3 and 4, where factor requirements were fixed. That assumption had strong consequences for the shapes of transformation curves and for the effects of trade on outputs and earnings. In the Ricardian model, the transformation curve was a straight line, and one trading country specialized completely. In the Heckscher–Ohlin model, the transformation curve had two straight-line segments and one full-employment output point, and a country starting at that point did not specialize at all.

This chapter introduces factor substitution into the Ricardian model. Factor requirements depend on factor prices. An increase in the relative price of labor, for example, leads employers to substitute capital for labor—to adopt more capital-intensive methods of production. The slope of the transformation curve changes with the output mix, as in Chapter 2, and the effects of trade on outputs, real earnings, and the income distribution are different from those in the simple Ricardian model. Thereafter, we put the modified model to work by examining the effects of economic growth on patterns of production, the terms of trade and gains from trade, and the income distribution.

The next chapter introduces factor substitution into the Heckscher–Ohlin model. Once again, the slope of the transformation curve changes with the output mix, and each point becomes a full-employment point. The effects of trade on real earnings are not drastically different from those predicted by the simple Heckscher–Ohlin model, but the new version of the model is more realistic. Factor prices never fall to zero, the Rybczynski theorem holds at every output point, and the model provides a very suitable framework for examining the effects of economic growth.

FACTOR PRICES AND FACTOR SUBSTITUTION

The Ricardian model in Chapter 3 was unrealistic in many ways, but one should have bothered you more than others. Wine and cloth were made by labor—nothing else. Yet wine cannot be made without grapes, and grapes cannot be grown without land. And cloth can be made in factories, small

shops, or cottages, but it cannot be woven without looms. More factors of production must be introduced.

Production with Specific Factors

Suppose that Britain has a fixed supply of labor, as in Chapter 3, but has other factors, too. It has fixed supply of land that is used to grow grapes for making wine. It has a fixed supply of capital that is invested in looms and other machines used in weaving cloth.[1] Labor is used by both industries and is perfectly mobile between them. Land and capital are *specific factors*. Land is used only to make wine; capital is used only make cloth; and the supply of each factor is fixed. A single firm in the cloth industry may be able to bid machines away from other firms in that industry, just as firms bid labor away from other firms, but it cannot bid them away from firms in the wine industry, because they are not used in that industry.

If the production of a gallon of wine required a fixed quantity of land and the production of a yard of cloth required a fixed quantity of capital, outputs would be fixed completely. Britain's transformation curve would degenerate into a single point. It would show the quantity of wine that could be made, given the quantity of land avail-

---

[1] These assumptions take us only part way to reality. Yarn is needed to make cloth, cotton to make yarn, and land to grow cotton. Furthermore, there must be an industry somewhere in the world that manufactures the machines used to make cloth. The need to grow cotton could be met by supposing that there is a fixed supply of land that can be used for this purpose but not for growing grapes, and it would not be hard to include an additional industry to make machines. When we move in this direction, however, new issues arise. What would happen if land that is used to grow cotton could also be used to grow grapes? What would happen if Britain could import cotton rather than grow its own? Advanced trade theory deals with these issues—the definition of comparative advantage and determination of the terms of trade in models that include "intermediate" goods.

able and the fixed requirement per gallon of wine, and the quantity of cloth that could be made, given the quantity of capital available and the fixed requirement per yard of cloth.[2]

This chapter, however, adopts a different supposition, which is used in most modern economic theory. There are many ways for firms to combine factors of production. If labor is cheap relative to land, a winery will use a large quantity of labor per acre of land. If labor becomes more expensive, the

---

[2] This statement assumes that Britain has enough labor to satisfy the needs of its wine and cloth industries. Suppose that 1 acre of land is required to make 1 gallon of wine, along with six workers, and that Britain has 20 acres. It can produce 20 gallons of wine but needs 120 workers to do so. Suppose that 2 machines are required to make 1 yard of cloth, along with 3 workers, and that Britain has 60 machines. It can produce 30 yards of cloth but needs 90 workers to do so. To use all its land and capital, then, Britain must have at least 210 workers.

winery will substitute land for labor and use less labor per acre of land. The factor intensity of each activity depends on the prices of the factors of production used in that activity.

Marginal Products and Employment

The implications of this supposition are shown in Figure 5-1, which describes the determination of employment in the wine industry. The curve MP_W measures the *marginal product* of labor in the wine industry. This is the additional wine output, measured in gallons, produced by employing an additional worker but holding all other things constant. The size of the marginal product of labor depends on the fixed quantity of land available and on the variable quantity of labor already employed by the industry. The marginal product of labor falls as employment rises in the wine industry. When employment is OL_1, for ex-

FIGURE 5-1 Demand for Labor in the Wine Industry The MP_W curve depicts the marginal product of labor in the wine industry. The marginal product falls as employment rises. The MP_W curve is also the demand curve for labor by the wine industry. When the real wage measured in wine is OV gallons, the demand for labor is OL_1 workers.

ample, the marginal product of labor is OV gallons; when employment rises to OL'_1, the marginal product falls to OV' gallons.

Strictly speaking, the marginal product of labor depends on the land intensity of the wine industry (its land-labor ratio). The larger the quantity of land per worker, the higher the marginal product of labor and the lower the marginal product of land. (The marginal product of land is well defined conceptually, even when the quantity of land is fixed. It is the increase in wine output that could be obtained if it were possible to increase the quantity of land, holding the quantity of labor constant.) This particular formulation is known as the *law of variable proportions*. It derives from an assumption made in Chapter 3 and carried over to this chapter. Returns to scale are constant in each industry. If land and labor inputs could be doubled, output would double, too, and the marginal products of labor and land would not change. When the labor input is doubled but the land input is kept constant, wine output rises but does not double. Furthermore, the marginal product of labor falls, and the marginal product of land rises. The changes in marginal products result from the fall in the land-labor ratio of the wine industry.

How much labor will the wine industry employ? A profit-maximizing firm will hire workers up to the point at which the marginal product of labor is equal to the real wage measured in terms of the firm's own output. This is shown algebraically in Note 5-1, and the logic of the argument is easy to illustrate numerically.

Suppose that the wage rate is $4 per worker, that the marginal product of labor is 3 gallons of wine when the firm employs 10 workers, and that the price of wine is $2 per gallon. By employing one more worker, the firm can earn $6 in additional revenue; it can produce 3 more gallons of

wine and sell them for $2 each. It can thus increase its profits by $2, because it has to pay only $4 for an additional worker. Therefore, the firm will hire an eleventh worker. When it does so, however, it reduces its land-labor ratio, and the marginal product of labor falls to 2 gallons. If it hires another worker, then, it can earn only $4 of additional revenue, and it cannot increase it profits, as it has to pay $4 for the worker. It has no incentive to hire a twelfth worker. In brief, the firm will hire labor up to the point at which

Wage rate = price of wine
$$\times \text{ marginal product of labor}$$

or

$$\frac{\text{Wage rate}}{\text{Price of wine}} = \text{marginal product of labor}$$

Returning to Figure 5-1, suppose that the real wage measured in wine is OV gallons. The wine industry will hire OL_1 workers.

When we know how much labor and land the wine industry uses, we know its output. Furthermore, we know the marginal product of land, which gives us the real rental rate for land measured in gallons of wine. If the marginal product of land were higher than the real rental rate, each firm in the industry would try to acquire more land. But the supply of land is fixed. Therefore, its rental rate would rise as firms bid against each other, until the real rental rate was equal to the marginal product of land.

Equilibrium in the Labor Market

To determine wine and cloth outputs together, the two industries' demand curves for labor must be put together in a single diagram to find the real wage at which the labor market is in equilibrium. The real wage determines employment in each industry and, therefore, the output of each industry.

Note 5-1

The production function of a firm in industry i is given by

$$x_i = f^i(L_i, K_i)$$

which says that output, x_i, depends on the amounts of labor, L_i, and capital, K_i, employed by the firm. In the notation of Note 2-1, the change in x_i is

$$dx_i = f^i_L \, dL_i + f^i_k \, dK_i$$

where f^i_L is the marginal product of labor and f^i_k is the marginal product of capital. Note that an increase in L_i reduces f^i_L and raises f^i_k, and an increase in K_i has the opposite effects.

The firm's profits, q_i, are the difference between its revenue and cost,

$$q_i = p_i x_i - (wL_i + rK_i)$$

where p_i is the price of its product, w is the wage rate, and r is the return to capital. The change in q_i is

$$dq_i = p_i \, dx_i - (w \, dL_i + r \, dK_i)$$

Changes in p_i, w, and r will also change

q_i, but these effects are omitted, because a competitive firm does not control p_i, w, or r. Replacing dx_i with the definition just given,

$$dq_i = p_i(f^i_L \, dL_i + f^i_k \, dK_i) - (w \, dL_i + r \, dK_i)$$
$$= (p_i f^i_L - w)dL_i + (p_i f^i_k - r)dK_i$$

When $p_i f^i_L > w$, an increase in L_i raises profit (it raises revenue by more than cost). But f^i_L will fall and f^i_k will rise, affecting the profitability of additional changes in L_i and K_i. To maximize profit, the firm must choose levels of L_i and K_i at which $p_i f^i_L - w = 0$ and $p_i f^i_k - r = 0$, as they are the levels at which $dq_i = 0$ (at which additional changes in L_i and K_i cease to be profitable). These conditions give

$$f^i_L = \frac{w}{p_i} \quad \text{and} \quad f^i_k = \frac{r}{p_i}$$

The marginal product of labor must equal the real wage expressed in x_i, and the marginal product of capital must equal the real return to capital.

This exercise is conducted in Figure 5-2. Employment is measured on the horizontal axis, as before, and the fixed quantity of labor in Britain is the distance $O\bar{L}$. The real wage is measured on the vertical axis, but using yards of cloth rather than gallons of wine.

The curve E_W is the demand curve for labor in the wine industry; it plots the demand for labor against the real wage measured in yards of cloth. It is obtained by dividing the relative price of cloth into the marginal product of labor given by the curve MP_W in Figure 5-1:

$$\frac{\text{Marginal product of labor}}{\text{Relative price of cloth}}$$
$$= \frac{\text{wage rate}}{\text{price of wine}} \times \frac{\text{price of wine}}{\text{price of cloth}}$$
$$= \frac{\text{wage rate}}{\text{price of cloth}}$$

When the real wage measured in cloth is OV yards, the wine industry demands OL_1 labor.

The curve E_C is the demand curve for labor in the cloth industry. It is the marginal-product curve for that industry, given the quantity of capital (machines) used by the industry, but is drawn to measure em-

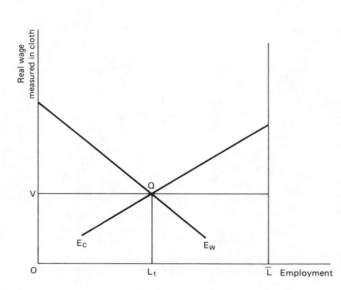

FIGURE 5-2 Equilibrium in the British Labor Market

The supply of workers is fixed at $O\bar{L}$. The E_W curve shows the demand for labor in the wine industry. It shows the marginal product of labor in that industry divided by the relative price of cloth and thus shows the marginal product measured in cloth. The E_C curve shows the demand for labor in the cloth industry. It shows the marginal product of labor in that industry measured in cloth. When labor is perfectly mobile within Britain, both industries must pay the same real wage. Therefore, the labor market is in equilibrium when OV is the real wage. The wine industry demands OL_1 workers; the cloth industry demands $\bar{L}L_1$ workers; the two demands add up to the supply.

ployment from $\bar{L}$. When the real wage in cloth is OV, the cloth industry demands $\bar{L}L_1$ labor.

Clearly, the real wage rate must be OV yards for the labor market to be in equilibrium. If the wage were higher than OV, the industries' demands for labor would be smaller than OL_1 and $\bar{L}L_1$, and the total demand would be smaller than the supply. The real wage would fall. If the wage were lower than OV, the industries' demands would be larger than OL_1 and $\bar{L}L_1$, and the total demand would exceed the supply. The real wage would rise. When the real wage is OV, we know employment in each industry and, therefore, the output of each industry, given the quantity of land used by the wine industry and the quantity of capital used by the cloth industry.

THE MODIFIED RICARDIAN MODEL

The point Q in Figure 5-2 corresponds to a point on Britain's transformation curve.

Starting from that point, the British economy cannot make more cloth without sacrificing wine and cannot make more wine without sacrificing cloth. The location of Q depends on four variables: the fixed supply of labor; the fixed quantities of land and capital that determine the marginal products of labor, given the technologies available to Britain; and the relative price of cloth, which is needed to convert the marginal-product curve MP_W in Figure 5-1 into the demand curve E_W in Figure 5-2.

Relative Prices and the Transformation Curve

To trace the whole transformation curve for Britain, we must ask what happens in the labor market when there is an increase in the relative price of cloth. The results are given by Figure 5-3.

The demand curve for labor in the wine industry shows the marginal product of labor divided by the relative price of cloth.

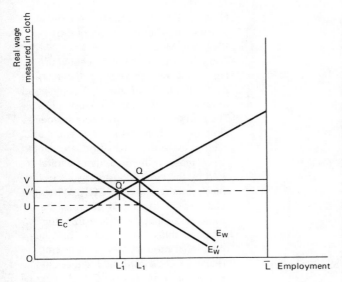

FIGURE 5-3 Effects of an Increase in the Relative Price of Cloth
The demand curve for labor in the wine industry is the marginal-product curve divided by the relative price of cloth. Therefore, an increase in the relative price of cloth shifts the demand curve downward from E_W to E'_W, displacing equilibrium from Q to Q'. Employment in the wine industry falls from OL_1 to OL'_1; employment in the cloth industry rises from $\overline{L}L_1$ to $\overline{L}L'_1$. The real wage measured in cloth falls from OV to OV'. But the real wage measured in wine rises, because the increase in the relative price of cloth exceeds the reduction in the real wage measured in cloth.

Therefore, an increase in that price shifts the curve downward from E_W to E'_W. The distance UV/OV measures the increase in the relative price of cloth. The pattern of employment changes. The marginal product of labor in the wine industry falls below the real wage, OV, when both are measured in cloth, and firms in the wine industry lay off workers. The real wage falls, because of excess supply in the labor market, and firms in the cloth industry hire more workers. The new equilibrium point is Q'. Employment in the wine industry falls from OL_1 to OL'_1, and employment in the cloth industry rises from $\overline{L}L_1$ to $\overline{L}L'_1$. Wine output falls and cloth output rises.

The movement from Q to Q' in Figure 5-3 traces a movement along Britain's transformation curve. But the shape of that curve is different from the curve in Chapter 3. It looks like Z_1Z_2 in Figure 5-4, being bowed outward (convex) rather than a straight line. A formal proof is given by Note 5-2, along with a new proof of the familiar assertion that the slope of the transformation curve is equal at each point to the relative price of cloth. A moment's

thought, however, should satisfy you on this point. When labor is transferred from wine to cloth production, the marginal product of labor falls in the cloth industry and rises in the wine industry. This is because the cloth industry becomes more labor intensive as it hires more workers, while the wine industry becomes less labor intensive as it lays off workers. As more and more labor is transferred, cloth output expands at a decreasing rate, wine output contracts at an increasing rate, and the transformation curve gets steeper.

The Haberler Theorem

How does the movement from Q to Q' in Figure 5-3 affect the real earnings of the factors of production? We have already seen that the real wage falls in terms of cloth, going from OV to OV'. It rises, however, in terms of wine. This can be shown in two ways. (1) The wage rate in terms of cloth falls by $V'V/OV$, and this decline is smaller than UV/OV, which measures the increase in the relative price of cloth. A yard of cloth purchases more wine than it

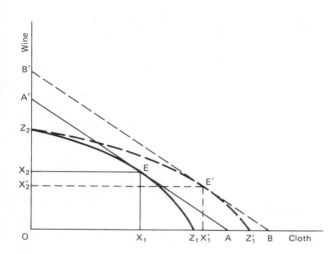

FIGURE 5-4 The British Economy in the Specific-Factor Version of the Ricardian Model
The labor-market equilibria shown in Figure 5-3 trace the transformation curve $Z_1 Z_2$. (Point Q in Figure 5-3 corresponds to point E on the transformation curve.) The transformation curve gets steeper as cloth output rises. Its slope is equal at each point to the relative price of cloth. An increase in the quantity of capital used by the cloth industry displaces the transformation curve to $Z_1' Z_2$. When the relative price of cloth is given by the slopes of the lines AA' and BB', the output point shifts from E to E'. The value of national product measured in cloth rises from OA to OB, and actual cloth output rises from OX_1 to OX_1', but actual wine output falls from OX_2 to OX_2'.

Note 5-2

When there is a fixed factor in an industry, the change in its output is given by the change in its use of the variable factor (labor) and by the marginal product of that factor. In the notation of Note 5-1,

$$dx_i = f_L^i \, dL_i$$

When labor is transferred between industries, then

$$\frac{dx_2}{dx_1} = \frac{f_L^2 \, dL_2}{f_L^1 \, dL_1} = -\frac{f_L^2}{f_L^1}$$

because $dL_2 = -dL_1$ when the total labor supply is fixed. As dx_2/dx_1 is the slope of the transformation curve (the rate at which x_2 output falls when x_1 output rises), that slope is equal absolutely to the ratio of marginal products. But f_L^1 falls as labor is transferred to the x_1 industry, and f_L^2 rises as labor is transferred from the x_2 industry. Therefore, the slope of the transformation curve increases as x_1 output rises.

Combining the previous equation with the condition given at the end of Note 5-1, that $f_L^i = w/p_i$,

$$\frac{dx_2}{dx_1} = -\frac{w/p_2}{w/p_1} = -\frac{p_1}{p_2}$$

The slope of the transformation curve is equal absolutely to the relative price of x_1 (the relative price of cloth in Figure 5-4).

did initially, and the increase in the purchasing power of cloth is large enough to raise the real wage in terms of wine, even though it falls in terms of cloth. (2) As employment in the wine industry drops from OL_1 to OL_1', that industry becomes less labor intensive. Therefore, the marginal product of labor rises in the wine industry until it is equal in equilibrium to the real wage measured in wine.

The decrease of employment in the wine industry tells us what happens to the real rental rate of land. The marginal product of land falls in the wine industry, which means that the real rental rate falls in terms of wine. And the purchasing power of wine falls, too, so that the real rental rate falls even farther in terms of cloth. The increase of employment in the cloth industry tells us what happens to the return to capital. The marginal product of capital rises in the cloth industry, which means that the real return rises in terms of cloth. And the purchasing power of cloth rises, too, so that the real return to capital rises even farther in terms of wine.

These findings can be summarized in what we shall call the Haberler theorem:[3]

A change in relative commodity prices raises the real earnings of the factor used specifically in the industry whose output price has risen and reduces the real earnings of the factor used specifically in the industry whose output price has fallen. The real earnings of the mobile factor (labor) fall in terms of the commodity whose price has risen and rise in terms of the commodity whose price has fallen.

This theorem is used to show how trade af-

fects the real earnings of land, capital, and labor in the specific-factor version of the Ricardian model.

Factor Supplies and the Transformation Curve

Figure 5-5 shows what happens when there is an increase in the supply of capital. The marginal product of labor rises in the cloth industry, because the industry becomes less labor intensive at each level of employment. Therefore, the demand curve for labor shifts upward from E_C to E_C', displacing equilibrium from Q to Q'. Employment in the cloth industry increases from $\bar{L}L_1$ to $\bar{L}L_1'$, and employment in the wine industry decreases from OL_1 to OL_1'. Cloth output rises due to the increase in the supply of capital and the resulting increase in employment. Wine output falls due to the decrease in employment.

Returning to Figure 5-4, Britain's transformation curve shifts from Z_1Z_2 to $Z_1'Z_2$. The distance OZ_1 rises to OZ_1', showing how the increase in the supply of capital would raise cloth output if all Britain's workers were employed in making cloth. The distance OZ_2 does not change, because an increase in the supply of capital cannot affect wine output when Britain does not produce any cloth. Let the relative price of cloth be equal to the slopes of the lines AA' and BB'. The economy will be at E initially, with cloth output at OX_1, wine output at OX_2, and the value of national product at OA measured in cloth. The increase in the supply of capital shifts the economy to E'. Cloth output rises to OX_1', wine output falls to OX_2', and national product rises to OB.

These output effects resemble those predicted by the Rybczynski theorem developed in connection with the Heckscher–Ohlin model. An increase in the supply of a specific factor raises the output of the industry using that factor and reduces the output of the other industry. This predic-

---

[3] Haberler did not prove this theorem completely but was among the first economists to examine the behavior of real earnings in the specific-factor model; see Gottfried von Haberler, *The Theory of International Trade* (London: William Hodge, 1936), ch. xii.

FIGURE 5-5   Effects of an Increase in the Supply of Capital Used in Cloth Production

An increase in the supply of capital used in making cloth raises the marginal product of labor in the cloth industry, shifting the demand curve for labor from E_C to E'_C, and displacing equilibrium from Q to Q'. Employment in the wine industry falls from OL_1 to OL'_1, reducing wine output, and employment in the cloth industry rises from $\bar{L}L_1$ to $\bar{L}L'_1$, raising cloth output. The real wage measured in cloth rises from OV to OV'.

tion holds for every set of commodity prices at which the economy produces some of both commodities.[4]

What are the effects on the earnings of the factors of production? There is, of course, an increase in the real wage measured in cloth. It rises from OV to OV' in Figure 5-5. Furthermore, the real wage rises in terms of wine as well, because relative prices have not changed. There is a decrease in the real rental rate for land measured in wine and cloth, because the wine industry becomes less labor intensive and the marginal product of land falls. There is a decrease in the real return to capital measured in wine and cloth, because the cloth industry becomes less labor intensive, too, and the marginal product of capital falls.

(The cloth industry uses more labor and more capital, but we can be sure that it becomes less labor intensive, because of the increase in the real wage measured in cloth. This necessarily indicates an increase in the marginal product of labor and, therefore, a decrease in the labor intensity of the cloth industry.)

These effects on earnings are different from those in Chapters 3 and 4. In the Ricardian and Heckscher–Ohlin models, real earnings cannot change unless commodity prices change. Yet real earnings changed in Figure 5-5 without any change in the relative price of cloth.

Factor Supplies and Trade

Suppose that Britain and Portugal have identical technologies and the same supplies of labor. Let Britain have more capital than Portugal, however, and Portugal more land than Britain. What can we say about trade between them? When the relative price of cloth is the same in the two countries, which happens with free trade,

---

[4] The output effects of an increase in the labor force are quite different. Outputs of cloth and wine rise together, by amounts that depend on the slopes of the demand curves for labor. (The marginal products of labor fall in both industries, reducing the real wage expressed in wine and cloth. The marginal products of land and capital rise, raising the real rental rate and real return to capital expressed in wine and cloth.)

Britain produces more cloth than Portugal, and Portugal produces more wine. If tastes are the same in the two countries, however, with unitary income elasticities of demand, their consumers will demand the same combinations of wine and cloth. Therefore, Britain must export cloth, and Portugal must export wine, just as they did in the simple Ricardian model.

How does trade affect the real earnings of land, capital, and labor? As Britain exports cloth, the relative price of cloth had to be lower in Britain before trade was opened. By implication, trade must raise that price in Britain and reduce it in Portugal, and the Haberler theorem tells the rest of the story. Trade must raise the real return to capital in Britain and reduce it in Portugal. Conversely, trade must reduce the real rental rate for land in Britain and raise it in Portugal. The effects on the real earnings of the specific factors are similar to those predicted by the Stolper–Samuelson theorem developed in connection with the Heckscher–Ohlin model. Capital is abundant in Britain, and land is abundant in Portugal. The opening of trade, then, raises the real earnings of the abundant specific factor and reduces the real earnings of the scarce specific factor.

The effects on real wages are more complicated. As trade raises the relative price of cloth in Britain, the real wage falls in terms of cloth but rises in terms of wine. As the relative price of cloth falls in Portugal, the real wage rises in terms of cloth but falls in terms of wine. When tastes are the same in the two countries, then, trade is beneficial to workers in one country but harmful to workers in the other. If workers spend most of their incomes on cloth, trade makes them worse off in Britain but better off in Portugal. (In the simple Ricardian model, by contrast, trade makes workers better off in both countries, regardless of their tastes. The real wage rises in each

country in terms of its import good and is constant in terms of its export good.)

In this example, trade is explained by differences in national endowments of specific factors rather than differences in technologies, using predictions about output that resemble those provided by the Rybczynski theorem. Furthermore, the effect of trade on the real earnings of the specific factors resemble those provided by the Stolper–Samuelson theorem. In consequence, many economists treat the specific-factor model as a version of the Heckscher–Ohlin model rather than a version of the Ricardian model. In the short run, they say, some factors of production are not mobile across industries. In the long run, all factors are perfectly mobile. Therefore, the specific-factor model can be used to describe the short-run behavior of an economy, and the factor-endowments model can be used to describe its long-run behavior.

ECONOMIC GROWTH IN THE MODIFIED RICARDIAN MODEL

In previous chapters, we used the Ricardian and Heckscher–Ohlin models to show why trade takes place, how the terms of trade are determined and the gains from trade distributed, and how trade affects the earnings of the factors of production. We did not ask how trade patterns are altered by changes in factor supplies—capital formation and population growth—or by technological change. But we have done most of the work needed to deal with these matters. Therefore, let us look at economic growth.

Economic growth can reflect changes in factor supplies, changes in the quality of capital or labor, and changes in the efficiency with which they are used. Changes in factor supplies are easiest to analyze, and we will focus on capital formation in order to minimize ambiguity. When numbers of workers and persons are constant, the principal measures of growth move in the same direction; an increase in total output raises output per worker and output per person.[5]

We will not take up the underlying reasons for capital formation, the motives for saving and investment. We will not ask what happens while it is taking place and raising the demands for capital equipment (the looms needed to weave cloth in this chapter and the mills and tractors needed to make steel and grow corn in the next chapter). In the spirit of earlier chapters,

[5] Population growth and technological change are examined in Chapter 6, using the Heckscher–Ohlin model.

we will concentrate on the long-run effects of capital formation by asking how an increase in the capital stock, optimally allocated among activities, affects the supplies of goods, the terms of trade and gains from trade, and the real earnings of the factors of production.

To answer this question systematically, however, we must subdivide it. First, we must ask how capital formation affects the output mix and distribution of domestic income in the growing country before it has affected the terms of trade. Second, we must ask how the change in the output mix affects the terms of trade and the distribution of the gains from trade. Finally, we must ask how the change in the terms of trade affects the distribution of domestic income.

FIGURE 5-6   Effects of Capital Formation in Britain on Outputs and Demands for Cloth and Wine
The British transformation curve is $Z_1 Z_2$. When the relative price of cloth is equal to the slope of AA', the output point is E, where cloth output is OX_1 and wine output is OX_2. Real national product is OA in terms of cloth. Consumption takes place at C, where the indifference curve U_1 is tangent to AA'. Britain exports ED cloth and imports DC wine. Capital formation shifts the transformation curve to $Z_1' Z_2$. When the relative price of cloth is unchanged and thus equal to the slope of BB', the output point is E', where cloth output rises to OX_1' and wine output falls to OX_2'. Real national product rises to OB in terms of cloth. Consumption takes place at C', where the indifference curve U_2 is tangent to BB'. Britain's export offer rises to $E'D'$ cloth, and its import demand rises to $D'C'$ wine.

FIGURE 5-7 Effects of Capital
Formation in Britain on the British
Income Distribution
Capital formation in Britain raises the
marginal product of labor in the cloth industry, shifting the demand curve for
labor from E_C to E'_C and displacing equilibrium from Q to Q'. Employment in
the wine industry falls from OL_1 to OL'_1,
and employment in the cloth industry
rises from $\bar{L}L_1$ to $\bar{L}L'_1$. The real wage measured in cloth rises from OV to OV'. The
increase in cloth output reduces the relative price of cloth, raising the demand
for labor in the wine industry. It is
shown here to rise from E_W to E'_W, displacing equilibrium to Q'' and restoring
employment in each industry to what it
was initially. The real wage rises to OV''
measured in cloth and is unchanged
when measured in wine.

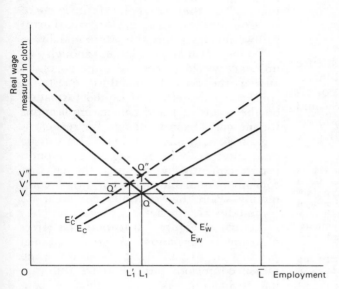

Effects on Outputs and Real Earnings at Constant Terms of Trade

We have already answered the first question completely when we used Figures 5-4 and 5-5 to show how a change in the capital stock affects the transformation curve and the labor market. They are reproduced for further work as Figures 5-6 and 5-7 and can be used to summarize our principal findings.

In Figure 5-6, the British transformation curve is Z_1Z_2 initially, and the relative price of cloth is given by the slope of the line AA'. The British economy produces at E, where cloth output is OX_1 yards and wine output is OX_2 gallons. An increase in Britain's capital stock shifts the transformation curve to Z'_1Z_2. When the terms of trade remain unchanged, the British economy produces at E', where cloth output rises to OX'_1 yards and wine output falls to OX'_2 gallons.

In Figure 5-7, labor-market equilibrium is at Q initially, where OL_1 workers are employed in the wine industry and $\bar{L}L_1$ are employed in the cloth industry, and the real wage in terms of cloth is OV yards. Capital formation raises the marginal product of labor in the cloth industry, shifting its demand curve from E_C to E'_C. and labor-market equilibrium is displaced to Q'. Employment in the wine industry falls to OL'_1, employment in the cloth industry rises to $\bar{L}L'_1$, and the real wage rises in terms of cloth to OV' yards, which means that it must rise in terms of wine as well, because relative prices have not changed.

The remaining results follow directly. As the real wage has risen in terms of wine and cloth, the marginal products of labor must be higher in the wine and cloth industries. Therefore, the marginal products of land and capital must be lower at Q' than at Q. Capital formation reduces the real rental rate for land and the real return to capital.[6]

Effects on the Terms of Trade and Gains from Trade

If Britain were too small to influence world prices, the story would end here. Capital formation in Britain would not affect the terms of trade, and Britain would appropriate the whole gain in welfare resulting from capital formation. In Figure

---

[6] These changes in the real earnings of the factors do not describe completely the changes in their *shares* (the changes in the income distribution). We can show what happens to the landlords' share. The amount of land is fixed and the real rental rate declines. Therefore, the real incomes of landlords fall. Furthermore, real national product rises. These events together reduce the landlords' share. But this is all we can say with certainty. The amount of labor is constant and the real wage rate rises, raising the real incomes of workers. But we do not know whether they rise by more or less than real national product. We cannot tell what happens to the workers' share. The amount of capital rises and the real return to capital falls, which means that the real incomes of capitalists can go up or down, and the change in their share is thoroughly ambiguous. Similar problems crop up later, which is why the analysis in the text concentrates on real earnings rather than factor shares.

5-6, British consumers would move from point *C* on the indifference curve U_1 to point *C'* on the higher indifference curve U_2. Consumers in the outside world (Portugal) would stay where they were initially.

When Britain is large enough to influence world prices, we must go on to answer the second and third questions, concerning the effect of capital formation on the terms of trade and its implications for the gains from trade and for real earnings in Britain and Portugal. This can be done most easily by making an assumption used frequently in economic theory, that consumers demand more of every commodity when their incomes rise (that no commodity is "inferior").

Return to Figure 5-6 to note the effect of capital formation on real national product in Britain. It starts at *OA* when measured in cloth and rises to *OB* with capital formation. As the number of consumers (persons) is constant here, consumers' incomes rise in Britain, and they demand more wine and cloth. But capital formation reduces wine output in Britain. Therefore, it generates an excess demand for wine matched by an excess supply of

FIGURE 5-8 Effects of Capital Formation in Britain on the British Offer Curve and Terms of Trade The British offer curve is *OJ* and the Portuguese offer curve is *OJ**. Equilibrium is established initially at *W*, where Britain imports *OZ* wine and exports *ZW* cloth. Britain's terms of trade (the relative price of cloth) are given by the slope of *OF*. Capital formation in Britain increases the British demand for wine imports to *OZ'* and the British supply of cloth exports to *Z'Y*. The British offer curve becomes *OJ'*, and equilibrium is displaced to *W'*. Britain's terms of trade are given by the slope *OF'* and have therefore deteriorated.

British wine imports
Portuguese wine exports

British cloth exports
Portuguese cloth imports

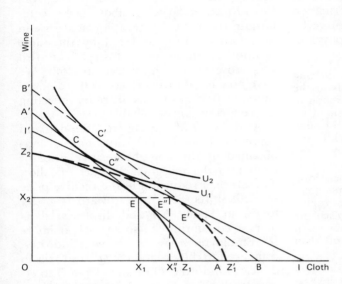

FIGURE 5-9 Effects of Capital
Formation in Britain on the Gains
from Trade
If the terms of trade were unaffected by
capital formation in Britain, remaining
equal to the slopes of AA' and BB',
British consumers would move from C
on the indifference curve U_1 to C' on
the higher indifference curve U_2. Capital formation would raise economic
welfare. If the terms of trade deteriorate
with capital formation, several outcomes are possible. In the case shown
here, the relative price of cloth falls
until it is equal to the slope of II', displacing the output point to E'' and the
consumption point to C''. As C'' lies on
the indifference curve U_1, the gains
from economic growth are offset exactly by the reduction in the gains from
trade due to the deterioration in the
terms of trade.

cloth at the initial terms of trade. The consumption point moves from C to C', raising
the British demand for wine imports from
DC to $D'C'$ and raising the supply of cloth
exports from ED to $E'D'$. (When consumers demand more wine and cloth, C' is
northeast of C, so the distance $D'C'$ must
exceed DC when output moves from E
to E'.)

The effects on Britain's terms of trade
are shown in Figure 5-8, using offer curves.
The British offer curve is OJ initially. The
Portuguese offer curve is OJ^*. The two
curves intersect at W, where Britain imports OZ gallons of wine and exports ZW
yards of cloth. Britain's terms of trade are
given by the slope of OF, passing through
W and measuring the relative price of
cloth. (The slope of OF in Figure 5-8 corresponds to the slope of AA' in Figure 5-6.)

As capital formation in Britain generates
an excess demand for wine and an excess
supply of cloth at the initial terms of trade,
Britain's demand for wine imports rises
from OZ to OZ', but Britain's supply of

cloth exports rises from ZW to $Z'Y$.[7] Therefore, the point Y must lie on the new
British offer curve, which is OJ'. Equilibrium in trade between Britain and Portugal is displaced to W', and Britain's terms
of trade deteriorate. They are given by the
slope of OF' passing through W', and OF'
is flatter than OF.

The effects on economic welfare in
Britain are analyzed in Figure 5-9. It is
based on Figure 5-6, showing once again
the shift in Britain's transformation curve
to $Z_1'Z_2$, the shift of the output point to E',
and the increase in real national product to
OB. Before capital formation in Britain,
consumers were at C on the indifference
curve U_1. If there were no change in
Britain's terms of trade, capital formation
would take consumers to C' on the indifference curve U_2. They would be better off.

---

[7] The distances OZ and OZ' in Figure 5-8 correspond to DC and $D'C'$ in Figure 5-6; the distances ZW
and $Z'Y$ correspond to ED and $E'D'$.

When the terms of trade deteriorate, however, consumers can be better or worse off.

Consider the new line II' in Figure 5-9. It is drawn to connect the transformation curve at E'' with the indifference curve U_1 at C'', and it serves to classify the possibilities:

1. If the slope of OF' in Figure 5-8, showing the actual terms of trade, corresponds to the slope of II' in Figure 5-9, the deterioration in the terms of trade is just large enough to offset completely the welfare gain from capital formation. British consumers are driven back to the indifference curve U_1. They do not gain or lose from capital formation.

2. If OF' is steeper than II', the deterioration in the terms of trade is not large enough to offset completely the welfare gain from capital formation. British consumers cannot reach the indifference curve U_2 in Figure 5-9 but reach one higher than U_1. They are better off than they were initially.

3. If OF' is flatter than II', the deterioration in the terms of trade more than offsets the welfare gain from capital formation. British consumers are driven back to an indifference curve lower than U_1. They are worse off than they were initially.

The third case is described as *immiserizing* growth.[8]

Additional Effects on Real Earnings

How does the deterioration in Britain's terms of trade affect the real earnings of labor, capital, and land? The answer is given by Figure 5-7. We have already seen

that capital formation raised the marginal product of labor in Britain's cloth industry, shifting the industry's demand curve from E_C to E'_C and displacing labor-market equilibrium from Q to Q'. Employment rose in the cloth industry and fell by the same amount in the wine industry. The real wage rose by VV' measured in cloth. We have now to add the effects of the deterioration in Britain's terms of trade, reflecting the reduction in the relative price of cloth.

At the start of this chapter, the demand curve for labor by the wine industry was obtained by dividing the relative price of cloth into the marginal product of labor. Therefore, a reduction in the relative price of cloth shifts that curve upward from E_W to E'_W in Figure 5-7 and displaces labor-market equilibrium to some such point as Q''. Employment rises in the wine industry, compared to the situation at Q', and falls in the cloth industry. (The shift from Q to Q' and on to Q'' in Figure 5-7 corresponds to the shift of the output point from E to E' and on to E'' in Figure 5-9.) The effects of the movement from Q' to Q'' are described completely by the Haberler theorem. The deterioration in the terms of trade reduces the real return to capital and raises the real rental rate for land, whether they are measured in wine or cloth. It raises the real wage measured in cloth, but reduces the real wage measured in wine.

Combining these effects with those involved in the movement from Q to Q', we

---

[8] Much work has been done on immiserizing growth—the circumstances in which it is likely to occur and its implications for trade policy. It is most likely to occur when the Portuguese demand for British cloth is inelastic and it is comparatively difficult for Britain to move from cloth to wine production. It has been shown, moreover, that immiserizing growth testifies to poor trade policy. It cannot occur when a country puts an "optimum" tariff on its imports, a notion defined precisely in Chapter 10. (Note that the increase in welfare which growth can confer will not be realized unless incomes are redistributed. We have already seen that capital formation reduces the real re-

turn to capital in Britain, and we are about to see that the deterioration in the terms of trade reinforces this effect. Therefore, a consumer whose income derives from the ownership of capital will be made worse off by growth, even when a "typical" consumer reaches an indifference curve higher than U_1. Hence, it is most accurate to say that growth has the potential to raise welfare, contingent on a redistribution of domestic income to compensate consumers whose incomes fall on account of reductions in the real earnings of the factors of production from which they derive their incomes.)

get clear-cut results for the return to capital. The real return was lower at Q' than at Q and is even lower at Q''. Therefore, capital formation in Britain reduces the real return to British capital, whether it is measured in wine or cloth. One other result is also clear. The real wage in terms of cloth was higher at Q' than at Q and is even higher at Q''. (It was OV initially and rises to OV''.) Therefore, capital formation in Britain raises the real wage in terms of cloth, the commodity that uses capital. But the real wage in terms of wine can rise or fall, depending on the size of the reduction in the relative price of cloth, and the effect on the real rental rate for land is likewise ambiguous.

The reasons for these ambiguities are shown by the special case depicted by Figure 5-7. Point Q'' has been placed vertically above the initial point Q, which says that the relative price of cloth falls by just enough to restore the initial pattern of employment.[9] In this special case, the marginal products of labor and land in the wine industry are the same as they were initially, because the land-labor ratio is the same. Capital formation does not affect the real wage or real rental rate when they are measured in wine. But it raises the real rental rate measured in cloth, because of the reduction in the relative price of cloth.

In this special case, then, these are the combined effects of capital formation shown by the movement from Q to Q'' in Figure 5-7:

	IN TERMS OF:	
Real Earnings of:	*Wine*	*Cloth*
Labor	Constant	Increase
Land	Constant	Increase
Capital	Decrease	Decrease

[9] By implication, wine output is what it was initially, because the same quantities of land and labor are used in wine production, but cloth output is larger, because more capital is used in cloth production along with the initial quantity of labor. (The special case depicted in

If the reduction in the relative price of cloth is larger than the reduction implied by the shift in the demand curve to E'_W, employment in the wine industry will exceed OL_1 workers. The real wage will fall in terms of wine (but will rise by more in terms of cloth), and the real rental rate for land will rise in terms of wine. If the reduction in the relative price of cloth is smaller than the reduction implied by the shift in the demand curve to E'_W, employment will not reach OL_1 workers. The real wage will rise in terms of wine (but will rise by less in terms of cloth), and the real rental rate for land will fall in terms of wine.

Effects on the Portuguese Economy

Capital formation in Britain can have important effects in Portugal, but only if it leads to a deterioration in Britain's terms of trade. If Britain is too small to influence world prices, the Portuguese economy is not affected.

A deterioration in Britain's terms of trade is, of course, an improvement in Portugal's terms of trade, and it raises economic welfare in Portugal. In effect, the deterioration in Britain's terms of trade redistributes from Britain to Portugal some of the welfare gains from capital formation.

The effects on real earnings are equally simple. They are described completely by the Haberler theorem. The real return to capital falls in Portugal, and the real rental rate rises, whether they are measured in wine or cloth. The real wage falls in terms of wine and rises in terms of cloth. Capital formation in Britain makes landlords better off in Portugal, makes capitalists worse off, and has an uncertain effect on Portuguese workers. If they consume much cloth and little wine, they benefit from capital forma-

Figure 5-7 is likewise depicted in Figure 5-9. At the output point E'', which corresponds to Q'', cloth output is OX''_1 and thus higher than it was at E, but wine output is OX_2 and thus the same as it was at E.)

tion in Britain. If they consume much wine and little cloth, they suffer.

Capital Formation in Portugal

We have dealt thus far with capital formation in Britain, the country that exports the commodity that uses capital. We found that it worsens the terms of trade of the growing country and gives rise to the possibility of immiserizing growth. Consider the effects of capital formation in Portugal, the country that imports the commodity that uses capital.

The effects on the output mix of the growing country are the same as before. The transformation curve for Portugal shifts outward in the manner described by Figures 5-6 and 5-9. If Portugal begins at a point such as E, capital formation moves it to a point such as E', where real national product is larger and cloth output is larger, too, but wine output is smaller. The increase in real national product raises consumers' incomes, and they demand larger quantities of wine and cloth. Accordingly, Portugal displays an excess demand for wine matched by an excess supply of cloth.

But Portugal exports wine and imports cloth. An excess demand for wine, then, reduces its supply of wine exports, and an excess supply of cloth reduces its demand for cloth imports. Portugal's offer curve shifts inward, instead of shifting outward as did the British offer curve in Figure 5-8. An inward shift of the Portuguese offer curve, however, has one effect in common with an outward shift of the British offer curve. It depresses the relative price of cloth.

By implication, capital formation in Portugal improves the Portuguese terms of trade, adding to the increase in economic welfare that results directly from economic growth. It cannot produce immiserizing growth. By worsening the British terms of trade, moreover, it reduces economic wel-

fare in Britain. Contrasting the effects of capital formation in Britain and Portugal:

Location of Capital Formation	ECONOMIC WELFARE	
	Britain	Portugal
Britain	Ambiguous	Increase
Portugal	Decrease	Increase

As capital formation reduces the relative price of cloth whether it occurs in Britain or Portugal, the effects on the income distributions are symmetrical. The changes in the real earnings of labor, land, and capital that take place in Portugal when capital formation occurs in Portugal are the same as those that took place in Britain when capital formation occurred in Britain. Similarly, the changes that take place in Britain when capital formation occurs in Portugal are the same as those that took place in Portugal when capital formation occurred in Britain.

SUMMARY

In the modified Ricardian model, one factor is specific to each industry. Another factor, labor, is mobile across industries. The real wage of labor in each industry is equal to its marginal product in that industry. The requirements of equilibrium in the labor market determine the allocation of the labor force and, therefore, the output of each industry. The effects of a change in relative prices are described by the Haberler theorem. An increase in the relative price of cloth raises employment in the cloth industry and reduces employment in the wine industry. Therefore, it raises the real wage in terms of wine but reduces it in terms of cloth. Furthermore, it raises the real return to capital, the factor specific to the cloth industry, and reduces the real rental rate for land, the factor specific to the wine industry.

An increase in the supply of one specific factor raises output in the industry using that factor and reduces output in the other industry. By implication, countries with different supplies of specific factors will have different transformation curves and will trade with one another. The country that is well supplied with capital will export cloth. The country that is well supplied with land will export wine.

The welfare effects of capital formation depend on the trade pattern. If the growing country imports the commodity that uses capital, the growing country gains, because capital formation improves its terms of trade, and the other country loses. If the growing country exports that commodity, it can gain or lose, depending on the size of the deterioration in its term of trade compared to the direct welfare-raising effect of capital formation, but the other country gains. Capital formation reduces the real return to capital in the growing country. Its effects on other real earnings, however, depend on the commodity in which they are measured and on the new employment pattern. The effects on real earnings in the other country are given by the Haberler theorem.

RECOMMENDED READINGS

The modern version of the specific-factor model is developed in Michael Mussa, "Tariffs and the Distribution of Income: The Importance of Factor Specificity, Substitutability, and Intensity in the Short and Long Run," *Journal of Political Economy,* 82 (November 1974).

On the use of the specific-factor model to describe short-run equilibrium and the factor-endowments model to describe long-run equilibrium, see Michael Mussa, "Dynamic Adjustment in the Heckscher–Ohlin–Samuelson Model," *Journal of Political Economy,* 86 (August 1978), and J. Peter Neary, "Short-Run Capital Specificity and the Pure Theory of International Trade," *Economic Journal,* 88 (September 1978).

For a different and interesting combination of specific-factor and factor-endowments models, see Kalyan K. Sanyal and Ronald W. Jones, "The Theory of Trade in Middle Products," *American Economic Review,* 72 (March 1982).

On conditions likely to produce immiserizing growth, see Jagdish Bhagwati, "Immiserizing Growth: A Geometrical Note," *Review of Economic Studies,* 25 (June 1985), reprinted in American Economic Association, *Readings in International Economics* (Homewood, Ill.: Richard D. Irwin, 1968), ch. 18.

6

FACTOR SUBSTITUTION AND THE HECKSCHER–OHLIN MODEL

INTRODUCTION

This chapter introduces factor substitution into the Heckscher–Ohlin model. It does not change the model to the same extent that it changed the Ricardian model. The main effect is to alter the shape of the transformation curve. Instead of having two straight-line segments and one full-employment output point, it becomes a smooth curve, and each point on the curve is a full-employment point. Nevertheless, the new version of the model allows us to explore more thoroughly the forms and effects of economic growth. We will be able to study capital formation, population growth, and a change in the efficiency of one industry.

ANOTHER WAY TO DEPICT FACTOR SUBSTITUTION

In Chapter 5, firms were able to combine various amounts of labor, the mobile factor, with fixed amounts of land or capital, the specific factors. In this chapter, by contrast, they are able to combine various amounts of labor with various amounts of capital, because both are mobile factors. The choices confronting a firm are described by *isoquants* like the curve I_C in Figure 6-1. Each point on I_C defines a combination of labor and capital that can be used to grow a single bushel of corn. (We will come back to the assumption that corn is grown with labor and capital rather than labor and land.)

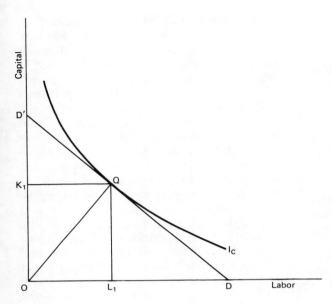

FIGURE 6-1 An Isoquant for the Corn Industry
Each point on the isoquant I_C shows a combination of labor and capital that can be used to produce a single bushel of corn. At Q, for example, OL_1 labor and OK_1 capital are used to grow 1 bushel. The slope of the isoquant is equal to the ratio of marginal products. The least-cost combination of labor and capital is given by the tangency between the isoquant and a line such as DD' whose slope is equal to the relative price of labor (the wage rate divided by the return to capital).

At Q in Figure 6-1, the firm uses OL_1 labor and OK_1 capital. To use less capital but hold corn output constant, the firm must use more labor. The curve I_C, however, makes a stronger statement. As the firm uses less and less capital, it must use increasingly large amounts of labor if it wants to hold corn output constant. The isoquant is bowed inward (concave).

This proposition is proved in Note 6-1. It follows from an assertion made in Chapter 5 that the marginal products of labor and capital depend on the capital-labor ratio, because the shape of the isoquant I_C depends on those marginal products. Suppose that the marginal product of labor is 2 bushels of corn and that the marginal product of capital is 4 bushels. If a firm reduces its use of capital by one unit, its output of corn will fall by 4 bushels, and it must hire 2 more workers to keep output constant. Along any isoquant,

Decrease in capital × marginal product of capital
　　= increase in labor × marginal product of labor

Therefore,

$$\frac{\text{Decrease in capital}}{\text{Increase in labor}} = \frac{\text{marginal product of labor}}{\text{marginal product of capital}}$$

The slope of the isoquant I_C, showing the rate at which capital can be replaced by labor without affecting output, is given by the ratio of marginal products. As production becomes more labor intensive, however, the marginal product of labor falls, the marginal product of capital rises, and the isoquant gets flatter.

Two more propositions follow from this one:

1. All corn isoquants will look just like I_C. To be precise, their slopes will equal the slope of I_C at points that lie on the same straight line drawn from the origin. Where they cross the line OQ, for example, all corn isoquants will have slopes equal to the slope of DD', which is tangent to I_C at Q.

2. A profit-maximizing firm will choose that factor combination at which the slope of an isoquant is equal to the relative price of labor. If the relative price of labor is given by the slope of

DD', the firm will go to Q, where DD' is tangent to I_C.

The first proposition follows from the fact that marginal products depend entirely on factor intensities. The slope of OQ measures the capital-labor ratio chosen by a firm that produces at Q. It uses OK_1 capital and OL_1 labor. The slope of OQ, then, determines the marginal products of labor and capital at all points on OQ, defining the slope of I_C at Q and the slopes of all other corn isoquants where they intersect OQ. The second proposition follows from a statement made earlier. A profit-maximizing firm uses those quantities of labor and capital at which the marginal product of labor is equal to the real wage and the marginal product of capital is equal to the real return. Therefore, we can substitute the real wage for the marginal product of labor and substitute the real return for the marginal product of capital:

$$\frac{\text{Decrease in capital}}{\text{Increase in labor}} = \frac{\text{real wage}}{\text{real return}}$$

$$= \frac{\text{wage rate}}{\text{price of corn}} \times \frac{\text{price of corn}}{\text{return to capital}}$$

$$= \frac{\text{wage rate}}{\text{return to capital}}$$

which is, of course, the relative price of labor.[1]

---

[1] This condition can be derived from the simple assumption that a firm will minimize the cost of producing any output. Suppose that the slope of DD' in Figure 6-1 is equal to the relative price of labor and that the firm begins by using OL_1 labor and OK_1 capital to produce a single bushel of corn. The total cost of producing that bushel will be OD' in terms of capital,

Total cost = (quantity of capital × return to capital)

+ (quantity of labor × wage rate)

and total cost in terms of capital will be

$$\frac{\text{Total cost}}{\text{Return to capital}} = \text{quantity of capital} +$$

$$\text{quantity of labor} \times \frac{\text{wage rate}}{\text{return to capital}}$$

Working back from this last proposition, let us see what we can say about the behavior of the firm when we know the shape of the corn isoquant and the relative price of labor. We know what point the firm will choose on a corn isoquant—the quantities of labor and capital it will use to grow the quantity of corn corresponding to that isoquant. Therefore, we know the capital-labor ratio or capital intensity of corn production, and it will be the same at each level of corn output, because it depends exclusively on the relative price of labor. We know the marginal products of labor and capital, because they depend on the capital intensity of corn production. Therefore, we know the real wage of labor and the real return to capital. Finally, we know that an increase in the relative price of labor will cause the firm to substitute capital for labor, raising the capital intensity of corn production at each output level. This will raise the real wage and reduce the real return to capital.

Allocating Capital

Labor can move freely from industry to industry. Capital can move, too, given enough time.

Before capital can be employed to manufacture steel, it must be invested in machinery and buildings. Call these invest-

But the quantity of capital is OK_1, the quantity of labor is OL_1, and the relative price of labor is $(L_1Q/L_1D) = (K_1D'/K_1Q) = (K_1D'/OL_1)$. Therefore,

$$\frac{\text{Total cost}}{\text{Return to capital}} = OK_1 + \left(OL_1 \times \frac{K_1D'}{OL_1} \right)$$

$$= OK_1 + K_1D' = OD'$$

Suppose that the firm attempted to reduce its total cost below OD'. It could not reach I_C. By implication, it cannot grow a bushel of corn at less cost than OD'. Suppose instead that it chose a point on I_C other than Q. The total-cost line passing through that point would lie above DD', and total cost in terms of capital would exceed OD'. The combination of labor and capital shown at Q is the least-cost combination when the relative price of labor equals the slope of DD'.

Note 6-1

Output is constant along any isoquant, which means that the change in output is zero. Repeating the second equation in Note 5-1,

$$dx_i = f^i_L \, dL_i + f^i_k \, dK_i = 0$$

Therefore,

$$f^i_k \, dK_i = -f^i_L \, dL_i$$

or

$$\frac{dK_i}{dL_i} = -\frac{f^i_L}{f^i_k}$$

The slope of the isoquant is equal (absolutely) to the ratio of marginal products.

When a firm maximizes profits, moreover, it equates the marginal product of labor to the real wage and the marginal product of capital to the real return. Therefore,

$$\frac{dK_i}{dL_i} = -\frac{w/p_i}{r/p_i} = -\frac{w}{r}$$

The firm chooses the point on its isoquant where the slope is equal (absolutely) to the relative price of labor (the wage rate divided by the return to capital).

---

ments "mills" for brevity. Before it can be employed to grow corn, it must be invested in some other form. Land is needed to grow corn, but must be improved by applying capital—cleared, irrigated, and fertilized—and must be worked with the help of machinery. Suppose that the supply of land is fixed, but that the supply available for growing corn depends on the amount of capital invested in it. Call these investments "tractors" for brevity.[2]

At any time, part of the economy's capital will be invested in mills, and the rest in tractors. The economy will resemble the modified Ricardian model examined in Chapter 5. It will have one mobile factor (labor) and two specific factors (mills and tractors). But capital can be reallocated

gradually. Mills and tractors depreciate with age and use. Their owners must set aside funds to replace them. If those funds are used in the amounts needed to maintain the numbers of mills and tractors, the supply of capital will not change, and its allocation will not change. This is what will happen in long-run equilibrium, when a dollar of capital earns the same return in each potential use—invested in a mill or invested in a tractor. If that equilibrium is disturbed, however, the number of mills and tractors will begin to change.

Let there be an increase in the relative price of corn. The Haberler theorem for the specific-factor model tells us what will happen in the short run. There will be an increase in the real return to tractors, the form of capital used specifically in growing corn, and a decrease in the real return to mills, the form used specifically in making steel. This will raise the rate of return to a dollar of capital invested in a tractor, compared to the rate of return to a dollar invested in a mill. Farmers will start to buy tractors faster than old ones wear out. They can obtain the funds they need to in-

---

[2] To be realistic, we might want to assume that the supply of land available for growing corn rises by smaller and smaller amounts as additional tractors are used to cultivate a fixed quantity of raw land, that the law of diminishing returns applies to investments in land. But we will assume for simplicity that the supply rises in proportion to the number of tractors, so the quantity of land used for growing corn can be represented by the quantity of capital invested in it.

crease their purchases by borrowing from firms that manufacture steel, because they can pay more for the use of those funds than steel producers can earn by replacing their old mills. There need be no change in the supply of capital—it is constant here—but the supply will be reallocated. The number of tractors will rise, and the number of mills will fall.

This way of looking at the role of capital is somewhat artificial, but it is more realistic than the approach adopted in many treatments of the Heckscher–Ohlin model. That approach assumes that there is a "machine" that can be used with equal ease to make steel or grow corn. The supply of capital is measured in machines and is freely transferable between the two activities. There is, of course, no such machine. But when we treat capital more realistically, we must be very clear about our findings. They hold only in the long run, when the supply of capital is allocated optimally between mills and tractors because the return to a dollar of capital is the same in both uses.

Equilibrium in the Factor Markets

Figure 6-2 shows one way to describe long-run equilibrium in an economy of this sort. The isoquant I_C shows how labor and capital (tractors) can be combined to grow corn. The isoquant I_S shows how labor and capital (mills) can be combined to make steel. Represent the relative price of labor by the slope of the line DD', and give the economy enough time to allocate capital optimally between mills and tractors. Corn will be grown by the method shown at C. The capital intensity of corn production is given by the slope of OC, showing how much capital is invested in tractors for every worker growing corn. Steel will be manufactured by the method shown at S. The capital intensity of steel production is given by the slope of OS, showing how much capital is invested in mills for every worker making steel. As OS is steeper than OC, steel is the capital-intensive commodity, as in Chapter 4. The shapes of the isoquants in Figure 6-2 generate this ordering of factor intensities at all sets of factor prices.

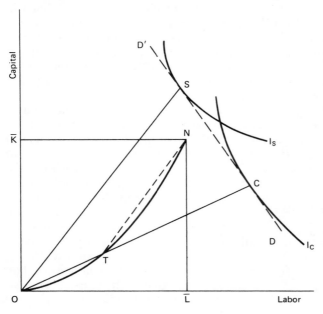

FIGURE 6-2 Fixed Factor Supplies and the Output Mix with Flexible Factor Intensities
Factor supplies are $O\overline{L}$ labor and $O\overline{K}$ capital. The relative price of labor is given by the slope of the line DD'. As that line is tangent to I_C at C, the slope of OC gives the capital-labor ratio in corn production. As it is tangent to I_S at S, the slope of OS gives the capital-labor ratio in steel production. Steel is more capital intensive than corn. The full-employment point is T, where the economy produces OT corn and NT steel. When factor intensities can vary, however, there are many full-employment points. All of them lie on the curve OTN.

The economy is endowed with $O\overline{L}$ workers and $O\overline{K}$ dollars of capital. Therefore, it can use both factors fully by producing at T. It can grow OT bushels of corn and can manufacture NT tons of steel. (The line NT is parallel to OS, measuring the capital intensity of steel production.) If factor requirements were fixed, T would be the only full-employment point. When factor requirements can vary, it is only one of many full-employment points that can be reached in the long run. They are the points on the curve OTN.

THE MODIFIED
HECKSCHER–OHLIN MODEL

To show how the Heckscher–Ohlin model behaves with factor substitution, we have first to show how market forces generate the curve OTN, and then use it to derive the transformation curve for an economy having $O\overline{L}$ labor and $O\overline{K}$ capital.

Factor Prices and Factor Intensities

The curve OTN is produced by the influence of factor prices on firms' decisions about factor intensities. Figure 6-3 shows what they do. The corn isoquant I_C is drawn as before. The steel isoquant I_S is inverted, and its origin is placed at N, so capital and labor used in making steel are measured from that point. Begin as before by letting the relative price of labor equal the slope of I_C at C and the slope of I_S at S. The capital intensity of corn production is given by the slope of OC, and the capital intensity of steel production is given by the slope of NS. Both factors of production will be fully employed if the economy winds up at T, producing OT bushels of corn and NT tons of steel. Now raise the relative price of labor by letting it equal the slope of I_C at C' and the slope of I_S at S'. The capital intensity of corn production is given by the slope of OC', and the capital intensity of steel production is given by the slope of NS'.

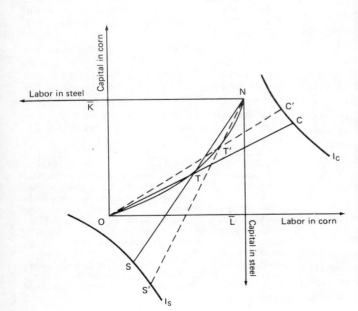

FIGURE 6-3 Factor Prices, Factor Intensities, and the Output Mix The corn isoquant I_C is drawn as in Figure 6-2. The steel isoquant I_S is inverted (the factors used in making steel are measured from N). When the relative price of labor equals the slopes of I_C at C and I_S at S, the full-employment point is T. When the relative price of labor equals the slopes of I_C at C' and I_S at S', the full-employment point is T', where corn output is higher and steel output lower. An increase in corn output raises the demand for labor and reduces the demand for capital, because corn is the labor-intensive commodity. The relative price of labor rises, causing both industries to substitute capital for labor (OC' is steeper than OC, and NS' is steeper than NS).

Both factors of production will be fully employed if the economy winds up at T', producing OT' corn and NT' steel. The points T and T' lie on the curve OTN, which shows the whole set of full-employment points.

When the economy moves from T to T', both industries become more capital intensive (OC' is steeper than OC, and NS' is steeper than NS). How can this happen when the supply of capital is fixed? A movement from T to T' raises the output of corn, the labor-intensive commodity, and reduces the output of steel, the capital-intensive commodity. This change in the output mix reduces the demand for capital, offsetting the shift by each industry to a more capital-intensive method of production.

The same point can be made by starting with a change in the output mix rather than a change in factor prices. Let there be an increase in corn output along with a decrease in steel output. The demand for labor rises, because corn is more labor intensive than steel, and this raises the relative price of labor. Farmers are induced to move along I_C from C to C', raising the capital intensity of corn production. Steel firms are induced to move along I_S from S to S', raising the capital intensity of steel production. Substitution of capital for labor takes place in each industry and makes way for the increase in the output of the labor-intensive commodity. With factor substitution, a change in the output mix leads to a change in factor prices that leads, in turn, to changes in factor intensities, which maintain equilibrium in the factor markets.

Deriving the Transformation Curve

There is a relationship between the curve OTN and the transformation curve. It is depicted in Figure 6-4. The lower part of this diagram shows what we have seen before: the fixed supplies of labor and capi-

tal, $O\overline{L}$ and $O\overline{K}$, and the curve OTN. It also shows the isoquants I_C and I_S that relate to the output levels obtained at T. The corn and steel isoquants are tangent to each other because the economy produces at T only when the slopes of I_C and I_S are equal to the relative price of labor, which means that the slope of I_C must equal the slope of I_S. The upper part of the diagram shows the transformation curve, Z_1QZ_2, that corresponds to the curve OTN.

The transformation curve can be derived from the information given in the lower part of the diagram:

1. If the economy specialized completely in growing corn, it would be at N in the lower part of the diagram, and its output would be some such quantity as OZ_1 bushels. (Point Z_1 is drawn deliberately to lie above N.)

2. If the economy specialized completely in making steel, it would be at O in the lower part of the diagram, and its output would be some such quantity as OZ_2 tons. (Point Z_2 is chosen arbitrarily.)

3. Draw the straight lines ON and Z_1Z_2, and note the relationship between them. If the economy produced at T', a point on ON, it would find itself at Q', the point on Z_1Z_2 that lies vertically above T'.[3]

4. Now go to T on OTN and move along the corn isoquant I_c until you reach ON at T'. As corn output is the same at every point on I_C and is also the same at T' and Q', corn output at T is OX_1 bushels.

5. Return to T to pick up the steel isoquant I_S, and move along it until you reach ON at T''.

---

[3] This relationship derives from the assumption that returns to scale are constant in both industries. Suppose that the economy produced at the point in the middle of ON, using half its labor and capital to grow corn and the rest to make steel. Its outputs would be half of OZ_1 and half of OZ_2, and it would be at the point in the middle of Z_1Z_2. Thus, movements along ON correspond to movements along Z_1Z_2. (Production at T' is feasible but inefficient. By moving along I_C from T' to T, the economy can keep corn output constant at OX_1 bushels but increase steel output at the same time. This is made clear by the next steps in the text.)

FIGURE 6-4 Equilibrium in Factor and Commodity Markets
When $O\bar{L}$ labor and $O\bar{K}$ capital are used to grow corn, output is OZ_1 bushels. When they are used to make steel, output is OZ_2 tons. Furthermore, output points on the straight line ON correspond to output points on the straight line Z_1Z_2, and this fact can be used to show the relationship between output points on the curve OTN and those on the transformation curve Z_1QZ_2. Start at T on OTN. Hold corn output constant by moving along the corn isoquant I_C until it intersects ON at T'. As T' corresponds to Q', corn output at T' and T is OX_1 bushels. Returning to T, hold steel output constant by moving along the steel isoquant I_S until it intersects ON at T''. As T'' corresponds to Q'', steel output at T'' and T is OX_2 tons. These are the outputs at Q on the transformation curve Z_1QZ_2.

As steel output is the same at every point on I_S and is also the same at T'' and Q'', steel output at T is OX_2 tons.

6. As OX_1 and OX_2 are the coordinates of Q, it is the point on the transformation curve Z_1QZ_2 that corresponds to T on the curve OTN.

The transformation curve is bowed outward, because changes in output involve changes in factor intensities that alter the marginal products of labor and capital. Furthermore, the slope of the transformation curve is equal in equilibrium to the relative price of corn.

Commodity Prices and Factor Prices

Figure 6-4 supplies a large amount of information about the behavior of the economy. Starting in the upper part of the diagram, set the relative price of corn equal to the slope of the transformation curve at Q. Corn output is OX_1 bushels, and steel output is OX_2 tons. Moving from Q to Q' and then from Q' to T', we can locate the corn isoquant I_C, where output is OX_1 bushels, and we can locate T by moving down I_C until we reach the curve OTN. The slope of I_C at that point tells us the relative price of labor, and the slopes of OT and NT tell us the capital intensities chosen by corn and steel producers. Those intensities, in turn, tell us the marginal products of labor and capital, which are equal to the real earnings of the factors. The real wage of labor measured in corn is equal to the marginal product of labor in the production of corn, and the real wage measured in steel is equal to the marginal product of labor in the production of steel. The real return to capital measured in corn is equal to the marginal product of capital in the production of corn, and the real return measured in steel is equal to the marginal product of capital in the production of steel.

How does the economy respond to an increase in the relative price of corn? The output point Q travels down the transformation curve, causing T to travel up the curve OTN. The relative price of labor rises, as in Figure 6-3, and both industries become more capital intensive. The marginal products of labor rise, raising the real wage of labor measured in corn or steel. The marginal products of capital fall, reducing the real return to capital measured in corn or steel. This proves the Stolper–Samuelson theorem for the modified version of the Heckscher–Ohlin model. An increase in the price of corn, the labor-intensive commodity, raises the real wage of labor and reduces the real wage of capital. (The theorem holds only in the long run, however, after the numbers of mills and tractors are fully adjusted to the new situation.)

The information obtained from Figure 6-4 is shown again in Figure 6-5, where relative prices and capital intensities are shown as distances rather than slopes. The curve CC' on the left side of this diagram shows how the capital intensity of corn production responds to the relative price of labor. When that price is OW, for example, the capital intensity of corn production is OK_1. When it is higher than OW, farmers substitute capital for labor, raising the capital intensity above OK_1. The curve SS' shows how the capital intensity of steel production responds to the relative price of labor. When that price is OW, the capital intensity of steel production is OK_2. Steel is more capital intensive than corn, and this is always true in Figure 6-5, because SS' and CC' do not cross. The curve HH' on the

right side of the diagram shows the relationship between the relative price of corn and the relative price of labor. When the relative price of corn is OP, the price of labor is OW. When the price of corn rises, so does the relative price of labor, and both industries become more capital intensive.

There is another way to use this diagram, however, and that is the main reason for presenting it. Suppose that an economy is endowed with $O\overline{K}$ capital per worker. If the relative price of corn is OP', the relative price of labor will be OW', and the economy will be at G', where all its labor and capital are used to manufacture steel (G' corresponds to Z_2 in Figure 6-4). If the relative price of corn is OP'', the relative price of labor will be OW'', and the economy will be at G'', where all its labor and capital are used to grow corn (G'' corresponds to Z_1 in Figure 6-4). Therefore, the segment $G'G''$ corresponds to the curve OTN in Figure 6-4 and to the transformation curve Z_1QZ_2. It shows how an economy endowed with $O\overline{K}$ capital per worker can allocate its labor and capital and how to identify the actual allocation. When the relative price of corn is OP, the economy will be at G. When that price is higher than OP, it will move to a point above G, producing more corn and less steel.[4]

Factor Endowments and the Transformation Curve

Before making further use of Figure 6-5, let us answer one more question. How does the economy respond to an increase in the supply of capital? The Rybczynski theo-

---

[4] When the relative price of corn falls below OP', the economy continues to produce at G', and the relative price of labor remains at OW'. This says that the curve HH' has no economic meaning for this economy when the relative price of corn is lower than OP' or higher than OP''. The relative price of labor gets stuck once the economy is completely specialized. It can go no lower than OW' and no higher than OW''.

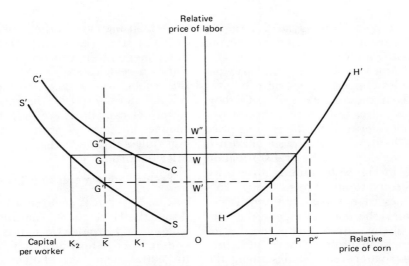

FIGURE 6-5 Commodity Prices, Factor Prices, and Factor Intensities
The curve *HH'* describes the relationship between the relative price of
corn and the relative price of labor. When the relative price of corn is
OP, the relative price of labor is *OW*. An increase in the relative price of
corn raises the relative price of labor. The curve *CC'* describes the relationship between the relative price of labor and the capital-labor ratio in
corn production. The curve *SS'* describes the corresponding relationship
in steel production. When the relative price of labor is *OW*, corn producers use OK_1 capital per worker, and steel producers use OK_2 capital
per worker. (Steel is more capital intensive than corn.) A country that
has $O\overline{K}$ capital per worker will produce at *G'* when the relative price of
corn is *OP'* (or lower); it will specialize completely in steel. It will produce at *G"* when the relative price of corn is *OP"* (or higher); it will specialize completely in corn. It will produce at *G* when the relative price
of corn is *OP*; it will produce some corn and some steel.

rem holds, but must be reformulated.
When factor requirements were fixed, that
theorem told us what would happen to the
full-employment point. When factor requirements vary, it tells us what happens to
the whole transformation curve.

In Chapter 4, where factor requirements
were fixed, the Rybczynski theorem was illustrated by Figure 4-3. Look back at that
diagram. The capital intensity of corn production was given by the slope of *OC*, the
capital intensity of steel production was
given by the slope of *OS*, and the slopes of
those lines were fixed by factor requirements. An increase in the supply of cap-
ital from $O\overline{K}$ to $O\overline{K}'$ shifted the full-

employment point from T to T', raising steel output from NT to $N'T'$ and reducing corn output from OT to OT'.

When factor requirements can vary, factor intensities depend on decisions by producers, given the relative price of labor. But we have already seen that the relative price of labor depends on the relative price of corn. When the relative price of corn is equal to the slope of the transformation curve at Q in Figure 6-4, the relative price of labor is equal to the slope of I_C at T. Factor intensities are not fixed, but they do not change unless there is a change in the relative price of corn. Accordingly, the shift of the full-employment point shown in Figure 4-3 can be reinterpreted as describing the shift of a point such as T in Figure 6-4 and, therefore, the shift of the output point Q, illustrating the shift of the whole transformation curve due to a change in the factor endowment. The point on the new transformation curve having the same slope as Q will lie to the northwest of Q. The value of national output will rise expressed in corn or steel, and steel output will rise, too, but corn output will fall.

Here again we see the major difference in behavior between the modified Ricardian model and the modified Heckscher–Ohlin model. In the modified Ricardian model, an increase in the supply of capital used in making cloth altered the real earnings of the factors of production even when there was no change in the relative price of cloth. It led to a reallocation of labor from wine to cloth production. As there was no change in the amount of land used for making wine, the marginal product of labor rose in that activity, raising the real wage, and the marginal product of land fell, reducing the real rental rate. With the increase in the real wage, moreover, cloth producers substituted capital for labor, reducing the marginal product of capital and its real return. In the Heckscher–Ohlin

model, an increase in the supply of capital does not affect real earnings unless it leads to a change in the relative price of corn. It causes a reallocation of capital along with the reallocation of labor, so factor intensities are not altered by the increase in the supply of capital. Therefore, there are no changes in marginal products or real earnings unless there is a change in the relative price of corn.

Factor Endowments and Trade

The Rybczynski theorem can be used to derive the Heckscher–Ohlin theorem, as in Chapter 4. Consider once again Manymen and Fewmen, which differ only in their factor endowments. As Manymen has more labor and less capital, the Rybczynski theorem tells us what will happen when the two countries' markets are unified by trade. As the relative price of corn will be the same in the two countries after trade is opened, Manymen will grow more corn and Fewmen will make more steel. As demand conditions are the same in the two countries, however, they will want to consume the same collections of commodities. Therefore, Manymen will export corn, the labor-intensive commodity, and Fewmen will export steel, the capital-intensive commodity.

The effects of trade are summarized by Figure 6-6. Manymen has $O\overline{K}_1$ capital per worker. Fewmen has $O\overline{K}_2$ capital per worker. Before trade is opened, the relative price of corn is OP_1 in Manymen, the relative price of labor is OW_1, and Manymen produces at M. The relative price of corn is OP_2 in Fewmen, the relative price of labor is OW_2, and Fewmen produces at F. The relative price of corn is lower in Manymen, and so is the relative price of labor. After trade is opened, the relative price of corn moves to some such level as OP, driving the relative price of labor to OW in both countries. Corn and labor become more expen-

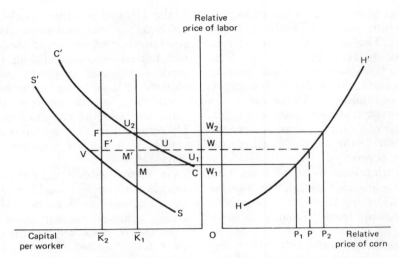

FIGURE 6-6 Free Trade Between Manymen and Fewmen
The capital-labor ratio is $O\overline{K}_1$ in Manymen and $O\overline{K}_2$ in Fewmen. Before
trade is opened, the relative price of corn is OP_1 in Manymen, the relative price of labor is OW_1, and Manymen produces at M. The relative
price of corn is OP_2 in Fewmen, the relative price of labor is OW_2, and
Fewmen produces at F. The real wage is higher in Fewmen, and the real
return to capital is higher in Manymen. When trade is opened, the relative price of corn goes to OP in both countries, and the relative price of
labor goes to OW. Manymen produces at M', growing more corn and
making less steel. Fewmen produces at F', growing less corn and making more steel. The real earnings of the factors have been equalized. The
real wage has fallen in Fewmen and risen in Manymen. The real return
to capital has risen in Fewmen and fallen in Manymen.

sive in Manymen but cheaper in Fewmen.
The output point for Manymen moves
from M to M', closer to the CC' curve and
farther from the SS' curve. The relative
price of corn rises in Manymen, which
moves along its transformation curve to
grow more corn and make less steel. The
output point for Fewmen moves from F to
F', in the opposite direction. The relative
price of corn falls in Fewmen, which moves
along its transformation curve to grow less
corn and make more steel.

Figure 6-6 illustrates another theorem.

Free trade can equalize the two countries'
factor prices. When the relative price of
labor is OW in Manymen and Fewmen,
their industries must have the same capital
intensities. The capital intensity of corn
output is given at U by the distance WU.
The capital intensity of steel output is given
at V by the distance WV. Thus, the marginal products of labor and capital must be
the same in the two countries, which means
that the factors' real earnings must be
equal, whether they are measured in corn
or steel.

The factor-price-equalization theorem is a strong result, and it depends on strong assumptions. This is a useful place to recapitulate. All markets must be perfectly competitive. Both countries must have access to the same technologies and must produce both commodities. There can be no trade barriers or transport costs. Returns to scale must be constant, and industries must differ in their factor intensities (there can be no factor reversals).

These assumptions are unrealistic. They serve nonetheless to highlight an interesting implication of the Heckscher–Ohlin model. Free trade tends to maximize world output.

Return to the pretrade situation in Figure 6-6. When the relative price of labor is OW_1 in Manymen and OW_2 in Fewmen, both industries are more capital intensive in Fewmen. The capital intensity of corn production, for example, is $W_1 U_1$ in Manymen and $W_2 U_2$ in Fewmen. Therefore, the marginal product of labor is lower in Manymen, and the marginal product of capital is lower in Fewmen.

Suppose that we could transfer factors of production from one country to the other. We could increase world output by moving labor from Manymen to Fewmen. Output would fall in Manymen but rise by more in Fewmen, because the marginal product of labor is higher in Fewmen. Similarly, we could increase world output by moving capital from Fewmen to Manymen. These transfers, however, would alter the marginal products. The marginal product of labor would rise in Manymen and fall in Fewmen; the marginal product of capital would fall in Manymen and rise in Fewmen. And once the gaps were closed completely, we could not increase world output by moving more factors around. World output would be maximized.

Look at the role of trade from this same standpoint. Under the strong assumptions of the Heckscher–Ohlin model, free trade will equalize marginal products. The marginal product of labor will rise in Manymen and fall in Fewmen, closing the gap between marginal products without any transfer of labor. The marginal product of capital will fall in Fewmen and rise in Manymen without any transfer of capital. Therefore, free trade maximizes world output. It is a perfect substitute for factor movements.

As factor-price equalization cannot be complete in the real world, free trade cannot maximize world output. Under much weaker assumptions than those made here, however, it does reduce differences between factor prices, narrowing the gaps between marginal products. Thus, it raises world output and is therefore a partial substitute for factor movements. This is another way to look at the gains from trade in the context of the Heckscher–Ohlin model.

ECONOMIC GROWTH IN THE HECKSCHER–OHLIN MODEL

As capital is used by both industries in the Heckscher–Ohlin model, we might expect the analysis of economic growth to be more complicated than it was in the modified Ricardian model. Fortunately, it is simpler, because the real earnings of the factors of production depend only on the terms of trade, and we do not have to worry about the commodity in which they are measured.

In the modified Ricardian model, labor was the only factor that moved between industries. Therefore, an increase in the relative price of cloth, inducing a shift of labor from wine to cloth production, increased the real wage in terms of wine but reduced it in terms of cloth. In the Heckscher–Ohlin model, labor and capital can move together, given enough time, and cause capital intensities to rise and fall together.

An increase in the relative price of corn, the labor-intensive commodity, shifts labor and capital from steel to corn production, raising the capital intensities of steel and corn outputs. It thus raises the marginal products of labor in both industries and reduces the marginal products of capital. The real wage rises and the real return to capital falls whether they are measured in corn or steel.

In what follows, then, it will not be necessary to mention the commodity used to measure real earnings. It will be necessary, however, to remember that the results hold only in the long run, when capital has been optimally allocated between the two industries.

We begin with capital formation; then we turn to other sources of economic growth.

Capital Formation in Fewmen

Consider the effects of capital formation in the capital-abundant country, Fewmen, which exports the capital-intensive commodity, steel. The output effects are given by the Rybczynski theorem. At commodity and factor prices prevailing initially, real national product will rise in Fewmen, steel output will rise, too, and corn output will fall.[5] But consumers in Fewmen will demand more corn and steel, so Fewmen will display an excess demand for corn matched by an excess supply of steel. Its offer curve will shift outward, because it exports steel, and its terms of trade will deteriorate. The story is the same one told by Figure 5-8 in

Chapter 5, with steel and corn put in place of cloth and wine, Fewmen put in place of Britain, and Manymen put in place of Portugal. Fewmen's offer curve will shift from OJ to OJ', displacing equilibrium from W to W'. The relative price of steel will fall, which worsens Fewmen's terms of trade.

The effects on economic welfare are much like those obtained when capital formation took place in Britain in the modified Ricardian model. If the relative price of steel falls far enough, Fewmen can experience immiserizing growth. The deterioration in its terms of trade can wipe out the welfare gain conferred by capital formation, because consumers can be driven to an indifference curve lower than the curve on which they started. Otherwise, Fewmen will gain from growth, but the gain will be smaller than the gain it would obtain if Fewmen were too small to influence world prices. By implication, Manymen is bound to gain. It will experience an improvement in its terms of trade.

How do real earnings change? They are not affected by capital formation until it reduces the relative price of steel. Once that happens, we can apply the Stolper–Samuelson theorem. A reduction in the relative price of steel depresses the real return to capital, the factor used intensively in making steel. It raises the real wage of labor, the factor used intensively in growing corn. Furthermore, these same things happen in Fewmen and Manymen whenever free trade equalizes the two countries' factor prices.

The effects of capital formation in Fewmen are summarized by Figure 6-7. Manymen has $O\overline{K}_1$ capital per worker, and Fewmen has $O\overline{K}_2$ before capital formation. The relative price of corn is OP in both countries and the relative price of labor is OW. Manymen produces at M, and Fewmen produces at F. Capital formation in Fewmen raises the quantity of capital per

---

[5] The shift in the transformation curve is much like the one shown in Figure 5-6 of Chapter 5, with steel put in place of cloth on the horizontal axis and corn in place of wine on the vertical axis. But there is one difference. As capital is used by both industries, capital formation increases the distance OZ_2 as well as the distance OZ_1. The whole curve shifts outward.

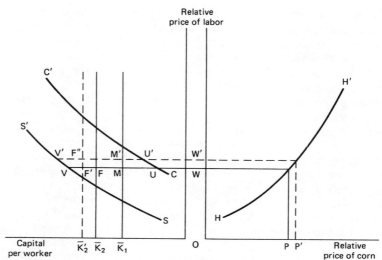

FIGURE 6-7 Effects of Capital Formation in Fewmen
Manymen has $O\overline{K}_1$ capital per worker, and Fewmen has $O\overline{K}_2$. With free
trade between them, the relative price of corn is OP in both countries,
and the relative price of labor is OW. Manymen produces at M, and
Fewmen produces at F. The capital intensity of corn production is WU,
and the capital intensity of steel production is WV. Capital formation in
Fewmen raises capital per worker to $O\overline{K}_2'$ and shifts that country's output
point from F to F', where it produces more steel and less corn. The reduction in corn output raises the relative price of corn to OP', and the
relative price of labor rises to OW'. The output point in Fewmen moves
from F' to F'', and the output point in Manymen moves from M to M'.
The capital intensities of corn and steel production rise to $W'U'$ and
$W'V'$, respectively, raising the marginal products of labor in both industries and countries and reducing the marginal products of capital. Real
wages rise and real returns to capital fall.

worker from $O\overline{K}_2$ to $O\overline{K}_2'$, shifting Fewmen's output point from F to F', where
Fewmen makes more steel and grows less
corn. The change in the output mix raises
the relative price of corn to some such level
as OP'. Therefore, it raises the relative
price of labor to OW' and shifts both countries' output points. Fewmen moves from
F' to F'', and Manymen moves from M to
M'. Both countries grow more corn and
make less steel to compensate for the shift
in Fewmen's output mix when it moved ini-

tially from F to F'. The capital intensity of
corn production rises from WU to $W'U'$ in
both countries, and the capital intensity of
steel production rises from WV to $W'V'$.
Real wages rise in both countries, and real
returns to capital fall.

Capital Formation in Manymen

You should be able to work out for yourself the effects of capital formation in
Manymen. The effects on relative prices
and real returns must be the same as when

capital formation took place in Fewmen. But Manymen imports steel, which means that a reduction in the relative price of steel is an improvement in Manymen's terms of trade. Accordingly, capital formation in Manymen cannot be immiserizing, and its welfare effects are unambiguous:

Location of Capital Formation	ECONOMIC WELFARE	
	Fewmen	Manymen
Fewmen	Ambiguous	Increase
Manymen	Decrease	Increase

This tabulation is identical to the one for the modified Ricardian model.

Growth in the Supply of Labor

The long-run effects of growth in the supply of labor are given by the Rybczynski and Stolper–Samuelson theorems. It increases the supply of the labor-intensive commodity in the growing country and decreases the supply of the capital-intensive commodity. Therefore, growth reduces the relative price of the labor-intensive commodity, worsening the terms of trade of the labor-abundant country. Furthermore, it raises the real return to capital in both countries and reduces the real wage. These effects are perfectly analogous to those obtained previously for capital formation. But a new problem has to be confronted. An increase in the supply of labor usually involves an increase in the number of consumers, and this affects the measurement of economic welfare.

When studying capital formation in Fewmen, we saw that it raised real national product, which cushioned the effect of the deterioration in Fewmen's terms of trade. As the number of consumers was constant, the increase in real national product raised consumers' incomes and led to an increase in economic welfare at the initial terms of trade. There had to be a large deterioration in the terms of trade before Fewmen could experience immiserizing growth. With an increase in the supply of labor and no change in the supply of capital, real national product rises by less than the number of consumers (workers), and consumers' incomes fall. Proof is offered in Note 6-2. Therefore, growth in the supply of labor reduces economic welfare at the initial terms of trade.

Accordingly, we come to dismal conclusions regarding the effects of growth in one country's population:

1. When population growth takes place in Manymen, the country that exports the labor-intensive commodity, it is bound to be immiserizing. The welfare-decreasing deterioration in Manymen's terms of trade is combined with a welfare-decreasing decline in consumers' incomes. (But Fewmen gains, as usual, because its terms of trade improve.)

2. When population growth takes place in Fewmen, the country that imports the labor-intensive commodity, it can still be immiserizing. The welfare-increasing improvement in Fewmen's terms of trade may not be large enough to offset the welfare-decreasing decline in consumers' incomes. (Manymen loses, moreover, because its terms of trade deteriorate.)

There is a difference, however, between the immiserizing growth that occurs with population growth and the sort that can occur with capital formation. Population growth is immiserizing in a closed economy; terms-of-trade effects can make matters worse or better, but they are not the primary cause of the welfare loss. Capital formation cannot be immiserizing in a closed economy; terms-of-trade effects are crucial for the outcome.

These assertions are illustrated in Figure 6-8, where outputs are divided by numbers of persons to show how capital formation and population growth affect the welfare

Note 6-2

The value of national product is the sum of payments to labor and capital:

$$y = wL + rK = r\left(\frac{w}{r} + \frac{K}{L}\right)L$$

Divide by N, the number of persons (consumers) to obtain income per capita:

$$y_c = \frac{y}{N} = r\left(\frac{w}{r} + \frac{K}{L}\right)\left(\frac{L}{N}\right)$$

Divide by p_i, the price of the ith commodity, to obtain real income per capita:

$$\frac{y_c}{p_i} = \frac{r}{p_i}\left(\frac{w}{r} + \frac{K}{L}\right)\left(\frac{L}{N}\right)$$

But r/p_i is the real return to capital measured in the ith commodity and equals the marginal product of capital in the ith industry. It cannot change without a change in the factor intensity of that industry resulting from a change in relative prices. Furthermore, w/r is the relative price of labor, and it cannot change without a change in commodity prices. The ratio of workers to persons, L/N, is a measure of labor-force participation, and we can assume that it is constant in the long run. Therefore, when relative prices are constant, real income per capita depends only on K/L, capital per worker in the economy. An increase in the supply of labor alone reduces K/L and thus reduces real income per capita. Increases in the supplies of labor and capital at the same rates keep K/L constant, and real income per capita does not change.

This note refutes a famous fallacy. Critics of the Heckscher–Ohlin model say that the factor-price-equalization theorem must be false, because incomes per capita are so different across countries. But factor-price equalization does not imply the equalization of incomes per capita. The w/r and r/p_i are equalized across countries, but not the L/N or K/L. In fact, differences in K/L are the basis for trade in the Heckscher–Ohlin model.

of the typical consumer. The transformation curve is $Z_1 Z_2$ initially in both parts of the diagram, and it is tangent at E to an indifference curve U_0.[6] Real output per capita is OA measured in corn, and is equal to real income per capita. Corn output per capita is OX_1 and is equal to corn consumption per capita in a closed economy. Steel

---

[6] The outputs shown by this transformation curve can be obtained from the equations at the bottom of Note 4-1. Factor L from the right side of each equation and divide both sides of each equation by N (population):

$$\frac{x_1}{N} = \frac{1}{D}\frac{L}{N}\left[b_2 - a_2\left(\frac{K}{L}\right)\right] \quad \text{and} \quad \frac{x_2}{N} = \frac{1}{D}\frac{L}{N}\left[a_1\left(\frac{K}{L}\right) - b_1\right]$$

where $D = a_1 b_2 - a_2 b_1 > 0$ when x_1 is the labor-intensive commodity (corn). Outputs per capita depend on L/N, defined in Note 6-2 as labor-force par-

ticipation, on K/L, the capital-labor ratio for the whole economy, and on the capital and labor requirements, a_i and b_i ($i = 1, 2$). Output per capita of the labor-intensive commodity falls with an increase in the capital-labor ratio, and output per capita of the capital-intensive commodity rises. The Rybczynski theorem applies to outputs per capita. Furthermore, Note 6-2 shows that real product per capita rises with an increase in the capital-labor ratio. (The curve U_0, incidentally, is an individual indifference curve, not a community indifference curve of the sort used elsewhere.)

FIGURE 6-8 Effects of Capital Formation and Population Growth in a Closed Economy

The transformation curve $Z_1 Z_2$ on the left side of the diagram shows outputs per capita of corn and steel. It is tangent to the indifference curve U_0 at E. Capital formation shifts the transformation curve outward to $Z_1' Z_2'$. If relative prices were unchanged, the output point would go to E', where corn output per capita falls from OX_1 to OX_1' and steel output per capita rises from OX_2 to OX_2'. Real product per capita increases from OA to OB measured in corn. As portions of $Z_1' Z_2'$ lie above U_0, the typical consumer can reach a higher indifference curve. Capital formation cannot be immiserizing in a closed economy. The situation is the same initially on the right side of the diagram. But population growth shifts the transformation curve inward to $Z_1' Z_2'$. If relative prices were unchanged, the output point would go to E', where corn output per capita rises from OX_1 to OX_1' and steel output per capita falls from OX_2 to OX_2'. Real product per capita decreases from OA to OB measured in corn. As $Z_1' Z_2'$ lies entirely below U_0, the typical consumer is driven to a lower indifference curve. Population growth is always immiserizing in a closed economy.

output per capita is OX_2 and is equal to steel consumption per capita.

The effects of capital formation are shown on the left side of the diagram, where the transformation curve shifts outward to $Z_1' Z_2'$. If the relative price of corn were constant, real product per capita

would rise to OB measured in corn, and the output point would shift to E'. The Rybczynski theorem holds for outputs per capita, so capital formation raises steel output per capita to OX_2' and reduces corn output per capita to OX_1'. As a portion of the new transformation curve lies above U_0, the typical consumer can move to a higher indifference curve. Capital formation raises welfare in a closed economy.[7]

The effects of population growth are shown on the right side of the diagram, where the transformation curve shifts *inward* to $Z_1' Z_2'$. If the relative price of corn were constant, real product per capita would fall to OB measured in corn, and the output point would shift to E'. Population growth reduces steel output per capita to OX_2' and raises corn output per capita to OX_1'. As the new transformation curve lies entirely below U_0, the typical consumer must move to a lower indifference curve. Population growth reduces welfare in a closed economy.

Growth in Supplies of Capital and Labor

What happens when the capital stock and population grow together? The long-run effects on economic welfare depend on their rates of growth. This can be shown clearly by treating the two cases already considered as limiting examples. When the supply of labor rises in Manymen, the country that exports the labor-intensive commodity, without any increase in the supply of capital, economic welfare falls in Manymen. It is reduced by the decline in consumers' incomes and the deterioration in the terms of trade. When the supply of capital rises instead, economic welfare rises in Manymen. It is raised by the increase in consumers' incomes and the improvement

in the terms of trade. But one more case deserves attention, because it introduces an important point.

Suppose that there is *balanced growth* in a single country. Capital formation and population growth proceed at the same rate. The whole economy will grow at that rate, but quantities per capita will not change. The closed economy described in Figure 6-8 will remain where it was to start, and the typical consumer will stay on the indifference curve U_0. An open economy, however, will demand more imports and offer more exports. (Imports per capita will not change, but total imports will grow with the increase in population.) The country's offer curve will shift outward, and its terms of trade will deteriorate. Balanced growth reduces economic welfare. Note that this result was obtained without knowing the trade pattern—whether the growing economy exported the labor-intensive or capital-intensive commodity.

You can extend this analysis easily. Suppose that there is balanced growth in Manymen and Fewmen but that the rate of growth is higher in Manymen. You should be able to show that the terms of trade will turn against Manymen, reducing economic welfare in Manymen and raising it in Fewmen.

An Improvement in Economic Efficiency

Consider, finally, the effects of a technological improvement. They depend on the nature of the improvement, the industry affected by it, and the country in which it occurs.

Increase the efficiency of steel production in Fewmen, the country that has its comparative advantage in steel. For simplicity, assume that the improvement is "factor neutral" in that it raises the efficiency with which the industry uses both capital and labor. It does not affect the cap-

---

[7] When consumers demand more of both commodities as their incomes increase, capital formation raises the relative price of corn. The increase in real product per capita from OA to OB raises the demands for corn and steel, but steel output rises and corn output falls as the output point goes from E to E'. There is thus an excess demand for corn that raises the relative price of corn. The final equilibrium position occurs on $Z_1' Z_2'$ to the southeast of E'. For analogous reasons, population growth reduces the relative price of corn.

ital intensity chosen by the industry at a particular set of factor prices.[8]

The increase of efficiency has two effects. First, it raises the quantity of steel that Fewmen can produce with each allocation of labor and capital. Second, it reduces the cost of producing a ton of steel by reducing labor and capital requirements. The two effects together shift the transformation curve in the manner shown by Figure 5-6 in Chapter 5, with steel put in place of cloth and corn in place of wine. The output-increasing effect of the increase in efficiency will shift the output point to the right; steel output will exceed OX_1 when corn output is OX_2. The cost-reducing effect will make the new transformation curve flatter at each point, which means that the point on the new curve having the same slope as the old one at E will be some point such as E', where steel output is larger than OX_1 but corn output smaller than OX_2. The result resembles the prediction made by the Rybczynski theorem. An increase in the efficiency of one industry raises real national product, raises the output of the industry affected, and reduces the output of the other industry when commodity prices are kept constant.

The welfare effects resemble those we encountered when studying capital formation in Fewmen. The increase in real national product generates an increase in consumers' incomes. (If prices did not change, consumers in Fewmen would move from C on the indifference curve U_1 to C' on the curve U_2.) But it raises Fewmen's demand

for corn imports, because domestic consumption rises and domestic production falls. Accordingly, the terms of trade move against Fewmen, and the welfare effect is ambiguous. An increase of efficiency in the export industry can reduce economic welfare if it leads to a large deterioration in the terms of trade. (There is, of course, an increase in welfare in Manymen, because its terms of trade improve.)

It is easy to work out other cases. Before leaving this example, however, note that an increase of efficiency differs in one important way from capital formation. By changing technology in Fewmen, it interferes with factor-price equalization. Figure 6-9 reproduces the initial free-trade equilibrium shown in earlier diagrams. Manymen has $O\overline{K}_1$ capital per worker, and Fewmen has $O\overline{K}_2$. With free trade between them, the relative price of corn is OP, and the relative price of labor is OW. The capital intensity of corn production is WU in both countries, and the capital intensity of steel production is WV. Therefore, real wages are the same in both countries, and so are real returns to capital. But an increase of efficiency in Fewmen's steel industry changes the relationship between the relative prices of labor and corn. The cost-reducing effect of the change in technology shifts the HH' curve outward in Fewmen. The new curve is $H_F H'_F$. If the relative price of labor remained at OW, the relative price of corn would rise to OP'.

With free trade between the two countries, however, prices have to be the same in Fewmen and Manymen, and we already know what happens. The relative price of corn rises, because of the increase in Fewmen's supply of steel exports and its demand for corn imports. It comes to rest at some such level as OP'' (higher than OP but lower than OP'). The relative price of labor rises to OW_1 in Manymen, raising the capital intensities of that country's indus-

---

[8] A factor-neutral improvement raises the marginal products of capital and labor to the same extent, shifting each isoquant inward without changing its shape. An improvement can be biased. It can raise one marginal product by more than the other and will then twist each isoquant when shifting it inward, affecting capital intensities and thus affecting the position of the SS' curve in Figure 6-9.

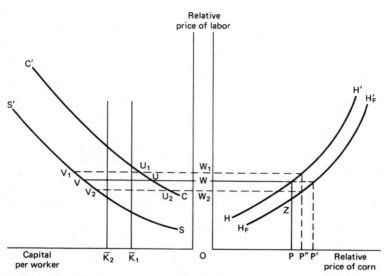

FIGURE 6-9   Effects of an Improvement in Efficiency in Fewmen's Steel Industry

The relative price of corn is *OP* initially, the relative price of labor is *OW*, the capital intensity of corn production is *WU*, and the capital intensity of steel production is *WV*. An increase of efficiency in Fewmen's steel industry shifts the curve connecting the relative price of labor to the relative price of corn. It was *HH'* initially (and this continues to be the relationship in Manymen). It is $H_F H_F'$ after the improvement. The relative price of corn would rise to *OP'* if the relative price of labor remained at *OW*. The improvement raises Fewmen's demand for corn imports and thus raises the relative price of corn to *OP"* in both countries. In Manymen, the relative price of labor rises to OW_1, the capital intensity of corn production rises to $W_1 U_1$, and the capital intensity of steel production rises to $W_1 V_1$. The real return to capital falls. In Fewmen, the relative price of labor falls to OW_2, the capital intensity of corn production falls to $W_2 U_2$, and the capital intensity of steel production falls to $W_2 V_2$. The real return to capital rises.

tries; the capital intensity of corn production goes to $W_1 U_1$, and the capital intensity of steel production goes to $W_1 V_1$. The marginal products of capital fall in both industries, and the real return to capital falls in Manymen. The relative price of labor falls to OW_2 in Fewmen, reducing the capital intensities of that country's industries; the capital intensity of corn production goes to $W_2 U_2$, and the capital intensity of steel production goes to $W_2 V_2$. The real return to capital rises in Fewmen. The increase of efficiency in Fewmen's steel industry has created a difference between the two countries' technologies, interfering with factor-price equalization.

SUMMARY

In the modified Heckscher–Ohlin model, factor intensities depend on factor prices. An increase in the relative price of labor causes firms to substitute capital for labor, making each industry more capital intensive. The requirements of equilibrium in the factor markets determine the relative price of labor and actual factor intensities. An economy can thus use its factors fully at each point on its transformation curve. All the theorems of the Heckscher–Ohlin model hold in the modified version of the model.

An increase in the relative price of corn raises corn output and the demand for labor, the factor used intensively in growing corn. Therefore, it raises the relative price of labor. The marginal product of labor rises, raising the real wage. The marginal product of capital falls, reducing the real return. These statements lead directly to the Stolper–Samuelson theorem. In a labor-abundant country, trade raises the real wage and reduces the real return to capital. In a capital-abundant country, trade raises the real return to capital and reduces the real wage.

An increase in the supply of one factor raises the output of the product intensive in that factor at each set of commodity prices. This is the Rybczynski theorem. It leads directly to the factor-proportions version of the Heckscher–Ohlin theorem. The country that has little capital per worker will export the labor-intensive commodity, and the country that has much capital per worker will export the capital-intensive commodity. Finally, the factor-price-equalization theorem holds in the modified version of the model, which clarifies its implications. By closing gaps between marginal products, free trade maximizes world output.

The welfare effects of capital formation are similar to those in the modified Ricardian model but must be stated differently. If the growing country imports the capital-intensive commodity, that country gains and the other country loses. If the growing country exports the capital-intensive commodity, it can gain or lose, but the other country gains. Capital formation reduces the real return to capital in both countries, regardless of the commodity in which it is measured, and raises the real wage.

Some of the effects of population growth are symmetrical to those of capital formation. But population growth is more likely to reduce economic welfare in the growing country. It generates immiserizing growth in a closed economy, and capital formation cannot. Therefore, population growth is necessarily immiserizing in an open economy unless the economy imports the labor-intensive good, so that its terms of trade improve, and the improvement is large enough to offset the welfare-reducing effect of population growth.

The effects of an increase in efficiency depend on its nature and the industry and country in which it occurs. In the simplest case, it raises the output of the affected industry and reduces the output of the other industry. Therefore, an increase of efficiency in the export industry can raise or lower welfare at home, because it worsens the terms of trade, but raises welfare abroad. An increase of efficiency in the import-competing industry raises welfare at home, by improving the terms of trade, but it lowers welfare abroad. The effects on real earnings likewise depend on the industry in which efficiency rises and they will be different at home and abroad, because an increase in efficiency interferes with factor-price equalization.

RECOMMENDED READINGS

The Heckscher–Ohlin model as a whole is described concisely by Harry G. Johnson, "Factor Endowments, International Trade, and Factor Prices," *Manchester School of Economic and Social Studies,* 25 (September 1957), reprinted in American Economic Association, *Readings in International Economics* (Homewood, Ill.: Richard D. Irwin, 1968), ch. 5.

The Stolper–Samuelson theorem was developed with flexible factor intensities in Wolfgang F. Stolper and Paul A. Samuelson, "Protection and Real Wages," *Review of Economic Studies,* 9 (November 1941), reprinted in American Economic Association, *Readings in the Theory of International Trade* (Philadelphia: Blakiston, 1949), ch. 15.

The factor-price-equalization theorem is set out clearly in Paul A. Samuelson, "International Factor-Price Equalisation Once Again," *Economic Journal,* 59 (June 1949), reprinted in American Economic Association, *Readings in International Economics* (Homewood, Ill.: Richard D. Irwin, 1968), ch. 3.

For a different treatment of the role of capital in the Heckscher–Ohlin model, see Peter B. Kenen, "Nature, Capital, and Trade," *Journal of Political Economy,* 73 (October 1965), reprinted in P. B. Kenen, *Essays in International Economics* (Princeton, N.J.: Princeton University Press, 1980).

On economic growth, trade, and welfare in the Heckscher–Ohlin model, see Harry G. Johnson, "Economic Development and International Trade," *Nationaløkonomist Tidskrift,* 97 (1959), reprinted in American Economic Association, *Readings in International Economics* (Homewood, Ill.: Richard D. Irwin, 1968), ch. 17.

The long-run behavior of the Heckscher–Ohlin model with capital formation and population growth is examined in Ronald Findlay, *International Trade and Development Theory* (New York: Columbia University Press, 1973), ch. 7.

The effects of trade on growth are surveyed in W. Max Corden, "The Effects of Trade on the Rate of Growth," in J. N. Bhagwati et al., eds., *Trade, Balance of Payments and Growth* (Amsterdam: North-Holland, 1971), ch. 6.

IMPERFECT COMPETITION AND INTERNATIONAL TRADE

INTERINDUSTRY AND INTRAINDUSTRY TRADE

The simple trade models examined thus far are very useful. They help us to understand how differences in national factor endowments lead countries to specialize in certain activities, how the pattern of specialization affects the real earnings of the factors of production, and how it tends to compensate for shortages of factors. Nevertheless, those models rely on assumptions that are inappropriate for dealing with certain important questions. Factors of production do not move from country to country, there are no economies of scale, and markets are perfectly competitive. For these and other reasons, those models are unable to explain two striking characteristics of the actual trade pattern. Pairs of countries that have very similar endowments trade heavily among themselves, and

there is two-way trade between most pairs of countries in most classes of commodities.

International factor mobility is taken up in Chapter 8, along with a closely related phenomenon, the prevalence of multinational production by a single firm. Imperfect competition and two-way trade are the main subjects of this chapter, and they also prove to be closely related.

We need not dwell at length on the frequency and magnitude of visible departures from perfect competition. In most major industrial countries, large parts of the manufacturing sector are dominated by very small numbers of companies. You can count on the fingers of one hand the numbers of automobile manufacturers in the United States, in Japan, or in Western Europe. And you can use the other hand to count the worldwide total of companies that manufacture large commercial aircraft.

These numbers often overstate the degree of concentration and thus understate the intensity of competition. The small number of firms in a single country must compete with foreign firms, not just among themselves. That indeed is one main gain from trade neglected in earlier chapters and emphasized here. Furthermore, the number of firms actually in business does not measure the intensity of competition when new firms are able to enter an industry. The threat of entry can deter monopolistic behavior. But competition is still far from perfect because there are significant barriers to entry. First, the products and technologies of existing firms are protected by patents. Second, those firms have cost and reputational advantages because they have acquired experience in making and marketing their products. Third, it can be very expensive to build and start up a new plant big enough to offer the economies of scale that established firms already enjoy. We will cite these barriers to entry when we study the effects of trade between two countries whose national markets have each been dominated by a single firm and when we study two-way trade in differentiated products—those that have similar factor requirements but differ in function, quality, or style.

The aims of this chapter can be restated in terms of a distinction that is increasingly popular among trade theorists. The models presented in previous chapters help us to explain interindustry trade: flows of goods with different factor requirements. Countries with large supplies of skilled labor tend to export sophisticated manufactures; those with large supplies of unskilled labor tend to export simple manufactures; and those with large supplies of land or natural resources tend to export agricultural commodities or resource-intensive goods. But those models do not help us to explain intraindustry trade: flows of goods with similar factor requirements. Countries that are large net exporters of sophisticated manufactures and, therefore, importers of simple manufactures, farm products, and raw materials also trade among themselves, exporting similar sophisticated products to each other.

The extent of intraindustry trade is impressive. Look at Table 7-1, which lists selected manufactures that appear on both sides of the trade accounts for the United States. It exports about $1 billion of automotive engines, but its imports are almost three times as large. It exports many types of machinery but imports every one of them. And it exports about $1.5 billion of books, records, disks, and tapes but imports about $1.4 billion.

The two-way trade in automotive engines testifies to the importance of multinational production, because most such engines are bought by the affiliates of the firm that makes them. Much intraindustry trade is also intrafirm trade. But that is a characteristic of such trade, not an explanation. Why do Japanese companies assemble cars in the United States, using engines manufactured in Japan? Factor requirements play a role, as they are not the same at all stages of production. Tariffs and other trade barriers are also important. But the big question still lies ahead. Why do Americans buy Japanese cars when they can buy less expensive American cars? For once, the obvious answer is also the right answer. The two countries' cars are not identical. And that answer covers many other cases. Clearly, American books and records are not identical to British, Dutch, or German books and records. Some cases are harder to explain, however, because the apparent differences in products are much smaller. We will soon see, in fact, that a

TABLE 7-1 Examples of Intraindustry Trade: Selected U.S. Exports and Imports of Manufactured Goods, 1984 (in millions of dollars)

Category	Exports	Imports
Motor vehicle engines	$1,000.4	$2,962.7
Harvesting machinery	635.9	323.9
Metal cutting machine tools	235.8	1,117.8
Welding equipment	206.6	198.6
Air-conditioning machinery	536.9	216.0
Forklift trucks	256.9	480.6
Ball and roller bearings	341.4	654.0
Line telephone equipment	833.8	1,983.3
Radio and TV transmitters	591.7	306.0
Insulated wire and cable	708.6	1,093.4
Electronic microcircuits	1,930.0	6,187.4
Batteries	294.4	322.4
Film	1,318.6	905.5
Printed books	662.0	468.4
Sound recordings, disks, and tapes	856.2	918.2

Source: United Nations, *Yearbook of International Trade Statistics,* 1984.

country may export and import identical varieties of the same basic product, because the domestic and foreign firms that make it will succeed in invading each other's national market. Let us study that case first, before looking at trade in differentiated products.

TRADE BETWEEN MONOPOLIZED NATIONAL MARKETS

Consider two companies, Edo in Japan and Acme in America, that manufacture industrial robots. Let them be identical in every way and face identical national markets. To keep the analysis simple, suppose that they have constant marginal costs but that the fixed costs of making robots, including the costs of design and development, are high enough to prevent additional firms from entering the robot market, so Edo and Acme will function as monopolists until trade is opened between their markets.

Equilibrium in the Closed Economies

Because the firms and markets are identical here, we can concentrate completely on one country's market, before and after trade is opened. The same things will happen in the other.

Figure 7-1 describes the American market before trade is opened. The American demand curve for robots is the curve *DD*. Although they are producers' goods, not consumers' goods, the demand curve for robots is downward sloping, because their use will spread as their prices fall. The corresponding marginal-revenue curve is *MR*. It is a straight line when *DD* is a straight line, but is twice as steep. Proof of this and other statements about Figure 7-1 are given in Note 7-1 (which handles a slightly more complicated case in which the two firms and markets are not identical). As the marginal cost of making a robot is constant here, the marginal-cost curve is the hori-

FIGURE 7-1 Acme's American Market Before Trade
The American demand curve for robots is *DD*, and the corresponding marginal-revenue curve is *MR* (which lies half way between *DD* and the vertical axis, because *DD* is a straight line). Acme's marginal-cost curve is *MC*, and its average-cost curve is *AC*. As *MR* = *MC* at *N*, Acme maximizes its profits by delivering *OA* robots to the American market. The price there is *OP*, Acme's total revenue is *OAFP*, its total cost is *OAVC* (*OANM* variable cost *plus* *MNVC* fixed cost), and profits are *CVFP*. Note that *OA* = *MN* = (1/2)*MH*.

Note 7-1

The American and Japanese demand curves for robots are

$$p_1 = a_1 - b_1(x_1 + x_1^*) \quad \text{and}$$
$$p_2 = a_2 - b_2(x_2 + x_2^*)$$

where p_1 and p_2 are the prices of robots in the American and Japanese markets, respectively, expressed in a common currency, x_1 and x_2 are the quantities sold by the American firm (Acme) in the two markets, and x_1^* and x_2^* are the quantities sold by the Japanese firm (Edo). Therefore, Acme's total revenues from the two markets are

$$R_1 = p_1 x_1 = [a_1 - b_1(x_1 + x_1^*)]x_1 \quad \text{and}$$
$$R_2 = p_2 x_2 = [a_2 - b_2(x_2 + x_2^*)]x_2$$

and Acme's marginal revenues are

$$MR_1 = a_1 - b_1(2x_1 + x_1^*) \quad \text{and}$$
$$MR_2 = a_2 - b_2(2x_2 + x_2^*)$$

Similarly, Edo's marginal revenues are

$$MR_1^* = a_1 - b_1(x_1 + 2x_1^*) \quad \text{and}$$
$$MR_2^* = a_2 - b_2(x_2 + 2x_2^*)$$

The two firms' marginal costs are constant and independent of the market in which output is sold (there are no transport costs). Therefore,

$$MC = c \quad \text{and} \quad MC^* = c^*$$

for Acme and Edo, respectively.

Before trade is opened, $x_1^* = x_2 = 0$. Setting each firm's marginal cost equal to its marginal revenue in its own market and solving for its sales, $\hat{x}_1 = (1/2b_1)(a_1 - c)$ and $\hat{x}_2^* = (1/2b_2)(a_2 - c^*)$. Substituting into the demand equations, $\hat{p}_1 = (1/2)(a_1 + c)$ and $\hat{p}_2 = (1/2)(a_2 + c^*)$. When $a_1 = a_2$, $b_1 = b_2$, and $c = c^*$, as in the text, $\hat{x}_1 = \hat{x}_2^*$ and $\hat{p}_1 = \hat{p}_2$. The two firms' profits are $N_1 = R_1 - cx_1 - k$ and zontal line *MC* (which also shows average variable cost). But there are fixed costs, too, so the average cost of making a robot is the downward-sloping line *AC*.

Because Acme can function as a monopolist before trade is opened, it will maximize its profits by producing the output at which marginal revenue is equal to marginal cost and selling that output in the American market. Thus, it produces *OA* robots and sells them at the price *OP*. Its total revenue is *OAFP*, its total cost is *OAVC* (*OANM* variable cost *plus MNVC* fixed cost), and its profits are *CVFP*. Note that Acme's strategy can be described without drawing the marginal-revenue curve, because we know that *MR* intersects *MC* at *N*, half way along *HM*. Therefore, marginal-revenue curves are omitted from subsequent diagrams.

The situation in the American market is replicated fully in the identical Japanese market, where Edo produces *OA* robots and sells them at *OP*.

The Opening of Trade

In previous models, a difference in prices was necessary and sufficient to generate trade. That was the law of comparative advantage. Trade will take place here, however, even though prices are the same in the two countries' markets. Edo will invade the American market, and Acme will invade the Japanese market.

Before we can show what they will do, however, we must deal with a problem that does not arise with perfect competition or with monopoly but is vital with *oligopoly*, where a few large firms dominate a market. With perfect competition, an individual

---

$N_2 = R_2 - c^* x_2^* - k^*$, where k and k^* are their fixed costs. Therefore,

$$\hat{N}_1 = (1/4b_1)(a_1 - c)^2 - k \text{ and}$$
$$\hat{N}_2 = (1/4b_2)(a_2 - c^*)^2 - k^*$$

When trade is opened, each firm will try to invade the other's market. We focus here on outcomes in the American market. (Those in the Japanese market will be symmetrical and indeed identical when demand and cost conditions are identical.) Setting each firm's marginal cost equal to its marginal revenue in the American market and solving for its sales, $x_1 = (1/2b_1)(a_1 - c) - (1/2)x_1^*$ and $x_1^* = (1/2b_1)(a_1 - c^*) - (1/2)x_1$, which are the equations for the firms' reaction curves in the American market. Solving them simultaneously for actual sales,

$$x_1 = (1/3b_1)(a_1 - 2c + c^*) \text{ and}$$
$$x_1^* = (1/3b_1)(a_1 - 2c^* + c)$$

So $x_1 - x_1^* = (1/b_1)(c^* - c)$. Acme's sales will be larger when Edo's costs are

higher. Replacing x_1 and x_1^* in the American demand equation, we obtain $p_1 = (1/3)(a_1 + c + c^*)$. Therefore,

$$p_1 - \hat{p}_1 = -(1/6)(a_1 - 2c^* + c)$$

But $(a_1 - 2c^* + c) > 0$ whenever $x_1^* > 0$ (whenever Edo stays in the American market). Hence, trade reduces the price of robots in the American market.

These results can be combined with those for Edo's market to calculate the two firms' profits. Take the case of identical demand and cost conditions, where $x_1 = x_1^* = x_2 = x_2^* = (1/3b)(a - c)$. Each firm has half of each national market, and $p_1 = p_2 = (1/3)(a + 2c)$. In this case, moreover

$$N_1 = N_2 = (2/9b)(a - c)^2 - k$$

and

$$N_1 - \hat{N}_1 = N_2 - \hat{N}_2 = -(1/9b)(a - c)^2 < 0$$

Both firms' profits fall.

FIGURE 7-2   Edo Enters the American Market

The demand curve *DD* and Acme's marginal-cost curve *MC* are reproduced from Figure 7-1 (but the latter is also Edo's marginal-cost curve and is labeled accordingly). Acme's initial position is also reproduced from Figure 7-1; it delivers *OA* robots to the American market at the price *OP*. Taking that level of Acme's shipments to be fixed, Edo will enter the American market. Its marginal-revenue curve (not drawn) starts at *F* and passes through *T*, the midpoint of *NH*, so Edo will ship *AE* robots to the American market, driving down the price to *OP'*. Edo's profits will rise by *NTGF'*, but Acme's profits will fall by *P'F'FP* until Acme changes the volume of its shipments.

firm does not worry about the behavior of other firms, because it is too small to elicit any action from them; it takes prices as given. With monopoly, the individual firm does not have to worry about the behavior of others, because there are no others. With oligopoly, by contrast, each firm is large enough to influence others and must forecast their behavior when planning any move of its own. How will the others respond? In this example, we use a simple supposition. Each firm expects its foreign rival to keep selling the same quantity of robots, even when its own behavior leads to a change in price.

The effects of this supposition on Edo's behavior are shown in Figure 7-2, which reproduces the main features of Figure 7-1

but adds one fact. The marginal-cost curve has been relabeled to remind us that Acme and Edo have the same marginal costs.[1] As Acme has been selling *OA* robots in the American market and Edo expects it to keep on doing so, Edo knows that it cannot sell robots there if the price remains at *OP*. At any lower price, however, it can invade the American market. In effect, Edo faces that portion of the American demand curve that lies to the right of the line *AF* and thus a marginal-revenue curve that starts at *F* and crosses the marginal-cost curve at *T*, half way along *NH*. Therefore, Edo will ship *AE* robots to the American market. This will drive down the price to *OP'*, but Edo's total profits will rise by *NTGF'*. Acme's profits will fall by *P'F'FP*,

[1] The *AC* curve has been dropped from Figure 7-2, along with the *MR* curve, even though Acme and Edo have the same average costs, because it is not immediately relevant to Edo's behavior. Edo has been covering its fixed costs (and making a profit) from its sales in Japan. The *AC* curve would tell us whether Acme can continue to cover its fixed costs from its sales in America and, by implication, whether Edo can continue to cover its fixed costs from its sales in Japan.

But that would not be useful information, because each firm will be selling in the other's market as well as its own. We do need to know that both firms can cover their fixed costs from their total sales when they reach equilibrium. Otherwise, the equilibrium will not be sustainable. (In this particular example, both firms can do so when one can, because their situations are identical, and both firms will take losses when one does. But we will ignore that last possibility.)

however, until it changes the volume of its sales.

Acme will be doing the same thing in the Japanese market that Edo is doing in the American market, so both firms face the same problem. What to do about the invasion of its domestic market?

We could use Figure 7-2 to show how Acme will respond, but that would be cumbersome, because we would have then to trace Edo's answer to Acme's response, and so on. It is easier to use new tools, known as *reaction curves,* and it is not hard to derive them. We start with Figure 7-3, which reproduces the demand curve DD and shows how Edo will behave when Acme has chosen its level of sales in the American market and Edo expects Acme to hold to that level.

Suppose that Acme decides to sell OA robots (which need not be the same as the quantity OA in Figure 7-2). Edo will face that part of the demand curve that lies to the right of the line AF and will go to T, half way along NH, just as it did in Figure 7-2. It will sell AE robots in the American market. Suppose that Acme decides to sell

OA' robots instead, driving down the price to OP'. Edo will face that part of the demand curve that lies to the right of the line $A'F'$ and will go to T', half way along $N'H$. It will sell $A'E'$ robots in the American market. What is the relationship between the changes in the two firms' sales? When Acme sells OA, Edo sells $(1/2)NH$. When Acme sells OA', Edo sells $(1/2)N'H$. Hence, the increase in Acme's sales, AA', leads Edo to change its sales by $(1/2)(N'H - NH)$. But $N'H = NH - NN'$ and $NN' = AA'$, so the change in Edo's sales is $(1/2)[(NH - AA') - NH] = -(1/2)AA'$. Edo's sales fall by half of any increase in Acme's sales. Reversing the procedure, we could start with an arbitrary level of sales by Edo, find Acme's sales, and show that Acme's sales in the American market will fall by half of any increase in Edo's sales. These are the statements made by the reaction curves in Figure 7-4.

Acme's reaction curve is AA. When Edo's shipments to the American market are zero, Acme sells OX_0 robots in that market. This was the quantity OA in Figure 7-2,

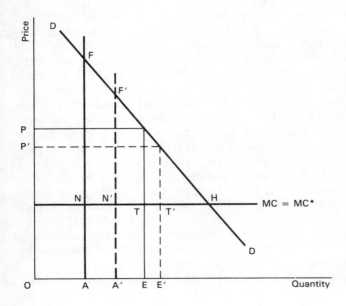

FIGURE 7-3 Deriving Edo's Reaction Curve
Let Acme deliver OA robots to the American market. Taking that level to be fixed, Edo will ship $(1/2)NH = NT = AE$ robots to the American market, and the price will be OP. Now let Acme deliver OA' robots. Taking that level to be fixed, Edo will ship $(1/2)N'H = N'T' = A'E'$ robots, and the price will be OP'. But $(1/2)N'H = (1/2)(NH - NN') = AE - (1/2)AA'$, so Edo will reduce its shipments by half of any increase in Acme's shipments.

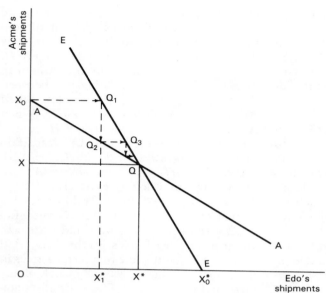

which measured Acme's sales when there
was no trade. As Edo starts to sell robots in
the American market, Acme reduces its
sales; they fall by half of every increase in
Edo's sales. Edo's reaction curve is *EE*. If
Acme sold no robots in the American market, Edo would sell OX_0^*. (This is likewise
the quantity *OA* in Figure 7-2, because the
two firms have the same marginal costs.) As
Acme starts to sell robots in that market,
Edo reduces its sales; they fall by half of every increase in Acme's sales.

It is easy to depict the opening of trade
and the subsequent adjustments made by
the two firms until they reach an equilibrium. As Acme was selling OX_0 robots
before trade was opened, Edo will go to Q_1
on its own reaction curve; it will start to sell
OX_1^* in the American market. (This is the
quantity *AA'* in Figure 7-2.) We have already seen, however, that Edo's sales drive
down the price of robots and Acme has
reason to alter its behavior. Because it assumes that Edo will hold its sales at OX_1^*,
Acme will go to Q_2 on its reaction curve, reducing its sales by half of Edo's initial sales.

And that will cause Edo to adjust its sales; it
will go to Q_3 and thus raise its sales by half
of the reduction in Acme's sales. Eventually, the two firms will reach Q, and they
will stay there once they get there, because
Acme has no cause to alter its sales when
Edo sells OX^* robots and Edo has no cause
to alter its sales when Acme sells OX robots.

The equilibrium at Q has two characteristics. First, the market is divided evenly between the two firms, because they have
identical costs. We will soon see that Acme's
sales would be larger and Edo's sales
smaller if Acme's costs were lower. Transport costs would also favor Acme by making it more expensive for Edo to deliver
goods to the American market. Second, the
price in the American market is lower at Q
than it was before the opening of trade.
This is because the volume of sales is
larger. The overall reduction in Acme's
sales, from OX_0 to OX, is only half as large
as the overall increase in Edo's sales, from
zero to OX^*, so total sales have increased by
half of Edo's sales.

The same diagram can be used to locate

equilibrium in the Japanese market. The story starts differently, with Edo selling OX_0^* robots and Acme selling none, but ends at the same equilibrium point, because demand and cost conditions are identical (and there are no transport costs).

We have thus told a rather strange tale. Prices were the same in the two markets before trade was opened, but that did not keep trade from starting. Furthermore, both countries export robots, and their intraindustry trade is perfectly balanced. Edo exports OX^* robots to the American market, Acme exports OX robots to the Japanese market, and these quantities are equal. In Note 7-1, moreover, we show that both companies wind up with lower profits, even though they were induced to invade each other's market by the prospect of raising their total profits. International trade has introduced an element of competition into the two countries' markets, undermining each firm's monopoly in its own national market, reducing prices in both markets, and reducing the firms' profits. Their profits do not fall to zero, as they would with perfect competition, but oligopolistic competition is better than none. It is not hard to show that the gains to consumers due to lower prices are larger than the losses to producers due to lower profits. Finally, our tale tells us why firms such as Edo and Acme are tempted to form market-sharing arrangements, called *cartels,* to protect their profits. If they could agree to stay out of each other's market or to divide their markets without letting total sales rise, prices and profits would not fall. But the gains from trade would be lost completely, which is why governments try to prohibit cartels.[2]

Shifting the Reaction Curves

Having learned how to derive reaction curves, what more can we do with them? They can be used to show how a difference in marginal costs or change in one country's costs alters an oligopolistic equilibrium and the trade flows that go with it. They can also be used to show what happens when a government subsidizes exports and the other government retaliates.

Return to Figure 7-3 and draw a new marginal-cost curve for Edo below the common curve shown in the diagram. When Acme sells OA robots, Edo's new sales point will lie on a line lower and longer than NH and thus to the right of T. When Acme sells OA' robots, Edo's new sales point will lie on a line lower and longer than $N'H$ and thus to the right of T'. At each and every level of Acme's sales, Edo will sell more robots in the American market. But faced with an increase in Acme's sales, Edo will still reduce its sales by half of the increase in Acme's sales. Therefore, Edo's reaction curve will lie to the right of the curve EE in Figure 7-4 but be parallel to it. Similarly, a reduction in Acme's marginal costs will shift its reaction curve. It will lie above the curve AA but be parallel to it. That is the shift shown in Figure 7-5, where Acme's curve moves from AA to $A'A'$, taking the equilibrium point to Q'.

When Acme's marginal costs are lower than Edo's, Acme sells more in the American market (OX' rather than OX), and Edo sells less ($OX^{*'}$ rather than OX^*). But total sales are larger than before, because Edo reduces its sales by half of the increase in Acme's sales, so the price of robots is lower. As the same things happen in the Japanese market, intraindustry trade is not perfectly balanced. Acme's exports to the Japanese market are larger than Edo's exports to the American market.

---

[2] In recent years, however, governments have actually sponsored them, or arrangements that resemble them. In Chapter 11, we will encounter "voluntary" export quotas that governments impose on their trading partners to protect their own producers and prop up their profits.

FIGURE 7-5 Effects of a
Reduction in Acme's Costs
A downward shift in Acme's marginal-
cost curve will increase that firm's
shipments to both markets for every
level of Edo's shipments. Acme's reaction curve will shift upward from
AA to *A'A'*, displacing equilibrium
from *Q* to *Q'*. Acme's shipments will
rise from *OX* to *OX'*, and Edo's shipments will fall from *OX** to *OX*'*.
The same changes will occur if the
American government subsidizes
Acme's exports.

Effects of Export Subsidies

Export subsidies are instruments of commercial policy, and it would be logical to
study them in Chapters 9 and 10, which
examine the instruments and uses of commercial policy. The tools are at hand, however, and we can use them right away.

To steer clear of certain complications,
including the welfare effects of price
changes on domestic robot buyers and the
need to distinguish between export subsidies and production subsidies, we change
the setting slightly. Suppose that American
and Japanese industries are fully supplied
with robots; they do not want more at any
price. But Brazilian industry is still in need
of robots, so the shipments shown in Figure
7-5 go only to Brazil, which does not produce any robots of its own.

When Acme and Edo have the same
marginal costs, their reaction curves are *AA*
and *EE*, as before, and an oligopolistic
equilibrium is established at *Q*. Acme and
Edo sell the same quantities of robots.
There is only one-way trade, however, be-

cause Brazil does not make or export
robots.

In this sort of situation, Acme's profits
from its sales to Brazil add to American national income.[3] Therefore, an American
government concerned to maximize American welfare will want to raise Acme's
profits. It can do so by offering Acme an
export subsidy that has the effect of reducing the marginal cost at which Acme can
deliver robots to the Brazilian market.[4]
Acme's reaction curve shifts upward, as in
Figure 7-5, raising Acme's exports and reducing Edo's exports. In Note 7-2, moreover, it is shown that a carefully chosen
subsidy will raise Acme's profits by more

---

[3] The rest of its export revenues do not, because
they represent costs of production and thus payments
to American factors of production that can be used in
other American industries.

[4] Acme could pursue this profit-raising strategy
without a government subsidy, merely by reducing the
price of its robots, but it would be exposed to losses if
Edo retaliated. By allowing the American government
to take the initiative, it shifts the risk of loss to the government.

than the government spends on the subsidy, which is necessary if there is to be an increase in American national income. (If the increase in profits were just as large as the amount spent on the subsidy, all of Acme's gain would be the taxpayers' loss, because they must provide the revenue needed for the subsidy, and there would be no increase in national income.)

Brazil's buyers of robots benefit from the American subsidy, because the increase in Acme's exports is twice as large as the decrease in Edo's exports, so the subsidy drives down the price of robots. But Japanese national income falls because Edo's profits fall; its sales are smaller and its price is lower. Therefore, the Japanese government will be tempted to retaliate by subsidizing Edo's exports.

If Japanese retaliation served merely to shift Edo's reaction curve in the way that the American subsidy shifted Acme's curve, we could conclude this story quickly. But that is not the case, because the American government will adjust its subsidy in response to the new Japanese subsidy. The interdependence between the two firms makes for interdependence between the two governments' policies. It is described in Figure 7-6 by two new reaction curves. The American curve is WW, and the Japanese curve is JJ. They are derived in Note 7-2, which shows that they are downward sloping. Policy competition does not cause the two governments to keep on raising their subsidies, leapfrogging over each other. Instead, one government cuts its subsidy when the other raises its subsidy. This is because an increase in a subsidy adds to the cost of the subsidy, which must be subtracted from the resulting increase in profit (if any) to measure the change in national income. In fact, an increase in one country's subsidy causes the other to cut its subsidy by one-quarter of the increase in the first country's subsidy. That is why JJ in Figure 7-6 is twice as steep as EE in Figure 7-4, while WW is half as steep as AA.

FIGURE 7-6 Policy Reaction Curves for Export Subsidies
The American policy reaction curve is WW, showing the optimal American export subsidy for every level of the Japanese subsidy. The Japanese policy reaction curve is JJ, showing the optimal Japanese export subsidy for every level of the American subsidy. When Japan does not subsidize Edo's exports to Brazil, the optimal American subsidy is OS_0. When America does not subsidize Acme's exports, the optimal Japanese subsidy is OS_0^*. When each government responds to the other's subsidy, however, they wind up at Z, where the subsidies are OS and OS^*. Note that OS is smaller than OS_0.

Note 7-2

Acme and Edo do not sell robots in America or Japan but sell them in Brazil, where the demand curve is

$$p = a - b(x + x^*)$$

The two firms' total and marginal revenues are obtained as in Note 7-1, and their (constant) marginal costs are set equal to their marginal revenues to obtain their sales: $x = (1/3b)(a - 2c + c^*)$ for Acme and $x^* = (1/3b)(a - 2c^* + c)$ for Edo, so $p = (1/3)(a + c + c^*)$. The firms' profits are

$$N = (1/9b)(a - 2c + c^*)^2 - k \text{ and}$$
$$N^* = (1/9b)(a - 2c^* + c)^2 - k^*$$

Suppose that their marginal costs are equal, however, apart from subsidies, s and s^*, given by their governments. (Since all outputs are exported in this example, these could be output or export subsidies.) Then

$$x = (1/3b)(a - c + 2s - s^*),$$
$$x^* = (1/3b)(a - c + 2s^* - s) \text{ and}$$
$$p = (1/3)(a + 2c - s - s^*)$$

So

$$N = (1/9b)(a - c + 2s - s^*)^2 - k \text{ and}$$
$$N^* = (1/9b)(a - c + 2s^* - s)^2 - k^*$$

Each country's subsidy raises its firm's sales and profits, but the other country's subsidy reduces them. Both subsidies reduce the price of robots in Brazil (so they raise the sum of the two firms' sales). But each country's subsidy is meant to raise its national income. Therefore, it must raise the profits of its country's firm by more than the amount of the subsidy. This gain is measured by

$$U = N - \hat{N} - sx \text{ and}$$
$$U^* = N^* - \hat{N}^* - s^*x^*$$

where $\hat{N}$ and $\hat{N}^*$ are the firms' profits when $s = s^* = 0$. Substituting into these definitions and simplifying,

$$U = (1/9b)[(a - c)(s - 2s^*) - (2s - s^*)(s + s^*)]$$
$$U^* = (1/9b)[(a - c)(s^* - 2s) - (2s^* - s)(s + s^*)]$$

The American government chooses that value of s that maximizes U, given the Japanese subsidy s^*, and the Japanese government behaves symmetrically. To replicate their behavior, we differentiate the equation for U with respect to s and the equation for U^* with respect to s^*, set the derivatives equal to zero, and solve for the subsidies:

$$s = (1/4)(a - c - s^*) \text{ and}$$
$$s^* = (1/4)(a - c - s)$$

These are the policy reaction curves in Figure 7-6.

Consider, first, a case in which Acme gets a subsidy and Edo does not. Then $s^* = 0$ and $s = (1/4)(a - c)$, so

$$U = (1/9b)(1/8)(a - c)^2 > 0 \text{ and}$$
$$U^* = -(1/9b)(7/16)(a - c)^2 < 0,$$

The subsidy to Acme raises American national income and reduces Japanese national income (by more than it raises American). A subsidy to Edo would have symmetrical effects.

Consider, next, a case in which both countries subsidize their firms. Solving the two subsidy equations simultaneously, $s = s^* = (1/5)(a - c)$, so the American subsidy is slightly smaller than when there was no Japanese subsidy, and $U = U^* = -(1/9b)(3/25)(a - c)^2 < 0$. The subsidies reduce both countries' national incomes. (They serve merely to cut the price of robots in Brazil and to raise both countries' exports, to the benefit of the Brazilian economy and the detriment of the American and Japanese.)

Where will the governments wind up once policy competition has begun? We start at the origin of Figure 7-6, where there are no subsidies, and assume that the American government acts first. It moves immediately to OS_0, the point on WW that shows what the American subsidy should be when there is no Japanese subsidy. But it provokes retaliation by the Japanese government, which moves to Z_1 on its reaction curve ZZ and introduces a subsidy equal to OS_1^*. The American government responds, and events unfold much as they did in Figure 7-4, where Acme and Edo were reacting to each other. Eventually, an equilibrium is reached at Z, where the American subsidy is OS, the Japanese subsidy is OS^*, and the two subsidies are equal in size (because the countries' firms have identical

the equilibrium level of the American subsidy is smaller than the initial level, which means that there must be an additional shift in Acme's reaction curve.

costs and compete in the same market). But

The final outcome for the firms is shown in Figure 7-7, which replicates most of Figure 7-5, including the initial shift in Acme's reaction curve from AA to $A'A'$. Because the equilibrium level of the American subsidy is lower than the initial level, Acme's reaction curve shifts inward from $A'A'$ to $A''A''$. But Edo's curve shifts outward from EE to $E''E''$ in response to the equilibrium Japanese subsidy, and the new reaction curves intersect at Q''. Both firms sell more robots than they did before the subsidies were introduced; Acme's sales rise from OX to OX'', and Edo's rise from OX^* to $OX^{*''}$.

FIGURE 7-7 Effects of Export Subsidies
When America subsidizes Acme's exports to Brazil, the firm's reaction curve shifts from AA to $A'A'$, raising American exports from OX to OX' and reducing Japanese exports from OX^* to $OX^{*''}$. When Japan retaliates, however, and the sequence of reciprocal adjustments is completed, the American subsidy will be lower than it was initially, shifting Acme's reaction curve to $A''A''$. But Edo's reaction curve will shift to the same extent, from EE to $E''E''$. Hence, both countries' exports will rise by the same amount, to OX'' and $OX^{*''}$.

In fact, they rise to the same extent, because the costs and subsidies are equal.

Clearly, Brazil is better off than it was before the subsidies; the fall in the price of robots has improved its terms of trade. But both exporting countries are worse off. Figure 7-8 shows what happens to them, using numbers obtained by assigning particular values to the coefficient in Note 7-2. The columns of Figure 7-8 represent the policy options open to the American government. The rows represent the options open to the Japanese government.[5] The first number in each cell is the change in American national income, compared with the situation in which there are no subsidies. The second is the change in Japanese national income.

Look first at the upper right-hand cell, which shows what happens when the American government subsidizes Acme but the Japanese government does not subsidize Edo. American national income rises by 50, and Japanese national income falls by 175. Look next at the lower right-hand cell, which shows what happens when the two governments reach the equilibrium de-

scribed by the point Z in Figure 7-6. The two countries' national incomes are 48 lower than they were before any subsidies, which means that retaliation has allowed Japan to make good much of the loss it suffered from the American subsidy and has "punished" America in the process by converting its gain into a loss.

A Strategic Analysis of Export Subsidies

In the diagrammatic analysis studied earlier, each government chose its own export subsidy on the supposition that the other government would not respond. That is how the American government chose its initial subsidy OS_0 in Figure 7-6, how the Japanese government got to Z_1, and how the two governments moved sequentially to the unsatisfactory equilibrium at Z. (It is unsatisfactory because both countries lose, but it is an equilibrium nevertheless, as neither government has any incentive to depart from it unilaterally. It is, in effect, a loss-minimizing equilibrium.) But this sequential process is not the only way in which governments can get themselves into trouble.

Suppose that the American and Japanese governments are trying to decide individually whether to subsidize their exports and will not be able to reverse their

---

[5] It should be remembered, however, that the size of the subsidy given by a government will depend on what the other government is doing. In effect, the size of the subsidy is chosen after the basic decision to subsidize and in light of the basic decision by the other government.

		American options	
		No subsidy	Subsidy
Japanese options	No subsidy	0, 0*	+50, −175*
	Subsidy	−175, +50*	−48, −48*

FIGURE 7-8 A Strategic Analysis of Export Subsidies
When one government subsidizes exports and the other does not, it will gain at the other's expense. When both governments subsidize exports, both will lose, but that is what they are likely to do.

decisions once they have announced them. (They can change the sizes of their subsidies but not the basic decisions to subsidize.) Suppose that both governments know the numbers in Table 7-8 and thus the effects on their national incomes of the four possible policy outcomes but do not know in advance what the other government will do. Both governments are still likely to subsidize their exports and wind up with losses.

Look at the situation from the American standpoint and you will see that it is safer to subsidize. If Japan decides not to subsidize, America will be better off if it has decided to subsidize; its national income will rise by 50 rather than remaining unchanged. If Japan decides instead to subsidize, America will still be better off if it has decided to subsidize; its national income will fall by 48 rather than falling by 175. But Japan must make similar calculations and will arrive at the same conclusion. Hence, both governments will subsidize their exports, and both will lose.

This is the "noncooperative" solution to a famous problem in game theory, known as the Prisoner's Dilemma. It takes its name from an example in which two prisoners are held incommunicado. Each knows that he will be released if he accuses the other and no accusation is made against him, that he will be punished severely if he is accused, and that both prisoners will be punished but less severely if they remain silent. Clearly, the prisoners should "cooperate" by remaining silent; both will be treated leniently. But one may accuse the other if he does not trust him. And when both do this, both will be punished severely.

Both governments would be better off, of course, if they did not subsidize their exports and could promise each other that they would not do so. And that is how governments sometimes behave. Export subsidies are prohibited by the General Agreement on Tariffs and Trade (GATT), except in special circumstances. The major industrial countries have also agreed to limit the size of the export credit subsidies given to less-developed countries. But these promises are broken frequently, and it is difficult to punish cheating. If the American and Japanese governments agreed not to subsidize their robot exports, but the American government broke its promise, Japan might find it hard to punish the American transgression, except by subsidizing its own exports. Agreements of this sort are especially fragile when many countries are involved; small countries can cheat without being punished, because the large countries do not want the whole agreement to unravel. Agreements tend to be more robust when the participating governments are linked by many other agreements; the threat to renounce many of those other agreements may prevent any government from violating one of them.

We have wandered rather far into a new subject, the *strategic analysis* of trade policy, and could explore it further. But we will come back to it in Chapter 11, when we look at retaliation against "optimal" tariffs and at a different sort of subsidy designed to help an industry "win" a race to discover and exploit a new technology. Let us turn, then, to another type of imperfect competition that can also lead to intraindustry trade.

TRADE WITH MONOPOLISTIC COMPETITION

In the first part of this chapter, Acme and Edo produced identical goods, and each had the whole domestic market to itself before trade was opened. Economies of scale kept other firms from entering their markets. Trade replaced monopoly with oligopoly. We turn now to monopolistic competition, in which each country's market is served by many firms, but each firm makes a different version or variety of the same basic good. Economies of scale are important here as well. They determine the number of varieties that each country will produce.

Equilibrium in the Closed Economy

To highlight the features of this model, suppose that widgets, the basic product, can be made in many shades. Think of them as lying along a line from light to dark. If there were no economies of scale in the widget industry, a very small country could produce every variety of widget. There could indeed be many firms making each variety, and the market for that variety would then be perfectly competitive. When there are significant economies of scale, fewer varieties will be produced, fewer firms will make them, and markets will be less than perfectly competitive.

A large body of literature deals with the way that firms will choose their places on the line between light and dark widgets. Their behavior will depend in part on consumers' preferences and on the consumers' willingness to substitute one type of widget

for another. In this example, we will assume that consumers are distributed evenly along the line; if every variety of widget were available and their prices were the same, the same number of consumers would buy each variety. But we will assume that our countries are too small to provide the whole range of varieties and that the varieties actually produced are spread out along the line, but with gaps between them, forcing some consumers to choose between buying no widgets at all and buying those that do not satisfy them perfectly. We will deal with two countries, France and Italy, that produce n varieties, but assume that France produces the odd-numbered varieties ($1, 3, 5, \ldots, 2n - 1$), while Italy produces the even-numbered varieties ($2, 4, 6, \ldots, 2n$). The initial situation will look like this:

Varieties produced in France / Varieties produced in Italy

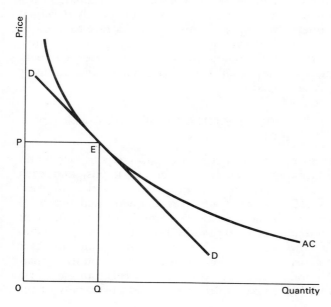

FIGURE 7-9 Equilibrium Under Monopolistic Competition
The curve *DD* is the domestic demand curve for the *j*th variety of widget. The curve *AC* is the average-cost curve for the only firm making that variety. The firm sells *OQ* widgets at price *OP*. Its total revenues are *OQEP* and are equal to its total costs. If the firm were making profits, additional firms would enter the widget industry to produce close substitutes for the *j*th variety, and the firm's demand curve would shift to the left until it was just tangent to its average-cost curve, causing the firm's profits to disappear.

There will be one firm producing each numbered variety, and each will have its own cluster of consumers.[7]

The situation of the typical firm in long-run equilibrium is shown by Figure 7-9. The firm produces the jth variety, its average-cost curve is AC, and its demand curve is DD. The shape of the average-cost curve reflects the assumption made earlier, that there are economies of scale in the production of widgets. The demand curve is downward sloping because the firm can acquire additional domestic customers by cutting its price. Some who have been buying the adjacent varieties, $j - 2$ and $j + 2$, will switch to the jth variety. The demand curve will be fairly flat if the adjacent varieties are close substitutes for the jth variety; a small reduction in the price of the jth variety will attract a large number of customers. Furthermore, the position of DD will depend on the prices of all other domestic varieties, but especially those of adjacent varieties. If an adjacent firm reduces its price and attracts additional customers, the demand curve for the jth variety will shift to the left. The size of the shift will depend on the number of consumers who abandon the jth variety when the price of another variety falls.

The firm will have marginal-cost and marginal-revenue curves, but we do not need them to describe the situation. We have merely to locate E, the point of tangency between DD and AC, where the firm produces OQ widgets and sells them at the price OP. Its total revenues are $OQEP$, and they equal the firm's total costs. If its total costs were higher, the firm would be making losses and would have to drop out of the industry; its customers would have to

move to other varieties. If its total costs were lower, it would be making profits and would attract additional firms to the widget industry. The new firms would produce near-by varieties, and the demand curve for the jth variety would shift to the left, reducing the firm's profits.

To sum up, France has n widget-making firms, and they produce the odd-numbered varieties. Italy has the same number of firms, but they produce the even-numbered varieties. Each firm in each country makes OQ widgets and sells them at the same price OP. Each country has the same number of consumers, and some of them would like to buy every sort of widget. Before trade is opened, however, French consumers can buy only odd-numbered widgets, and Italian consumers can buy only even-numbered widgets.

The Opening of Trade

Trade serves a very simple function in this model. It fills the gaps in the menu of widgets available to French and Italian consumers. But this can have a number of consequences. First, it will rearrange each country's consumption. Second, it may rearrange each country's production. Third, it may stimulate consumption and production.

The first effect is easily explained without an additional diagram. When consumers are evenly distributed and are given the opportunity to buy odd-numbered widgets and even-numbered widgets, half of those who used to buy odd-numbered widgets will switch to even-numbered widgets, and vice versa. Looking at the outcome from the standpoint of the jth firm, it will lose half its customers to the newly adjacent foreign firms making varieties $j - 1$ and $j + 1$ but will gain just as many customers from them. Therefore, it will continue to produce OQ widgets and obtain the price OP but will start to export half of its out-

---

[7] There are technical difficulties with this linear arrangement of varieties and firms. The firm at each end of the line will have only one close competitor, and all others will have two, but the linear arrangement is a convenient approximation.

put. Looking at the outcome in terms of trade flows, France will export half its output of odd-numbered widgets, Italy will export half its output of even-numbered widgets, and there will be balanced trade in widgets.

The second and third effects, which modify this outcome, reflect the indirect results of the change in the menu of widgets available to French and Italian consumers. Before trade was opened, the ability of the jth firm to attract additional customers was limited by the two-digit distance between the jth variety of widget and the closest substitutes available domestically, $j - 2$ and $j + 2$. After trade is opened, its ability is increased, because there is only a one-digit distance between the jth variety and the closest substitutes, $j - 1$ and $j + 1$, which come from the other country. Furthermore, consumers who did not buy widgets before will return to the widget market, attracted by the richer menu of varieties. The

immediate effects are shown in Figure 7-10, where the demand curve shifts from DD to $D'D'$. It gets flatter because there are closer substitutes for the jth variety; it shifts upward because there are more consumers in the widget market.

The firm will see this as an opportunity to raise its output and move to a point such as E', where its output is OQ' and its price is OP'. Its total revenues will be $OQ'E'P'$, its total costs will be $OQ'FC$, and its profits will be $CFE'P'$. But every other firm will see things the same way and try to raise its output, so the prices of adjacent varieties will fall and the demand curve for the jth variety will shift to the left. A new long-run equilibrium will be established when the demand curve is $D*D*$, which is tangent to AC at $E*$. The firm will produce $OQ*$ widgets, its price will be $OP*$, and its profits will be zero, just as they were before trade. But important gains accrue to consumers, who consume more widgets at lower prices.

FIGURE 7-10   Effects of Trade on Monopolistic Competition When Varieties Become Closer Substitutes Before trade, *DD* is the domestic demand curve for the *j*th variety of widget, and *AC* is the average-cost curve for the only firm making that variety. Output is *OQ*, and price is *OP*, as in Figure 7-9. Trade makes additional varieties available, shifting the demand curve to *D'D'*. It gets flatter because the firm can gain more customers by cutting its price and shifts upward because there are more customers in the market. The firm moves from *E* to *E'*, where its total revenues are *OQ'E'P'*, its total costs are *OQ'FC*, and its profits are *CFE'P'*. But all other firms are doing the same thing, so all demand curves shift to the left. A new long-run equilibrium is established at *E**, where profits have vanished, output is *OQ**, and price is *OP**.

The increase in widget consumption will be due in part to the increase in demand resulting from the increase in the number of consumers—the return of those who were not buying widgets before trade was opened. But it will be due in part to another phenomenon—a reduction in the total number of varieties produced and thus the number of firms in the two countries together. Each of the remaining firms will produce more widgets and will thus be able to exploit more fully the economies of scale in widget production.

How does this reduction come about? Initially, each country's consumers had a menu comprising n varieties. The opening of trade doubled the number, allowing some consumers to pick a widget better suited to their preferences. But ask yourself what you would do if offered a variety quite close to your ideal type or one that was somewhat farther away but priced at OP^* rather than OP. You might choose the cheaper widget, and that is what has happened in Figure 7-10. Think of the outcome this way: before trade, France produced n odd-numbered varieties and Italy produced n even-numbered varieties; after the opening of trade and all of the resulting adjustments, France produces varieties 1, 4, 7, and so on while Italy produces varieties 2.5, 5.5, 8.5, and so on. The number of varieties is larger than n but smaller than $2n$, and they are 1.5 digits apart, closer than they were before trade but farther apart than they would be without any rearrangement of production. Consumers benefit from more choice and from lower prices, because costs will fall.

The second and third effects do not cancel the first. When industries producing differentiated goods are identical apart from the varieties produced, intraindustry trade will still be balanced. Each country, however, will export a larger quantity of each remaining variety.

EMPIRICAL WORK ON INTRAINDUSTRY TRADE

Quantitative work on intraindustry trade underscores the importance of the variables featured in the theoretical models we have studied.

The level of intraindustry trade is usually measured by this index:

$$T = 1 - \frac{|x_{ijk} - x_{jik}|}{x_{ijk} + x_{jik}}$$

where x_{ijk} is the value or volume of the ith country's exports to the jth country in the kth product group, and x_{jik} is the trade flow in the opposite direction. This index is zero when trade goes only one way (when $x_{ijk} = 0$ or $x_{jik} = 0$); it is one when trade is perfectly balanced (when $x_{ijk} = x_{jik}$).[8]

One of the most ambitious empirical studies, covering 38 countries and 152 product groups, is summarized in Table 7-2. It tries to explain the value of T for each bilateral trade flow.

The first five variables listed in the table pertain to the general characteristics of the trading countries, and all of them have the expected effects. Models of monopolistic competition suggest that countries with high incomes can be expected to engage heavily in intraindustry trade, because their consumers will spend large fractions of their incomes on sophisticated manufac-

---

[8] Returning to Table 7-1, we can compute T for U.S. trade in records, tapes, and disks:

$$T = 1 - \frac{|856.2 - 918.2|}{856.2 + 918.2} = 1 - \frac{62.0}{1774.4} = 0.965$$

which says that trade in this product group comes close to being pure intraindustry trade. The average value of T for trade in manufactured goods lies between 0.55 and 0.75 for most major industrial countries; see David Greenaway and Chris Milner, *The Economics of Intra-Industry Trade* (Oxford: Blackwell, 1986), Table 5-3. Most statistical studies, including the one summarized in Table 7-2, adjust the value of T for imbalances in the countries' total trade.

TABLE 7-2   Country and Product Characteristics Affecting Levels of Intraindustry Trade Between Pairs of Countries

Characteristic	Effect
Average of countries' incomes per capita	Positive
Difference in incomes per capita	Negative
Average of countries' total incomes	Positive
Difference in total incomes	Negative
Average trade orientation of countries	Positive
Distance between countries	Negative
Common border between countries	Positive
Common language between countries	Positive[a]
Membership in common trade bloc	Positive
Product differentiation within industry	Positive[b]
Economies of scale for firms in industry	Negative
Industrial concentration in industry	Negative
Multinational production by firms in industry	Negative[c]
Average tariff level for industry	None
Tariff dispersion within industry	Negative

Source: Bela Balassa and Luc Bauwens, "Intra-Industry Specialization in a Multi-Country and Multi-Industry Framework," World Bank Development Research Department, Discussion Paper DRD116, December 1984, Table 1. Effect is shown as "none" when not significant at the 0.05 level.

[a] Positive for English, French, German, and Portuguese but not for Spanish or Scandinavian languages.

[b] Three measures were used simultaneously: an index of export prices (unit values) within the industry, an index of dispersion for profits, and the level of advertising expenditure. All three had positive effects.

[c] Two variables were used simultaneously: a measure of income received from foreign affiliates by firms in the industry and a measure of their trade with foreign affiliates. Both had negative effects. (A third variable, representing the influence of special provisions in the U. S. tariff schedule favoring offshore assembly, had the expected positive effect.)

tured goods, which tend to be most sharply differentiated. Conversely, countries with different income levels can be expected to have different tastes and thus to engage in less intraindustry trade. Similarly, large countries can be expected to produce many varieties of manufactured goods, and levels of national income are used to represent size. Finally, countries that are outwardly oriented, with low trade barriers, are also shown to participate heavily in intraindustry trade.

The next four variables relate to the characteristics of the bilateral relationship between each pair of countries. Distance discourages intraindustry trade, because transport costs tend to reduce each country's share of the other's market; this hap-

pens in the model of pure national monopoly that leads to oligopolistic competition and can also be expected to happen in models of monopolistic competition. Information should flow freely between countries with a common border or common language, and this should promote intraindustry trade, because each country's consumers should be thoroughly familiar with the range and variety of goods available from the other countries. Membership in a common trade bloc, such as the European Community, also encourages intraindustry trade.

The last six characteristics relate to the industries and product groups rather than the countries. Measures of product differentiation have the positive effect predicted by models of monopolistic competition. Economies of scale and industrial concentration appear to have perverse effects. In both models examined in this chapter, economies of scale provided the barriers to entry that led to intraindustry trade. Furthermore, industrial concentration should produce the mutual penetration of national markets that took place in the model of oligopolistic competition. But there are forces working in the opposite direction, and they appear to dominate. When there are significant economies of scale or large firms in an industry, there are opportunities for standardization as well as differentiation, and standardization leads to specialization rather than intraindustry trade. The extent of multinational production can likewise cut two ways. On the one hand, it displaces trade, because firms that produce locally for a particular market do not have to export to it. On the other hand, it creates trade, because firms that produce locally often import parts and components from plants in other countries. (Trade in automotive engines is an example.) In this particular study, the trade-displacing effect appears to dominate. Finally, tariffs and other trade barriers might be expected to limit intraindustry trade, but their effects are weak in this and other studies.

SUMMARY

Models with perfectly competitive markets cannot explain two-way trade within a single product group. Yet this intraindustry trade accounts for a large portion of all international trade, especially in manufactured goods. Models with imperfect markets are needed to explain it.

When two countries' domestic markets are monopolized, the opening of trade intensifies competition; oligopoly replaces monopoly, reducing prices and profits. Producers lose but consumers gain, and the gains are larger than the losses. Trade can occur even when the countries' firms produce identical goods and sell them at identical prices.

When two countries' markets are characterized by monopolistic competition involving differentiated products, the opening of trade raises the number of varieties available. It can also reduce the number produced in each country, along with the number of producers, allowing the survivors to exploit economies of scale and thus reduce their costs. Trade is beneficial for both of these reasons.

Under conditions of imperfect competition, there are incentives for governments to subsidize their exports, to capture more of the profits from foreign markets. When other governments retaliate, however, there are losses all around, and binding agreements may be needed to keep the process from starting.

Finally, it must be remembered that models of imperfect competition can explain intraindustry trade but cannot by themselves explain why some countries are net exporters of certain manufactures, net importers of others, and net exporters or importers of other goods. Those models must be combined with others, such as the modified Ricardian model or Heckscher—Ohlin model, to explain the whole trade pattern.

RECOMMENDED READINGS

The model of oligopolistic competition developed in this chapter is based on the model in James A. Brander, "Intra-Industry Trade in Identical Commodities," *Journal of International* *Economics*, 11 (February 1981); the model of monopolistic competition is based on the model in Paul R. Krugman, "Increasing Returns, Monopolistic Competition, and International Trade,"

Journal of International Economics 9 (November 1979).

A good survey of recent theoretical work is provided in David Greenaway and Chris Milner, *The Economics of Intra-Industry Trade* (Oxford: Blackwell, 1986), chs. 2–3; for a more comprehensive and rigorous treatment, see Elhanan Helpman, "Increasing Returns, Imperfect Markets, and Trade Theory," in R. W. Jones and P. B. Kenen, eds., *Handbook of International Economics* (Amsterdam: North-Holland, 1984), ch. 7.

Models of trade with imperfect competition have been used to reexamine many issues in trade policy. See, for example, Paul R. Krugman, "Import Protection as Export Promotion," in H. Kierzkowski, ed., *Monopolistic Competition and International Trade* (Oxford: Oxford University Press, 1984), ch. 11.

For a survey of recent research on strategic aspects of trade policy, see Gene M. Grossman and J. David Richardson, *Strategic Trade Policy: A Survey of Issues and Early Analysis,* Special Papers in International Economics 15 (Princeton, N.J.: International Finance Section, Princeton University, 1983); for contrasting views on the same subject, see Paul R. Krugman, ed., *Strategic Trade Policy and the New International Economics* (Cambridge, Mass.: MIT Press, 1986), chs. 2–4, and Avinash Dixit, "How Should the United States Respond to Other Countries' Trade Policies?" in R. M. Stern, ed., *U.S. Trade Policies in a Changing World Economy* (Cambridge, Mass.: MIT Press, 1987), ch. 6.

CHAPTER

8

TRADE
AND FACTOR
MOVEMENTS

PERSPECTIVES AND OBJECTIVES

The introduction to this book, describing the scope and method of international economics, said that it would focus on the nation-state as the basic unit of analysis but would measure the welfare of the typical consumer. This was the procedure adopted in Chapters 5 and 6 to study the effects of economic growth. When examining capital formation, we compared the sizes of two changes affecting the welfare of a typical consumer in the growing country, the change in real income measured at initial prices and the change in the terms of trade caused by the shift in the output mix. We saw that capital formation can be immiserizing when the growing country exports the capital-intensive good, because the welfare-raising effect of the increase in real income may not be large enough to offset the welfare-reducing effect of the deterioration in the terms of trade.

When dealing with movements of capital or labor from one country to another, it makes less sense to focus on the nation-state and typical consumer. It is difficult, in fact, to define the typical consumer, because factor movements can involve movements of consumers, too. When workers move from Portugal to Britain, how should they be classified? As British consumers or Portuguese consumers? When capital moves from Britain to Portugal, should we reclassify the owners of that capital? Even when these questions can be answered clearly, so as to define the typical consumer in each country, the concept can obscure interesting issues. Why do many countries limit immigration? There are, of course, political and cultural reasons. To get at the economic reasons, however, we must distinguish the effects of immigration on the incomes of the immigrants from its effects on the incomes of all others, not average the effects on immigrants and others.

We will continue to concentrate on long-run changes in outputs and incomes that can be identified only when a factor movement is completed and all factors of production are optimally allocated in each economy. But we will classify them differently. First, we will look at the effects on global output, defined by the sum of the outputs of the *host* and *source* countries, to see how factor movements affect the efficiency of the world economy. Second, we will look at the distributional effects defined by the changes in the incomes of three groups of persons: those who move (or move their capital) from source to host country, those who reside initially in the host country, and those who remain behind in the source country. It will be important, moreover, to look separately at effects on the earnings of labor, capital, and land in each country. They will not change uniformly.

Although it adopts a different classification of welfare effects, this chapter follows the same general approach adopted to study economic growth. It concentrates on capital movements, which are easier to analyze than labor movements. It looks at the effects of factor movements in both models used before, the modified Ricardian model and Heckscher–Ohlin model.

It is easy to find reasons for factor movements in the modified Ricardian model and equally easy to analyze their consequences. We can ask how they alter outputs and earnings when there are no other changes in the countries concerned, then ask how they influence patterns of employment, and conclude by asking how the changes in employment affect real earnings in the host

and source countries. We will see that factor movements are *self-limiting* in the modified Ricardian model. The changes in earnings induced in each country remove the incentives for factors to move.

It is harder to find reasons for factor movements in the Heckscher–Ohlin model, because free trade can equalize factor prices, depriving capital and labor of any economic incentive to leave one country for another. We must introduce an impediment to factor-price equalization to drive a wedge between factor prices. But the effects of the resulting factor movements depend on the nature of the impediment. In some cases, factor movements remove the impediment itself, allowing trade to equalize the countries' factor prices and ending the incentives for factors to move. In other cases, factor movements cannot remove the impediment, and the movements will continue unabated until they have eliminated trade itself.

The chapter will go on to deal with some questions that emerge from the formal analysis of factor movements but are not answered fully by it. Why do firms engage in *multinational production*, putting plants in many countries rather than one country? What are the effects on the countries involved? When firms and individuals reside in one country but earn incomes in another, what principles should govern the taxation of that income? How should those principles be implemented?

CAPITAL MOVEMENTS IN THE MODIFIED RICARDIAN MODEL

Recall the main characteristics of Britain and Portugal. They have the same quantities of labor, but Britain has more capital than Portugal, and Portugal has more land than Britain. When their technologies and tastes are the same and there is free trade between them, Britain exports cloth and Portugal exports wine. Yet free trade does not equalize the countries' factor prices. When their stocks of capital differ greatly, the marginal product of capital will be lower in Britain's cloth industry, so the real return to capital will be lower in Britain, whether measured in cloth or wine.[1] There is thus an incentive for capital to move from Britain to Portugal.

Primary Effects of a Capital Movement

The initial situation is described by Figure 8-1. The curve AC shows the relationship between the marginal product of capital in Britain's cloth industry and the quantity of capital in Britain, given the number of workers in the industry. When the quantity of capital is OK_1, the marginal product of capital is OR yards of cloth, which measures the real return to capital in terms of cloth. Therefore, the owners of capital earn $OR \times OK_1$, or $ORBK_1$ yards of cloth. The curve A^*C^* shows the relationship prevailing in Portugal, given the number of workers in its cloth industry. (The British curve is higher and flatter than the Portuguese curve, because more workers are employed in Britain's cloth industry.) When the quantity of capital is OK_2 in Portugal, the marginal product of capital is OR^* yards of cloth, and the owners of capital earn OR^*PK_2 yards of cloth.

An additional point about marginal-product curves is important here. The area under any marginal-product curve measures the total product of the industry. When the supply of capital is OK_1 in Britain, cloth output is $OABK_1$ yards. By implication, the workers in the British cloth industry earn RAB yards of cloth, the difference between total output and the payment made to the owners of capital. In Portugal, cloth output is OA^*PK_2 yards, and the workers in the Portuguese industry earn R^*A^*P yards of cloth.

When the real return to capital is lower in Britain, owners of capital have an incentive to transfer some to Portugal. The primary effects show up in Figure 8-1. Suppose that K_1K_1' of British capital is transferred to Portugal, reducing the supply of capital to OK_1' in Britain and raising the supply to OK_2' in Portugal (i.e., $K_1K_1' = K_2K_2'$). Five effects follow directly.

First, the transfer eliminates completely the difference between marginal products in Britain and Portugal. The marginal product of capital rises in Britain from OR to OR'. It falls in Portugal from OR^* to OR'. (A transfer smaller than K_1K_1' would reduce the difference but not eliminate it.) Therefore, the factor movement is self-limiting. By closing the gap between marginal products and thus the difference

---

[1] We can prove this assertion by invoking the results of capital formation obtained from the special case in Chapter 5, where the real wage remained constant in Britain when measured in wine. Let the marginal products of capital be the same initially in Britain and Portugal. Let there be capital formation in Britain. The real return to capital falls in both countries but falls farther in Britain. The proof is in three steps: (1) Marginal products in a particular industry depend only on the industry's capital-labor ratio. If the marginal products of capital are equal in the countries' cloth industries, the capital-labor ratios must be equal, too, which means that the marginal products of labor must be equal. By implication, real wages must be equal, whether measured in wine or cloth. (2) Capital formation in Britain raises each country's real wage measured in cloth, but by more in Britain. Otherwise, the real wage measured in wine could not remain constant in Britain while falling in Portugal, and that is what happened in Chapter 5. (3) When the real wage rises by more in Britain, however, the marginal product of labor must rise by more in Britain's cloth industry. Therefore, the marginal product of capital must fall by more in Britain's cloth industry and be lower thereafter in Britain than in Portugal.

between real returns, it removes the incentive for owners of capital to transfer any more.

Second, the transfer raises global cloth output, increasing the efficiency of the world economy. Output falls in Britain from $OABK_1$ to $OAB'K_1'$, decreasing by $K_1'B'BK_1$ yards of cloth. But output rises in Portugal from $OA*PK_2$ to $OA*P'K_2'$, increasing by $K_2'P'PK_2$ yards of cloth. The increase in Portuguese output is larger than the decrease in British output. Global output rises by $\frac{1}{2}(K_1K_1' \times RR*)$ yards of cloth, where K_1K_1' is the capital transfer and $RR*$ is the initial gap between marginal products.[2] If there were no such gap, a capital transfer from Britain to Portugal would not raise global output. Without the gap, however, the owners of capital would not move it, because rates of return would not differ. Putting the same point in general terms, a factor movement activated by a difference in real returns raises the efficiency of the world economy whenever the difference in real returns reflects a difference in marginal products.

Third, the transfer of capital raises the incomes of its owners, even though it eliminates the gap between marginal products. The owners earned $K_1'EBK_1$ in Britain, and $K_2'P'FK_2$ in Portugal. Their incomes rise by $HP'FG$ yards of cloth.

Fourth, the transfer redistributes income in Britain from labor to capital. As the marginal product of capital rises in Britain, the owners of the capital remaining in Britain earn an additional $RR'B'E$ yards of cloth (i.e., $RR' \times OK_1'$). Labor loses even more, however, because British cloth output falls. Labor's income falls from RAB to $R'AB'$, a decrease of $RR'B'B$ yards of cloth. This loss exceeds the gain to the owners of capital by $EB'B$ yards of cloth, which is part of the decrease in British cloth output. By implication, British labor has reason to oppose the capital movement (and the British government cannot compensate labor by taxing the gain accruing to capital, because the gain is smaller than labor's loss).

Fifth, the transfer redistributes income in Portugal from capital to labor. As the marginal product of capital falls in Portugal, the earnings of the owners of capital initially in Portugal fall by $R'R*PF$ yards of cloth (i.e., $R'R* \times OK_2$). Labor gains even more, however, because Portuguese cloth output rises. Labor's income rises from $R*A*P$ to $R'A*P'$, an increase of $R'R*PP'$ yards of cloth. This gain exceeds the loss to the owners of capital by FPP' yards of cloth, which is part of the increase in Portuguese cloth output. Portuguese labor has reason to favor the capital movement.

Secondary Effects of a Capital Movement

These five results, however, were derived with the help of a drastic simplification. The positions of the curves AC and $A*C*$ depend on the initial levels of employment in the countries' cloth industries, yet our previous work with the modified Ricardian model told us that a change in the supply of capital leads to a reallocation of labor. When allowance is made for this effect, the capital transfer shown in Figure 8-1 turns out to be too small to eliminate the gap between marginal products, and the increase in global

---

[2] The decrease in British output can be written as $K_1'EBK_1 + EB'B$. The increase in Portuguese output can be written as $K_2'HGK_2 + HP'FG + FPP'$. But $K_1'EBK_1 = K_2'GHK_2$ (because $K_1K_1' = K_2K_2'$), so the increase in Portuguese output exceeds the decrease in British output by $HP'FG + FPP' - EB'B$. But $HP'FG$ can be written as $GH \times GF$, while FPP' can be written as $\frac{1}{2}(FP' \times FP)$, and $EB'B$ can be written as $\frac{1}{2}(EB \times EB')$. Furthermore, $GH = FP' = K_2K_2' = K_1K_1' = EB$, while $GF = RR' = EB'$, and $FP = R'R*$. Therefore, the increase in Portuguese output exceeds the decrease in British output by $(K_1K_1' \times RR') + \frac{1}{2}(K_1K_1' \times R'R*) - \frac{1}{2}(K_1K_1' \times RR')$ or $\frac{1}{2}(K_1K_1' \times RR') + \frac{1}{2}(K_1K_1' \times R'R*)$. This gives the expression in the text, because $RR' + R'R* = RR*$, the gap between marginal products.

FIGURE 8-1 Effects of Transferring Capital from Britain to Portugal Before Adjustments in Employment

The curve AC gives the marginal product of capital in Britain's cloth industry. With OK_1 capital invested in that industry initially, the marginal product is OR. As the area under any marginal-product curve measures the total product, cloth output is $OABK_1$. Payments to capital total $ORBK_1$, and payments to labor total RAB. When $K_1 K_1'$ capital is transferred to Portugal, raising the marginal product to OR', cloth output falls by $K_1'B'BK_1$, payments to capital remaining in Britain rise by $RR'B'E$, and payments to labor fall by $RR'B'B$. The curve A^*C^* gives the marginal product of capital in Portugal's cloth industry. With OK_2 capital invested in the industry initially, the marginal product is OR^*. Cloth output is OA^*PK_2, payments to capital total OR^*PK_2, and payments to labor total R^*A^*P. When $K_2 K_2'$ (= $K_1 K_1'$) capital is transferred to Portugal, reducing the marginal product to OR', cloth output rises by $K_2'P'PK_2$, payments to capital initially in Portugal fall by $R'R^*PF$, and payments to labor rise by $R'R^*PP'$. Payments to the capital transferred from Britain to Portugal rise by $HP'FG$, from $K_1'EBK_1$ in Britain to $K_2'P'FK_2$ in Portugal.

output understates the efficiency gain conferred by the transfer (and thus understates to a greater extent the gain conferred by a transfer large enough to close the gap completely).

These assertions are confirmed by Figure 8-2, which traces the effects of a capital transfer on the countries' labor markets.

The point B defines equilibrium in Britain's labor market before the transfer of capital. The real wage measured in cloth is OV_1 yards, OL_1 workers are employed in the wine industry, and $\overline{L}L_1$ are employed in the cloth industry. Wine and cloth outputs are measured by the areas under the demand curves (because they are marginal-product

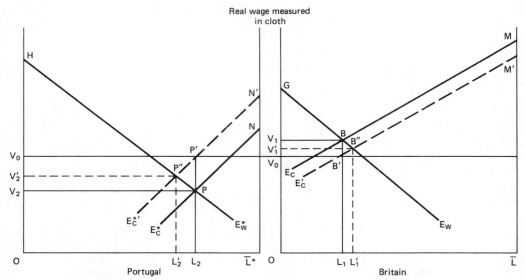

FIGURE 8-2 Effects of Transferring Capital from Britain to Portugal After
Adjustments in Employment

Initially, OL_1 workers are employed in Britain's wine industry and $\bar{L}L_1$ in
its cloth industry; the real wage is OV_1 in terms of cloth. The transfer of
capital shown in Figure 8-1 shifts the demand curve for labor downward. The marginal product of labor falls to OV_0, and cloth output falls
by $B'BMM'$. Initially, OL_2 workers are employed in Portugal's wine industry and $\bar{L}*L_2$ in its cloth industry; the real wage is OV_2 in terms of
cloth. The transfer of capital shifts the demand curve for labor upward.
The marginal product of labor rises to OV_0, and cloth output rises by
$PP'N'N$. If labor markets were in equilibrium at B' and P, the transfer
would equalize the real returns to capital by equalizing the marginal
products of labor and thus the marginal products of capital. But the
labor-market equilibria are displaced to B'' and P''. Therefore, the marginal product of labor falls to OV'_1 in Britain and rises to OV'_2 in Portugal, leaving a gap between the real returns to capital. A larger transfer of
capital is needed to equalize real returns.

curves), but wine output is measured by its
cloth equivalent at the free-trade prices
prevailing initially. Thus, cloth output is
$\bar{L}MBL_1$ yards in Britain, and the cloth
equivalent of wine output is $OGBL_1$. The
point P defines equilibrium in Portugal's
labor market. The real wage measured in
cloth is OV_2 yards, OL_2 workers are em-

ployed in the wine industry, and $\bar{L}*L_2$ are
employed in the cloth industry. Cloth output is $\bar{L}*NPL_2$ yards, and the cloth equivalent of wine output is $OHPL_2$ yards.

The real wage expressed in cloth is
higher in Britain than in Portugal, because
the marginal product of labor is higher in
Britain's cloth industry. Recall that mar-

ginal products in a particular industry depend on factor proportions in that industry. As the marginal product of capital is lower initially in Britain than in Portugal, the capital-labor ratio must be higher in Britain's cloth industry, which means that the marginal product of labor must likewise be higher.

The transfer of capital from Britain to Portugal induced by the gap between rates of return is shown in Figure 8-2 by shifting the demand curves for labor. The capital stock falls in Britain, reducing the marginal product of labor in Britain's cloth industry and shifting its demand curve for labor downward from E_C to E_C'. The capital stock rises in Portugal, raising the marginal product of labor in Portugal's cloth industry and shifting its demand curve upward from E_C^* to $E_C^{*'}$. These shifts have been drawn carefully to satisfy two requirements. First, the capital transfer in Figure 8-1 was just large enough to equalize the marginal products of capital in the countries' cloth industries at the initial levels of employment. Therefore, it must equalize the marginal products of labor. Holding employment at $\bar{L}L_1$ in Britain's cloth industry and at $\bar{L}^*L_2$ in Portugal's cloth industry, the shifts in the curves must bring the marginal products of labor to the common level OV_0 in Figure 8-2. Second, the capital transfer raised Portuguese cloth output by more than it reduced British cloth output. In Figure 8-2, then, the area $PP'N'N$, which measures the increase in Portuguese cloth output at the initial level of employment, must be larger than the area $B'BMM'$, which measures the corresponding decrease in British cloth output.

The new points B' and P', however, are not equilibrium points. If the real wage falls in Britain from OV_1 to OV_0, the wine industry will demand more labor, driving up the real wage. If the real wage rises in Portugal from OV_2 to OV_0, the wine indus-

try will demand less labor, driving down the real wage. Equilibrium in Britain's labor market must be established at B'', with L_1L_1' workers moving from the cloth to the wine industry. Equilibrium in Portugal's labor market must be established at P'', with L_2L_2' workers moving from the wine to the cloth industry. What are the implications?

The real wage rises in Britain to OV_1' yards of cloth and falls in Portugal to OV_2' yards of cloth. The difference between real wages has been reduced but not eliminated. Therefore, the transfer of capital has not eliminated the difference between the marginal products of capital. This proves the first assertion made previously that the transfer required to remove the gap is larger than the one in Figure 8-1.

Figure 8-2 was constructed to reflect the primary effect of the capital transfer on global cloth output ($PP'N'N$ is bigger than $B'BMM'$). But it also shows secondary changes in outputs that augment the gain in efficiency. In Britain, the labor-market adjustments reduce cloth output by an extra $L_1B'B''L_1'$ yards, but raise the cloth equivalent of wine output by $L_1BB''L_1'$ yards. Thus, the cloth value of real product rises in Britain by $B'BB''$ yards. In Portugal, the labor-market adjustments reduce the cloth equivalent of wine output by $L_2PP''L_2'$ yards, but raise cloth output itself by an extra $L_2P'P''L_2'$ yards. Thus, the cloth value of real product rises in Portugal by $PP'P''$ yards. Therefore, the increase in global output is larger than the one in Figure 8-1. (The decrease in the cloth value of British output is $B'BB''$ yards smaller than $B'BMM'$, and the increase in the cloth value of Portuguese output is $PP'P''$ larger than $PP'N'N$.)

The more complicated story told by Figure 8-2 does not contradict any basic lesson taught by Figure 8-1. A larger capital transfer would eliminate completely the difference between real wages and, therefore, the difference between real returns to capital. That transfer, moreover, would raise global output by more than the amount in Figure 8-2 (which is already larger than the amount in Figure 8-1). Furthermore, the labor-market changes shown in Figure 8-2 do not alter fundamentally the results obtained before concerning the earnings of labor and capital. The owners of capital remaining in Britain gain from the capital transfer, because the real return to capital rises. British labor loses, however, because the real wage falls. But Figure 8-2 brings in an additional effect. The owners of land gain in Britain, because the increase in employment in the wine industry raises the real rental rate. Conversely, the owners of land lose in Portugal, because the decrease in employment in the wine industry reduces the real rental rate.

Three more points should be made before ending this discussion. First, Figure 8-2 relaxed one assumption made in Figure 8-1, that patterns of employment are fixed in the two countries, but did not relax another. The output changes shown by Figure 8-2 could alter relative prices (the terms of trade), which would alter the distributions of gains and losses within and between the two countries. Second, a transfer of capital from Britain to Portugal large enough to equalize the marginal products of capital will also equalize the marginal products of labor and the marginal products of land. It will thus *maximize* the efficiency of the world economy. There is no need to transfer any other factor. (This conclusion, however, depends on two basic assumptions: that returns to scale are constant, so marginal products depend only on factor proportions, and that technologies are the same in all countries.) Finally, a transfer of capital does not undermine the basis for trade. As Portugal has more land than Britain, it will continue to produce

more wine, even when marginal products have been equalized. As Britain has more capital, even after the transfer, it will continue to produce more cloth.[3]

CAPITAL MOVEMENTS IN THE HECKSCHER–OHLIN MODEL

In the modified Ricardian model, factor movements are required to equalize marginal products and thus maximize global efficiency. Trade alone cannot do so. In the Heckscher–Ohlin model, factor movements may not be needed. Trade alone can equalize marginal products and maximize efficiency, because it can equalize factor prices.

The factor-price-equalization theorem, however, depends on the long list of assumptions given at the end of Chapter 6. All markets must be perfectly competitive, and trade must unify markets completely; there can be no transport costs, tariffs, or other trade barriers. All countries must produce a common set of traded commodities, and the number of commodities in that set must be no smaller than the number of factors of production; in the two-country, two-commodity, two-factor case, one country cannot specialize completely in a single commodity. Production functions must be the same in all countries, must display constant returns to scale, and must not give rise to reversals in factor intensities when factor prices change.

---

[3] When marginal products are equalized in Britain and Portugal, their wine industries will have the same land-labor ratios, and their cloth industries will have the same capital-labor ratios. But Portugal has more land than Britain, which means that its wine industry must employ more workers to go with its larger supply of land. At the start, moreover, we assumed that Britain and Portugal have the same quantities of labor. Therefore, Portugal must employ less labor and less capital in its cloth industry, and Britain must have more capital than Portugal, even after the transfer.

These are strong assumptions, and they have strong consequences. On the one hand, they give us a good reason for favoring free trade—for wanting to remove all trade barriers. Free trade maximizes global efficiency. On the other hand, they deprive us of any economic explanation for factor movements. Free trade will equalize real earnings, and differences in real earnings are the main economic motivation for factor movements.

To generate and analyze factor movements in the Heckscher–Ohlin model, we must modify one of the assumptions, in order to produce a situation in which trade cannot equalize factor prices, then trace the consequences of that situation. Two examples will illustrate this strategy. In the first, a tariff will interfere with the unification of markets, preventing factor-price equalization. A capital movement will occur in response to the resulting difference in real returns, and it will eliminate trade completely. In the second, factor intensities will be reversed; corn will be labor intensive in one country but capital intensive in the other. This will prevent factor-price equalization and induce a capital movement. But the capital movement will not eliminate trade. Instead, it will eradicate the factor reversal, allowing trade to equalize factor prices.

Effects of a Tariff

We will study tariffs systematically in Chapter 9 and see how they affect prices, outputs, and trade flows. We will find that a tariff on Fewmen's corn imports raises the relative price of corn in Fewmen but lowers it in Manymen. This is the situation shown in Figure 8-3. As usual, Manymen begins with $O\overline{K}_1$ capital per worker, and Fewmen begins with $O\overline{K}_2$. In the initial free-trade equilibrium, the relative price of corn is OP in both countries, the relative price of labor

is OW, and factor intensities are the same in the two countries' industries. (The capital intensity of steel production, for example, is WV capital per worker.) By implication, the marginal products of capital and labor are the same in both countries, and their real earnings are the same, whether they are measured in corn or steel.

When Fewmen imposes a tariff on its corn imports, the relative price of corn rises to OP_2 in that country, and the relative price of labor rises to OW_2. Fewmen moves to F, producing more corn and less steel than it did with free trade, and firms adopt more capital-intensive methods of production. (The capital intensity of steel production rises from WV to W_2V_2.) In Manymen, however, the relative price of corn falls to OP_1, and the relative price of labor falls to OW_1. Manymen moves to M, producing less corn and more steel, and firms adopt less capital-intensive methods. (The capital intensity of steel production falls from WV to W_1V_1.) The gap between capital intensities implies a gap between marginal products and, therefore, a gap between real returns. The real return is lower in Fewmen, whether it is measured in corn or steel. Therefore, capital will move from Fewmen to Manymen, reducing the quantity in Fewmen below $O\overline{K}_2$ per worker and raising it in Manymen above $O\overline{K}_1$ per worker.

If owners of capital are sufficiently responsive to the gap between real returns, they will continue to transfer capital to Manymen until the gap has vanished. This cannot occur, however, until all other gaps have vanished—the gaps between marginal products, factor intensities, relative prices of labor, and relative prices of corn. But the gap between relative prices cannot vanish until trade has vanished. For as long as any corn flows from Manymen to Fewmen, crossing Fewmen's tariff, the relative price of corn must be higher in Fewmen. The

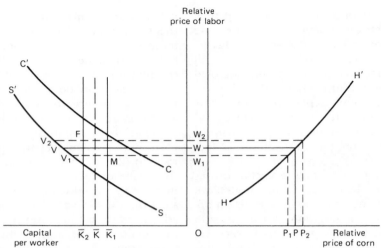

FIGURE 8-3 Factor Movement Induced by a Tariff

Manymen has $O\overline{K}_1$ capital per worker, and Fewmen has $O\overline{K}_2$. Under free trade, the relative price of corn is OP, and the relative price of labor is OW in each country. Both countries produce both commodities, but Manymen exports corn and Fewmen exports steel. If Fewmen imposes a tariff on its corn imports, the relative price of corn will rise to OP_2 in Fewmen, raising the relative price of labor to OW_2 and causing Fewmen to produce at F. The relative price of corn will fall to OP_1 in Manymen, reducing the relative price of labor to OW_1 and causing Manymen to produce at M. The real return to capital will be higher in Manymen, attracting capital from Fewmen and driving both countries' factor endowments closer to $O\overline{K}$ capital per worker. This process cannot end while trade continues, because trade across the tariff will continue to separate the countries' commodity and factor prices. The process can end only when the capital movement has eliminated trade by eliminating the difference between the countries' endowments.

two countries' commodity prices cannot be equalized until the influence of the tariff has been eliminated, and this can happen only when trade has been eliminated.

How does the transfer of capital eliminate trade? As capital moves from Fewmen to Manymen, it reduces the difference between their factor endowments. At some point in the process, determined in part by the level of the tariff, the difference in endowments becomes too small to furnish any basis for trade, and trade comes to an end. But the capital movement continues even

after that. Going back to our earlier work on the opening of trade, recall how we proved the Heckscher–Ohlin theorem. When demand conditions are the same in Manymen and Fewmen but factor endowments are not, relative prices will differ before trade is opened. That is the situation here just after trade has ended. When relative prices differ, however, marginal products also differ, and the capital movement continues. It cannot cease until the countries' endowments have become identical. In Figure 8-3, the capital stock in Fewmen must fall from $O\overline{K}_2$ per worker to some such level as $O\overline{K}$, and the capital stock in Manymen must rise from $O\overline{K}_1$ per worker to that same level $O\overline{K}$.

Suppose that the two countries reach $O\overline{K}$, ending the capital transfer. What would happen if Fewmen repealed its tariff? Nothing. Trade would not resume, because there is no basis for it. Manymen and Fewmen are the same in all significant respects and cannot gain from trade. In the Heckscher–Ohlin model, then, trade and factor movements are perfect substitutes. When free trade equalizes factor prices, maximizing global efficiency, factor movements are not needed and do not take place. When trade is restricted, however, factor movements are required to maximize efficiency, and they wipe out trade.[4]

Note finally the effects of the capital transfer on the real earnings of labor and capital. By keeping the relative price of corn in Fewmen above its free-trade level, a tariff raises the real wage above its free-trade level and depresses the real return to capital. The capital transfer reduces the real wage and raises the real return to the capital remaining in Fewmen. If you were a worker in Fewmen, then, you would oppose the transfer. The situation is sym-

---

[4] There are two qualifications to this proposition. (1) If there are impediments to factor movements as well as trade, factor movements may not wipe out trade completely. In Figure 8-3, the capital movement will drive the capital-labor ratios closer to $O\overline{K}$ but will stop before they reach $O\overline{K}$. The remaining difference between endowments may be large enough for trade to continue. The outcome depends on the cost of moving goods (the level of the tariff) compared to the cost of moving factors. (2) Those who move their capital from Fewmen to Manymen may not move with it. If they remain behind in Fewmen, the income they earn on their capital in Manymen must be brought back to Fewmen, and this requires trade. Manymen must sell some of its output to Fewmen to pay for the services of capital from Fewmen. This trade, however, is not the sort that we have studied heretofore. Manymen will export corn *and* steel rather than exporting corn and importing steel.

metrical in Manymen. The tariff keeps the relative price of corn below its free-trade level, depressing the real wage and raising the real return to capital. The capital transfer raises the real wage and reduces the real return to the capital initially in Manymen. If you were a worker in Manymen, you would favor the transfer.

Effects of a Factor Reversal

In Figure 8-3 and earlier diagrams, the SS' and CC' curves did not intersect. Steel was more capital intensive than corn at all sets of factor prices. In Figure 8-4, the two curves cross at Y, reversing the factor intensities. When the relative price of labor is below OW, steel is more capital intensive than corn; when it is OW_1, for example, the capital intensity of steel production is W_1V_1, and the capital intensity of corn production is W_1U_1. When the relative price of labor is above OW, corn is more capital intensive than steel; when it is OW_2, for example, the capital intensity of steel production is W_2V_2, and the capital intensity of corn production is W_2U_2. The shape of the HH' curve reflects this reversal. When the relative price of labor is below OW, so that steel is more capital intensive than corn, an increase in the relative price of labor raises the cost of producing corn compared to the cost of producing steel, and this raises the relative price of corn. When the relative price of labor is above OW, so that factor intensities are reversed, an increase in the relative price of labor raises the cost of producing steel compared to the cost of producing corn, and this reduces the relative price of corn.

Technologies determine the shapes of the SS' and CC' curves, excluding or allowing these reversals. But factor endowments affect the actual result. When Manymen and Fewmen have capital stocks smaller than $O\overline{K}$ per worker, steel will be more cap-

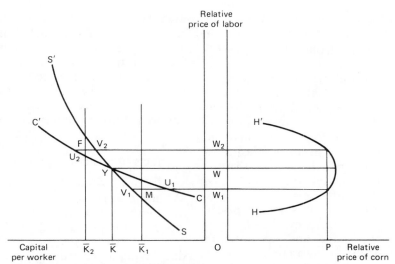

FIGURE 8-4   Factor Movement Induced by a Factor Reversal
When the relative price of labor is lower than OW, steel is more capital
intensive than corn, and an increase in the relative price of labor is associated with an increase in the relative price of corn. When the relative
price of labor is higher than $O\overline{W}$, corn is more capital intensive than
steel, and an increase in the relative price of labor is associated with a
decrease in the relative price of corn. Manymen has $O\overline{K}_1$ capital per
worker, and Fewmen has $O\overline{K}_2$. When the relative price of corn is OP,
the relative price of labor is OW_1 in Manymen, which produces at M,
but the relative price of labor is OW_2 in Fewmen, which produces at F.
As the real return to capital is higher in Manymen, capital will move
from Fewmen to Manymen. The movement will continue until the two
countries' endowments lie on the same side of $O\overline{K}$ (until capital per
worker is higher than $O\overline{K}$ in Manymen or lower than $O\overline{K}$ in Fewmen).
The factor reversal will be eliminated, allowing trade to equalize the
countries' factor prices.

ital intensive than corn in both countries;
when they have stocks larger than $O\overline{K}$, corn
will be more capital intensive than steel. In
both cases, the trade pattern is easy to predict. In the first case, the country with the
larger capital stock will export steel; in the
second case, that country will export corn.
In both cases, moreover, free trade can
equalize factor prices and there is no need
or incentive for capital to move. Factor reversals occur and complicate the problem
only when factor endowments straddle $O\overline{K}$.

When Manymen has $O\overline{K}_1$ capital per
worker, less than $O\overline{K}$, steel is the capital-
intensive commodity at all points on Many-
men's transformation curve. When Few-
men has $O\overline{K}_2$ capital per worker, more than
$O\overline{K}$, corn is the capital-intensive commodity
at all points on Fewmen's transformation
curve. It is therefore impossible to forecast
the trade pattern merely by examining factor endowments. Looking at the situation
in Manymen, we would be tempted to predict that it will import steel, because it has

less capital per worker and steel is the capital-intensive commodity. But looking at the situation in Fewmen, we would be tempted to predict that it will import steel, too, because it has more capital per worker and steel is the labor-intensive commodity. The two predictions would be inconsistent. Both countries cannot import steel. More important for present purposes, free trade cannot equalize factor prices.

Suppose that the relative price of corn is OP in the initial free-trade equilibrium. The relative price of labor must be OW_1 in Manymen, and it produces at M, where the capital intensity of steel output is $W_1 V_1$ and the capital intensity of corn output is $W_1 U_1$. The relative price of labor must be OW_2 in Fewmen, and it produces at F, where the capital intensity of steel output is $W_2 V_2$, and the capital intensity of corn output is $W_2 U_2$. Both capital intensities are higher in Fewmen. Therefore, the marginal products of capital are lower in Fewmen, and the real return is lower there. Free trade does not equalize factor prices, and capital will flow from Fewmen to Manymen in response to the gap between real returns.

As the flow of capital will not cease until it has closed the gap, it has to eliminate the factor reversal. Here are two ways in which this can happen:

1. Capital per worker can fall below $O\overline{K}$ in Fewmen before it has risen to that level in Manymen. Steel will become more capital intensive than corn in both countries. Fewmen will export steel, because it continues to have more capital per worker, and Manymen will export corn.

2. Capital per worker can rise above $O\overline{K}$ in Manymen before it has fallen to that level in Fewmen. Corn will become more capital intensive than steel in both countries. Fewmen will export corn, because it continues to have more capital per worker even in this instance, and Manymen will export steel.

The actual outcome will depend on the initial situation and on the sizes of the coun-

tries. If $O\overline{K}_2$ is close to $O\overline{K}$ but $O\overline{K}_1$ is far away, and the countries have the same quantities of labor, the capital movement is likely to drive $O\overline{K}_2$ below $O\overline{K}$, producing the first outcome. In both cases, however, the capital movement serves the same basic purpose. It permits trade to equalize factor prices, rather than eliminating trade itself, so free trade can maximize global efficiency.[5]

When factor movements are induced by factor reversals, they can have drastic effects on the trade pattern. If Fewmen exports corn initially, the first outcome will switch the trade pattern completely. Steel will become more capital intensive than corn in both countries, and Fewmen will export steel instead of corn. If Fewmen exports steel initially, the second outcome will switch the trade pattern. Corn will become more capital intensive than steel in both countries, and Fewmen will export corn.

We do not have to know the trade pattern, however, or the way that it evolves, to predict the change in the relative price of corn. As corn is capital intensive in Fewmen when it produces at F, the fall in Fewmen's capital stock decreases its corn output and increases its steel output, pursuant to the Rybczynski theorem. As steel is capital intensive in Manymen when it produces at M, the rise in Manymen's capital stock increases its steel output and decreases its corn output. Steel outputs rise in both countries, and corn outputs fall. Therefore, the capital transfer raises the relative price of corn. If you were a worker in Fewmen, you would oppose the capital transfer, because an increase in the relative price of corn drives Fewmen downward on the HH' curve, reducing the relative price

---

[5] There is a third possibility. Both countries could wind up with $O\overline{K}$ capital per worker and would have identical transformation curves (which would be straight lines, like those in Chapter 3). There would be no basis for trade.

of labor and the real wage. If you were a worker in Manymen, you would favor the transfer, because an increase in the relative price of corn drives Manymen upward on the *HH'* curve, raising the real wage.

CAPITAL MOVEMENTS AS TRANSFERS OF CLAIMS

In all our work thus far, international capital movements have altered stocks of capital equipment. In the Heckscher–Ohlin model, for example, Manymen ends up with more mills to make steel and more tractors to grow corn, and Fewmen ends up with fewer mills and tractors. There are two ways of making these adjustments, by shipping equipment from one country to the other or financing internal changes in supplies.

When the return to capital is higher in Manymen, that country's firms can afford to borrow at interest rates higher than Fewmen's firms can pay. Hence, residents of Fewmen will lend to firms in Manymen rather than firms in Fewmen. Manymen's firms will be able to acquire additional mills or tractors, and Fewmen's firms will be forced to run down their holdings. If mills and tractors can be shipped from one country to the other, firms in Manymen will buy them from firms in Fewmen. If they cannot be transferred, the adjustment process is more complicated. New mills and tractors must be manufactured in Manymen, using factors of production ordinarily employed to make steel and grow corn. To maintain its consumption of steel and corn, Manymen must export less corn to Fewmen and import more steel. But fewer mills and tractors are needed in Fewmen to replace those that wear out, and Fewmen can divert factors of production to make more steel and grow more corn. It can export more steel to Manymen and import less corn. When mills and tractors are not

traded, flows of other goods adjust, permitting the countries involved in a capital transfer to alter their stocks of mills and tractors.[6]

A capital movement, however, need not alter stocks of capital goods (mills and tractors in the Heckscher–Ohlin model). It may serve merely to accommodate a change in consumption. Suppose that Manymen suffers a drought that reduces its corn crop temporarily. The relative price of corn will rise on world markets, but something else may happen, too. Residents of Manymen may borrow from residents of Fewmen to compensate for the loss of real income resulting from the drought. This is an international capital movement, even though it does not affect stocks of capital equipment. Residents of Manymen will issue bonds to residents of Fewmen, mortgaging a portion of their country's future output in exchange for some of Fewmen's current output. Alternatively, residents of Manymen may sell shares to residents of Fewmen, transferring the ownership of firms in Manymen and thus the future earnings of those firms; mills and tractors in Manymen will come under foreign control without any change in location or quantity.

This example leads to a general statement about the nature of capital movements:

---

[6] In Chapter 12, we will derive this equation:

$$\text{Investment} - \text{saving} = \text{imports} - \text{exports}$$

When Manymen invests more in mills and tractors but saving does not change, Manymen must import more, export less, or both. It need not import mills and tractors, but will then have to import more or export less of other commodities so as to produce more mills and tractors. The resulting gap between imports and exports will be filled by borrowing or transferring securities. The same sort of thing will happen in a case described below, when Manymen suffers a drought and its corn crop fails. In that case, the gap between imports and exports will correspond to a reduction in saving—a fall in output and income without a fall in consumption—rather than an increase in investment.

International capital movements are transfers of claims that raise the future income of the country that acquires them.

The country that issues the claims can use the proceeds to buy or build capital goods or to consume more currently than it can produce. The claims themselves may convey some information about the issuer's intentions, but this is not always the case.

The many forms that capital movements can take are shown by Table 8-1, which lists the claims on other countries held by U.S. residents and the claims on the United States held by foreigners. The numbers are large and have changed dramatically in the

1980s. At the end of 1980, U.S. residents held almost $607 billion of claims and foreigners held almost $501 billion. The difference between the totals, known as the net investment position, was $106 billion. This difference says that gross capital outflows from the United States were larger in previous decades than gross capital inflows into the United States. In the 1980s, however, the net investment position turned negative. Capital outflows were large, raising the claims of U.S. residents by $361 billion through 1986, but capital inflows were very much larger, raising the claims of foreigners by $831 billion. This striking change was due largely to the budget and trade deficits of the United States,

TABLE 8-1 International Investment Position of the United States, 1980 and 1986 (billions of dollars)

Type of Claim	1980	1986
Claims held by U. S. residents	606.9	1,067.9
Held by U. S. government		
Monetary reserves[a]	26.8	48.5
Loans and other claims	63.5	89.5
Held by other U. S. residents		
Direct investments	215.4	259.9
Foreign bonds	43.5	80.2
Foreign stocks	19.2	50.9
Other claims		
Reported by U. S. banks	203.9	506.4
Reported by U. S. corporations, etc.	34.7	32.6
Claims held by foreigners	500.8	1,331.5
Held by foreign governments		
U. S. government securities	118.2	177.4
Other claims	57.9	63.4
Held by other foreigners		
Direct investments	83.0	209.3
U. S. government securities	16.1	96.0
Corporate and other bonds	9.5	142.1
Corporate stocks	64.6	167.4
Other claims		
Reported by U. S. banks	121.1	449.2
Reported by U. S. corporations, etc.	30.4	26.7
Net investment position (claims by U. S. residents *less* claims by foreigners)	106.0	−263.6

Source: U. S. Department of Commerce, *Survey of Current Business,* June 1987. Detail may not add to total because of rounding.

[a] Includes U. S. gold stock valued at statutory price.

but a full explanation must be postponed until we have examined the relationship between them and the roles of capital movements and of the exchange rate in maintaining that relationship. The table is important here because it shows the wide variety of capital movements.

Claims and liabilities of governments bulk large in Table 8-1. At the top of the table, for example, we find the foreign claims of the U.S. government. It held about $48 billion of monetary reserves at the end of 1986 and about $90 billion of loans and other claims on foreigners. The reasons for holding monetary reserves are examined in Chapter 12. The other claims of the U.S. government include loans to European countries for economic reconstruction after World War II, more recent loans to less-developed countries to finance their development, loans by the Export-Import Bank to finance U.S. exports, and subscriptions to international institutions such as the World Bank. Later in the table, we find that foreign governments held $177 billion of U.S. government securities and $63 billion of other claims, including large deposits with U.S. banks. These claims are the monetary reserves that other countries hold in dollars, reflecting the dominant role of the dollar in the international monetary system.

Claims held by corporations, financial institutions, and individuals take three forms: direct investments, portfolio investments, and loans to finance capital formation or consumption.

Direct investments by U.S. firms totaled almost $260 billion at the end of 1986. They reflect the growth of multinational production. American companies own factories and other facilities in many foreign countries. General Motors, for example, has plants in Canada, Britain, Germany, Spain, Australia, Brazil, Mexico, and two dozen other countries. Some of these facilities serve foreign markets, producing goods and services that the parent companies would otherwise export from the United States. Some serve the U.S. market, producing raw materials, parts and components, and finished goods for use or sale in the United States. The figures in the table are the amounts spent by American firms to build or buy foreign facilities. Foreign direct investments in the United States have increased hugely in recent years, rising from $83 billion in 1980 to $209 billion in 1986, and the trade names of the firms involved are household words. Honda is Japanese, Volkswagen is German, Shell is Dutch, Nestlé is Swiss, and Michelin is French.

Portfolio investments are holdings of stocks and bonds designed to earn dividends and interest rather than exercise control over plants and other productive facilities. At the end of 1986, Americans held about $131 billion of foreign stocks and bonds, and foreigners held about $405 billion of American securities. The very large size of foreign holdings, compared to American holdings, is linked to the budget and trade deficits mentioned earlier, but there was a similar (though smaller) difference in 1980, before those deficits emerged. There are many reasons, including the size of the American economy. American firms are larger than their foreign counterparts and issue larger quantities of stocks and bonds, and there are active markets for those securities, making it easy to buy and sell them. Furthermore, American firms must disclose more information than most other countries' firms, which makes it easier for investors to assess their risks and prospects.

Some of the "other claims" in Table 8-1 represent portfolio investments, too. Claims of foreign residents reported by U.S. banks include deposits and short-term securities held by foreign banks and corporations, and some of the corresponding claims of U.S. residents represent deposits held at foreign banks. But most of the claims reported by U.S. banks are the banks' own loans to foreigners. These loans began to grow in the 1960s but became much larger in the 1970s, when many foreign countries borrowed heavily to deal with financial problems brought on by higher oil prices. We will say more about them when we look at the events that led to them and examine the issues posed by present levels of indebtedness.

MULTINATIONAL PRODUCTION AND TRANSNATIONAL TAXATION

The multinational company is not a new phenomenon. Some American firms had plants in other countries before World War I. Singer Sewing Machine and the Ford Motor Company are well-known examples. The phenomenon became much more common after World War II, however, and it is hard to find a major company today that does not have affiliates in other countries.

The U.S. government gathers detailed data on the foreign affiliates of American firms and the U.S. affiliates of foreign firms. A summary is reproduced in Table 8-2, showing total assets, total sales, and numbers of employees, classified by region and activity.

The assets of the foreign affiliates of American firms came close to $840 billion in 1985, a figure more than three times as large as the figure for direct investments in Table 8-1. This is because the figures in Table 8-2 relate to the total assets of the foreign affiliates, whereas those in Table 8-1 relate to the amounts provided by the parent companies. Foreign affiliates of American firms raise some of their capital by issuing securities and borrowing from banks; they do not rely entirely on their

parents. Measured by assets, sales, and employment, the foreign affiliates of U.S. firms are concentrated heavily in manufacturing and are also concentrated in developed countries (Western Europe, Canada, and Japan), which have the largest markets. The distributions are somewhat different for the U.S. affiliates of foreign firms. Most of them come from other developed countries but manufacturing is less important than trade, finance, and real estate, when measured by assets and sales (but not by employment). Foreign direct investment in the United States has included large purchases of commercial property, including office buildings, shopping centers, and hotels, and foreign firms are active in a wide range of financial activities, including insurance and banking.

The large size of the sales by foreign affiliates of U.S. firms is made clear by some simple comparisons. Here are some comparisons with U.S. exports in 1985:

Category	Sales by Affiliates	U.S. Exports
Total (billions)	$898	$213
To Europe	440	60
To Canada	139	47
Manufactured goods	388	130

Total sales by affiliates were four times as large as total exports, and sales of manufactured goods were almost three times as large.

Two more comparisons are illuminating. Sales of manufactured goods by firms in the United States, including both domestic and export sales, were valued at $2,279 billion in 1985 and were just slightly less than six times as large as sales of manufactured goods by the foreign affiliates of U.S. firms. Firms engaged in manufacturing employed 19.3 million workers in the United States; foreign affiliates in manufacturing employed 4.4 million workers in

TABLE 8-2   Multinational Investment and Production, 1985 (assets and sales in billions of dollars, employment in thousands of workers)

Category	Assets	Sales	Employment
Foreign affiliates of U. S. firms	$837.9	$898.0	6,426
Location of affiliate			
Europe	357.4	440.2	2,764
Canada	118.0	138.6	903
Other developed countries[a]	102.5	125.2	757
Latin America	160.3	94.7	1,234
Other developing countries	86.2	92.9	735
International and unallocated	13.4	6.4	32
Industry of affiliate			
Manufacturing	305.1	388.2	4,355
Petroleum	183.4	261.0	335
Trade	68.3	131.1	464
Finance and real estate[b]	208.3	31.8	141
Other	72.8	85.9	1,131
U. S. affiliates of foreign firms	736.2	630.1	2,854
Location of parent			
Europe	354.4	335.5	1,806
Canada	114.7	77.2	528
Japan	63.6	152.1	209
All other countries	203.5	65.3	311
Industry of affiliate			
Manufacturing	170.1	185.4	1,439
Petroleum	76.5	76.8	125
Trade	96.0	277.0	776
Finance and real estate[b]	352.5	61.1	147
Other	41.1	29.8	367

Source: U. S. Department of Commerce, *Survey of Current Business,* May, June 1987. Detail may not add to total because of rounding.

[a] Japan, Australia, New Zealand, and South Africa.

[b] Excludes banking.

other countries. Thus, one foreign worker was employed by an affiliate for every four workers employed in the United States.

Many American firms derive more than a quarter of their earnings from their foreign affiliates, including Coca-Cola, Colgate-Palmolive, Dow Chemical, Ford Motors, General Electric, IBM, United Technologies, and Xerox. Note that a number of these firms produce goods containing new technologies (IBM and Xerox, among others) and many manufacture goods with well-known names (Coca-Cola, Colgate-Palmolive, and Ford). This point will come up again.

Reasons for Multinational Production

Why do firms acquire or build facilities in other countries rather than expand their facilities at home? Simple reasons come to mind and fit some cases easily.

You cannot produce oil in countries without oil fields. You cannot produce copper or aluminum in countries without ores. Firms in extractive industries will go where they can find the minerals they need. Similar arguments can be adduced to explain the international migration of manufacturing. A firm producing labor-intensive goods will migrate to labor-abundant countries, where labor costs are low even after allowing for differences in productivity. A firm producing goods that have high shipping costs, such as processed foods and household supplies that are bulky compared to their value, will build plants close to its large markets. A firm that faces a high tariff or some other barrier limiting its access to a major foreign market can sometimes leap over it by building a plant on the other side, even when costs of production are higher there.

These explanations are helpful, but they are incomplete. They say that there will be concentrations of economic activity in certain places and something about the type of activity undertaken in each place. They do not explain why foreign firms will be involved. Why were the oil fields of the Middle East developed by foreign companies (American, British, Dutch, and French) rather than local companies? Why are foreign firms able to exploit local advantages, such as natural resources, abundant labor, proximity to markets, or the protection afforded by tariffs, more effectively than local firms?

Clearly, multinational firms must have competitive advantages over local firms. They may have easier access to capital from home or foreign sources. They may be subsidized by their own governments. But other advantages are more important. Scanning the names of the companies listed earlier, it is not hard to spot them. Some firms have technological advantages— better products, better processes, or combinations of the two. Other firms have well-known product lines. They began the development of foreign markets by small-scale exports from plants at home, then turn to multinational production when their markets become large enough to permit the exploitation of economies of scale.

An explanation of multinational production must focus on the same phenomena that were used in Chapter 7 to explain intraindustry trade. Differentiated products, technological advantages, and economies of scale give large, established firms a competitive advantage over their local counterparts. (Returning to the case considered in that chapter, an Italian firm may find that it is cheaper to make widgets in France, for sale in Italy as well as France. It is firmly entrenched in both markets, becauses its widgets are different from those of French and other Italian producers.) A firm's advantages may not be permanent, but they last long enough for the firm to exploit effectively the special features of the local environment—access to raw materials, low labor costs, and protected markets.

Costs and Benefits of Multinational Production

The rapid growth of multinational production has led to much controversy and many policy problems. Multinational firms encounter vocal criticism in host and home countries alike, and some of the criticism that used to be leveled at U.S. firms in other countries is now being leveled at foreign firms in the United States.

Viewed from a cosmopolitan perspective, the advantages of multinational production appear to dominate the disadvantages. The activities of multinational firms tend to increase the efficiency and flexibility of the world economy by making resource use and, therefore, trade patterns, more sensitive to relative costs. When costs rise in one country compared to others, all firms have the same incentive to find alternative sources of supply. But multinational firms may be able to move faster and farther than others. A firm that does not have foreign affiliates must start by searching for new suppliers and must then place orders with them. (It must also weigh the costs of breaking relations with old suppliers, which it might want to reestablish if cost conditions changed again.) Multinational firms do not have these problems. They can switch orders and production from one affiliate to another. Furthermore, they are apt to keep close watch on trends in costs and prices, because they do business in many locations and make comparisons all the time.

This flexibility is not unlimited. A multinational firm may hesitate to close down a plant in a high-cost country or lay off workers, because it fears punitive action by the country's government. Managers of multinational firms emphasize considerations of this sort, and some observers have therefore concluded that multinational firms are actually insensitive to cost conditions and may therefore interfere with appropriate adaptations. But testimony can be marshalled on the other side. Labor leaders claim that multinational firms have unusual bargaining power in wage negotiations precisely because they *can* close plants when labor costs get out of line and relocate production without interrupting it. As usual, the truth lies between extremes. Multinational firms have more flexibility than localized producers but less than their critics and admirers believe. On balance, then, they probably contribute to global efficiency by raising the responsiveness of outputs and trade flows to changes in comparative costs and by fostering the international mobility of capital, technology, and managerial talent.

Governments express concerns much like those of labor leaders, because multinational firms can act in ways that limit the governments' autonomy in pursuing national policy objectives. The development of multinational banking, for example, has enhanced the international mobility of capital, and we will see in Chapter 15 that high capital mobility reduces the effectiveness of monetary policy under pegged exchange rates and of fiscal policy under floating

rates. Furthermore, "footloose" firms can frustrate a government's attempt to regulate or tax domestic business more heavily than it is regulated or taxed in other countries, because the firms can move to more congenial environments. This option is most readily available to a multinational firm because of its experience in linking plants and markets at distant points around the world.

Multinational firms do not always have to move in order to minimize the impact of cross-country differences in policy regimes. They can manipulate *transfer prices*, the prices at which goods pass from plant to plant within a single firm. A firm with an affiliate in a high-tax country can instruct it to charge low prices for goods sold to affiliates in low-tax countries. When the goods are sold again to final buyers, with or without additional processing, the profits accrue to the affiliates in the low-tax country and escape taxation by the high-tax country. Some goverments try to regulate transfer pricing, but they rarely have enough information to do it effectively.

Trade policies can have unexpected consequences when multinational firms are involved. A tariff imposed to protect domestic firms from foreign competition may attract foreign firms to the domestic economy. This happened in the 1960s when U.S. firms built plants in Europe to serve the large internal market created by formation of the European Economic Community (EEC). (Tariffs were not raised in that instance, but U.S. and other firms outside Europe were placed at a disadvantage compared to European firms and sought to overcome it by investing in Europe.) When outsiders jump over trade barriers by building plants inside, the barriers may still protect the incomes of the factors used intensively by the protected industry; they will to the extent that the foreigners' plants employ those same factors intensively. But the barriers will cease to protect the incomes of domestic firms and their stock-holders, which is often the main policy objective.

This example illustrates one more phe-nomenon. Differences between national policies may cause firms to *become* multina-tional. Here is another illustration. Large American banks became multinational in the 1960s and 1970s, establishing branches in London and other financial centers, to escape the effects of interest-rate ceilings and other domestic regulations that placed them at a competitive disadvantage when bidding for foreign deposits and making foreign loans. The migration of the banks had two effects. First, it put pressure on the U.S. authorities to relax or remove the re-strictions that were causing the banks to migrate. Second, it led the U.S. authorities to permit the establishment of Interna-tional Banking Facilities (IBFs) in the United States, which domestic and foreign banks can use to conduct international business without satisfying some of the re-quirements imposed on banks that operate within the United States.

When firms operate in many countries, another hard problem arises. Governments clash over jurisdiction. Several clashes have occured because of efforts by the United States to limit trade with the Soviet Union. Washington has tried to impose its regula-tions on the operations of U.S. firms in Eu-rope, and European governments have ob-jected strongly. The French affiliate of a U.S. firm, they argue, must obey French law but lies beyond the normal reach of U.S. law. A famous clash occurred in 1979, after Iranian militants seized the American embassy in Teheran. The United States in-structed U.S. banks to freeze the accounts of their Iranian depositors, including those at foreign branches of U.S. banks. The British government objected, maintaining that the London branches of U.S. banks are subject only to its orders, not those of Washington.

Additional concerns are heard in certain host countries, where critics charge that foreign firms impair economic and political independence. When asked what they mean, some critics retreat into rhetoric about neocolonialism and the subversion of indigenous values. Others are more pre-cise. Multinational firms, they say, resist guidance or control by host-country gov-ernments, interfering with the execution of national policies and development plans, and are able to evade host-country taxes by manipulating transfer prices. Multinational firms, they say, exploit their host coun-tries' natural resources unfairly. They per-petuate an "unequal" division of labor by mining raw materials in less-developed countries but processing them in developed countries. They use their bargaining power to wring one-sided concessions from host-country governments, paying too little for the raw materials they take away, and de-prive future generations of their rightful inheritance by taking them away too rapidly.[7] These concerns about exploita-tion, transfer pricing, and the depletion of raw materials have been expressed for many years in countries ranging from Canada to Australia and from Venezuela to Nigeria. Governments have responded by canceling petroleum and mining conces-sions, requiring local participation in the new affiliates of foreign firms, and taking over foreign affiliates. Saudi Arabia, Ven-ezuela, Iran, and Libya have taken over the affiliates of foreign oil companies, paying full or partial compensation. Mexico took them over decades ago, provoking a long and bitter dispute with the United States.

---

[7] This complaint invokes an important proposition. The more oil that we lift today, the lower the current price and the higher the future price (because less oil will be available in the future). There is, then, an opti-mal rate of extraction that depends on current and fu-ture demands and on the weights that consumers attach to future income compared to current income.

In home countries, critics charge that multinational companies act in ways that weaken the domestic economy. Labor unions charge that multinational firms destroy jobs when they go abroad, whether to serve foreign markets or bring goods back home. These complaints are easy to understand but hard to evaluate. Workers who lose their jobs when a company closes a plant in Michigan or California and opens one in Spain or South Korea cannot be blamed for saying that the company has destroyed their jobs. Companies reply, however, that it is too costly to serve foreign markets from home-country plants—that they could not have saved their workers' jobs even if they had not opened plants abroad. They say that they protect domestic jobs, moreover, when they import low-cost parts from their foreign affiliates to overcome import competition in finished products. Economists looking at these issues call attention to indirect effects neglected by workers and companies alike. The building of a plant abroad can raise foreign incomes and augment the demand for exports from the home country. This effect is often overlooked because the additional exports are manufactured by a different company and the jobs they create are located in a different town or region. Furthermore, the full effects of multinational production on employment and wage rates depend on the factor intensities of the goods involved—those produced in the plants that are closed and those for which foreign demand is raised.

Problems of Transnational Taxation

One additional issue deserves study here, because it grows directly from our work on capital movements and introduces a distinction we will need again. Who should tax incomes arising from capital movements, including those arising from direct investments, and what tax rates should be chosen?

Most governments claim and exercise the right to tax incomes generated in their countries. This right is rarely contested. It arises in part from the basic relationship between taxes collected and services supplied. The relationship is loose. A government that takes a dollar of your income does not necessarily give you a dollar's worth of services. Yet those who live and work within a country or hold property protected by its laws do receive some value for their taxes.

Applying this principle pervasively, most governments claim tax jurisdiction over all individuals and firms inside their borders, including the local affiliates of foreign firms. Typically, they tax those affiliates just as they tax domestic firms. Some treat them preferentially, however, to attract foreign capital, and some have been known to discriminate against them, despite attempts by the home countries' governments to prevent discrimination. (The United States combats discrimination by writing tax treaties with other governments in which each party promises "national treatment" to the other's citizens and companies; it undertakes to treat them as if they were domestic.)

The main problem in transnational taxation has to do with the rights of the *home* country. Should it tax the foreign earnings of its own citizens, including those remitted by the foreign affiliates of domestic firms? Most countries claim and exercise this right, too, saying that they furnish protection and services to *all* their citizens, even those abroad, and they give additional reasons. If foreign countries' tax rates were lower than their own and they did not tax their citizens' foreign earnings, those citizens might have inappropriate incentives to invest and earn incomes in other countries rather than invest at home.

Once we concede this possibility, however, another question must be answered. What is an "inappropriate" incentive? The answer depends on the government's perspective. In Chapter 1, we encountered two perspectives, cosmopolitan and national. They can be applied to transnational taxation.

Consider a competitive model of the sort used earlier to study the effects of capital movements. (We can use a modified Ricardian model or a Heckscher–Ohlin model. It does not matter here.) The real return to capital in each country will equal the marginal product of capital, so real returns can be used to measure the effects of capital movements on each country's output and on global output.

If governments adopt a cosmopolitan perspective and thus seek to maximize global output regardless of its distribution, they will not want to discourage capital movements that occur in response to differences in real returns. When the return to capital is higher in country A than country B, a capital movement from country B to country A will raise output in country A by more than it reduces output in country B. Therefore, it will raise global output. Conversely, governments will want to discourage capital movements that do not reflect differences in real returns, because they will reduce global output. Those movements may occur, however, when there are significant differences in tax rates.

Suppose that $100 of capital can earn $10 in each country but that tax rates are different. The income tax is 50 percent in country A and 20 percent in country B, and country A does not tax its citizens' foreign-source incomes. Here is what a citizen of country A can earn:

Investment of $100 in Country A

Income before tax	$10
Tax paid to country A (50 percent)	5
Income after tax	5

Investment of $100 in Country B

Income before tax	$10
Tax paid to country B (20 percent)	2
Income after tax	8

There is an "inappropriate" incentive for the citizens of country A to invest in country B.

What tax policy should country A adopt to get rid of this incentive? It should impose its own tax rate on its citizens' incomes from country B but give them a *credit* for taxes they pay to country B. This is proved algebraically in Note 8-1 and illustrated by this calculation:

Investment of $100 in Country B

Income before tax	$10
Tax paid to country B (20 percent)	2
Tax paid to country A	
Provisional tax (50 percent)	5
Less: Credit for tax paid to country B	2
Actual tax	3
Income after tax	5

This tax regime is *neutral* from a cosmopolitan standpoint, because after-tax earnings are the same in both countries when pretax earnings are the same.

If the government of country A adopts a national perspective and thus seeks to maximize its own country's income, it will want to discourage its citizens from investing in country B unless investments there add more to the national income of country A than do investments in country A itself. As taxes paid to country B add nothing to the national income of country A, the government of country A will not want its citizens to invest abroad unless they can earn more *after* paying taxes to country B than they can earn *before* paying taxes on income earned at home.

Note 8-1

When citizens of country A invest in that country, they earn r_A on each dollar and pay taxes to country A at the rate t_A. Their after-tax return is $r_A(1 - t_A)$. When they invest in country B, they earn r_B on each dollar and pay taxes to country B at the rate t_B. Because they reside in country A, however, they owe taxes to that country, too, and the rate they pay is t'_A, so their after-tax return is $r_B(1 - t_B - t'_A)$. Define the difference between the after-tax returns:

$$D = r_b(1 - t_B - t'_A) - r_A(1 - t_A)$$

Citizens of country A will invest in country B whenever D is positive. What rate t'_A should country A adopt, given the other two tax rates?

If the government of country A seeks to maximize global income, it should encourage its citizens to invest in country B whenever r_B exceeds r_A. Therefore, it should impose the rate t_A on its citizens' earnings from country B but allow them to *credit* taxes paid to country B against taxes owed to country A. They will then pay $r_B t'_A = r_B t_A - r_B t_B$ to country A, so $t'_A = t_A - t_B$. Substituting into the definition of D,

$$D = r_B[1 - t_B - (t_A - t_B)] - r_A(1 - t_A)$$
$$= (r_B - r_A)(1 - t_A)$$

D will be positive, inducing investment in country B, whenever r_B exceeds r_A.

If the government of country A seeks to maximize its country's own national income, it should encourage its citizens to invest in country B only when $r_B(1 - t_B)$ exceeds r_A, because an investment in country B adds only $r_B(1 - t_B)$ to national income in country A. It should impose the rate t_A on its citizens' earnings from country B but allow them to *deduct* taxes from those earnings paid to country B before they calculate the taxes owed to country A. They will pay $r_B t'_A = r_B(1 - t_B)t_A$ to country A, so $t'_A = (1 - t_B)t_A$, which is higher by $t_B(1 - t_A)$ than the value of t'_A obtained previously. Substituting into the definition of D,

$$D = r_B[1 - t_b - (1 - t_B)t_A] - r_A(1 - t_A)$$
$$= [r_B(1 - t_B) - r_A](1 - t_A)$$

D will be positive, inducing investment in country B, only when $r_B(1 - t_B)$ exceeds r_A.

Suppose that $100 of capital can earn $8 in country A and $10 in country B and that tax rates are the same as before (50 percent in country A and 20 percent in country B). Here is what a citizen of country A can earn:

Investment of $100 in Country A

Income before tax	$8
Tax paid to country A (50 percent)	4
Income after tax	4

Investment of $100 in Country B

Income before tax	$10
Tax paid to country B (20 percent)	2
Income after tax	8

Citizens of country A will want to invest in country B, but the government of country A will not want them to do so, because an investment in country B adds only $8 to the national income of country A, no more than an investment in country A itself.

What tax policy should country A adopt? A credit for taxes paid to country B will not achieve its objective. Income after tax from an investment in country B would be $5, as before, $1 more than income after tax from an investment in country A, and citizens of country A would be encouraged to invest in country B. Therefore, country A should impose its own tax rate on its citizens' incomes from country B but give a *deduction* rather than a credit for taxes paid to country B. This is proved in Note 8-1 and illustrated by this calculation:

Investment of $100 in Country B

Income before tax	$10
Tax paid to country B (20 percent)	2
Tax paid to country A	
Income from country B	10
Less: Deduction of tax paid to country B	2
Income taxable by country A	8
Actual tax (50 percent)	4
Income after tax	4

This regime is neutral from the standpoint of country A, because after-tax earnings are the same when earnings from country A before taxes are equal to earnings from country B after foreign taxes.

What is the actual tax policy of the United States? It is cosmopolitan, not national, in that it allows investors to credit foreign taxes paid against taxes due to the U.S. government. In fact, it goes farther. A firm with earnings from a foreign affiliate may not have to pay U.S. taxes on those earnings when it reinvests them in its affiliate. Tax payments are *deferred* until income is brought home. By reinvesting its foreign-source income in its foreign affiliate, then, a firm can obtain what amounts to an interest-free loan from the U.S. Treasury. The size of this implicit subsidy, however, depends on the size of the difference between U.S. and foreign tax rates. When those rates are equal, the firm does not owe any tax to the U.S. government, thanks to the tax credit, and there is no subsidy. As corporate tax rates in other industrial countries are not very different from U.S. rates, the subsidy is small.

SUMMARY

When analyzing international factor movements, we must distinguish effects on the factors that move from effects on those remaining in the source country and those residing initially in the host country. In the modified Ricardian model, for example, a capital movement raises the real return to the capital that moves and to capital remaining in the source country, but reduces the return to capital residing initially in the host country. (It reduces the real wage and raises the rental rate in the source country, but raises the real wage and reduces the rental rate in the host country.) When factor movements are induced by differences in real earnings, which are due in turn to differences in marginal products, factor movements raise global output, contributing to global efficiency. They raise output in the host country by more than they reduce it in the source country.

To induce and analyze factor movements in the Heckscher–Ohlin model, we must modify the assumptions of the model to keep trade from equalizing factor prices. The effects of the factor movements, however, depend on the particular impediment introduced to separate factor prices. A tariff can cause factor movements that wipe out all trade; the host and source countries will wind up with identical factor endowments. A reversal of factor intensities, by contrast, can cause factor movements that are self-limiting; they eliminate the factor reversal, allowing trade to equalize factor prices. In both cases, however, factor movements have the same effects on real earnings. A capital movement raises the real return to the capital that moves and to capital remaining in the source country, but reduces the return to capital invested initially in the host country. (It reduces the real wage in the source country and raises it in the host country.)

The results summarized thus far come from cases in which capital movements are linked in the long run with capital formation. The capital stock rises in the host country and falls in the source country. These are special cases. Capital movements take place whenever residents of one country acquire claims on residents of another. Those who issue the claims are mortgaging future income to step up current spending. They may engage in capital formation or additional consumption.

When firms in one country buy or build facilities in another, the capital movement is described as direct investment. It leads to multinational production. Explanations for this phenomenon emphasize competitive advantages enjoyed by large firms—superior technologies and well-known product lines—that give them a head start in competition with local firms. Multinational pro-

duction raises the efficiency and flexibility of the international economy but gives rise to many problems, because it limits the ability of governments to pursue independent policies and can lead to serious jurisdictional conflicts. In host countries, moreover, multinational firms are accused of resisting indigenous policies, manipulating transfer prices to minimize taxes, and using their bargaining power to obtain one-sided concessions from host-country governments. In home countries, they are accused of taking plants and jobs abroad and weakening trade unions.

When firms and individuals earn incomes abroad, their governments must decide how to tax them. What allowances should be made for taxes paid to foreign governments? If governments adopt a cosmopolitan perspective and thus seek to maximize global income, they should allow their citizens to credit foreign taxes paid against taxes owed at home. If they adopt a national perspective and seek to maximize domestic incomes, they should be less generous and grant deductions rather than credits.

RECOMMENDED READINGS

The effects of capital movements are studied from the standpoint of host countries in G. D. A. MacDougall, "The Benefits and Costs of Private Investment from Abroad," *Economic Record*, Special Issue (March 1960), reprinted in American Economic Association, *Readings in International Economics* (Homewood, Ill.: Richard D. Irwin, 1968), ch. 10.

The causes and effects of factor movements in the Heckscher–Ohlin model are examined in Robert A. Mundell, "International Trade and Factor Mobility," *American Economic Review*, 57 (June 1957), reprinted in American Economic Association, *Readings in International Economics* (Homewood, Ill.: Richard D. Irwin, 1968), ch 7.

On movements of labor rather than capital, see Peter B. Kenen, "Migration, the Terms of Trade, and Economic Welfare in the Source Country," in J. N. Bhagwati et al., eds., *Trade, Balance of Payments and Growth* (Amsterdam: North-Holland, 1971), ch. 11, reprinted in P. B. Kenen, *Essays in International Economics* (Princeton, N.J.: Princeton University Press, 1980).

The reasons for multinational production are reviewed in Richard E. Caves, *International Trade, International Investment, and Imperfect Markets* (Princeton, N.J.: International Finance Section, Princeton University, 1974). On the roles of tariffs and taxes in decisions by multinational firms, see Thomas Horst, "The Theory of the Multinational Firm: Optimum Behavior Under Different Tariff and Tax Rates," *Journal of Political Economy*, 79 (September 1971).

On U.S. attitudes and policies toward multinational firms, see C. Fred Bergsten, Thomas Horst, and Theodore H. Moran, *American Multi-*

nationals and American Interests (Washington, D.C: Brookings Institution, 1978); for a critical review of effects on host countries, see Stephen Hymer, "The Efficiency (Contradictions) of Multinational Corporations," *American Economic Review,* 60 (May 1970).

Less technical but more controversial views about multinational firms are found in Richard J. Barnet and Ronald E. Müller, *Global Reach* (New York: Simon & Schuster, 1974), and Robert Gilpin, *U.S. Power and the Multinational Corporation* (New York: Basic Books, 1975).

CHAPTER

9

THE INSTRUMENTS OF TRADE POLICY

INTRODUCTION

The trade models developed in earlier chapters illustrated two basic propositions. Under competitive conditions, free trade can maximize the value of global output. Furthermore, free trade is beneficial to each participating country. It relaxes the constraints imposed by a country's endowment of labor, capital, and natural resources, permitting its households to consume a collection of commodities better than any collection the country can produce.

Look around the world, however, and you will find that every country uses import tariffs, and many use other trade barriers as well. In most countries, moreover, important economic and political groups want more protection. Is something wrong with the case for free trade?

The answer to this question has two parts. Some arguments for protection are fallacious and easily refuted by economic analysis, but they have a peculiar immunity to logic and evidence. Economists can answer the protectionists' arguments, but warnings about "cheap foreign labor" and the "imperatives of national security" have great popular appeal. Other arguments for protection stand up to analysis. Free trade may be best from a global standpoint but not from a national standpoint. In certain circumstances, tariffs can be used to redistribute the gains from trade, increasing the welfare of one country at the expense of others. Tariffs can also be used to redistribute income within a single country and to compensate for defects in domestic markets.

The Hardiest Fallacy

The oldest and hardiest fallacy says that tariffs are needed to protect domestic workers against cheap foreign labor. Its advocates have lots of numbers about low foreign wages, and the numbers are accurate enough. But they draw the wrong inference from those numbers. We have, in fact, already encountered the answer to that inference.

In Chapter 3, we saw how wage rates are determined in the simple Ricardian model. When wages in Britain and Portugal were exactly equal before trade was opened, the prices of wine and cloth were higher in Britain than in Portugal, because British labor was less efficient. Wages had to fall in Britain and rise in Portugal for Britain to specialize in cloth and Portugal to specialize in wine. The wage changes were achieved by the process of adjustment to the opening of trade, which translates comparative advantage into market prices. Protectionists who make alarming comparisons between high wages in the United States and low wages elsewhere do not allow for the crucial relationship between wages and economic efficiency. Differences in wage rates, they assert, make for unfair competition. Those differences, however, are produced by competition, and trade cannot occur without them when levels of efficiency differ greatly.

Some versions of the argument are more subtle. Low wage rates, it is said, may testify to low levels of efficiency in an economy as a whole, but efficiency may be very high in its export industries. The methods used to make textiles in Hong Kong and Singapore are similar to those used in the United States, yet wages are much lower in those countries, even in their textile industries. Surely, textile workers in the United States are exposed to unfair competition. The answer should be obvious enough. Textile workers in the United States suffer from intense foreign competition, but it is not unfair competition. It is competition that has to be tolerated if countries are to realize the gains from trade.

Return to the example used in Chapter 3. Workers in Portugal's cloth industry could be expected to complain of unfair competition from Britain. The British cloth industry was less efficient than the Portuguese industry, but the gap between levels of efficiency was smaller than the gap between the countries' wage rates. If this were not so, however, Britain could not export cloth. To realize the gains from trade between the two economies, cloth output must contract in Portugal in the face of British competition, and wine output must contract in Britain in the face of Portuguese competition. We have seen, moreover, that the gains from trade based on these adjustments are large enough to compensate those who are injured by them.

The logic of this argument is impeccable. Yet it gives little comfort to textile workers in the United States. Some have lost their jobs on account of competition from Hong Kong, Singapore, and other countries. More jobs would be lost if tariffs and other trade barriers were removed completely. Some who lose their jobs have trouble finding new ones. Some suffer in other important ways. They lose seniority and thus job security. Until recently, many even lost their pension rights. Some may have to move from one city to another in search of new jobs and take large losses when they sell their homes. Furthermore, those who keep their jobs may take cuts in real wages, and the wage cuts may not be confined to workers in import-competing industries. In the modified Ricardian model, the opening of trade reduces the real wage measured in terms of the export good, and the reduction occurs throughout the economy. In the Heckscher–Ohlin model, it reduces the real wage, whether measured in terms of the export good or the import-competing good, whenever the export good is more capital intensive than the import-competing good. Reductions in tariffs have these same effects.

Economists who make the strong case for free trade do not always pay adequate attention to these and other costs, and they weaken their case by neglecting them. It is not enough to demonstrate that the gains from trade can compensate for adjustment costs and for the permanent income losses suffered by some groups. It is important to devise ways of making compensation. This problem is taken up in Chapter 11, which looks at techniques that have been developed to help those who have been hurt by tariff cuts and shifts in patterns of comparative advantage.

Tariffs and the National Defense

Another hardy argument for protection appeals to the needs of national defense, the importance of maintaining domestic industries able to produce armaments in case of war. This argument goes back to Adam Smith:

There seem, however, to be two cases in which it will generally be advantageous to lay some burden upon foreign [industry] for the encouragement of domestic industry.

The first is, when some particular sort of industry is necessary for the defence of the country. The defence of Great Britain, for example, depends very much upon the number of its sailors and shipping. The act of navigation, therefore, very properly endeavours to give the sailors and shipping of Great Britain the monopoly of the trade of their own country. . . .

The act of navigation is not favourable to foreign commerce, or to the growth of that opulence which can arise from it. . . . As defence, however, is of much more importance than opulence, the act of navigation is, perhaps, the

wisest of all the commercial regulations of England.[1]

The same argument is made today to justify large subsidies received by merchant ships that fly the U.S. flag, although the connection between national security and the health of the maritime industry was somewhat tenuous even when Smith accepted it and is more tenuous today. The argument, moreover, is easily abused. Here is the language used by Congress some years ago, in legislation instructing the president to impose trade barriers for reasons of national security:

the President shall, in the light of the requirements of national security and without excluding other relevant factors, give consideration to domestic production needed for projected national defense requirements, the capacity of domestic industries to meet such requirements, existing and anticipated availabilities of the human resources, products, raw materials, and other supplies and services essential to the national defense, the requirements of growth of such industries and such supplies and services including the investment, exploration, and development necessary to assure such growth, and the importation of goods in terms of their requirements, availabilities, character, and use as those affect such industries and the capacity of the United States to meet security requirements. In the administration of this section, the . . . President shall further recognize the close relation of the economic welfare of the Nation to our national security, and shall take into consideration the impact of foreign competition on the economic welfare of individual domestic industries; any substantial unemployment, decrease in revenues of government, loss of skills, or investment, or other serious effects resulting from the displacement of any domestic products by excessive imports shall be considered. . . .

---

[1] Adam Smith, *The Wealth of Nations*, 1776, bk. iv, ch. ii. The second exception admitted by Smith is the case for a compensatory revenue tariff, mentioned later in this chapter.

Fortunately, the president did not apply all these criteria. Had he done so, he might have been obliged to restrict all sorts of imports—from cameras and cars to textiles and toys—because of their effects on employment, revenues, and so on. The legislation was invoked to limit oil imports. World oil prices were low at that time, and the United States had spare capacity. By limiting imports, it was argued, and keeping domestic oil prices above world prices, import restrictions would encourage exploration in the United States, adding to domestic oil reserves. In the event, the restrictions had perverse effects. They tended to accelerate the exploitation of domestic oil fields by more than they fostered the discovery of new fields.

What would Adam Smith say about the language adopted by Congress? He was quick to denounce self-serving arguments and would surely ask whether Congress was wrapping the flag around all sorts of industries that want protection against import competition but contribute little to the national defense. He would probably concede, moreover, that import restrictions can do less today for the national defense than in his own time. The case for protecting "essential" industries depends on their ability to convert to arms production after war breaks out. Smith wanted to be sure that Great Britain would have shipyards to build men-of-war and trained sailors for their crews. Congress wanted to be sure that the United States would have the plants to manufacture tanks and planes. There are two objections.

One objection is strategic. Under present and foreseeable circumstances, the United States might have to fight two sorts of wars, a limited war on foreign soil or a global war for survival. The first sort, limited in area and in the range of weapons used, is not likely to require massive mobilization of do-

mestic industry. The second sort would not give it time to mobilize. It would be ended quickly and terribly by weapons put in place before it began—by a thermonuclear exchange.

The other objection is tactical. Concede for the sake of analysis that the United States might have the need and time for industrial mobilization once a war had started. Experience during World War II suggests that the conversion of civilian firms may not be the best method. The United States built a huge cargo fleet after the war began and was able eventually to launch ships faster than German submarines could sink them. The shipyards that built them were new ones, however, and used mass-production methods that older shipyards could not adopt easily. Furthermore, firms that did convert to arms production sometimes proved to be less efficient than new firms that grew up beside them. Several years ago, the watch industry argued that it needed protection because the watchmaker's skills are required to manufacture fuses and other precision goods used by the military. But Defense Department studies showed that watchmakers did these jobs less efficiently than workers trained expressly to perform them.

Go one step farther. Concede the case for maintaining "essential" industries to meet future military needs. Tariffs to protect them from import competition are not the right way to maintain them. A tariff has two main effects. It encourages domestic production and discourages domestic consumption. The consumption effect reduces economic welfare, and the welfare loss is borne by those who consume the peacetime products of the protected industry. Therefore, the tariff is an inequitable instrument. Buyers of watches should not be required to bear the costs of maintaining the watchmaker's skills in the interests of national security. The costs of national defense should be borne by the nation as a whole, not by one group of consumers. Furthermore, the tariff is an inefficient instrument. Subsidies to domestic producers make more sense, because they do not distort consumers' choices.

The needs of national security cannot be neglected, and there are important instances in which events abroad, including wars, could impair the national security of the United States and damage its economy. If the oil fields of the Persian Gulf were shut down suddenly, the world economy could suffer hugely. The United States could be hurt directly, because it depends on imported oil. It could be hurt indirectly, because the world economy could contract sharply. Trade theory warns us, however, that self-sufficiency may be the wrong reply. It makes more sense to import oil than to divert scarce resources to the search for oil in the United States or develop substitutes for oil regardless of their cost. The short-run effects of a crisis in the Persian Gulf should be met by drawing down oil reserves during the time required to cut consumption and switch to imports from other foreign sources. The United States has adopted this approach. It holds a Strategic Petroleum Reserve, financed by the federal government, to protect itself against interruptions of supply.

Tariffs as Second-Best Policy Instruments

Many other noneconomic reasons are given for protecting domestic industries. National prestige may be just as potent as national defense in rallying support for protection. How else can we explain the costly efforts of small, poor countries to develop their own international airlines? Let us turn, however, to arguments that make a modicum of economic sense, those that

would use tariffs and other trade restrictions to influence the distribution of the gains from trade or correct for defects in domestic markets.

These are subtle arguments. To illustrate and analyze them, we need to know how tariffs and other trade barriers affect domestic and foreign prices and, by way of prices, production and consumption. In each instance, moreover, we should seek to determine whether there are better ways to achieve the policy objective. Recall an objection to the use of tariffs to maintain domestic output in "essential" industries. Tariffs are inefficient because they distort consumers' choices, reducing economic welfare. The same point can be made about most other arguments for tariffs. We can usually find a better way to reach the objective. Trade barriers tend to be *second-best* policy instruments and may be only third best in some cases.

The rest of this chapter will show how tariffs and other trade barriers affect prices, production, and consumption. We will start by looking at the market for a single commodity, just as we did when we analyzed the gains from trade, and will go on as we did before, by using offer curves to look at effects on the whole economy. The next chapter will examine the ways that tariffs can affect the distribution of the gains from trade and the distribution of domestic income, how they can compensate for defects in domestic markets, and how they can foster the growth of an "infant" industry.

TARIFFS, QUOTAS, AND OTHER TRADE CONTROLS

Governments have many trade-policy instruments. Some are used to raise revenue or influence the terms of trade. Some are used to limit imports. Some are used to promote exports.

Tariffs can be used for various purposes. They can raise revenue rather than limit imports. The clearest cases are those in which tariffs are imposed on imported commodities that are not produced domestically. Some European countries, for example, have tariffs on coffee and other tropical products. The same intent is clear when an imported commodity is taxed at the same rate as its domestic counterpart. Taxes on imported wine, liquor, and tobacco products are good examples of these compensatory tariffs. Without them, the taxes on domestic goods would handicap domestic producers. A number of countries use tariffs on exports to raise revenue or improve their terms of trade. This practice is common in less-developed countries, which rely on tariffs because they are easy to collect. (The U.S. Constitution prohibits the United States from using export tariffs. Southern states feared that the federal government would finance itself by putting export tariffs on tobacco and other Southern products.) Most tariffs, however, are protective in purpose and effect. They are meant to stimulate production in import-competing industries.

Tariffs affect quantities by affecting prices. Subsidies operate in the same way, and they are sometimes used to stimulate exports. The General Agreement on Tariffs and Trade (GATT), the basic code of conduct governing trade policies, attempts to outlaw export subsidies. This is because subsidies can cancel the protective effects of existing import tariffs (and because they can lead to competitive subsidization of the welfare-reducing sort illustrated in Chapter 7). But the prohibition is not fully effective. Many countries subsidize exports indirectly. They offer export credits at low interest rates, treat export earnings preferentially when taxing business profits, and subsidize production in export industries instead of giving outright export subsidies.

Import quotas operate directly on quantities rather than affecting them indirectly by altering prices. A quota is an absolute limitation on the volume of imported goods. At one time, the United States used quotas to limit oil imports under the legislation quoted earlier. It has quotas on several agricultural commodities covered by domestic price supports. If there were no such quotas, it would not be possible to support the domestic prices of farm products without also supporting their world prices, and the benefits of price supports could not be confined to domestic farmers.

Like other schemes that ration quantities directly, quotas interfere with economic efficiency; price changes reflecting changes in scarcity cannot have their usual effects on quantities. Furthermore, quotas are hard to administer fairly. If you happen to be at the head of the line when "tickets" are handed out, giving you a share of an import quota, you will reap windfall profits. If you are the one who hands them out, you may be tempted to grab some profits for yourself. Quotas breed corruption. If quotas are distributed to foreign suppliers, using base-period market shares, old suppliers obtain an advantage over new suppliers, even when the new suppliers are more efficient. Because they interfere with efficiency and produce inequities, quotas are prohibited by the GATT. But there are important exceptions to the prohibition, including one invoked by the United States to justify its quotas on farm products. Furthermore, several countries have persuaded their trading partners to impose "voluntary" export restrictions, which resemble import quotas in most of their effects (apart from the distribution of the windfall profits).

Tariffs, subsidies, and quotas are fairly transparent. Although it may be hard to measure their effects on prices, outputs, and trade flows, it is not hard to detect their purposes. Other forms of intervention are less transparent.

Most countries regulate products and processes for reasons of health, safety, and environmental quality, and they regulate imports for the same reasons. All too often, however, the regulations are written or administered in ways that discriminate against imported goods so that the regulations become protective. Restrictions on imports of meat products and plants, adopted to keep out diseases and pests, are used to protect domestic farmers. Rules about packaging and labeling are used to make it costly for foreign producers to enter domestic markets.

Governments grant significant advantages to domestic firms when buying goods and services for themselves. These may be the most important barriers to trade. Gov-

ernments are the biggest buyers of many manufactured goods, especially in countries where mass transportation, communications, and electricity are provided by the public sector. They buy motor vehicles, locomotives, telephones, and power plants, along with military hardware. In the United States, federal and state agencies give preferential treatment to domestic firms bidding for government contracts. A foreign firm can win a contract only if the lowest domestic bid exceeds the lowest foreign bid by more than a fixed margin, and the margins are very high, compared to tariff rates. They are fixed at 50 percent under some federal programs, a number more than twice the typical tariff rate shown later in Table 9-1. Matters are worse in many foreign countries; contracts can be awarded without bidding, and even when

TABLE 9-1   Nominal and Effective Tariff Rates After Reductions Negotiated in the Tokyo Round

Product Group	UNITED STATES		EUROPEAN COMMUNITY		JAPAN	
	Nominal	Effective	Nominal	Effective	Nominal	Effective
Agriculture, forestry, etc.	1.8	1.9	4.9	4.1	18.4	21.4
Food, beverages, and tobacco	4.7	10.2	10.2	17.8	25.4	50.3
Textiles	9.2	18.0	7.2	8.8	3.3	−2.4
Apparel	22.7	43.3	13.4	19.3	13.8	42.2
Leather products	4.2	5.0	2.0	−2.2	3.0	−14.8
Footwear	8.8	15.4	11.6	20.7	15.7	50.0
Wood products	1.7	1.7	2.5	1.7	0.3	−30.6
Furniture and fixtures	4.1	5.5	5.6	11.3	5.1	10.3
Paper and paper products	0.2	−0.9	5.4	8.3	2.1	1.8
Printing and publishing	0.7	0.9	2.1	−1.0	0.1	−1.5
Chemicals	2.4	3.7	8.0	11.7	4.8	6.4
Petroleum and petroleum products	1.4	4.7	1.2	3.4	2.2	4.1
Rubber products	2.5	2.0	3.5	2.3	1.1	−5.0
Nonmetallic mineral products	5.3	9.2	3.7	6.5	0.5	−0.5
Glass and glass products	6.2	9.8	7.7	12.2	5.1	8.1
Iron and steel	3.6	6.2	4.7	11.6	2.8	4.3
Nonferrous metals	0.7	0.5	2.1	8.3	1.1	1.7
Metal products	4.8	7.9	5.5	7.1	5.2	9.2
Nonelectrical machinery	3.3	4.1	4.4	4.7	4.4	6.7
Electrical machinery	4.4	6.3	7.9	10.8	4.3	6.7
Transport equipment	2.5	1.9	8.0	12.3	1.5	0.0
Miscellaneous manufactures	4.2	5.8	4.7	6.6	4.6	7.3

Source: Alan V. Deardorff and Robert M. Stern, "The Effects of the Tokyo Round on the Structure of Protection," in R. E. Baldwin and A. O. Krueger, eds., *The Structure and Evolution of Recent U. S. Trade Policy* (Chicago: University of Chicago Press, 1984), Tables 10-1 through 10-3.

competitive bids are solicited, margins of preference are not fixed or publicized. To complicate the problem of the foreign bidder, specifications can be rigged deliberately to favor domestic firms.

Some countries have exchange controls that regulate their citizens' use of foreign currencies. Some have established state trading companies to sell certain exports and buy certain imports. All of these arrangements can be used to protect domestic industries, even when this is not their main aim.

Although tariffs are transparent, compared to these devices, their influence on trade flows can depend on decisions made at dockside by the customs inspector. A product may be taxed at a high or low rate, depending on the manner in which it is classified. How will the inspector classify a wooden box filled with chocolates? Is it a wood product or a food product? As the box is probably worth more than the candy, the inspector is likely to treat it as a wood

product. He must go farther, however, and decide what sort of wood product. And decisions made by one inspector are not binding on the next. You may get your first box through as a wood product, only to be told that the next one is a food product and subject to a higher tariff.

EFFECTS OF A TARIFF WITH A CONSTANT WORLD PRICE

At the start of Chapter 2, we used a simple diagram to study the effects of trade in a single market. The same diagram can be used to study the principal effects of a tariff.

Effects in a Single Market

In Figure 9-1, the demand curve for cameras is D_H, and the domestic supply curve is S_H. If there is no trade at all, equilibrium will be established at E. If there is free trade and the foreign supply curve is

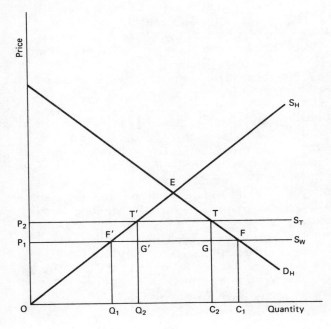

FIGURE 9-1 Effects of a Tariff in a Single Market
In the initial free-trade equilibrium, domestic consumers buy OC_1 at the price OP_1 determined by the foreign supply curve, S_W. Domestic producers supply OQ_1, and imports are $Q_1 C_1$. An import tariff raises the domestic price to OP_2, so domestic consumers buy OC_2, domestic producers supply OQ_2, and imports fall to $Q_2 C_2$. The consumption effect of the tariff is $C_1 C_2$. The production (protective) effect is $Q_1 Q_2$. The two together measure the restrictive effect. The government collects $P_1 P_2$ of tariff revenue on each imported unit, or $G'GTT'$ in total tariff revenue.

S_w, equilibrium will be established at F. The domestic price will equal the world price, OP_1. Domestic consumption will be OC_1, domestic production will be OQ_1, and imports will be $Q_1 C_1$ (equal to $F'F$).

Suppose that the importing country imposes a tariff at an *ad valorem* (percentage) rate equal to $P_1 P_2 / OP_1$. As the foreign supply curve is perfectly elastic, the world price will stay at OP_1. But the domestic price will rise to OP_2. Domestic consumption will fall to OC_2, domestic production will rise to OQ_2, and imports will fall to $Q_2 C_2$ (equal to $G'G$). The *consumption effect* of the tariff is $C_1 C_2$. The *production effect* is $Q_1 Q_2$ and is also called the *protective effect*. The two together measure the *restrictive effect*, the amount by which the tariff reduces import volume. The government collects $P_1 P_2$ of tariff revenue on each imported camera, which means that it collects $G'GTT'$ in total tariff revenue. At this point in our work, we will assume that all such revenue is returned to households; the government reduces other taxes or raises transfer payments, so tariffs do not cut consumers' incomes.

What are the effects on economic welfare? Consumer surplus falls by $P_1 FTP_2$. Producer surplus rises by $P_1 F'T'P_2$. The

---

Note 9-1

In Figure 9-1, the welfare loss is $F'G'T'$ *plus* FGT. But $F'G'T'$ equals $\frac{1}{2}(G'T' \times F'G')$, and FGT equals $\frac{1}{2}(GT \times FG)$. Furthermore, $G'T' = GT = P_1 P_2$, and $P_1 P_2$ is tp_w, where t is the ad valorem tariff rate and p_w is the world price OP_1. Finally, the sum of $F'G'$ and FG measures the reduction in import volume, $Q_1 Q_2$ *plus* $C_1 C_2$, denoted by dM hereafter. Thus, the welfare loss is $\frac{1}{2}dM\, tp_w$.

In Figure 9-3, the welfare loss to the exporting country is $KP_0 P_1 D$ *plus* KDN. But $KP_0 P_1 D$ equals $(P_0 P_1 \times P_0 K)$, where $P_0 P_1$ measures the reduction in the world price, denoted by dp_w hereafter, and $P_0 K$ is OM_2, the new import volume, denoted by M' hereafter. Therefore, $KP_0 P_1 D$ equals $M'\, dp_w$. Furthermore, KDN equals $\frac{1}{2}(KD \times DN)$ or $\frac{1}{2}(P_0 P_1 \times M_1 M_2)$, where $P_0 P_1$ is dp_w, as before, and $M_1 M_2$ is dM, the reduction in import volume. Thus, KDN equals $\frac{1}{2}dM dp_w$. The loss to the exporting country, then, is $M'dp_w + \frac{1}{2}dM dp_w$, or $(M' + \frac{1}{2}dM)dp_w$.

The welfare loss to the importing country is $F'G'T'$ *plus* FGT *less* $KP_0 P_1 D$. We have already seen that $KP_0 P_1 D$ is $M'dp_w$. Furthermore, $F'G'T'$ equals $\frac{1}{2}(G'T' \times F'G')$ or $\frac{1}{2}(P_1 P_2 \times Q_1 Q_2)$, while FGT equals $\frac{1}{2}(GT \times FG)$ or $\frac{1}{2}(P_1 P_2 \times C_1 C_2)$. The two together are thus equal to $\frac{1}{2}(Q_1 Q_2 + C_1 C_2)P_1 P_2$ or $\frac{1}{2}dM\, P_1 P_2$. In this instance, however, $P_1 P_2$ is not tp_w, as it was in Figure 9-1. It is $OP_2 - OP_1$, where OP_2 is the new domestic price, $(1 + t)(p_w - dp_w)$, while OP_1 is the old world price, p_w. Therefore, $P_1 P_2$ is $t(p_w - dp_w) - dp_w$, so $\frac{1}{2}dM\, P_1 P_2$ can be written as $\frac{1}{2}dM[t(p_w - dp_w) - dp_w]$. The loss to the importing country, then, is $\frac{1}{2}dM[t(p_w - dp_w) - dp_w] - M'\, dp_w$.

The welfare loss for the world as a whole is the sum of the losses to the trading countries. Canceling common terms, it works out to be $\frac{1}{2}dM\, t(p_w - dp_w)$. This expression resembles that obtained for Figure 9-1, where there was no loss to the exporting country, but uses the new world price rather than the old world price.

difference is $F'FTT'$. But $G'GTT'$ of this loss is offset by returning tariff revenue to households, so the net loss is reduced to $F'G'T'$ plus FGT. The area $F'G'T'$ is the welfare loss associated with the protective effect; the area FGT is the loss associated with the consumption effect. The total welfare loss is related to the restrictive effect of the tariff. Note 9-1 shows that it is equal to $\frac{1}{2} dM\ tp_w$, where dM is the reduction in import volume (Q_1Q_2 plus C_1C_2 in Figure 9-1), t is the tariff rate, and p_w is the world price OP_1.

Comparing Tariffs and Quotas

Figure 9-1 can be used to compare an import quota with an import tariff. Start again with free trade and suppose that the government imposes a quota that has the same restrictive effect as the tariff analyzed in Figure 9-1. It limits the volume of imports to Q_2C_2. The domestic price must rise to OP_2 to clear the domestic market. Domestic production will rise to OQ_2, imports will be Q_2C_2, and the two together will equal domestic consumption, which falls to OC_2. The consumption and protective effects of the quota are identical to those of the tariff when the two devices are equally restrictive.

There is, of course, one difference between the quota and the tariff. The tariff yields $G'GTT'$ in tariff revenue. The quota does not yield any. The revenue equivalent, $G'GTT'$, goes as a windfall profit to importers standing at the head of the line when tickets are handed out. Under the assumption adopted previously, however, this difference is relatively unimportant. When the government returns its tariff revenue, consumers as a group get back what they pay out. When a quota is used instead of a tariff, importers collect what consumers pay out, but importers are consumers, too. Therefore, the welfare loss with the quota is $F'G'T'$ plus FGT, just as it was with the tariff.

The equivalence between a quota and a tariff breaks down in two instances: when markets are not perfectly competitive and when the various demand and supply curves are subject to random shifts. Such random shifts need not affect the *expected* levels of production and consumption. Under a tariff, however, shifts in the foreign supply curve cause domestic output to fluctuate. Under a quota, they do not. (Furthermore, random fluctuations have different consequences for expected welfare under tariffs and quotas.)

Effects in General Equilibrium

When the foreign supply curve is perfectly elastic, as in Figure 9-1, the foreign offer curve is a straight line. The implications are developed in Figure 9-2, which shows trade between Britain and Portugal when Britain is much larger than Portugal. The British offer curve is the straight line OJ, and the Portuguese offer curve is OJ^*. The free-trade equilibrium occurs at W. The relative price of cloth in Portugal must equal its world price, which is given by the slope of the British offer curve. Portugal imports OV cloth and exports WV wine. When Portugal imposes an import tariff, the relative price of cloth in Portugal rises by the full amount of the tariff. Assume that the tariff rate is $W'Z'/Z'V'$ so that the relative price of cloth in Portugal is given by the slope of the line OJ_T. (For proof that $W'Z'/Z'V'$ measures the Portuguese tariff on cloth, see Note 9-2.) At that new price, Portuguese consumers will demand OV' cloth imports, and their outlay will be worth $W'V'$ wine. The Portuguese government will collect tariff revenue worth $W'Z'$ wine.

To locate the equilibrium point in trade between Britain and Portugal, recall what we learned in Chapter 2. A country's demand for imports is its excess demand for the imported good; its supply of exports is its excess supply of the export good; and

FIGURE 9-2 Effects of a Tariff in a Two-Commodity
World When One Country Is Small
The Portuguese offer curve is *OJ**. The British offer curve is *OJ* and is a
straight line in this example, indicating that Portugal is too small to
influence British prices. In the initial free-trade equilibrium, Portugal imports *OV* cloth in exchange for *VW* wine. The relative price of cloth in
Portugal is given by the slope of Britain's offer curve. When Portugal imposes a tariff on cloth imports, the relative price of cloth in Portugal is
given by the (steeper) slope of the line *OJ*$_T$. The tariff rate is *W'Z'/Z'V'*.
Equilibrium in Portugal is displaced from *W* to *W'*. Portugal's supply of
wine exports is *V'W'*, and its demand for cloth imports is *OV'*. Equilibrium in trade with Britain is displaced to *Z'* or *Z"*, depending on the
disposition of the tariff revenue. That revenue is *Z'W'*. If it is spent on
wine, equilibrium is displaced to *Z'*; if it is spent on cloth, equilibrium
is displaced to *Z"*.

the value of the one must equal the value
of the other when a country's spending is
equal to its income. When Portuguese consumers demand *OV'* cloth imports, Portuguese producers must offer *W'V'* wine
exports. When British producers are asked
to supply *OV'* cloth exports, moreover,
British consumers must receive *V'Z'* wine
imports, because *Z'* lies on Britain's offer
curve *OJ*. All these requirements are met,

however, when tariff revenue worth *W'Z'*
wine is used by the Portuguese government
or by Portuguese consumers to buy that
quantity of wine. The excess supply of wine
is reduced from *W'V'* to *Z'V'*. This is the
quantity that British consumers have to receive if British producers are to offer *OV'*
cloth exports.

What would happen if Portugal's tariff
revenue were spent on cloth instead of

Note 9-2

The price of cloth in Britain is p_1. Its price in Portugal is p_1^* and differs from the price in Britain by the amount of the tariff, t^*, imposed by Portugal. Therefore,

$$p_1^* = (1 + t^*)p_1$$

There is no tariff on wine, so its price, p_2, is the same in both countries. Dividing both sides of the price equation by p_2,

$$p^* = \frac{p_1^*}{p_2} = (1 + t^*)\frac{p_1}{p_2} = (1 + t^*)p$$

where p^* is the relative price of cloth in Portugal, and p is its relative price in Britain.

In Figure 9-2, Portuguese consumers make payments worth $W'V'$ wine for OV' cloth imports, so p^* is $W'V'/OV'$. British producers receive payments worth $Z'V'$ wine for OV' cloth exports, so p is $Z'V'/OV'$. Accordingly,

$$\frac{W'V'}{OV'} = (1 + t^*)\frac{Z'V'}{OV'}$$

and

$$W'V'/Z'V' = 1 + t^*$$

But $W'V' = W'Z' + Z'V'$, so that $W'V'/Z'V' = 1 + W'Z'/Z'V'$. Therefore $t^* = W'Z'/Z'V'$, as stated in the text.

wine? The effects are trivial in this example. Suppose, for simplicity, that the Portuguese government does the buying directly, rather than remitting the tariff revenue to Portuguese consumers. As it can purchase British cloth at world prices, without paying its own tariff, it can use tariff revenue worth $W'Z'$ wine to buy $W'Z''$ cloth. Portugal's demand for cloth imports rises to OV'' when the government's demand is included, and Portugal must offer $Z''V''$ wine in order to purchase that quantity of cloth, because Z'' lies on Britain's offer curve. But that is exactly what Portugal will offer, because $Z''V''$ equals $W'V'$, which measures the excess supply of wine in Portugal when the tariff revenue is not used to buy wine.[2]

Figure 9-2 does not show explicitly the protective and consumption effects of the tariff. (The protective effect is implied, however, because there is an increase in the relative price of cloth, which stimulates Portuguese cloth output.) It does show the restrictive effect explicitly. With free trade, Portuguese cloth imports were OV yards. With a tariff, they fall to OV'' yards when the revenue is spent on cloth and to OV' yards when it is spent on wine. Furthermore, the story told by Figure 9-2 is more comprehensive than that told by Figure 9-1. By showing what happens to relative prices, it describes reactions in the wine market as well as in the cloth market.

Nevertheless, the story is incomplete, because it does not take account of three complications:

1. The protective effect of any single tariff depends on many other tariffs. It is especially important to take account of tariffs on raw materials purchased by the industry being studied.

2. A tariff can affect the terms of trade when the foreign offer curve is not perfectly elastic. A change in the terms of trade has important wel-

---

[2] When part of the revenue is used to buy wine and the rest to buy cloth, equilibrium in trade between Britain and Portugal takes place at a point on OJ lying between Z' and Z''.

fare implications and can also influence the sizes of the protective and consumption effects.

3. When a tariff alters the terms of trade, its full effects depend on the way the revenue is spent. If it is spent mainly on the export good, the improvement in the terms of trade can be big enough to reduce the domestic price of the imported good, causing a perverse protective effect.

These propositions are easy to illustrate when taken one at a time.

NOMINAL AND EFFECTIVE TARIFFS

Consider an economy that manufactures iron using domestic coal and imported ore. Suppose that it uses 1 ton of coal and 2 tons of ore to manufacture a ton of iron. The economy is small in world markets and faces these fixed foreign prices:

Iron	$100 per ton
Coal	35 per ton
Ore	20 per ton

If the country has no tariffs, the costs of the materials needed to make iron will total $75 per ton. Therefore, the iron industry will suffer losses if wage and other factor costs total more than $25 per ton.

What happens when the country imposes a 50 percent tariff on imported iron? The domestic price of iron will rise from $100 to $150 per ton, and the iron industry will not suffer losses unless wage and other factor costs total more than $75 per ton. Putting the same point differently, a 50 percent tariff on imported iron is equivalent to a 200 percent tariff on the *value added* by the iron industry. It raises the amount available for meeting wage and other factor costs from $25 to $75 per ton, an increase of $50 or 200 percent. The tariff rate on value added is known as the *effective* rate for the iron industry. It can be

very different from the nominal (ordinary) rate on imported iron.

What happens however, when the country imposes a 50 percent tariff on imported ore together with the tariff on imported iron? The costs of the materials required to make iron will rise to $95 per ton, and the iron industry will suffer losses if wage and other factor costs total more than $55 per ton. The addition of the tariff on imported ore reduces the effective rate for the iron industry from 200 to 120 percent. It raises the amount available for meeting wage and other factor costs from $25 to $55 per ton, an increase of only $30 or 120 percent.

Two points emerge from these calculations. First, we should concentrate on effective rates when asking how tariffs affect profits and production in domestic industries. Second, the effective rate for a particular industry depends on the nature of its costs and on a variety of nominal rates, those on the outputs of the industry itself and those on its inputs.

The formula employed to calculate effective rates is derived in Note 9-3. It shows what we have just discovered. The effective rate will rise with the nominal rate on an industry's output. It will fall with an increase in the nominal rates on an industry's inputs.[3]

How large are the differences between effective and nominal tariffs? Data for the United States, Europe, and Japan were re-

---

[3] Here is how to apply the formula in Note 9-3 to the case of the iron industry: The value of t is 50 percent (the nominal rate on iron). The value of t_i is zero for coal (there is no tariff), and the value of c_i is 0.35. The value of t_i for ore is 50 percent, and the value of c_i is 0.40. Therefore, the effective rate for iron is

$$T = \frac{50 - [(0 \times 0.35) + (50 \times 0.40)]}{1 - (0.35 + 0.40)}$$
$$= \frac{50 - 20}{0.25} = 120$$

which is the number obtained in the text.

Note 9-3

An imported commodity, x, is produced by labor, L, whose wage is w, and capital, K, whose rate of return is r, using intermediate goods in amounts denoted by y_i. The world price of the commodity is p, and the world prices of the intermediate goods are p_i. Under competitive conditions,

$$px = wL + rK + \Sigma\, p_i y_i$$

Value added in the production of x is defined by

$$V = wL + rK = px - \Sigma\, p_i y_i$$

Let a_i be the fixed amount of y_i required per unit of output, so that $y_i = a_i x_i$ and

$$V = (p - \Sigma\, p_i a_i)x$$

Define value added per unit of output as

$$v = \frac{V}{x} = p - \Sigma\, p_i a_i$$

Impose a tariff, t, on imports of x and tariffs, t_i, on imports of the intermediate goods. Value added per unit of output becomes

$$v' = (1 + t)p - \Sigma\, (1 + t_i)p_i a_i$$
$$= v + (tp - \Sigma\, t_i p_i a_i)$$

so $v' - v = tp - \Sigma t_i p_i a_i$. Dividing this difference by v, we obtain the effective rate of protection, T, for the x industry:

$$T = \frac{v' - v}{v} = \frac{tp - \Sigma\, t_i p_i a_i}{p - \Sigma\, p_i a_i} = \frac{t - \Sigma\, t_i c_i}{1 - \Sigma\, c_i}$$

where $c_i = (p_i a_i / p)$, the share of the ith intermediate good in the price of x. Subtracting t from both sides of this equation,

$$T - t = \frac{\Sigma\, (t - t_i)c_i}{1 - \Sigma\, c_i}$$

When all t_i equal t (a uniform tariff), the effective rate equals the nominal rate. When many t_i are higher than t, the effective rate is lower than the nominal rate. When many t_i are lower than t, the effective rate is higher.

produced in Table 9-1. Effective rates are higher than nominal rates in a large majority of cases, because tariffs on outputs are higher than tariffs on inputs. They are more than three times as high for apparel and footwear in Japan and for nonferrous metals in Europe; they are about twice as high for food, beverages, and tobacco in the United States and Japan, for textiles and apparel in the United States, for furniture in Japan and Europe, and for steel in Europe. They are lower in some instances, however, because tariffs on inputs are higher than tariffs on outputs, and effective rates are negative in nine cases. The structure of protection damages these industries; they would be better off with free trade. Instances of this sort crop up quite frequently in the tariff schedules of less-developed countries, where tariffs on iron and steel and other inputs are so high that the industries dependent on those inputs are handicapped severely.

The calculation of effective rates was popular some years ago, when the concept of effective protection was still new. It has lost popularity for two reasons. First, the formula used to calculate effective rates is based on several restrictive assumptions that are not easy to relax. It assumes that the country under study is small in world markets—that its tariffs do not alter world prices. It assumes that the industry under study is unable to substitute one input for another—that the coefficients in the formula are fixed. It neglects the influence of quotas, subsidies, and other trade controls that may be more important than some nominal tariffs in determining effective rates. Second, there have been significant advances in the design, estimation, and solution of large econometric models that shed light directly on protective effects. Those models show what happens in each and every industry when one nominal tariff is raised or reduced, and this is what we really want to know. The concept of effective protection is still needed, however, to warn against errors in analysis and policy. It warns that the influence of any tariff depends on many other tariffs. It warns that an increase in the nominal tariff on one product can reduce the effective tariff on another product. By implication, we cannot give one industry more protection without the risk of taking some away from another.

EFFECTS OF A TARIFF WITH A VARIABLE WORLD PRICE

To study the effects of tariffs on the terms of trade and the consequences for economic welfare, we start with a single market, then use offer curves to look at the effects in general equilibrium.

Effects in a Single Market

In Figure 9-3, the domestic demand curve for cameras is D_H, on the right side of the diagram, and the domestic supply curve is S_H. The foreign supply curve is S_W, on the left side of the diagram. The domestic and foreign supply curves are used to build the aggregate supply curve, S_A, on the right side of the diagram. Faced with

the price OP_1, domestic producers go to F' on the supply curve S_H, offering OQ_1 cameras, and foreign producers go to N on the supply curve S_W, offering OM_1 cameras. The sum of these quantities is given at F on the aggregate supply curve. It is the quantity OC_1. Clearly, equilibrium occurs at F under free trade, and the equilibrium price is OP_1. The quantity demanded by domestic consumers is equal to the sum of the quantities supplied by domestic and foreign producers.

The introduction of a tariff is more complicated here than in Figure 9-1. It can be explained with the aid of the foreign supply curve, and then represented by drawing a new aggregate supply curve. Suppose that the tariff is imposed at the ad valorem rate P_2P_0/OP_0 (equal to HK/KM_2). If the domestic price of a camera rises to OP_2, the tariff on each camera will be P_0P_2, and foreign producers will receive OP_0 per camera. They will go to K on their supply curve, offering OM_2 cameras. The introduction of the tariff can be represented by shifting the foreign supply curve upward from S_W to S_T. The curve S_W shows the quantity supplied at the price received by foreign producers; the curve S_T shows the quantity supplied at the price paid by domestic consumers. When foreign producers are at K on S_W, they will be at H on S_T. The shift in the foreign supply curve, however, must be matched by a shift in the aggregate supply curve. It shifts leftward from S_A to S_A'. (The horizontal distance between S_A and S_A' equals the horizontal distance between S_W and S_T. At the price OP_1, for instance, the shift is FE, which equals NL.)

The shift in the aggregate supply curve to S_A' is the one we need to determine the effects of the tariff. The tariff displaces equilibrium from F to T. The domestic price rises to OP_2, and the foreign price falls to OP_0. Domestic consumers demand OC_2 cameras, domestic producers supply

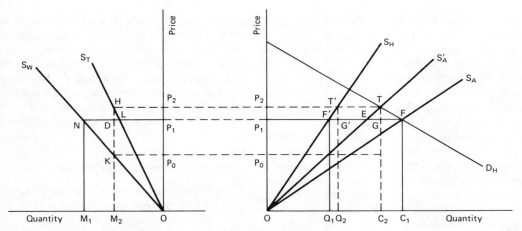

FIGURE 9-3 Effects of a Tariff in a Single Market When
Foreign Supply Is Not Perfectly Elastic
The domestic demand curve is D_H, and the domestic supply curve is S_H.
The foreign supply curve is S_W, and the aggregate supply curve is
S_A ($P_1 F' + P_1 N = P_1 F$). The initial free-trade equilibrium is at F, where
S_A intersects D_H. World and domestic prices are OP_1, and total domestic
consumption is OC_1. Domestic producers supply OQ_1, and foreign producers supply OM_1. A tariff displaces the foreign supply curve to S_T (the
tariff rate is HK/KM_2) and thus displaces the aggregate supply curve to
S_A'. Equilibrium is displaced to T, and the domestic price rises to OP_2.
Domestic consumption falls to OC_2. Domestic producers supply OQ_2,
and foreign producers supply OM_2. The consumption effect is $C_1 C_2$, and
the corresponding welfare loss is FGT. The production (protective) effect
is $Q_1 Q_2$, and the corresponding welfare loss is $F'G'T'$. The restrictive
effect is the sum of the two and equals $M_1 M_2$. The world price falls to
OP_0. This is the terms-of-trade effect, and the corresponding welfare loss
is KDN. The government collects $P_0 P_2$ of tariff on each unit imported, or
$KP_0 P_2 H$ of total tariff revenue.

OQ_2, and foreign producers supply OM_2.
The government collects $KP_0 P_2 H$ of tariff
revenue ($P_0 P_2$ per camera *times* OM_2 cameras). The consumption effect of the tariff
is $C_1 C_2$, the protective effect is $Q_1 Q_2$, and
the restrictive effect is $M_1 M_2$. The welfare
effects follow directly.

Look first at the effect on foreign producers. They lose $KP_0 P_1 N$ of producer
surplus, due to the reduction in the world
price from OP_1 to OP_0. This loss can be
rewritten as $KP_0 P_1 D$ *plus* KDN, where
$KP_0 P_1 D$ is the tariff revenue "extracted"
from foreign producers by the reduction in
the world price and KDN is the terms-of-
trade effect on foreign supply.

Look next at the domestic effects. The
decrease in consumer surplus is $P_1 FTP_2$; it
can be rewritten as $P_1 GTP_2$ *plus* FGT. The
increase in producer surplus is $P_1 F'T'P_2$; it
can be rewritten as $P_1 G'T'P_2$ *less* $F'G'T'$.
The difference between them is a loss of

$G'GTT'$ *plus* FGT *plus* $F'G'T'$. But tariff revenue is KP_0P_2H, which can be rewritten as KP_0P_1D *plus* DP_1P_2H. Furthermore, DP_1P_2H is equal to $G'GTT'$.[4] Therefore, the welfare loss works out at FGT *plus* $F'G'T'$ *less* KP_0P_1D. It is the sum of the losses associated with the consumption and protective effects *less* the portion of the tariff revenue extracted from the foreigner. There can thus be a welfare gain rather than a loss when the reduction in the world price is large enough, because the amount of revenue extracted from the foreigner depends on the size of this price reduction.

What happens to world welfare in this example? The change is the sum of the changes in national welfare. When they are added up, moreover, the revenue term KP_0P_1D drops out, leaving a welfare loss equal to KDN *plus* FGT *plus* $F'G'T'$. This is the sum of the losses associated with the terms-of-trade effect on foreign supply, the consumption effect, and the protective effect. Note 9-1 shows that the loss can be measured by $\frac{1}{2}dM\,t(p_w - dp_w)$, where dM is the reduction in import volume measured by M_1M_2, t is the tariff rate, p_w is the initial world price measured by OP_1, and dp_w is the reduction in the world price measured by P_1P_0.

These measurements illustrate an important point discussed more thoroughly in Chapter 10. Free trade need not be the best regime from the standpoint of a single country. If the country is large enough to influence its import prices and, therefore, its terms of trade, it may be able to raise its economic welfare above the free-trade level by imposing an "optimum" tariff. By doing so, however, it interferes with global efficiency, reducing world welfare.

Note that this last formulation connected the reduction in the price of the imported good with an improvement in the terms of trade. To establish this connection, we must look beyond the market for that single good to see how a tariff and the pattern of expenditure influence the market for the export good. We must use offer curves.

Effects in General Equilibrium

In Figure 9-4, the British offer curve is OJ, the Portuguese offer curve is OJ^*, and free-trade equilibrium occurs at W. The relative price of cloth is given in both countries by the slope of the line OP_W. Portugal imports OV cloth and exports VW wine.

Suppose that Portugal imposes an import tariff at the rate $W'Z'/Z'V'$ and spends the tariff revenue on wine. The relative price of cloth rises in Portugal; it is given by the slope of the line OP_H. The Portuguese economy is displaced to W', where Portuguese consumers demand OV' cloth imports and Portuguese producers supply $V'W'$ wine exports. The relative price of cloth falls in Britain; it is given by the slope of the line OP_F. The British economy is displaced to Z', where British producers supply OV' cloth exports and British consumers demand $Z'V'$ wine imports. The diagram describes equilibrium in trade between Britain and Portugal, but only because the tariff revenue is used entirely to buy wine. That revenue is worth $W'Z'$ wine. When it is spent on wine, the supply of wine exports is cut by $W'Z'$, falling to $Z'V'$, and is thus equal to the demand for wine imports. The wine market clears, and so does the cloth market.

The tariff improves Portugal's terms of trade by reducing the relative price of cloth in the outside world, the price at which Portugal buys cloth from Britain. The tariff protects the Portuguese cloth industry by raising the relative price of cloth inside

---

[4] This is because $DP_1P_2H = OM_2 \times P_1P_2$, while $G'GTT' = Q_2C_2 \times P_1P_2$, and $OM_2 = Q_2C_2$ (as both of them measure the quantity of imports).

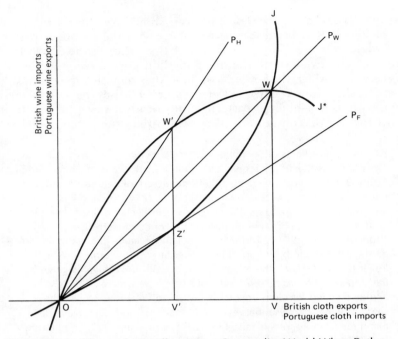

FIGURE 9-4 Effects of a Tariff in a Two-Commodity World When Both Countries Are Large

The Portuguese offer curve is OJ^*. The British offer curve is OJ. In the initial free-trade equilibrium, Portugal imports OV cloth in exchange for VW wine. The relative price of cloth is given in both countries by the slope of OP_W. When Portugal imposes a tariff on its imports and spends the tariff revenue on wine, the relative price of cloth is given in Portugal by the (steeper) slope of OP_H. It is given in Britain by the (flatter) slope of OP_F. The tariff rate is $W'Z'/Z'V'$. Equilibrium in Portugal is displaced from W to W', where Portugal's supply of wine exports is $V'W'$ and its demand for cloth imports is OV'. Tariff revenue is $Z'W'$ measured in wine. Because that revenue is spent entirely on wine, Portugal's offer of wine exports is reduced to $V'Z'$. Equilibrium in Britain is displaced to Z', where Britain's supply of cloth exports is OV' and its demand for wine imports is $V'Z'$.

Portugal, the price at which Portuguese producers sell their cloth output. (The welfare effects of the tariff are examined in Chapter 10.)

When Portugal was too small to influence its terms of trade, the spending of the tariff revenue did not influence the final outcome. The relative price of cloth in Portugal rose by the full amount of the tariff. When Portugal is large enough to influence its terms of trade, the spending of the revenue is very important. It affects the size of the change in the terms of trade and, therefore, the change in the relative price of cloth in Portugal, the change that gives protection to the Portuguese cloth industry. That price rises in Figure 9-4, but by less than in Figure 9-2, because Portugal's terms of trade improve.

There are two ways to illustrate the importance of the way in which the revenue is spent. (1) We can show how relative prices change along with the spending pattern when the tariff rate is held constant. (2) We can show how the tariff rate must change along with the spending pattern when one relative price is held constant. The first method goes directly to the point at issue, but the requisite diagram is complicated. Figure 9-5 uses the second method. It fixes the relative price of cloth in Portugal, which fixes the protective effect of the tar-

FIGURE 9-5   Effects of Spending Patterns

The offer curves and price lines OP_F and OP_H are drawn as they were in Figure 9-4, showing the effects of a Portuguese tariff when the tariff revenue is spent on wine. The tariff rate is $W'Z'/Z'V'$, equilibrium in Portugal occurs at W', and equilibrium in Britain occurs at Z'. When the tariff revenue is spent on cloth instead, the price of cloth rises in both countries. Alternatively, Portugal can obtain the same change in the domestic price of cloth by imposing a lower tariff. If the tariff is set at the lower rate $W'U/UV'$, the relative price of cloth in Portugal is given by the slope of OP_H, as before. Portugal's supply of wine exports is $V'W'$, and its demand for cloth imports is OV'. Tariff revenue is UW' measured in wine. Because that revenue is spent on cloth, Portugal's demand for cloth imports is raised by $W'Z''$, becoming OV''. Equilibrium in Britain is displaced to Z'', where Britain's supply of cloth exports is OV'' and its demand for wine imports is $V''Z''$.

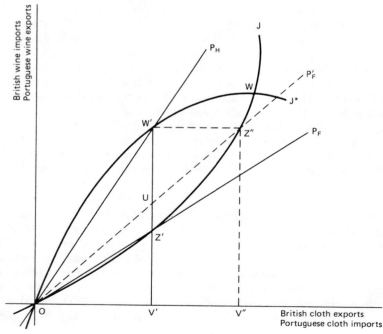

iff, and asks how the tariff rate must change when the revenue is spent on cloth instead of wine.

The offer curves OJ and OJ^* are drawn as before, along with the price lines OP_H and OP_F, giving the relative prices of cloth in Portugal and Britain when the tariff revenue is spent on wine, as in Figure 9-4. The new price line, OP_F' shows what happens to the relative price of cloth in Britain (the Portuguese terms of trade) when the tariff revenue is spent on cloth and the tariff rate is adjusted to prevent the relative price of cloth from changing in Portugal.

The tariff rate required for this purpose is $W'U/UV'$, which is lower than the rate $W'Z'/Z'V'$. As the relative price of cloth in Portugal is still given by the slope of the line OP_H, the Portuguese economy goes to W', where consumers demand OV' cloth imports and producers supply $V'W'$ wine exports. As the relative price of cloth in Britain is equal to the slope of the new line OP_F', the British economy goes to Z'', where producers supply OV'' cloth exports and consumers demand $Z''V''$ wine imports. The tariff revenue, however, is worth $W'U$ wine, which can be employed to buy $W'Z''$ cloth. (Remember that the Portuguese government does not have to pay its own tariff on cloth; it can import cloth at the world price, given by the slope of OP_F'.) When all the revenue is spent on cloth, then, the demand for cloth imports rises from OV' to OV'' and is equal to the British supply of cloth exports. The cloth market clears, and so does the wine market.

The outcome in Figure 9-5 is different in two ways from the outcome in Figure 9-4. The tariff rate is lower, and the change in the terms of trade is smaller. There is a simple explanation. When the Portuguese government spends its revenue on cloth, it raises the global demand for cloth and thus raises the price of cloth in both Britain and Portugal. (It raises both countries' prices because they can differ

only by the tariff rate.) Therefore, it reduces the improvement in Portugal's terms of trade but gives more protection to Portuguese cloth producers. If the government does not want to give them more protection, it can reduce the tariff rate.

The same point can be made in another way. When the Portuguese government spends its revenue on wine, it drives up the price of wine, increasing the improvement in Portugal's terms of trade but decreasing the amount of protection given to Portuguese cloth producers. There is, in fact, one case in which the producers are injured, not aided, by the tariff: when the revenue is spent on wine and the British demand for wine imports is inelastic.

This perverse case is illustrated by Figure 9-6. When the British demand for wine imports is inelastic, Britain's offer curve bends backward.[5] The free-trade equilibrium is at W, and the relative price of cloth is given by the slope of OP_W. When Portugal imposes a tariff at the rate $W'Z'/Z'V'$ and spends the revenue on wine, the Portuguese economy moves to W', and the relative price of cloth in Portugal is given by the slope of OP_H. It is lower than it was with free trade, which means that cloth output falls in Portugal. The reason is the large improvement in the terms of trade. It is given by the slope of OP_F, which is much flatter than OP_W.

---

[5] When the demand for a product is inelastic, an increase in its price reduces the quantity demanded but raises the amount spent on the product. In Figure 9-6, increases in the relative price of wine are shown by drawing flatter price lines from the origin. (An increase in the relative price of wine is a decrease in the relative price of cloth.) On the backward-bending segment of OJ, price increases reduce the quantity of wine imported by Britain but raise the cloth equivalent of the payment for it. When the relative price of wine corresponds to the slope of OP_W, the quantity imported is WV, and the payment is worth OV cloth. When the relative price of wine corresponds to the slope of OP_F, the quantity imported falls to $Z'V'$, but the payment is worth OV' cloth.

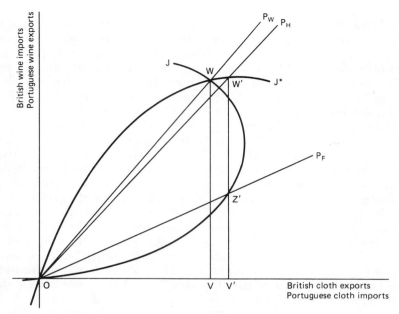

FIGURE 9-6   A Perverse Case

In the neighborhood of the free-trade equilibrium at *W*, the British offer curve *OJ* bends backward. The British demand for wine imports is inelastic. When Portugal imposes a tariff on its cloth imports and spends the revenue on wine, the relative price of cloth can move perversely in Portugal, reducing cloth output rather than raising it. When the tariff rate is *W'Z'/Z'V'* and the revenue *W'Z'* is spent on wine, Portugal's export offer is *V'Z'*. Equilibrium in Britain is established at *Z'*, and the British price line is *OP_F*. As usual, the relative price of cloth falls in Britain. Equilibrium in Portugal is established at *W'*, and the Portuguese price line is *OP_H*. As *OP_H* is flatter than *OP_W*, the free-trade price line, the relative price of cloth falls in Portugal, too. Therefore, the tariff works perversely to reduce Portuguese cloth output.

SUMMARY

Many popular arguments for tariffs are fallacious. Differences in wage rates, for example, do not justify protection. They are required for trade to take place when there are differences in productivity. Tariffs can protect domestic industries essential for the national defense, but this argument is not compelling; the maintenance of a mobilization base may not be helpful in the nuclear age. Furthermore, protection is the wrong way to maintain that base if it is required. Tariffs tax consumers of the peacetime products of the protected industries rather than distributing the costs across the whole population. It would be more equitable and efficient to use production subsidies.

This last point can be made against many other arguments, even those that are analytically sound. Because they distort consumers' choices, tariffs are second-best policy instruments compared to other ways of redistributing income, increasing output in domestic industries, or promoting economic growth. Tariffs are better instruments, however, than most other trade controls, because they are less rigid and more transparent. Quotas are formally equivalent to tariffs under perfectly competitive conditions, but quotas do not allow imports to increase when domestic demand rises, and they give windfall profits to the quota holders.

Tariffs have two important effects. By raising the domestic price of the imported commodity, they raise the production of domestic substitutes (the protective effect) and reduce domestic demand (the consumption effect). Both effects impose welfare losses on the domestic economy. Tariffs have a third effect when the country imposing them is large enough to influence world prices. They can improve its terms of trade. When they do so, however, they impose welfare losses on the outside world, and these are always larger than the welfare gains extracted from foreign suppliers. As a consequence, there is a loss to the world as a whole. The size of the improvement in the terms of trade varies with the way that the revenue is spent. It is largest when the revenue is spent on the export good. In that case, however, the improvement in the terms of trade may be large enough to reverse the protective effect of the tariff.

To measure the protective effects of tariffs, we must examine the whole tariff schedule. The protective effects increase with the sizes of the tariffs on products that compete with an industry's output. The effects decrease with the sizes of the tariffs on products that it purchases. The net effects can be approximated by the effective rate for the industry. This rate can be higher or lower than the nominal rate. It can even be negative, in which case the industry would be better off with complete free trade.

RECOMMENDED READINGS

This chapter has concentrated on import tariffs, but export tariffs have identical effects on relative prices and on outputs. See Abba P. Lerner, "The Symmetry between Import and Export Taxes," *Economica*, 3 (August 1936), reprinted in American Economic Association, *Readings in International Economics* (Homewood, Ill.: Richard D. Irwin, 1968), ch. 11.

On comparing tariffs with quotas when markets are not perfectly competitive, see Jagdish Bhagwati, *Trade, Tariffs, and Growth* (Cambridge, Mass.: MIT Press, 1969), ch. 9; on comparing them when demand and supply curves are subject to random shocks, see Michael D. Pelcovits, "Quotas Versus Tariffs," *Journal of International Economics*, 6 (November 1976).

The use of quotas and other nontariff trade barriers is surveyed in Robert E. Baldwin, *Nontariff Distortions of International Trade* (Washington, D.C.: Brookings Institution, 1970).

For ways of extending and applying the concept of effective protection, see W. Max Corden, "The Structure of a Tariff System and the Effective Protective Rate," *Journal of Political Economy*, 74 (June 1966), reprinted in J. N. Bhagwati, ed., *International Trade: Selected Readings* (Cambridge, Mass.: MIT Press, 1981), ch. 9.

Effective rates for less-developed countries are given in Bela Balassa, "Effective Protection in Developing Countries," in J. N. Bhagwati et al., eds., *Trade, Balance of Payments and Growth* (Amsterdam: North-Holland, 1971), ch. 14.

Attempts have been made to measure the welfare costs of trade restrictions using the concepts of consumer and producer surplus. For an example, see Stephen P. Magee, "The Welfare Effects of Restrictions on U.S. Trade," *Brookings Papers on Economic Activity*, 1972(3); for a compilation of recent calculations, see Gary Clyde Hufbauer and Howard F. Rosen, *Trade Policy for Troubled Industries*, Policy Analyses in International Economics, 15 (Washington, D.C.: Institute for International Economics, 1986).

CHAPTER
10
THE USES
OF TRADE POLICY

INTRODUCTION

This chapter examines four arguments for tariffs. Unlike those discussed at the start of Chapter 9, these arguments stand up to rigorous analysis. But tariffs turn out to be second-best instruments. The same policy objectives can be reached by methods that do not reduce economic welfare or are less costly in this respect. These are the four arguments:

1. A tariff can improve the terms of trade and thus redistribute the gains from trade.

2. A tariff can change factor prices and thus redistribute income within a single country.

3. A tariff can correct for distortions in domestic markets, such as rigid wage rates, and thus contribute to economic efficiency.

4. A tariff can protect an infant industry until it is able to compete effectively at free-trade prices.

Thereafter, we examine a combination of the infant–industry argument with the case for subsidies discussed in Chapter 7. It shows what can happen when subsidies are used to help domestic firms win a race for leadership in a new technology.

The chapter concludes with an introduction to the theory of *customs unions*. These are international agreements in which the participating countries exempt their partners' exports from all tariffs and adopt a common external tariff on goods from the outside world. The United States is a customs union. So is the European Economic Community.

TARIFFS AND THE DISTRIBUTION OF THE GAINS FROM TRADE

In Chapter 9, we saw that an import tariff can raise economic welfare when it reduces the price paid to the foreigner. Some of the tariff revenue is "extracted" from the foreigner, and it can be large enough to offset the welfare losses resulting from the protective and consumption effects of the tariff.

The proposition can be put more strongly. Any country big enough to affect its terms of trade can impose an *optimum tariff* that raises economic welfare above its free-trade level. The size of the tariff de-

pends in part on domestic demand conditions and on the shape of the foreign offer curve.

A Special Case

This strong form of the proposition is easy to prove when a country is completely specialized, because its output mix is not affected by the tariff. Let us return to the simple Ricardian model, where Britian specialized completely in cloth and imported its wine from Portugal. The situation seen from the British standpoint is shown in Figure 10-1. The British transformation curve is BB', and Britain produces at B.

FIGURE 10-1 The Optimum Tariff with Complete Specialization

The British transformation curve is BB'. The Portuguese offer curve is BJ^*. The free-trade equilibrium occurs at W, where the price line BP_W cuts the Portuguese offer curve and is also tangent to the British indifference curve U_1. The relative price of cloth is given in both countries by the slope of BP_W. Britain specializes completely in cloth, producing OB, and exports VB cloth in exchange for VW wine. As U_1 is tangent to the price line but not to the Portuguese offer curve, there is a higher indifference curve, U_2 that is tangent to the offer curve. Britain can reach it by imposing a tariff. The new price of cloth is given in Portugal by the slope of BP_F, which is steeper than BP_W. Britain improves its terms of trade. The new price of cloth in Britain is given by the slope of U_2 at the new equilibrium point, W'. It is the slope of HH', which is flatter than BP_F. The relative price of cloth is lower in Britain (the relative price of wine higher), and the difference between the countries' prices measures the British tariff.

The Portuguese offer curve is BJ^*. It is drawn with its origin at B and its axes parallel to those of the diagram. Free-trade equilibrium occurs at W, where the price line BP_W cuts the Portuguese offer curve and is also tangent to U_1, a British indifference curve. Britain produces OB cloth, consumes OV, and exports VB. It imports VW wine.

Because the indifference curve U_1 is tangent to the price line BP_W rather than the Portuguese offer curve, it is not the highest indifference curve accessible to Britain. The highest curve is U_2, which is tangent to the Portuguese offer curve at W'. If Britain can reduce its wine imports from VW to $V'W'$, it can reach U_2 at W'.

Britain can employ an import quota for this purpose. It can also use the tariff that has the same effect on imports. To measure this optimum tariff, we need to know what prices will move the two countries to W'. To bring the Portuguese economy to W', the relative price of cloth in Portugal must equal the slope of the line BP_F. To bring the British economy to W', the relative price of cloth in Britain must equal the slope of U_2 and, therefore, the slope of the line HH'. The gap between those prices is the optimum tariff, the one which will maximize welfare in Britain. It is derived algebraically in Note 10-1.

Note 10-1

An equation developed in Note 9-2 can be adapted to measure the optimum tariff. When Britain imposes a tariff on Portuguese wine,

$$p^* = (1 + t)p$$

where p is the relative price of cloth in Britain, p^* its relative price in Portugal, and t is the tariff rate. Therefore,

$$t = \frac{p^* - p}{p} \quad \text{or} \quad t = \frac{p^*}{p} - 1$$

In Figure 10-1, p^* is given by the slope of BP_F and p by the slope of HH'. In Figure 10-2, p^* is given by the slope of TT' and p by the slope of HH'.

The optimum tariff rate is related to the elasticity of Portuguese demand for British cloth. Portugal's offer curve can be viewed as Britain's total-revenue curve; it shows how much wine Britain can earn by exporting cloth to Portugal. In Figure 10-2, Britain's total revenue is $W'V'$ wine when it exports $V'Q'$ cloth.

Therefore, Britain's average revenue is $W'V'/V'Q'$, which equals the slope of TT' and thus equals p^*. Britain's marginal revenue is the slope of Portugal's offer curve, which equals the slope of HH' and thus equals p. Therefore, the ratio of average to marginal revenue is p^*/p, which equals $1 + t$. That same ratio, however, is related to e_d, the elasticity of demand:

$$\frac{\text{Average revenue}}{\text{Marginal revenue}} = \frac{e_d}{e_d - 1}$$

Hence, $(1 + t) = [e_d/(e_d - 1)]$, and $t = 1/(e_d - 1)$. Note that $t > 0$ only when $e_d > 1$. Britain's optimum-tariff point must lie on the elastic portion of Portugal's demand curve. A country using its market power to maximize economic welfare behaves much like an ordinary monopolist using its market power to maximize profits. Both operate on the elastic portions of the demand curves for their products.

The General Case

When Britain does not specialize completely in cloth, a tariff will change its output mix. This does not undermine the proof, but it complicates the diagram.

The left side of Figure 10-2 shows the free-trade situation seen from the British standpoint. The British transformation curve is BB', and Britain produces at Q. Its cloth output is OX_1, and its wine output is OX_2. The Portuguese offer curve is QJ^*. It is drawn with its origin at Q. Equilibrium occurs at W, where the relative price of cloth is given by the slope of the line FF', which is tangent to the British transformation curve at Q and to a British indifference curve at W. Once again, U_1 is not the

FIGURE 10-2 The Optimum Tariff with Incomplete Specialization
The free-trade equilibrium is shown on the left. The British transformation curve is BB', and the Portuguese offer curve is QJ^*. Britain produces at Q, where the slope of the price line FF' equals the slope of its transformation curve. Its cloth output is OX_1, and its wine output is OX_2. Britain consumes at W, where the slope of FF' equals the slope of the indifference curve U_1. It exports QV cloth and imports VW wine, which match the quantities that Portugal imports and exports when the price line cuts the Portuguese offer curve at W. The optimum-tariff equilibrium is shown on the right. The relative price of cloth is given in Britain by the slopes of the price lines HH'. Britain produces at Q', where the slope of the (solid) line HH' equals the slope of its transformation curve. As HH' is flatter than FF', the relative price of cloth has fallen in Britain, reducing its cloth output to OX_1' and raising its wine output to OX_2'. Britain consumes at W', where the slope of the (dashed) line HH' equals the slope of the indifference curve U_2. It exports $Q'V'$ cloth and imports $V'W'$ wine, which match the quantities that Portugal imports and exports when it faces the price line TT'. As TT' is steeper than FF', Britain has improved its terms of trade. As U_2 is tangent to the Portuguese offer curve, Britain has chosen the optimum tariff.

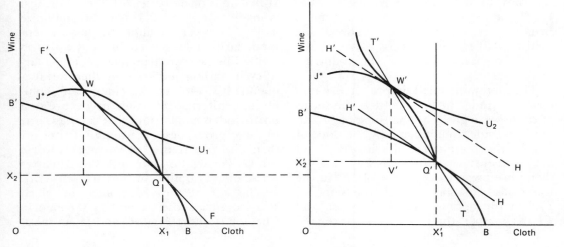

highest indifference curve accessible to Britain. But it is not easy to locate that curve in this particular diagram. The optimum tariff will reduce the relative price of cloth in Britain, moving the output point along the transformation curve. The output point, however, serves as the origin for the Portuguese offer curve, which means that the offer curve has to move, too. The diagram begins to disintegrate as soon as we disturb it.

The optimum-tariff situation is not hard to draw, however, once it has been located. It is shown on the right side of Figure 10-2. The relative price of cloth in Britain is given by the slopes of the two lines HH'. The output point is Q', where the solid line HH' is tangent to the British transformation curve. Cloth output has fallen to OX_1', in response to the reduction in the relative price of cloth, and wine output has risen to OX_2'. The consumption point is W', where the dashed line HH' is tangent to the indifference curve U_2. The Portuguese offer curve is $Q'J^*$, with its origin at Q', and it is also tangent to U_2 at W'. Hence, U_2 is the highest indifference curve that Britain can reach. The relative price of cloth in Portugal is given by the slope of the line TT'. It is the price that brings the Portuguese economy to W', where Portugal supplies $V'W'$ wine exports and thus meets Britain's demand for wine imports. The British tariff rate is given as before, by the gap between the slopes of the countries' price lines.

The optimum tariff improves Britain's terms of trade. In Figure 10-1, the terms of trade were given by the slope of BP_W in the free-trade situation and by the slope of BP_F in the optimum-tariff situation, and BP_F is steeper than BP_W. In Figure 10-2, they were given by the slope of FF' in the free-trade situation and by the slope of TT' in the optimum-tariff situation, and TT' is steeper than FF'. Therefore, the optimum-tariff argument is sometimes called the terms-of-trade argument.

Do not be misled by this name. An improvement in the terms of trade is necessary to increase economic welfare. But it is not sufficient for that purpose. Remember a point made in Chapter 9, in connection with Figure 9-3. A tariff can reduce the welfare of the country imposing it even when some of the revenue is "extracted" from the foreigner. Look closely at Figure 10-1. If the terms-of-trade line were steeper than BP_F, it would intersect the Portuguese offer curve below W'. It might even intersect that curve below the point where the offer curve is cut by the indifference curve U_1. In that case, of course, the tariff would put Britain on an indifference curve lower than U_1, and Britain would be worse off than it was with free trade. The tariff rate must be chosen carefully. Bigger is not necessarily better.

Retaliation

Thus far, we have ignored the possibility of retaliation. When Britain imposes its optimum tariff, economic welfare falls in Portugal. The reason is familiar. Any departure from free trade reduces world welfare. If Britain is made better off, then, Portugal is made worse off. Portugal can minimize its loss, however, by imposing its own optimum tariff, taking account of the British tariff. The two countries may get into a tariff cycle, raising and lowering their rates sequentially, without reaching an equilibrium. Alternatively, they may move to a tariff-ridden equilibrium that can have one of three properties: (1) Britain is better off than with free trade, but Portugal is worse off. (2) Portugal is better off, but Britain is worse off. (3) Both countries are worse off.

The last of these outcomes, in which both countries lose, resembles the one in Chapter 7, where America and Japan subsidized their robot exports to Brazil, and can be interpreted in the same manner.[1] Both governments know that their citizens will suffer welfare losses if they reach this sort of tariff-ridden equilibrium. When they do not trust each other, however, both will be tempted to use tariffs. To preserve free trade or a less restrictive tariff-ridden regime, the governments must make a binding agreement to refrain from starting the process. This may be one reason why governments participate in the General Agreement on Tariffs and Trade (GATT), which prevents them from raising their tariffs unilaterally.

The Inefficiency of the Optimum Tariff

The optimum-tariff argument is analytically sound. A tariff can be used to redistribute the gains from trade. But it is a second-best policy instrument for that purpose. As tariffs and other trade barriers reduce world welfare, they are inefficient ways to influence its distribution. Suppose that Britain gave notice to Portugal that it was about to adopt its optimum tariff. Portugal could threaten to retaliate, but it has another option. It can offer to pay Britain an annual "bribe" just large enough to put British consumers on the indifference curve U_2, the curve they would reach with the optimum tariff. The bribe would redistribute world welfare without reducing it, and Portugal would suffer a welfare loss smaller than what it would endure if Britain adopted its optimum tariff.

---

[1] The two examples are very similar indeed, because the example in Chapter 7 can be modified to generate the three possibilities listed above. Both countries lose in that particular example because they produce identical robots under identical cost conditions. Under less symmetrical circumstances, one country could gain and the other could lose when both used export subsidies.

There is, of course, a practical objection. It would be hard for the Portuguese government to carry out its promise. Its citizens would probably object, urging retaliation instead. National self-esteem would probably dominate national self-interest. The first-best policy would not be feasible, and Britain could increase its welfare only by imposing its optimum tariff.

In the next three cases, however, it is easy to define and use a first-best policy. The cases deal with domestic policy objectives and, thus, the domain of a single government. The treatment of each case will emphasize the welfare costs of using a tariff by showing how another policy instrument can be used instead. In each case, moreover, the country imposing the tariff will be too small to influence its terms of trade. This assumption will exclude optimum-tariff gains and thus focus attention on the welfare costs involved. (It will also exclude the perverse case described in Figure 9-6 of Chapter 9. A tariff will not lower the domestic price of the import-competing product.)

TARIFFS AND THE DISTRIBUTION OF DOMESTIC INCOME

A tariff can be used to alter the income distribution within a single economy, because it can affect the real earnings of labor, capital, and land. Its impact, however, depends on the structure of the economy.

Effects in the Modified Ricardian Model

In Chapter 5, on the modified Ricardian model, the effects of a change in relative prices on the real earnings of the factors of production were summarized by the Haberler theorem. It can be applied directly to describe the effects of a tariff. When Britain imposes a tariff on its wine imports, the relative price of wine rises in

Britain. The owners of land gain, because land is used in making wine, and the owners of capital lose, because capital is used in making cloth. The effects on British workers depend, of course, on the commodity in which the real wage is measured. The real wage rises in terms of cloth and falls in terms of wine.

These outcomes are reviewed in Figure 10-3, along with some that we have not seen before. The curve E_C is the demand

curve for labor used in making cloth; it measures the marginal product of labor at each level of employment in Britain's cloth industry. The curve E_W is the demand curve for labor used in making wine; it measures the marginal product of labor in Britain's wine industry divided by the relative price of cloth. Let the free-trade equilibrium occur at F, where the real wage measured in cloth is OV in both industries, OL_1 workers are employed in the wine in-

FIGURE 10-3 Effects of a Tariff on the Income Distribution When Some Factors Are Not Mobile

Under free trade, labor-market equilibrium in Britain occurs at F, where the real wage measured in cloth is OV in both industries. When Britain imposes a tariff on wine imports, the demand curve for labor by the wine industry shifts upward by the amount of the tariff, from E_W to E_W'. (The tariff rate is VV'/OV.) If labor is completely immobile, employment remains at OL_1 in the wine industry, and equilibrium is displaced to T. The real wage measured in wine does not change in the wine industry; the real wage measured in cloth rises by the full amount of the tariff, going from OV to OV'. The real wage measured in cloth does not change in the cloth industry; the real wage measured in wine falls by the full amount of the tariff. If labor is perfectly mobile, equilibrium is displaced to T', and employment in the wine industry rises to OL_1'. The real wage measured in cloth rises in both industries but by less than the amount of the tariff, going from OV to OV''; the real wage measured in wine falls in both industries.

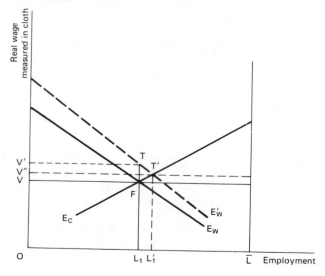

dustry, and $\bar{L}L_1$ workers are employed in the cloth industry.

When Britain imposes a tariff on its wine imports, the relative price of wine rises in Britain, reducing the relative price of cloth. The demand curve E_C is not affected, but the demand curve E_W shifts upward to E'_W. The size of the shift, measured by $V'V/OV$, is equal to the ad valorem tariff.[2]

Consider first a case we have not seen before. Suppose that there is *no* labor mobility. Employment in the wine industry is fixed at OL_1, fixing the marginal products of labor and land used in making wine. Employment in the cloth industry is fixed at $\bar{L}L_1$, fixing the marginal products of labor and capital used in making cloth. A tariff cannot influence *own* real earnings, those measured in terms of the goods produced by the factors earning them, because own real earnings are equal to marginal products. The tariff can affect *cross* real earnings, those measured in terms of the other good, because it affects relative prices.

Let us spell this out. Although the earnings of the land and labor used in making wine are fixed in terms of wine, they rise together in terms of cloth, because of the fall in the relative price of cloth. In Figure 10-3, labor-market equilibrium for the wine industry is shifted from F to T, raising the real wage measured in cloth by the full amount of the tariff, from OV to OV'. The earnings of the capital and labor used in making cloth do not change when mea-

sured in cloth; labor-market equilibrium for the cloth industry remains at F, and the real wage measured in cloth remains at OV. They fall together, however, when measured in wine, because of the increase in the relative price of wine.

Consider next the case studied in Chapter 5. When labor is perfectly mobile in Britain, the tariff leads to equilibrium at T'. The real wage rises in terms of cloth, going to OV''. It falls in terms of wine, however, because $V'V''/OV$ is smaller than $V'V/OV$, which measures the increase in the relative price of wine (because it measures the tariff rate). Employment rises in the wine industry, increasing the marginal product of land, which raises the real rental rate for land, measured in wine or cloth. Employment falls in the cloth industry, decreasing the marginal product of capital, which reduces the real return to capital, measured in wine or cloth.

Effects in the Heckscher–Ohlin Model

In Chapter 6, on the Heckscher–Ohlin model, the effects of a change in relative prices on the real earnings of the factors of production were summarized by the Stolper–Samuelson theorem. An increase in the relative price of corn raised the real wage of labor, the factor used intensively in growing corn, and reduced the real return to capital. But the theorem depended on the basic assumption that all factors can move freely from industry to industry, which means that it can hold only in the long run, because it takes time to transform capital from mills into tractors.

The Stolper–Samuelson theorem was developed initially to answer the question with which we are dealing here. How does a tariff influence the income distribution in the Heckscher–Ohlin model? As corn is the labor-intensive commodity, Manymen is the labor-abundant country, and tastes are the same in Manymen and Fewmen, we know

---

[2] Using notation developed earlier, the free-trade wage, OV, can be written as f_L^w/p, where f_L^w is the marginal product of labor in the wine industry (and does not change until employment changes), while p is the relative price of cloth in Britain. With free trade, however, p is equal to p^*, the relative price of cloth in Portugal (and p^* does not change at all, as Britain is too small to influence its terms of trade). When Britain imposes a tariff, $p^* = (1 + t)p$, as shown in Note 10-1, so $p = p^*/(1 + t)$. The new wage, OV', is $f_L^w(1 + t)/p^*$. Therefore, $(OV' - OV)/OV = V'V/OV$ $= \{[f_L^w(1 + t)/p^*] - (f_L^w/p^*)\}/(f_L^w/p^*) = t$.

that Manymen exports corn and imports steel. By implication, Manymen can use an import tariff to redistribute income from labor to capital. A tariff raises the relative price of steel in Manymen. Over the long run, then, it raises the real return to capital and reduces the real wage of labor. Fewmen can employ a tariff for the opposite purpose. By raising the relative price of corn in Fewmen, a tariff raises the real wage of labor and reduces the real return to capital, redistributing income from capital to labor.

The Crucial Role of Factor Mobility

Before looking at the costs of relying on a tariff to influence the income distribution, note that the exercises just conducted make very different forecasts about attitudes toward tariffs:

1. When there is no factor mobility whatsoever, your attitude should depend entirely on the industry from which you obtain your income, not the nature of that income. If you earn your income from the British wine industry, whether it be rental or wage income, you should favor an import tariff. It will raise your real income by raising your cross real earnings. If you earn your income from the British cloth industry, you should oppose it.

2. When labor is perfectly mobile but land and capital are not, your attitude should depend in part on the nature of your income, not the industry from which you obtain it. If you own land in Britain, you should favor an import tariff. If you own capital in Britain, you should oppose it. If you are a worker in Britain, your attitude should depend in part on the way you spend your income. If you dress much and drink little, you should favor a tariff, because it will raise the real wage in terms of cloth but reduce the real wage in terms of wine. If you dress little and drink much, you should oppose it.

3. When all the factors of production are perfectly mobile, as in the Heckscher–Ohlin model, your attitude should depend entirely on the nature of your income, not the industry from which you obtain it nor the way you spend it. If you own capital in Manymen, you should

favor a tariff. If you are a worker in Manymen, you should oppose it.

We will return to these differences in Chapter 11 when looking at the sources of political support for tariffs and other trade barriers.

Welfare Costs and Alternative Policies

To measure the welfare costs of a tariff and compare them with the costs of another policy, let us look again at the modified Ricardian model and examine the goods-market equilibria shown in Figure 10-4. Britain's transformation curve is BB', and Britain's terms of trade are given by the slope of the line FF'. In the initial free-trade situation, the output point is Q, where BB' is tangent to FF' (Q corresponds to F in Figure 10-3); the consumption point is C, where the indifference curve U_2 is tangent to FF'.

When Britain imposes an import tariff to redistribute income, the relative price of wine rises in Britain, reducing the relative price of cloth. Represent the new relative price of cloth by the slope of the lines HH'. The output point moves to Q', where the transformation curve is tangent to the solid line HH' (Q' corresponds to T' in Figure 10-3). The consumption point moves to C', where the indifference curve U_0 is tangent to the dashed line HH' and where the line EE', parallel to FF', connects Q' with C'.[3] The tariff reduces welfare because U_0 is lower than U_2.

There are other ways to redistribute income that avoid or reduce the welfare loss. The first-best policy for this purpose goes directly to the heart of the matter. If Britain wants to redistribute income from owners of capital to owners of land, the re-

---

[3] As Britain cannot influence its terms of trade, the lines FF' and EE' stand for the Portuguese offer curve. The displacement of FF' to EE', then, corresponds to the displacement of the Portuguese offer curve from Q to Q' in the two parts of Figure 10-2.

FIGURE 10-4 Comparing a Tariff with a Production Subsidy
Britain's terms of trade are given by the slope of FF'. Under free trade, Britain produces at Q on the transformaton curve BB' and consumes at C on the indifference curve U_2. Cloth output is OX_1, and wine output is OX_2. A tariff on wine imports raises the relative price of wine in Britain (reduces the relative price of cloth). Represent this effect by the slope of HH'. Britain will produce at Q', where cloth output is OX_1' and wine output is OX_2', and will trade along EE' (parallel to FF') until it reaches C', where the slope of the indifference curve U_0 equals the slope of the dashed line HH'. A subsidy to wine production financed by a tax on cloth production can have the same effect on the output point. The slope of HH' can be taken to represent the effects on prices received by British producers, causing them to move to Q'. The prices paid by British consumers, however, are given by the slopes of FF' and EE', just as they were under free trade. Therefore, Britain will trade to C'', where the slope of the indifference curve U_1 is equal to the slope of EE'. As U_1 lies above U_0, the subsidy reduces economic welfare by less than the tariff.

sult of the tariff in this instance, it should raise taxes on income from capital and reduce taxes on income from land. This policy would leave production at Q, avoiding the protective effect. It would leave consumption at C, avoiding the consumption effect. Therefore, it would leave economic welfare at the free-trade level.

The next-best policy would tax cloth output and subsidize wine output, changing the net prices received by producers. It would set the ratio of those prices equal to the slope of HH', moving the output point to Q'. The rental rate for land would rise, the return to capital would fall, and real income would be redistributed just as it is by the tariff. But the prices paid by British consumers would not change, and the ratio of those prices would still equal the slopes of FF' and EE'. The consumption point would move to C'', where the indifference curve U_1 is tangent to EE'. As U_1 lies between U_0 and U_2, the tax-subsidy scheme would cause a smaller welfare loss than the tariff. There would be a welfare-reducing protective effect, but no consumption effect.

In this particular case, the tariff is a third-best policy. It is dominated by income-tax adjustments and by a tax-subsidy scheme. The ranking illustrates an important proposition that applies in other cases, too:

To minimize the welfare loss or to maximize the welfare gain associated with a particular policy objective, intervention should take place at the point closest to the policy objective.

If the government seeks to change the income distribution, it should alter income taxes. If it seeks to change the composition of production, it should tax or subsidize production. If it seeks to change the composition of consumption, it should tax or subsidize consumer purchases. It should not tax or subsidize imports or exports unless it seeks to change the level or pattern of foreign trade.

TARIFFS AND DOMESTIC DISTORTIONS

An economy can differ in many ways from models used heretofore. Markets may not be perfectly competitive. Product and factor prices may be rigid in nominal or real terms. Uncertainty may influence decisions by producers and consumers. Some products and processes may damage health or the environment.

These possibilities have led economists to look for ways of using tariffs and other trade controls to compensate for welfare-reducing distortions in the economy. They have spent much time modeling the distortions themselves and ranking policies to deal with them. The technique and conclusions can be illustrated by analyzing the effects of a rigid real wage in the modified Ricardian model.

Introducing the Rigid Wage

The British labor market is shown again in Figure 10-5. Before the opening of trade, equilibrium occurs at D, where the real wage is $O\overline{V}$ measured in cloth. Employment is OL_1 in the wine industry and $\overline{L}L_1$ in the cloth industry. The opening of trade reduces the relative price of wine in Britain, raising the relative price of cloth, and the demand curve for labor in the wine industry shifts downward from E_W to E'_W. When the real wage is flexible, equilibrium is displaced to F, and the real wage falls to OV^*. Employment falls to OL_1^* in the wine industry and rises to $\overline{L}L_1^*$ in the cloth industry. When the real wage is rigid in terms of cloth, however, it remains at $O\overline{V}$. Employment falls in the wine industry to OL_1^i but remains at $\overline{L}L_1$ in the cloth industry. There is unemployment amounting to DF' workers.

The output and welfare effects of wage rigidity are shown in Figure 10-6. Before trade, equilibrium occurs at Q, where the transformation curve BB' is tangent to the indifference curve U_0. The relative price of cloth is given by the slope of U_0 at Q. Trade is opened by introducing the price line FF', steeper than U_0 at Q. The relative price of cloth rises in Britain.

When the real wage is flexible, the output point moves along BB' to Q^*. Cloth output rises from OX_1 to OX_1^*, corresponding to the increase in employment in the

FIGURE 10-5 Effects of Trade and a Tariff on Labor-Market Equilibrium When the Real Wage Is Rigid

Before trade, E_C is the demand curve for labor in the British cloth industry, and E_W is the demand curve in the British wine industry. Equilibrium occurs at D, where the real wage is $O\overline{V}$ measured in cloth. Trade raises the relative price of cloth in Britain, shifting E_W downward to E_W'. If the real wage is flexible, it falls to OV^*, and equilibrium occurs at F, where employment in the wine industry falls from OL_1 to OL_1^*, and employment in the cloth industry rises from $\overline{L}L_1$ to $\overline{L}L_1^*$. If the real wage is rigid at $O\overline{V}$, however, employment in the wine industry falls farther to OL_1', and employment in the cloth industry remains at OL_1. There is unemployment. A tariff on wine imports raises the relative price of wine and shifts the wine industry's demand curve from E_W' to E_W'', raising employment to OL_1''. It does not affect employment in the cloth industry (so it cannot establish equilibrium at F). A tariff could shift the demand curve all the way to E_W, raising employment to OL_1 and eliminating unemployment. But the relative price of wine would return to what it was before trade, and trade would be eliminated. A wage subsidy could take the labor market to F, offsetting the effects of wage rigidity. The requisite subsidy measured in cloth would be $V^*\overline{V}$ per worker in both industries.

cloth industry shown by Figure 10-5. Wine output falls from OX_2 to OX_2^*, corresponding to the decrease in employment in the wine industry. Britain trades along FF' to

some such point as C^*, on an indifference curve higher than U_0.

When the real wage is rigid, Britain cannot move along BB'. As employment in the

FIGURE 10-6 Effects of Trade on Economic Welfare When the Real Wage Is Rigid

Before trade, Britain produces and consumes at Q, on the transformation curve BB' and the indifference curve U_0. When trade is opened, the terms of trade are given by the slope of FF'. If the real wage is flexible, production moves to Q^*, where cloth output rises to OX_1^* and wine output falls to OX_2^*, and Britain trades along FF' to some such point as C^*, on an indifference curve higher than U_0. If the real wage is rigid, cloth output cannot rise, and wine output falls all the way to OX_2'. The production point is Q', and Britain trades along EE' (parallel to FF') to some such point as C', on an indifference curve lower than U_0. The opening of trade can reduce economic welfare. If employment is subsidized in both industries, firms can reach Q^*, the point reached when the real wage is flexible, and welfare losses are replaced by welfare gains.

cloth industry remains at $\overline{L}L_1$ in Figure 10-5, cloth output remains at OX_1 in Figure 10-6. As employment in the wine industry falls to OL_1' in Figure 10-5 (a level lower than OL_1^*), wine output falls to OX_2' in Figure 10-6 (a level lower than OX_2^*). The new production point is Q', and Britain trades along EE', parallel to FF', to some such point as C'. This point will be on an indif-

ference curve lower than U_0 if the output loss QQ' is large. When the real wage is rigid, free trade can reduce economic welfare.

Correcting the Effects of a Rigid Wage

A tariff can be used to deal with this problem. A tariff on wine imports will raise the relative price of wine in Britain, reducing the relative price of cloth. In Figure 10-5, then, it shifts the demand curve for the wine industry from E'_W to E''_W. The tariff cannot affect employment in the cloth industry; it remains at $\overline{L}L_1$, because the rigid real wage remains at $O\overline{V}$. But it raises employment in the wine industry from OL'_1 to OL''_1.

The implications for output and welfare are shown in Figure 10-7, which repro-

FIGURE 10-7   Effects of a Tariff on Economic Welfare When the Real Wage Is Rigid

The production points Q, Q', and Q^* are reproduced from Figure 10-6. With free trade and a rigid wage, Britain produces at Q', rather than Q^*, and it trades along EE' to C', on an indifference curve below U_0 (the curve reached before trade is opened). By raising wine output above OX'_2, a tariff can raise economic welfare above the levels reached at C'. If it raises wine output to OX''_2 (the level corresponding to employment at OL''_1 in Figure 10-5), it shifts the production point to Q'', and Britain can trade along TT' (parallel to FF' and EE') until it reaches a point such as C'', where the indifference curve U_1 is tangent to HH', whose slope is equal to the relative price of cloth in Britain. As U_1 is higher than U_0, the tariff raises welfare above the level reached before trade was opened. As U_1 is lower than the indifference curve tangent to FF' at C^*, however, the tariff cannot raise welfare to the level that would be reached by subsidizing employment to produce at Q^*.

duces from Figure 10-6 the output points Q, Q^*, and Q' and the consumption points C^* and C'. The increase in employment in the wine industry is shown by the increase in wine output from OX'_2 to X''_2. The output point moves from Q' to Q'', and Britain trades along the line TT', parallel to EE' and FF', until it reaches C'' on the indifference curve U_1. The slope of that indifference curve at C'', shown by the slope of the line HH', measures the relative price of cloth in Britain. The gap between the slopes of HH' and TT' measures the tariff rate on wine imports. As U_1 is higher than U_0, the tariff has converted the welfare loss into a welfare gain. British consumers are better off with the tariff than they were before the opening of trade and much better off than they were with free trade.

Looking back at Figure 10-5, note that some workers are still unemployed in Britain. Unemployment is reduced from DF' with free trade to DF'' with a tariff, but it is not eradicated. Britain could achieve full employment by raising its tariff until E'_W shifted all the way back to E_W, restoring labor-market equilibrium at D. In this case, however, the relative price of cloth in Britain would be what it was before trade was opened, which means that the tariff would eliminate all trade. The output point in Figure 10-7 would go all the way from Q' to Q, where the relative price of cloth in Britain would equal the slope of the indifference curve U_0. Britain would consume at Q, and economic welfare would return to its pretrade level. As in the optimum-tariff case, a bigger tariff is not better, even though it could eliminate unemployment.[4]

------

[4] That would be the best tariff policy if it were not possible to find an output point Q'' from which Britain could trade to an indifference curve higher than U_0. All points such as C'' could be on indifference curves lower than U_0. Under these circumstances, Britain would have to impose the tariff that brought the output point back to Q, eliminating both trade and unemployment.

As the tariff cannot stimulate employment in Britain's cloth industry, it cannot establish labor-market equilibrium at F in Figure 10-5, the point that would be reached with a flexible real wage. That is why it cannot eliminate unemployment and raise economic welfare at the same time. Furthermore, the tariff has a costly consumption effect. Because consumers' choices are governed by the slope of the price line HH' in Figure 10-7, they go to C'' on U_1 rather than a point on an indifference curve tangent to TT'. As usual, the tariff is a second-best policy.

Can Britain find a form of intervention that does not have these defects, involving intervention closer to the problem? As wage rigidity arises in the labor market, intervention in that market can give better results. Return to Figure 10-5 and suppose that the government subsidizes firms for hiring labor. Let the subsidy be $V^*\overline{V}$ per worker, measured in cloth, which reduces the cost of hiring a worker from $O\overline{V}$ to OV^*. That is what the cost would be with wage flexibility, and labor-market equilibrium will be established at F. The output point will move to Q^* in Figure 10-7, and Britain can trade along FF' to C^*. It can reap the full gains from trade.

TARIFFS AND ECONOMIC TRANSFORMATION

Most standard arguments for tariffs call for permanent departures from free trade. One group calls for temporary deviations to help an economy make large changes in the structure of production. There are three important versions of this case for protection.

One version is associated with the problems of senescent industries. Because they have old plants and products, they are especially vulnerable to import competition.

They ask for time to modernize their plants and introduce new products. Labor unions ask for the same sort of help so that reductions in employment can be achieved by retirements (attrition) rather than dismissals. This version of the argument is examined more fully in Chapter 11, along with alternatives to the use of tariffs.

Two other versions of the argument are associated with the problems of infant industries. These are industries that give promise of competing successfully with imports if they are given help to grow. The first version relies on the promise that young industries can reap economies of scale. The second relies on the promise that they can reap economies of experience. Both versions were advanced by Alexander Hamilton in his *Report on Manufactures*, urging industrial development in the United States and tariffs to promote it.

Economies of Scale

The argument invoking economies of scale is based on strong assumptions about the way that costs of production vary with output. Costs rise steeply for a while, but start to fall once output becomes large enough to justify the use of mass-production methods. As a tariff can raise the outputs of import-competing firms, it can be used to capture economies of scale. Once firms are on the downward-sloping parts of their cost curves, the tariff can be removed. The argument can be put in another way. Tariffs can reserve domestic markets for domestic products until those markets are big enough to absorb output levels that confer economies of scale. At that point, domestic firms will not need protection. They may indeed begin to export.

This argument makes most sense analytically when the economies of scale attach to the industry as a whole rather than the individual firm. When the economies of scale attach to the firm, it can capture them by expanding its own output until costs start to fall. It can undercut its domestic competitors and does not need a tariff. When the economies of scale attach to the industry as a whole, the firm cannot capture them by itself. Consider firms that assemble finished products from parts supplied by other firms, and suppose that mass-production methods can reduce the costs of making the parts. A single firm that expands its output of the finished product cannot induce its suppliers to use mass-production methods; its demand for parts is not large enough. If all such firms expand, however, they can induce their suppliers to adopt those methods and thus reduce the costs of parts and of the finished product. In this example, economies of scale attaching to the firms that make the parts show up as economies of scale to the industry that assembles them. As firms that make the parts move along their downward-sloping cost curves, firms that assemble the parts experience a downward shift in their cost curves. A tariff on the finished product would be effective here.

This version of the infant-industry argument has been invoked to justify protection in less-developed countries, including many countries in Latin America. They have used tariffs too freely, however, without asking whether the industries protected by them can capture significant economies of scale. A number of countries have shifted recently from import substitution to export promotion, but they have found it hard to dismantle their import restrictions. Protected industries have enough political influence to block trade liberalization. As a consequence, promising export industries have been handicapped by tariffs and other restrictions on imported equipment and materials. They suffer from negative effective protection. Nevertheless, the change in strategy has been successful in several countries. Growth rates have accelerated.

Economies of Experience

The argument invoking economies of experience is based on the notion of *learning by doing*. An infant industry may be less efficient than an older industry because it lacks seasoned managers, skilled workers, and reliable suppliers of equipment and materials. Therefore, protection may be justified temporarily, until the industry matures, cuts back its costs, and can compete with imports. Recent statements of this argument put much emphasis on the time and money needed to train workers, invoking the point made in Chapter 4 that labor skills are important determinants of comparative advantage.

This last version of the argument amounts to the assertion that temporary tariffs can induce a permanent outward shift of the transformation curve, leading to an increase in output that raises welfare in the future by more than the tariff reduces welfare currently. Consider the economy depicted by Figure 10-8. Its transformation curve is AA' initially, and it produces at Q_1, where the slope of its transformation curve is equal to the slope of F_1F_1', which gives the relative price of coffee on the world market. It moves along F_1F_1' to some such point as C_1, exporting coffee and importing trucks. When it imposes a tariff on trucks, the relative price of coffee in the domestic market is given by the slope of a line such as H_1H_1', flatter than F_1F_1'. The production point will move to Q_1', where the country produces more trucks and less coffee. Economic welfare falls because consumers move to some such point as T_1, which lies on a lower indifference curve than C_1. With the passage of time, however, productivity will rise in the domestic truck industry, because the increase in output fostered by the tariff encourages learning by doing. The transformation curve will shift outward to AA'', and the output point will move to Q_2', where AA'' is tangent to H_2H_2'. When the tariff is removed, the output point will move to Q_2, where AA'' is tangent to F_2F_2'. Truck output will fall but will still be higher than at Q_1. Accordingly, consumers can move to some such point as C_2, where welfare is higher than at C_1.

Alternatives to Infant-Industry Protection

There are several answers to these arguments for tariffs. Some come from history, others from trade theory.

It is not easy to choose appropriate candidates for infant-industry protection. If it is granted too freely, it will go to industries that cannot reap economies of scale or economies of experience. Even when it is confined to promising candidates, it can hurt other industries, as in many less-developed countries, where import substitution has handicapped export promotion. Once they get protection, moreover, few industries give it up willingly. They do not want to suffer reductions in output like the one described in Figure 10-8 by the movement from Q_2' to Q_2.

There are better ways to help an infant industry. A production subsidy is better than a tariff. It goes closer to the policy objective, an increase in domestic output, and does not have welfare-reducing consumption effects. Production subsidies, however, may not go close enough to the basic problem.

Suppose that a firm can expect to cut costs by training its managers and workers. It should be able to borrow in the capital market to cover the training costs and other losses suffered in infancy and repay what it borrows when it reaches maturity. If capital markets are competitive and lenders are not heavily averse to risk, the interest rate at which the firm can borrow will reflect the social rate of return on capi-

FIGURE 10-8 The Infant-Industry Argument

A country faces fixed terms of trade equal to the slope of $F_1 F'_1$. Before imposing a tariff, it produces at Q_1 on the transformation curve AA'. It trades to a point such as C_1, where an indifference curve would be tangent to $F_1 F'_1$. It exports coffee and imports trucks. An import tariff shifts production to Q'_1, where AA' is tangent to the domestic price line $H_1 H'_1$. The economy trades along a line with the same slope as $F_1 F'_1$ to a point such as T_1, where an indifference curve would be tangent to the line having the same slope as $H_1 H'_1$. The tariff raises the production of trucks but reduces welfare (T_1 lies on an indifference curve lower than C_1). With the passage of time, however, protection increases the efficiency of firms or factors engaged in making trucks. The transformation curve shifts outward to AA'', and production moves to Q'_2. When the tariff is removed, production moves to Q_2, where the output of trucks is lower than at Q'_2, but higher than at Q'_1 or Q_1. The economy trades along $F_2 F'_2$ to C_2 and reaches an indifference curve higher than it did initially.

tal, the value of the firm's marginal product to the economy at large. A firm that cannot afford to borrow at that competitive interest rate does not have a strong claim to protection or any other help from the government. The real resources absorbed by the firm can be used more efficiently elsewhere in the economy, by firms that can afford to pay the competitive interest rate because they can expect to earn the social rate of return.

There are two important exceptions to this argument, but they do not justify the use of tariffs. First, capital markets may not be perfectly competitive, and a firm may be forced to pay more than the social rate of return or be unable to borrow at all. When this is the case, however, the government should make loans to the infant industry rather than protect or subsidize its output. Second, a firm may be reluctant to borrow because it cannot expect to recover the costs of training workers. Once they have been trained, the workers may take jobs with other firms. If labor markets were perfectly competitive, the firm could expect to recover its costs by paying lower wages to trainees—by shifting the costs of training to the workers themselves. But labor-market imperfections and minimum-wage laws get in the way. In this case, however, the government should subsidize training rather than protect the industry involved.

Extending the Argument to New Products

In Chapter 7, two national monopolists, Edo and Acme, sold robots to Brazil, and the exporters' governments, Japan and America, backed them with subsidies. That framework can be used to illustrate an interesting variant of the infant-industry argument that has been attracting much attention.

Suppose that the two firms are trying to develop a new type of robot, that they are bound to succeed eventually, that the first firm to succeed will capture the whole Brazilian market, and that the two firms are evenly matched. Let the value of that market be $10 billion, measured by the profits to be made over the life of the new product, and that each firm is spending $1 billion on research and development. On these assumptions, each firm (and country) will value that market at $4 billion (the value of the market *times* the probability of winning the race *less* the firm's spending on research, or $10 billion *times* 0.5 *less* $1 billion). This number is shown in the upper left-hand box of Figure 10-9, where governments do not help to develop the new robot. If the American government gives Acme $1 billion for additional research, however, it can raise the probability that Acme will win. Suppose that it rises from

		American options	
		No subsidy	Subsidy
Japanese options	No subsidy	4, 4*	5.5, 1.5*
	Subsidy	1.5, 5.5*	3, 3*

FIGURE 10-9 Outcomes of a Race to Develop a New Robot
The first number in each cell is the increase in American national income resulting from the policy configuration; the second (with asterisk) is the increase in Japanese national income. Each number is the value of the market *times* the probability of winning it *less* the expenditure on research.

0.5 to 0.75. The value of the market from the American standpoint will increase to $5.5 billion ($10 billion *times* 0.75 *less* $2 billion of total spending on research), and the value seen from the Japanese standpoint will decrease to $1.5 billion ($10 billion *times* 0.25 *less* $1 billion).[5] These numbers are shown in the upper right-hand box of Figure 10-9, where America subsidizes research and Japan does not. Since the situation is symmetrical here, the same numbers appear in the lower left-hand box, where Japan subsidizes research and America does not. Finally, the numbers in the lower right-hand box reflect the outcome when both firms are subsidized. They are evenly matched again, but $1 billion of additional expenditure on research must be deducted from the value that each country attaches to the Brazilian market.

Clearly, the governments have reason to agree that they will not subsidize research. If they do not trust each other, however, both will act defensively and subsidize their firms. If America decides not to subsidize, the value of the market stands at $4 billion when Japan makes the same decision and at $1.5 billion when Japan subsidizes. If America decides to subsidize, the value of the market stands at $5.5 billion when Japan does not subsidize and at $3 billion when Japan subsidizes. When America cannot be sure that Japan will not subsidize, it makes sense for America to subsidize Acme. But Japan will make the same com-

parisons and come to the same conclusion, so both governments will subsidize and wind up in the lower right-hand box.

This example is far too simple. It ignores the effects of subsidies on the probability that the discovery will in fact be made, focusing instead on the probability that one firm will make it.[6] It also ignores the difficult problem of deciding which firm to subsidize, because we have assumed that there is just one firm in each country. But it highlights the risk of competitive behavior by governments, which is very similar to the risk they court when they subsidize output or use an optimum tariff.

THE THEORY OF CUSTOMS UNIONS

Customs unions were defined in the introduction to this chapter. They are intriguing analytically, because they can be studied from several points of view—from the standpoint of each member separately, the membership collectively, outside countries, and the world as a whole. They are important historically and politically, because they have played major roles in the formation and consolidation of nation-states.

The Constitution of the United States established a customs union. Congress was given the power to "regulate Commerce with foreign Nations, and among the several States," and the states were denied the right to "lay any Imposts or Duties on Im-

---

[5] As additional research raises the value of the market from Acme's own standpoint, we must ask why it does not spend more on research without help from the American government. The most plausible answer is similar to an argument made above, that Acme cannot expect to cover all its expenditure. This would happen if it could not patent its discovery or could expect to lose scientists and engineers to other American firms that were willing to pay high salaries for their skills and knowledge of the work in progress in Acme's laboratories.

[6] Suppose that the probability of making the discovery is 0.4 when there are no subsidies, rather than an absolute certainty, and that the firms are still evenly matched. The value of the market from America's standpoint is $1 billion ($10 billion *times* 0.4 *times* 0.5 *less* $1 billion). Suppose that the probability of making the discovery rises to 0.8 when both governments subsidize research. The value of the market from America's standpoint rises to $2 billion ($10 billion *times* 0.8 *times* 0.5 *less* $2 billion). It pays for both governemts to subsidize.

ports or Exports . . ."[7] Bismarck used a customs union, the *Zollverein,* to bring the petty states of Germany under Prussian dominance. The Treaty of Rome, signed in 1958, established the European Economic Community, also known as the Common Market, as a step toward the economic and political unification of Europe. In each instance, the customs union was a means to a larger end, but it had important economic consequences of its own.

The first rigorous analysis of customs unions was undertaken by Jacob Viner, an American economist who made many contributions to trade theory. He identified two ways in which a customs union can affect trade patterns and resource allocation:

There will be commodities . . . which one of the members of the customs union will now newly import from the other but which it formerly did not import at all because the price of the protected domestic product was lower than the price at any foreign source plus the duty. This shift in the locus of production as between the two countries is a shift from a high-cost to a lower-cost point, a shift which the free-trader can properly approve, as at least a step in the right direction, even if universal free trade would divert production to a source with still lower costs.

There will be other commodities which one of the members of the customs union will now newly import from the other whereas before the

customs union it imported them from a third country, because that was the cheapest possible source of supply even after payment of duty. The shift in the locus of production is not now as between the two member countries but as between a low-cost third country and the other, high-cost, member country. This is a shift of the type which the protectionist approves, but it is not one which the free-trader who understands the logic of his own doctrine can properly approve.[8]

Viner called the first phenomenon *trade creation* and the second, *trade diversion.* When trade creation is dominant, he said, a union raises the welfare of its members collectively and raises world welfare, too. One member of the union may suffer a welfare loss, but the gain to the other will exceed that loss. Outside countries must suffer welfare losses, but the gain to the union will exceed them. When trade diversion is dominant, by contrast, a union may reduce the welfare of its members collectively and must reduce the welfare of the whole world.

Much of the large literature on customs unions that developed in the wake of Viner's contribution was concerned with rectifying three defects. Viner did not show how to weigh trade creation against trade diversion. Furthermore, the distinction between them tends to break down when we drop an assumption implicit in his reasoning, that all goods are produced under constant returns to scale. Finally, his analysis took no account of the consumption effects that played so large a role elsewhere in this chapter.

The main lines of the amended analysis can be illustrated with tools used before to study the effects of tariffs. Let us look at a customs union between Britain and Portugal, focusing on trade in wine.

---

[7] In *Hood* vs. *Du Mond* (336 U.S. 525, 1949), Supreme Court Justice Jackson noted that "The sole purpose for which Virginia initiated the movement which ultimately produced the constitution was 'to take into consideraton the trade of the United States; to examine the relative situations and trade of the said states; to consider how far a uniform system in their commercial relations may be necessary to their common interest and their permanent harmony' and for that purpose the General Assembly of Virginia in January of 1786 named commissioners and proposed their meeting wth those from other states. . . . The desire of the Forefathers to federalize regulation of foreign and interstate commerce stands in sharp contrast to their jealous preservation of power over their internal affairs. No other federal power was so universally assumed to be necessary, no other state power was so readily relinquished."

[8] J. Viner, *The Customs Union Issue* (New York: Carnegie Endowment for International Peace, 1950), p. 43.

A Special Case

Figure 10-10 shows a case in which the customs union leads to trade diversion. The British demand curve for wine is D_H, and the domestic supply curve is S_H. The supply curve for wine imports from Portugal is S_F^*, and the supply curve for wine imports from the rest of the world (ROW) is S_F. Before formation of the customs union, Britain imposes an import tariff at the rate $P_H P_W / O P_W$. The tariff displaces the supply curve for imports from Portugal to S_T^* and the supply curve for imports from the ROW to S_T. The price of wine in Britain is OP_H. Domestic consumption is OC, domes-

tic production is OQ, and imports are QC. Portugal supplies OM_1^*, and the ROW supplies the remainder, Britain's tariff revenue is $GHTK$.

When Britain and Portugal form a customs union, wine imports from Portugal enter Britain duty free. This means that S_F^* is the relevant supply curve, as Portuguese producers receive the price of wine in Britain, rather than the British price *less* the tariff. If the union adopts the British tariff on wine imports, the supply curve for imports from the ROW remains at S_T. In this particular case, the price of wine in Britain does not change. Accordingly,

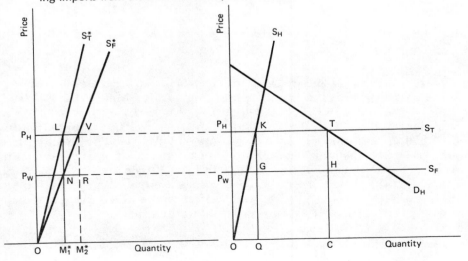

FIGURE 10-10   Trade Diversion in a Customs Union
The British demand curve for wine is D_H, and the domestic supply curve is S_H. The supply curve for imports from Portugal is S_F^*, and the supply curve for imports from the rest of the world (ROW) is S_F. Britain imposes a tariff at the rate of $P_H P_W / O P_W$, so the price of wine in Britain is OP_H. Domestic consumption is OC, domestic production is OQ, and imports are QC. Portugal supplies OM_1^*, and the rest of the imports come from the ROW. Britain's tariff revenue is $GHTK$. Britain and Portugal form a customs union so that imports from Portugal enter Britain tariff free. The union adopts the British tariff on imports from the ROW. As the price in Britain does not change, there are no changes in British consumption, production, or imports. But imports from Portugal rise to OM_2^*, displacing imports from the ROW. This is pure trade diversion.

British consumption remains at OC, domestic production remains at OQ, and total imports remain at QC. Imports from Portugal rise, however, from OM_1^* to OM_2^*, displacing an equal quantity of imports from the ROW. As imports from Portugal pay no tariff, Britain's tariff revenue falls by P_WRVP_H.

Why does this case illustrate trade diversion? The resource cost of extra imports from Portugal can be measured by the area under the Portuguese supply curve. It is $M_1^*NVM_2^*$. The real resource cost of the imports they displace is the corresponding area under the ROW supply curve. It is $M_1^*NRM_2^*$, which is smaller by NVR than the cost of the extra imports from Portugal. The customs union diverts demand from a low-cost source to a high-cost source. In this particular case, moreover, the increase in total resource cost measures the welfare loss to the world as a whole. Consider the various welfare effects.

As the price of wine in Britain is constant, along with levels of production and consumption, there are no changes in consumer or producer surplus. There is a loss of tariff revenue, however, equal to P_WRVP_H, and it is the welfare loss to

Britain. Note 10-2 shows that this loss can be measured by $(M_P + dM_P)tp_w$, where M_P is the initial level of imports from Portugal measured by OM_1^*, dM_P is the change in imports from Portugal measured by $M_1^*M_2^*$, t is the tariff rate, and p_w is the world price OP_W.

There is an increase in Portuguese producer surplus on account of the increase in exports to Britain and in the price paid to Portuguese suppliers. It is equal to P_WNVP_H, and it measures the welfare gain to Portugal. Note 10-2 shows that it can be written as $(M_P + \frac{1}{2}dM_P)tp_w$.

The welfare effect on the members collectively is the sum of the effects on them individually. Therefore, it is the British loss, P_WRVP_H, *less* the Portuguese gain, P_WNVP_H, and is thus a loss of *NVR*. Note 10-2 shows that it can be written as $\frac{1}{2}dM_Ptp_w$.

As the world price of wine is constant, there are no changes in consumer or producer surplus in the ROW. Therefore, there are no welfare effects.

The welfare effect on the whole world is the sum of the welfare effects on the union and on the ROW. In this particular case, it equals the loss to the union.

Note 10-2

In Figure 10-10, the welfare loss to Britain is P_WRVP_H, which can be written as $(P_WP_H \times P_WR)$. But P_WP_H is tp_w, where t is the tariff rate and p_w is the world price, while P_WR is OM_2^* or $M_P + dM_P$, where M_P is OM_1^*, the initial level of imports from Portugal, and dM_P is $M_1^*M_2^*$, the change in that level. Therefore, the welfare loss is $(M_P + dM_P)tp_w$. The welfare gain to Portugal is P_WNVP_H, which can be written as P_WNLP_H *plus* NVL. But

P_WNLP_H is $(P_WP_H \times P_WN)$, where P_WN equals OM_1^*, while NVL is $\frac{1}{2}(P_WP_H \times LV)$, where LV equals $M_1^*M_2^*$. Therefore, the welfare gain to Portugal is $(M_P + \frac{1}{2}dM_P)tp_w$. The welfare effect on the union as a whole is the sum of the effects on Britain and Portugal, which is a loss of $\frac{1}{2}dM_Ptp_w$. As there is no welfare effect on the ROW, this is also the effect on world welfare.

To measure the welfare effects of the union comprehensively, we would have to look at the market for cloth, as well as the market for wine. If circumstances were the same in the cloth market, the results would be symmetrical to those obtained from Figure 10-10. Britain would gain, Portugal would lose, and the union would lose. There would be no effect on the ROW, which means that the effect on the whole world would be the loss to the union. Taking the two markets together, we come close to the results obtained by Viner. When a union leads to trade diversion, one or both of the members must lose, the union as a whole must lose, and the world as a whole must lose.

A More General Case

Trade creation takes place whenever the formation of a customs union reduces high-cost domestic production in one of the member countries. For this to happen, however, the formation of the union must reduce the domestic price of the product, and there are at least two ways in which a union can do that. First, the members can agree on a common external tariff lower than the previous national tariff. Second, the displacement of imports from the outside world can reduce the world price of the imported product and thus depress the domestic price. The second possibility is more interesting. It involves an improvement in the union's terms of trade, which redistributes world welfare in favor of the union. It is harder to illustrate, however, because the supply curve for the rest of the world must be upward sloping, and there are many components to the change in welfare. Let us therefore concentrate on the first possibility.

Figure 10-11 reproduces the initial situation shown in Figure 10-10. Before formation of the union, Britain produces OQ, consumes OC, and imports QC, with OM_1^*

coming from Portugal and the remainder from the ROW. Britain's tariff rate is $P_W P_H / O P_W$, and its tariff revenue is $GHTK$. When Britain and Portugal form a customs union, they adopt a common external tariff at the lower rate $P_W P_H' / O P_W$, and the price of wine in Britain falls to OP_H'. Therefore, British consumption rises to OC', domestic production falls to OQ', and imports rise to $Q'C'$. As imports from Portugal pay no tariff, they rise to OM_2^*, and this involves trade diversion, because the additional imports from Portugal are produced at higher cost than imports from the *ROW*. But imports from the ROW can rise or fall, depending on the size of the increase in total British imports and of the increase in imports from Portugal. They rise in Figure 10-11, where $Q'Q$ *plus* CC', the increase in total imports, is larger than $M_1^* M_2^*$, the increase in imports from Portugal. The increase in total British imports reflects the usual consumption and production effects, and the production effect involves trade creation, because the imports that displace domestic output are produced at lower cost, whether they come from Portugal or the ROW. The new level of tariff revenue is $G'H'T'K'$ *less* $P_W R'V'P_H'$, which is the revenue lost by admitting imports from Portugal without tariff.

The welfare effect in Britain has three components. Consumer surplus rises by $P_H'T'TP_H$. Producer surplus falls by $P_H'K'KP_H$. The difference between these components is $AK'K$ *plus* $BT'T$ *plus* $ABTK$. The third component is the change in tariff revenue, which is $G'H'T'K'$ *less* $P_W R'V'P_H'$ *less* $GHTK$, and this difference is $G'GAK'$ *plus* $H'HBT'$ *less* $P_W R'V'P_H'$ *less* $ABTK$. Adding the two differences, we obtain the change in British welfare, which is $(AK'K$ *plus* $BT'T)$ *plus* $(G'GAK'$ *plus* $H'HBT')$ *less* $P_W R'V'P_H'$. Note 10-3 writes this as $(dM_P + dM_W)(t - \frac{1}{2}dt)p_w - (M_P + dM_P)(t - dt)p_w$, where M_P is the initial level of imports from Portugal and dM_P is the

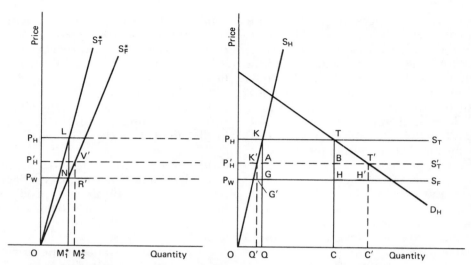

FIGURE 10-11 Trade Creation and Trade Diversion in a Customs Union

The situation initially is the same as in Figure 10-10. When Britain and Portugal form a customs union, however, they adopt a new, lower tariff on imports from the outside world. It is $P'_H P_W/OP_W$, and it reduces the price of wine in Britain to OP'_H. British consumption rises by CC', and British production falls by $Q'Q$. British imports from Portugal rise from OM^*_1 to OM^*_2 (an increase smaller than in Figure 10-10 because of the lower tariff level).

change in that level, dM_W is the change in imports from the ROW, t is the initial tariff rate, dt is the change in the rate, and p_w is the world price. The first expression is necessarily positive, because it is the product of two positive terms multiplied by the world price. The first term is the change in total British imports, and they always rise. The second term is the difference between the initial tariff and half the tariff cut and is positive because the tariff cut cannot exceed the tariff. But the second expression is necessarily positive, because it is also the product of two positive terms multiplied by the world price. The first term is the level of imports from Portugal, and the second is the level of the common external tariff. As the change in British welfare is the difference between the two expressions,

Britain can either gain or lose from the formation of the union.

The welfare effect in Portugal has only one component, the increase in producer surplus, $P_W NV'P'_H$, so Portugal gains from the formation of the union. Note 10-3 shows that the welfare gain can be measured by $(M_P + \frac{1}{2} dM_P)(t - dt) p_w$.

The welfare effect on the union is the sum of the effects on Britain and Portugal: $(dM_P + dM_W)(t - \frac{1}{2}dt) p_w - \frac{1}{2}dM_P (t - dt) p_w$. This can be positive or negative because it is the difference between two positive expressions. Therefore, the union can gain or lose. But Note 10-3 shows that the welfare effect on the union is positive whenever there is an increase in imports from the ROW. That is a way of saying that the union will gain when the trade-creating

Note 10-3

In Figure 10-11, the welfare effect on Britain is $(AK'K$ plus $BT'T)$ plus $(G'GAK'$ plus $H'HBT')$ less $P_W R'V'P_H'$. But $AK'K$ is $\frac{1}{2}(P_H P_H' \times Q'Q)$, $BT'T$ is $\frac{1}{2}(P_H P_H' \times CC')$, $G'GAK'$ is $(P_W P_H' \times Q'Q)$, $H'HBT'$ is $(P_W P_H' \times CC')$, and $P_W R'V'P_H'$ is $(P_W P_H' \times OM\frac{*}{2})$. Furthermore, $P_H P_H'$ equals dtp_w, where dt is the reduction in the tariff rate and p_w is the world price, $P_W P_H'$ equals $(t - dt)p_w$, where t is the initial tariff rate, and $Q'Q$ and CC' add up to the change in total British imports, $dM_P + dM_W$, where dM_P is the change in M_P, the initial level of imports from Portugal, and dM_W is the change in M_W, the initial level of imports from the outside world. Finally, $OM\frac{*}{2}$ equals $M_P + dM_P$. Therefore, the welfare effect on Britain is $\frac{1}{2}(dM_P + dM_W)\ dt\ p_w + (dM_P - dM_W) \times (t - dt)p_w - (M_P + dM_P) \times (t - dt)p_w$, which simplifies to $(dM_P + dM_W)(t - \frac{1}{2}dt)p_w - (M_P + dM_P)(t - dt)p_w$. The welfare effect on Portugal is $P_W NV'P_H'$, which is $(P_W P_H' \times OM_1^*) + \frac{1}{2}(P_W P_H' \times M_1^* M\frac{*}{2})$, or $(M_P + \frac{1}{2}dM_P) \times (t - dt)p_w$. The welfare effect on the union is the sum of the effects on Britain and Portugal, or $(dM_P + dM_W) \times (t - \frac{1}{2}dt)p_w - \frac{1}{2}dM_P(t - dt)p_w$. But this can be rewritten as $\frac{1}{2}dM_P tp_w + dM_W(t - \frac{1}{2}dt)p_w$, which is positive whenever dM_W is positive (when imports from the *ROW* rise).

and consumption effects dominate the trade-diverting effects.

As in the previous example, the welfare gain or loss to the union is the gain or loss to the whole world, because there is no change in ROW welfare when the world price is constant.

SUMMARY

The four uses of trade policy reviewed in this chapter show that tariffs can achieve important economic aims but are rarely first-best policy instruments.

A country large enough to influence world prices can use a tariff to improve its terms of trade and capture larger gains from trade at the expense of other countries. The size of its optimum tariff depends on the shape of the foreign offer curve. If other countries retaliate, however, the one that initiates the process may wind up worse off than with free trade. Furthermore, the departure from free trade reduces world welfare, which means that

there must be a less costly way to redistribute welfare. It is possible in principle to "bribe" a country to dissuade it from imposing an optimum tariff.

A tariff can be used to redistribute income internally. If all factors of production are immobile internally, a tariff will benefit the factors employed in the import-competing industry and harm those employed in the export industry. Real earnings in the import-competing industry will rise in terms of the export good, and real earnings in the export industry will fall in terms of the import-competing good. If some factors are mobile and others are not, as in the modified Ricardian model, the Haberler theorem applies. A tariff will raise the real earnings of the factor specific to the import-competing industry and reduce those of the factor specific to the export industry. It will raise the real earnings of the mobile factor (labor) in terms of the export good but reduce them in terms of the import-competing good. If all factors are mobile internally, as in the

Heckscher–Ohlin model, the Stolper–Samuelson theorem applies. A tariff will raise the real earnings of the factor used intensively in the import-competing industry and reduce those of the factor used intensively in the export industry. In all cases, however, a tariff is the third-best way to redistribute income. Income taxes are the first-best way; they do not distort production or consumption. Production taxes and subsidies are the second-best way; they distort production but do not distort consumption.

When a country's commodity or factor markets do not function perfectly, free trade may reduce economic welfare. When real wages are rigid, for example, the opening of trade can cause unemployment, and the resulting welfare loss can exceed the welfare gain obtainable through trade. By raising employment in the import-competing industry, a tariff can reduce the welfare loss resulting from the rigid wage. But it cannot compensate completely for a rigid wage, and it distorts consumers' choices. It would be better for the government to intervene at a point closer to the basic problem by subsidizing firms to hire workers at the rigid wage.

There is sometimes a case for using tariffs to help infant industries that can expect to cut their costs by reaping economies of scale or learning from experience. But the argument is frequently abused in practice, and there are better ways to help an infant industry. When analyzed closely, moreover, the infant-industry argument turns into a statement about capital markets. If an industry gives promise of being competitive when it grows up, it should be able to borrow during its infancy. If it cannot do so, because of imperfections in the capital market, the government should give it credit rather than protection. There is likewise a case for promoting exports of new products by subsidizing research and development. Competition among governments, however, can lead to welfare losses, as in the case of ordinary export subsidies and the use of an optimum tariff.

When countries form a customs union, they impose no tariffs on imports from the other members and impose a common tariff on imports from the outside world. The welfare effects on the world as a whole depend on the production and consumption effects. A union is more likely to raise the welfare of its members and raise world welfare when the production effects are trade creating rather than trade diverting—when goods from low-cost sources replace goods from high-cost sources.

RECOMMENDED READINGS

On optimum tariffs and retaliation, see Tibor de Scitovszky, "A Reconsideration of the Theory of Tariffs," *Review of Economic Studies*, 9 (Summer 1942), reprinted in American Economic Association, *Readings in the Theory of International Trade* (Philadelphia: Blakiston, 1949).

For more on retaliation, see Harry G. Johnson, "Optimum Tariffs and Retaliation," *Review of Economic Studies*, 21 (1953–54), reprinted in H. G. Johnson, *International Trade and Economic Growth* (London: George Allen & Unwin, 1958), ch. 2.

On tariffs and the income distribution, see the paper by Mussa listed at the end of Chapter

5 and the paper by Stolper and Samuelson listed at the end of Chapter 6.

There has been much work on tariffs and other policies to deal with domestic distortions. Three papers are especially relevant to the treatment in this chapter: Harry G. Johnson, "Optimal Trade Intervention in the Presence of Domestic Distortions," in R. E. Caves et al., eds., *Trade, Growth and the Balance of Payments* (Chicago: Rand McNally, 1965); Jagdish N. Bhagwati, "The Generalized Theory of Distortions and Welfare," in J. N. Bhagwati et al., eds., *Trade, Balance of Payments and Growth* (Amsterdam: North-Holland, 1971), ch. 4; and Richard

A. Brecher, "Optimum Commercial Policy for a Minimum-Wage Economy," *Journal of International Economics*, 4 (May 1974). All three are reprinted in J. N. Bhagwati, ed., *International Trade: Selected Readings* (Cambridge, Mass.: MIT Press, 1981), chs. 11–13.

The infant-industry argument is dissected in R. E. Baldwin, "The Case Against Infant-Industry Tariff Protection," *Journal of Political Economy*, 77 (May/June 1969).

The modern theory of customs unions is surveyed in R. G. Lipsey, "The Theory of Customs Unions: A General Survey," *Economic Journal*, 70 (September 1960), reprinted in American Economic Association, *Readings in International Economics* (Homewood, Ill.: Richard D. Irwin, 1968), ch. 16.

Recent contributions to customs-union theory are reviewed and extended in P. J. Lloyd, "3 × 3 Theory of Customs Unions," *Journal of International Economics*, 12 (February 1982).

CHAPTER

11

THE POLITICAL ECONOMY
OF
INTERNATIONAL TRADE

INTRODUCTION

Chapters 9 and 10 reviewed the major arguments for restricting trade. Trade restrictions usually turn out to be inefficient instruments. Nevertheless, governments continue to use them, and many new trade barriers have been erected recently. This chapter looks at the reasons. It starts with a brief history of tariff policy in the United States and Europe, leading up to the years of trade liberalization after World War II. It turns next to the problem of injury from import competition and the retreat from trade liberalization that started in the 1970s. It also examines special problems in trade policy, including those arising from domestic farm policies and difficulties faced by the less-developed countries.

TARIFF THEORY AND TARIFF HISTORY

At one time or another, every tariff argument has been invoked in debates about trade policy. Tariff history is also the history of tariff theory, showing how theory can affect policy.

Divergent Trends: 1815–1860

The infant-industry argument was very popular in the United States during the first half of the nineteenth century. The country had just started its industrial development, and its new manufacturers sought protection from foreign competition. In Great Britain, distributional arguments for tariffs were used for the opposite purpose, to justify reductions in existing tariffs. The

United States was moving toward protection. Great Britain was moving toward free trade.

The United States had taxed imports from the start. But its early tariffs, though protective in effect, were designed mainly to raise revenue for the federal government. Because there was no income tax, the government relied on excise taxes, and tariffs were the most important. Import tariffs were fairly easy to collect; one had merely to police the ports and coastline. It would have been even easier to tax the country's major exports, cotton and tobacco, but the Southern states that grew them had insisted that the U.S. Constitution prohibit export taxes. They feared that the federal government would be dominated by the more populous Northern states and would pay its bills by taxing Southern produce.

After the War of 1812, however, manufacturers in New England and the Middle Atlantic states demanded additional protection. Transatlantic trade had been disrupted for more than a decade. Jefferson's Embargo had tried to prevent the impressment of American sailors by keeping them from going to sea and had cut off imports of British textiles and hardware. The embargo and the War of 1812 were equivalent to *prohibitive* tariffs on imported manufactures. With the coming of peace and resumption of trade, British goods began again to cross the Atlantic, and American producers lost ground. Despite opposition from the South, which wanted to import cheaper foreign manufactures, Congress imposed higher tariffs on textiles in 1816 and on iron, cutlery, and glass in 1824.

The North–South controversy over tariffs reached a peak in 1828. Southern Congressmen tried to outmaneuver their Northern opponents by amending a pending tariff bill; they added high tariffs on raw wool and other crude materials, hoping that Northern manufacturers, who

used those materials, would reject the whole bill. But the strategem failed and the bill became law. Its effect is shown clearly in Figure 11-1. Tariff rates soared, and the bill was promptly dubbed the Tariff of Abominations. It inspired South Carolina's Ordinance of Nullification, which proclaimed a state's right to abrogate federal legislation, asserting that "the tariff law of 1828, and the amendment to the same of 1832, are null and void and no law, nor binding upon this State, its officers and citizens." The constitutional issue was not settled until the Civil War, but the furor over tariff policy died down with the passage of a compromise in 1833.

In the 1840s, the federal government developed an embarrassing budget surplus, and Congress cut tariffs to reduce tax revenues. The average rate of duty fell toward 25 percent as tariffs were cut sharply in 1846 and again in 1857. But the United States was still out of step with Europe, which was moving faster toward free trade.

The free-trade movement started in Great Britain as part of a broader assault on the powers of the aristocracy. It sought to end the political dominance of the rural gentry, who were the main beneficiaries of the tariffs on imported grain, known as the Corn Laws. As in the United States, the debate about tariff policy was entangled in constitutional questions, including the issue of Parliamentary reform. But the free-trade movement was also inspired by the arguments of classical economists. It invoked the *allocative* argument for free trade that Adam Smith had formulated 50 years before and David Ricardo had refined just before the debate about the Corn Laws:

Under a system of perfectly free commerce, each country naturally devotes its capital and labour to such employments as are most beneficial to each. This pursuit of individual advantage is admirably connected with the universal good of the whole. By stimulating industry, by

FIGURE 11-1   Average U.S. Tariff Rates on Dutiable Imports
Legislation raising U.S. tariffs is usually reflected in an increase in the
average rate, and legislation reducing them is usually reflected in a decrease. *Source:* U.S. Department of Commerce, Bureau of the Census, *Historical
Statistics of the United States,* and *Statistical Abstract of the United States,* 1986,
1987.

rewarding ingenuity, and by using most ef-
ficaciously the peculiar powers bestowed by nature, it distributes labour most effectively and
most economically. . . . It is this principle which
determines that wine shall be made in France
and Portugal, that corn shall be grown in America and Poland, and that hardware and other
goods shall be manufactured in England.[1]

The free-trade movement relied even
more heavily on a *distributive* argument

---

[1] David Ricardo, *On the Principles of Political Economy and Taxation,* 1817, ch. vii. Ricardo had attacked
the Corn Laws in an earlier work, *An Essay on the
Influence of a Low Price of Corn on the Profits of Stock,*
published in 1815, which set out the *distributive* argument discussed shortly.

against the Corn Laws, an argument that
can be extracted from the modified Ricardian model developed in Chapter 5. Suppose that Great Britain produces corn
using land and labor and produces hardware using capital and labor. Land and
capital are specific factors, but labor is perfectly mobile between industries. Suppose
that Great Britain imports corn and has a
tariff on it. Finally, assume that workers
consume corn but little or no hardware, an
assumption used frequently by classical
economists. If Great Britain removed its
tariff on corn, the relative price of corn
would fall. Therefore, landlords' rents
would fall in terms of cloth and hardware,

and capitalists' profits would rise. Workers' wages would rise in terms of corn and fall in terms of hardware, but workers would gain because they consume mainly corn. Ricardo and his colleagues went farther, saying that workers would gain in *two* ways. First, free trade would raise real wages directly by making corn cheaper. Second, it would increase the demand for labor by raising profits and encouraging investment.

Great Britain had started toward free trade in the eighteenth century, and the Tory government continued the process after the Napoleonic Wars. It abolished tariffs on many raw materials without provoking the rural gentry, who did not produce those materials. During the next decade, however, attention turned to grain, a more explosive issue. In 1842, the Tory government of Sir Robert Peel refused to repeal the Corn Laws, taking the side of the gentry. But the Irish famine of 1845–1846 forced Peel to reverse himself and allow larger imports of grain. He suspended the Corn Laws in 1845 and split the Tory party by repealing them permanently a year later.

The Triumph and Decline of Free Trade: 1860–1914

To move farther toward free trade, Great Britain turned to diplomacy. In the Cobden–Chevalier Treaty of 1860, Britain and France agreed to *reciprocal* tariff cuts, including a reduction in British taxes on French wines. The French, in turn, negotiated tariff treaties with other European countries and with the *Zollverein*, the German customs union.

The treaties of 1860–1870 had two effects. First, they made new tariff cuts, enlarging world markets. Second, they generalized tariff cuts that countries had already made, because they included the *most-favored-nation clause*, the key provision in commercial treaties, under which the

parties give each other *all* of the concessions that they give to any other country.[2] Under this clause, France gave the *Zollverein* the concessions given to Great Britain under the Cobden–Chevalier Treaty. The *Zollverein* was not obliged to make concessions in return but had to give France all of the concessions it had given or would give to other countries.

Within 10 years, however, the free-trade movement was defeated by shifts in political and economic circumstances. The 1870s witnessed a sharp change in European views concerning the benefits and costs of colonies. Imperialist sentiment had died down after the Napoleonic Wars, and no new colonies were acquired during the next 50 years, apart from French acquisitions in North Africa. In the early 1870s, however, European governments started again to scramble for tropical real estate. The partition of Africa was completed in two decades, and there was new rivalry in the Near East and Orient. Bellicose nationalism captured European politics and soon led to the use of tariffs to protect domestic industries, especially those needed to make armaments.

At about the same time, European agriculture began to face new competition, as railroads and steamships brought wheat from the United States, Argentina, and Russia to compete with German and French grain. Germany had long been an exporter of grain but became an importer when farm prices fell. European farmers and landlords had favored free trade, like their counterparts in the American South,

---

[2] The name of the clause is a bit misleading. It sounds like a promise of preferential treatment. It is instead a promise that no *other* country will be given preferential treatment (i.e., that the partner will receive treatment no less favorable than that given to any other country). The clause is the basis of modern commercial diplomacy and appears in the General Agreement on Tariffs and Trade (GATT) discussed later in this chapter.

but changed their minds when they encountered import competition. The balance of political power swung toward protection.

The tide turned first in Germany in 1879. Six years earlier, Bismarck had abolished the tariff on imported iron and announced that tariffs on iron products would be abolished soon. He was forced to backtrack, however, when landlords in Prussia and farmers in Bavaria united to support manufacturers in the Ruhr and Rhineland. Bismarck introduced a new tariff law in 1879, giving more protection to industry and agriculture.

German protectionists invoked the infant-industry argument. In fact, a German, Friedrich List, produced the most elaborate version of that argument. List had lived in the United States and was impressed by the growth of American industry behind high tariff walls. He returned to Germany a passionate advocate of protection. List conceded that free trade is best from a cosmopolitan standpoint, but he said that a nation should not be guided by allocative arguments until it has developed its domestic industries and can export manufactures instead of raw materials. Only then can it prosper by benefiting fully from the international division of labor.

List's views about the gain from trade are easily refuted. Countries such as Denmark, Australia, and New Zealand export agricultural products but have higher living standards than many other countries. Furthermore, List's argument contains a contradiction. If all countries tried to export manufactures, the terms of trade would turn against them; the prices of raw materials would rise, and some countries would find it advantageous to export them. Nevertheless, List's argument won the day in Germany.

France was quick to follow Germany. Manufacturers and farmers united to reverse the low-tariff policies of Napoleon III and enact the Meline Tariff of 1892 designed to promote industrial development. The French economy grew rapidly thereafter, but the Meline Tariff cannot take credit. It may instead have handicapped the iron and steel industry, by levying a high tax on coal and thus raising the costs of producing iron. In the language of Chapter 9, the tariff on coal reduced the effective tariff on iron.

The resurgence of protectionism was followed by tariff warfare. In 1902, for example, Germany raised its tariffs to increase its bargaining power, and it peppered its tariff schedule with artificial distinctions to conserve its power. To distinguish Swiss from Danish cattle, the 1902 tariff had a separate category applying to "brown or dappled cows reared at a level of at least 300 metres above sea level and passing at least one month in every summer at an altitude of at least 800 metres." As Danish cattle cannot graze at those altitudes, German negotiators were able to reduce the German tariff on Danish cattle without automatically reducing the tariff on Swiss cattle *via* the most-favored-nation clause.

American tariffs did not come down as far as European tariffs and they turned upward earlier. In 1861, Congress passed the Morrill Tariff Act, raising rates on iron and steel products; in 1862 and 1864, it raised other duties. The new rates were not meant to be protective but merely to deny foreign producers an unfair advantage over domestic producers. To finance the Civil War, Congress had imposed high excise taxes on many domestic products and raised tariffs to offset them. When the war ended, however, government spending fell, and the domestic taxes were allowed to lapse, but the wartime tariffs were not repealed. Therefore, they came to be highly protective. In 1890, moreover, the McKinley Tariff raised rates to a postwar peak. (They were brought down slightly during Grover Cleveland's second term, when control of Congress passed briefly to the Democrats, but a Republican Congress raised them again in 1897.)

After 1900, the Republican party seemed to edge away from the extreme protectionism that had been one of its chief tenets. Its 1908 platform declared that

the true principle of protection is best maintained by the imposition of such duties as would equalize the difference between the cost of production at home and abroad, together with a reasonable degree of profit.

This formula looked rather reasonable and was reflected in the Payne–Aldrich Tariff of 1909, which cut some duties slightly. But trade theory points to an obvious flaw in this "scientific" principle. Differences in costs of production are the very basis for trade, and a tariff designed to offset them will therefore prohibit trade, except in farm products which need special climates, and in raw materials which can be produced only where nature put them. If costs of production are equalized, transport costs will usually suffice to prohibit trade in manufactures.

Collapse and Reconstruction: 1914–1939

On the eve of World War I, the Wilson administration cut tariffs sharply and added many items to the "free list," including iron, coal, wool, lumber, and newsprint. But the war, the peace settlement, and shortsighted policies disrupted trade patterns and burdened many countries with heavy debts, and protectionist pressures began to build up everywhere.

The peace settlement lengthened Europe's frontiers by more than 12,000 miles by cutting up the Hapsburg Empire into a half-dozen states—Austria, Czechoslovakia, Hungary, and the rest—and tariff walls were built along the new borders. Great Britain had sold foreign assets during the war to pay for imports of arms and food and was therefore deprived of earnings

that had offset the gradual decline in the competitive position of British industry. Furthermore, Britain and France had borrowed heavily in the United States to pay for war materiel, and Germany was saddled with huge reparation payments by the Versailles Treaty. In the United States, industries that had expanded during the war feared foreign competition with the coming of peace. Farmers were apprehensive, too, not only in the United States but in many other countries. They had been encouraged to grow large crops during the war, confronted intense competition after it ended, and experienced adverse terms of trade throughout the 1920s.

One by one, governments erected new trade barriers. Some raised their tariffs. Others used quotas and other nontariff barriers. The new nations of Central Europe led the way but were not alone. Germany imposed high tariffs on farm products in 1925. Countries in Latin America, burdened by debts and adverse terms of trade, applied tariffs and quotas more freely than before. Britain abandoned free trade in 1919 and succumbed completely to protectionism in 1931, amidst the worldwide economic crisis.

The United States should have lowered its tariffs after World War I to allow other countries to earn the dollars they needed to service their debts. Instead, Congress voted to increase tariffs during the first postwar recession. The Fordney–McCumber Tariff of 1922 was designed to help farmers, but it also helped "war babies" such as the chemicals industry. Eight years later, Congress passed the Hawley–Smoot Tariff, once called the "Holy-Smoke Tariff" by a student with keener insight than memory. Hearings on tariff reform began in 1929, concerned once again with helping farmers. But then the economy started its sickening slide into the Great Depression, and one industry after another demanded protection to stimulate domestic production.

When the new tariff bill came before Congress, there was an orgy of logrolling. Congressmen traded votes, seeking higher tariffs for their own constituents, and when they were done, the United States had the highest tariff in its history.

The early 1930s gave birth to more trade barriers. Shut out of American markets by the Hawley-Smoot Tariff and concerned to defend their domestic economies from the spread of the depression, governments restricted imports. Each in turn frustrated its neighbors' efforts; a cut in one country's imports was, of course, a cut in other countries' exports. As a result, world trade recovered less vigorously than world production. Indeed, it was a drag on recovery rather than a stimulant. World imports in 1938 were only half as large as they had been in 1928.

U.S. tariffs started to decline after 1932. Part of the reduction was due to the increase in prices that took place during recovery. Many U.S. tariffs were *specific* duties, fixed in cents per pound, dollars per dozen, and so on; when the prices of dutiable products rose, their *ad valorem* (percentage) equivalents fell.[3] But some of the reduction in U.S. tariffs reflected a major turnabout in policy. Seeking ways to stimulate production and employment, the Roosevelt administration turned to world markets, launching a campaign to cut trade barriers so as to expand U.S. exports.

In 1934, President Roosevelt asked Congress for the power to negotiate bilateral trade agreements. The United States would cut its tariffs by as much as 50 percent in return for equivalent cuts by other countries. The president told Congress

A resumption of international trade cannot but improve the general situation of other countries, and thus increase their purchasing power. Let

us well remember that this in turn spells increased opportunity for American sales. . . . Legislation such as this is an essential step in the program of national economic recovery which the Congress has elaborated during this past year.

Roosevelt promised that reciprocal tariff cuts would not hurt American producers by opening domestic markets to competitive imports. In effect, he foreswore the allocative gains from freer trade; he was looking instead for the output and employment effects of expanded exports. Having made a mess of tariff policy in 1930, when the legislative process got out of control, and deeply worried about the Depression, Congress gave the president the power he requested.

The United States negotiated 31 reciprocal trade agreements before World War II and extended its concessions to many other countries under the most-favored-nation clause. The Trade Agreements Program resembled the network of trade treaties that spread out from France after 1860. Unlike that earlier network, it did not bring the world close to free trade. But it helped to arrest the worldwide increase in trade barriers that was choking world trade. Furthermore, it broke an historic pattern. After every other major war, U.S. tariffs rose, but the Trade Agreements Program held them down after World War II.

THE MULTILATERAL APPROACH TO TRADE LIBERALIZATION

During World War II, governments put strict controls on trade and payments to keep their citizens from spending foreign currencies needed to buy food and war materiel. Many carried their controls into the postwar period to save scarce foreign currencies for reconstruction. Early in the war, however, they began to draw up plans for liberalizing peacetime trade and payments. Even before fighting ceased, they estab-

---

[3] A $2 tariff on a $20 product works out at 10 percent ad valorem; if the price of the product rises to $40, the tariff falls to 5 percent ad valorem.

lished two new institutions, the International Monetary Fund (IMF) and the International Bank for Reconstruction and Development (IBRD), commonly known as the World Bank, to manage the monetary system and encourage international lending. They also made plans to reduce trade barriers.

The American Initiative: Universality and GATT

The wartime planners drew on American experience with the Trade Agreements Program but tried to correct its flaws. Under that program, for example, bargaining took place bilaterally and thus sequentially, and governments were fearful of making large tariff cuts because they had to hoard their bargaining power. Therefore, the wartime planners adopted a *multilateral* approach. When bargaining takes place multilaterally and thus simultaneously, each participant can keep track of the concessions it is likely to receive, those it will receive directly in exchange for its own and those it will receive indirectly under the most-favored-nation clause. The prewar program, moreover, had dealt mainly with tariffs, and the wartime planners wanted to eliminate quotas and other nontariff barriers that countries had erected during the Depression and the war. Quotas block imports absolutely, preventing price changes from affecting trade patterns, and they had been used in the 1930s to nullify negotiated tariff cuts by keeping out the imports attracted by the tariff cuts. Therefore, the wartime planners tried to design a comprehensive approach to trade liberalization.

The new approach found its first expression in wartime agreements between the United States and Great Britain—the Atlantic Charter and the Lend-Lease Agreement under which the United States gave aid to Britain before its own entry into the war. It was then embodied in a charter for

an International Trade Organization (ITO) to be affiliated with the United Nations. But the charter was not ratified by the U.S. Senate, and the ITO never came into being. Its charter had antagonized foes of international cooperation, who charged that the ITO would meddle in domestic economic matters. It had disappointed advocates of cooperation, who warned that no country would be bound by the rules because exceptions and qualifications had swamped the principles.

In 1947, however, the major trading countries agreed on rules for reducing tariffs and convened the first of many tariff-cutting conferences. That agreement has survived and is known as the General Agreement on Tariffs and Trade (GATT). Its heart is the most-favored-nation clause, under which each tariff bargain made at a GATT meeting is extended to all members. Its rules discourage withdrawals of concessions, because countries injured by a increase in a member's tariffs are entitled to retaliate by withdrawing concessions made to the offending member. (Unfortunately, the practices and language of GATT perpetuate an ancient fallacy. Because governments have to contend with protectionist pressures, they treat reductions in their tariffs as concessions made to foreigners, rather than achievements for their own consumers and for the efficient use of their own resources. Mercantilist notions about national advantage interfere with clear thinking about comparative advantage.)

The rules of GATT outlaw discriminatory practices and prohibit the use of import quotas except by countries experiencing balance-of-payments problems or by those imposing comparable quotas on domestic producers—crop ceilings on farmers, for example, imposed in conjunction with domestic price-support programs. There are exceptions, moreover, for less-developed countries which permit them to protect infant industries. In addition,

GATT members have drawn up codes of conduct to deal with dumping, subsidies, and other "unfair" practices. These are discussed later in this chapter.

Congress passed another Trade Agreements Act in 1945, authorizing the president to cut U.S. tariffs in GATT negotiations, and five rounds of bargaining were completed between 1947 and 1961. The largest cuts were made in 1947 and 1948, and they are reflected in Figure 11-1. They used up most of the president's powers, however, and Congress became increasingly reluctant to give him more when it was asked periodically to extend the Trade Agreements Act.

When President Roosevelt proposed the Trade Agreements Program in 1934, he promised that no injury would befall American industry. Accordingly, an *escape clause* was written into bilateral trade agreements in the 1930s, allowing the United States to withdraw tariff cuts when American firms were injured by imports. President Truman promised to continue this practice when he asked for more tariff-cutting powers in 1945. But Congress was not satisfied, and the president had to introduce formal procedures for dealing with injury from import competition. The Tariff Commission (now known as the International Trade Commission) would hold hearings whenever American producers charged that tariff cuts had exposed them to injury. When it found evidence of injury, it would recommend a higher tariff or some other way to limit imports. The president could set aside its recommendations, but this would put him on the defensive, because he would be seen to be allowing injury.

In the 1950s, however, protectionist pressures intensified in the United States. With the reconstruction of war-damaged industries in Europe and Japan, American producers began to experience vigorous foreign competition for the first time in decades. Furthermore, a major political shift had occurred in Congress, reminiscent of the shifts in Germany and France during the 1870s. Industrial development had spread to the South, and Southern Congressmen began to retreat from their historic opposition to high tariffs. In 1951, Congress wrote an escape clause into the Trade Agreements Act itself, tightening procedures and listing criteria that the Tariff Commission should employ when judging a complaint of injury from import competition:

> In arriving at a determination . . . the Tariff Commission, without excluding other factors, shall take into consideration a downward trend of production, employment, prices, profits, or wages in the domestic industry concerned, or a decline in sales, an increase in imports, either actual or relative to domestic production, a higher or growing inventory, or a decline in the proportion of the domestic market supplied by domestic producers.

An increase in imports was to be regarded as a *measure* of injury, not just a cause, and it did not have to be an absolute increase. A company could ask for additional protection if its sales had grown but imports had grown faster.

In 1955 and 1958, Congress broadened the escape clause and made it harder for the president to reject advice from the Tariff Commission. It also passed the National Defense Amendment quoted in Chapter 9. Furthermore, a number of tariffs were raised in response to recommendations by the Tariff Commission. But trade policy was not a front-page issue in the United States until developments in Europe raised its importance and led to a new round of liberalization.

The European Initiative: Regionalism and the EEC

Soon after the end of World War II, the United States made an unprecedented commitment to the reconstruction of Western Europe, the Marshall Plan. At the same time, it urged European governments to combine their economic and political resources in pursuit of an age-old dream, a United States of Europe. Washington was concerned to strengthen Europe against the threat of Soviet aggression and also to bind Germany into a democratic federation so that it could never again wage war against its neighbors.

At first, the Europeans adopted a *sectoral* approach to economic integration. They established the European Coal and Steel Community, making for free trade in coal and steel and creating a supranational agency to regulate pricing policies and commercial practices. Then they changed their tactics and began to work for a full-fledged customs union. In 1957, six continental countries, France, Germany, Italy, the Netherlands, Belgium, and Luxembourg, signed the Treaty of Rome, establishing the European Economic Community (EEC), or Common Market. They agreed to eliminate all barriers to internal trade and adopt a common external tariff. They also agreed to harmonize domestic policies, lift restrictions on internal movements of labor and capital, and unify eventually their monetary systems. In other words, they wrote a blueprint for comprehensive economic integration, not just for a customs union.

For many Europeans, and Washington as well, ultimate political unification was the chief rationale for the EEC. But its members also hoped to reap economic benefits. They expected to intensify internal competition and thus foster more efficient resource use. They expected to capture economies of scale often associated with large markets and thus strengthen European firms vis-à-vis their large American competitors. The transition was not painless. There was rapid progress initially, and the customs union was completed in 1968,

two years ahead of schedule. But the history of the EEC has been punctuated by disputes and crises. The first crisis occurred in 1963, when France vetoed a British application for membership, and this issue was not resolved until 1973, when Great Britain and two other countries joined the EEC.[4] Disagreements about agricultural policy have caused several crises.

The Treaty of Rome called for a Common Agricultural Policy (CAP) that would ensure a "fair" standard of living for farmers. But farmers are powerful politically in Europe, and it was hard for governments to agree on levels of farm prices and on the financing of price supports. The CAP did not come into being until 1968, when the governments adopted uniform prices for farm products and *variable levies* on imports that keep world prices from undercutting higher suport prices in the EEC. A central fund pays for the price-support programs and subsidizes exports of surplus commodities. Support prices have risen rapidly, however, inflating the costs of the CAP, and some countries have paid much more for the program than their farmers have received. More controversy lies ahead.

The United States encouraged the creation of the EEC but was concerned about its economic effects. Its common external tariff was not higher than the separate national tariffs of its member countries (it was, in fact, an average of those tariffs). Nevertheless, it threatened to divert demand from American exports. Previously,

---

[4] In 1988, Belgium, Denmark, France, Germany, Greece, Ireland, Italy, Luxembourg, the Netherlands, Portugal, Spain, and the United Kingdom were members. The European Economic Community, the Coal and Steel Community, and the European Atomic Energy Authority have been unified and are known as the European Communities (EC). The EC is governed by a commission appointed by the member countries, but important decisions must be approved by a Council of Ministers, in which each country can exercise a veto, in fact if not in law. A European Parliament is elected directly by the voters of the member countries, but it has only limited powers.

exports from the United States to France paid the same French tariff as exports from Germany or Italy; once the EEC was formed, however, goods from Germany and Italy paid no tariff, while goods from the United States had to pay the common external tariff. There was concern about the CAP, too, because it could reduce European imports of American farm products.

The United States had two options. It could treat the EEC as a threat and respond by retreating farther into protection. Alternatively, it could treat the EEC as an opportunity and respond by reviving trade liberalization.

The American Response: The Kennedy Round

In 1961, the Kennedy administration chose trade liberalization and asked Congress for new legislation. A year later, Congress passed the Trade Expansion Act, which gave the president broader tariff-cutting powers than earlier laws. In previous negotiations, the United States had bargained on a product-by-product basis; henceforth, it could make more sweeping offers. The president could cut *all* tariff rates in half if the EEC and other countries were willing to make similar across-the-board cuts. Furthermore, the Trade Expansion Act modified the basic "no injury" rule that had limited the process of trade liberalization.

First, it tightened the criteria that the Tariff Commission was to use when deciding whether domestic producers had been injured. An increase of imports, by itself, would no longer be regarded as a form of injury. The commission was authorized to "take account of all economic factors which it considers relevant," but told to pay particular attention to the "idling of productive facilities, inability to operate at a level of reasonable profit, and unemployment or underemployment." Furthermore, peti-

tioners had to show that "increased imports have been the major factor in causing, or threatening to cause, such injury," and that the increase in imports was "in major part" the result of tariff cuts.

Second, it introduced a new way to deal with injury. Instead of raising tariffs, the president could give *trade adjustment assistance* directly to companies and workers. Companies could obtain tax benefits and low-cost loans to diversify or modernize their operations. Workers could receive supplementary unemployment benefits and assistance in finding new jobs. The benefits for workers are listed in Table 11-1 (which also shows how they were liberalized by the Trade Act of 1974). We will look at experience with adjustment assistance later in this chapter. The main point to note here is the change in principle. Instead of renouncing the allocative gains from trade by restricting imports, the new law sought to capture them by encouraging shifts in the uses of capital and labor. Adjustment assistance can also be viewed as an attempt to compensate those who are hurt by trade liberalization—to redistribute some of the gains from freer trade along lines mentioned frequently in earlier chapters.

New GATT negotiations, known as the Kennedy Round, got under way soon after passage of the Trade Expansion Act but were not completed until 1967. They were interrupted by internal crises in the EEC, and their success was in doubt until the very end, because of disputes between the Europeans and Americans. Disputes about the tariff-cutting process were resolved by an agreement that countries could submit *exceptions lists* showing those tariffs they would not reduce by the full 50 percent that was the target for the Kennedy Round, and most of the subsequent tariff bargaining focused on those lists. Disputes about agricultural issues were harder to resolve, because the Europeans had just adopted the CAP and were not ready to modify it,

TABLE 11.1 Benefits to Workers Under Adjustment Assistance Programs

Item	Trade Act of 1962	Trade Act of 1974
Finding of eligibility Requirement for individual eligibility	International Trade Commission Employment in 78 of prior 156 weeks and with affected firm in 26 prior of prior 52 weeks	Department of Labor Employment with affected firm in 26 of prior 52 weeks
Cash payments	65% of previous weekly earnings but not more than 70% of average weekly earnings in manufacturing	70% of previous weekly earnings but not more than 100% of average weekly earnings in manufacturing
Benefit period	Up to 52 weeks (65 if worker over age 60)	Up to 52 weeks (78 if worker over age 60)
Other benefits Job training and counseling	No special services but access to all other federal programs	Same
Job search allowance	None	$500 maximum
Relocation payments	Reasonable and necessary expenses plus 2.5 times average weekly earnings in manufacturing	80% of reasonable and necessary expenses plus 3.0 times worker's own average weekly wage

Source: Adapted from George R. Neumann, "Adjustment Assistance for Trade Displaced Workers," in D. B. H. Denoon, ed., *The New International Economic Order* (New York: New York University Press, 1979).

while the United States wanted to maintain its share of Europe's grain market. The two sides agreed to disagree so that the Kennedy round would not break down.

In the end, the Kennedy Round was quite successful in reducing tariffs on manufactured products. Two-thirds of the reductions were as large as 50 percent and covered the major industrial countries. Average tariffs on manufactures fell by about 33 percent (because of the exceptions lists, which kept the average cut below 50 percent). But many trade problems had still to be faced, and protectionist pressures were building up again.

Broadening Liberalization: The Tokyo Round

Soon after the Kennedy Round, Congress began to consider bills that would have put import quotas on many products, from textiles to steel. Forty years of trade liberalization were threatened by a new outbreak of congressional initiatives, reminiscent of the 1930 outbreak that led to the Hawley–Smoot Tariff.

The Johnson and Nixon administrations tried at first to mollify the protectionists by negotiating "voluntary" restrictions on Japanese and other exports to the United States. In 1971, however, the Nixon administration adopted a different strategy. In the midst of a monetary crisis described later in this book, it called for a new round of GATT negotiations aimed at trade practices "unfair" to the United States, and it promised to pay particular attention to the concerns of American farmers. In the Trade Act of 1974, Congress gave the president more bargaining power and made other changes in trade policy. Workers were given easier access to adjustment assistance. Companies seeking relief from import competition were no longer required to show that imports are the major cause of their problems or that increased imports are due to tariff cuts.

A GATT meeting in Tokyo in 1973 agreed to an ambitious agenda. There were to be more tariff cuts, special efforts to liberalize trade in farm products, an attempt to reduce nontariff barriers and prepare

TABLE 11-2   Average Tariff Rates Before and After the Tokyo Round

Category	All Industrial Countries[a]	United States	European Community	Japan[b]
Raw materials				
Before	0.8	0.9	0.7	1.5
After	0.3	0.2	0.2	0.5
Percentage cut	*64.0*	*77.0*	*69.0*	*67.0*
Semimanufactures				
Before	5.7	4.5	5.8	6.6
After	4.0	3.0	4.2	4.6
Percentage cut	*30.0*	*33.0*	*27.0*	*30.0*
Finished manufactures				
Before	9.8	8.0	9.7	12.5
After	6.5	5.7	6.9	6.0
Percentage cut	*34.0*	*29.0*	*29.0*	*52.0*
All industrial products				
Before	7.1	6.4	6.6	5.5
After	4.7	4.4	4.7	2.8
Percentage cut	*34.0*	*31.0*	*29.0*	*49.0*

Source: International Monetary Fund, *Developments in International Trade Policy,* 1982, Table 49. Averages are weighted by imports.

[a] Austria, Canada, Finland, Japan, Norway, Sweden, Switzerland, the United States, and the EEC.

[b] Tariff rates are those to which Japan agreed in the Kennedy and Tokyo Rounds. Between the two rounds, however, Japan made unilateral tariff cuts, and the actual reductions to which Japan agreed in the Tokyo Round were therefore smaller than those shown here, averaging about 25 percent for all industrial products.

codes of conduct that would bar unfair trade practices, and an effort to give "special and differential" treatment to exports from the less-developed countries. The Tokyo Round lasted until 1979 and covered a large part of its agenda.[5] Some of its successes and failures are examined in subsequent sections of this chapter, which deal with unfair trade practices, agricultural trade, and the special problems of less-developed countries. We concentrate here on the reductions in tariffs and nontariff barriers.

The tariff cuts were similar in form and size to those in the Kennedy Round. They

are summarized in Table 11-2. Cuts were made across the board, using a formula designed in part to meet complaints made by the Europeans at the start of the Kennedy Round; it called for the largest cuts in the highest tariffs. Had the formula been applied mechanically, it would have cut tariffs by 60 percent, a more ambitious target than the Kennedy Round had adopted. As in that earlier round, however, each country proposed exceptions, and average tariff rates on manufactured goods fell by only 34 percent, a figure close to the average for the Kennedy Round, even though the Tokyo target cut was bigger.

Attempts have been made to estimate the employment effects of the tariff cuts. One of them is summarized in Table 11-3. Reductions in U.S. tariffs will raise U.S. imports and will therefore reduce employment in import-competing domestic indus-

---

[5] At first, the negotiations were known as the Nixon Round, but they were rechristened after the president's resignation. They are known officially as the Multilateral Trade Negotiations (MTN).

TABLE 11-3 Trade and Employment Effects of Tariff Reductions in the Tokyo Round: Results for the United States When Exchange Rates Adjust to Balance Trade Changes

Sector	TRADE (in millions of dollars)			EMPLOYMENT (in thousands of jobs)		
	Exports	Imports	Net	Exports	Imports	Net
All sectors	2,900	2,900	0	147.9	148.2	−0.3
Primary agriculture	47	7	39	6.2	2.9	3.3
Mining	−4	8	−12	1.5	1.7	−0.2
Manufacturing	2,858	2,885	−27	92.6	95.8	−3.2
Services	—	—	—	47.6	47.8	−0.2

Source: U.S. Department of Labor, Bureau of International Labor Affairs, *Trade and Employment Effects of Tariff Reductions Agreed to in the MTN*, 1980, Table C.1. Employment changes in each sector include those induced by tariff cuts on products made by other sectors.

tries (and in industries that sell them raw materials, parts, and services). But reductions in other countries' tariffs will raise U.S. exports and thus raise employment in export industries. To focus on compositional effects and the resulting need to reallocate resources, the study assumes that exchange-rate adjustments will prevent any change in the overall trade balance, so the increase in aggregate exports will balance the increase in aggregate imports. It looks at the resulting changes in employment in the major sectors of the U.S. economy.

Because the trade balance cannot change in this particular study, the change in total employment is tiny, a loss of 300 jobs. But the study predicts large shifts in employment within and between sectors. Cuts in other countries' tariffs on farm products will create an additional 3,300 jobs in American agriculture, but the number of jobs in manufacturing will fall. What will happen within manufacturing? Answers are given in Table 11-4. Large numbers of jobs will be created in some industries, such as those producing office equipment and aircraft, but there will be job losses in other industries, including those producing textiles and apparel. Few gains and losses, however, are as large as 1 percent of the total labor force in the affected industry.

In Chapter 9, we saw that tariffs are more transparent than most other trade barriers, yet decisions made at dockside about classification and valuation can affect the duties that importers must pay. Uncertainty about valuation can be a greater barrier to trade than the level of the tariff rate. One of the new GATT codes of conduct deals with this problem. It calls for the use of prices "actually paid or payable" when valuing goods for tariff purposes. Therefore, it prohibits a controversial practice followed by the United States, use of an American selling price (ASP) to calculate duties on certain commodities.

Chapter 9 called attention to another problem. Governments discriminate against foreign firms when buying goods and services for themselves. In the United States, for example, a foreign firm can win a federal contract only when the lowest bid by a domestic firm exceeds the foreigner's bid by some percentage. For military procurement, the allowable cost margin is as high as 50 percent. In many other countries, contracts have been awarded without bidding, and even when there was competitive bidding, cost margins were not fixed.

During the Tokyo Round, American negotiators pressed for a code of conduct on government procurement, because govern-

TABLE 11-4   Employment Effects of Tariff Reductions in the Tokyo Round: Detail for Selected Manufacturing Industries in the United States

Industry	CHANGE IN NUMBER OF JOBS			Net Change as Percentage of Industry Labor Force
	Exports	*Imports*	*Net*	
Office machinery	9,572	2,345	7,227	2.25
Electrical components	11,793	3,393	8,400	1.96
Aircraft and parts	10,158	5,077	5,081	0.94
Electrical machinery	3,552	1,609	1,943	0.43
Paper products	2,566	1,086	1,480	0.31
Chemicals	2,762	1,899	863	0.28
Metalworking machinery	2,920	2,369	551	0.16
Printing and publishing	3,801	2,066	1,735	0.16
Scientific instruments	3,160	2,738	422	0.13
Nonferrous metals	2,043	1,761	282	0.07
Miscellaneous fabricated metal products	2,151	2,664	−513	−0.10
Primary iron and steel	3,514	4,585	−1,071	−0.12
Rubber and miscellaneous plastics	1,781	2,932	−1,151	−0.17
Electrical lights and wiring	2,281	2,863	−582	−0.27
Lumber products	1,378	2,973	−1,595	−0.27
Radio and television equipment	3,771	5,745	−1,978	−0.33
Furniture	406	2,495	−2,089	−0.40
Apparel	698	8,737	−8,039	−0.56
Fabrics, yarn, and thread	1,777	5,303	−3,526	−0.60
Stone and clay products	791	5,234	−4,452	−0.90
Miscellaneous manufacturing	2,010	10,230	−8,220	−1.84

Source: U.S. Department of Labor, Bureau of International Labor Affairs, *Trade and Employment Effects of Tariff Reductions Agreed to in the MTN,* 1980, Tables C.2 and C.3. Industries in which change due to exports or imports exceeds 2,000 jobs; employment changes in each industry include those induced by tariff cuts on products made by other industries (and sectors).

ments buy large quantities of goods in which the United States has a comparative advantage, such as electronic and transportation equipment, and a new code was drafted after hard bargaining. In countries whose governments adopt the code, specified lists of government agencies must employ competitive bidding and cannot discriminate against firms from other countries whose governments apply the code on a comparable basis. But the code does not cover military procurement or purchases by state and local governments, and most governments do not apply the code to state-owned entities, such as telephone and electricity companies and airlines and railroads. The code makes a start, however, and can be widened gradually.

THE RETREAT FROM TRADE LIBERALIZATION

By launching the Tokyo Round and promising to win "fair" treatment for American producers, the Nixon administration kept Congress from imposing import quotas. During and after the Tokyo Round, however, there was a worldwide retreat from liberal trade policies. Responding to complaints of injury from imports and of unfair practices by foreigners, governments imposed import quotas, persuaded other countries to accept "voluntary" export restraints, and subsidized domestic industries. They promised repeatedly to refrain from using trade controls but broke their promises with increasing frequency.

In 1981, Japanese exports of automobiles were restricted or restrained by countries that account together for two-thirds of those exports, including the United States. In 1982, the United States put quotas on imports of steel from Europe, and the European Community extended or tightened its restrictions on steel imports from Japan, Brazil, Korea, and a dozen other countries. Acting independently of the EEC, France announced that Japanese video recorders would have to pass through a single customs house in the town of Poitiers, where they would be inspected individually. And most of the developed countries maintained or imposed import quotas on textiles and apparel from ¹ess-developed countries.

Why have protectionist pressures mounted so sharply? Why have governments responded by imposing quotas and other nontariff barriers?

Import Competition and Protectionist Pressures

To a significant extent, the new protectionism testifies to the success of trade liberalization. Economies have become more open and more sensitive to global competition. But it also testifies to the poor performance of the world economy in the 1970s and early 1980s. Growth rates of gross national product fell sharply in the major industrial countries:

Year	United States	Europe	Japan
1963–1972	4.0	4.4	10.5
1973–1977	3.0	2.8	4.1
1978–1982	1.3	1.6	4.3
1983–1987	3.5	2.1	3.6

Unemployment rates rose in most countries and rose very steeply in Europe, where the rate reached an average of 10.8 percent in 1986 (compared with 7.0 percent in the United States). When economies grow slowly, adjustments are difficult. Those who lose jobs or markets because of changes in demand, technology, or comparative advantage have trouble finding new ones. Therefore, they seek to protect themselves from dislocation, and they find it easier to mobilize support for actions against their foreign competitors than remedies for other causes of their plight. Furthermore, firms compete aggressively for export markets when domestic markets shrink or stagnate, which makes it even easier for their foreign competitors to mobilize domestic political support for new trade restrictions.

In brief, changes in trade flows are often symptomatic rather than the main cause of an industry's problems, and this was true in two very prominent cases. Yet action against imports was taken in both.

The American steel industry has faced serious problems for many years. The demand for steel has grown slowly, because some of the largest steel-using industries have had troubles too, including the automobile industry, and because steel is being replaced by lighter metals and plastics. The industry has also found it costly to modernize, so productivity has risen more slowly than in other countries. Firms have retired many of their older mills, reducing excess capacity, but too many of the remaining mills are also obsolete. The European industry has had most of the same problems, and both have been exposed to new competition from less-developed countries that have started to export steel.

The American industry began to seek protection in the 1960s and was increasingly successful. In 1968, Japan and several European countries were persuaded to impose "voluntary" export restraints on basic carbon steel. In 1976, Japan accepted an *orderly marketing agreement* on stainless and other specialty steels. Nevertheless, the industry sought additional relief, saying that foreign firms were dumping steel in the American market, selling it below its normal market price. The Carter administration responded by devising a mechanism that was to put a floor beneath the prices of imported steel products and was successful temporarily in holding down imports.

In the early 1980s, however, a worldwide recession cut production deeply in most major steel-producing countries, and mills were working far below capacity. And the end of the recession did not solve the problems of American producers. For reasons examined in later chapters, the dollar began to *appreciate* hugely, which reduced the dollar prices of foreign steel products relative to those of domestic products, and imports rose. The American industry filed for relief under the escape clause and filed numerous complaints against dumping by foreign producers and subsidies by foreign governments. Some of these complaints were dismissed but others were found to be valid, and the United States threatened to impose higher tariffs—antidumping duties to offset abnormally low foreign prices and countervailing duties to offset foreign subsidies. Rather than confront these higher tariffs, the European Community agreed in 1982 to limits exports of steel products to the United States and thus reduce Europe's share of the American market. Quotas were imposed on other steel products in 1983, when the International Trade Commission found that the industry was being injured by them, and the Reagan administration adopted a "comprehensive" approach to steel imports when another such finding was made in 1984.

The president rejected the specific recommendations of the International Trade Commission but announced a program to deal with "unfair" competition, aimed at limiting imports to 18.5 percent of the American market. Exporting countries whose sales to the United States have "surged" in recent years were invited to sign bilateral agreements with the United States, limiting their shares of the American market in exchange for promises by U.S. producers that they would cease to file complaints of unfair competition. Agreements have been signed with many countries, including Japan, Brazil, Mexico, and South Korea. Furthermore, the United States has broadened and extended its 1982 agreement with the European Community.

Europe has also been limiting its steel imports, as part of a "steel crisis plan" initiated in 1977 and designed to support domestic prices and reduce excess capacity. Unlike the United States, it has imposed production quotas on domestic mills and given subsidies to firms that agree in principle to phase out excess capacity. Trade in steel has become very tightly controlled by a network of bilateral restrictions, some of them administered by importing countries and others administered by exporting countries.

The American automobile industry provides another illustration of the widespread tendency to limit imports when domestic firms have been slow to adjust to changing circumstances. In 1980, the United Auto Workers and Ford Motor Company petitioned the International Trade Commission to recommend relief from import competition. The Commission turned them down, ruling that the problems of their industry were due largely to the shift in demand to small, fuel-efficient cars induced by the increase in gasoline prices which the industry had failed to anticipate. But the industry would not take no for an answer. It appealed to the Carter administration, which authorized large payments to workers under the Trade Adjustment Assistance program but refused to limit imports, despite the introduction of bills in Congress that would have imposed quotas on Japanese cars.

In the face of mounting congressional pressure, however, the Reagan administration began talks with Japan that led to an agreement in 1981. Japan would limit its exports to 1.68 million cars per year, a number 8 percent below actual exports in 1981. The agreement was renewed annually until 1985, though the number of cars was raised to 1.82 million during the final year. When it expired, however, Japan announced that it would continue to limit its exports, hoping to discourage restrictive legislation.[6]

The automobile case has several interesting features. First, it appears to contradict conventional trade theory. In 1980, the union and the second-largest firm took the same side of the trade question, asking for relief from import competition. Most trade models, by contrast, predict that labor and capital will take opposite sides. Second, it shows how trade barriers can cause large shifts in the location of production and can change the nature of the product itself. Finally, it shows how costly those restrictions can be.

In the two-factor, two-sector Heckscher–Ohlin model, trade policies that benefit one factor of production are bound to hurt the other. When a country imports capital-intensive goods, an increase in tariffs raises the real return to capital throughout the economy and reduces the real wage. Therefore, owners of capital should favor protection, regardless of the industry in which they have invested, and workers should oppose protection, regardless of the industry in which they are employed.

In the modified Ricardian model, trade policies benefit some specific factors, injure others, and have mixed effects on labor, the mobile factor. An increase in tariffs raises the real return to capital invested in the import-competing industry and reduces its real return in the export industry. The effect on labor depends in part on workers' tastes, because a tariff raises the real wage in terms of the export product but lowers it in terms of the import-competing product.

In the world described by the Heckscher–Ohlin model, unions and companies should disagree decisively about protection. In the world described by the modified Ricardian model, two outcomes are possible: (1) If workers consume large quantities of import-competing goods, they will be hurt by higher tariffs, and unions should oppose protection, together with companies in the export sector. They should thus disagree with companies in the import-competing sector. (2) If workers consume large quantities of export goods, they will benefit from higher tariffs, and unions should favor protection, together with companies in the import-competing sector. They should disagree with companies in the export sector. In both instances, however, unions should agree among themselves; they should not divide along industry lines.

As a matter of fact, unions and companies agree far more frequently than they disagree. Here are the results of a study by Stephen Magee[7] based on congressional hearings:

Industries in which unions and companies agreed about trade policy		19
Favored protection	14	
Opposed protection	5	
Industries in which unions and companies disagreed about trade policy		2

[6] The Japanese authorities may have also wanted to prevent some Japanese firms from raising their shares of the American market at the expense of others; by continuing to limit automotive exports on a firm-by-firm basis, it could stabilize their shares and avoid an intensification of competition among Japanese producers.

[7] Stephen P. Magee, "Three Simple Tests of the Stolper–Samuelson Theorem," in P. Oppenheimer, ed., *Issues in International Economics* (London: Oriel Press, 1978), Tables 3 and 5.

The evidence is thus inconsistent with the forecast made by the Heckscher–Ohlin model; unions and companies agreed overwhelmingly on trade policy. But the evidence is likewise inconsistent with the forecast made by the modified Ricardian model, because unions were not unanimous. They tended to divide along industry lines:

Unions favoring protection		16
In import-competing industries	11	
In export industries	5	
Unions opposing protection		5
In import-competing industries	1	
In export industries	4	

The evidence may favor a version of the modified Ricardian model discussed briefly in Chapter 10, in which *all* factors of production, including labor, are somewhat immobile (specific). In such a model, an increase in tariffs will raise the real incomes of labor and capital employed in import-competing industries and reduce the real incomes of labor and capital employed in export industries.[8]

An important event in recent years, due partly to the 1981 agreement on Japanese cars, was the transfer of Japanese production to the United States. Honda has built an assembly plant in Ohio, Nissan has built one in Tennessee, Toyota as embarked on a joint venture with General Motors to make cars in California, and other plants are due to open soon. Since 1979, foreign manufacturers have committed almost $2 billion to automotive investments and partnerships in the United States. Further-

more, the 1981 agreement led Japanese firms to change their cars substantially. Because the limit on exports to the United States was stated in terms of vehicles, not values, it encouraged Japanese firms to export larger cars on which they could earn bigger profits and to include as standard features many that used to be optional. One study calculates that these changes raised the prices of Japanese cars by an average of $1,032 per car while the agreement was in force.[9] And the changes should be viewed as welfare-reducing quality improvements insofar as they narrowed the range of choice available to American consumers and forced them to buy options they did not really want.

This welfare-worsening quality change is only one small part of the total cost borne by American consumers. Table 11-5 is drawn from a compilation of studies that show how costly protection can be. It includes estimates for steel and cars, just considered, textiles and apparel, considered later, and some of the other products that have been given special protection in recent years. The costs reflect the higher prices paid for imported goods and those paid for domestic goods because trade barriers have permitted American producers to raise their prices on goods that compete with imports. The figure for automobiles, $105,000 per job saved, is lower than other estimates for the auto industry, because methodologies differ from study to study, and it is also lower than the figures for several other industries. But even the lowest number in the table is higher than the annual income of the worker whose job was saved, and some of the numbers are very much higher.

---

[8] There is another possibility, that unions enjoy some monopoly power and can therefore expect to capture for their members part of the increase in their employers' profits conferred by a tightening of import restrictions.

[9] Charles Collyas and Steven Duneway, "The Cost of Trade Restraints: The Case of Japanese Automobile Exports to the United States," *International Monetary Fund Staff Papers,* 34 (March 1987), Table 10.

TABLE 11-5 Cost to the American Consumer of Special Protection for
Selected Industries

Industry	Year in Which Program Began	ANNUAL COST TO CONSUMERS Total (in millions)	Per Job Saved
Specialty steel	1976	520	1,000,000
Nonrubber footwear	1977	700	55,000
Color TV sets	1977	420	42,000
Bolts, nuts and large screws	1979	110	550,000
Automobiles	1981	5,800	105,000
Textiles and apparel	1982	27,000	42,000
Carbon steel	1982	6,800	750,000
Motorcycles	1983	104	150,000

Source: Gary C. Hufbauer, Diane T. Berliner, and Kimberly A. Elliott, *Trade Protection in the United States: 31 Case Studies* (Washington, D.C.: Institute for International Economics, 1986), Tables 1.1 and 1.2.

Trade Adjustment Assistance

If workers were perfectly mobile and other factors of production were not, workers would not be badly hurt by trade liberalization or import competition. Tariff cuts, for example, would raise their real incomes in terms of import-competing goods and lower them in terms of export goods. But these effects would be rather small compared to the costs that workers bear because they are not perfectly mobile. They experience unemployment before they are rehired or move on to new jobs, and their new jobs, when they find them, may pay lower wages.

There are two groups of obstacles to labor mobility. First, there are obstacles to *occupational* mobility. Jobs are not alike, and workers cannot move from job to job without learning new skills. Second, there are obstacles to *geographic* mobility. Table 11-4 predicts that the Tokyo Round will create 5,000 jobs in the aircraft industry and eliminate 4,000 in the apparel industry. But most of the aircraft industry is on the West Coast, and much of the apparel industry is on the East Coast. Workers cannot always move from job to job, even when they have the necessary skills, without also moving

from place to place, and moving is expensive in both monetary and nonmonetary terms. Furthermore, workers who change jobs may lose many benefits, including the seniority that is frequently crucial for future job security. Most workers want to stay where they are, with the same firm in the same place.

In the early 1960s, many labor unions continued to favor trade liberalization, because their members had not started to experience import competition or were heavily involved in export production. But other unions had begun to demand protection. Trade adjustment assistance was introduced in 1962 to win their support for the Trade Expansion Act and the forthcoming Kennedy Round. But it did not work as well as its advocates had promised, and it was not successful politically. One labor leader called it "burial insurance," and the U.S. labor movement turned sharply to protectionism in the 1970s.

The trade adjustment assistance program had two defects. First, it was hard for workers to qualify for benefits. Second, the program helped to maintain workers' incomes when they lost their jobs but was not very effective in promoting adjustment.

TABLE 11-6 Trade Adjustment Assistance

Item	Trade Act of 1962[a]	TRADE ACT OF 1974[b]	
		1975–1980	1981–1985
Workers certified (number)	53,899	1,313,349	179,689
Benefit payments (millions)	$45	$2,455	$1,719
Firms certified (number)	36	972	1,624
Technical assistance (millions)	$1	$53	$80
Financial assistance (millions)[c]	$40	$272	$112

Source: Robert Z. Lawrence and Robert E. Litan, *Saving Free Trade* (Washington, D.C.: The Brookings Institution, 1986), Table 3-6.

[a] Figures for workers are for period from October 1962 through March 1975 (when the 1974 Trade Act took effect); figures for firms omit the first few years of the program).

[b] Figures are for periods from April 1975 through September 1980 and from October 1980 through April 1985 (for workers) and August 1985 (for firms).

[c] Includes loans, loan guarantees, and grants.

Under the program introduced in 1962, workers and companies had to prove to the International Trade Commission that they had been hurt by import competition resulting from earlier tariff reductions; they had to satisfy the tight criteria introduced by the Trade Expansion Act. Those criteria made good sense but had an unintended consequence. Few workers and companies could meet them completely, so trade adjustment assistance was not given a fair test and could not accumulate political support. The history of the program is summarized by Table 11-6. From 1962, when it was introduced, to 1974, when it was modified, the International Trade Commission certified fewer than 54,000 workers, who received only $45 million in benefits, and the program for companies was even smaller.

This first defect was corrected by the Trade Act of 1974, which transferred adjustment assistance for workers from the International Trade Commission to the Department of Labor and made access easier (see Table 11-1). Many more workers received assistance, and outlays rose hugely. (Much of the increase in numbers and dollars is explained by the certification of auto workers; although they failed to persuade

the International Trade Commission that they had been injured by import competition, they qualified for trade adjustment assistance under the rules administered by the Department of Labor.)

There have been several studies of the program, including one that interviewed some 950 workers who received trade adjustment assistance (TAA) and compared their histories with those of workers who received ordinary unemployment insurance (UI) benefits.[10] It tends to confirm the assertion made previously, that adjustment assistance compensated workers for the costs of unemployment but was less effective in fostering adjustment by training workers or finding them new jobs. The incomes of unemployed workers were maintained at three quarters of the levels earned before the workers lost their jobs. But TAA recipients were unemployed for longer periods than UI recipients and more likely to drop out of the labor force. They were less likely to change occupations or industries

---

[10] J. David Richardson, "Trade Adjustment Assistance Under the United States Trade Act of 1974: An Analytical Examination and Worker Survey," in J. N. Bhagwati, ed., *Import Competition and Response* (Chicago: University of Chicago Press, 1982).

when they found new jobs, and they were more likely to take pay cuts. Finally, TAA recipients received less training than UI recipients; only one in 30 took job training in 1975–1979, and only one in 200 received a job-search allowance. Recipients made more use of these services in the early 1980s, but there was a decline in the number of workers finding jobs after training. The number of workers certified for benefits also fell in the 1980s, although the number of firms rose, because the Reagan administration tightened the standards for workers. (It likewise reduced the level of benefits in its effort to curtail domestic programs; workers could receive TAA benefits only after their UI benefits had been exhausted, and their weekly TAA benefits could not exceed their weekly UI benefits.)

CURRENT ISSUES IN TRADE POLICY

The recent history of U.S. trade policy has featured four developments that call for more attention: the more extensive use of quotas, some of them administrated by the United States but most of them administered by its trading partners; complaints about unfair foreign competition; a change in the nature but not the severity of conflict over trade in agricultural goods; and proposals for reducing barriers to trade in various services.

The Growing Use of Quotas

During the first seven years of the TAA program, the International Trade Commission did not certify a single worker for benefits. Tight criteria were largely to blame, but there may be another reason. Many of the workers for whom the program had been designed originally, in the textile, apparel, and shoe industries, were being protected by new trade restrictions.

In 1957, the United States sought to limit textile imports by persuading Japan to impose voluntary export restraints. But imports from other countries, especially Hong Kong, began to replace imports from Japan, and the United States called for an international agreement on trade in cotton textiles. A short-term agreement was concluded in 1961, put on a long-term basis in 1962, and replaced in 1974 by a comprehensive scheme covering all textiles and known as the Multifibre Agreement (MFA). Its stated objective is

to ensure the expansion of trade in textile products, particularly for the developing countries, and progressively to achieve the reduction of trade barriers and the liberalization of world trade in textile products while, at the same time, avoiding disruptive effects on individual markets and on individual lines of production in both importing and exporting countries.

In fact, the MFA serves as an "umbrella" under which importing countries negotiate bilateral agreements with exporting countries to limit trade in textiles and apparel on a country-by-country, product-by-product basis. The United States and EC have agreements of this type with more than twenty other countries, mainly less-developed countries.

The MFA has not stopped trade from growing or kept the less-developed countries from raising their share of world exports (it grew from 22 percent in 1973 to 31 percent in 1983). But the latest set of orderly marketing agreements may slow trade down. In a recent agreement with Hong Kong, for example, the United States limited the yearly growth of imports to 0.5 percent on two-thirds of the products covered and to 2.0 percent on the remaining products.

The less-developed countries object strongly to the way that the MFA has been interpreted. They charge that the developed countries have failed to fulfill the long-term objective of liberalizing trade in textiles and apparel, and that the MFA violates the spirit of the GATT because it is discriminatory. They are right but are not likely to achieve their aims. The industry is too important in too many countries. It is, in fact, the largest industrial employer in the world and accounts for more than 10 percent of total industrial employment in the developed countries.

The MFA established an important precedent. In the Trade Act of 1974, Congress authorized the use of orderly marketing agreements instead of higher tariffs to deal with injury from import competition, and large parts of world trade are now covered by them or by voluntary export restraints. They have been applied widely by the United States and the European Community, not only to textiles, apparel, and footwear but also to automobiles, iron and steel, television sets, other electronic products, and many agricultural commodities. Table 11-7 shows how much trade they cover but understates their coverage because it does not include the most recent restrictions on trade in steel (or an agreement between Japan and the United States to regulate trade in microchips). Note that

the restrictions apply very heavily to the exports of less-developed countries, a point made again by Table 11-8, which summarizes information from three Asian countries on quantitative barriers that limit their access to the world's major markets.

These restrictions are particularly worrisome. First, they are more rigid than tariffs because they do not allow changes in relative costs to influence trade patterns. If an exporter's costs of production fall, the volume of its exports cannot rise, nor can it capture part of the ongoing growth of demand in the importing country unless the restrictions on its exports are cast in terms of market share. Second, they tend to be discriminatory because they are usually imposed on a country-by-country basis. The United States and the European Community do not restrict each other's exports of textiles and apparel, but both restrict imports from the less-developed countries. For this reason, incidentally, quotas tend to spread; countries not covered initially expand their exports at the expense of those that are covered, until quotas are applied to them too. Third, quotas are often applied outside the GATT framework, just as they were in the 1930s to limit or nullify the ef-

TABLE 11-7   Shares of Imports Subject to Nontariff Barriers, 1985

Category	United States	European Community	Japan
Agricultural goods	11.5	37.8	33.8
From industrial countries	11.7	46.7	35.7
From developing countries	11.8	27.5	30.2
Manufactured goods	5.8	10.1	5.4
From industrial countries	2.7	5.7	5.5
From developing countries	14.4	21.4	5.4

Source: Bela Balassa and Constantine Michaelopoulos, *Liberalizing World Trade* (Washington, D.C.: World Bank, 1985), Table 3. Figures for the United States make no allowance for the continuation by Japan of limitations on automobile exports or the imposition of additional restrictions on steel imports in 1986; figures for imports from industrial and developing countries may not average to worldwide figures because the latter also include imports from Eastern Europe.

TABLE 11-8   Quantitative Restrictions Reported by Three Exporting Countries

Restrictions Imposed by	Reported by India	Reported by Korea	Reported by the Philippines
Canada	Textiles, apparel, footwear; leather garments	Textiles, footwear; leather garments	Coffee, sugar, beer
EC and member countries	Textiles, apparel, footwear; iron and steel	Textiles, silk fabrics, footwear; newsprint; iron and steel; radios and TV sets; semiconductors; watches; toys	Coffee, fruit, sugar, tobacco; textiles; tableware; ceramics
Japan	Footwear	Fish, fruit, seaweed products; textiles, apparel, silk and silk products; leather goods; chemicals; cosmetics	Fish, fruit, oilseeds, tobacco; footwear
United States	Apparel	Textiles; iron and steel	Textiles

Source: International Monetary Fund, *Trade Policy Issues and Development,* 1985, Tables 76–78. Restrictions include all quotas, voluntary export restraints, administrative guidance (practiced by France and Japan), and outright prohibitions, regardless of the reason for them. Antidumping and countervailing duties are omitted.

fects of tariff cuts under the Trade Agreements Program. As a consequence, they are not supervised or made to comply with international guidelines, and they undermine the authority of the GATT as the watchdog of the trading system.

Subsidies and Dumping

When the American steel industry brought charges against foreign firms and governments, the U.S. government had to consider them. Under U.S. law, the Commerce Department must look into the facts, and the International Trade Commission must determine the extent of injury to domestic firms. If there is adequate evidence to support a charge of dumping or the use of subsidies, and domestic firms are being hurt, additional tariffs must be imposed (antidumping duties in the one case and countervailing duties in the other).

A prohibition against export subsidies was written into the original GATT, for a reason given in Chapter 9. When governments cut their tariffs or promise not to raise them, they are entitled to expect that other governments will not nullify the effects of the remaining tariffs, which is what export subsidies can do. If the United States has a 10 percent tariff on imported steel, but Brazil gives a 10 percent export subsidy to its steel industry, Brazilian steel will enter the United States at its free-trade price, and the American steel industry will not be protected. Widespread use of export subsidies could undermine the framework for trade liberalization established by the GATT and lead to tariff warfare.

But many countries subsidize their exports indirectly. Examples listed in Chapter 9 included low interest rates on export credits, preferential tax treatment for profits from exports, and output subsidies to export industries (typically in the form of wage subsidies and investment incentives). These practices were not prohibited by the GATT, and they have spread widely. Furthermore, most governments use subsidies to achieve domestic goals—to aid depressed communities or regions, encourage adaptation or modernization in declining industries, retrain unemployed workers, reduce environmental hazards, and encourage research and development. Some of the European subsidies that prompted the complaint by the American steel industry were part of the crisis plan adopted by the EC to modernize the European steel industry. They were not outright export subsidies.

During the Tokyo Round, governments drafted a new code on export subsidies. It broadens the GATT prohibition against export subsidies and tries to deal with domestic subsidies that have similar effects. Such subsidies, it says, may injure an industry in another country or nullify GATT benefits accruing to another country. Governments are not denied the right to use them but must try to avoid adverse effects on other countries' industries. Governments affected by other countries' subsidies, including domestic subsidies, can still impose countervailing duties when their domestic producers are injured.[11]

A prohibition against dumping—selling below normal market price—was included in the GATT because dumping is regarded as a *predatory* practice. By selling at low prices, even taking losses, a strong company can drive weaker rivals out of business and increase its market power. Low prices are good for consumers in the short run, but consumers may lose out in the long run, when the predator exploits its market power. Like many other unfair practices, however, predatory dumping is hard to identify. Companies may charge low export prices for many benign reasons, not to drive competitors out of business.

---

[11] Two sorts of export subsidies are still permitted. Governments may subsidize exports of farm products unless these give their exports "more than an equitable share of world trade" in those products, and a less-developed country may subsidize its manufactured exports but "should endeavor to enter into a commitment to reduce or eliminate export subsidies when the use of such export subsidies is inconsistent with its competitive development needs."

Two tests of dumping are employed by U.S. law and the GATT code:

For the purpose of this Code a product is to be considered as being dumped, i.e., introduced into the commerce of another country at less than its normal value, if the export price of the product . . . is less than the comparable price, in the ordinary course of trade, for the like product when destined for consumption in the exporting country. . . .

When there are no sales of the like product in the ordinary course of trade in the domestic market of the exporting country or when, because of the particular market situation, such sales do not permit a proper comparison, the margin of dumping shall be determined by a comparison with . . . the cost of production in the country of origin plus a reasonable amount for administrative, selling and any other costs and for profits.

The flaws in the two tests are easy to illustrate by cases in which exporters would violate them without having any predatory purpose.

Consider a firm that sells its product in two markets and tries to maximize its long-run profits. Suppose that it has constant costs of production but faces a downward-sloping demand curve in each market. Its situation is described by Figure 11-2. The firm's marginal-cost curve is MC. The demand curve in its home market is AR_h, and the corresponding marginal-revenue curve is MR_h. The demand curve in its export market is AR_f, and the marginal-revenue curve is MR_f. The firm will maximize its total profits when its sales in each market equate the marginal revenue from that market with the firm's (constant) marginal cost. Therefore, it will sell OQ_h in the home market by setting its domestic price at OP_h, and it will sell OQ_f in the export market by setting its export price at OP_f. The firm is not a predator. The prices OP_h and OP_f are long-run profit-maximizing prices. Nevertheless, the firm is violating the first test in the GATT code, because its export price is

FIGURE 11-2 Dumping by a Firm with Monopoly Power
A firm has constant costs of production, so that its marginal-cost curve is
the horizontal line *MC* in each panel of the diagram. The firm has
monopoly power in each market and will therefore maximize profits
when its sales in that market equate marginal revenue with marginal
cost. The panel on the left represents the firm's home market; the demand curve is AR_h, the marginal-revenue curve is MR_h, and the firm will
sell the quantity OQ_h at the price OP_h. The panel in the center represents the firm's export market; the demand curve is AR_f, the marginal-
revenue curve is MR_f, and the firm will sell OQ_f at the price OP_f. As OP_f
is lower than OP_h, the firm will be accused of dumping, even though it
is not exporting at a loss to undercut foreign competitors. If forced to
charge the same price in both markets, it would operate in the manner
described by the panel on the right. The curve AR_c is the (horizontal)
sum of the home and foreign demand curves, and MR_c is the marginal-
revenue curve. The firm will sell OQ_c and charge OP_c. (It will sell OQ_h'
in the home market and OQ_f' in the export market.) The price OP_c is
below the profit-maximizing home price OP_h but above the profit-
maximizing export price OP_f.

lower than the price it charges normally in
its home market.[12]

---

[12] A firm cannot charge different prices in two
markets unless there are barriers to trade between
them. If goods could be shipped freely from one market to the other, someone would buy the firm's products in its export market and ship them back for sale
in the firm's home market. There are, of course, such
barriers, including transport costs and tariffs. (In this
instance, tariffs protect the firm against itself by shel-
tering its home market from the firm's own goods.)

What would the firm do if it could not
"dump" its product? It would add up the
demand curves AR_h and AR_f to obtain the
consolidated demand curve AR_c and the
corresponding marginal-revenue curve
MR_c. It would then sell OQ_c and charge the
price OP_c. (It would sell OQ_h' in its home
market and OQ_f' in its export market.) Note
that OP_c is higher than OP_f and lower than
OP_h. In this instance, the GATT rule
against dumping has the odd effect of

hurting the firm's foreign customers but helping its domestic customers.

The cost-of-production test has a different defect. It penalizes firms that follow the right short-run pricing rule when demand is depressed temporarily. Consider a firm that has high fixed costs of production typical of steel firms and those in other capital-intensive industries. When demand is depressed by a recession or events in the firm's own industry, the firm may be unable to cover its full costs. It should not shut down, however, if it can cover its *variable* costs and have a bit left over to meet some of its fixed costs. If it shut down completely, it would still have to cover all its fixed costs (by borrowing or drawing down cash balances). If it goes on operating, even at low prices, and can cover some fixed costs, it will minimize its losses. Nevertheless, the firm could be accused of dumping because its export prices would be lower than its total unit costs. (The law tries to deal with this possibility by saying that a foreign firm must sell below cost for an "extended time" before being accused of dumping, but the time allowed may be too short to draw the distinction effectively.)

Complaints and actions against dumping have become common in recent years. From 1974 through 1979, the European Community received about 26 complaints per year; from 1980 through 1984, it received about 41 per year. In the same two periods, the United States received 18 per year and 56 per year, respectively. On both sides of the Atlantic, moreover, action was taken in an increasing percentage of cases; in the EC, the percentage rose from 56 to 81 between the two periods. Complaints about subsidies have grown too, with many of them aimed at Japanese practices.

Japan's Ministry of Trade and Industry (MITI) is accused of *industrial targeting:* selecting new products for Japan to export, then choosing and helping companies to make them. MITI does try to guide industrial development, with particular attention to the use of new technologies, but has made some big mistakes, and its influence is probably exaggerated by foreigners who do not understand that MITI is trying to compensate for some of the shortcomings of the Japanese economy:

Most Japanese high-technology companies obtain their financing from banks and government finance agencies, which tend to be very conservative, rather than from the equity markets. In the United States . . ., venture capitalists compete with each other to turn [new] technology into new products, signaling to the rest of the economy that this is an area of potential rewards. MITI plays an equivalent role in Japan, signaling to bankers and corporations through its "visions," as its plans are called, that it favors certain investments. . . .

The cooperative R&D projects sponsored by MITI . . . are similarly misperceived, according to this view. The Japanese educational system, combined with lifetime employment guarantees, produces researchers who are not as well-rounded in their technical background as U.S. personnel. . . . [The] movement of personnel among firms, and the informal exchanges that are typical among employees in U.S. high-technology firms, do not occur in Japan. Technological cross-pollination has been central to U.S. advance. In order to imitate it, MITI has encouraged firms to participate in cooperative research. . . .

Government subsidies to Japanese industry, either through credit or the tax system, have been relatively small. In both Europe and the United States, subsidy programs are much larger. Moreover, the larger Japanese subsidies go to declining industries. . . .

The principal function of Japanese targeting has been to prevent foreign access to a [local] market until the domestic industry has reached the point at which it no longer needed this level of protection. Even here, however, the role of the government should not be overstated.[13]

---

[13] Congressional Budget Office, *The GATT Negotiations and U.S. Trade Policy* (Washington, D.C., 1987), pp. 53–55.

Yet foreign firms complain frequently about hidden barriers to access. Some probably reflect cultural and institutional differences between Japan and other industrial societies that baffle foreigners trying to do business in Japan. Others reflect official and business practices that discriminate against imports. The government and trade associations apply quality and safety standards that foreigners find unnecessarily rigid, and goods that are tested abroad must be tested again in Japan. The government has been slow to apply and extend the GATT code on government procurement, and companies frequently favor local suppliers. American manufacturers of microchips say that their Japanese markets dried up as soon as Japanese chips became available. (In another celebrated case, Japanese baseball teams refused to use imported bats, although Japanese bats tended to break frequently.)

Japan has undertaken to dismantle some of these hidden barriers, but progress has been slow, and some studies warn that the results may not be very large. Japan has a comparative advantage in manufactures and must run a large trade surplus in manufactures if it is to import raw materials.

Farmers and Foreign Trade

Twenty years ago, international disputes about farm policies focused on barriers to trade in grain, meat, cheese, and other temperate-zone products, used by the United States and Europe to prop up the domestic prices of those products. Washington was particularly fearful that the European Community's Common Agricultural Policy would reduce the American farmers' share of European markets. These issues have not been resolved, but new ones have attracted more attention. High prices for farm products have created huge surpluses in Europe, and the EC has been us-ing export subsidies to sell them to other countries. American and European farmers are competing in third countries' markets more intensely than in each other's markets, and the problem is compounded by the fact that many food-importing countries, such as India, have become self-sufficient in many products. There have been famines in Africa, but there is no global shortage of food.

Let us look first at the origins of the problem—domestic agricultural policies in the United States and Europe.

In the United States, the Commodity Credit Corporation (CCC) makes loans to farmers that can be repaid in cash or kind. When market prices are below official support prices, farmers will repay in kind by turning their crops over to the CCC. At one time, support prices for wheat, cotton, tobacco, and many other products were higher than prices in world markets, and the United States restricted imports to hold down the costs of its farm programs. If imports had entered U.S. markets freely, domestic prices would have fallen, and farmers would have turned more crops over to the CCC.

The situation has changed. Table 11-9 contrasts the prices of farm products in the United States, Europe, and Japan by comparing domestic (supported) prices with world (unsupported) prices. In the United States, the domestic prices of coarse grains, meat, and poultry have been roughly equal to world prices, and the price of wheat has not been much higher than the world price. There has been no need to limit imports. The United States continues to impose quotas on imported cotton, peanuts, sugar, butter, and cheese and has import fees on sugar. But it claims to be more sinned against than sinner, because other countries' policies are more restrictive. The prices of most farm products in Europe have been higher than their world prices,

TABLE 11-9   Agricultural Protection in Major Industrial Countries: Ratios of Domestic Producer Prices to World Prices, 1980–1982

Commodity	United States	European Community	Japan
Wheat	1.15	1.25	3.80
Coarse grains	1.00	1.40	4.30
Rice	1.30	1.40	3.30
Beef and lamb	1.00	1.90	4.00
Pork and poultry	1.00	1.25	1.50
Dairy products	2.00	1.75	2.90
Sugar	1.40	1.50	3.00
Weighted average	1.16	1.54	2.44

Source: World Bank, *World Development Report*, 1986, Table 6.1; EC figures omit Greece, Portugal, and Spain. In the United States, consumer prices for wheat and rice were below producer prices (and equal in fact to world prices), but consumer prices for dairy products and sugar were approximately equal to producer prices; in the EC, the consumer price for sugar was above the producer price, but there were no other significant gaps; in Japan, many consumer prices were below producer prices, especially for wheat and coarse grains.

thanks to the Common Agricultural Policy, and Japanese prices have been very much higher.[14]

Some effects of the CAP are shown in Table 11-10. In 1968–1969, the EC countries were self-sufficient in rye and poultry but net importers of many other products. Ten years later, they had reached self-sufficiency in five more product groups, and they had large surpluses of several commodities, including wheat, butter, and sugar. And the trend continued in the early 1980s, leading the EC to promote its agricultural exports by using export subsidies. Such subsidies are not prohibited by the GATT code unless a government uses them aggressively to cut into other countries' market shares. But that is what the EC has been accused of doing, to dispose of surplus grain and dairy products. Coming together with other developments, includ-

---

[14] When world prices fell in the mid-1980s, more gaps opened up between U.S. domestic prices and world prices, but the European and Japanese gaps got bigger, minimizing the change in the comparative situation.

ing the appreciation of the dollar, which made American farm products more expensive for foreigners, the intensification of competition in world markets reduced the American farmers' market share. Look at Table 11-11, which shows what has happened in the grain market. European shares have risen and American shares have fallen.

The domestic costs of the CAP have grown hugely, partly because of rising export subsidies. Total spending on the CAP increased by more than 12 percent per year from 1977 to 1987 and amounts to about two-thirds of the EC budget. It lies at the heart of recent arguments in the EC concerning benefits and burdens of membership. Furthermore, the trade-policy side of the CAP is bound to produce more friction between the EC and the United States, which must count on increasing its exports of farm products to reduce its very large trade deficit and is subsidizing its own exports on a larger scale.

Progress toward more liberal trade in farm products probably requires a new ap-

TABLE 11-10 Self-sufficiency of the European Community in Selected Agricultural Products: Ratios of Domestic Production to Domestic Consumption

Commodity	1968–1969	1978–1979	1981–1982
Wheat	94	108	109
Rye	100	108	127
Corn	45	60	73
Sugar	82	124	144
Cheese	98	103	107
Butter	91	111	122
Beef and veal	90	100	103
Poultry	101	105	110

Source: International Monetary Fund, *Developments in International Trade Policy*, 1982, Table 45, and *Trade Policy Issues and Development*, 1985, Table 42.

proach to the underlying domestic problem. For as long as governments maintain farmers' incomes by propping up farm prices, they will have to limit imports and subsidize exports. The United States has made some progress on this front. It has shifted partially from price supports and CCC loans to direct *deficiency payments* to keep farmers' incomes from falling. But the costs of its farm programs have been rising even faster than those of the EC.

TABLE 11-11 Shares of World Trade in Grain

Commodity and Country	1980–1981	1985–1986
Wheat		
United States	44.5	29.4
Canada	18.1	19.8
Australia	11.3	18.8
European Community	16.7	18.4
Argentina	4.1	7.2
All other	5.3	6.4
Coarse grains		
United States	64.2	43.6
Argentina	13.2	11.6
European Community	5.5	9.6
China	0.0	8.5
Canada	5.1	7.0
All other	12.0	19.7

Source: Congressional Budget Office, *The GATT Negotiations and U.S. Trade Policy*, 1987, Table 6.

Trade in Services

When we think about international trade, we usually concentrate on trade in goods. In 1986, however, the United States earned $51 billion from sales of services, other than the services of capital, which earn dividends and interest; this amount was almost 23 percent of its receipts from exports of goods and services combined. Some $16 billion came from foreign travel in the United States, including passenger fares paid by foreigners to U.S. carriers, and $15 billion more came from other transport services. Fees and royalties accounted for $7 billion, and $13 billion came from other services.

Here is a partial list of business services that governments have submitted to the GATT in connection with forthcoming negotiations on the liberalization of trade in services: advertising, auditing, legal, and other professional services; air transport; banking and related financial services; construction and engineering services; data processing; film distribution; franchising and leasing; hotels, restaurants, and other travel services; insurance; maritime transport; motion picture distribution; securities and commodity trading; and telecommunications. American businessmen have become increasingly interested in reducing barriers to trade in services and have been joined by European and Japanese businessmen.

Barriers to trade in services, however, are different from barriers to trade in goods. Most services are not subject to tariffs or quotas. They are subject instead to various restrictions deeply imbedded in domestic legislation. Some of them are outright prohibitions; foreign ships, for example, cannot carry cargoes from one American port to another, and American ships must be used to carry goods sold or subsidized by the U.S. government. Foreign banks and other financial institutions cannot set up branches in many countries or are barred from certain lines of business. Foreign insurance companies cannot sell policies to other countries' citizens. Accountants, engineers, and other professionals cannot sell their services in foreign countries, even to the local affiliates of their own countries' firms. Many services are closely regulated. International air transport, for example, is governed by a network of bilateral agreements. One country's airlines can use another country's airports only if the other's airlines are given reciprocal rights; fares and frequencies are tightly controlled; and foreign carriers are not allowed to carry passengers between domestic destinations or fly from one foreign country to another.

In other instances, the absence of adequate protection is the most serious problem. Many American firms complain that their copyrights and trademarks are not protected by foreign governments—a problem affecting not only the producers of books, recorded music, and video tapes, but also the producers of computer software and fashionable clothing. Furthermore, producers of motion pictures and television programs complain of discrimi-

nation by foreign distributors and TV networks, which favor local films and programs.

As barriers to trade in services take so many forms, it will be hard for governments to use familiar bargaining techniques when trying to liberalize trade in services. And the problem is made more complicated because some countries have many barriers and others have very few. In fact, those that seek to sell more services, including the United States, are already more open to trade in services than are those to which they want to expand their sales. It will be hard to define reciprocity and even harder to achieve it.

Yet the need for liberalizing is growing more urgent, especially for the United States and other advanced economies that expect to experience intensified competition from developing countries that are starting to acquire a comparative advantage in manufacturing. They must assert their own comparative advantage in advanced technologies, especially in information processing.

The politics of the situation also argue for liberalized trade in services. As American manufacturers encounter more competition in their export and domestic markets, they may become increasingly dissatisfied with the fruits of traditional trade liberalization. Political support for freer trade and opposition to protectionism will have to come not only from consumers, who pay the costs of trade restrictions, but also from the service sector, which can look forward to large benefits from liberalization.

Therefore, the United States is likely to pursue three new objectives in future GATT negotiations: (1) extension of the *right of establishment* and the *principle of national treatment,* so foreigners can set up businesses in other countries and be treated as though they were citizens of those countries, rather than suffer discrimination with regard to their activities, tax treatment, and standing in local courts; (2) agreements much like GATT codes to deal with the special problems of particular sectors, especially the information-processing industries; and (3) adequate copyright and trademark protection for all forms of intellectual property.

TRADE AND ECONOMIC DEVELOPMENT

At a number of points in this chapter, we touched on the trade problems of the less-developed countries. We saw that new trade barriers imposed by the advanced industrial countries have been particularly harmful to the less-developed countries. They have been the chief targets of the MFA, and some of them were hard hit by the new steel quotas. It is not easy for old producers to make room for new competitors; they are more likely to lash back than to move aside. Their resistance, however, has made it harder for the less-developed countries to change their own policies— to abandon inward-looking development strategies based largely on infant-industry protection in favor of outward-looking strategies based on export growth and trade liberalization.

In Chapters 5 and 6, we examined the effects of economic growth on a country's foreign trade but not the other side of the relationship, the effects of trade on growth. Those effects may be more important, however, with extensive policy implications. Trade played a large role in the nineteenth century. It served as an "engine of growth" for many countries, including the United States, shaping their factor endowments and furnishing investment opportunities for foreign as well as domestic capital. John Henry Williams put the point this way:

The development of international trade has been a process in which the countries outside the centre have owed the development of their trade, and indeed their very existence, to the movement, not merely of goods but of capital, labour, and enterpreneurship from the centre; and the centre countries have in turned owed their further development primarily to this movement. Western Europe created the modern world and was in turn remade by it. Any theory of international trade that does not approach the subject-matter in this way must have very serious limitations as a guide to policy.[15]

Another economist, Ragnar Nurkse, dwelt on the same theme:

The industrial revolution happened to originate on a small island with a limited range of natural resources, at a time when synthetic materials were yet unknown. In these circumstances economic expansion was transmitted to less-developed areas by a steep and steady increase in Britain's demand for primary commodities which those areas were well suited to produce. Local factors of production overseas, whose growth may in part have been induced by trade, were thus largely absorbed in the expansion of profitable primary production for export. On top of this, the center's increasing demand for raw materials and foodstuffs created incentives for capital and labor to move from the center to outlying areas, accelerating the process of growth-transmission from the former to the latter.[16]

Most economists continue to believe that trade is the most promising engine of growth for less-developed countries, and they argue that the doctrine of comparative advantage applies with particular force to those countries, which should attempt to make the best possible use of their very scarce skills and capital.

---

[15] John H. Williams, *Trade, Not Aid: A Program for World Stability* (Cambridge, Mass.: Harvard University Press, 1953), p. 10.

[16] Ragnar Nurkse, "Patterns of Trade and Development," in *Equilibrium and Growth in the World Economy* (Cambridge, Mass.: Harvard University Press, 1961), p. 285.

For many years, however, economists and governments in less-developed countries rejected this advice. They argued that their countries are quite different from the young economies of the nineteenth century. The United States, Canada, and Australia had temperate climates and unusual factor endowments—vast quantities of land and small amounts of labor. They could therefore supply cotton, wheat, and other staples needed at the center of the world economy. Furthermore, the new countries of the nineteenth century were peopled by recent immigrants from Europe, who brought with them attitudes and institutions conducive to the growth of a modern economy. Many less-developed countries of our day, by contrast, are tropical or semitropical and densely populated, and they have different institutions and traditions.

Trade patterns, it was argued, are different today from those of the nineteenth century. Production at the center of the world economy tends to be resource saving instead of resource using, and synthetics have replaced many raw materials. Furthermore, the trade policies of the center countries are less liberal than are those of the nineteenth century, which had no Multifibre Agreement, no Common Agricultural Policy, and no EC quota on Brazilian steel.

Finally, many less-developed countries did not welcome private foreign capital because it had colonial overtones. Nor were they willing to serve forever as suppliers of raw materials. They feared the instability of raw-materials prices and wanted to draw back from export dependence. Above all, they identified economic development with industrialization, adopting the doctrines of Friedrich List, and sought to build modern factories to symbolize their independence and assert their maturity. Most countries in Asia and Latin America engaged in systematic *import substitution* by offering extrava-

gant levels of protection, and they neglected exports.

These policies seemed at first to have great promise but ran into diminishing returns eventually. Opportunities for import substitution were exhausted, and economies were saddled with high-cost industries producing in small, inefficient plants. Therefore, some governments began to look for export opportunities. Singapore and Hong Kong relied on large supplies of low-cost labor and specialized in labor-intensive products—textiles, apparel, shoes, and light electronics. Korea and Brazil began in this manner but went on to develop heavier industries—automobiles, shipbuilding, steelmaking, and so on—and some of them subsidized their exports extensively.

These outward-looking strategies have been quite successful. In 1973, manufactured exports from the less-developed countries accounted for only 6.8 percent of manufactured imports by the developed countries; in 1983, they accounted for 11.3 percent. Furthermore, countries that adopted outward-looking strategies tended to grow faster than did other less-developed countries. Table 11-12 summarizes an elaborate study by the World Bank that classified the trade regimes of less-developed countries and looked at their rates of growth. Most countries grew more slowly in 1973–1983 than in 1963–1973, but countries that followed outward-looking strategies did better in both periods.

In the era of inward-looking development, the less-developed countries were exempted from GATT rules that outlaw the use of quotas and other nontariff barriers, because they were using them for import substitution. They also sought relief from any obligation to reduce their tariffs in exchange for tariff cuts made by the developed countries. They succeeded for the most part in obtaining special treatment. When they began to export manufactured

TABLE 11-12 Growth Rates of Per Capita Output in Countries
Classified by Trade Regime

Trade Regime	1963–1973		1973–1983	
	Number	Growth Rate	Number	Growth Rate
Strongly outward oriented	3	7.4	3[a]	6.1
Moderately outward oriented	10	3.7	8[b]	1.8
Moderately inward oriented	12	2.5	16[c]	0.7
Strongly inward oriented	16	1.7	14[d]	−1.0

Source: World Bank, *World Development Report*, 1987, Figure 5.3.

[a] Hong Kong, Korea, and Singapore.

[b] Brazil, Chile, Israel, Malaysia, Thailand, Tunisia, Turkey, and Uruguay.

[c] Cameroun, Colombia, Costa Rica, El Salvador, Guatemala, Honduras, Indonesia, Ivory Coast, Kenya, Mexico, Nicaragua, Pakistan, Philippines, Senegal, Sri Lanka, and Yugoslavia.

[d] Argentina, Bangladesh, Bolivia, Burundi, Dominican Republic, Ethiopia, Ghana, India, Madagascar, Nigeria, Peru, Sudan, Tanzania, and Zambia.

goods, however, they started to concentrate on other countries' policies, to ask for freer access to the markets of developed countries, as well as the right to subsidize their exports.

They won what seemed to be a major victory in 1968, at the second meeting of the United Nations Conference on Trade and Development (UNCTAD), when the developed countries agreed to introduce a Generalized System of Preferences (GSP) for manufactured imports from less-developed countries. In 1973, moreover, at the start of the Tokyo Round, the developed countries promised to provide "a better balance as between developed and developing countries" in sharing the gains from trade liberalization and "special and more favorable treatment" for developing countries. Unfortunately, both victories turned out to be small.

We have already seen how preferences work, but called them by another name. In Chapter 10, we studied the effects of a customs union between two small countries. Look back at Figure 10-10, where Britain was importing wine from Portugal and

from the rest of the world (ROW). Britain's demand curve was D_H, its supply curve was S_H, and the world price was OP_W. Britain's tariff was $P_H P_W / OP_W$, which raised the price of wine in Britain to OP_H and shifted the Portuguese supply curve from S_F^* to S_T^*. Britain produced OQ wine, consumed OC, and imported QC. It imported OM_1^* from Portugal and the balance from the rest of the world. The diagram was drawn to describe the effects of a customs union between Britain and Portugal, but it also tells the story of preferential treatment. When Portuguese wine is granted duty-free access to the British market, the relevant supply curve for Portugal is S_F^*, rather than S_T^*, and Portuguese wine exports rise to OM_2^*. This is, we said, a case of pure trade diversion, because additional Portuguese exports displace those of the ROW. But there are gains to Portugal from preferential treatment—an increase in export earnings ($P_W NLP_H$ plus $M_1^* LVM_2^*$) and in economic welfare ($P_W NVP_H$).

Each major industrial country introduced its own version of the GSP, and most of them were limited. Under the U.S. version, eligible imports enter duty free, but many important products are not eligible (textiles, apparel, shoes, watches, and several other "import-sensitive" goods). Furthermore, eligible quantities are limited on a country-by-country and product-by-product basis, and some items have been "graduated" from the program to make room for exports from less-advanced countries. In practice, then, GSP benefits are fairly small.

The less-developed countries pressed hard for these preferences but were disappointed by them. They were likewise disappointed by the Tokyo Round. Cuts in tariffs on their exports were much smaller than average, and some will not mean much. Tariff cuts on manufactured goods, taken as a group, averaged 34 percent, but cuts on goods exported by the less-developed countries averaged only 26 percent. In many cases, moreover, cuts that did take place will not be effective in stimulating exports by the less-developed countries. The goods in question are covered by the MFA and other quantitative barriers.

To complicate matters, the developed countries are beginning to criticize the trade policies followed by less-developed countries, particularly those that have made rapid progress in manufacturing. It may be time, they say, for countries like Brazil and Mexico to conform more fully to GATT rules and codes of conduct, even to agree to partial reciprocity in any future round of tariff bargaining. Furthermore, less-developed countries are finding it increasingly difficult to agree among themselves on trade-policy problems. Those that have grown rapidly are being asked to open their own markets and relinquish their preferences to help those who want to catch up. The international politics of trade are getting as complicated as the domestic politics.

THE URUGUAY ROUND

As protectionist pressures mounted in the 1980s and new policy problems came to the fore, governments began to consider the starting of a new GATT round. They knew that it could not be completed for several years but hoped that, once negotiations had begun, they could halt the building of new trade barriers and even agree to dismantle some old ones. The Tokyo Round had helped to contain protectionist pressures, because governments were able to promise that they would deal with their industries' problems during the negotiations and could thus avoid unilateral measures.

After many meetings devoted to planning future meetings, agreement was reached at a meeting in Uruguay to hold a new round of trade negotiations, which will therefore be known as the Uruguay Round. Governments pledged to take no unilateral measures that would disrupt the new negotiations and adopted an ambitious agenda. There will be new tariff cuts, including cuts by some of the less-developed countries, an attempt to solve the problems of trade in farm products, completion of a code to regulate ways of dealing with injury from import competition, and a first attempt to liberalize trade in services.

The governments agreed to examine frankly the domestic origins of international disputes about agricultural trade—ways of making agricultural production more responsive to market forces and protecting farmers' incomes without supporting prices. They did not agree fully on ways of dealing with the recent growth of "illegal" trade barriers—quotas and voluntary export restrictions that fall outsides the GATT framework—or ways of liberalizing trade in services. The talks on trade in services will follow a "parallel track" simultaneous with but separate from the Uruguay

Round. The agreement to look frankly at farm policies was made at the insistence of the United States. The agreement to deal with services separately and tentatively was made at the insistence of Brazil, India, and other less-developed countries, which want to protect their own service industries.

The negotiations will not be completed until 1990 and may not achieve all of their objectives. Only time will tell, moreover, whether the negotiating process will help to hold protectionist pressures at bay.

SUMMARY

There have been long swings in national trade policies. In the United States, tariffs rose sharply during the first three decades of the nineteenth century, fell for the next three, but rose rather steadily from the start of the Civil War until the eve of World War I. Great Britain, by contrast, moved rapidly toward free trade during the first half of the nineteenth century, a process that was dramatized by the repeal of the Corn Laws, and did not lapse back into protection until the Depression of the 1930s. France and Germany participated briefly in the movement toward free trade, which spread out from Britain by way of trade treaties containing the most-favored-nation clause, but they raised their tariffs during the last quarter of the century, when French and German farmers encountered import competition and joined with factory owners to demand protection.

After World War I, tariffs rose sharply on both sides of the Atlantic, and American tariffs reached their peak in 1930 with the passage of the Hawley–Smoot Tariff. In addition, many countries started to use quotas and other controls to protect their economies against the spread of the depression. Trade liberalization began again, however, when the Roosevelt administra-

tion started the Trade Agreements Program. It was interrupted by World War II, but resumed in 1947 with the signing of the General Agreement on Tariffs and Trade and first rounds of GATT negotiations. During the 1950s, protectionist pressures in the United States slowed down trade liberalization, but it regained momentum with the formation of the European Economic Community, the passage of the Trade Expansion Act, and the Kennedy Round of tariff cuts. In the 1970s, trade liberalization took a new tack. In the Tokyo Round, governments attempted to reduce nontariff barriers along with tariffs, and agreed on codes of conduct dealing with purchases by governments themselves and with subsidies and dumping.

But protectionist pressures built up in the 1960s and became more intense in the 1970s, as economic growth slowed down and unemployment rose. In the United States, large industries and labor unions began to experience import competition and sought protection, despite the introduction of trade adjustment assistance and of informal trade controls on many manufactured products. Those controls became more formal as pressures mounted. Imports of textiles and apparel are restricted by country and product under the Multifibre Agreement. Japan was obliged to limit its exports of automobiles. The EC countries accepted similar restraints on their steel exports to the United States and put new restrictions on their own steel imports.

Internal and international politics complicate trade policies. Most industrial countries support their farmers' incomes by policies that lead them to limit imports and also tempt them to subsidize exports. At one time, the United States was criticized severely for following these practices. Today, the EC comes in for most of the criticism, because of its Common Agricultural

Policy. The less-developed countries are injured and angered by the trade policies of developed countries. They were promised preferences, which turned out to be small, and were promised special treatment in the Tokyo Round but did not get much. All these issues will come up again in the Uruguay Round, which will also attempt to liberalize trade in services.

RECOMMENDED READINGS

On trade-policy debates in the United States from 1815 to 1930, see Frank W. Taussig, *The Tariff History of the United States* (New York: Capricorn, 1964); on the free-trade movement in Europe, see Charles P. Kindleberger, "The Rise of Free Trade in Western Europe, 1820–1874," *Journal of Economic History*, 35 (March 1975).

The politics of trade policy in the United States are examined in I. M. Destler, *American Trade Politics: System Under Stress* (Washington, D.C.: Institute for International Economics, 1986), and Robert E. Baldwin, *The Political Economy of U.S. Import Policy* (Cambridge, Mass.: MIT Press, 1985).

Trade adjustment assistance is discussed in C. Michael Aho and Thomas A. Bayard, "Costs and Benefits of Trade Adjustment Assistance," in R. E. Baldwin and A. O. Krueger, eds., *The Structure and Evolution of Recent U.S. Trade Policy* (Chicago: University of Chicago Press, 1984), ch. 5.

For a more formal and rather unusual analysis of dumping, see Wilfried Ethier, "Dumping," *Journal of Political Economy*, 90 (June 1982).

For a comprehensive review of trade relations between the United States and Japan, see C. Fred Bergsten and William R. Cline, *The United States-Japan Economic Problem*, Policy Analyses in International Economics, 13 (Washington, D.C.: Institute for International Economics, 1985).

The policies of less-developed countries are reviewed in Anne O. Krueger, "Trade Policies in Developing Countries," in R. W. Jones and P. B. Kenen, eds., *Handbook of International Economics* (Amsterdam: North-Holland, 1984), ch. 12. On the contrast between inward-looking and outward-looking trade regimes, see World Bank, *World Development Report* (Washington, D.C., 1987).

Trade preferences are examined in Tracy Murray, *Trade Preferences for Developing Countries* (New York: John Wiley, 1977). See also Andre Sapir and Lars Lundberg, "The U.S. Generalized System of Preferences and Its Impacts," in R. E. Baldwin and A. O. Krueger, eds., *The Structure and Evolution of Recent U.S. Trade Policy* (Chicago: University of Chicago Press, 1984), ch. 6.

12

THE BALANCE OF PAYMENTS
AND
FOREIGN-EXCHANGE MARKET

INTRODUCTION

When dealing with the microeconomics of the open economy, we concentrated on the allocation of resources and distribution of income. We saw how international transactions and disturbances affect the way that an economy confronts the problems of efficiency and equity. When dealing with the macroeconomics of the open economy, we will concentrate on the utilization of resources. We shall see how international transactions and disturbances affect the way that an economy confronts the problem of stability. We will deal with these questions:

1. How do international transactions affect output and price levels, money stocks, interest rates, and other variables important in macroeconomic theory and policy?

2. How do international transactions affect the freedom and effectiveness with which gov-

ernments can use monetary and fiscal policies, the main instruments of macroeconomic policy, to achieve and maintain economic stability?

3. How do international monetary arrangements, especially exchange-rate arrangements, influence our answers to these questions?

These are complicated issues, and we will devote eight chapters to them.

Introducing International Transactions

The first question asks how international transactions should be introduced into macroeconomic models of the closed economy. Can we merely add them to standard models or must we reach within those models to revise substantially the basic behavioral relationships determining consumption, investment, interest rates, wages, and prices? For many years, economists were content to open up our models by adding international transactions, without reworking the basic relationships, but we have found that this is not enough. Trade and other transactions with the outside world affect pervasively the internal workings of an economy, even one like the U.S. economy, with smaller international transactions in relation to its size than those of most other countries.

It is impossible, for example, to analyze completely the effects of a change in a country's exchange rate without allowing for *feedback effects* on its domestic economy. Some feedback effects are direct. The change in the foreign demand for a country's exports resulting from an exchange-rate change will affect aggregate demand in domestic markets and will thus affect output, income, and the price level. The income and price changes will go on to affect the domestic demand for foreign (imported) goods; the price changes will also affect the foreign demand for domestic (exported) goods. Some feedback effects are indirect but can be more important than the direct effects. A change in the exchange rate can induce financial flows that influence conditions in asset markets and can thus affect interest rates. In consequence, they can affect saving and investment in ways that alter aggregate demand, the supply of exports, and the demand for imports.

Analyzing Macroeconomic Policies

The second question posed at the outset asks how international interdependence limits or modifies national autonomy in the execution of economic policy. The problem has two aspects. On the one hand, an open economy has an additional policy target. Its international transactions must be balanced over time. This requirement may limit its freedom to pursue other important targets. On the other hand, the instruments of macroeconomic policy function differently in open than in closed economies.

To complicate matters, monetary and fiscal policies operate quite differently when exchange rates are pegged than when they are flexible. In a small open economy with a pegged exchange rate, monetary policy cannot have any permanent effect on output, employment, or prices. In an economy with a flexible exchange rate, by contrast, monetary policy can have larger effects than in a closed economy, because it affects the exchange rate itself. Furthermore, the effectiveness of monetary policy is influenced jointly by exchange-rate arrangements and the degree of financial integration—the tightness of the links between national markets for bonds and other securities. Under pegged exchange rates, tight links between national markets raise the speed at which monetary policy loses its influence. Under flexible exchange rates, tight links enhance the influence of monetary policy.

These assertions about monetary policy are proved in subsequent chapters. They are introduced here to show why we must consider carefully the third question posed earlier about the implications of international monetary arrangements. That question, however, has many more dimensions. We must ask how exchange-rate arrangements affect the functioning of fiscal policies. We must ask how they affect the way that external shocks impinge on the domestic economy: what happens with pegged and flexible exchange rates when there is a change in the foreign demand for a country's exports or the foreign inflation rate.

Cosmopolitan and National Perspectives Once Again

The international monetary system must be studied from a cosmopolitan perspective as well as from a national perspective. A simple example makes this clear. If the German government decides to peg the U.S. dollar price of the Deutsche mark, using techniques described in this chapter, it will automatically peg the Deutsche mark price of the U.S. dollar. If it fixes the price of its currency at $0.50 per Deutsche mark, it will fix the price of the U.S. dollar at DM 2 per dollar. Putting the point in general terms, a world with n countries has only $n - 1$ independent exchange rates. If every government other than the U.S. government pegs the dollar price of its own currency, the price of the dollar will be pegged automatically in terms of every foreign currency.

This example is a matter of arithmetic, but it raises a major problem in political economy. Governments can come into conflict if they try simultaneously to pursue independent exchange-rate policies. The conflict can show up in foreign-exchange markets if governments intervene at cross purposes. It can show up at the highest political level when inconsistencies become apparent, and the conflict can then interfere with international relationships of great diplomatic and strategic importance.

How can international monetary arrangements avoid conflicts of this sort? We will use this question as an organizing principle in Chapter 19, when we review international monetary history. We will see that the United States did not try to pursue an independent exchange-rate policy in the first decades following World War II. Because of its great economic strength and comparative self-sufficiency, it was content to be the nth country in the system. During that period, moreover, the dollar became the main international currency. It became the international *unit of account*, in that foreign governments used it to define their exchange rates. It became the international *means of payment*, in that foreign governments used it when they intervened in foreign-exchange markets to keep exchange rates close to their official values. It became an international *store of value*, in that foreign governments held dollars as

reserves, to be used when they had to stabilize exchange rates and thus to finance their balance-of-payments deficits.

The central role of the dollar came under political attack in the 1960s, when the United States began to have balance-of-payments problems of its own. The French president, Charles de Gaulle, castigated the United States for abusing the "exorbitant privilege" conferred by the special role of the dollar. Matters were made worse a few years later when an American Secretary of the Treasury told foreign officials that "the dollar is our currency but your problem." Serious difficulties arose, moreover, when the U.S. government decided that the United States could no longer be the nth country and started to pursue an active exchange-rate policy. There were dramatic changes in international monetary arrangements, which have not yet ended.

What Lies Ahead

A number of new terms have appeared in this introduction, such as *intervention* on foreign-exchange markets, *reserves* that countries hold to finance intervention, and *balance-of-payments* problems, and the text has referred repeatedly to pegged and flexible exchange rates. Before answering the questions with which this chapter started, we must pause for definitions. We have indeed a larger task—to understand how international transactions fit into balance-of-payments accounts, how those accounts relate in turn to conditions in foreign-exchange markets, and how transactions in those markets affect the banking system.

BALANCE-OF-PAYMENTS ACCOUNTS

A country's balance-of-payments accounts summarize its dealings with the outside world. To introduce the concepts and conventions used in those accounts, we will construct a hypothetical balance-of-payments table for the United States. Then we will consider ways of balancing the cash flows that show up at the bottom of the table.

The balance-of-payments table is usually divided into two main parts, and each part has subdivisions:

I. *The Current Account* shows flows that affect directly the national-income accounts and includes
Exports and imports of merchandise
Exports and imports of services
Inflows and outflows of investment income
Grants, remittances, and other transfers
II. *The Capital Account* shows flows that affect directly the national balance sheet and includes
Direct investments by foreign firms in their U.S. affiliates and by U.S. firms in their foreign affiliates
Portfolio investments, which include
Net purchases by foreigners of U.S. securities and net lending to U.S. residents
Net purchases by U.S. residents of foreign securities and net lending to foreigners
Changes in cash balances, which include
Changes in balances held by banks and other foreign-exchange dealers, resulting from current and capital transactions
Changes in reserves held by official institutions, resulting from intervention on foreign-exchange markets

All transactions are classified as credits (+) or debits (−). The method of classification may seem puzzling at first but is based on a few simple principles. If you accept them at face value, rather than trying to attach deep meaning to them, you should have no trouble. Clear your mind of the notion that credits are good and debits bad. This notion is silly, as every transaction appears *twice* in the balance-of-payments table, once as a credit and once as a debit.

The Current Account

Merchandise exports appear in the first instance as credit items, because they give rise to claims on the outside world that foreigners must discharge by payments to the United States. Merchandise imports appear in the first instance as debit items because they give rise to claims by the outside world that U.S. residents must discharge by payments to foreigners.

Exports and imports of services are treated analogously. When a foreign airline pays for baggage handling and aircraft maintenance at Kennedy Airport in New York, it is doing much the same thing as a foreign firm that buys machinery in the United States. It is using the services of American factors of production and incurring an obligation that must be discharged by a payment to the United States. When American tourists buy tickets from that foreign airline, they are doing much the same thing as an American firm that buys steel in Brazil. They are using the services of foreign factors of production and incurring an obligation that must be discharged by a payment from the United States. (Exports and imports of services are sometimes described as *invisible* trade, because they cannot be seen to cross the border but have the same effects as visible merchandise trade. Some of the more important services were described in Chapter 11.)

Inflows and outflows of investment income are put in the current account because they share two characteristics with exports and imports of goods and services. First, they give rise to claims that must be discharged by payments. Second, they reflect the use by one country of another country's capital, a factor of production, and add to the national income of the country owning it. A dividend paid to a U.S. company by its Spanish affiliate is an inflow of investment income and appears in the first instance as a credit item; it represents compensation for the use in Spain of U.S. capital, and it adds to U.S. national income. Interest paid by the U.S. Treasury to the Saudi Arabian Monetary Authority, which holds U.S. Treasury bills, is an outflow of investment income; it represents compensation for the use in the United States of Saudi capital, and it adds to Saudi national income.

All the credit items described thus far represent foreign payments to domestic factors of production. American exports of goods and services correspond to American spending on current output in the United States, and they measure the immediate impact of foreign demand on production and employment in the United States. American imports of goods and services correspond to American spending on current output in other countries, and they measure the immediate impact of American demand on production and employment in the outside world. Flows of investment income do not measure effects of demand in one country on output and employment in another. Nevertheless, inflows represent additions to U.S. national income earned by American capital "working" in other countries, and outflows represent additions to other countries' national incomes earned by foreign capital "working" in the United States.

Grants, remittances, and other transfers, which appear at the foot of the current account, do *not* represent additions to income. As their names imply, they represent redistributions of income. When the U.S. government makes a grant for disaster relief or military aid, it transfers income from U.S. residents to the residents or government of another country. (Pension payments appear here, too, because they likewise represent transfers of income rather than payments for current factor services.) Transfers are included at this point so that the current-account balance, discussed later, will reflect accurately the net change

in U.S. claims on the outside world. If wheat shipped to Bangladesh for famine relief was included in merchandise exports (as a credit) but the corresponding grant was not included in the current account (as a debit), we would mistakenly infer that the shipment had increased U.S. claims on the outside world.

There is another way to look at credits and debits, which is useful when we turn to the capital account. Credits give rise to U.S. claims on foreigners that must be discharged by foreign payments to Americans. Therefore, we can think of credits as creating a foreign demand for dollars in the foreign-exchange market. Debits give rise to foreign claims on the United States that must be discharged by American payments to foreigners. Therefore, we can think of debits as creating an American demand for foreign currencies in the foreign-exchange market. The correspondence is not perfect. Some Americans may choose to be paid in foreign currencies, and some foreigners may choose to be paid in dollars. But it is close enough to be useful in sorting out debits and credits.

The Capital Account

Every transaction in the current account is an income-related flow. Every transaction in the capital account is an asset-related flow. Those that add to U.S. claims on foreigners are described as capital outflows and appear as debits. Those that add to foreign claims on the United States are described as capital inflows and appear as credits.[1]

These conventions are hard to assimilate. Two devices can be helpful. We can think in terms of trade in paper—deeds to real property, corporate securities, and

---

[1] Transactions that add to U.S. claims on foreigners are sometimes described as capital exports, but this terminology can be confusing. (It describes a debit as an export.) We will avoid it.

various debt instruments. When an American company acquires a plant in Spain, it is "importing" the deed to the plant. When an American pension fund buys bonds in Tokyo, it is "importing" securities. In each instance, the "importer" must make payment to a foreigner, just like an importer of merchandise or services. Alternatively, we can look at matters from the standpoint of the foreign-exchange market. When a company acquires a plant in Spain, it adds to the American demand for Spanish pesetas. When a pension fund buys shares on the Tokyo Stock Exchange, it adds to the American demand for Japanese yen. Conversely, when a Canadian insurance company buys bonds in New York, the transaction adds to foreign claims on the United States and appears as a credit in the U.S. balance of payments. It is an "export" of securities, and it adds to the foreign demand for dollars.

We have already studied the first type of transaction in the capital account. Direct investments are transactions that create, extend, or facilitate control over productive facilities in other countries. They are the building blocks of multinational enterprises, and we examined them in Chapter 8. (Notice, however, that U.S. direct investments include *all* increases in the claims of U.S. firms on their foreign affiliates. When Ford makes a loan to its British affiliate to finance the affiliate's purchase of steel from Belgium, the loan appears as a direct investment, even though there is no increase in productive capacity owned or controlled by Ford.)

All other transactions in claims to property, equities, and debt instruments appear as portfolio investments. These are *arm's-length* transactions between independent entities. They are undertaken for financial or commercial reasons—to earn income, to capture capital gains or hedge against losses, and to finance trade in goods and services. They do not create or facilitate

control. Portfolio investments take many forms. Corporations issue stocks and bonds abroad, and they borrow from foreign banks. Insurance companies, pension funds, and other institutional investors buy foreign securities to diversify their assets. Governments borrow from international institutions, other governments, and commercial banks.

The cash component of the capital account does not appear separately in the actual balance-of-payments table for the United States. Its contents are scattered across the portfolio component and can be pulled together only with some difficulty. Nevertheless, it is helpful conceptually to collect in one place all changes in bank balances and similar cash flows. They are crucial to the functioning of foreign-exchange markets and interpretation of the balance-of-payments accounts.

Recording Individual Transactions

Balance-of-payments accounts are built on the principles of double-entry bookkeeping. Each transaction appears twice, once as a credit and once as a debit. Most transactions appear for the first time in the current or capital account and appear for the second time in the cash component of the capital account.

A German firm that buys machinery from the United States can pay for it by running down its dollar balance at an American bank or by buying dollars from a German bank and thus running down the bank's dollar balance. Alternatively, it can obtain credit from the manufacturer or borrow dollars from a bank in the United States.[2] In each case, the export of machin-

---

[2] It can also borrow dollars from a foreign bank—from a German bank in Frankfurt or its branch in Luxembourg, from the London branch of an American bank or, for that matter, the London branch of a Brazilian bank. These possibilities will be examined in Chapter 20, which reviews the growth of international bank lending and the Eurocurrency markets.

ery will appear first as a credit in the current account. If the firm runs down its dollar balance or that of a German bank, the second entry will be a debit in the cash component of the capital account. If it borrows from its American supplier or an American bank, the second entry will be a debit in the portfolio component of the capital account. In both instances, however, the debit will testify to an increase in the *net* claims of the United States, the difference between gross claims and gross liabilities. If the firm runs down its dollar balance or

that of a German bank, it will reduce gross U.S. liabilities to foreigners. If it borrows instead, it will raise gross U.S. claims on foreigners.

These principles are illustrated in Table 12-1, which is a hypothetical balance-of-payments table for the United States. It lists seven transactions, worked out step by step:

(a) An American firm buys $240,000 worth of tin from a Malaysian company. It pays with pounds bought with dollars from a New York bank.

TABLE 12-1 Hypothetical Balance of Payments for the United States (thousands of dollars)

Item	Credit	Debit
Merchandise exports and imports		
Tin from Malaysia (a)		240
Antibiotics to Venezuela (b)	300	
Jet aircraft to India (g)	200	
Service exports and imports		
Shipping (c)	50	
Investment income		
Profit from German subsidiary (d)	75	
Balance on current account	385	
Direct investment		
Plant in Spain (f)		400
Portfolio investment		
U. S. Government loan (g)		200
Sale by foreigners of U. S. securities (e)		175
Cash component[1]		
Increase (+) in dollars held by foreign banks		
Venezuelan bank (b)		300
German bank (d)		75
Spanish bank (f)	400	
Net increase (+)	25	
Increase (−) in foreign currencies held by U. S. banks		
New York bank in pounds (a)	240	
Chicago bank in pounds (c)		50
Boston bank in yen (e)	175	
Net increase (−)	365	
Balance on capital account		385

[1] Note carefully the signs of the items in the cash component. As increases in U. S. liabilities to foreigners are credit items in the capital account, increases in the dollar balances of foreign banks show up as credits (+) in the cash component, and decreases show up as debits (−). As increases in U. S. claims on foreigners are debit items in the capital account, increases in the foreign-currency balances of U. S. banks show up as debits (−) in the cash component, and decreases show up as credits (+).

The purchase of tin appears as a merchandise import in the current account. The transfer of pounds to pay for it appears in the cash component of the capital account. The purchase of tin is a debit because it gives rise to a foreign claim on the United States. The transfer of pounds is a credit because it discharges the foreign claim by reducing the foreign-currency holdings of the U.S. bank that supplied the pounds. How will the transaction be executed? The American firm will write a check for $240,000 (plus a small commission) against its own bank account, hand the check over to the New York bank, and receive a *draft* for the equivalent in pounds. (If the exchange rate is $1.60 per pound, the draft will be for £150,000.) The American firm will endorse the draft to the Malaysian firm, which will sell it to its own bank in Kuala Lumpur and obtain the equivalent of £150,000 in Malaysian ringitt. The bank in Kuala Lumpur will send the draft to London, where the British bank on which it was drawn will deduct £150,000 from the pound (sterling) balance of the New York bank that issued it.

(b) An American firm sells $300,000 worth of antibiotics to Venezuela. It is paid with dollars bought from a bank in Caracas.

The sale of antibiotics appears as a merchandise export in the current account. The transfer of dollars to pay for it appears in the cash component of the capital account. The sale of antibiotics is a credit because it gives rise to a U.S. claim on the outside world. The dollar transfer is a debit because it discharges the U.S. claim by reducing the dollar holdings of the bank in Caracas. In this case, the Venezuelan importer will buy a $300,000 draft from the bank in Caracas, paying with a check for the equivalent in Venezuelan bolivares. The importer will endorse the draft to the U.S. firm supplying the antibiotics, and the firm will deposit the draft in its own bank

account. Finally, the draft will be sent to the New York bank where the bank in Caracas keeps its dollar balance, and $300,000 will be deducted from that balance.

(c) A British firm pays $50,000 to lease an American ship that will carry frozen beef from Buenos Aires to Liverpool. It pays with pounds bought from a British bank.

This transaction is similar to an export sale. The American owner of the ship provides a service using U.S. resources. Therefore, the rental fee appears as a credit in the current account. If the British firm pays in pounds and the American recipient sells them to a bank in Chicago, the transaction appears as a debit in the cash component of the capital account. It raises the pound (sterling) balance of the Chicago bank, adding to U.S. claims on foreigners.

(d) The German subsidiary of a U.S. firm remits $75,000 in profits in its U.S. parent. It pays with dollars bought from a German bank.

This transaction is also similar to an export sale. The parent company in the United States is being paid for the services of capital and technology put to work in Germany, and the payment appears as a credit in the current account. The offsetting entry appears in the cash component of the capital account, where the dollar holdings of the German bank fall by $75,000. This is, of course, a debit, because there is a reduction in foreign claims on the United States.

(e) A Canadian insurance company sells $175,000 of IBM stock to an American investor and uses the proceeds to buy bonds in Tokyo. It employs a Boston bank to execute the whole transaction.

Both parts of this transaction appear in the capital account. The sale of stock appears as a debit in the portfolio component of the capital account, reflecting a reduction in foreign claims on the United States—in foreign holdings of American securities. The Canadian insurance company, however, needs Japanese yen to purchase bonds in Tokyo and buys them from the Boston bank handling the transaction. Its purchase of yen appears as a credit in the cash component of the capital account, reflecting a reduction in U.S. claims on the outside world—in the foreign-currency (yen) holdings of the Boston bank.

(f) An American company spends $400,000 to build a new factory in Spain. It uses a Spanish bank to execute the foreign-exchange transaction.

This transaction appears in the balance-of-payments table even though no goods, services, or securities cross the U.S. border. Both parts appear in the capital account. The building of the factory is a direct investment and appears as a debit in the capital account. It is, in effect, an "import" of the title to the plant. The payment for the plant appears as a credit in the cash component. The U.S. company must buy pesetas from a Spanish bank, and the bank builds up its dollar holdings with the U.S. bank where it keeps its dollar balance.

(g) The Export-Import Bank, an agency of the U.S. government, lends $200,000 to the Indian government to pay for jet aircraft purchased from an American manufacturer.

This transaction does not appear in the cash component of the capital account, because the dollars lent to India come back immediately to pay for the jet aircraft. The export of aircraft appears as usual as a credit in the current account. The loan increases the claims of the United States and appears as a debit in the portfolio component of the capital account.

Totaling the entries in Table 12-1, we find that credits are equal to debits. There is $385,000 *surplus* on current account, and it is matched by a $385,000 *deficit* on capital

account. This equality must always hold, because every transaction enters twice, once as a credit and once as a debit.[3] By grouping certain credits and debits, however, we can learn a lot about a country's international transactions.

THE CURRENT ACCOUNT AND NATIONAL INCOME

The current-account surplus in Table 12-1 says that trade in goods and services and investment-income flows contributed more to the national income of the United States than to the national incomes of other countries. Furthermore, it says that the United States "paid its way" in the world. Indeed, it did more. It increased its claims on the outside world. In Chapter 8, we examined the international investment position of the United States. In Table 12-2, we see how the seven balance-of-payments transactions affect that position. A current-account surplus is necessarily reflected by an increase in domestic claims on the outside world, a decrease in foreign claims on the domestic

[3] In actual balance-of-payments accounts, there is usually a gap between recorded credits and debits, and it is covered by an item called errors and omissions. The gap arises because the accounts are not built up transaction by transaction, with each entered twice. They are built up from data on each *type* of transaction. Data on trade flows are collected when goods cross the frontier; data on services are collected from shippers, travelers, and others who supply or purchase services; data on capital flows are collected from companies, securities dealers, banks, and other institutions. There are errors in each category, and large errors in some categories. Data on services and investment income are hard to collect, and data on investments are likewise incomplete. If you purchase foreign stocks and bonds through a broker in London or Zurich, the statisticians in Washington will not know it. They may catch the corresponding transfer of bank balances (a credit) but not the transfer of securities (a debit). Statisticians are often asked how much of the gap measured by errors and omissions is due to statistical error and how much is due to statistical omission. The question betrays misunderstanding. The errors-and-omissions entry is an accounting device; it is not a measure of statistical *quality*.

TABLE 12-2   Changes in the International
Investment Position of the United States
(thousands of dollars)

Assets held by U. S. residents	+235
Held by U. S. government	
Loans and other claims	+200
Held by other U. S. residents	
Direct investments	+400
Foreign securities	—
Claims reported by U. S. banks	−365
Assets held by foreigners	−150
Held by foreign governments	—
Held by other foreigners	
Direct investments	—
U. S. securities	−175
Claims reported by U. S. banks	+25

Note: In Table 12-1, increases in assets held by
U. S. residents were debits (−), and their signs are reversed here; increases in assets held by foreigners
were credits (+), and their signs are the same here.
The decrease in U. S. claims reported by U. S. banks is
the decrease in the banks' own deposits with foreign
banks; the increase in foreign claims reported by U. S.
banks is the increase in the deposits of foreign banks.

economy, or a combination of the two, as in
Table 12-2.

Remember an earlier warning, however,
that credits are not "good" or debits "bad"
from any economic point of view. A
current-account surplus represents an addition to national income, but an attempt to
run a current-account surplus may not be a
good way to stimulate income and employment. In Chapter 10, we saw that a tariff
could be used to raise employment when
the real wage was rigid. But a tariff is an
inefficient instrument; it is inferior to a
production or wage subsidy, because of its
consumption effects. Furthermore, it is a
"beggar-my-neighbor" remedy for unemployment, because it can reduce employment in other countries and provoke retaliation. An attempt to run or raise a
current-account surplus is likewise inefficient and uncertain. The methods used
may interfere with economic efficiency and
reduce welfare even though they raise output and employment. They may also re-

duce employment in the outside world,
which is unneighborly and can also invite
retaliation.

Another point will come up in Chapter
13. Although a current-account surplus
says that trade in goods and services and
investment-income flows have added more
to income at home than abroad, an increase
in a current-account surplus does not necessarily reflect an increase in domestic
income. It may be the result of a fall in domestic income that has reduced the demand for imports.

Finally, a current-account surplus says
that the domestic economy is not spending
its whole income. To see why this is so, we
must open up the basic relationship used in
national-income accounts.

In a closed economy, there are three
sources of demand for domestic output:
consumption (C), government spending
(G), and domestic investment (I). Therefore,

$$Y = C + G + I \qquad (1)$$

where Y is gross national product.[4] In an
open economy, there is an additional
source of demand and an additional source

---

[4] In what follows, we continue to interpret Y as
gross national product. In an open economy, however,
it is sometimes important to distinguish between gross
domestic product and gross *national* product. Gross domestic product (GDP) is the value of output originating within a country's borders. Gross national product
(GNP) is the value of output accruing as gross income
to its residents. If a country pays investment income to
foreigners, who own capital used in that country,
those payments must be deducted from GDP to measure GNP, the value of the product going to residents.
If a country employs foreign workers who are not
counted as permanent residents, their wages must
likewise be deducted from GDP to obtain GNP. (As we
will go on using Y to mean GNP rather than GDP, exports of goods and services in equation (2) must be
deemed to include investment income earned from
foreigners, and imports must be deemed to include investment income paid to foreigners. The difference
between them in equation (3) will measure the
current-account balance. Proofs of these statements
are not difficult but need not detain us.)

of supply. Exports of goods and services (X) constitute the additional source of demand or claim on domestic output. Imports of goods and services (M) supplement supplies in domestic markets. Therefore, the open-economy equation is

$$Y + M = C + G + I + X \qquad (2)$$

Rearranging this equation,

$$X - M = Y - (C + G + I) \qquad (3)$$

Define domestic absorption (A) as the sum of consumption, government spending, and investment, so that

$$X - M = Y - A \qquad (4)$$

But X *minus* M is the current-account balance when there are no transfers (we neglect them here), while Y *minus* A is the gap between output (income) and absorption (expenditure). Therefore, equation (4) says that a country with a current-account surplus is not absorbing all its own output. It is using some to build up claims on the outside world.

Rich countries can afford to do this. Poor countries cannot. They should indeed be trying to acquire additional resources for capital formation in order to promote economic development. Therefore, they should run current-account deficits and build up debt to the outside world. This is what most less-developed countries do. The United States did it, too, for most of the nineteenth century. It borrowed in foreign financial markets, mainly London, to finance its own development, especially the building of the railroads, and ran persistent current-account deficits.

A current-account deficit does not become worrisome if it can be financed on acceptable terms and the proceeds of the borrowing are used well. A country can run into trouble, however, if it has to cover its current-account deficit by short-term borrowing (or running down reserves) and must then repay its debts before it can eliminate its deficit. It can also run into trouble if it has to borrow at high interest rates or refinance its debts at interest rates higher than those at which it borrowed initially. Finally, it can run into trouble if it fritters away borrowed resources by consuming rather than investing them. Its capital stock will not rise rapidly enough to yield the "growth dividend" it needs to repay debt.

The connections among borrowing, consumption, and investment can be illustrated here by carrying the algebra one step farther. Recall another basic statement made in national-income accounts. Income can be used for three purposes: consumption (C), tax payments (T), and saving (S). Thus,

$$Y = C + T + S \qquad (5)$$

This statement is true for open economies as well, and it can be used to replace Y in equation (3):

$$\begin{aligned} X - M &= (C + T + S) - (C + G + I) \\ &= (S - I) + (T - G) \qquad (6) \end{aligned}$$

A current-account surplus ($X > M$) must be matched by a private-sector surplus ($S > I$) or a public-sector surplus ($T > G$). A current-account deficit must be matched by a private-sector deficit or a public-sector deficit.[5]

When a country starts to run a current-account deficit, a thoughtful observer will want to look at the right side of equation (6) to see whether there has been a decrease in saving, increase in investment, or increase in the budget deficit. There is reason to worry about the country's long-term prospects if the onset of a current-account deficit reflects smaller saving or a larger budget deficit. In both cases, the country is

---

[5] In a closed economy, X and M vanish, so $(S - I) + (T - G) = 0$. If the government balances its budget, moreover, $T = G$, so $S - I = 0$ and $S = I$. Saving must equal investment, the assertion made in elementary macroeconomic models.

borrowing abroad or running down its foreign assets to sustain or raise consumption, whether by the private or the public sector. There is less cause to worry when the onset of a current-account deficit reflects an increase in investment. In this case, the country is building up its capital stock more quickly and, therefore, increasing its future output.

All of these issues will come up again when we look at the debt problems of the less-developed countries and at the current-account deficits of the United States.

CASH FLOWS AND THE FOREIGN-EXCHANGE MARKET

A country that runs a current-account surplus, building up net claims on the outside world, is adding to its wealth. However, we must pay attention to the composition of those claims. Look again at Table 12-1. The United States added to its income-producing claims (the direct investment in Spain and the loan to India). It also redeemed a claim previously held by a foreigner (the Canadian investment in IBM stock). In the process, however, foreign banks built up their cash balances with U.S. banks by $25,000, and U.S. banks ran down their cash balances with foreign banks by $365,000. Let us look more closely at these changes in cash balances.[6]

---

[6] Some economists treat these changes as a measure of the overall surplus or deficit in the balance of payments. In this particular instance, they would say that the United States has a deficit of $390,000, the sum of the increase in its monetary liabilities to foreigners and the decrease in its own monetary assets. (Starting at the top of Table 12-1, the current-account surplus, at $385,000, is too small to cover the net increase in "nonmonetary" claims, at $775,000, leaving a deficit of $390,000.) This definition, however, is less useful than one given later, which measures the surplus or deficit in the balance of payments by changes in *official* monetary assets and liabilities (i.e., official reserves).

Banks supplied the currencies required for most of the transactions in Table 12-1. In the first transaction, for example, a New York bank sold $240,000 worth of pounds to the American firm purchasing tin from Malaysia. In other words, the banks served as foreign-exchange dealers. Looking at matters from this standpoint, we can treat changes in the banks' cash balances as changes in their inventories. And when we see a change in any dealer's inventory, we are bound to ask whether the dealer will try to reverse it.

It is easy to concoct cases in which banks will not want to reverse a change in their cash balances. When interest rates in the United States are higher than in other countries, banks and other foreign-exchange dealers will want to hold more dollars and fewer pounds, marks, and yen. Foreign banks might be quite happy with the $25,000 increase in their dollar balances caused by their dealings with their customers, and U.S. banks might likewise be happy with the $365,000 decrease in their foreign-currency balances. When banks and other dealers expect the dollar to appreciate (to become more valuable in terms of other currencies), they will want to hold more dollars. In this case, too, they might be happy with the changes shown in Table 12-1.

There are limits, however, to the changes that banks can tolerate. If they do not have adequate inventories of foreign currencies, they cannot satisfy their customers' requirements and cannot continue to function effectively as foreign-exchange dealers. In normal circumstances, then, banks may try to reverse large changes in their inventories.

It is useful at this point to distinguish between two parts of the foreign-exchange market. Heretofore, we have been concerned with the "retail" market, where banks meet the needs of their customers.

Most transactions in that market take place at exchange rates (prices) posted by the banks, though large customers can sometimes shop around to get more favorable rates. When banks want to adjust their inventories, however, they turn to the "wholesale" market, where foreign-exchange dealers do business with each other. This market is nothing more than a network of telephone connections linking the banks' trading rooms. But it is like any other wholesale market. Variations in demand and supply lead to price changes.

Suppose that the Boston bank listed in Table 12-1 wants to rebuild its holdings of yen, which fell by the equivalent of $175,000 when it sold yen to the Canadian insurance company. The bank will place a bid in the wholesale market, saying how many yen it wants to buy and the price it is willing to pay. Its bid for yen is also an offer of dollars, and the price it is bidding for yen is therefore the price it is asking for dollars.

If it can find a seller at its quoted price, the Boston bank will make a contract right away. Suppose that it finds a Seattle bank that wants to sell yen. The Boston bank will deliver dollars to the Seattle bank, which will deliver yen to the Boston bank. The transfer of dollars can take place anywhere in the United States—on the books of a New York bank, for example, where the Boston and Seattle banks keep working balances. The transfer of yen can take place in Tokyo or some other trading center such as New York or London, where banks can hold foreign-currency deposits.

There may be no other bank, however, willing to sell yen at the price quoted by the Boston bank. The bank will have then to raise its bid until it finds a buyer (or decides to withdraw temporarily from the market). This is how exchange rates change in the wholesale market, and rates in the retail market follow them closely. But it is not the end of the story. It is time to introduce the fundamental distinction between flexible and pegged exchange rates.

MONETARY ARRANGEMENTS AND THE ADJUSTMENT PROCESS

When no one comes forward to offer yen at the exchange rate quoted by the Boston bank, there is an *excess demand* for yen (an excess supply of dollars) in the foreign-exchange market. Under a system of flexible exchange rates, the yen will *appreciate* (the dollar will *depreciate*). Under a system of pegged exchange rates, governments will intervene to stabilize rates. The Japanese government will sell yen in exchange for dollars to meet the excess demand and prevent the yen from appreciating. The excess demand for yen will show up as an increase in the Japanese government's dollar holdings. Those holdings are described as *reserves,* and changes in reserves are frequently used to measure the *overall* surplus or deficit in the balance-of-payments accounts:

A country is said to have a surplus in its balance of payments if there is an increase in the difference between its official reserves and its liabilities to foreign official institutions. It is said to have a deficit if there is a decrease.

The surplus or deficit measured this way is sometimes called the balance on official settlements. In this particular example, the Japanese balance of payments displays a surplus, measured by the increase in Japanese reserves, and the U.S. balance of payments displays a deficit, measured by the increase in U.S. liabilities to the Japanese government.

At the end of World War II, governments adopted arrangements resembling a system of pegged exchange rates. The arrangements were not as simple or mechanical as those we use below to illustrate a pegged-rate system. The pegs were not permanent. From time to time, a government *devalued* its currency, decreasing its official value; less frequently, a government *revalued* its currency, increasing its official value. Furthermore, most governments interfered systematically with the changes in money supplies that play a central role in balance-of-payments adjustment under pegged exchange rates.

In 1971, the pegged-rate system broke down. Two years later, after unsuccessful attempts to rehabilitate it, the major industrial countries went over to arrangements resembling a system of flexible exchange rates. Once again, the arrangements were not as simple as those described in the next section. Some countries continued to peg their currencies. Others intervened from time to time to combat erratic fluctuations in exchange rates or reduce the speed with which they were changing.

The monetary systems described and examined more thoroughly in subsequent chapters should be regarded as prototypes of actual exchange-rate regimes. They will help us to identify and analyze the main ingredients of the adjustment process and the problems that arise under each regime.

Adjustment Under Flexible Exchange Rates

Under a system of flexible exchange rates, prices of currencies fluctuate freely in response to changes in demand and supply. There can be large fluctuations from week to week and month to month, as in Figure 12-1, which shows dollar exchange rates for seven major currencies. There can be long swings in rates, as in Figure 12-2, which shows movements in the foreign-currency value of the U.S. dollar measured by trade-weighted averages of national exchange rates.

Changes in flexible exchange rates are normally initiated by banks' attempts to regulate their inventories. But the inventory changes to which they are reacting reflect more fundamental forces—changes in demand and supply that come from households, firms, and financial institutions that buy and sell goods, services, and assets. When the Boston bank attempted to buy yen to rebuild its inventory and drove up the value of the yen in terms of the dollar, it was responding to the demand for yen that came from the Canadian insurance company.

Changes in exchange rates, moreover, modify behavior by households, firms, and financial institutions. They alter demands for goods, services, and assets whose prices are denominated in different currencies. An appreciation of the yen in terms of the dollar makes Japanese goods and services more expensive for American households and firms, which will reduce their purchases. The corresponding depreciation of the dollar in terms of the yen makes American goods and services less expensive for Japanese households and firms, which will raise their purchases. The fall in American purchases will reduce the demand for yen in the foreign-exchange market; the rise in Japanese purchases will raise the demand for dollars.

This process of adjustment is described by Figures 12-3 and 12-4. The left side of Figure 12-3 shows the American demand for yen. The price of the yen is measured in dollars on the vertical axis; the quantity of yen demanded is measured on the horizontal axis. The demand curve DD is negatively sloped because an appreciation of the yen (an increase in its dollar price) raises the dollar prices of Japanese goods and services, reducing the American demand for them and thus the American demand for yen. When the price of the yen is OP dollars, the quantity demanded is OU. When the yen appreciates to OP' dollars, the

FIGURE 12-1 Movements in Exchange Rates

Scales have been chosen so that increases represent depreciations of the U.S. dollar against other currencies and decreases represent appreciations. *Source:* International Monetary Fund, *IMF Survey*, February 22, 1988.

quantity demanded falls to *OU'*. The position of the American demand curve depends on prices in Japan and the United States, income in the United States, and all other variables affecting American demands for Japanese goods, services, and assets. The right side of Figure 12-3 shows the Japanese demand curve for dollars. The price of the dollar is measured in yen on the vertical axis; the quantity of dollars demanded is measured on the horizontal axis. The demand curve *D*D** is negatively sloped for the same reason that *DD* is negatively sloped. When the dollar price of the yen is *OP* on the left side, the yen price of the dollar is *OR* on the right side, and the Japanese demand for dollars is *OV*. When the yen appreciates to *OP'* on the left side, the dollar depreciates to *OR'* on the right side, and the Japanese demand for dollars rises to *OV'*. The position of the Japanese demand curve depends on prices and other variables affecting Japanese demands for American goods, services, and assets.

The two demand curves in Figure 12-3 cannot be used directly to determine the market-clearing exchange rate between the yen and dollar. Their axes measure

FIGURE 12-2   Average Values of the Dollar in Terms of Foreign Currencies, 1971–1987
Scales have been chosen so that increases represent appreciations of the U.S. dollar against an average of 15 other currencies. The values of the individual foreign currencies are weighted by total U.S. trade (exports *plus* imports) with the corresponding countries. Measures of this sort are described as indexes of effective exchange rates. *Source:* Morgan Guaranty Trust, *World Financial Markets* (various issues).

different things. But the Japanese demand curve for dollars can be used to derive a Japanese supply curve of yen, which can be combined with the American demand curve for yen to determine the exchange rate. The supply of yen is the quantity that Japanese will offer when they bid for dollars:

Supply of yen = demand for dollars × yen per dollar

When the dollar price of the yen is *OP*, the yen price of the dollar is *OR*, and the supply of yen is *OR* × *OV* or *OVFR* yen. When the dollar price of the yen rises to *OP'*, the yen price of the dollar falls to *OR'*, and the

supply of yen is *OR'* × *OV'*, or *OV'F'R'* yen. The quantity of yen supplied can rise or fall when the price of the yen rises. It rises when *OV'F'R'* is larger than *OVFR*, which happens when the demand curve *D*D** is elastic. It falls when *OV'F'R'* is smaller than *OVFR*, which happens when *D*D** is inelastic.

In Figure 12-4, we copy the demand curve for yen from the left side of Figure 12-3 and add the supply curve of yen derived in the manner just described. The supply curve *SS* is positively sloped when the Japanese demand curve *D*D** is elastic;

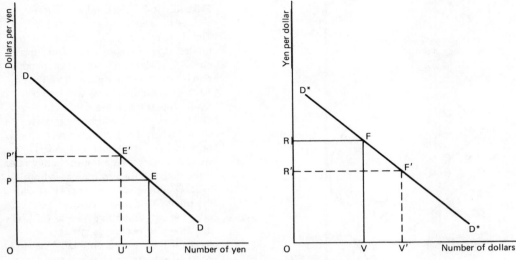

FIGURE 12-3   Demand Curves for Yen and Dollars
The curve *DD* on the left shows the American demand for yen. The
price of the yen is measured on the vertical axis, and the quantity demanded on the horizontal axis. An appreciation of the yen from *OP* to
OP' reduces the quantity demanded from *OU* to *OU'*. The curve *D*D**
on the right shows the Japanese demand for dollars. The price of the
dollar is measured on the vertical axis, and the quantity demanded on
the horizontal axis. The appreciation of the yen from *OP* to *OP'* shown
on the left appears on the right as a depreciation of the dollar from *OR*
to *OR'*, and the quantity demanded rises from *OV* to *OV'*. The Japanese
demand curve *D*D** can be used to derive a supply curve for yen.
When the dollar price of the yen is *OP*, so that the yen price of the dollar is *OR*, Japanese supply *OVFR* yen. When the yen appreciates, to *OP'*
so that the dollar depreciates to *OR'*, Japanese supply *OV'F'R'* yen.

an increase in the price of the yen raises
the quantity supplied. The supply curve is
negatively sloped when *D*D** is inelastic;
an increase in the price reduces the quantity supplied. The demand and supply
curves intersect at *E*. This point gives the
exchange rate that clears the foreign-
exchange market.[7] When the price of the

yen is *OP*, Americans demand *OU* yen, and
Japanese supply them.

To see how flexible exchange rates function, consider the effects of an increase in
the American demand for Japanese goods.
It will raise the American demand for yen
and shift the demand curve from *DD* to
D'D'. American banks may run down their

---

[7] We will call it a market-clearing rate, rather than
an equilibrium rate, because *E* may not denote a full-
fledged equilibrium. We will soon see that exchange
rates can affect domestic prices and other variables.
When this happens, the curves *DD* and *SS* will move to
new positions, changing the market-clearing exchange

rate. We should not describe *E* as an equilibrium point
(and *OP* as an equilibrium exchange rate) unless we
are sure that the effects of the exchange rate have
worked themselves out in each country so that the exchange rate will be self-perpetuating.

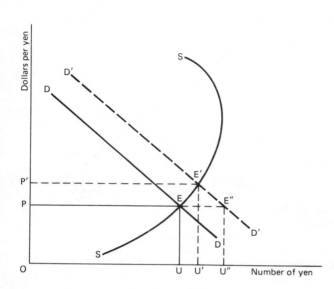

FIGURE 12-4   Demand and Supply Curves for Yen
The demand curve *DD* is copied from the left side of Figure 12-3. The supply curve *SS* is derived from the demand curve *D*D** on the right side of Figure 12-3. (The supply curve will be positively sloped when the demand curve *D*D** is elastic; it will be negatively sloped when the demand curve is inelastic.) As *DD* and *SS* intersect at *E*, *OP* will be a market-clearing exchange rate. If the demand for yen increases from *DD* to *D'D'*, there will be excess demand at the price *OP*. Under a flexible exchange rate, the yen will appreciate to *OP'*. Under a pegged exchange rate, governments will have to supply *UU"* yen to keep it from appreciating. The distance *UU"* is the surplus in the Japanese balance of payments measured in yen. The area *UEE"U"* is the deficit in the American balance of payments measured in dollars.

holdings of yen to satisfy their customers, but they will have to replenish those holdings eventually and enter the foreign-exchange market to buy yen. There will be an excess demand for yen equal to *UU"* at the initial exchange rate *OP*, and the yen will start to appreciate. As it does so, however, Americans will reduce their purchases from Japan, moving along *D'D'* from *E"* toward *E'*, and Japanese will raise their purchases from the United States, moving along *SS* from *E* towards *E'* (i.e., moving along *D*D** in Figure 12-3 from *F* toward *F'*). When they meet at *E'*, the excess demand for yen is eliminated, and the exchange rate is stabilized at *OP'*.

Adjustment under Pegged Exchange Rates

Under a system of pegged exchange rates, banks regulate their inventories much as they do with flexible rates, but their purchases and sales of currencies can have only small effects on exchange rates. Governments announce and maintain official prices for their currencies, known as *parities*, and keep market prices close to those official prices. When there is a pegged rate between the dollar and yen, and the Boston bank begins to bid for yen, one of the two governments will intervene in the foreign-exchange market. It will prevent the yen from appreciating by providing the yen demanded by the bank and accepting the dollars offered.

The immediate effects of intervention show up in the balance-of-payments accounts. Table 12-3 reproduces a summary of the cash component shown in Table 12-1 and adds a new transaction:

(h) The Boston bank buys $175,000 worth of yen, and the U.S. Treasury supplies them, drawing on its balance with the Bank of Japan.

The Boston bank's purchase appears as a debit in the cash component (an increase in

TABLE 12-3   Cash component of the Balance of Payments for the United States (thousands of dollars)

Item	Credit	Debit
Increase (+) in dollars held by foreign banks		
Transactions (a) through (g)	25	
Increase (−) in foreign currencies held by U. S. banks		
Transactions (a) through (g)	365	
Boston bank in yen (h)		175
Net increase (−)	190	
Increase (−) in U. S. reserve assets		
Balance in yen with Bank of Japan (h)	175	

foreign currencies held by U.S. banks). The U.S. Treasury's sale appears as a credit on a new line, showing changes in official reserves.

The two new entries have no net effect on the cash component or capital account. Changes in official reserves, however, have particular significance. First, they differentiate a pegged-rate system from a flexible-rate system. Second, they can have important consequences for money supplies. This is why changes in reserves are used to measure overall surpluses and deficits in the balance-of-payments accounts. In this particular case, the United States has an overall deficit because it has lost reserves. Note that there can be no balance-of-payments surplus or deficit under freely flexible exchange rates. Changes in reserves do not occur unless some government intervenes to influence exchange-rate behavior.

Intervention can be shown in Figure 12-4. Suppose that the dollar price of the yen is pegged officially at OP. When DD and SS intersect at E, the foreign-exchange market clears without intervention, and there is no surplus or deficit in the balance of payments. When DD shifts to $D'D'$, however, there is an excess demand for yen, and one of the governments must intervene to keep the exchange rate pegged at OP. It must sell UU'' yen and take up $UEE''U''$ dollars.

If the U.S. authorities intervene, U.S. reserves will fall by UU'' yen, and the U.S.

deficit will be $UEE''U''$ dollars. There will be no change in Japanese reserves, but Japan will still show a balance-of-payments surplus of UU'' yen. The reduction in U.S. reserves appears in the Japanese cash account as a reduction in Japanese liabilities to a foreign official institution, which is treated as being equivalent to an increase in Japanese reserves. (If the Japanese authorities intervene, Japanese reserves will rise by $UEE''U''$ dollars, and the Japanese surplus will be UU'' yen. There will be no change in U.S. reserves, but the United States will still show a deficit in its balance of payments, because the increase in Japanese reserves appears in the U.S. cash account as an increase in U.S. liabilities to a foreign official institution and is treated as being equivalent to a decrease in U.S. reserves.)

When exchange rates are pegged permanently, they cannot contribute to the adjustment process. What can take their place? Clearly, the demand and supply curves in Figure 12-4 must be made to move. The demand curve must be driven to the left or the supply curve to the right, until they intersect on the line PE''. They will then eliminate the excess demand for yen and the need for intervention, without any change in the exchange rate.

Many forces can contribute to this process. The mix will depend in part on the reasons for the initial increase in the American demand for yen. But money-supply changes induced by intervention will play a key role. The American money supply will fall, raising American interest rates, reducing American income and absorption, and reducing prices in the United States. The Japanese money supply will rise, reducing Japanese interest rates, raising Japanese income and absorption, and raising prices in Japan. All these events will contribute to the requisite shifts in the demand and supply curves. They are examined in subsequent chapters. This introduction concludes by showing why official intervention affects the American money supply.

Intervention and the Money Supply

When the U.S. Treasury sells yen to a Boston bank to keep the dollar from depreciating, it will receive instructions from the Boston bank to place the yen at the Japanese commercial bank where the Boston bank holds its balance. The Boston bank will receive instructions from the Treasury to place the corresponding dollars in the Treasury's account at the Federal Reserve Bank of Boston. Therefore, the Treasury will instruct the Bank of Japan to transfer $175,000 worth of yen to the Japanese commercial bank, and the Boston bank will instruct the Federal Reserve Bank of Boston to transfer $175,000 to the Treasury's account. The Federal Reserve Bank will deduct $175,000 from the Boston bank's *member-bank balance,* its account at the Federal Reserve Bank, and add that amount to the Treasury's account.

The U.S. Treasury will hold more dollars and fewer yen. These are the changes in its balance sheet (measured in thousands of dollars):

U.S. TREASURY

Assets		Liabilities
Reserves (yen) at Bank of Japan	−175	
Balance at FRB of Boston	+175	

The Federal Reserve Bank of Boston has larger liabilities to the U.S. Treasury but smaller liabilities to the Boston commercial bank:

FEDERAL RESERVE BANK OF BOSTON

Assets	Liabilities	
	Treasury balance	+175
	Member-bank balance of Boston Bank	−175

The Boston commercial bank has fewer dollars on deposit with the Federal Reserve Bank but more yen in its account with a Japanese bank:

BOSTON COMMERCIAL BANK

Assets		Liabilities
Member-bank balance at FRB of Boston	−175	
Balance (yen) at Japanese bank	+175	

The most important change, however, is yet to come.

The member-bank balance held by the Boston bank at the Federal Reserve Bank is part of the cash reserve that it must hold against its own deposit liabilities.[8] If that balance falls, and the bank does not have any excess reserves, it must cut back its loans and investments to replenish its cash reserves. Summarizing the complicated process that will follow, the reduction in one bank's member-bank balance can lead to a contraction in the money supply many times as large, with the size of the multiple depending on the quantity of excess reserves held by the whole banking system and the *reserve requirement* imposed by the

---

[8] Unfortunately, two sorts of reserves are involved in this exercise and appear again in subsequent chapters. First, there are the currency and other international reserves of official institutions (the Treasury's holdings of yen in this example). Second, there are the cash reserves of commercial banks (the member-bank balance of the Boston bank in this example). The two are quite different and must not be confused.

Federal Reserve System. If banks have no excess reserves and the reserve requirement is 20 percent, the reduction in the Boston bank's member-bank balance will lead to a fivefold reduction in the American money supply.

A similar process will occur in Japan but will run the other way. When the Bank of Japan transfers yen to a Japanese commercial bank at the request of the U.S. Treasury, it adds to the commercial bank's cash reserves, and the bank can start to increase its loans and deposits. The Japanese money supply will start to grow.

Adjustment Under the Gold Standard

If currencies were pegged to gold, as they were before World War I, exchange rates would be pegged too, and money-supply changes would take place automatically, without official intervention in foreign-exchange markets.

Under the gold standard, each government defined the value of its currency in grains or ounces of gold metal, then stood ready to buy and sell gold in exchange for its currency. Some governments went farther, issuing gold coins, but this was not vital. The gold-standard mechanism worked as well when governments issued paper money in exchange for gold, so that any change in official gold holdings caused an equal change in paper money outstanding.

When currencies were pegged to gold and governments were willing to deal in gold with private citizens as well as with other governments, gold could be used to trade one currency for another, and an implicit exchange rate was established between each pair of currencies. If the French franc was redeemable in gold at 140 francs per ounce, and the U.S. dollar was redeemable at $35 per ounce, $35 could be used to buy an ounce of gold, which could be used in turn to buy 140 francs. Therefore, a dollar would buy

4 francs. Actual exchange rates could fluctuate a bit, because governments charged small commissions, and traders had to pay the costs of shipping gold from one country to another. When an exchange rate ran outside the boundaries set by those commissions and costs, however, someone could profit by engaging in *arbitrage*.

An *arbitrageur* would buy gold with the currency that was priced below its gold parity in the foreign-exchange market, sell the gold for the currency that was priced above its gold parity, and then sell the second currency for the first. Suppose that the franc rose from $0.25 to $0.28 and that it cost $0.10 in commissions and freight to ship an ounce of gold from New York to Paris. An arbitrageur could buy 1,000 ounces of gold from the U.S. Treasury and ship them to Paris at a total cost of $35,100 ($35,000 for the gold and $100 in other costs). He could sell the gold to the Bank of France for 140,000 francs and could then sell the francs for dollars in the foreign-exchange market for $0.28 × 140,000 or $39,200. His profit would be $39,200 *less* $35,100 or $4,100. The arbitrageur would earn nearly 12 percent on capital in a matter of days! In the process, moreover, the arbitrageur would help to reduce the price of the franc by selling francs for dollars at the end of this three-part transaction and thus help to keep the actual exchange rate close to its gold parity. Finally, arbitrage would alter national money supplies. In this example, there is an increase in the supply of francs and a decrease in the supply of dollars, which are needed in the longer run for balance-of-payments adjustment.

Every so often, someone calls for a return to the gold standard. But practice was messier than theory, even in the nineteenth century. Governments went on and off the gold standard, back and forth between pegged and flexible exchange rates. Furthermore, they interfered with the money-supply effects that gold flows were supposed to produce automatically. Most economists are therefore convinced that the gold standard is no better or worse than most other methods of pegging exchange rates.

SUMMARY

The macroeconomic analysis of open economies is concerned with the effects of international transactions on output, employment, and the price level and the effects of these in turn on the balance of payments and exchange rate. It is also concerned with the implications of openness and exchange-rate arrangements for the functioning of monetary and fiscal policies.

A country's international transactions are described in its balance-of-payments accounts. Purchases and sales of goods and services appear in the current account, as do investment-income flows. Credit items in the current account are those that raise domestic income; debit items are those that raise foreign income. Purchases and sales of real and financial assets appear in the capital account, along with changes in cash balances, including officially held balances described as reserves. Credit items in the capital account (capital inflows) are those that increase foreign claims on the economy or decrease domestic claims on foreigners; debit items (capital outflows) are those that decrease foreign claims or increase domestic claims.

All transactions appear twice in the balance-of-payments accounts, once with each sign. Therefore, total credits equal total debits, and the balances on current and capital accounts always add up to zero. It is useful, however, to single out changes in official reserves to measure the overall surplus or deficit in the balance of payments. They reflect official intervention in foreign-exchange markets to peg or influence exchange rates. Under a freely floating exchange rate, there can be no such surplus

or deficit because there is no intervention. Under a pegged exchange rate, the surplus or deficit measures the amount of official intervention that was needed to prevent the rate from changing.

Most transactions that appear in balance-of-payments accounts show up in the foreign-exchange market. Typically, those that appear as credits are reflected in the foreign demand for the domestic currency, and those that appear as debits are reflected in the domestic demand for foreign currency. These demands, moreover, depend on the exchange rate. A depreciation of the domestic currency reduces the domestic demand for foreign currency by raising the domestic-currency prices of foreign goods, services, and assets. It raises the foreign demand for the domestic currency by reducing the foreign-currency prices of domestic goods, services, and assets. The foreign demand for the domestic currency can be expressed as the foreign supply of foreign currency, which can be used together with the domestic demand to identify the market-clearing exchange rate.

Under a flexible exchange rate, the domestic currency will depreciate in response to an excess demand for foreign currency. The depreciation, in turn, will reduce the domestic demand for foreign goods, services, and assets, curbing the demand for foreign currency, and will raise the foreign demand for domestic goods, services, and assets, boosting the supply of foreign currency. These adjustments will eliminate the excess demand. Under a pegged exchange rate, official intervention will prevent any change in the exchange rate, but it will initiate monetary changes that also eliminate the excess demand. The domestic money supply will fall, reducing domestic expenditure and, therefore, the domestic demand for foreign currency. The foreign money supply will rise, stimulating foreign expenditure and, therefore, the foreign demand for the domestic currency. A gold standard is a way to peg exchange rates and induce these monetary changes automatically.

Transactions that appear in the current account of the balance of payments also appear in the national-income accounts. Exports add to the demand for domestic goods and services. Imports supplement supplies on domestic markets. The current-account balance is equal to the difference between output and absorption. It is also equal to the sum of two internal balances, the private-sector surplus (saving *less* investment) and the public-sector surplus (tax revenue *less* government spending).

RECOMMENDED READINGS

Some matters covered in this chapter are treated more thoroughly in subsequent chapters, and lists of readings are appended to those chapters. Here are readings that deal with balance-of-payments accounts, the foreign-exchange market, and the links between them:

On the problem of defining surpluses and deficits in the balance-of-payments accounts, see *The Balance of Payments Statistics of the United States: Report of the Review Committee for Balance of Payments Statistics* (Washington, D.C.: Government Printing Office, 1965), ch. 9.

Several years ago, the U.S. government decided not to publish any measure of surplus or deficit; for reactions and comments, see Robert M. Stern et al., *The Presentation of the Balance of Payments: A Symposium* (Princeton, N.J.: International Finance Section, Princeton University, 1977).

On the functioning of foreign-exchange markets, see Roger M. Kubarych, *Foreign Exchange Markets in the United States* (New York: Federal Reserve Bank of New York, 1983).

On experience under the gold standard, see Richard N. Cooper, "The Gold Standard: Historical Facts and Future Prospects," *Brookings Papers on Economic Activity,* 1982 (1).

CHAPTER
13
INCOMES
AND THE
CURRENT ACCOUNT

ELEMENTS IN THE
ADJUSTMENT PROCESS

In Chapter 12, demand and supply curves were used to show how balance-of-payments adjustment is reflected in the foreign-exchange market. Under a flexible exchange rate, movements along the demand and supply curves play the leading role. Under a pegged exchange rate, movements of the curves themselves play the leading role.

To review the main lines of the analysis, consider the effects of an increase in the domestic demand for foreign goods, services, or assets. It raises the domestic demand for foreign currencies, depleting dealers' inventories. Dealers enter the foreign-exchange market to reconstitute those inventories and cause an outward shift in the demand curve for foreign currency. There is an excess demand for for-

eign currency at the initial exchange rate and, therefore, an excess supply of domestic currency.

If the exchange rate is flexible, the domestic currency depreciates. Foreign goods, services, and assets become more expensive in domestic markets, because the currency needed to buy them has become more expensive, and domestic buyers cut back their purchases, reducing the domestic demand for foreign currency. Domestic goods, services, and assets become cheaper in foreign markets, and foreign buyers step up their purchases, raising the foreign demand for domestic currency. These events show up as movements along the demand and supply curves.

If the exchange rate is pegged, an excess demand for the foreign currency must be met by official intervention. One or both of the governments concerned must sell the foreign currency, meeting the excess demand, and thus buy the domestic currency, absorbing the excess supply. Such intervention typically reduces the cash reserves of domestic banks and raises those of foreign banks. The domestic money supply contracts, depressing aggregate domestic demand and reducing the domestic demand for imports. The foreign money supply expands, stimulating aggregate foreign demand and raising the foreign demand for imports. The demand for the foreign currency falls, and the demand for the domestic currency rises, even though there is no change in the exchange rate. These events show up as shifts of the demand and supply curves.

But these are not the only elements in the adjustment process. A complete analysis must look first at the underlying cause of the increase in demand for the foreign currency.

Suppose that it is caused by a change in tastes—a switch in domestic demand from domestic to foreign goods. This will depress aggregate domestic demand, which will reduce the domestic demand for imports. Similarly, it will raise aggregate foreign demand, which will raise the foreign demand for imports. The income effects of the disturbance will work directly to reduce the excess demand for the foreign currency caused by the initial change in tastes.

Suppose that the increase in demand for the foreign currency is caused by a change in asset preferences—a switch by domestic asset holders from domestic to foreign bonds. As they sell domestic bonds, the prices of those bonds will fall and thus raise the domestic interest rate. This will depress aggregate domestic demand, which will reduce the domestic demand for imports. As asset holders buy foreign bonds, the prices of those bonds will rise and thus reduce the foreign interest rate. That will stimulate aggregate foreign demand and raise the foreign demand for imports. Once again, the income effects of the disturbance will re-

duce the excess demand for the foreign currency caused by the disturbance.

Therefore, we must trace carefully the ramifications of a disturbance, showing its direct effects on demand and supply conditions in the foreign-exchange market and its effects on all other variables that can impinge indirectly on that market. The character of the adjustment process will depend on the nature of the disturbance, the exchange-rate regime, the extent of integration between home and foreign markets, especially between asset markets, and the policies adopted by the governments concerned in response to the internal effects of the disturbance. It would be tiresome to trace in such detail all the effects of every disturbance, but it is not necessary. We can learn a great deal by looking at a few disturbances and at a small number of responses to them.

This chapter and the next will concentrate on two disturbances, *switches* in demand between home and foreign goods and *shifts* in the level of aggregate demand. They will also concentrate on two responses, income effects and price effects, which are the chief ingredients of the adjustment process affecting the current account. Thereafter, Chapter 15 will examine capital flows and interest-rate effects and combine them with income and price effects to describe the workings of domestic policies in an open economy. Chapter 16 will examine the influence of expectations on capital movements and exchange rates.

STRATEGIC SIMPLIFICATIONS

In recent work on the balance of payments and exchange-rate behavior, economists have emphasized the implications of economic integration. When national economies are tightly linked, events in one country's markets for goods and assets are influenced heavily by events in other countries' markets. Prices and interest rates are determined jointly at home and abroad, and national policies have rather limited effects on the domestic economy. There has been a tendency, moreover, to focus on long-run equilibria, where wage rates have adjusted fully to changes in the demand for labor, and stocks of assets, including money, have adjusted fully to the corresponding flows.

These analytical strategies reflect recent experience, notably the discovery that national price levels are strongly affected by price changes in international markets. Increases in the world price of oil afford the most dramatic examples. Those strategies likewise reflect recent developments in macroeconomic theory, which has come to stress, too strongly perhaps, the limited effectiveness of economic policy, even in a closed economy. Some economists argue that a change in monetary policy cannot have any permanent effect on the real side of the economy—on output or employment. Going farther, some say that a policy change cannot even have temporary effects unless it comes as a surprise to the private sector (or workers, firms, and households are constrained by contractual arrangements that prevent them from adjusting their behavior right away). This new view depends in part on the strong assumption that workers, firms, and households have *rational expectations;* they anticipate correctly the economy's response to any disturbance or policy change and neutralize the consequences by their own behavior.

Some of this new work will be examined later, in chapters that present macroeconomic models where markets are very closely integrated. Those chapters will not adopt the central thesis of the "new" macroeconomics, that policies are neutralized by private behavior. Nevertheless, they will show that economic integration can dilute the effects of monetary and fiscal policies, even in the absence of rational expec-

tations, or cause their effects to wear off eventually.

For a while, however, we will adopt an older and simpler approach. We will add international transactions to a closed economy without changing to any significant degree the ways in which its markets work. Furthermore, we will concentrate on the short or medium run, in which wages and prices tend to be rigid and stocks of assets do not change appreciably. Let us state these suppositions more precisely.

The Size of the Foreign Sector

Foreign transactions will be small compared with the size of the national economy, and it will be small compared with the world economy. Putting these assumptions very strongly,

1. Home and foreign prices will be fixed, and thus unaffected by disturbances or policies or by the balance-of-payments adjustment process set in motion by those disturbances and policies. The price effects studied in the next chapter will come from changes in exchange rates, not in the home prices of home goods or foreign prices of foreign goods.

2. The economy itself will be too small to influence aggregate demand, output, or employment in the outside world. In other words, we will disregard the *foreign repercussions* of domestic events.

The first assumption is unrealistic, even as an approximation to short-run price rigidity. It is very useful, however, because it allows us to equate nominal with real changes. When a disturbance raises gross national product at current prices, we will be able to say that it raises *real* gross national product to the same extent and, by implication, raises domestic employment. The second assumption is less extreme but clearly inappropriate for studying relationships among large economies like those of the United States, Western Europe, and

Japan. We will therefore abandon it later in this chapter, when we look at interactions between national economies.

Intervention and Sterilization

Official intervention in foreign-exchange markets will not affect national money supplies. We will ignore temporarily the money-supply effects of surpluses and deficits invoked in Chapter 12 and in the opening paragraphs of this chapter. But we will take them up again in Chapter 15, where they will play a major role in explaining the long-run effects of monetary and fiscal policies, and they will be vital in Chapter 17, which presents the *monetary approach* to balance-of-payments theory.

There are two ways to insulate the money supply from the effects of intervention. First, we can pretend that the amounts of intervention are too small to have much cumulative impact in the short or medium run. Second, we can assume that central banks *sterilize* the money-supply effects of intervention.

When a central bank sells foreign currency and thus buys domestic currency to keep the domestic currency from depreciating, it reduces the cash reserves of domestic banks, and triggers a contraction of the money supply. To replenish the banks' cash reserves and prevent that contraction, the central bank can make an open-market purchase of domestic bonds. When a central bank buys foreign currency and thus sells domestic currency to keep the domestic currency from appreciating, it can prevent an expansion of the money supply by making an open-market sale of domestic bonds.

The mechanics of sterilization can be illustrated easily by extending an example used in Chapter 12, where a Boston bank bought yen for dollars and the U.S. Treasury intervened to keep the dollar from depreciating. The main monetary consequence was, of course, the $175,000 reduction in the member-bank balance of the Boston commercial bank; this was the effect that could trigger a contraction of the American money supply. To offset it completely, the Federal Reserve System can buy $175,000 of government bonds on the open market, paying with a check drawn on itself (i.e., on the Federal Reserve Bank of Boston). To keep matters simple, suppose that the seller of the bonds deposits the check with the same commercial bank that was involved in the original foreign-exchange transaction. That bank will credit the seller's account and send the check on to the Federal Reserve Bank, which will credit the commercial bank's member-bank balance.

Let us look at the changes in the balance sheet of the Federal Reserve Bank, beginning with those shown in Chapter 12. After the U.S. Treasury has intervened in the foreign-exchange market, the Federal Reserve Bank of Boston has larger liabilities to the Treasury but smaller liabilities to the Boston commercial bank:

FEDERAL RESERVE BANK OF BOSTON

Assets	Liabilities	
	Treasury balance	+175
	Member-bank balance of Boston Bank	−175

The open-market purchase in the bond market adds to its assets and its liabilities:

FEDERAL RESERVE BANK OF BOSTON

Assets		Liabilities	
U.S. government bonds	+175	Member-bank balance of Boston bank	+175

Consolidating the two transactions,

FEDERAL RESERVE BANK OF BOSTON

Assets		Liabilities	
U.S. government bonds	+175	Treasury balance	+175

There is no net change in the member-bank balance of the Boston commercial bank and, therefore, no cause for a contraction of the money supply.

When domestic and foreign financial markets are closely integrated, central banks may not be able to engage in sterilized intervention, which means that they cannot conduct independent monetary policies when they peg exchange rates. This possibility is examined in Chapter 15. In this and the next chapter, however, we will assume that central bank can engage in sterilization. Indeed, we will go farther. We will assume that they have enough monetary independence, even under pegged exchange rates, to regulate interest rates by open-market operations.[1] Therefore, the interest rate will be treated here as the chief instrument of monetary policy; it will be used to influence aggregate demand and, at times, to influence capital movements.

INCOME, IMPORTS, AND THE MULTIPLIER

In Chapter 12, we looked briefly at the national-income accounts for an open economy. Exports of goods and services were added to consumption, investment, and government spending to define aggregate demand in the domestic market, and imports of goods and services were subtracted from aggregate demand to define gross national product. Using the same notation as before,

$$Y = C + I + G + X - M \qquad (1)$$

---

[1] To raise its country's interest rate, a central bank will make an open-market sale. The sale will reduce the supply of money but raise the supply of bonds available to the public. Accordingly, it will reduce bond prices, raising the interest rate.

We also saw that the current-account balance is equal to the sum of two domestic balances:

$$X - M = (S - I) + (T - G) \qquad (2)$$

The first term on the right side is the private-sector balance, the difference between saving and investment; the second is the public-sector balance, the difference between tax revenue and government spending.

The discussion in Chapter 12 did not distinguish between nominal and real amounts; it derived the equations shown here without saying whether the variables in them are measured at current or constant prices. In this chapter, they are measured at constant prices, because we have assumed that prices do not change. Therefore, they refer to quantities produced, consumed, and traded. Furthermore, a second assumption made before, that there are no foreign repercussions, allows us to show how production and employment are determined in a small open economy.

We will start with the familiar case of a closed economy but will introduce some new notation and use methods slightly different from those found in elementary textbooks. We will then be able to identify clearly the effects of opening the economy.

The Multiplier for a Closed Economy

A closed economy has no exports or imports ($X = M = 0$). Therefore, equation (2) can be rewritten as

$$S = I + (G - T) \qquad (3)$$

To simplify it further, use D to define the public-sector (budget) deficit,

$$D = G - T$$

so that

$$S = I + D \qquad (3a)$$

Finally, convert equation (3a) into a statement about changes,

$$dS = dI + dD \qquad (4)$$

where dS is the change in saving, and so on.

In closed and open economies alike, saving rises with income and with the interest rate, denoted here by r, but can also change *autonomously* (i.e., for reasons unrelated to behavior of the other variables under study). Therefore,

$$dS = sdY + S_r\,dr + dS^a \qquad (5)$$

Here, s is the *marginal propensity to save*, the fraction of any increase in income that goes to saving rather than consumption, S_r is the increase in saving induced by an increase in the interest rate, and dS^a is an increase in saving that takes place autonomously, for reasons unrelated to changes in income and the interest rate.[2]

Investment depends on many variables, including the size of the capital stock, the intensity with which it is utilized, and the rate at which it depreciates. It also depends on the interest rate, which is the only variable included here,

$$dI = I_r\,dr + dI^a \qquad (6)$$

where I_r is the decrease in investment induced by an increase in the interest rate, and dI^a is an autonomous increase in investment (taking account implicitly of all other variables that affect investment). Note that I_r is negative, whereas S_r is posi-

tive. An increase in the interest rate reduces investment but raises saving.

The size of the budget deficit depends on many decisions and events, decisions about tax rates and government spending and events affecting the whole economy. An increase in income, for example, raises tax revenues even when tax rates are fixed. It is hard to forecast the budget deficit, let alone control it. But we will assume that it is controlled completely, that D changes only when the government decides to change it. Politicians would laugh—or cry—at this assumption, but it is the easiest way to put fiscal policy into the analysis.

Returning to equation (4), substitute the right sides of equations (5) and (6) for the changes in saving and investment:

$$sdY + S_r\,dr + dS^a = I_r\,dr + dI^a + dD \qquad (4a)$$

Move $S_r\,dr$ and dS^a to the right side of this equation and divide both sides by the marginal propensity to save:

$$dY = \left(\frac{1}{s}\right)[(dI^a - dS^a) + dD - (S_r - I_r)\,dr] \qquad (7)$$

Finally, simplify equation (7) by defining two new terms:

$$dA^a = dI^a - dS^a$$
$$dA^g = dD - (S_r - I_r)\,dr$$

The first term is the autonomous change in domestic expenditure (absorption); it will be positive when there is an autonomous increase in investment larger than the autonomous increase in saving. (By definition, an autonomous increase in saving is independent of income, and it must therefore be matched by a reduction in consumption. That is why it reduces autonomous expenditure.) The second term is the change in domestic expenditure induced by government policies. It will be positive when the government raises its budget deficit (runs a

---

[2] In many models, saving is made to depend on disposable income (income after taxes) rather than total income. That specification may be more realistic, but it complicates the exposition in ways that are not needed for our work. The specification used in equation (5) has two implications. First, an increase in taxes is reflected fully by a decrease in consumption, rather than falling partly on consumption and partly on saving. Second, an increase in government spending matched by an increase in taxes has no effect on income; the "balanced-budget multiplier" is zero. (In Chapter 18, saving will depend on wealth in addition to income and the interest rate.)

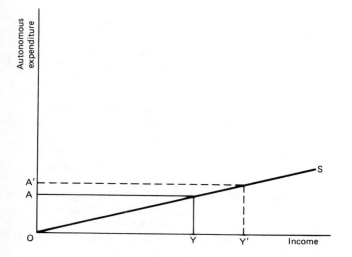

Autonomous expenditure

FIGURE 13-1 Income Determination in a Closed Economy
The slope of *OS* is the marginal propensity to save. When autonomous and policy-induced expenditures total *OA*, income is *OY*. When they rise to *OA'*, income rises to *OY'*.

less restrictive fiscal policy) or when the central bank reduces the interest rate (runs a less restrictive monetary policy). Putting these terms into equation (7),

$$dY = \left(\frac{1}{s}\right)(dA^a + dA^g) \qquad (7a)$$

This formulation may look new, because of the notation, but makes a familiar statement. Output, income, and employment, represented by Y, increase by a *multiple* of any autonomous or policy-induced increase in expenditure. The *multiplier* is $1/s$, and it is larger than 1 because s is smaller than 1.[3]

The story told by equation (7a) is illustrated in Figure 13-1. The line *OS* describes the relationship between changes in saving and changes in income; its slope equals the marginal propensity to save. When autonomous and policy-induced expenditures add up to *OA*, income is *OY*. When they rise to *OA'*, income rises to *OY'*. The in-

crease in income, *YY'*, is larger than the increase in autonomous expenditure, *AA'*.

The Multiplier for an Open Economy

When analyzing an open economy, we must work with equation (2), containing X and M, exports and imports of goods and services. It can be rewritten as

$$S + M = I + D + X \qquad (2a)$$

Converting it into a statement about changes,

$$dS + dM = dI + dD + dX \qquad (8)$$

which contains the changes in imports and exports in addition to the terms in equation (4), for the closed economy.

A country's imports of goods and services depend on prices at home and abroad, the exchange rate, and the country's income. But prices are held constant here, and we will hold the exchange rate constant temporarily. Therefore, the change in imports of goods and services can be written as

$$d\dot{M} = mdY + dM^a \qquad (9)$$

where m is the *marginal propensity to import*,

---

[3] Equation (7a) may look more familiar when put differently. Write $c + s = 1$, where c is the marginal propensity to consume. As $s = 1 - c$, equation (7a) becomes

$$dY = \left(\frac{1}{1-c}\right)(dA^a + dA^g)$$

the fraction of any increase in income that is spent on imports, and dM^a is an autonomous increase in imports. Note that an autonomous increase in imports reduces the domestic demand for domestic goods. Because it takes place independently of income and saving, it cannot affect absorption. When absorption is unchanged, however an increase in the demand for imports necessarily involves a switch in demand from home to foreign goods.

A country's exports of goods and services depend on prices, the exchange rate, and foreign income. Therefore, our price and exchange-rate assumptions allow us to write

$$dX = m^*dY^* + dX^a \qquad (10)$$

where m^* is the foreign marginal propensity to import, dY^* is the change in foreign income, and dX^a is an autonomous increase in exports, a switch in foreign demand from foreign to home goods.

Returning to equation (8), substitute the right sides of equation (5) and (6) for the changes in saving and investment, and substitute the right sides of equations (9) and (10) for the changes in imports and exports:

$$(sdY + S_r dr + dS^a) + (mdY + dM^a)$$
$$= (I_r dr + dI^a) + dD + (m^*dY^* + dX^a) \qquad (8a)$$

Move $S_r\, dr$, dS^a, and dM^a to the right side of this equation, collect the income terms, and divide both sides by the sum of the marginal propensities to save and import:

$$dY = \left(\frac{1}{s+m}\right)[(dI^a - dS^a) + dD$$
$$- (S_r - I_r)\, dr + (dX^a - dM^a) + m^*dY^*] \qquad (11)$$

This equation can be simplified by using the expressions for autonomous and policy-induced changes in expenditure and by in-

troducing one additional expression:

$$dN^a = (dX^a - dM^a) + m^*dY^*$$

This is the autonomous change in the current-account balance—in net exports of goods and services. It contains the autonomous switches in domestic and foreign demands and the income-induced change in foreign demand. (We can treat that income-induced change as being autonomous here because we have assumed that the domestic economy is too small to influence income in the outside world.) Putting this expression into equation (11),

$$dY = \left(\frac{1}{s+m}\right)(dA^a + dA^g + dN^a) \qquad (11a)$$

This equation differs in two ways from equation (7a), its closed-economy counterpart. First, the multiplier is $1/(s+m)$, which is smaller than $1/s$. There are two "leakages" from the domestic income stream, one into saving and the other into imports. Second, there is an additional influence on income—the autonomous change in net exports reflecting switches in domestic and foreign demand (and changes in foreign income).

Income Changes and the Current Account

How do income changes affect the current-account balance? Use N to denote the current-account balance,

$$N = X - M \qquad (12)$$

so that

$$dN = dX - dM \qquad (13)$$

Use the right sides of equations (9) and (10) to replace the changes in imports and exports:

$$dN = (m^*dY^* + dX^a)$$
$$- (mdY + dM^a) = dN^a - mdY \qquad (13a)$$

Finally, use the right side of equation (11a) to replace the change in income,

$$dN = dN^a - m\left(\frac{1}{s + m}\right)(dA^a + dA^g + dN^a)$$

(13b)

which can be rewritten as

$$dN = \left(\frac{s}{s + m}\right)dN^a - \left(\frac{m}{s + m}\right)(dA^a + dA^g)$$

(13c)

This equation makes two statements:

1. An autonomous increase in net exports improves the current-account balance. The improvement, however, is smaller than the autonomous increase itself; it is multiplied by $s/(s + m)$. The autonomous increase in net exports raises domestic income, which means that it raises imports, reducing the improvement in the current-account balance.

2. An autonomous or policy-induced increase in domestic expenditure worsens the current-account balance. By raising income, it raises the demand for imports.

These results are illustrated in Figure 13-2, which builds on Figure 13-1. The slope of OS is the marginal propensity to save. The slope of OF is the sum of the marginal propensities to save and import. (The difference between their slopes is therefore the marginal propensity to import.) When OE is the sum of autonomous and policy-induced expenditures, including the autonomous component of net exports, income is OY. When that sum rises to OE', income rises to OY'. The increase in income, YY', is smaller than in Figure 13-1, because the multiplier is $1/(s + m)$ rather than $1/s$. The line NX shows the relationship between income and net exports (the current-account balance); its slope is equal in absolute value to the marginal propensity to import. When the autonomous component of net exports is ON and income is OY, the current account is exactly balanced.

When income rises from OY to OY', net exports are affected, but we must know why income rises if we are to know *how* they are affected. When EE' represents an autonomous or policy-induced increase in domestic expenditure (like AA' in Figure 13-1), net exports fall to OB'. The increase in income raises imports, driving the current account into deficit. But when EE' represents an autonomous increase in net exports, a switch in domestic or foreign expenditure from foreign to home goods, NX shifts upward to $N'X'$ (NN' equals EE'), and net exports rise to OB''. The switch in expenditure raises net exports, driving the current account into surplus. But that surplus is smaller than the autonomous increase in net exports, because income rises, raising imports. (The autonomous increase is NN', which is equal to $B'B''$, but the surplus is OB'', which is smaller than $B'B''$.)

This last example makes a point noted in Chapter 12. The nature of balance-of-payments adjustment depends in part on the exchange-rate regime, but it also depends on the type of disturbance involved. Turning the previous example around, consider an autonomous switch in expenditure from home to foreign goods. Taken by itself, this would reduce net exports by the full amount of the switch in expenditure. But the actual reduction will be smaller, because domestic income falls and reduces the demand for imports. The fall in income induced by the autonomous decrease in net exports contributes to balance-of-payments adjustment.

The same point is made in Figure 13-3, which shows what happens in the foreign-exchange market. A switch in expenditure from American to foreign goods increases the American demand for foreign currency. The demand curve for yen shifts outward from DD to $D'D'$, producing an excess demand for yen at the initial exchange rate, OP, and a corresponding ex-

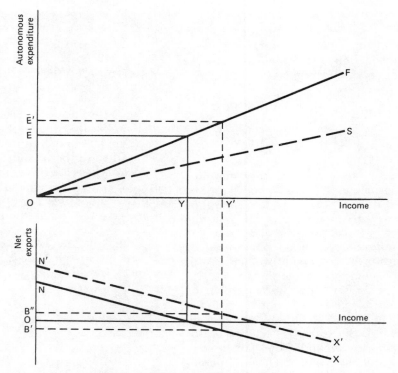

FIGURE 13-2 Income Determination in an Open Economy
The slope of *OS* is the marginal propensity to save. The slope of *OF* is
the sum of the marginal propensities to save and import. When *OE* is the
sum of autonomous and policy-induced expenditures, including autonomous net exports, income is *OY*. When the sum rises to *OE'*, income rises to *OY'* (by less than in Figure 13-1). The line *NX* shows the
relationship between income and net exports; its slope is equal (absolutely) to the marginal propensity to import. When income is *OY*, net exports are zero. When *EE'* is an autonomous or policy-induced increase
in domestic expenditure, net exports fall to *OB'*. When *EE'* is an autonomous increase in net exports (a switch in expenditure from foreign
to home goods), *NX* shifts upwards to *N'X'* (*NN'* equals *EE'*), and net
exports rise to *OB"*.

cess supply of dollars. The excess demand
for yen is *UU'*. The excess supply of dollars is *UEE'U'*, which also measures the autonomous decrease in net exports and the
current-account deficit that would appear
initially in the American balance of payments. But American income falls, reduc-

ing the demand for imports and the demand for yen. The demand curve for yen
drops back to *D"D"*, cutting the excess demand for yen to *UU"* and the excess supply
of dollars to *UEE"U"*.

Income changes of this sort contribute to
balance-of-payments adjustment, but they

Note 13-1

Using equation (11) in the text, write the change in U.S. income as

$$dY_1 = \left(\frac{1}{s_1 + m_1}\right)m_2 dY_2$$
$$+ \left(\frac{1}{s_1 + m_1}\right)(dA_1^a + dA_1^g + dN_1^a)$$

where s_1 and m_1 are the marginal propensities to save and import for the United States, m_2 is the marginal propensity to import for Japan, dY_2 is the change in Japanese income, dA_1^a and dA_1^g are autonomous and policy-induced changes in U.S. expenditure, and dN_1^a is the autonomous change in U.S. net exports. This last term, however, can be written as $dN_1^a = dX_1^a - dM_1^a = dX_1^a - dX_2^a$, where dX_1^a is an autonomous increase in U.S. exports reflecting a switch in Japanese demand from Japanese to U.S. goods, and dX_2^a is an autonomous increase in Japanese exports reflecting a switch in U.S. demand from U.S. to Japanese goods. Therefore, $dN_2^a = -dN_1^a$, and this result can be used when writing the change in Japanese income,

$$dY_2 = \left(\frac{1}{s_2 + m_2}\right)m_1 dY_1$$
$$+ \left(\frac{1}{s_2 + m_2}\right)(dA_2^a + dA_2^g - dN_1^a)$$

where s_2 is the marginal propensity to save for Japan, and dA_2^a and dA_2^g are autonomous and policy-induced changes in Japanese expenditure.

The equations for dY_1 and dY_2 can be solved simultaneously,

$$dY_1 = \frac{1}{H}[(s_2 + m_2)(dA_1^a + dA_1^g)$$
$$+ m_2(dA_2^a + dA_2^g) + s_2 dN_1^a]$$

$$Y_2 = \frac{1}{H}[(s_1 + m_1)(dA_2^a + dA_2^g)$$
$$+ m_1(dA_1^a + dA_1^g) - s_1 dN_1^a]$$

where $H = s_1 m_2 + s_2 m_1 + s_1 s_2$. An increase in U.S. expenditure ($dA_1^a > 0$ or $dA_1^g > 0$) raises both countries' incomes; so does an increase in Japanese expenditure. A switch in demand between the countries' goods ($dN_1^a \gtrless 0$) raises income in one country and lowers income in the other.

Using equation (13a) in the text, write the change in the U.S. current-account balance:

$$dN_1 = (dX_1^a + m_2 dY_2) - (dX_2^a + m_1 dY_1)$$
$$= dN_1^a + m_2 dY_2 - m_1 dY_1$$

Inserting the solutions for dY_1 and dY_2 given previously,

$$dN_1 = \frac{1}{H}[s_1 m_2(dA_2^a + dA_2^g)$$
$$- s_2 m_1(dA_1^a + dA_1^g) + s_1 s_2 dN_1^a]$$

An increase in Japanese expenditure improves the U.S. current-account balance; it raises incomes in both countries but raises Japanese imports by more than U.S. imports. An increase in U.S. expenditure has the opposite effect. Finally, a switch in demand to U.S. goods improves the U.S. current-account balance, even though it raises U.S income and reduces Japanese income. The reduction in Japanese income contributes to balance-of-payments adjustment but cannot complete it.

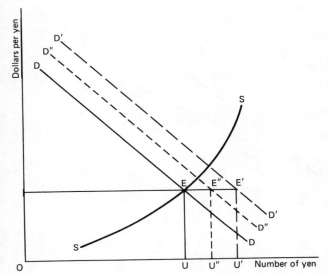

FIGURE 13-3 Switch in Expenditure from Home to Foreign Goods
A switch in American expenditure from home to foreign goods increases the demand for foreign currency (yen) in the foreign-exchange market. The demand curve for yen shifts from *DD* to *D'D'*. The excess demand for yen is *UU'*, and the excess supply of dollars is *UEE'U'* (which also measures the autonomous change in net exports). But the switch in expenditure reduces American income, reducing the demand for imports and for foreign currency. The demand curve for yen falls to *D"D"*. The excess demand for yen drops to *UU"*, and the excess supply of dollars drops to *UEE"U"*.

are too small to do the whole job. In Figure 13-2, an increase in income offset part of the autonomous increase in net exports, but it left a current-account surplus equal to *OB"*. In Figure 13-3, a decrease in income offset part of the autonomous decrease in net exports, but it left a current-account deficit equal to *UEE"U"*.

These results raise two questions: (1) What would happen if we took account of income changes in the outside world? Would they do the rest of the job, eliminating completely surpluses and deficits that are reduced but not removed by changes in one country's income? (2) What should be done to deal with surpluses and deficits if they are not removed completely by automatic income changes? The first question can be answered briefly, using a two-country model. The answer to the second will take up the rest of this chapter and all of the next.

A TWO-COUNTRY MODEL

The United States is not a small country. Therefore, a switch in American expendi-

ture from home to foreign goods will raise income in Japan and thus raise the Japanese demand for imports. In Figure 13-3, the supply curve *SS* will shift outward, as Japanese consumers demand additional imports and offer more yen to buy more dollars. This shift in the supply curve will reduce the excess demand for yen, which will fall below *UU"*. It will therefore reduce the excess supply of dollars, which will fall below *UEE"U"*. But the imbalance will not disappear completely. The increase in Japanese income makes an additional contribution to the adjustment process but cannot eradicate the American current-account deficit.

Adjustment with Interdependent Incomes

A formal proof of this assertion is given in Note 13-1, which derives equations for the changes in the two countries' incomes and their current-account balance. Illustrations are given in Figures 13-4 and 13-5.

The curve I_1I_1 in Figure 13-4 shows how, income in the United States depends

FIGURE 13-4 An Autonomous Increase in U.S. Expenditure in a Two-Country Model

The curve $I_1 I_1$ shows how U.S. income depends on Japanese income; when Japanese income is OY_2, U.S. income must be OY_1. The curve $I_2 I_2$ shows how Japanese income depends on U.S. income; when U.S. income is OY_1, Japanese income must be OY_2. The two countries' incomes are thus given at Q. The curve BB describes the sets of income levels at which the current account is balanced; the U.S. current account is in surplus above the curve and in deficit below the curve. An autonomous increase in U.S. expenditure shifts $I_1 I_1$ to $I_1' I_1'$; if there were no change in Japanese income, U.S. income would rise to OY_1^0. The new equilibrium point is Q', where U.S. income is OY_1', Japanese income is OY_2', and the U.S. current account is in deficit (because Q' lies below BB). The increase in U.S. income is $Y_1 Y_1'$, which is larger than $Y_1 Y_1^0$, the increase that would occur in a small-country model, because the increase in Japanese income raises U.S. income by raising U.S. exports.

on income in Japan; an increase in Japanese income raises U.S. income by raising the Japanese demand for U.S. exports. The position of the curve depends on autonomous expenditure in the United States and on the autonomous component of net exports. (In Figure 13-2, EE' of additional autonomous expenditure raised income by YY'. In Figure 13-4, it would shift the $I_1 I_1$ curve to $I_1' I_1'$ and raise U.S. income by $Y_1 Y_1^0$ if there were no change in Japanese income.) The slope of the $I_1 I_1$

curve depends on the marginal propensities to save and import for the United States and on the marginal propensity to import for Japan.[4] The curve I_2I_2 shows how income in Japan depends on income in the United States; an increase in U.S. income raises Japanese income by raising the U.S. demand for Japanese exports. Its position depends on autonomous expenditure in Japan and on the autonomous component of net exports. Its slope depends on the marginal propensities to save and import for Japan and on the marginal propensity to import for the United States.

The two countries' incomes are given at Q, because it is the only point where income levels are consistent. When Japanese income is OY_2, the I_1I_1 curve says that U.S. income must be OY_1. When U.S. income is OY_1, the I_2I_2 curve says that Japanese income must be OY_2.

The BB curve shows how the two countries' incomes affect the U.S. current account. Its position depends on the autonomous component of net exports. Its slope depends on the countries' marginal propensities to import. The current account is balanced at all points on BB.[5] At points above BB, the U.S. current account is in surplus (the Japanese account is in deficit); Japanese income is higher, relative to U.S. income, than it is along the BB curve, so Japanese imports are too large

to balance the U.S. current account. At points below BB, the U.S. current account is in deficit (the Japanese is in surplus); Japanese income is lower, relative to U.S. income, so Japanese imports are too small to balance the U.S. current account.

There is a basic conceptual difference between the countries' income curves and the BB curve. The income curves depict direct relationships between the two countries' incomes; when U.S. income is OY_1 Japanese income must be OY_2. The BB curve shows the relationship between the two countries' incomes, taken together, and a third variable, the current-account balance. The two countries' incomes are always given by points such as Q, where I_1I_1 and I_2I_2 intersect, but the BB curve does not have to pass through those points, because the current account does not have to balance at all times. (It does pass through Q in Figure 13-4, but that is for simplicity, not by necessity.)

What happens when there is an autonomous increase in U.S. expenditure? The I_1I_1 curve shifts outward to $I_1'I_1'$. The other curves do not shift. If the United States were a small country, unable to affect incomes in the outside world, U.S. income would rise to OY_1^0, and the United

---

[4] The curve I_1I_1 comes from the first equation for U.S. income in Note 13-1. Increases in A_1^q, A_1^g, and N_1^q would raise U.S. income, Y_1, by the small-country multiplier, $1/(s_1 + m_1)$, if they did not influence Japanese income; that is why they shift I_1I_1 to the right. An increase in Japanese income, Y_2, raises U.S. income by the small-country multiplier *times* the Japanese marginal propensity to import; that is why the slope of I_1I_1 depends on the U.S. marginal propensity to save and on the U.S. and Japanese marginal propensities to import. The curve I_2I_2 comes from the first equation for Japanese income in Note 13-1, and its properties are similar to those of I_1I_1. It is easy to show that I_1I_1 is steeper than I_2I_2 and that the curve BB, discussed later, lies between I_1I_1 and I_2I_2.

[5] The BB curve is based on the first equation for the U.S. current-account balance in Note 13-1. As net exports are zero all along BB, set $dN_1 = 0$ and solve that equation for the change in Japanese income required to keep the current account balanced when there is a change in U.S. income or an autonomous change in net exports:

$$dY_2 = \frac{m_1}{m_2} dY_1 - \frac{1}{m_2} dN_1^q$$

An increase in U.S. income requires an increase in Japanese income to raise the demand for U.S. exports and balance the current account. Therefore, BB is positively sloped. An autonomous increase in U.S. net exports would put the U.S. current account in surplus if it did not increase U.S. income, and elimination of the U.S. surplus would require a reduction in Japanese income to reduce the Japanese demand for U.S. exports. Therefore, an autonomous increase in net exports shifts BB downward.

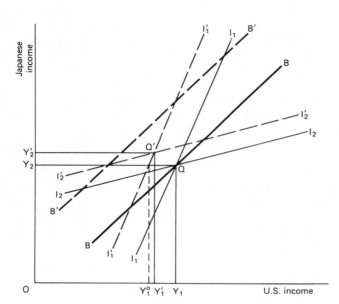

FIGURE 13-5   An Autonomous Switch
in Expenditure from Home to Foreign
Goods
In the initial equilibrium at Q, U.S. income is OY_1, Japanese income is OY_2, and the current account is balanced (because BB is drawn through Q). A switch in expenditure from U.S. to Japanese goods shifts the U.S. income curve from $I_1 I_1$ to $I_1' I_1'$. If there were no change in Japanese income, U.S. income would fall to OY_1^0. But the switch in expenditure also shifts the Japanese income curve from $I_2 I_2$ to $I_2' I_2'$, so the new equilibrium point is Q', where U.S. income is OY_1' and Japanese income is OY_2'. The decrease in U.S. income is not as large as in the small-country case, because the increase in Japanese income raises the demand for U.S. exports. The switch in expenditure, however, shifts the BB curve all the way to $B'B'$, and Q' lies below $B'B'$. Therefore, the U.S. current account is in deficit in the new equilibrium.

States would have a current-account deficit. (The results would be the same as in Figure 13-2.) As the United States is not a small country, incomes are affected in the outside world. The new equilibrium lies at Q', where $I_1'I_1'$. intersects $I_2 I_2$. Japanese income rises to OY_2', raising the demand for U.S. exports, and thus raises U.S. income further, all the way to OY_1'. The multiplier for a large economy is bigger than the multiplier for a small economy. But Q' lies below BB, which says that the United States continues to run a current-account deficit. Note 13-1 shows that the increase in Japanese income reduces the deficit but does not make it disappear completely.

Figure 13-5 deals with a more complicated case, a switch in expenditure from U.S. to Japanese goods, There are shifts in all three curves. The U.S. income curve shifts inward from $I_1 I_1$ to $I_1' I_1'$, because the switch in expenditure reduces the demand for U.S. goods. (If the United States were a small country, U.S. income would fall to OY_1^0.) The Japanese income curve shifts upward from $I_2 I_2$ to $I_2' I_2'$, because the switch in expenditure raises the demand for Japanese goods. The current-account curve shifts upward from BB to $B'B'$, because the switch in expenditure would drive the U.S. current account into deficit if there were no changes in the two countries' incomes.[6]

---

[6] The size of the upward shift in the current-account curve can be derived from the equations for that curve and for the income curves. It can be shown that $B'B'$ must intersect $I_1'I_1'$, vertically above Q and must intersect $I_2'I_2'$, horizontally across from Q.

The new equilibrium is at Q', the intersection of $I_1'I_1'$ and $I_2'I_2'$. Income falls to OY_1' in the United States, by less than it would if there were no increase in Japanese income. Income rises to OY_2' in Japan, by less than it would if there were no decrease in U.S. income. The contraction of U.S. income is limited by the increase in Japanese income and the resulting increase in the Japanese demand for U.S. goods; the expansion of Japanese income is limited by the decrease in U.S. income and the resulting decrease in the U.S. demand for Japanese goods. But the U.S. current account moves into deficit. The shift in the current-account curve is bigger than the shifts in the income curves, and Q' lies below $B'B'$, the curve on which the U.S. current account would be balanced after the autonomonous switch in expenditure.

We have thus answered the first question posed above, concerning the effects of income changes in the outside world. Although they contribute to the adjustment process, they cannot eliminate imbalances completely.

Measuring Interdependence

Econometric models of national economies rarely allow explicitly for the interdependence of national incomes. Best guesses about exports are fed into the models, not produced by the models themselves. In recent years, however, national models have been put together to show how disturbances and policy changes in one country affect other countries' incomes. The results of one such effort are shown in Table 13-1, which deals with changes in government spending. The numbers are not exactly comparable to the income multipliers in Note 13-1. They show third-year effects of the policy changes rather than the full multiplier effects; they include effects of changes in the countries' prices resulting from the changes in their incomes; and they include effects that come from changes in third countries' incomes. (The change in German income, for example, caused by a change in U.S. fiscal policy includes the effect on German income of the changes in the incomes of all the other

TABLE 13-1 Interdependence Among the Seven Economic Summit Countries: Income Changes Induced by Fiscal-Policy Changes (measured by third-year percentage changes in real gross national product)

Country Where Fiscal Policy Changes	*EFFECT ON INCOME IN:*						
	United States	*Japan*	*Germany*	*France*	*United Kingdom*	*Italy*	*Canada*
United States	*3.29*	0.53	0.37	0.44	0.70	0.34	1.41
Japan	0.03	*2.38*	0.16	0.18	0.17	0.11	0.18
Germany	0.00	0.24	*1.77*	0.84	0.33	0.56	0.18
France	0.03	0.11	0.32	*2.63*	0.23	0.30	0.09
United Kingdom	0.01	0.14	0.26	0.38	*0.65*	0.22	0.15
Italy	0.00	0.12	0.34	0.53	0.17	*1.68*	0.12
Canada	0.09	0.11	0.11	0.12	0.09	0.07	*1.84*

Source: John F. Helliwell and Tim Padmore, "Empirical Studies of Macroeconomic Interdependence," in R. W. Jones and P. B. Kenen, eds., *Handbook of International Economics* (Amsterdam: North-Holland, 1985), ch. 21. The estimates are those reported for the EPA model, which gives somewhat larger effects to U.S. fiscal policy than do most other models. (It likewise gives lower estimates of the effects of foreign fiscal policies on U.S. income and an unusually low estimate of the own-country multiplier for the United Kingdom.)

countries included in the model.) Nevertheless, the numbers are indicative of the degree to which events in a single country affect incomes elsewhere.

How do we read this table? Let there be an increase in government spending in the United States. Set it equal to 1 percent of real gross national product. The effect on U.S. income is shown on the first line of the table, in the column for the United States. Real gross national product rises by 3.29 percent. The effect on Japanese income is shown on the same line, in the column for Japan. Real gross national product rises by 0.53 percent. The own-country effects are italicized so that you can spot them easily. They are larger than the cross-country effects. But some of the cross-country effects are impressive, especially those of U.S. fiscal policy and, within Europe, those of German fiscal policy. Interdependence is far from negligible.

These linked simulations can be very useful. When governments exchange official forecasts, they frequently find that their forecasts are not mutually consistent. Each country has projected an increase in its exports different from the other countries' forecasts of their imports. When the relevant national models are linked, they make consistent forecasts, not only of trade flows but also of incomes. Here is an example. The Japanese econometric model that was combined with other national models to generate the numbers in Table 13-1 can be used by itself to estimate the change in Japanese income resulting from an increase in Japanese government spending. The second-year increase in income turns out to be 12 percent lower than the estimate obtained when the Japanese model is combined with other countries' models. When run by itself, the Japanese model cannot include the increase in Japanese income induced by the increase in Japanese exports resulting from increases in other countries' incomes.

COMPLETING THE ADJUSTMENT PROCESS

Since income changes at home and abroad are not large enough to eradicate current-account deficits, we must turn to the second question posed earlier. What should be done about those deficits?

A current-account deficit can be financed by adopting policies capable of attracting a capital inflow—by borrowing abroad in one way or another. It can be met by intervention in the foreign-exchange market—by running down reserves. But these are not apt to be permanent solutions. A country that continues to run a current-account deficit may find it increasingly difficult to borrow abroad; its creditors may start to doubt the country's ability to manage its debts. A country cannot run down reserves indefinitely because it will run out of them.

Therefore, a country with a current-account deficit may have to eliminate it sooner or later. It can tighten its monetary or fiscal policy to reduce domestic expenditure and thus reduce its imports. It can devalue its currency to switch expenditure from foreign to home goods. Alternatively, it can let market forces take the lead in reducing or switching expenditure. If it stops sterilizing reserve losses, its money stock will shrink when it intervenes to support its currency, and that will cut expenditure. If it stops intervening altogether, its currency will depreciate, and that will switch expenditure.

Postponing until Chapter 14 an explanation of the way that a change in the exchange rate can switch expenditure, let us examine the underlying choice between reducing and switching expenditure as ways to end a current-account deficit, using the equations for a small economy developed earlier in this chapter.

Introducing the Theory of Optimal Policy

Consider an economy with a pegged exchange rate that starts out in a blissful state. Its income, Y, is at the full-employment level, defined as some desired fraction of the labor force or a level consistent with long-run price stability. This condition is described hereafter as *internal balance*. Its net exports, N, are zero or are matched exactly by autonomous capital flows (flows that can be expected to continue indefinitely and are not affected by domestic policies). In other words, there is no deficit or surplus in the country's balance of payments. This condition is described hereafter as *external balance*.

The government of this lucky country will want to prevent any change in income. An increase would cause inflation; a decrease would cause unemployment. It will also want to prevent any change in net exports. An increase would produce a balance-of-payments surplus; a decrease would produce a deficit.

Suppose that the initial situation is disturbed by an autonomous increase in domestic expenditure ($dA^a > 0$). Income rises and net exports fall, as shown by equations

(11a) and (13c) and by Figure 13-2. What can the government do to restore internal and external balance? It can, of course, restore external balance by adopting policies to switch expenditure from foreign to home goods. This strategy, however, would drive the economy farther from internal balance, because it would add to the increase in income.[7] Therefore, the government should restore internal balance by using monetary or fiscal policy, or the two together, to bring domestic expenditure down to its initial level. By doing so, moreover, it will bring net exports back to their initial level. It will restore external balance as well as internal balance.

Suppose that the initial situation is disturbed by an autonomous decrease in net exports ($dN^a < 0$). Income and net exports fall. The government can restore external balance by reducing domestic expenditure. But that is the wrong strategy in this instance; it reduces income and drives the economy farther from internal balance. It can restore internal balance by raising expenditure. But that is a bad strategy, too; it raises net exports and drives the economy farther from external balance. Therefore, the government should adopt an expenditure-switching policy. By reversing the autonomous reduction in net exports, it can restore external and internal balance.

These examples illustrate a general principle. There is an *optimal pairing* of dis-

---

[7] Using equation (13c), set $dN = 0$ and solve for the autonomous switch in expenditure that would exactly offset an autonomous change in domestic expenditure:

$$dN^a = \frac{m}{s} dA^a$$

Using equation (11a), compute the effect on income:

$$dY = \frac{1}{s + m}(dA^a + dN^a)$$

$$= \frac{1}{s + m}\left[dA^a + \left(\frac{m}{s}\right)dA^a\right] = \frac{1}{s}dA^a$$

which is larger than the change in income caused by the autonomous change in expenditure. (It is, in fact, equal to the change in income that takes place in a closed economy, because the expenditure-switching policy offsets the leakage into imports.) The same method can be used to prove assertions made later concerning the effects of policy-induced expenditure changes designed to achieve internal or external balance in the face of an autonomous switch in expenditure.

turbances and policy responses. Facing an autonomous change in expenditure, a government can restore internal and external balance by an expenditure-changing policy. Facing an autonomous switch in expenditure, it should adopt an expenditure-switching policy.

Complications in the Two-Country Case

The same principle applies in the two-country model outlined earlier, but the applications are more complicated. We must distinguish between policy responses that are optimal from a global standpoint and those that are optimal only from a national standpoint. Algebraic illustrations are offered in Note 13-2. A diagrammatic illustration is offered in Figure 13-6.

As in earlier diagrams, the two economies begin at Q. Income is OY_1 in the United States and OY_2 in Japan, and the current account is balanced. The situation is disturbed, however, by an autonomous increase in U.S. expenditure, and the U.S. income curve shifts to $I_1^0 I_1^0$, just as in Figure 13-4. Incomes rise to OY_1^0 and OY_2^0, and the U. S. current account moves into deficit, because the new equilibrium point, Q^0, lies below BB.

We can see at once the globally optimal response. By tightening monetary or fiscal policy, the United States can reduce domestic expenditure, shifting the U.S. income curve back to $I_1 I_1$. This strategy restores internal balance in both countries and restores external balance for both together. Suppose, however, that the United States does nothing. What options are open to Japan?

Japan can restore internal balance by tightening its monetary or fiscal policy. It can shift its own income curve from $I_2 I_2$ to $I_2^i I_2^i$ and thus bring its income back to OY_2. By doing so, moreover, it brings the United States closer to internal balance; U.S. in-

come falls from OY_1^0 to OY_1^i. But the new equilibrium point, Q^i, lies farther from the BB curve. An expenditure-changing policy for internal balance carries both economies farther from external balance. Alternatively, Japan can restore external balance by relaxing its monetary or fiscal policy. It can shift its income curve from $I_2 I_2$ to $I_2^* I_2^*$, so that the new equilibrium point, Q^*, lies on the BB curve. By doing so, however, it takes both economies farther from internal balance: U.S. income rises to OY_1^*, and Japanese income rises to OY_2^*. These options, then, are not globally optimal. They are not even nationally optimal for Japan.

The best strategy for Japan is an expenditure-switching policy. By changing the exchange rate between the yen and dollar, or letting it adjust automatically under the influence of market forces, Japan can achieve internal and external balance. It can *insulate* the Japanese economy and balance of payments from the effects of a change in foreign expenditure. A proof is given in Note 13-2 (it could be given in Figure 13-6, but the diagram gets cluttered). The proof also shows that the strategy is not globally optimal, because it raises U.S. income, driving the United States farther from internal balance. It can be argued, however, that the U.S. government has itself to blame, for failing to adopt the globally optimal policy, a reduction in U.S. expenditure.

Consider one more case, an autonomous switch in expenditure from U.S. to Japanese goods. We saw in Figure 13-5 that this disturbance reduces U.S. income, raises Japanese income, and drives the U.S. balance of payments into deficit. The optimal response from a global standpoint is, of course, a U.S. or Japanese policy to switch expenditure back again. Expenditure-changing policies are not optimal, even from a national standpoint. If the United States raises domestic expenditure to restore internal balance, it will drive its bal-

FIGURE 13-6 Effects of Japanese Expenditure Policies.

An autonomous increase in U.S. expenditure shifts the U.S. income curve from $I_1 I_1$ to $I_1^0 I_1^0$, raising U.S. income to OY_1^0, raising Japanese income to OY_2^0, and driving the U.S. current account into deficit (because Q^0 lies below BB). To restore internal balance by changing domestic expenditure, Japan must tighten its monetary or fiscal policy to shift its income curve from $I_2 I_2$ to $I_2^i I_2^i$. The new equilibrium point is Q^i, where Japanese income returns to OY_2. U.S. income falls to OY_1^i but its current-account balance moves farther into deficit (because Q^i is farther from BB). To restore external balance by changing domestic expenditure, Japan must relax its monetary or fiscal policy to shift its income curve to $I_2^* I_2^*$. The new equilibrium point is Q^*, which lies on BB. But both countries move farther from internal balance. Income rises to OY_1^* in the United States and to OY_2^* in Japan.

Note 13-2

Let there be an autonomous increase in U.S. expenditure ($dA_1^q > 0$). The effects on U.S. and Japanese incomes are given by the third and fourth equations in Note 13-1, and the effect on the current-account balance is given by the final equation. The optimal response from a global standpoint is a policy-induced reduction in U.S. expenditure ($dA_1^g = -dA_1^q$). It can restore internal balance in both countries and external balance, too ($dY_1 = dY_2 = dN_1 = 0$). If the United States fails to adopt that policy, Japan has three options:

(1) An expenditure-changing policy for internal balance can be defined by

setting $dY_2 = 0$ and solving the Japanese income equation for the requisite change in Japanese expenditure; it is $dA_2^g = -[m_1/(s_1 + m_1)] dA_1^q$. This policy reduces U.S. income, but not by enough to restore internal balance in the United States. Substituting the solution for dA_2^g into the U.S. income equation,

$$dY_1 = \frac{1}{H}\left[(s_2 + m_2)dA_1^q - m_2\left(\frac{m_1}{s_1 + m_1}\right)dA_1^q\right]$$

$$= \frac{1}{s_1 + m_1} dA_1^q$$

This is the same change in U.S. income that was given for a small economy by equation (11a), because Japanese income has not been allowed to change. Furthermore, the policy worsens the external imbalance, because Japanese imports cannot rise when Japanese income does not change. The resulting change in the current-account balance is the same as the change for a small economy given by equation (13c). This policy is not globally optimal and not nationally optimal even for Japan, which is driven farther from external balance.

(2) An expenditure-changing policy for external balance can be defined by setting $dN_1 = 0$ and solving the current-account equation for the requisite change in Japanese expenditure; it is $dA_2^g = (s_2 m_1/s_1 m_2)dA_1^q$. As this change has the same sign as the autonomous change in U.S. expenditure, it increases the changes in both countries' incomes, driving them farther from internal balance.

(3) An expenditure-switching policy for internal balance can be defined by setting $dY_2 = 0$ and solving the Japanese income equation for the requisite switch in expenditure; it is $dN_1^q = (m_1/s_1)dA_1^q$. The same result is obtained by setting $dN_1 = 0$ and solving the current-account equation. The expenditure-switching policy that restores internal balance also restores external balance. Therefore, this policy is nationally optimal for Japan. It is not globally optimal, however, because it increases the change in U.S. income. (The signs of dN_1^q and dA_1^q are the same, and they appear with the same signs in the U.S. income equation.)

Let there be an autonomous switch in U.S. expenditure ($dN_1^q \gtrless 0$). The optimal response from a global standpoint is a U.S. or Japanese policy to switch expenditure back again. Expenditure-changing policies are not globally or nationally optimal. Consider the options open to the United States. (Those open to Japan have symmetrical effects.)

(1) An expenditure-changing policy for internal balance is defined by setting $dY_1 = 0$; it is $dA_1^g = -[s_2/(s_2 + m_2)]dN_1^q$. This policy increases the external imbalance (because dA_1^g and dN_1^q have opposite signs and appear with opposite signs in the current-account equation). It also increases the change in Japanese income (the reason is the same). Therefore, Japan is driven farther from internal balance, and both countries are driven farther from external balance.

(2) An expenditure-changing policy for external balance is defined by setting $dN_1 = 0$; it is $dA_1^g = (s_1/m_1)dN_1^q$. This policy is not nationally optimal for the United States. It increases the change in U.S. income (because dA_1^g and dN_1^q have the same signs and appear with the same signs in the U.S. income equation). But it restores internal balance in Japan:

$$dY_2 = \frac{1}{H}(m_1 dA_1^g - s_1 dN_1^q)$$
$$= \frac{1}{H}\left[\left(\frac{s_1}{m_1}\right)m_1 dN_1^q - s_1 dN_1^q\right] = 0$$

When used to deal with an autonomous switch in expenditure, an expenditure-changing policy for external balance is nationally optimal in an *altruistic* sense. It restores internal balance in the *foreign* country!

ance of payments into deeper deficit. If it reduces domestic expenditure to restore external balance, it will carry its economy farther from internal balance. Japan faces a symmetrical dilemma. Nevertheless, an odd result appears in Note 13-2. If the United States reduces expenditure to achieve external balance, it will bring Japanese income back to its initial level. Japan will enjoy external and internal balance. An expenditure-changing policy for external balance is nationally optimal but in an *altruistic* way. It confers internal balance on the *foreign* economy.

National Policies and International Polemics

When exchange rates are pegged and difficult to change, governments cannot easily achieve the switches in expenditure that are optimal globally or nationally for dealing with certain disturbances. (There are other ways to switch expenditure, including tariffs, but these have real welfare costs and can provoke retaliation.) The resulting policy conflicts can cause nasty arguments.

If one country's spending changes autonomously and its government fails to correct the situation by modifying its domestic policies, other countries will experience internal and external problems that they cannot solve completely by changing their own policies. They will confront the dilemmas faced by Japan in Figure 13-6 and will therefore demand a change in policy by the country in which the disturbance arose. It is the only country that can adopt a globally optimal response.

An autonomous switch in expenditure can cause trouble, too. Each government will want the other to adopt an expenditure-changing policy for external balance—the policy with the altruistic feature mentioned earlier. Japan may thus wait for the United States to act, the United States may wait for Japan, and each will blame the other for its plight. Yet blame is hard to fix because of the nature of the disturbance and the dilemma that both countries face.

These examples are too simple to explain completely the disputes of recent years, especially those involving U.S. policies. The disputes have been compounded by the effects of capital flows produced by monetary and fiscal policies. Nevertheless, these simple examples show how controversies can arise among major countries whose economies and policies are interdependent.

SUMMARY

This chapter has developed the theory of income determination for an open economy, beginning with a country that is too small to affect other countries' incomes. Throughout the chapter, prices were fixed, the exchange rate was pegged, and the country's central bank sterilized reserve flows and used its control of the money supply to regulate the interest rate. Changes in the interest rate represented changes in monetary policy. Changes in taxes represented changes in fiscal policy. The two together were described as expenditure-changing policies.

Using the basic equations of national-income accounting and simple behavioral relationships connecting a country's income with its demands for home and foreign goods, we can derive the national-income multiplier for an open economy and an additional equation linking the current-account balance to autonomous changes and switches in expenditure. The multiplier is smaller for an open economy than for a closed economy, because there are two leakages from the income stream, one into saving and the other into imports. An autonomous or policy-induced increase in expenditure raises income and worsens the current-account balance. An autonomous switch in expenditure from foreign to home goods raises income, too, but improves the current-account balance. The increase in income induced by an autonomous switch in expenditure raises the demand for imports and reduces the improvement in the current-account balance, but it does not eliminate the whole improvement.

When we allow for changes in other countries' incomes, an autonomous increase in domestic expenditure leads to a larger increase in domestic income, because it raises other countries' incomes and imports. An autonomous switch in expenditure, however, leads to a smaller increase in domestic income, because it reduces other countries' incomes and imports. Even in this multicountry case, however, automatic income changes cannot eliminate completely the current-account deficit or surplus produced by an autonomous disturbance.

A country confronting an autonomous increase in domestic expenditure can restore internal and external balance by an expenditure-reducing policy—a tightening of monetary or fiscal policy. A country confronting an autonomous switch in expenditure can restore internal and external balance by an expenditure-switching policy—a change in the exchange rate. These policies are optimal from national and global standpoints. Other policies may be optimal from a national standpoint but not a global standpoint. Confronting an autonomous change in foreign expenditure, a government can restore internal and external balance by an expenditure-switching policy. A change in its exchange rate will insulate its economy from the external disturbance, but it will drive the foreign country farther from internal balance. Confronting an autonomous switch in expenditure, a government cannot restore internal and external balance by an expenditure-changing policy. But by using such a policy to restore external balance, it can restore internal balance in the other country.

RECOMMENDED READINGS

The subjects treated in this chapter are examined at greater length in James E. Meade, *The Balance of Payments* (London: Oxford University Press, 1951), pts. I–IV.

On the multiplier and its uses, see Lloyd A. Metzler, "Underemployment Equilibrium in International Trade," *Econometrica,* 10 (April 1942); for a more thorough geometric treatment of the two-country case, see Romney Robinson, "A Graphical Analysis of the Foreign Trade Multiplier," *Economic Journal,* 62 (September 1952).

The vital distinction between shifts and switches in expenditure comes from a famous paper by Harry G. Johnson, "Towards a General Theory of the Balance of Payments," in H. G. Johnson, *International Trade and Economic Growth* (Cambridge, Mass.: Harvard University Press, 1961), reprinted in American Economic Association, *Readings in International Economics* (Homewood, Ill.: Richard D. Irwin, 1968), ch. 23.

The problems of policy interdependence are explored more thoroughly in Chapters 19 and 20, and additional readings are listed there.

14

EXCHANGE RATES AND THE CURRENT ACCOUNT

INTRODUCTION

At several points in the previous chapter, changes in exchange rates were said to cause switches in expenditure. This chapter furnishes the explanation and explores its implications for the theory of economic policy. It uses the basic assumptions of the previous chapter. Home and foreign prices are fixed. The economy is too small to influence incomes in other countries. The central bank sterilizes the effects of intervention in the foreign-exchange market and uses its control of the money supply to regulate the interest rate.

The first section of the chapter works through the expenditure-switching effect of a change in the exchange rate. It sets out the *elasticities approach* to the analysis of exchange-rate changes. The next section looks at the implications for incomes and prices at home and abroad. This takes us to

the *absorption approach* and the role of the exchange rate as a policy instrument. The chapter ends with a brief look at the way that a flexible exchange rate would behave in the sort of model used throughout the chapter.

THE ELASTICITIES APPROACH

In Chapter 12, which introduced exchange-rate theory, we were already dealing with switches in expenditure. When changes in exchange rates led to movements along demand and supply curves for currencies, they reflected switches in demands between home and foreign goods.[1]

---

[1] Another form of switching is emphasized in some accounts. A depreciation of the domestic currency tends to raise the domestic prices of *traded* goods relative to those of *nontraded* goods. Therefore, it switches domestic demand from traded to nontraded goods,

Additional conditions must be satisfied, however, before we can be sure that a depreciation or devaluation of the domestic currency will improve the current-account balance and raise domestic income, as was asserted in the previous chapter.

The Marshall–Lerner–Robinson Condition

One such condition involves the price elasticities of the domestic and foreign demands for imports. It is known as the Marshall–Lerner–Robinson condition, after three economists who derived it independently.

Consider two countries in which internal prices and income are constant. Neglect trade in services and investment-income

---

releasing additional goods for export, as well as reducing imports. Symmetrical effects occur in the outside world. Some say that this is the most important expenditure-switching effect, because the prices of traded goods are determined in international markets and cannot be affected by changing the exchange rate. The form of substitution does not matter much, however, when we are dealing with the broad macroeconomic effects of an exchange-rate change. We have merely to show that there is *some* form of substitution, so that a change in the exchange rate *can* switch expenditure.

flows so that the current-account balance equals the trade balance, and assume that trade is balanced initially. The Marshall–Lerner–Robinson (MLR) condition makes this statement:

A depreciation or devaluation of a country's currency will improve its current-account balance if the sum of the price elasticities of domestic and foreign demands for imports is larger than unity.

This condition is derived algebraically in Note 14-1. It is illustrated diagrammatically in Figure 14-1.

The upper panels of Figure 14-1 show demand curves for exports and imports plotted against prices in domestic currency. The lower panels show them plotted against prices in foreign currency. The home-currency price of exports, p_1, is constant. Therefore, the supply curve S_1 in the upper left panel is perfectly elastic and cannot shift. Its foreign-currency counterpart, however, depends on the exchange rate, π. The supply curve in that panel is also infinitely elastic, but it shifts downward as π rises. The foreign-currency price of im-

---

Note 14-1

To derive the MLR condition, define the trade balance as

$$N = p_1 c_1^* - \pi p_2^* c_2$$

Here, p_1 is the home-currency price of the home (export) good, and c_1^* is the quantity demanded by foreign consumers; p_2^* is the foreign-currency price of the foreign (import) good, and c_2 is the quantity demanded by domestic consumers; and π is the exchange rate in units of home currency per unit of for-

eign currency. But the change in any product, ab, can be written as $ab(\dot{a} + \dot{b})$, where $\dot{a}$ is (da/a), the proportionate change in a. Therefore, the change in N is

$$dN = p_1 c_1^* (\dot{p}_1 + \dot{c}_1^*) - \pi p_2^* c_2 (\dot{\pi} + \dot{p}_2^* + \dot{c}_2)$$

The foreign demand for the home good depends on the prices of home and foreign goods and on foreign income, all expressed in foreign currency; the domestic demand for the foreign good depends on those same prices and on domestic income, expressed in home currency. Formally, $c_1^* = g^*(p_1^*, p_2^*, Y^*)$ and $c_2 = g(p_1, p_2, Y)$ where $p_1^* = (p_1/\pi)$ and $p_2 = \pi p_2^*$, while Y^* and Y are foreign and home incomes.

The change in c_1^* can therefore be written as

$$dc_1^* = g_1^* dp_1^* + g_2^* dp_2^* + g_Y^* dY^*$$

where g_1^* is the change in c_1^* induced by a small change in p_1^*, and so on. (As quantity demanded normally falls when the price of a good rises but rises when incomes rise, $g_1^* < 0$, and $g_Y^* > 0$. The sign of g_2^* is uncertain.) Let e_1^* be the *own*-price elasticity of the foreign demand for the home good, let e_2^* be its *cross*-price elasticity, and let e_Y^* be its income elasticity:

$$e_1^* = -g_1^*(p_1^*/c_1^*) > 0,$$

$$e_2^* = g_2^*(p_2^*/c_1^*) \gtrless 0,$$

$$e_Y^* = g_Y^*(Y^*/c_1^*) > 0$$

The previous equation can then be rewritten as

$$c_1^* = -e_1^* \dot{p}_1^* + e_2^* \dot{p}_2^* + e_Y^* \dot{Y}^*$$

where c_1^* is the proportionate change in the foreign demand for the home good. Similarly, the change in c_2 can be written as

$$c_2 = e_1 \dot{p}_1 - e_2 \dot{p}_2 + e_Y \dot{Y}$$

where e_1 is the *cross*-price elasticity of the domestic demand for the foreign good, e_2 is its *own*-price elasticity, and e_Y is its income elasticity. But the change-in-product rule says that $\dot{p}_1^* = \dot{p}_1 - \dot{\pi}$, and $\dot{p}_2 = \dot{p}_2^* + \dot{\pi}$. Substituting these expressions for $\dot{p}_1^*$ and $\dot{p}_2$ into the equations for c_1^* and c_2, and using those equations to replace c_1^* and c_2 in the equation for the change in N,

$$dN = p_1 c_1^*[\dot{p}_1 - e_1^*(\dot{p}_1 - \dot{\pi}) + e_2^* \dot{p}_2^* + e_Y^* \dot{Y}^*]$$
$$- p_2^* c_2[\dot{\pi} + \dot{p}_2^* + e_1 \dot{p}_1 - e_2(\dot{p}_2^* + \dot{\pi}) + e_Y \dot{Y}]$$

In the text, however, the MLR condition is stated under three restrictions: Trade is balanced initially ($p_1 c_1^* = \pi p_2^* c_2$). Home and foreign prices are constant ($\dot{p}_1 = \dot{p}_2^* = 0$). Incomes are constant ($\dot{Y}^* = \dot{Y} = 0$). Imposing these restrictions on the previous equation,

$$dN = p_1 c_1^*(e_1^* \dot{\pi} - \dot{\pi} + e_2 \dot{\pi})$$
$$= p_1 c_1^*(e_1^* + e_2 - 1)\dot{\pi}$$

As e_1^* is the price elasticity of the foreign demand for imports and e_2 is the price elasticity of the domestic demand for imports, the last statement embodies the MLR condition. A devaluation or depreciation of the domestic currency ($\dot{\pi} > 0$) improves the current-account balance ($dN > 0$) when the sum of the elasticities of demand is larger than unity. Hereafter, we write $e_\pi = e_1^* + e_2 - 1$, so that $e_\pi > 0$ satisfies the MLR condition.

ports, p_2^*, is constant, too, so the supply curve S_2 in the lower right panel is perfectly elastic and cannot shift. Its home-currency counterpart, however, depends on π. It shifts upward as π rises.

The curve D_1 in the lower left panel is the demand curve for the home country's exports (i.e., the foreign demand curve for imports). It is plotted against the price that the foreign consumer faces. That price begins at Oa, and the quantity demanded is Oc. Therefore export receipts in foreign currency begin at $Oabc$. A depreciation or devaluation of the domestic currency raises π and reduces the price facing foreign consumers. Let it fall to Oa', shifting the sup-

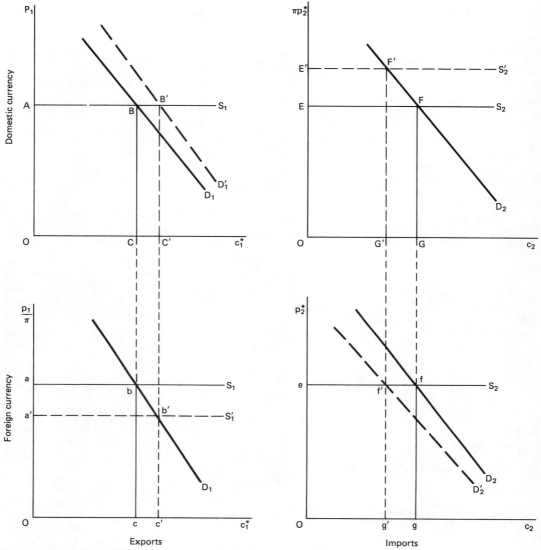

FIGURE 14-1 Effects of a Devaluation on the Current-Account Balance

The upper panels show prices and outlays in home currency. When the home-currency price of exports is OA, the foreign demand is OC, and export proceeds are $OABC$. When the home-currency price of imports is OE, the domestic demand is OG, and import payments are $OEFG$. Let $OABC$ equal $OEFG$ initially. The lower panels show prices and outlays in foreign currency. When the foreign-currency price of exports is Oa, the foreign demand is Oc, and export proceeds are $Oabc$. When the foreign-currency price of imports is Oe, the domestic demand is Og, and import payments are $Oefg$. When $OABC$ equals $OEFG$, then $Oabc$ equals $Oefg$. A devaluation or depreciation of the domestic currency reduces the foreign-currency price of exports from Oa to Oa', raising quantity from Oc to Oc'. Export proceeds in foreign currency become $Oa'b'c'$. Domestic suppliers see this as an increase in demand, an outward shift in the demand curve from D_1 to D_1' in the upper export panel. Quantity rises by CC' (equal to cc'), and export proceeds in home currency rise to $OAB'C'$. The devaluation raises the home-currency price of imports from OE to OE', reducing quantity from OG to OG'. Import payments in home currency become $OE'F'G'$. Foreign suppliers see this as a decrease in demand, an inward shift in the demand curve from D_2 to D_2' in the lower import panel. Quantity falls by gg' (equal to GG'), and import payments in foreign currency fall to $Oef'g'$. Let the elasticity of D_1 be unity (so that $Oa'b'c'$ equals $Oabc$); export receipts are constant in foreign currency. Let the elasticity of D_2 be greater than zero (so that $Oef'g'$ is smaller than $Oefg$ because gg' is not zero); import payments fall in foreign currency. The current-account balance improves in foreign currency.

ply curve downward from S_1 to S_1'. Foreign consumers move along D_1, and export volume rises to Oc'. Export receipts in foreign currency go to $Oa'b'c'$. This outcome is translated into domestic currency in the upper left panel. The export price remains at OA in domestic currency, so the supply curve does not shift. But export volume rises to OC' (CC' equals cc'). Seen from the standpoint of domestic suppliers, the outcome is an outward shift in the demand curve from D_1 to D_1', an increase in sales, and an increase in home-currency receipts from $OABC$ to $OAB'C'$.

The curve D_2 in the upper right panel is the domestic demand curve for imports plotted against the price that the domestic consumer faces. That price begins at OE, and the quantity demanded is OG. Import payments in domestic currency begin at $OEFG$. A depreciation or devaluation of the domestic currency raises the home-currency price. Let it rise to OE', shifting the supply curve upward from S_2 to S_2'. (The ratio OE'/OE must equal absolutely the ratio Oa'/Oa, because both ratios measure the same change in π.) Domestic consumers move along D_2, and import volume falls to OG'. Import payments in domestic currency go from $OEFG$ to $OE'F'G'$. This outcome is translated into foreign currency in the lower right panel. The import price remains at Oe in foreign currency, so the supply curve does not shift. But import volume falls to Og' (gg' equals GG'). Seen from the standpoint of foreign suppliers, the outcome is an inward shift in the demand curve from D_2 to D_2', a decrease in sales, and a decrease in their foreign-currency receipts to $Oef'g'$.

Let trade be balanced initially ($OABC$ equals $OEFG$, and $Oabc$ equals $Oefg$). Suppose that the price elasticity of the foreign demand curve is 1 in the neighborhood of point b. The revenue-reducing effect of the decrease in price is exactly equal to the revenue-raising effect of the increase in

quantity, and export revenues remain constant in foreign currency ($Oa'b'c'$ equals $Oabc$). Suppose that the price elasticity of the domestic demand curve is greater than zero. The quantity of imports falls (gg' is not zero), reducing import payments in foreign currency ($Oef'g'$ is smaller than $Oefg$). The values chosen for the two price elasticities satisfy the MLR condition (their sum is greater than unity), and the depreciation or devaluation improves the current-account balance measured in foreign currency.

What about the balance measured in domestic currency? It must also improve. When export proceeds are unchanged in foreign currency, their value in home currency must rise in proportion to the change in the exchange rate ($OAB'C'/OABC$ must equal OE'/OE). When import payments fall in foreign currency, they may rise or fall in domestic currency ($OE'F'G'$ can be larger or smaller than $OEFG$), but they cannot rise in proportion to the change in the exchange rate ($OE'F'G'/OEFG$ must be smaller than OE'/OE). Therefore, export proceeds must rise by more than the largest possible increase in import payments ($OAB'C'$ must exceed $OE'F'G'$ when $OABC$ equals $OEFG$ initially).

Figure 14-1 can be used to work through other cases. Suppose, for example, that the price elasticity of domestic demand is 1 and that the elasticity of foreign demand is greater than zero, assumptions that also satisfy the MLR condition. It is easy to show that import payments will be constant in domestic currency, export receipts will rise, and the current-account balance will improve, regardless of the currency in which it is measured.[2]

---

[2] It can also be shown that the current-account balance measured in foreign currency will improve by a larger amount if it begins in deficit, and this is an important result. A country is more likely to devalue its currency when it has a deficit. Return to the example analyzed in the text. When the elasticity of foreign

The MLR condition is a sufficient condition for an improvement in the current-account balance. It is not a necessary condition. If supply curves are not infinitely elastic, as they were in Figure 14-1, a depreciation or devaluation of the domestic currency can improve the current-account balance even when demand elasticities are too low to satisfy the MLR condition.

But the MLR condition appears to be satisfied for most major industrial countries. Estimates of price elasticities are shown in Table 14-1. In all but the British case, the elasticities of domestic and foreign demand sum to numbers much larger than unity. There is just one difficulty. These elasticities relate to long-run responses; they describe the effects of an exchange-rate change after enough time has passed for consumers and producers to work through old commitments and find new suppliers and customers. The short-run elasticities are lower and do not always satisfy the MLR condition. Therefore, the current-account balance may trace a J-shaped curve through time, getting worse before it improves in response to a depreciation or devaluation.

This J-curve effect poses no serious problem when a government devalues a pegged exchange rate, provided the government has enough reserves to finance the temporary deterioration of the current-account balance. It does pose a problem for the functioning of a flexible exchange rate. If the current account gets worse when the domestic currency depreciates, the currency may go on depreciating under the

TABLE 14-1 Price Elasticities of Demand for the Seven Economic Summit Countries

Country	Price Elasticities of Demand for Imports	
	Domestic	*Foreign*
Canada	1.30	0.79
France	1.08	1.31
Germany	0.88	1.11
Italy	1.03	0.93
Japan	0.78	1.11
Britain	0.65	0.48
United States	1.66	1.41

Source: Robert M. Stern et al., *Price Elasticities in International Trade* (London: Macmillan, 1976), Table 2.2.

Note: These are "consensus" estimates, based on many studies, rather than the outcomes of one study. Estimates from individual studies vary widely, depending on the concepts, econometric methods, price data, and time periods employed.

pressure of excess supply in the foreign-exchange market. The market may be unstable. If this instability is to be avoided, the foreign-exchange market must be inhabited by speculators farsighted enough to know that exchange-rate movements tend to go too far and that profits can therefore be made by purchasing a currency that has been depreciating, because it will appreciate when the current account begins to improve. Their purchases will limit the depreciation. (The perverse response of the exchange rate due to the J-curve effect is one of several ways in which a flexible rate can *overshoot* its long-run value. Others are discussed later.)

Nominal and Real Exchange Rates

The main limitations of the elasticities approach reside in the assumptions about prices and incomes that were used to derive the MLR condition. In Figure 14-1, a depreciation of the domestic currency improved the current-account balance because it affected relative prices. It raised the home-currency price of the foreign (imported) good relative to that of the

---

demand is 1, $Oa'b'c'$ equals $Oabc$; there is no change in foreign-currency export proceeds. But foreign-currency import payments fall by $g'f'fg$, which is gg' times Oe. Furthermore, gg'/Og is equal to the elasticity of domestic demand, e_2, *times* the exchange-rate change: $gg'/Og = -e_2(EE'/OE)$. Therefore, $gg' = -e_2(Og)(EE'/OE)$, while $gg' \times Oe = -e_2(Og \times Oe) \times (EE'/OE)$, and $g'f'fg = -e_2(Oefg) \times (EE'/OE)$. The reduction in import payments increases absolutely with the size of $Oefg$, the initial import bill.

domestic (exported) good, inducing domestic consumers to switch from foreign to domestic goods. It lowered the foreign-currency price of the domestic good relative to that of the foreign good, inducing foreign consumers to switch in that same direction. A change in the *nominal* exchange rate, the price of foreign currency in terms of domestic currency, altered the *real* exchange rate, the price of foreign output in terms of domestic output.

A country's real exchange rate can be defined as the relative purchasing power of domestic output,

$$v = \frac{\pi p_2^*}{p_1}$$

where v is the real exchange rate, π is the nominal exchange rate, p_2^* is the foreign-currency price of the foreign (imported) good, and p_1 is the home-currency price of the domestic (exported) good. (The real exchange rate is thus the *reciprocal* of the terms of trade.)

Note 14-2 shows that the MLR condition relates fundamentally to the effect of a

---

Note 14-2

To show that the current-account balance depends on the real exchange rate, not the nominal rate, recall the foreign demand function in Note 14-1:

$$c_1^* = g^*(p_1^*, p_2^*, Y^*)$$

But quantities demanded depend fundamentally on relative prices and real incomes. Therefore, a uniform change in p_1^*, p_2^* and Y^* should not affect c_1^*, because it does not affect relative prices or foreign real income. Algebraically,

$$c_1^* = g^*(\lambda p_1^*, \lambda p_2^*, \lambda Y^*)$$

which says that the uniform change, λ, in all nominal variables does not alter c_1^*. When a demand function takes this form, however, we can show that $p_1^* g_1^* + p_2^* g_2^* + Y^* g_Y^* = 0$, which can be used in turn to show that $e_2^* = e_1^* - e_Y^*$. Working with the domestic demand function, we can likewise show that $e_1 = e_2 - e_Y$.

Substituting these expressions into the next-to-last equation of Note 14-1,

$$dN = p_1 c_1^*[\dot{p}_1 - e_1^*(\dot{p}_1 - \dot{\pi})$$
$$+ (e_1^* - e_Y^*)\dot{p}_2^* + e_Y^* \dot{Y}^*] - \pi p_2^* c_2[\dot{\pi} + \dot{p}_2^*$$
$$+ (e_2 - e_Y)\dot{p}_1 - e_2(\dot{p}_2^* + \dot{\pi}) + e_Y \dot{Y}]$$

Setting $p_1 c_1^* = \pi p_2^* c_2$ and grouping terms,

$$dN = p_1 c_1^*[(e_1^* + e_2 - 1)(\dot{\pi} + \dot{p}_2^* - \dot{p}_1)$$
$$+ e_Y^*(\dot{Y}^* - \dot{p}_2^*) - e_Y(\dot{Y} - \dot{p}_1)]$$

The real exchange rate, however, is $v = \pi p_2^*/p_1$, so $\dot{v} = \dot{\pi} + \dot{p}_2^* - \dot{p}_1$. Furthermore, foreign real income is $y^* = Y^*/p_2^*$, so $\dot{y}^* = \dot{Y}^* - \dot{p}_2^*$, and domestic real income is $y = Y/p_1$, so $\dot{y} = \dot{Y} - \dot{p}_1$. Substituting $\dot{v}$, $\dot{y}^*$, and $\dot{y}$ into the previous equation,

$$dN = p_1 c_1^*[(e_1^* + e_2 - 1)\dot{v} + e_Y^* \dot{y}^* - e_Y \dot{y}]$$

A devaluation or depreciation of the domestic currency improves the current-account balance when the MLR condition is satisfied, the devaluation or depreciation is not offset by movements in domestic and foreign prices that prevent the real exchange rate from changing, and real incomes are constant.

change in the real exchange rate. A change in the nominal exchange rate can affect the current-account balance only by changing the real exchange rate. That is what happened throughout Chapter 13, where p_1 and p_2^* were constant, but it is easy to build cases in which prices are not constant.

One such case arises when real wage rates are completely rigid—when workers have the market power to raise the money wage in a manner that offsets completely each increase in the cost of living, or when the money wage is *indexed* automatically to the cost of living. Suppose that the real wage is fixed institutionally in terms of the imported good. Furthermore, suppose as before that domestic output (income) is kept constant, keeping the marginal product of labor constant and thus fixing the real wage in terms of the domestic good. To put these assumptions precisely, let w be the money wage rate. Then $w/\pi p_2^*$ will be constant at some level $\bar{w}_2$ when the real wage is fixed institutionally in terms of the imported good, and w/p_1 will be constant at some level $\bar{w}_1$ when the marginal product of labor is fixed by keeping output constant. Dividing $\bar{w}_1$ by $\bar{w}_2$

$$\frac{\bar{w}_1}{\bar{w}_2} = \frac{w/p_1}{w/\pi p_2^*} = \frac{\pi p_2^*}{p_1} = v$$

The real exchange rate will be constant when the real wage is constant. Any change in the nominal exchange rate will be offset completely by a change in the money wage that prevents the real rate from changing, and the change in the nominal exchange rate cannot affect the current-account balance even when the MLR condition is satisfied.[3] But the real rate cannot be constant when all prices are kept constant; an increase in π will raise v unless p_1 rises or

p_2^* falls. Accordingly, the constant-price assumption used to derive the MLR condition rules out rigidity in the real wage. Conversely, rigidity in the real wage contradicts the constant-price assumption.

Another problem needs attention. The expenditure-switching effects of a depreciation or devaluation increase the total demand for the domestic good and decrease the total demand for the foreign good. These demand changes can have two consequences. First, they can raise prices at home and reduce them abroad and thus erode the initial switch in expenditure by cutting down the change in the real exchange rate. Second, they can raise real income at home and reduce it abroad and thus offset part of the initial switch. In both cases, they will reduce the improvement in the current-account balance.

The demand-increasing effect of a depreciation or devaluation was predicted by equations (11a) and (13c) in Chapter 13. Those equations were derived under our constant-price assumption, which allowed a depreciation or devaluation to affect the real exchange rate and produce a switch in expenditure. The switch is equivalent to an autonomous increase in net exports $(dN^a > 0)$. Therefore, it raises real income, Y, and the ultimate improvement in the current-account balance is only a fraction, $s/(s + m)$, of the initial expenditure-switching effect.

The same demand-increasing effect can be detected in Figure 14-1. That diagram was constructed by assuming that incomes are constant. But interest rates and taxes are also constant (they are treated as policy variables), so total consumption is constant in each country. When consumption is constant, moreover, a change in spending on

---

[3] The same problem arises when the real wage is fixed institutionally in terms of a price index containing both domestic and foreign goods. Define a *geometric* price index, $p_i = p_1^a(\pi p_2^*)^{1-a}$, where a and $1 - a$ are the weights attached to the home-currency prices of the domestic and foreign goods, and define $\bar{w}_i = w/p_i$. Then, $\bar{w}_1/\bar{w}_i = (\pi p_2^*/p_1)^{1-a} = v^{1-a}$. The real exchange rate is still rigid when $\bar{w}_1$ and $\bar{w}_i$ are fixed.

one good must be matched by an equal but opposite change in spending on the other. This last statement points to a contradiction lurking in Figure 14-1.

Look first at expenditure on the home good measured in home currency. Foreign expenditure on that good rises by $CBB'C'$, and this amount is proportional to the exchange-rate change. Domestic expenditure on the foreign good can rise or fall ($OE'F'G'$ can be bigger or smaller than $OEFG$, depending on the elasticity of the domestic demand for imports). But it cannot rise by an amount proportional to the exchange-rate change, because of the reduction in the quantity demanded. By implication, domestic expenditure on the home good cannot fall by an amount proportional to the exchange-rate change. Thus, foreign expenditure on the home good must rise by more than the largest possible decrease in domestic expenditure, and there must thus be an increase in *total* expenditure on that good, which is an increase in the quantity demanded when the domestic price is constant.

Look next at expenditure on the foreign good measured in foreign currency. Domestic expenditure falls by $g'f'fg$. Foreign expenditure is constant, because there is no change in foreign spending on the domestic good ($Oa'b'c'$ equals $Oabc$ when the elasticity of foreign demand is unity). Accordingly, there must be a decrease in *total* expenditure on the foreign good, which is a decrease in the quantity demanded when the foreign price is constant.

Therefore, Figure 14-1 does contain a contradiction. It was constructed by assuming that incomes and prices are constant at home and abroad, but they cannot stay constant when a depreciation or devaluation improves the current-account balance. Demand for the home good rises and demand for the foreign good falls. There must then be an increase in domestic output (income) or in the price of the home good to clear the market for the home good. There must be a decrease in foreign output (income) or in the price of the foreign good to clear the market for the foreign good.

When prices change to clear goods markets, the outcome is the first result mentioned previously, a smaller switch in expenditure, because the real exchange rate does not change by as much as the nominal exchange rate. When outputs and incomes change to clear those markets, the outcome is the second result, an income-induced change in trade flows that offsets some of the switch.

In some situations, there can be *no* switch in expenditure and no improvement in the current-account balance, because there can be no change in the real exchange rate. Recall the Ricardian model in Chapter 3, where employment was fixed at its full-employment level and the terms of trade were determined in international markets. A depreciation or devaluation of the Portuguese currency cannot affect the real exchange rate. It raises the money wage and price level in Portugal, reduces them in Britain, and has no effect on the current-account balance. Similar results obtain in the simple monetary model examined in Chapter 17.

THE ABSORPTION APPROACH AND OPTIMAL POLICY

Three conclusions follow from this close analysis of the events that lie behind Figure 14-1:

1. A change in the exchange rate *is* the appropriate policy response to an autonomous switch in expenditure.

2. For that very reason, however, a depreciation or devaluation designed to improve the current-account balance can drive economies away from internal balance.

3. Departures from internal balance induced by an exchange-rate change can undermine the

effectiveness of the exchange-rate change, by altering home and foreign prices in ways that reduce the size of the change in the real exchange rate.

The third conclusion has attracted much attention recently. Modern economies are very sensitive to inflationary shocks, which can be prolonged and amplified by wage-price dynamics. Once started, moreover, an inflation is hard to stop. It sets up expectations of continuing inflation that permeate behavior in labor and goods markets. A single change in the exchange rate can start a *vicious circle*. It raises costs, prices, and wages, which leads to the need for another depreciation, which touches off another round of cost, price, and wage increases, and so on.

These tendencies can be contained by restrictive monetary and fiscal policies. Even in the absence of such tendencies, however, there is a fundamental problem that can be stated as the basic postulate of the absorption approach:

When resources are fully employed, a change in the nominal exchange rate cannot affect the current-account balance unless absorption is adjusted to accommodate the expenditure-switching effect of the exchange-rate change.

Using language introduced in Chapter 12, an improvement in the current-account balance calls for an increase in the private-sector surplus (the difference between saving and investment) or an increase in the public-sector surplus (a decrease in the budget deficit).

This proposition generates two strands of analysis. The first was developed by economists who sought to show that a change in the exchange rate can affect absorption automatically and that the automatic changes in absorption are the chief way in which an exchange-rate change improves the current-account balance. Some argued that a devaluation reduces real income by worsening the terms of trade and that the reduction in real income will reduce expenditure (absorption). Others argued that devaluation raises the price level, which will reduce expenditure by raising the amounts that households want to save or raising the amounts of money that they want to hold. (The cash-balance version of this argument is central to the monetary approach presented in Chapter 17.)

The second strand of analysis was developed by economists who held that the absorption approach was complementary to the elasticities approach, rather than a substitute for it. They constructed policy-oriented models to show how monetary and fiscal policies must be adjusted to make room for the expenditure-switching effects of an exchange-rate change—to make sure that the MLR condition can translate a depreciation or devaluation into an improvement in the current-account balance. That is the tack taken in the rest of this chapter.

Optimal Policy Once Again

Consider the small open economy examined in Chapter 13. Its prices are fixed or change only slowly when it moves away from internal balance. Its government pegs the exchange rate but is free to change the peg, to devalue or revalue the domestic currency from time to time. Its central bank controls the money supply to regulate the domestic interest rate.

Such a country is described by Figure 14-2. The vertical axis measures the restrictiveness of expenditure policy, which rises with the tax rate and the interest rate. An upward movement along the vertical axis represents a tightening of fiscal or monetary policy, which reduces policy-induced expenditure. The horizontal axis measures the nominal exchange rate and thus measures the real rate, too, because goods

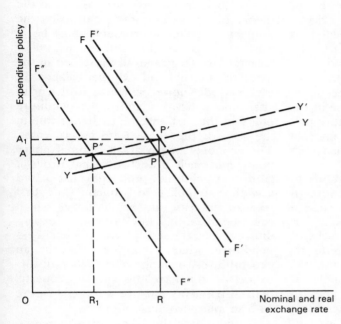

FIGURE 14-2 Policy Responses to an Autonomous Change in Expenditure and an Autonomous Switch in Expenditure

Points on the curve YY show combinations of expenditure policy and the exchange rate that maintain internal balance. Points on the FF curve show combinations that maintain external balance. The economy starts at the policy point P. An autono-mous increase in expenditure shifts the internal-balance. The economy starts at the policy point P. An autonomous increase in expenditure shifts the internal-ture policy must be tightened from OA to OA_1, but the exchange rate need not change. An autonomous switch in expenditure to domestic goods that shifts the internal-balance curve to Y'Y' will shift the external-balance curve to F"F". The new policy point is P", where expenditure policy need not change but the domestic currency must be revalued from OR to OR_1.

prices do not change without prolonged departures from internal balance. The YY curve shows how the exchange rate can be combined with expenditure policy to maintain internal balance. It is upward sloping because a devaluation switches domestic and foreign demands to domestic goods and requires a more restrictive expenditure policy to reduce absorption and restore internal balance. There is unemployment above the YY curve and inflationary pressure below it. The FF curve shows how the exchange rate can be combined with expenditure policy to maintain external balance. It is downward sloping because a devaluation improves the current-account balance and requires a less restrictive expenditure policy to raise imports and restore external balance. There are balance-of-payments surpluses above the FF curve and deficits below it. The intersection of

the YY and FF curves at P defines an optimal policy combination conferring internal and external balance.[4]

---

[4] To obtain the YY curve, set $Y = Y^t$, where Y^t is the income level required for internal balance. Then $dY = dY^t$. But dY is given by equation (11a) in Chapter 13, with one modification. Separate the autonomous change in net exports into two components: $dN^a = dN^{a'} + dN^{a''}$, where $dN^{a'}$ is truly autonomous and $dN^{a''}$ is the expenditure-switching effect of an exchange-rate change:

$$dN^{a''} = (p_1 c_1^*) e_\pi (d\pi/\pi)$$

where e_π is the expression for the MLR condition in Note 14-1. Set dY^t equal to the modified argument of equation (11a) and solve for the policy-induced change in expenditure:

$$dA^g = -(p_1 c_1^*) e_\pi (d\pi/\pi) - dA^a - dN^{a'} + (s + m)dY^t$$

As $e_\pi > 0$ (the MLR condition is satisfied), A^g must fall with a rise in π, which means that the tax rate or interest rate must rise and the YY curve must be upward sloping. (A^g must likewise fall with a rise in A^a or $N^{a'}$ but must rise with a rise in Y^t.) To obtain the FF curve,

An autonomous increase in domestic expenditure shifts *YY* upward, because a more restrictive expenditure policy is needed to maintain internal balance. It shifts *FF* upward, too, because a more restrictive expenditure policy is likewise needed to maintain external balance. In fact, the curves shift up together, to *Y'Y'* and *F'F'*, displacing *P* to *P'* and reproducing a result we encountered before. When an economy experiences an autonomous increase in expenditure, a tightening of expenditure policy from *OA* to *OA*₁ can maintain internal and external balance without a change in the exchange rate.

An autonomous switch in expenditure to domestic goods (or an increase in foreign expenditure) shifts *YY* upward, because a more restrictive expenditure policy is needed to maintain internal balance. Let it go to *Y'Y'*, just as it did before. This disturbance, however, shifts *FF* downward, because a less restrictive expenditure policy is needed for external balance. It goes to *F"F"*, displacing *P* to *P"*, and thus reproduces another result encountered earlier. When an economy experiences an autonomous switch in expenditure, a change in the exchange rate from *OR* to *OR*₁ can

---

set $N + K = 0$, where N is the current-account balance and K is an autonomous capital inflow. When $N + K = 0$, the economy is in external balance (there is no balance-of-payments surplus or deficit). Then $dN + dK = 0$, where dN is given by equation (13c) in Chapter 13 modified in the same way as equation (11a). Replace dN with the modified argument of equation (13c) and solve for the policy-induced change in expenditure:

$$dA^g = (p_1 c_1^*)\left(\frac{s}{m}\right)e_\pi(d\pi/\pi) - dA^a$$
$$+ \left(\frac{s}{m}\right)dN^{a'} + \left(\frac{s+m}{m}\right)dK$$

As $e_\pi > 0$, A^g must rise with a rise in π, which means that the tax rate or interest rate must fall and the *FF* curve must be downward sloping. (A^g must likewise rise with a rise in $N^{a'}$ or K, but must fall with a rise in A^a.) Note that the *FF* curve gets flatter as the economy becomes more open (i.e., as m increases).

---

maintain internal and external balance without a change in expenditure policy.

Both episodes illustrated in this diagram appear to violate a basic proposition in the theory of economic policy. Normally, the number of policy instruments must be at least as large as the number of policy targets. Two targets are represented in the diagram, internal and external balance. In each episode, however, it was sufficient to alter one policy instrument—expenditure policy in the first and the exchange rate in the second. But these were special cases. The economy began at an optimal policy point, and each disturbance that drove it from that point had properties that paired it with one policy instrument. The first was an increase in expenditure, which could be offset by a more restrictive expenditure policy; the second was a switch in expenditure, which could be offset by an expenditure-switching policy. When disturbances do not have this special property, both instruments must be adjusted. Figure 14-3 supplies two illustrations.

Suppose that the labor force increases. The target level of income rises, because income and output must be raised to maintain full employment. The *YY* curve shifts to *Y'Y'*, as a less restrictive expenditure policy is needed for internal balance, but the *FF* curve stays in place. The policy point goes from *P* to *P'*. There must be an easing of expenditure policy from *OA* to *OA*₁, and the domestic currency must be devalued from *OR* to *OR*₁.

Suppose that capital inflows increase permanently. Net exports must be reduced to maintain external balance. The *FF* curve shifts to *F'F'*, as a less restrictive expenditure policy is needed for external balance, but the *YY* curve stays in place, and the policy point goes from *P* to *P"*. The domestic currency must be revalued from *OR* to *OR*₂, and expenditure policy must be eased from *OA* to *OA*₂ (which can be larger or smaller than *OA*₁).

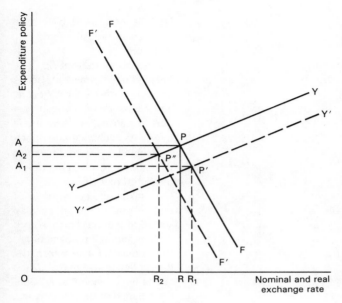

FIGURE 14-3 Policy Responses to Changes in Target Levels of Income and the Current-Account Balance

The economy begins at the policy point P, in internal and external balance. An increase in the labor force raises the target level of income, shifting the internal-balance curve to $Y'Y'$. The policy point goes to P', where expenditure policy must be eased to OA_1 and the domestic currency must be devalued to OR_1. An increase in capital inflows requires a reduction in net exports, shifting the external-balance curve to $F'F'$. The policy point goes to P'', where expenditure policy must be eased to OA_2 and the domestic currency must be revalued to OR_2.

The Assignment Problem

When working with Figure 14-2, we were able to pair each disturbance with a policy instrument. When working with Figure 14-3, it is tempting to pair targets with instruments. If the labor force grows, for example, it seems natural to say that expenditure policy should be used to raise income and exchange-rate policy should be used to prevent a deterioration in the balance of payments. But the pairing of targets and instruments is tricky. It is known as the *assignment problem,* and it is solved by using a rule that its author, Robert Mundell, described as the principle of effective market classification:

> Each policy instrument should be assigned to the target variable on which it has the greatest relative effect.

The use of this principle is illustrated by Figure 14-4, which deals with a somewhat artificial case in which instruments are adjusted sequentially.

Let the economy begin at P_0, above the YY and FF curves. It has unemployment and a balance-of-payments surplus. Assign to the manager of the exchange rate the task of maintaining external balance. Assign to the manager of expenditure policy the task of maintaining internal balance. Assume arbitrarily that the manager of the exchange rate is the first to act.

To pursue external balance, the manager of the exchange rate will revalue the domestic currency from OR_0 to OR_1, taking the economy back to the FF curve. But there is still unemployment, because the economy remains above the YY curve. To pursue internal balance, the manager of expenditure policy will therefore ease expenditure policy from OA_0 to OA_1, taking the economy back to the YY curve. The balance of payments moves into deficit, because the new policy point P_1 lies below the FF curve. Accordingly, the domestic currency must be devalued from OR_1 to OR_2, and this will trigger another change in expenditure policy, taking the policy point to

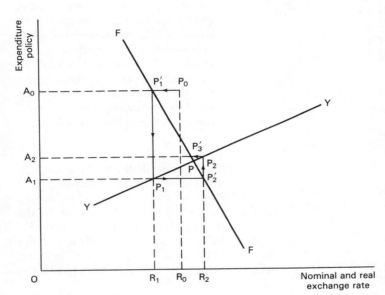

FIGURE 14-4 A Stable
Assignment of Instruments
to Targets
The economy starts at P_0.
There is unemployment, because P_0 is above the YY curve,
and a balance-of-payments surplus, because it is above the FF
curve. As exchange-rate policy
is assigned to external balance,
its manager revalues the domestic currency from OR_0 to
OR_1, taking the economy to
P_1'. As expenditure policy is assigned to internal balance and
there is still unemployment at
P_1', its manager eases expenditure policy from OA_0 to OA_1,
taking the economy to P_1. But
the balance of payments is in
deficit there, so the domestic
currency is devalued from OR_1
to OR_2, taking the economy to
P_2' and producing inflationary
pressure. Expenditure policy is
then tightened from OA_1 to
OA_2, taking the economy to
P_2. The policy path is the cob-
web that leads to the optimum
policy point P. The assignment
is stable.

P_2. The policy path is described by the *cob-web* P_0, P_1', P_1, P_2', P_2, and so on and con-verges on P, the intersection of the YY and FF curves.

This decentralized procedure seems wasteful. The exchange rate goes up and down. So does expenditure. To move di-rectly to the optimal point P, however, policymakers must possess all the informa-tion needed to construct the YY and FF curves and to know where those curves lie. Policymakers do not claim to know this much. But they can most certainly recog-nize a balance-of-payments surplus or defi-cit, incipient unemployment, and incipient

inflation. By pairing their policy instru-ments with the symptoms of departures from policy targets, they can wend their way through the cobweb in Figure 14-4 without knowing the whole structure of the economy or being able to identify precisely the nature of the disturbances affecting it.

It is essential, however, to get the assign-ment right. In Figure 14-4, exchange-rate policy is assigned to external balance and expenditure policy to internal balance. This is the conventional assignment, but it is the right assignment only because the FF curve is steeper absolutely than the YY curve. If the sizes of the slopes were reversed, the conventional assignment would be un-stable. The policy point would move far-ther and farther from *P*. This would hap-pen in a very open economy, with a marginal propensity to import larger than its marginal propensity to save. As the mar-ginal propensity to import rises, expendi-ture policy acquires more influence over the balance of payments; a change in in-come has a larger effect on imports. When the marginal propensity to import is very large, the principle of effective market classification says that expenditure policy should be assigned to external balance and the exchange rate assigned to internal bal-ance.

THE BEHAVIOR OF A FLEXIBLE EXCHANGE RATE

In the story told by Figure 14-4, the ex-change rate was pegged and thus adjusted periodically. The same sort of diagram can be used to describe the behavior of a flexible exchange rate. The exchange rate

is the price that clears the foreign exchange market. Throughout this chapter, more-over, the only flows that cross the market are those which come from the current account and autonomous capital move-ments. Accordingly, the *FF* curve can be re-garded as the market-clearing curve for the foreign-exchange market. It becomes the source of information about the behavior of a flexible exchange rate.

In Figure 14-5, the economy begins at P_0, but this point has to lie on the initial *FF* curve. The economy cannot leave the *FF* curve, even momentarily, because the bal-ance of payments cannot be in surplus or deficit with a freely flexible exchange rate. An autonomous increase in capital inflows shifts *FF* to *F'F'*, as before, because it re-quires an appreciation of the domestic cur-rency to clear the foreign-exchange mar-ket. The exchange rate moves at once from OR_0 to OR_1, as the foreign-exchange mar-ket does the job previously assigned to a policymaker. But there is unemployment in the new situation, as the policy point P_1' lies above *YY*, and expenditure policy must be

FIGURE 14-5 Behavior of a Flexible Exchange Rate
When the exchange rate is flexible, the economy cannot depart from its external-balance curve, and the ini-tial policy point, P_0, must lie on that curve. An autonomous increase in the capital inflow shifts the curve to *F'F'*, moving the economy immedi-ately to P_1', because the domestic currency appreciates from OR_0 to OR_1. An easing of expenditure policy from OA_0 to OA_1, designed to achieve internal balance, takes the economy to P_2', because the domes-tic currency depreciates from OR_1 to OR_2. The economy converges to P by successively smaller movements up and down the *F'F'* curve.

eased to restore internal balance. Suppose that it is eased immediately from OA_0 to OA_1, the full amount required to achieve internal balance at the exchange rate OR_1. The economy does not move to P_1, as in Figure 14-4. It moves along the $F'F'$ curve directly to P_2', because the domestic currency depreciates immediately from OR_1 to OR_2. Unemployment is replaced by inflationary pressure, and expenditure policy must then be tightened from OA_1 to OA_2. The policy path is P_0, P_1', P_2', and so on, rather than a cobweb. Nevertheless, the policy point converges to P.

In this diagram, the slopes of YY and FF describe reactions to the way that expenditure policy is managed. If the marginal propensity to import is low, YY is flatter than FF, and the economy converges to P even under the extreme assumption that expenditure is changed by the very large amounts needed to achieve internal balance at the existing exchange rate, without regard to the effect on the exchange rate itself. The economy will oscillate but not explosively. If the marginal propensity to import is high, however, YY will be steeper than FF, and the economy cannot converge to P when expenditure is managed in this fashion. It will oscillate explosively.

But policymakers are not as dumb as those who inhabit this diagram. They can take account of exchange-rate changes resulting from their actions. Because an increase in expenditure raises imports and causes the domestic currency to depreciate, it has two effects on income: a direct expenditure-raising effect and an indirect expenditure-switching effect. By taking account of the indirect effect as well as the direct effect, policymakers can use small changes in expenditure to maintain internal balance. They can therefore prevent explosive oscillations. (Matters become more difficult, however, when exchange-rate changes have long-lagged effects on the current account, producing a J-curve and making it hard to predict the ultimate expenditure-switching effect of each change in the exchange rate.)

SUMMARY

Using the assumptions made in Chapter 13 concerning incomes, prices, and policies, one can show how an exchange-rate change will switch expenditure. But several conditions must be satisfied.

The Marshall–Lerner–Robinson condition is the basis of the elasticities approach to the analysis of exchange-rate changes. A devaluation or depreciation of the domestic currency improves the current-account balance when the price elasticities of domestic and foreign demands for imports sum to a number larger than unity. Statistical evidence suggests that this condition is satisfied for most major countries, although there may be difficulties in the short run.

When the MLR condition is satisfied, however, a devaluation or depreciation raises income at home and reduces it abroad, and these income changes have expenditure effects that diminish the improvement in the current-account balance. If home and foreign prices are rigid, the expenditure effects will operate by way of the multiplier process. If home and foreign prices are flexible, they will operate by raising prices at home and reducing them abroad, and these changes will limit the change in the real exchange rate brought about by a devaluation or depreciation of the nominal exchange rate.

These findings lead directly to the basic postulate of the absorption approach. A devaluation or depreciation will not improve the current-account balance unless absorption is adjusted to make room for the expenditure-switching effects of an exchange-rate change. This postulate has inspired attempts to show that a devaluation or depreciation reduces absorption automatically. It has also led to the development of policy-oriented models showing how monetary and fiscal policies must be used jointly with exchange-rate changes to maintain internal and external balance— that the absorption and elasticities approaches are complementary.

Policy models can also be used to show how each policy instrument should be assigned to a policy target. To obtain an optimal policy combination by successive approximations, each instrument should be assigned to the target on which it has the greatest relative effect. We would therefore expect the exchange rate to be used for external balance and expenditure policies to be used for internal balance. In highly open economies, however, with large marginal propensities to import, the conventional assignment should be reversed.

The same policy models can be used to describe the behavior of a flexible exchange rate. Because it clears the foreign-exchange market automatically, it is in effect assigned to external balance. The principle that dictates policy assignments under a pegged exchange rate can then be employed to forecast an economy's reactions to the way that expenditure policies are used. In a very open economy with a flexible exchange rate, large changes in monetary or fiscal policy can cause explosive oscillations if the policy changes are made without allowing for their exchange-rate effects.

RECOMMENDED READINGS

Some readings recommended at the end of Chapter 13, including the book by Meade and the article by Johnson, deal with issues covered in this chapter. Here are additional suggestions:

The derivation of the Marshall–Lerner–Robinson condition in Figure 14-1 comes from a paper by Gottfried Haberler, "The Market for Foreign Exchange and the Stability of the Balance of Payments," *Kyklos,* 3 (1949); that paper also shows how supply elasticities affect the outcome and the importance of the MLR condition for the stability of the foreign-exchange market. For more on these issues, see Arnold C. Harberger, "Currency Depreciation, Income and the Balance of Trade," *Journal of Political Economy,* 58 (February 1950), reprinted in American Economic Association, *Readings in International Economics* (Homewood, Ill.: Richard D. Irwin, 1968), ch. 21.

On the expenditure-switching effects of exchange-rate changes in a variety of models and the importance of wage flexibility, see Neil Bruce and Douglas D. Purvis, "The Specification and Influence of Goods and Factor Markets in Open-Economy Macroeconomic Models," in R. W. Jones and P. B. Kenen, *Handbook of International Economics* (Amsterdam: North-Holland, 1985), ch. 16; on exchange-rate changes and wage-price dynamics, see Marian E. Bond,

"Exchange Rates, Inflation, and Vicious Circles," *International Monetary Fund Staff Papers,* 27 (December 1980).

Lags in the adjustment process and other complications are examined in Paul R. Krugman and Richard E. Baldwin, "The Persistence of the U.S. Trade Deficit," *Brookings Papers on Economic Activity,* 1987 (1).

The absorption approach is implicit in Meade's analysis but is set out explicitly by Sidney S. Alexander, "Effects of Devaluation on a Trade Balance," *International Monetary Fund Staff Papers,* 2 (April 1952), reprinted in American Economic Association, *Readings in International Economics* (Homewood, Ill.: Richard D. Irwin, 1968), ch. 22.

For the effects of exchange-rate changes on saving and absorption, see Svendt Laursen and Lloyd A. Metzler, "Flexible Exchange Rates and the Theory of Employment," *Review of Economics and Statistics,* 32 (November 1950); and the reformulation by Lars E. O. Svensson and Assaf Razin, "The Terms of Trade, Spending, and the Current Account," *Journal of Political Economy,* 91 (February 1983).

On the assignment problem and the principle of effective market classification, see Robert A. Mundell, "The Monetary Dynamics of International Adjustment under Fixed and Flexible Exchange Rates," *Quarterly Journal of Economics,* 74 (May 1960), reprinted in R. A. Mundell, *International Economics* (New York: Macmillan, 1968), ch. 11.

For a more sophisticated analysis, in which policy instruments are adjusted gradually and simultaneously rather than by jumps and sequentially, see Richard N. Cooper, "Macroeconomic Policy Adjustment in Interdependent Economies," *Quarterly Journal of Economics,* 83 (February 1969).

CHAPTER
15

INTEREST RATES AND THE CAPITAL ACCOUNT

THE ISSUES

The theory of balance-of-payments adjustment in Chapters 13 and 14 was developed in the 1950s, when many countries had tight controls on international capital movements. Therefore, the theory said very little about the capital account. It emphasized income and exchange-rate changes affecting the current account. Questions were raised occasionally about the effects of autonomous capital flows on the policies required for internal and external balance. But economists did not pay much attention to the role of capital flows in the adjustment process or the implications of capital mobility for choosing optimal policies.

During the 1950s and 1960s, capital controls were liberalized, and other changes in the economic environment reduced the risks and costs of capital movements. There

was thus an increase in capital mobility, and balance-of-payments theory began to take notice. Two economists, J. Marcus Fleming and Robert Mundell, made large contributions, and the model used in the next section of this chapter is known as the Fleming–Mundell model.

More work was needed in the 1970s because of another change in the monetary system, the shift from pegged to flexible exchange rates in 1973. Having shown how capital movements can affect the adjustment process and the behavior of a flexible exchange rate, economists had next to show how a flexible exchange rate can affect capital movements.

When exchange rates are flexible, an investor must answer two questions before choosing between domestic and foreign assets: (1) Are rates of return higher at home or abroad? (2) Which way will the exchange rate go? Suppose that an asset denominated in foreign currency bears a higher rate of return than a comparable asset denominated in domestic currency. Before deciding to buy the foreign asset and hold it for a year, you must forecast the exchange rate at which you can expect to bring your money home. If the price of the foreign currency will be lower a year from now, your loss on the exchange-rate change can swamp your profit on the simple difference between rates of return. Thus, analyses of capital movements must take account of ways in which investors form expectations about exchange rates and of the uncertainty surrounding those expectations. Both can affect capital movements and the behavior of a flexible exchange rate.

Asset holders, however, are not the only ones affected by the possibility of exchange-rate changes. Trade takes time. A firm that signs a contract to sell goods to a foreigner and agrees to take payment in the foreigner's currency may not be paid for many months, until the goods have been delivered. How can the firm protect itself against a change in the exchange rate? There are several ways, but one of them involves the *forward* foreign-exchange market. The firm can sell foreign currency in that market at a price determined now, but will not deliver it to the buyer in exchange for domestic currency until a stated future date.

This chapter and the next look at many issues and arrangements produced by international capital mobility, by expectations and uncertainty about exchange rates, and by transactions in the forward market. This chapter introduces capital movements into that simple balance-of-payments model constructed in earlier chapters, converting it into the Fleming–Mundell model. It uses the model to reexamine the theory of optimal policy developed in Chapters 13 and 14. The assumptions with which we begin are similar to those used before. The domestic economy is small, and the central

bank sterilizes the effects of intervention in the foreign-exchange market. Expectations and uncertainty are ignored. Later in this chapter, however, we drop the assumption about sterilization to show that the workings of monetary and fiscal policies are strongly affected by the exchange-rate regime and by international capital mobility. We will prove an assertion made at the beginning of this book, that monetary policy loses its effectiveness under a pegged exchange rate and acquires additional effectiveness under a flexible rate, and that these results are intensified by capital mobility.

The next chapter introduces expectations and uncertainty and shows how they affect capital mobility and the behavior of a flexible exchange rate. We will see that expectations about future exchange rates can have large effects on present rates. Under certain circumstances, they can even determine present rates completely. We will examine transactions in the forward market to see how traders and investors can *hedge* against uncertainty and how the forward market can be used for speculation.

THE FLEMING–MUNDELL MODEL

In Chapters 13 and 14, monetary and fiscal policies were lumped together. They were described as expenditure policies, because they were used to regulate absorption, which is how they influenced the balance of payments. When capital movements are sensitive to interest rates at home and abroad, we cannot lump those policies together. Both policies continue to influence absorption and affect the current account by affecting imports, but monetary policy affects the capital account, too. By raising the domestic interest rate, the central bank can encourage capital inflows, discourage capital outflows, and improve the balance of payments. Two propositions follows: (1)

When monetary policy is combined with a flexible exchange rate, the risk of instability is intensified. (2) A government can use monetary and fiscal policies to pursue external and internal balance without using the exchange rate simultaneously. These two points are made by the Fleming–Mundell model.

Interest Rates and Capital Flows

Let us go back to the economy studied earlier. It is too small to influence incomes and prices in other countries. It is likewise too small to influence their interest rates. Domestic prices are fixed, as before, and the central bank controls the domestic interest rate.

In language used extensively hereafter, domestic and foreign bonds are *imperfect substitutes* viewed from an investor's standpoint. If the domestic interest rate rises and the foreign rate does not, an investor will switch partially from foreign to domestic bonds but not completely from one to the other. Therefore, the switch in demand for bonds will not be large enough to obliterate the interest-rate difference, and the central bank can influence the domestic interest rate by open-market operations. It can raise the domestic rate by open-market sales, which increase the supply of domestic bonds and decrease the money supply. It can reduce the rate by open-market purchases, which decrease the supply of bonds and increase the money supply.

In the Fleming–Mundell model, moreover, a permanent interest-rate difference causes a permanent capital flow. Suppose that the central bank raises the domestic interest rate. It makes domestic bonds more attractive, compared with foreign bonds, causing domestic and foreign investors to build up their holdings of domestic bonds. In the Fleming–Mundell model, they continue to build them up for as long as the interest-rate incentive persists, and the ad-

ditional flow demand for domestic bonds shows up as a continuing capital inflow.

This flow formulation is illustrated in Figure 15-1. Interest rates are shown on the vertical axis and capital flows on the horizontal axis. The foreign interest rate is fixed at Or^*. When the domestic interest rate is equal to the foreign rate, there is no net capital flow. When the domestic rate is raised to Or_1, there is a continuing capital inflow equal to OK_1. When the domestic rate is reduced to Or_2, there is a continuing capital outflow equal to OK_2.

The slope of the KK curve depends on the degree of substitutability between domestic and foreign bonds. If there were no substitutability whatsoever, the curve would be vertical. An interest-rate difference could not lead investors to switch between domestic and foreign bonds; it would not cause a capital flow. If there were perfect substitutability, the curve would be horizontal. The tiniest interest-rate difference would lead investors to switch completely from one bond to the other, which would drive the interest-rate difference back to zero. The central bank would have no control over the domestic interest rate. When there is imperfect substitutability, the KK curve is upward sloping. The central bank retains control over the domestic interest rate, and the size of the continuing capital flow depends on the interest-rate difference.[1]

The flow formulation in the Fleming–Mundell model has been strongly criticized, and the critics have produced more sophisticated formulations. In Chapter 18, for example, an increase in the domestic interest rate will generate a one-time shift in asset holdings from foreign to domestic bonds,

---

[1] The higher the degree of substitutability, however, the larger are the open-market operations required to maintain a given interest-rate difference and sustain the corresponding capital flow. In Chapter 16, substitutability is related to investors' attitudes toward risk.

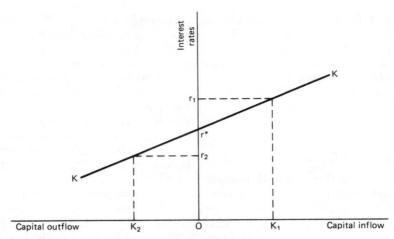

FIGURE 15-1 Interest Rates and Capital Flows
The *KK* curve shows the relationship between interest rates and capital flows in the Fleming–Mundell model. When the foreign interest rate is fixed at *Or**, the capital flow depends on the domestic interest rate. When it is raised to *Or₁*, there is a net inflow equal to *OK₁*. When it is reduced to *Or₂*, there is a net outflow equal to *OK₂*. The slope of *KK* depends on the substitutability between domestic and foreign bonds. When they are close substitutes, *KK* is quite flat. A small difference between domestic and foreign interest rates causes a large switch in demand between domestic and foreign bonds and thus a large capital flow.

causing a temporary capital flow. The Fleming–Mundell model is still useful, however, especially for short-run analysis, and most of the policy conclusions drawn from it have been shown to hold in models with more complex formulations.

Capital Mobility and Exchange-Rate Flexibility

How do capital movements affect the behavior of a flexible exchange rate? The greater their sensitivity to interest-rate differences, the greater is the likelihood of the instability mentioned in Chapter 14 in connection with Figure 14-5.

Figure 15-2 is another version of that diagram, with the interest rate replacing expenditure policy on the vertical axis. Interest rates and exchange rates that con-

fer internal balance are shown by the Y_iY_i curve, which is a variant of the YY curve used in Chapter 14. It is upward sloping because a devaluation or depreciation of the domestic currency switches expenditure to the domestic good and requires an increase in the interest rate to offset it (assuming that there is no change in fiscal policy). Interest rates and exchange rates that confer external balance are shown by the F_iF_i curve, which is a variant of the FF curve used in Chapter 14. It is downward slopping because a depreciation of the domestic currency improves the current account and requires a decrease in the interest rate to offset it.[2]

---

[2] To obtain the Y_iY_i curve in Figure 15-2 and the UU curve in Figure 15-3, reproduce the equation for the YY curve from footnote 4 of Chapter 14. omitting

The $Y_i Y_i$ curve shows the combinations of the interest rate and exchange rate required for internal balance. The $F_i F_i$ curve shows the combination required for external balance. High capital mobility makes the $F_i F_i$ curve flatter absolutely than the $Y_i Y_i$ curve. When the exchange rate is flexible, the economy cannot depart from the $F_i F_i$ curve. Growth in the labor force shifts the $Y_i Y_i$ curve to $Y_i' Y_i'$ because a lower interest rate is needed to raise income and employment. As there is then unemployment at the initial point P, the central bank reduces the interest rate from Or_0 to Or_1, but the economy moves directly to P', because the domestic currency depreciates from OR_0 to OR_1. As there is inflationary pressure at P', the central bank raises the interest rate to Or_2, but the economy moves directly to P'' because the currency appreciates to OR_2. The policy path is P, P', P'', and so on, and does not converge to $P*$.

for simplicity the autonomous changes and switches in expenditure:

$$dA^g = -(p_1 c_1^*)e_\pi(d\pi/\pi) + (s + m) dY^t$$

Then reproduce from Chapter 13 the definition of the policy-induced change in expenditure, omitting for simplicity the change in government expenditure (so that $dD = -dT$):

$$dA^g = -dT - (S_r - I_r) dr$$

where $(S_r - I_r) > 0$ because an increase in r raises saving and reduces investment. Substituting into the YY equation and solving for the change in r,

$$dr = [1/(S_r - I_r)][(p_1 c_1^*)e_\pi(d\pi/\pi) - dT - (s + m) dY^t]$$

The $Y_i Y_i$ curve in Figure 15-2 is obtained by plotting the change in r against the change in π (and is thus upward sloping). The UU curve in Figure 15-3 is obtained by plotting the change in r against the change in T (and is thus downward sloping). Note that both curves shift downward with an increase in Y^t, the target level of income. To obtain the $F_i F_i$ curve in Figure 15-2 and the XX curve in Figure 15-3, reproduce the equation for the FF curve from footnote 4 of Chapter 14, making the same omissions and making the change in the capital inflow depend on the change in the interest-rate difference, $dK = k(dr - dr^*)$, so that

$$dA^g = (s/m)(p_1 c_1^*)e_\pi(d\pi/\pi) + [(s + m)/m]k(dr - dr^*)]$$

Substituting for the change in A^g and solving for the change in r,

$$dr = -[1/(S_r - I_r + K_r)][(s/m)(p_1 c_1^*)e_\pi(d\pi/\pi) + dT - (K_r) dr^*]$$

where $K_r = [(s + m)/m]k$. The $F_i F_i$ curve in Figure 15-2 is obtained by plotting the change in r against the change in π (and is thus downward sloping). The XX curve in Figure 15-3 is obtained by plotting the change in r against the change in T (and is also downward sloping). Note that both curves shift upward with an increase in r^*, the foreign interest rate. Note further that the UU curve is steeper than the XX curve because the change in r produced by a change in T is $-[1/(S_r - I_r)]$ in the case of the UU curve but only $-[1/(S_r - I_r + K_r)]$ in the case of the XX curve.

A lower interest rate has two effects on the balance of payments. It worsens the current account by raising absorption and imports. It worsens the capital account by inducing investors to switch from domestic to foreign bonds. Therefore, the slope of the F_iF_i curve is affected by two characteristics of the economy that do not affect the slope of the Y_iY_i curve: the marginal propensity to import and the interest sensitivity of capital movements. As increase in either makes the F_iF_i curve flatter. It diminishes the size of the reduction in the interest rate needed to offset a depreciation of the domestic currency. (If domestic and foreign bonds were perfect substitutes, the F_iF_i curve would be horizontal and the domestic interest rate could not be different from the foreign rate.)

In Chapter 14, the external-balance curves were steeper absolutely than the internal-balance curves. We assumed that the marginal propensity to import was smaller than the marginal propensity to save and that capital movements were not affected by the interest rate. In Figure 15-2, the external-balance curve is flatter absolutely than the internal-balance curve, because we assume that capital movements are highly sensitive to interest rates. This can introduce the sort of instability mentioned but not illustrated in Chapter 14.

Because a flexible exchange rate clears the foreign-exchange market automatically, it is assigned implicitly to external balance, and monetary policy must then be assigned to internal balance. When F_iF_i is flatter than Y_iY_i, however, the central bank must be careful. If it does not take adequate account of the exchange-rate change resulting from a change in monetary policy, it can cause explosive oscillations in the exchange rate and domestic income.

Let there be growth in the labor force once again, raising the income level required for internal balance. The Y_iY_i curve shifts downward to $Y_i'Y_i'$, saying that the in-terest rate should be reduced to stimulate aggregate demand. If it is cut immediately from Or_0 to Or_1, the interest rate needed for internal balance at the initial exchange rate, the policy point moves at once from P to P', because the exchange rate goes from OR_0 to OR_1. Unemployment gives way to inflationary pressure (P' is below $Y_i'Y_i'$), and the central bank must tighten monetary policy. If it raises the interest rate to Or_2, the rate needed for internal balance at the new exchange rate, OR_1, the policy point moves to P'', because the exchange rate goes to OR_2. Inflationary pressure gives way to unemployment, and the central bank must alter its policy again. The policy path is P, P', P'' and so on, and the economy moves farther and farther from P^*, where $Y_i'Y_i'$ intersects F_iF_i.

This instability does not condemn exchange-rate flexibility but reminds us of a point made in Chapter 14. The central bank must not focus exclusively on domestic targets, disregarding the influence of monetary policy on the exchange rate. Clearly, this warning is made more important by the introduction of capital mobility.

Why not use fiscal policy for internal balance? We will soon see that fiscal policy loses its effectiveness when the exchange rate is flexible and capital mobility is high. Under a pegged exchange rate, however, high capital mobility opens up a new possibility.

Capital Mobility and Optimal Policy Under a Pegged Exchange Rate

When monetary and fiscal policies have different effects on the balance of payments, they can be assigned to different targets, using the principle of effective market classification defined in Chapter 14. As monetary policy has extra influence on the balance of payments, because of its effect on capital flows, it can be assigned to external balance, and fiscal policy can then be assigned to internal balance. The two targets can thus be achieved without changing the exchange rate.

This strategy is illustrated in Figure 15-3. Monetary policy is represented by the domestic interest rate, measured on the vertical axis. Fiscal policy is represented by the tax rate, measured on the horizontal axis. The *UU* curve shows how monetary and fiscal policies can be combined to maintain internal balance. It is downward sloping because an increase in the tax rate reduces domestic expenditure and requires an offsetting decrease in the interest rate. There is unemployment above *UU* and inflationary pressure below it. The *XX* curve shows how the two policies can be combined to maintain external balance. It is downward sloping, too, because an increase in the tax rate improves the balance of payments by reducing imports and likewise requires an offsetting decrease in the interest rate. There is a balance-of-payments surplus above *XX* and a deficit below it.

If capital movements were not sensitive to interest rates, the *UU* and *XX* curves would be identical. Monetary and fiscal policies would affect the balance of payments only by affecting absorption, and there would be no way to distinguish between them, apart from their different effects on the composition of aggregate demand, an important issue for domestic

FIGURE 15-3 Fiscal and Monetary Policies for Internal and External Balance

The *UU* curve shows the tax rates and interest rates that maintain internal balance. It is downward sloping because a decrease in the interest rates is needed to offset an increase in the tax rate. The *XX* curve shows the tax rates and interest rates that maintain external balance. It is downward sloping for the same reason, but it is flatter than the *UU* curve, because a smaller decrease in the interest rate is needed for external balance than for internal balance. The interest rate affects capital flows and thus has an additional influence on the balance of payments. An increase in the labor force calls for an increase in income to maintain internal balance; the *UU* curve shifts to *U'U'*, and the policy point shifts from *P* to *P'*. The tax rate must be cut to stimulate aggregate demand and increase employment. The interest rate must be raised to attract a capital inflow and thus offset the increase in imports produced by the increase in aggregate demand.

purposes but not here. When capital movements are sensitive to interest rates, the *XX* curve is flatter than the *UU* curve. To see why, assume that the economy begins in internal and external balance and raise the tax rate arbitrarily. Absorption will fall, reducing imports, and the balance of payments will move into surplus. Next, reduce the interest rate by enough to restore absorption to its initial level (move along the *UU* curve to maintain internal balance). Imports will return to their initial level, but the balance of payments will move from surplus to deficit because the interest-rate reduction will cause a capital outflow. Putting the point differently, the reduction in the interest rate required to restore external balance is smaller than required to restore internal balance, making *XX* flatter than *UU*.

Suppose that the economy starts at *P*, the optimal policy point. Let the labor force grow, raising the income level needed for internal balance. The *UU* curve shifts downward to *U'U'*. Less restrictive policies are needed to maintain internal balance. The policy point goes to *P'*, which says that the tax rate should be reduced from Ot_0 to Ot_1 so as to stimulate income and employment, and the interest rate should be raised from Or_0 to Or_1 so as to induce the capital inflow needed for external balance (to offset the increase in imports resulting from the increase in income).

This policy assignment is stable. Tell the finance ministry to use the tax rate for internal balance. Tell the central bank to use the interest rate for external balance. When the labor force grows, producing unemployment, the finance ministry will cut the tax rate from Ot_0 to Ot_0'. This will restore internal balance, but the balance of payments will move into deficit. The central bank will raise the interest rate from Or_0 to Or_0' to restore external balance, and unemployment will reappear. The finance ministry will cut the tax rate again, producing a

new deficit in the balance of payments, and the central bank will raise the interest rate again. The policy point will move to *P'* eventually.[3]

The assignment, however, may not work well in the long run. The first reason, mentioned earlier, has to do with the effect of an interest-rate difference. It may not produce a permanent capital flow but merely a one-time switch in demand between foreign and domestic bonds. In that case, the central bank would have to raise the interest rate over and over again to produce a continuing capital inflow—to induce investors to make repeated shifts from foreign to domestic bonds. The second reason has to do with interest payments. These were left out of the model developed in earlier chapters and were not put back when capital flows were added. When they are included in the current-account balance, monetary policy affects it in a way that diminishes the case for assigning monetary policy to external balance. An increase in the domestic interest rate raises interest payments to foreigners on those domestic bonds that they held initially, and the capital inflow induced by a higher rate adds further to those payments. Taken together, these effects reduce the net improvement in the balance of payments resulting from an increase in the interest rate. Indeed, the balance of payments can deteriorate.[4] In any case, reliance on high

---

[3] There is one difference between this stepwise movement and that in Figure 14-4, where expenditure policy and the exchange rate were adjusted sequentially. The policy instruments, income, and the balance of payments all move *monotonically* in Figure 15-3 (i.e., without oscillating).

[4] Let the domestic interest rate be 10 percent initially, and suppose that foreigners hold $1 billion of domestic bonds. Interest payments start at $100 million. Raise the interest rate to 12 percent and suppose that this induces a $200 million increase in foreign holdings of domestic bonds. Interest payments rise eventually to $144 million ($1.2 billion *times* 12 percent), worsening the current-account balance by $44

domestic interest rates to maintain external balance involves large interest income payments to the outside world and corresponding income losses to the domestic economy.

CAPITAL MOBILITY, EXCHANGE RATES, AND DOMESTIC POLICIES

Under a flexible exchange rate, capital movements affect the domestic economy directly. Whenever they produce exchange-rate changes, they have expenditure-switching effects on income, output, and employment (and can also alter domestic prices, triggering a wage-price spiral). Under a pegged exchange rate, capital movements do not affect the economy directly but can affect it indirectly by altering the money supply, interest rates, and so on. With high capital mobility, indeed, the central bank will be unable to control the money supply and will then lose control of the domestic interest rate.

It is time to examine this possibility by abandoning the assumption introduced in Chapter 13, that the monetary effects of official intervention are sterilized completely. Let us go to the opposite extreme by assuming that there is *no* sterilization. Capital mobility acquires important implications for the workings of monetary and fiscal policies, but those implications

---

million. As the capital inflow is $200 million (the increase in foreign holdings of domestic bonds), the balance of payments improves by only $156 million. Now change one number. Suppose that foreigners start out with $10 billion of domestic bonds, so interest payments start at $1 billion. With the increase in the interest rate, they rise to $1.224 billion ($10.2 billion *times* 12 percent), worsening the current-account balance by $224 million. The balance of payments deteriorates by $24 million! (The two effects mentioned in the text can guarantee disaster when put together. If the interest rate must be raised repeatedly to produce a continuing capital inflow and each increase worsens the current-account balance by raising interest payments, the balance of payments must deteriorate sooner or later.)

depend crucially on the exchange-rate regime.

New Tools

Two new tools of analysis are helpful in tracing these implications. They are the *IS* and *LM* curves in Figure 15-4.

The *IS* curve shows how the interest rate affects real income in a small economy with fixed domestic prices. It is downward sloping because a reduction in the interest rate stimulates aggregate demand, raising real income. It will be fairly flat—the increase in income will be large—when aggregate demand is very sensitive to the interest rate or when the multiplier is large (the marginal propensities to save and import are low). The position of the *IS* curve depends on all of the other variables affecting aggregate demand. Two are important here. A depreciation or devaluation of the domestic currency shifts the curve to the right, because it switches expenditure from foreign to home goods. A tax cut shifts it in the same direction because it raises expenditure.

The *LM* curve shows the relationship between income and the interest rate required for monetary equilibrium. The demand for money increases as income rises, because transactions rise with income. It decreases as the interest rate rises, because holders of money are induced to switch from cash to interest-bearing assets (bonds) when they can earn more on those assets. When the supply of money is fixed by central-bank policy, monetary equilibrium can be maintained only when the demand-raising effect of an increase in income is offset by the demand-reducing effect of an increase in the interest rate. This is the relationship shown by the *LM* curve, which is thus upward sloping. The position of the curve depends on the supply of money. An increase in the money supply shifts it downward because a lower interest rate is

FIGURE 15-4 Monetary Policy Under a Pegged Exchange Rate
This *IS* curve shows how a change in the interest rate affects real income. Its slope depends on the interest sensitivity of domestic expenditure and the size of the multiplier. Its position depends on the exchange rate and tax rate. The *LM* curve shows the relationship between income and the interest rate required for monetary equilibrium. It is upward sloping because the demand for money rises with income and falls with the interest rate, so an increase in the interest rate is needed to offset an increase in income. Its position depends on the supply of money. An increase in the money supply shifts it from *LM* to *L'M'*, displacing equilibrium from E_0 to E_1. Income rises from OY_0 to OY_1, and the interest rate falls from Or_0 to Or_1. In an open economy with a pegged exchange rate, however, these income and interest-rate changes drive the balance of payments into deficit, reducing the money supply. The *LM* curve moves back to its initial position, and the effects of monetary policy wear off. They wear off faster with high capital mobility, because the initial reduction in the interest rate leads to a larger balance-of-payments deficit.

needed to maintain monetary equilibrium at each and every income level.

In earlier exercises, we represented changes in monetary policy by changes in the domestic interest rate. In the rest of this chapter, we represent them by changes in the money supply. An easier monetary policy is represented by raising the money supply and shifting the *LM* curve downward. A tighter policy is represented by reducing the money supply and shifting the curve upward. A balance-of-payments deficit is also represented by shifting the curve upward, because a deficit reduces official reserves and thus reduces the money supply when the central bank does not engage in sterilization. In each exercise that follows, we will assume that the balance of payments is in equilibrium at the initial levels of income and the interest rate; this will keep the money supply from changing until we introduce a policy change.

Monetary Policy Under a Pegged Exchange Rate

Under a pegged exchange rate, the domestic effects of monetary policy wear off eventually when the central bank does not sterilize reserve flows, and they wear off faster with high capital mobility. This is the story told by Figure 15-4.

The economy begins at E_0, where the IS and LM curves intersect. Income is OY_0, and the interest rate is Or_0. Let the central bank make an open-market purchase, increasing the money supply and shifting the LM curve downward to $L'M'$. The economy is displaced to E_1. Income rises to OY_1, and the interest rate falls to Or_1. This is the permanent result for a closed economy. It is the initial result in an open economy with a pegged exchange rate. An increase in income worsens the current account, and a decrease in the interest rate worsens the capital account. The balance of payments moves into deficit, and reserves start to fall. If the central bank sterilized reserve flows indefinitely, the economy would remain at E_1. Otherwise, the money supply will start to fall and must go on falling until the balance-of-payments deficit is eliminated. Accordingly, the money supply must return eventually to what it was before the open-market purchase, taking the LM curve back to its starting point. Income must return to OY_0, the interest rate must return to Or_0, and the effects of monetary policy must wear off completely.

Capital mobility is important here mainly for the speed at which the economy returns to its starting point. With no capital mobility, the balance-of-payments deficit is equal to the current-account deficit induced by the increase in income. With the introduction of capital mobility, the deficit is raised by the capital outflow resulting from the reduction in the interest rate, and the money supply falls faster. Capital mobility accelerates the process by which the economy "exports" the additional money created by an open-market purchase.

In the limiting case of *perfect capital mobility* (i.e., perfect substitutability between domestic and foreign bonds), monetary policy has no influence whatsoever in a small economy, not even temporarily. The domestic interest rate cannot fall in Figure 15-4, because it must equal the foreign rate, and the economy must stay at E_0. By implication, the LM curve must snap back immediately after an open-market purchase. The whole effect of the open-market purchase is offset instantaneously by a capital outflow. Investors buy foreign bonds to replace the domestic bonds purchased by the central bank, and the central bank loses reserves equal in amount to its additional holdings of domestic bonds. The money supply does not change.

Fiscal Policy Under a Pegged Exchange Rate

The workings of fiscal policy are described in Figures 15-5 and 15-6. The initial effect of tax a cut is shown in both diagrams by shifting the IS curve to $I'S'$. Equilibrium is displaced from E_0 to E_1. Income rises from OY_0 to OY_1, and the interest rate rises from Or_0 to Or_1. This is, again, the permanent result for a closed economy, or for an open economy in which the central bank sterilizes reserve flows. It is not the whole story when those flows affect the money supply. In the fiscal-policy case, however, the rest of the story depends crucially on capital mobility, which affects the *direction* in which variables move, not merely the speed at which they move. Outcomes with no and low mobility are shown in Figure 15-5. Outcomes with perfect and high mobility are shown in Figure 15-6.

FIGURE 15-5   Fiscal Policy Under a Pegged Exchange Rate with Low
Capital Mobility
A tax cut shifts the *IS* curve to *I'S'*, displacing equilibrium from E_0 to E_1.
Income rises from OY_0 to OY_1, and the interest rate rises from Or_0 to
Or_1. With no capital mobility, the deterioration in the current account
drives the balance of payments into deficit, and the money supply falls.
The *LM* curve goes gradually to *L'M'*, displacing equilibrium to E_2,
where income is back to its initial level and the balance-of-payments
deficit has ended. The effects of fiscal policy wear off gradually. With
low capital mobility, the increase in the interest rate from Or_0 to Or_1 induces a capital inflow that offsets part of the deterioration in the current
account, reducing the balance-of-payments deficit. It is brought to an
end, moreover, at a point on the *I'S'* curve between E_1 and E_2, where
income is between OY_0 and OY_1 and the interest rate is between Or_1 and
Or_2. The current account stays in deficit, but the deficit is covered by a
continuing capital inflow. Reserves and the money supply are stabilized.
The effects of the tax cut are reduced in the long run but do not wear off
completely.

When there is no capital mobility, the
long-run outcome resembles the outcome
after a change in monetary policy, because
income returns eventually to OY_0. A tax cut
produces a balance-of-payments deficit; it is
equal to the current-account deficit induced by the initial increase in income. Reserves fall, reducing the money supply, and
the *LM* curve moves gradually upward. It
cannot stop moving until the payments
deficit has ended, which means that it must
move to *L'M'* in Figure 15-5, where income is brought back to OY_0 and the
current-account deficit is eliminated. The
interest rate rises to Or_2 and "crowds out"
enough domestic spending to offset the
stimulus provided by the tax cut. The effect of fiscal policy wears off completely.

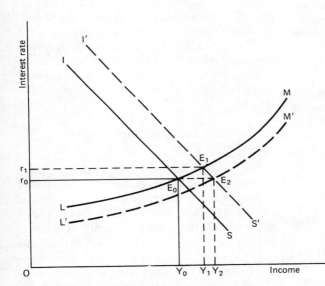

FIGURE 15-6 Fiscal Policy Under a Pegged Exchange Rate with High Capital Mobility

The initial effects of a tax cut are the same as before. The *IS* curve shifts to *I'S'*, raising income from OY_0 to OY_1, and raising the interest rate from Or_0 to Or_1. With high capital mobility, however, the capital inflow induced by the higher interest rate is larger than the deterioration in the current account, and the balance of payments moves into surplus. The money supply rises, driving the *LM* curve downward. With perfect capital mobility, it would drop immediately to *L'M'*, because the interest rate would remain at Or_0. The equilibrium point would be displaced to E_2, and income would rise to OY_2. Otherwise, the balance-of-payments surplus is brought to an end at a point on the *I'S'* curve between E_1 and E_2, where income is between OY_1 and OY_2 and the interest rate is between Or_0 and Or_1. The current account remains in deficit, as before, and the deficit is covered by a capital inflow. But the effects of the tax cut are reinforced by high capital mobility.

When capital mobility is low, fiscal policy raises income permanently but by less than the increase to OY_1. The initial increase in the interest rate induces a capital inflow that offsets part of the current-account deficit. Therefore, the balance-of-payments deficit is smaller initially, and it is brought to an end before income is reduced all the way to OY_0. In Figure 15-5, the *LM* curve comes to rest at a point on $I'S'$ somewhere between E_1 and E_2. The permanent level of income lies between OY_1 and OY_0, and the permanent level of the interest rate lies between Or_1 and Or_2. There is still a current-account deficit, because income is above OY_0, but the remaining deficit is offset by the larger capital inflow induced by the additional increase in the interest rate. The

effect of fiscal policy is reduced but does not disappear.[5]

Clearly, there is some degree of capital mobility that would keep the economy at E_1 permanently. The capital inflow induced by the increase in the interest rate to Or_1 would just match the current-account deficit induced by the increase in income to OY_1. When capital mobility is lower, the re-

---

[5] Note that this outcome resembles closely the outcome in Figure 15-3, where fiscal policy was used for internal balance and monetary policy was used for external balance. In that example, however, the outcome was obtained immediately; the money supply was reduced abruptly by an open-market sale. In this example, it is obtained by a gradual reduction in the money supply produced by a transitory balance-of-payments deficit.

sults are those described by Figure 15-5. When capital mobility is higher, the results are those described by Figure 15-6.

Start with the limiting case of perfect capital mobility. The domestic interest rate cannot change because it must equal the foreign rate, and this means that the tax cut must take the economy all the way to E_2, raising income to OY_2. By implication, the capital inflow must be very large, because it must produce a balance-of-payments surplus large enough to shift the LM curve downward immediately to $L'M'$ and prevent the domestic interest rate from rising. The increase in income is large, too, because there is no increase in the interest rate to "crowd out" the stimulus provided by the tax cut. In general, high capital mobility makes fiscal policy more effective. The interest rate rises initially, as it did in Figure 15-5, but the increase induces a capital inflow larger than the current-account deficit. The balance of payments move into surplus, as in the case of perfect capital mobility, and the money supply grows. The LM curve moves downward and comes to rest at a point on $I'S'$ between E_1 and E_2. The permanent level of income lies between OY_1 and OY_2, and the permanent level of the interest rate lies between Or_0 and Or_1. (There is a permanent deficit on current account, but it is exactly offset by a capital inflow, as it was with low capital mobility.)

Let us sum up. When the exchange rate is pegged and the central bank does not sterilize reserve flows, these three statements hold:

1. If there is no capital mobility, the effects of monetary and fiscal policies wear off completely.

2. As capital mobility rises, the effectiveness of monetary policy is reduced more speedily. With perfect capital mobility, monetary policy is completely ineffective.

3. As capital mobility rises, the effectiveness of fiscal policy is restored. With high capital mo-

bility, the total effect of fiscal policy is larger than its initial effect.

All three propositions however, abstract from the effects of capital flows on interest-income payments,[6] and the third proposition depends crucially on the underlying assumption of the Fleming–Mundell model, that an interest-rate difference induces a continuing capital flow. If capital flows taper off eventually, the effects of fiscal policy must wear off, too. The economy must start to run a balance-of-payments deficit in the wake of a tax cut, and it must move eventually to E_2 in Figure 15-5. Income must fall back to what it was before the tax cut.

Monetary Policy Under a Flexible Exchange Rate

Under a pegged exchange rate, the position of the LM curve is determined in part by the balance of payments. If the central bank does not sterilize reserve flows, it cannot control the money supply. Under a flexible exchange rate, there are no reserve

---

[6] To illustrate the implications of interest-income payments, consider the effects of an increase in the money supply that reduces the domestic interest rate initially. Asset holders will sell domestic bonds and buy foreign bonds (there will be a capital outflow on the way to the new long-run equilibirum). Interest payments to foreigners will fall because of the change in bond holdings, and this will improve the current-account balance. Therefore, the long-run equilibrium cannot be at E_0 in Figure 15-4. The permanent level of the interest rate must be Or_0, just as it was before; otherwise, capital flows would continue in the Fleming–Mundell model, and the level of interest payments would go on changing. But the permanent level of income must be higher than OY_0, because the economy must run a permanent trade deficit just large enough to match the reduction in interest payments and thus bring the current account into balance. (In effect, the IS curve will shift slightly to the right, because the reduction in interest payments will raise the permanent level of income.) Monetary policy will then have a small effect on income, even in the long run. The statements made later about flexible exchange rates have to be amended in similar ways when allowance is made for interest-income payments.

flows, and the position of the *LM* curve is determined completely by monetary policy. This is one basic difference between the two regimes, and it is often used as an argument for exchange-rate flexibility. But there is another difference. Under a pegged exchange rate, the position of the *IS* curve is determined by domestic economic conditions, including fiscal policy. Under a flexible exchange rate, its position depends in part on the real exchange rate, which affects the division of expenditure between domestic and foreign goods. Both differences are relevant for the workings of domestic policies under pegged and flexible exchange rates.

A flexible exchange rate enhances the effectiveness of monetary policy, and capital mobility compounds the increase in effectiveness. These propositions are illustrated in Figure 15-7.

An open-market purchase shifts the *LM* curve downward to *L'M'*, just as with a pegged exchange rate, and equilibrium is displaced from E_0 to E_1. Income rises immediately from OY_0 to OY_1, and the interest rate falls from Or_0 to Or_1. This is the outcome for a closed economy but not for an open economy with a flexible exchange rate, not even initially. Something more must happen right away. Because an increase in income raises imports, and a decrease in the interest rate causes a capital outflow when there is any capital mobility, the domestic currency must depreciate to clear the foreign-exchange market. The expenditure-switching effect of the depreciation shifts the *IS* curve to some such position as *I'S'*. The equilibrium point goes to E_2, and income rises to OY_2. As the size of the shift in the *IS* curve depends on the size of the depreciation, which increases with the size of the capital outflow, high capital mobility adds to the increase in in-

FIGURE 15-7 Monetary Policy Under a Flexible Exchange Rate

An increase in the money supply shifts the *LM* curve to *L'M'*, displacing equilibrium from E_0 to E_1. The domestic currency depreciates at once, even in the absence of capital mobility, because an increase in income from OY_0 to OY_1 raises imports. The expenditure-switching effect of the depreciation shifts the *IS* curve to some such position as *I'S'*, displacing equilibrium to E_2 and raising income to OY_2. Capital mobility strengthens this effect, because the reduction in the interest rate induces a capital outflow, causing a larger depreciation of the domestic currency. With perfect capital mobility, the interest rate must stay at Or_0, and equilibrium is displaced to E_3. The *IS* curve shifts all the way to *I"S"*, and income rises all the way to OY_3. Under a flexible exchange rate, monetary policy is effective permanently, and capital mobility raises its effectiveness.

come. Look at the limiting case of perfect capital mobility. The interest rate must stay at Or_0, which means that the *IS* curve must shift all the way to $I''S''$. Income must rise to OY_3.

Fiscal Policy Under a Flexible Exchange Rate

A flexible exchange rate can reduce the effectiveness of fiscal policy, and high capital mobility is to blame. The reasons are shown in Figure 15-8. A tax cut shifts the *IS* curve to $I'S'$, as in Figures 15-5 and 15-6, displacing equilibrium from E_0 to E_1. This is again the outcome for a closed economy, but not for an open economy with a flexible exchange rate. We must al-

low for the change in the exchange rate, and the outcome depends on the degree of capital mobility. When there is no mobility or low mobility, the domestic currency depreciates. (The current account deteriorates because of the increase in income, and the capital inflow, if any, is too small to cover the deterioration.) The expenditure-switching effect of the depreciation amplifies the shift in the *IS* curve, taking it beyond $I'S'$ to some such position as $I_1'S_1'$. Income rises to OY_1'. The flexible exchange rate adds to the income-raising effect of the tax cut, making fiscal policy more effective. When there is perfect mobility or high mobility, however, the domestic currency appreciates. (The current account deteriorates, but the capital inflow is more than

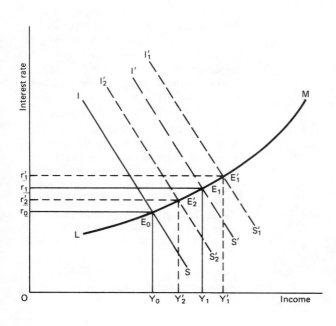

FIGURE 15-8 Fiscal Policy Under a Flexible Exchange Rate

A tax cut shifts the *IS* curve to $I'S'$, displacing equilibrium from E_0 to E_1. Income rises from OY_0 to OY_1, and the interest rate rises from Or_0 to Or_1. With no capital mobility or low mobility, the domestic currency must depreciate at once. The expenditure-switching effect of the depreciation shifts the *IS* curve to some such position as $I_1'S_1'$, displacing equilibrium to E_1' and raising income permanently to OY_1'. The tax cut is more effective. With high capital mobility, the domestic currency must appreciate instead, because of the large capital inflow induced by the increase in the interest rate. The expenditure-switching effect shifts the *IS* curve to some such position as $I_2'S_2'$, displacing equilibrium to E_2' and reducing income to OY_2'. The tax cut is less effective. With perfect mobility, the interest rate must stay at Or_0, and the appreciation of the domestic currency must be large enough to drive the *IS* curve back to its starting point. There is no increase in income, and the tax cut is completely ineffective.

sufficient to cover the deterioration.) The expenditure-switching effect of the appreciation limits the shift in the *IS* curve, taking it to some such position as $I\frac{1}{2}S\frac{1}{2}$. Income rises but only to OY'_2. With perfect mobility, fiscal policy is completely ineffective. Because the interest rate must stay at Or_0, the economy must stay at E_0. By implication, the appreciation of the domestic currency must snap the *IS* curve right back to its starting point, and income cannot change at all.

The outcomes under a flexible exchange rate can be summarized most easily by starting with perfect capital mobility:

1. With perfect capital mobility, the effectiveness of monetary policy is maximized, but fiscal policy is deprived of any effect on the domestic economy.
2. As capital mobility falls, the effectiveness of monetary policy diminishes, but its effect on income is always larger than the initial effect obtained with a pegged exchange rate and complete sterilization.
3. As capital mobility falls, the effectiveness of fiscal policy grows, and its effect on income can be larger than the initial effect.

Note that *all* these results depend in part on the Fleming–Mundell supposition about the permanence of capital flows. If capital movements taper off, the influence of monetary policy is reduced gradually, but the permanent change in income is larger nonetheless than the change to OY_1 in Figure 15-7; the domestic currency must still depreciate to eliminate the current-account deficit. The influence of fiscal policy is raised gradually, and the permanent change in income is also larger than the change to OY_1 in Figure 15-8, because of the depreciation of the domestic currency.

SUMMARY

When capital movements are sensitive to interest rates, monetary policy acquires additional influence on the balance of payments and on the behavior of a flexible exchange rate. It is therefore necessary to amend the theory of economic policy developed in Chapter 14. Under a flexible exchange rate, for example, capital mobility adds to the risk of instability. When monetary policy is used to achieve internal balance and the central bank does not take account of the large exchange-rate changes that occur with high capital mobility, there can be explosive oscillations in income and the exchange rate.

Under a pegged exchange rate, moreover, monetary policy can be used to maintain external balance and fiscal policy used to maintain internal balance. The two targets can be reached simultaneously without changing the exchange rate, and the policy assignment is stable. But there are two objections to this strategy. An increase in the domestic interest rate induced by a tightening of monetary policy may merely produce a one-time switch in investors' portfolios, rather than an ongoing capital inflow, and will not improve the balance of payments permanently. Furthermore, an increase in the interest rate can lead to a progressive deterioration in the current-account balance, because it raises interest payments to the outside world, and the deterioration in the current-account balance will offset more and more of the capital inflow induced by the higher interest rate.

Capital mobility has additional effects on the workings of domestic economic policies. These are seen most clearly when we drop the assumption that central banks sterilize the money-supply effects of official intervention in the foreign-exchange market.

If the exchange rate is pegged and there is no capital mobility, the domestic effects of monetary and fiscal policies must wear off eventually. A tightening of monetary policy leads to an inflow of reserves that gradually undermines the tightening of policy. A tax increase has similar effects in the long run. As capital mobility rises, the effectiveness of monetary policy is reduced more speedily, and it has no influence whatsoever with perfect capital mobility. By contrast, the effectiveness of fiscal policy is enhanced by capital mobility, and the permanent effects of fiscal policy are larger with high mobility than its initial effects with no mobility.

If the exchange rate is flexible and there is no capital mobility, the effectiveness of fiscal policy is reinforced; a tax cut induces a depreciation of the domestic currency, and the expenditure-raising effect of the

tax cut is supplemented by the expenditure-switching effects of the depreciation. When capital mobility is high, however, the effectiveness of fiscal policy is low; a tax cut induces an appreciation of the domestic currency by producing a large capital inflow. Fiscal policy is utterly ineffective with perfect capital mobility. The consequences for monetary policy go the other way. It is always more effective with a flexible rate than with a pegged rate, and its effectiveness is enhanced by capital mobility.

RECOMMENDED READINGS

The Fleming–Mundell model owes its name to one paper by Fleming and two by Mundell: J. Marcus Fleming, "Domestic Financial Policies Under Fixed and Under Floating Exchange Rates," *International Monetary Fund Staff Papers*, 9 (November 1962), reprinted in J. M. Fleming, *Essays in International Economics* (Cambridge, Mass.: Harvard University Press, 1971), ch. 9; Robert A Mundell, "The Appropriate Use of Monetary and Fiscal Policy Under Fixed Exchange Rates," *International Monetary Fund Staff Papers*, 9 (March 1962), and "Capital Mobility and Stabilization Policy Under Fixed and Flexible Exchange Rates," *Canadian Journal of Economics and Political Science*, 29 (November 1963), reprinted in R. A. Mundell, *International Economics* (New York: Macmillan, 1968), chs. 16, 18.

For a survey and synthesis of the subsequent literature on optimal economic policy, with particular attention to capital mobility, see Marina v. N. Whitman, *Policies for Internal and External Balance* (Princeton, N.J.: International Finance Section, Princeton University, 1970).

Recent contributions include Jeffrey Sachs, "Wages, Flexible Exchange Rates, and Macroeconomic Policies," *Quarterly Journal of Economics*, 94 (June 1980), which shows how wage rigidity alters the effects of the exchange-rate regime on the workings of monetary and fiscal policies; see also Richard C. Marston, "Stabilization Policies in Open Economies," in R. W. Jones and P. B. Kenen, eds., *Handbook of International Economics* (Amsterdam: North-Holland, 1985), ch. 17, which synthesizes a large body of recent work.

For a survey of quantitative work on international capital mobility, see Ralph C. Bryant, "Empirical Research on Financial Capital Flows," in P. B. Kenen, ed., *International Trade and Finance: Frontiers for Research* (New York: Cambridge University Press, 1975); also Peter B. Kenen, *Capital Mobility and Financial Integration: A Survey* (Princeton, N.J.: International Finance Section, Princeton University, 1976), ch.2.

CHAPTER

16

EXPECTATIONS, EXCHANGE RATES, AND THE CAPITAL ACCOUNT

INTRODUCTION

Most investments are uncertain because they must be based on forecasts about future earnings, and these can be wrong. Foreign investments are especially uncertain, because they involve forecasts about changes in exchange rates, as well as forecasts about earnings. International capital movements do not depend only on interest-rate differences. They depend in addition on investors' expectations about changes in exchange rates, and they are affected by attitudes toward risk, by an investor's willingness to make commitments in an uncertain world.

This chapter introduces expectations and uncertainty into the analysis of capital movements. It begins by showing how exchange-rate expectations affect an investor's choice between foreign and domestic bonds. It turns next to uncertainty and its

implications for capital mobility. Thereafter, we look at speculation in the foreign-exchange market, which connects the actual exchange rate today with expectations about future exchange rates. Speculation can contribute to exchange-rate stability, but its contribution depends in part on its profitability. Finally, we look at the forward foreign-exchange market. Traders and investors use that market to protect themselves against exchange-rate risk. Speculators use it to place "bets" on their views about the future by deliberately incurring exchange-rate risk. Therefore, the forward market allows traders and investors to shift risk to speculators.

EXPECTATIONS AND RATES OF RETURN

Let there be two bonds, a domestic bond bearing an interest rate r and denominated in domestic currency, and a foreign bond bearing an interest rate r^* and denominated in foreign currency. The exchange rate between the two currencies is π, the number of units of domestic currency needed to buy a unit of foreign currency. To keep matters simple, suppose that r and r^* are known in advance and that the two bonds are identical in all other ways—maturity, likelihood of default, and the rest.

The Open Interest Differential

If you invest a unit of domestic currency in the domestic bond, you can expect to come out with $1 + r$ units of that currency after a year. If you invest a unit of domestic currency in the foreign bond, you will obtain $1/\pi$ foreign-currency units of that bond and can therefore expect to come out with $(1/\pi)(1 + r^*)$ units of foreign currency after a year. This is where exchange-rate expectations enter the story. To compare the two returns, you must forecast the exchange rate that is likely to prevail a year from now. Denote that *expected* exchange rate by π^e and use it to convert the foreign-currency return on the foreign bond. It is $(1/\pi)(1 + r^*)\pi^e$ units of domestic currency.

Use u to define the difference between the returns that you can expect to receive:

$$u = \frac{1}{\pi}(1 + r^*)\pi^e - (1 + r) \qquad (1)$$

This is known as the *open interest differential* between foreign and domestic investments. If you are totally indifferent to risk, the possibility of being wrong about the future exchange rate, you will buy the foreign bond whenever u is positive.

The equation for u can be simplified by defining a new term, $\hat{\pi}$, the expected rate of change of the exchange rate:

$$\hat{\pi} = \frac{\pi^e - \pi}{\pi} \qquad (2)$$

A positive value of $\hat{\pi}$ signifies an expectation that the domestic currency will depreciate during the coming year; a negative value signifies an expectation that it will appreciate. As $\pi^e = (1 + \hat{\pi})\pi$, equation (1) can be rewritten as

$$\begin{aligned} u &= (1 + r^*)(1 + \hat{\pi}) - (1 + r) \\ &= (r^* - r) + (1 + r^*)\hat{\pi} \qquad (1a) \\ &\approx (r^* - r) + \hat{\pi} \end{aligned}$$

because $(1 + r^*)\hat{\pi}$ is approximately equal to $\hat{\pi}$.

There are two ways to look at equation (1a). Viewed from the perspective of an investor concerned primarily with the advantage of holding one bond instead of the other, it says that an additional gain or loss can come from investing in the foreign bond. It is the capital gain or loss resulting from a change in the exchange rate. Viewed from the perspective of a speculator concerned primarily with the advantage of holding one currency instead of the other, the equation says that an additional gain or loss can come from purchasing the foreign currency in the belief that $\hat{\pi}$ is positive. It is the interest gained or lost by holding the foreign bond.[1]

But perspectives do not matter fundamentally. An investor who buys the foreign bond is also a speculator; part of the return expected from that purchase depends on $\hat{\pi}$, the investor's forecast of the change in the exchange rate. A speculator who buys the foreign currency is also an investor;

---

[1] Both interpretations are based on the supposition that investors and speculators measure gains and losses in domestic currency. They will be concerned, however, with the *real* values of their assets, not *nominal* values in domestic or foreign currency. Real values depend in turn on the prices of the goods they consume. When we deal with real values, however, the analysis grows complicated, because we must take account of expectations about prices, as well as expectations about exchange rates, and the main conclusions do not differ hugely from those in the text, which continues to deal with nominal values.

part of the return expected from that purchase depends on the interest rate that can be earned by holding foreign-currency assets. Whenever u is positive, moreover, an investor-speculator will want to hold *some* foreign-currency assets. We can show this most clearly by rearranging equation (1a):

$$u \approx (r^* + \hat{\pi}) - r \qquad (1b)$$

The first term is the rate of return expected on the foreign bond; the second is the rate of return on the domestic bond. If the first is larger than the second, regardless of the reason, an investor-speculator will hold some foreign bonds. Furthermore, an increase in u will raise the demand for the foreign bond and reduce the demand for the domestic bond. It will thus cause a capital flow from the domestic to the foreign economy, raising the demand for foreign currency in the foreign-exchange market.

An Illustration

As equation (1a) plays an important role in much of this chapter, let us illustrate its use. Suppose that the U.S. interest rate is 8 percent, that the British interest rate is 6 percent, and that the current exchange rate is $1.75 per pound. You are an American investor and calculate your wealth in dollars. You expect the dollar to depreciate (the pound to appreciate) to $1.85 per pound during the coming year. You should therefore invest in British bonds, even though they pay a lower interest rate. You will sacrifice 2 percent in interest by investing in British bonds. If you are right about the future exchange rate, however, you will gain 10 cents on every pound invested in British bonds, and 0.10/1.75 is 5.7 percent, which is 3.7 percent more than the interest you will sacrifice. Working with equation (1b), r^* is 6 percent, r is 8 percent, and $\hat{\pi}$ is 5.7 percent, so

$$u \approx (6.0 + 5.7) - 8.0 = 11.7 - 8.0 = 3.7$$

You can go farther, by borrowing dollars at 8 percent in the United States, buying pounds at $1.75, and investing the pounds in Britain at 6 percent. If the exchange rate goes to $1.85 a year from now, as expected, the transaction will cost you 2 percent in interest but give you a 5.7 percent capital gain on the exchange-rate change when you sell pounds to pay back the dollars you borrowed. There are thus many ways to exploit an open interest differential. Whenever u is positive, however, they all involve purchases of pounds now and sales of pounds later.

UNCERTAINTY AND ATTITUDES TOWARD RISK

In the previous example, you forecast an appreciation of the pound from $1.75 to $1.85 during the coming year and decided to buy pounds, because the expected gain from the exchange-rate change was larger than the sacrifice of interest income. But you can be wrong about the exchange rate.

Errors, Uncertainty, and Risk

Suppose that interest rates are the same in the United States and Britain, so that there are no interest gains or losses. You believe that there is a 75 percent chance that the pound will appreciate from $1.75 to $1.90 per pound during the coming year but a 25 percent chance that it will depreciate from $1.75 to $1.70 per pound. The expected exchange rate, π^e, is $1.85 per pound, as before. It is defined formally as a weighted average of the possibilities with their probabilities used as weights:

$$\pi^e = (0.75 \times \$1.90) + (0.25 \times \$1.75)$$
$$= \$1.85$$

It makes sense for you to buy some British bonds. When interest rates are equal, u is equal to $\hat{\pi}$, and $\hat{\pi}$ is still 0.10/1.75, or 5.7

percent. You will earn more, of course, if the pound appreciates to $1.90; the gain will be 0.15/1.75, or 8.6 percent. You will incur a loss, however, if the pound depreciates to $1.70; the loss will be 0.05/1.75, or 2.8 percent. Accordingly, you may not want to invest your whole portfolio in British bonds. Your exposure to the risk of loss rises with the fraction invested in those bonds.[2]

What will you do if you believe that there is a 75 percent chance that the pound will appreciate to $2.05 per pound but a 25 percent chance that it will depreciate to $1.25 per pound? The expected exchange rate is still $1.85 per pound:

$$\pi^e = (0.75 \times \$2.05) + (0.25 \times \$1.25)$$
$$= \$1.85$$

so $\hat{\pi}$ is still 5.7 percent. Nevertheless, an investment in British bonds is more risky. Your gain can be as large as 0.30/1.75, or 17.1 percent, but your loss as large as 0.50/1.75, or 28.6 percent. You may still want to hold some British bonds but to limit your exposure more stringently.

Two propositions can be drawn from these illustrations: (1) The open interest differential measures the expected gain or loss from shifting to the foreign bond. (2) The size of the shift, however, may be influenced by the uncertainty surrounding investors' expectations, depending on investors' attitudes toward risk.

Risk Neutrality and Open Interest Parity

Some investors may be perfectly *risk neutral*, utterly indifferent to uncertainty. When

the open interest differential favors investment in Britain, those investors will shift completely into British bonds, regardless of the risk of loss. In other words, they will be guided only by expected gains and losses and can therefore be said to treat domestic and foreign bonds as perfect substitutes.

If most investors were risk neutral, however, an open interest differential could not last long. By shifting massively to British bonds, investors would drive up the prices of those bonds and drive down the prices of U.S. bonds, reducing the British interest rate and raising the U.S. rate. With a flexible exchange rate, moreover, the pound would appreciate immediately in response to the demand for pounds reflecting the demand for British bonds. This would reduce $\hat{\pi}$ (unless the expected exchange rate, π^e, kept pace with the current rate, π). The movements in r^*, r, and $\hat{\pi}$ would not cease until the open interest differential fell to zero.

When the differential is zero, of course, equation (1a) asserts that

$$\hat{\pi} = r - r^* \qquad (3)$$

This condition is called *open interest parity*. It says that the expected change in the exchange rate is exactly equal to the interest-rate difference, and it has two implications. First, it repeats in slightly different form a statement made before about monetary policy. If investors treat domestic and foreign bonds as perfect substitutes because they are risk neutral, the central bank cannot control the domestic interest rate unless it can influence exchange-rate expectations. If r^* and $\hat{\pi}$ are given, r is also given. Second, the condition provides a way to measure market views about the future exchange rate. If the U.S. interest rate is 8 percent and the British interest rate is 6 percent, the numbers used before, the typical investor-speculator must expect the dollar to depreciate by 2 percent. But investors may not be risk neutral.

---

[2] To see why π^e is defined as the weighted average of the possibilities, suppose that you could "bet" repeatedly on those possibilities. You would make an 8.6 percent gain on 75 percent of your "bets" but would lose 2.8 percent on 25 percent. Your average gain would be $(0.75 \times 8.6) - (0.25 \times 2.8)$, or 5.7 percent, and you would come out ahead in the long run. You could suffer a series of losses, however, that could put you out of business. That is why you might not invest your whole portfolio in British bonds.

FIGURE 16-1 Portfolio Selection by a Risk-Averse Investor
The curve *DI* shows how the expected return and riskiness of a portfolio
change with its composition. When the whole portfolio is invested in the
domestic bond, the return is *OD* and the standard deviation is zero;
when it is invested in the foreign bond, the return is *OF* and the standard deviation is $O\overline{S}$; when it is divided between the two bonds, the
return is *OV* and the standard deviation is *OS*. The indifference curves
show that an investor's welfare rises with an increase in the return and
falls with an increase in the standard deviation; *U'* represents a higher
level of welfare than *U*. Facing the set of returns and risks given by the
line *DI*, the investor goes to *Q*, as *U* is the highest attainable indifference curve. An increase in the foreign interest rate raises the open interest differential from *DF* to *DF'* and shifts *DI* to *DI'*. The investor goes to
Q', as *U'* is the highest attainable indifference curve. The return rises
from *OV* to *OV'*, and the standard deviation rises from *OS* to *OS'*. As
the latter cannot rise without an increase in the fraction of the portfolio
invested in the foreign bond, that fraction is higher at *Q'* than at *Q*.

Risk Aversion and Portfolio Selection

If investors are *risk averse* rather than
risk neutral, an open interest differential
can persist indefinitely. It will still induce a
shift from one bond to the other, but the
shift will be limited by exchange-rate risk
and the degree of risk aversion. This proposition is illustrated in Figure 16-1. The
vertical axis shows the expected return on a
portfolio containing domestic and foreign
bonds. When the whole portfolio is in-

vested in the domestic bond, the expected return is $v_h = (1 + r)$, which is given in the diagram by the distance OD. When the whole portfolio is invested in the foreign bond, the expected return is

$$v_f = (1 + r^*)(1 + \hat{\pi})$$

which is given by the distance OF. Note that

$$OF - OD = FD = v_f - v_h \approx u$$

When a fraction n of the whole portfolio is invested in the foreign bond, the expected return is a weighted average of v_h and v_f:

$$v = nv_f + (1 - n)v_h$$
$$= v_h + n(v_f - v_h) = v_h + nu$$

It is given in the diagram by the distance OV, so that $OV = OD + nFD$, which says that $n = VD/FD$. When n is 0.5, for instance, V lies halfway between D and F.

The horizontal axis of Figure 16-1 measures the riskiness of the portfolio from the standpoint of an investor whose wealth is denominated in domestic currency. Riskiness depends on the dispersion of the possibilities that underlie investors' expectations and on their exposure to that dispersion. In technical terms, it can be measured by the *standard deviation* of the return on the portfolio, a term defined precisely in Note 16-1. When the whole portfolio is invested in the domestic bond, there is no exchange-rate risk because there is no exposure; the standard deviation is zero. When the whole portfolio is invested in the foreign bond, exchange-rate risk is maximized because exposure is maximized; the standard deviation is $O\bar{S}$ and can get no larger.[3] What happens when a fraction of

the total portfolio is invested in the foreign bond? Note 16-1 shows that the standard deviation rises at a constant rate with the fraction n invested in the foreign bond. Therefore, the standard deviation is $OS = nO\bar{S}$. When n is 0.5, then, S lies halfway between O and $\bar{S}$. The line DI represents the simple relationship between expected return and riskiness. When riskiness is measured by the standard deviation, DI is a straight line, because OV and OS rise at constant rates when n increases.

The indifference curves in Figure 16-1 show how a risk-averse investor looks at opportunities involving uncertainty about the future exchange rate. Clearly, the investor is better off with a high return and low standard deviation. Therefore, points on the indifference curve U' are better than points on U. Furthermore, a risk-averse investor wants the expected return OV to rise at a growing rate to offset successive increases in risk. Therefore, the indifference curves get steeper as OS increases. The curves are drawn, however, to reflect one more assumption. The slope of U' at Q'', vertically above Q, is the same as the slope of U at Q. The investor's willingness to sacrifice return for safety, a lower standard deviation, does not vary with OV.

Faced with the tradeoff between return and risk represented by the line DI, a risk-averse investor will go to Q, because U is the highest attainable indifference curve. Given the open interest differential shown by FD and the way that risk rises with n, the investor will choose the value of n at which the expected return on the investor's

---

[3] This last statement is not strictly true. An investor can borrow at home in order to invest abroad. When that happens, the fraction n will exceed 1, and the standard deviation will exceed $O\bar{S}$. To keep matters simple, however, we say no more about this possibility. (Note that a domestic investor will hold no foreign bonds when OD is larger than OF in Figure 16-1. The safest portfolio will be the most profitable. In that same circumstance, however, a foreign investor will hold some domestic bonds. We should therefore be working with two diagrams, one for the domestic investor whose wealth is denominated in domestic currency and another for the foreign investor whose wealth is denominated in foreign currency. When the open interest differential is positive, as in Figure 16-1, the domestic investor will take a risky position and the foreign investor will take a safe position. When the differential is negative, the domestic investor will take a safe position and the foreign investor will take a risky position.)

Note 16-1

Suppose that an investor believes that there is a probability p_1 that the domestic currency will depreciate by $\hat{\pi}_1$ percent and a probability p_2 that it will depreciate by $\hat{\pi}_2$ percent, where $p_1 + p_2 = 1$. The expected depreciation is

$$\hat{\pi} = p_1\hat{\pi}_1 + p_2\hat{\pi}_2$$

Let $u \approx r^* + \hat{\pi} - r > 0$, as in the text.

The definition of the expected return follows directly,

$$
\begin{aligned}
v &= n[p_1(1 + r^*)(1 + \hat{\pi}_1) \\
&\quad + p_2(1 + r^*)(1 + \hat{\pi}_2)] + (1 - n)(1 + r) \\
&= n(1 + r^*)[1 + (p_1\hat{\pi}_1 + p_2\hat{\pi}_2)] \\
&\quad\quad\quad\quad\quad\quad\quad + (1 - n)(1 + r) \\
&= n(1 + r^*)(1 + \hat{\pi}) + (1 - n)(1 + r) \\
&= v_h + nu
\end{aligned}
$$

where n is the fraction of the investor's portfolio invested in the foreign bond and v_h is the (riskless) return on the domestic bond. Note that an increase in r^* raises u, which raises v when $n > 0$.

If the domestic currency does indeed depreciate by $\hat{\pi}_i$ ($i = 1, 2$), the actual return on the portfolio will differ from the expected return by

$$
\begin{aligned}
e_i &= [n(1 + \hat{\pi}_i)(1 + r^*) + (1 - n)(1 + r)] \\
&\quad - [n(1 + \hat{\pi})(1 + r^*) + (1 - n)(1 + r)] \\
&= n(1 + r^*)(\hat{\pi}_i - \hat{\pi}) \approx n(\hat{\pi}_i - \hat{\pi})
\end{aligned}
$$

This is why the portfolio is risky when $n > 0$. Its riskiness can be measured by its standard deviation,

$$
\begin{aligned}
\sigma_v &= \sqrt{p_1 e_1^2 + p_2 e_2^2} \\
&\approx n\sqrt{(p_1 p_2)(\hat{\pi}_1 - \hat{\pi}_2)^2} = n\overline{\sigma}_v
\end{aligned}
$$

where $\overline{\sigma}_v$ is the value of σ_v when the whole portfolio is invested in the foreign bond (and thus equals $O\overline{S}$ in Figure 16-1). Note that $\overline{\sigma}_v$ depends on the forecasts $\hat{\pi}_1$ and $\hat{\pi}_2$ and their probabilities, that σ_v rises as n rises, given the value of $\overline{\sigma}_v$, and that an increase in r^* does not affect σ_v (because it does not affect $\overline{\sigma}_v$).

portfolio is OV and the standard deviation is OS.

How will the investor respond to an increase in the foreign interest rate? Note 16-1 shows that an increase in r^* raises the expected return by raising u but does not change the standard deviation. In Figure 16-1, then, an increase in the differential from FD to FD' shifts DI to DI', and the investor goes to Q' on the higher indifference curve U'. The indifference curves are "stacked up" vertically, however, so Q' must lie to the northeast of Q. The return on the portfolio rises from OV to OV', and the standard deviation rises from OS to OS'. But the standard deviation cannot rise unless there is an increase in exposure to

exchange-rate risk, the fraction n invested in the foreign bond. By implication, an increase in the foreign interest rate induces a risk-averse investor to substitute foreign for domestic bonds but not to move completely out of domestic bonds.

EXPECTATIONS AND EXCHANGE-RATE BEHAVIOR

Investors' expectations about future exchange rates strongly affect the current exchange rate. Some economists even say that short-term fluctuations in the actual exchange rate are due mainly to revisions in investors' expectations, reflecting the arrival of new information about forces that will influence exchange rates. But the effects of changes in expectations depend importantly on attitudes toward risk.

Another Look at the Foreign-Exchange Market

These statements are illustrated in the next three diagrams, which give us a new way to look at the foreign-exchange market. In Figure 16-2, the actual exchange rate is measured on the vertical axis; purchases and sales of foreign currency are measured on the horizontal axis. The *ED* curve describes the *excess demand* for foreign currency coming from investor-speculators. The *ES* curve describes the *excess supply* coming from all other market participants.

The *ES* curve can be derived from the ordinary supply and demand curves introduced in Chapter 12. At some exchange rate, *OP*, the total supply of foreign currency coming from foreign buyers of domestic goods and services will equal the total demand coming from domestic buyers of foreign goods and services. Excess supply will be zero. Suppose that the domestic currency depreciates. The supply of foreign currency will rise as foreign buyers of domestic goods and services increase their purchases, and the demand for foreign currency will fall as domestic buyers of foreign goods and services decrease their purchases. Excess supply will be positive. Accordingly, the *ES* curve slopes upward. (The slope of the *ES* curve depends on the Marshall–Lerner–Robinson condition. Whenever it is satisfied, a depreciation of the domestic currency improves the current-account balance and thus raises the excess supply of foreign currency.)

The position of the *ED* curve depends on interest rates and expectations. When the open interest differential is zero, investors will not want to buy foreign bonds.

Therefore, they will not want to buy foreign currency. Excess demand will be zero. A special case is shown in Figure 16-2. Let foreign and domestic interest rates be equal. The open interest differential will be zero if investors expect the exchange rate to be constant—if *OP* is equal to π, the actual exchange rate, and is also equal to π^e, the expected future rate, so that $\hat{\pi}$ is zero. The slope of the *ED* curve depends on the riskiness of foreign investment and the degree of risk aversion. Suppose that the domestic currency appreciates without affecting the expected exchange rate—that π falls but π^e remains at *OP*. Since $\hat{\pi}$ becomes positive, the open interest differential becomes positive, too. Investors will expect the domestic currency to depreciate and will buy foreign currency in order to buy foreign bonds, so excess demand will be positive. When investors are risk averse, however, they will not switch completely into foreign bonds, and their demand for foreign currency will be limited. Accordingly, the *ED* curve slopes downward. The greater the uncertainty about the expected rate and the higher the degree of risk aversion, the steeper is the *ED* curve.

Effects of a Change in the Foreign Interest Rate

Before showing how a revision of investors' expectations affects the actual exchange rate, let us see how an increase in the foreign interest rate affects the situation. Start with the special case in Figure 16-2. Interest rates are equal initially, and the expected exchange rate is *OP*. If the actual exchange rate is also equal to *OP*, excess demand will be zero and excess supply will be zero, too. Therefore, the actual exchange rate must be *OP*. It is the market-clearing rate.

An increase in the foreign interest rate leads investors to buy foreign bonds and

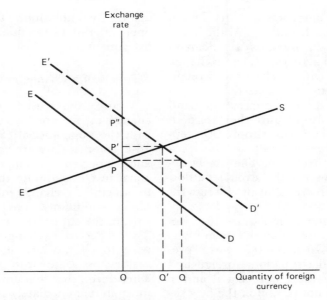

FIGURE 16-2 Effects of an Increase in the Foreign Interest Rate

The *ED* curve shows the excess demand for foreign currency coming from investor-speculators. When foreign and domestic interest rates are equal and the actual and expected exchange rates are both equal to *OP*, the *ED* curve will cross the vertical axis at *P*. The open interest differential will be zero, and excess demand will be zero. If the actual exchange rate falls below *OP* without affecting the expected rate, the open interest differential will be positive, and investors will demand more foreign currency. The *ES* curve shows the excess supply of foreign currency coming from all other market participants. At some exchange rate, *OP*, the total supply of foreign currency coming from foreign buyers of domestic goods and services will equal the total demand for foreign currency coming from domestic buyers of foreign goods and services. If the actual exchange rate rises above *OP*, total supply will increase, total demand will decrease, and excess supply will be positive. When the actual exchange rate is *OP*, excess demand is equal to excess supply, because both are zero. Therefore, *OP* is the market-clearing rate. If there is an increase in the foreign interest rate and it does not affect the expected exchange rate, the demand curve will shift from *ED* to *E'D'*. The open interest differential will be positive and investors will demand *OQ* of foreign currency at the initial exchange rate. Excess demand will exceed excess supply, and the actual exchange rate will go to *OP'* to clear the foreign-exchange market.

thus buy foreign currency. It shifts the demand curve from ED to $E'D'$. At the initial exchange rate, OP, investors will demand OQ of foreign currency.[4] The exchange rate must go to OP' to clear the foreign-exchange market; the domestic currency must depreciate to reduce excess demand and raise excess supply until they are both equal to OQ'. (The excess supply OQ' represents the current-account surplus produced by the depreciation. The excess demand OQ' represents the capital outflow produced by the increase in the foreign interest rate.)

The two situations in Figure 16-2 can be compared by examining the open interest differential. Open interest parity prevailed in the initial situation; foreign and domestic interest rates were equal and $\hat{\pi}$ was zero. It does not prevail in the new situation. If the actual exchange rate could go to OP'', it would reduce excess demand to zero. Open interest parity would prevail, because $\hat{\pi}$ would be large enough to offset the increase in the foreign interest rate. But the actual exchange rate goes only to OP', which does not eliminate excess de-

---

[4] There are two ways to look at this shift: (1) It can be treated as a rightward shift, showing the amount of foreign currency that investors will demand at the initial exchange rate. (2) It can be treated as an upward shift, showing the change in the actual exchange rate that would have to take place to eliminate the open interest differential and reduce excess demand to zero. When the open interest differential is zero, equations (2) and (3) say that

$$\hat{\pi} = \frac{\pi^e - \pi}{\pi} = r - r^*, \text{ so } \pi^e = [1 + (r - r^*)]\pi$$

and

$$\pi = \frac{\pi^e}{1 + (r - r^*)}$$

When r^* rises but r and π^e do not change, the actual exchange rate must come to exceed the expected rate. Investors must be made to expect an appreciation of the domestic currency large enough to offset the new difference between r^* and r. This can happen, however, only if the domestic currency depreciates immediately.

mand. By implication, there must be an open interest differential favoring foreign investment.

Effects of a Change in Expectations

Figure 16-3 illustrates the impact of a change in investors' expectations. It starts with the same special case used in Figure 16-2. Interest rates are equal and the actual and expected exchange rates are both equal to OP. Suppose that investors come to anticipate a change in fundamental economic conditions. They predict a *future* shift in the supply curve from ES to E^*S^*. The expected exchange rate must go at once to OP^*, which is the rate that investors associate with the E^*S^* curve. Therefore, the investors' demand curve must shift immediately from ED to E^*D^*; investors must expect the domestic currency to depreciate, and $\hat{\pi}$ becomes positive, producing an open interest differential that favors foreign investment. The actual exchange rate must go at once to OP', which is the rate that clears the foreign-exchange market when the demand curve is E^*D^* and the supply curve is still ES. The domestic currency must depreciate immediately when it is expected to depreciate eventually. The immediate depreciation is caused by the capital outflow OQ' produced by the open interest differential. (The outflow is matched by the current-account surplus induced by the depreciation, as in Figure 16-2.)

If investors are right about the supply curve and it does shift to E^*S^* eventually, the market-clearing exchange rate will go to OP^*. At that point, actual and expected exchange rates will be equal once again, the open interest differential will be zero, and the capital outflow will cease. If investors are wrong about the supply curve and it does not shift at all, they will revise their expectations. (The persistence of the current-account surplus OQ' will tell them

FIGURE 16-3 Effects of a Change in Expectations

Foreign and domestic interest rates are equal initially and the actual and expected exchange rates are *OP*. When investors anticipate a future shift in the supply curve from *ES* to *E*S**, the expected exchange rate goes to *OP**, the rate associated with the supply curve *E*S**. Therefore, the investors' demand curve goes at once to *E*D**, driving the actual exchange rate to *OP'*, which is the market-clearing rate when the demand curve is *E*D** and the supply curve is still *ES*. If investors are right, and the supply curve shifts to *E*S**, the exchange rate will go to *OP** eventually. If investors are wrong, and the supply curve remains at *ES*, investors will have to revise their expectations; the demand curve will return to *ED*, and the exchange rate will return to *OP*. When investors fail to anticipate a shift in the supply curve, the exchange rate remains at *OP* until the shift takes place. At that time, the rate goes to *OP"*, which is the market-clearing rate when the demand curve is still *ED* and the supply curve is *E*S**. But investors have then to revise their expectations, taking the demand curve to *E*D** and driving the exchange rate to *OP** eventually.

to do so.) The demand curve will shift back to *ED* eventually and the exchange rate will return to *OP*.

Figure 16-3 is drawn on two suppositions: that the shift in the supply curve is fully anticipated and that investors are risk averse. What happens when the shift is not anticipated? What happens when investors are risk neutral?

Speculation, Stability, and Profitability

When investors anticipate the shift in the supply curve from *ES* to *E*S** and they are correct, their behavior is stabilizing, and they make profits. Their behavior is stabilizing because it drives the exchange rate from *OP* to *OP'* and thus in the direction of *OP**, the rate that must prevail in the long run. Investors make profits because they buy foreign currency at the price OP' and sell it thereafter at the higher price OP^*. When investors anticipate a shift in the supply curve and turn out to be wrong, their behavior is destabilizing and they take losses. It is destabilizing because it drives the exchange rate to OP' when the rate should stay at OP. Investors take losses because they buy foreign currency at the price OP' and sell it later at the lower price OP.

When investors fail to anticipate a shift in the supply curve, their demand curve does not shift, and the exchange rate stays at OP temporarily. When the shift in the supply curve takes place, the domestic currency depreciates to OP'', the rate that clears the foreign-exchange market when the demand curve is still ED and the supply curve is E^*S^*. (The depreciation is produced by the current-account deficit resulting from the shift in the supply curve. It induces a matching capital inflow OQ'' because investors expect the exchange rate to return to OP and sell foreign currency.) If the shift in the supply curve is permanent, however, investors will revise their expectations eventually (helped this time by the current-account deficit OQ''). The demand curve will move to E^*D^*, driving the exchange rate to OP^*. Once again, investors behave in a destabilizing way and take losses. Their behavior is destabilizing because it delays the necessary change in the exchange rate. Investors take losses because they sell foreign currency at the price OP'' and buy it later at the price OP^*.

There would thus appear to be a systematic link between the profitability of speculation and its contribution to exchange-rate stability. Milton Friedman put it this way:

People who argue that speculation is generally destabilizing seldom realize that this is largely equivalent to saying that speculators lose money, since speculation can be destabilizing in general only if speculators on the average sell when the currency is low in price and buy when it is high.[5]

But be careful about the conclusion you draw from this quotation. Some economists have taken it to mean that speculation will *always* be stabilizing: destabilizing speculators will be driven out of business because they will take losses, and they will thus leave the market to stabilizing speculators, those who make profits and prosper in the long run. Friedman saw the flaw in this interpretation; he warned that "professional speculators might on average make money while a changing body of amateurs regularly lost larger sums."[6]

In recent years, economists have advanced another reason for believing that speculation will be stabilizing. It is the *rational expectations hypothesis*, which says that all decision makers, including speculators, process information about the future using an accurate model of the whole economy. They may make mistakes from time to time, because they do not have enough information or cannot distinguish information from mere rumor. But they will be right on average, because they use an accurate model, so speculation will tend to be stabilizing.[7]

---

[5] Milton Friedman, "The Case for Flexible Exchange Rates," in *Essays in Positive Economics* (Chicago: University of Chicago Press, 1953), p. 175.

[6] Ibid., pp. 175–176. He went on to argue, however, that the presumption favors stabilizing speculation. If private speculation were destabilizing, he said, governments could engage in stabilizing speculation and make large sums of money. But this is equivalent to supposing "that government officials risking funds that they do not themselves own are better judges of the likely movements in foreign-exchange markets than private individuals risking their own funds."

[7] The rational expectations hypothesis does not rule out instability completely. In fact, it typically gives rise to a multiplicity of paths for the economy, and decision makers may be unable to choose the stable path. If they choose an unstable path, they will produce a "speculative bubble" that must burst eventually but is destabilizing in the short run because it drives the economy away from its long-run equilibrium.

This hypothesis is attractive analytically and appealing intellectually. If we could not believe that economic decisions are based on rational calculations, we would have grave doubts about the optimality of resource allocation in a market economy. But watch out for a leap in logic. Advocates of the rational expectations hypothesis identify rightness with rationality and go on to identify wrongness with *ir*rationality. This is an invalid inference. It is vital to distinguish between ways in which decision makers form their expectations about rapidly changing market prices, such as stock prices and exchange rates, and ways in which they make infrequent but major decisions about building a factory, entering a new market, and so on. When making the first type of decision, it may be necessary to use rules of thumb to process information; when making the second type of decision, there is time to collect and process information carefully. Those who must use rules of thumb are not behaving irrationally, and

we would expect them to learn from experience and improve their rules, or to switch from one rule to another when the economic situation changes. But rules of thumb may be wrong in a particular instance, and speculation in the foreign-exchange market can be destabilizing, not because market participants are irrational but because they must act quickly.

Risk Neutrality Once Again

Suppose that investors are risk neutral rather than risk averse. The tiniest open interest differential will lead them to demand huge quantities of foreign currency, because they will try to switch completely to the foreign bond. The excess demand curve becomes horizontal, as in Figure 16-4. When investors expect the supply curve to shift in the future from ES to E^*S^*, the demand curve will shift immediately from ED to E^*D^*, and the market-clearing exchange rate will go at once to OP^*. (The

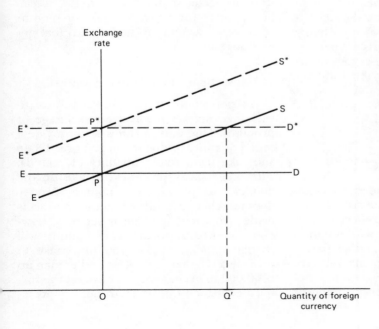

FIGURE 16-4 Effects of a Change in Expectations When Investors Are Risk Neutral
When investors are risk neutral, the *ED* curve becomes horizontal. If investors anticipate a future shift in the supply curve from *ES* to *E*S***, their demand curve goes at once to *E*D***, because the expected exchange rate goes to *OP**. The actual exchange rate goes at once to *OP**, because it is the market-clearing rate when the demand curve is *E*D*** and the supply curve is still *ES*, and the rate remains at *OP** even after the supply curve has shifted to *E*S***.

capital outflow will be *OQ'*.) There will thus be no further change in the exchange rate when the supply curve actually shifts.

When investors are risk neutral, then, expectations about the future exchange rate determine the actual exchange rate completely. In Figure 16-4, the change in the expected rate drives the actual rate directly from *OP* to *OP**. The responses of other market participants affect the size of the resulting capital flow but not the change in the exchange rate. When investors are risk averse, by contrast, expectations influence the actual exchange rate but do not determine it by themselves. In Figure 16-3, the change in the expected rate from *OP* to *OP** drove the actual rate from *OP* to *OP'*. The change in the actual rate depended in part on the change in the expected rate, but also on the way that other participants responded to events in the foreign-exchange market—on the slope of the *ES* curve.

The same point can be put differently. When investors are risk neutral, expectations are completely self-fulfilling. The actual exchange rate goes immediately to *OP** in Figure 16-4 and does not change again when the supply shifts. When investors are risk averse, expectations are partially but not completely self-fulfilling. The exchange rate went immediately to *OP'* in Figure 16-3. It did not go to *OP** until the supply curve shifted.

THE FORWARD FOREIGN-EXCHANGE MARKET

In the discussion just concluded, investors were exposed to exchange-rate risk. Therefore, the demand curve *ED* reflected their attitudes toward risk as well as their forecasts about the exchange rate. Other participants in the foreign-exchange market were not exposed to risk because they did not take *positions* in foreign currency. Domestic

buyers of foreign goods and services paid for them immediately and bought foreign currency when they needed it. Foreign buyers of domestic goods and services behaved in the same way. Therefore, the supply curve *ES* did not reflect attitudes toward risk or expectations; it reflected the influence of the actual exchange rate on demands for goods and services.

In many cases, however, goods and services are delivered long after they are ordered, and payments are not made until deliveries take place. Accordingly, someone is exposed to risk. An American firm that agrees to pay for British goods in pounds faces the risk that the pound will appreciate in terms of the dollar between the day when goods are ordered and the day when payment must be made. A British firm that agrees to be paid in dollars faces the same risk. But firms that acquire trade claims or obligations can find ways to *hedge* against exchange-rate risk. An American firm that agrees to pay for British goods in pounds can buy pounds right away and hold them until it needs them. Alternatively, it can buy pounds for delivery weeks or months from now by going to the forward foreign-exchange market.

Transactions in the Forward Market

A transaction in the forward foreign-exchange market involves an exchange of promises. One party promises to provide a stated quantity of dollars on an agreed date and take up a stated quantity of pounds. The other party promises to take up the dollars and provide the pounds. Money does not change hands when the contract is made. An exchange rate is set now, however, at which dollars and pounds will change hands later. If you undertake to provide $175,000 in 90 days and to take up £100,000 in exchange, you have set the forward exchange rate at $1.75 per pound.

Clearly, your willingness to make this contract will depend on your forecast of the spot exchange rate 90 days from now, the rate you would have to pay if you delayed your purchase. If you expect the spot rate to be $1.80, you have an incentive to buy pounds forward at $1.75 per pound. But your willingness to do so will also depend on interest rates in Britain and the United States, because they determine the cost of hedging by purchasing pounds now and holding them for 90 days, which is the alternative to a forward purchase. To purchase pounds now, you must give up (or borrow) dollars now. The cost of hedging will therefore depend on the interest rate you can earn on pounds compared to the rate you can earn on dollars (or must pay to borrow them). Finally, your willingness to make a forward contract will depend on your attitude toward risk.

Let us look more carefully at the ways of hedging against exchange-rate risk. The spot exchange rate is $1.75 per pound today. An American firm buys British goods and agrees to pay £200,000 when they are delivered 90 days from now. It incurs a £200,000 obligation to its supplier. Suppose that the firm borrows $350,000 from its bank, uses the dollars to buy pounds, and invests the pounds for 90 days. The £200,000 obligation remains but is offset by a £200,000 claim, the pounds bought with the borrowed dollars. The firm has hedged its foreign-currency position. It has replaced a net liability in pounds with a net liability in dollars, the $350,000 it owes to its bank. Suppose that the firm goes to the forward market instead and that the forward rate is $1.75 per pound. The firm undertakes to provide $350,000 in 90 days in exchange for the £200,000 it will need. The £200,000 obligation is offset by the other party's promise to deliver pounds, and the firm has hedged its foreign-currency position. It has again replaced a net liability in pounds with a net liability in dollars, represented by its promise to deliver dollars.

Investors use the forward market to avoid exchange-rate risk. Let the British interest rate be higher than the U.S. rate. An investor wants to take advantage of the higher British rate but does not want to face exchange-rate risk. Suppose that the investor starts out with $700,000, that the spot exchange rate is $1.75 now, and that the British interest rate is 6 percent. The investor can acquire £400,000 now and can therefore expect to have £424,000 a year from now. The investor can avoid exchange-rate risk by selling the £424,000 now on the forward market.

Finally, speculators use the forward market. Let the forward exchange rate be $1.75 per pound. A speculator believes that the spot exchange rate will be $1.80 per pound 90 days from now. The speculator will buy pounds forward at $1.75 in the hope of selling them 90 days from now at $1.80 and thus making a five-cent profit on each pound. Note that this form of speculation does not tie up cash. Transfers take place only after 90 days have passed, when the speculator turns over dollars in exchange for pounds and sells the pounds for dollars at the then-current spot rate.

Forward Rates and Interest Rates

When we looked at the behavior of an investor-speculator choosing between foreign and domestic bonds, we worked through a comparison that led to the open interest differential and open parity condition. An investor who chooses between those bonds but plans to avoid exchange-rate risk by going to the forward market must work through a similar comparison.

The investor can buy $1/\pi$ foreign-currency units of the foreign bond with one unit of domestic currency and can thus expect to have $(1/\pi)(1 + r^*)$ units of foreign currency when the bonds mature. To avoid exchange-rate risk, the investor can sell foreign currency now at the forward foreign-exchange rate, π^f. Therefore, an investment in the foreign bond is worth $(1/\pi)(1 + r^*)\pi^f$ units of domestic currency. Alternatively, the investor can buy the domestic bond and can thus earn $1 + r$ of domestic currency. Use c to define the difference between these two returns:

$$c = \frac{1}{\pi}(1 + r^*)\pi^f - (1 + r) \qquad (4)$$

This is the *covered interest differential*. When it is positive, an investor will buy foreign currency at the spot rate π in order to buy foreign bonds, but will also sell foreign currency at the forward rate π^f to avoid exchange-rate risk. In the language of the forward market, the investor will engage in *covered interest arbitrage.* [8]

We can simplify equation (4). Use δ to define the *forward premium* on the foreign currency, the difference between its forward and spot prices measured in relation to its spot price:

$$\delta = \frac{\pi^f - \pi}{\pi} \qquad (5)$$

As $\pi^f = (1 + \delta)\pi$, by definition, equation (4) can be rewritten as

$$c = \frac{1}{\pi}(1 + r^*)(1 + \delta)\pi - (1 + r)$$
$$= (r^* - r) + (1 + r^*)\delta \qquad (4a)$$
$$\approx (r^* - r) + \delta$$

because $(1 + r^*)\delta$ is approximately equal to δ.

There are two ways of looking at the covered interest differential, just as there were two ways of looking at the open differential. Investors concerned mainly with earning income on their bonds will read equation (4a) as saying that an additional gain or loss can come from purchasing the foreign bond. There is an additional gain when δ is positive—when the foreign currency is selling at a premium on the forward market. There is a loss when δ is negative—when the foreign currency is selling at a discount. Traders in the foreign-exchange market will read equation (4a) as saying that profits made from *swaps* between spot and forward markets must be adjusted for interest-rate differences. When δ is positive, a foreign-exchange trader will be inclined to buy foreign currency spot and sell it forward. The profit from this swap will be larger than δ when r^* is higher than r, because the trader will be holding foreign currency rather than domestic currency while waiting to deliver

---

[8] The same sort of calculation will govern a firm's choice between the two ways of hedging a commercial obligation. Suppose that the firm can borrow dollars at the interest rate r, can buy pounds immediately at the spot rate π, and can invest the pounds at the interest rate r^*. For every pound needed in the future, the firm has to buy $1/(1 + r^*)$ pounds now and spend $\pi[1/(1 + r^*)]$ dollars. But it will incur $(1 + r)$ dollars of debt, including interest, for each dollar borrowed to buy pounds. Therefore, the dollar cost of hedging in this way is $\pi[1/(1 + r^*)](1 + r)$ dollars per pound needed in the future. The dollar cost of hedging in the forward market is, of course, the forward rate, π^f, because it is the dollar cost of purchasing a pound for future delivery. Define the difference between the two dollar costs:

$$c^* = \pi^f - \pi[1/(1 + r^*)](1 + r)$$

If c^* is positive, it is cheaper to buy pounds with borrowed dollars. If c^* is negative, it is cheaper to use the forward market. But the expression for c^* can be rewritten. Multiply both sides by $1 + r^*$ and divide by π:

$$(1/\pi)(1 + r^*)c^* = (1/\pi)(1 + r^*)\pi^f - (1 + r) = c$$

Thus, the firm will buy pounds forward when the covered differential is negative. (When the covered differential is zero, the firm will have no reason to prefer one way of hedging over the other. Under assumptions made later, moreover, the differential *will* be close to zero. Therefore, we will not go far wrong when we assume that firms rely completely on the forward market to hedge their positions.)

the foreign currency. The profit will be smaller than δ and can turn into a loss when r^* is lower than r.

When the open interest differential was positive, risk-neutral investors sought to shift completely to the foreign bond. In the process, however, they drove that differential to zero. When the covered differential is positive, risk-averse investors may want to shift completely, too, and strong market forces will keep c close to zero. When they are strong enough to keep c at zero, equation (4a) asserts that

$$\delta = r - r^* \qquad (6)$$

This condition is called *covered interest parity*. It says that the forward premium on the foreign currency is exactly equal to the difference between interest rates, and no profits can be made from arbitrage. (The process may not go that far, however, because covered arbitrage is not totally risk free. By selling foreign currency forward, an investor avoids exchange-rate risk but incurs another risk. The other party to the forward contract may not honor its commitment. Default risk replaces exchange-rate risk.)

The open and covered interest differentials look much alike, and both are used to show how capital movements respond to interest rates. The two are very different in character, however, because $\hat{\pi}$ and δ are different. The term $\hat{\pi}$ involves a comparison between the actual spot exchange rate prevailing today and the expected future rate. It is surrounded by uncertainty. The term δ involves a comparison between the spot and forward rates prevailing today. It is not surrounded by uncertainty, because both rates are known now.

Spot and forward exchange rates were shown in Figure 1-2. Look back and find those for the pound on Tuesday, February 9, 1988. The spot rate was $1.750 per pound, and the 90 day forward rate was

$1.739 per pound. Therefore, δ was $-0.011/1.75$, which works out to be a discount of about 0.6 percent per quarter or 2.4 percent per year. At that same time, the interest rate on interbank loans in pounds was 9.375 percent, and the rate on loans in dollars was 6.750 percent. Hence

$$c = (9.375 - 6.750) - 2.4 = 2.625 - 2.4$$
$$= 0.225$$

A bank having access to the interbank market could earn a much higher interest rate by lending in pounds than in dollars, but when it came to hedge its position by selling pounds forward, it would find the advantage of lending in pounds greatly diminished—less than a quarter of one percent.[9]

DETERMINANTS OF THE FORWARD RATE

A realistic model of the forward market would be inhabited by firms that hedge commercial claims and obligations, investors who engage in covered interest arbitrage, and speculators who bet on expectations about future exchange rates. It would not include all firms, because some do not hedge (or do so by borrowing and other methods rather than the forward

---

[9] The rates used in this comparison are those that banks must pay to borrow funds from other banks in the Eurocurrency markets. Rates on other transactions can be quite different. On February 9, 1988, for example, the British Treasury bill rate was 8.75 percent, and the U.S. Treasury bill rate was 5.75 percent, so

$$c = (8.75 - 5.75) - 2.4 = 3.0 - 2.4 = 0.6$$

There was a slightly larger covered differential favoring the purchase of British Treasury bills. All such transactions, moreover, must be adjusted for transactions costs, which vary with the type and size of the transaction, and allowance must also be made for the ways in which various national tax systems treat interest earnings, interest costs, and gains and losses made in foreign-exchange transactions.

market). It would not include all investors, because some do not cover their positions; they are investor-speculators of the sort encountered earlier in this chapter. It would not include all speculators, because some have other ways to place their bets. But the essential features of the forward market can be captured by a very simple model:

1. All firms engaged in foreign trade hedge in the forward market. Trade is balanced, however, so the demand for forward contracts coming from one country's firms always equals the supply of forward contracts coming from the other's firms, and commercial hedging drops out of the model.

2. All investors cover their foreign-currency positions. Therefore, international capital movements depend on the covered interest differential. Interest rates are equal initially, however, so that the investors' demand for forward contracts depends exclusively on δ, the forward premium on the foreign currency. When δ is positive, investors sell foreign currency forward; when δ is negative, they buy it.

3. All speculators operate in the forward market. When their estimate of $\hat{\pi}$ is larger than the market value of δ, they buy foreign currency forward. If they are right about $\hat{\pi}$, they make profits; foreign currency bought forward now can be sold at a higher spot rate later. When their estimate of $\hat{\pi}$ is smaller than the market value of δ, they sell foreign currency forward.

4. The spot exchange rate is pegged, and the balance of payments is in equilibrium initially. Therefore, events in the forward market which impinge on the spot market show up as changes in official reserves rather than changes in the spot exchange rate. When investors demand foreign currency spot in order to buy foreign bonds, the foreign central bank intervenes to prevent its country's currency from appreciating, and its reserves rise. In ordinary circumstances, moreover, $\hat{\pi}$ will be zero. It can differ from zero only when speculators come to believe that the central bank is going to devalue or revalue its currency—to change the peg at which it intervenes in the spot market.[10]

This model is set out in Figure 16-5. The forward premium on the foreign currency, δ, is measured on the vertical axis. Forward purchases and sales of foreign currency are measured on the horizontal axis. The *FD* curve shows the forward demand for foreign currency coming from speculators. It is drawn on two suppositions, that $\hat{\pi}$ is zero initially and that speculators are risk averse. When $\hat{\pi}$ is zero, speculators' purchases depend entirely on the forward premium. They buy it forward when it goes to a discount (when δ is negative); they sell it forward when it goes to a premium (when δ is positive). When speculators are risk averse, their positions depend on the riskiness of speculation as well as the expected profit, and *FD* is downward sloping. (If speculators were risk neutral, their positions would not be limited by riskiness, and *FD* would be horizontal.) The *FS* curve shows the forward supply of foreign currency coming from investors. When interest rates are equal initially, investors' sales of foreign currency depend on the forward premium. They sell foreign currency forward when it goes to a premium and buy foreign currency forward when it goes to a discount.[11]

---

accompanied by a change in π^e produces a change in $\hat{\pi}$, affecting the position of the *FD* curve in Figure 16-5. Therefore, it affects the equilibrium position in the forward market.

[11] When investors engage in covered interest arbitrage, they avoid exchange-rate risk completely. We noted earlier, however, that investors face another risk. Someone may default on a forward contract. Accordingly, the *FS* curve is fairly flat but not horizontal. Investors are risk averse and do not shift completely to the foreign bond when δ is positive. If covered interest arbitrage were riskless in all respects, the *FS* curve would be horizontal. (Figure 16-5 differs importantly from earlier diagrams that dealt with the spot market. In Figure 16-5, distances along the vertical axis measure δ and $\hat{\pi}$, the forward premium and the expected rate of change in the spot exchange rate. In earlier diagrams, by contrast, vertical distances measured π and π^e, the *levels* of the actual and expected spot rates. Figure 16-5 could be drawn in terms of π, π^f, and π^e, the levels of the spot rate, forward rate, and expected spot rate, but would be rather cluttered.)

---

[10] If the spot rate were flexible, we would have to analyze simultaneously the behavior of the spot and forward rates. This is not hard conceptually but difficult diagrammatically. Any change in π that is not

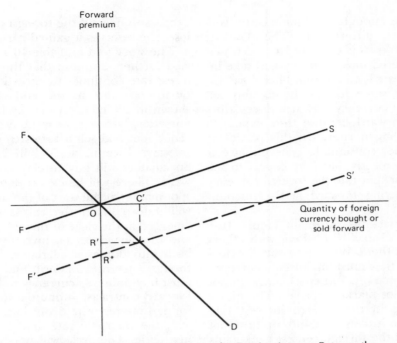

FIGURE 16-5   Effects of an Increase in the Foreign Interest Rate on the Forward Market

The *FS* curve shows the quantity of foreign currency that investors sell forward to engage in covered interest arbitrage. When foreign and domestic interest rates are equal, investors sell foreign currency forward when it goes to a premium. The *FD* curve shows the quantity of foreign currency that speculators buy forward. When $\hat{\pi}$ is zero, speculators buy foreign currency forward when it goes to a discount. When interest rates are equal and $\hat{\pi}$ is zero, the *FS* and *FD* curves intersect at zero, and the forward premium is zero. An increase in the foreign interest rate lowers the investors' supply curve from *FS* to *F'S'*; they will buy foreign bonds and will cover their positions by selling foreign currency forward. The foreign currency will go to a discount, *OR'*, at which investors want to sell *OC'* foreign currency forward and speculators want to buy that same quantity forward.

Effects of a Change in the Foreign Interest Rate

When interest rates are equal and $\hat{\pi}$ is zero, the *FS* and *FD* curves intersect at zero, and the forward premium must be zero. That is the initial situation in Figure 16-5. What happens when the foreign interest rate rises? The covered interest differential becomes positive when δ starts at zero, and the investors' supply curve shifts from *FS* to *F'S'*. Investors want to buy foreign bonds and want therefore to sell foreign currency forward. The market-clearing value of δ goes to *OR'*. This discount on the foreign currency, however, is not large enough to eliminate the covered interest differential. (The discount that would do so is OR^*, because it would restore covered interest parity and take investors' sales back to zero.) Therefore, investors buy some foreign bonds and sell OC' foreign currency forward. Speculators buy OC' forward because they expect to gain by selling it later. (In this particular example, they continue to believe that $\hat{\pi}$ is zero, which means that they expect to sell at a constant spot rate the foreign currency they are buying forward at the discount OR'.)

The transactions shown in Figure 16-5 are listed in Table 16-1, along with others that go with them. When investors buy foreign bonds, they must buy foreign currency in the spot market. But speculators do not enter the spot market, not yet. Therefore, the increase in the foreign interest rate gives rise to excess demand in the spot market, and the foreign central bank gains reserves. When investments and forward contracts mature, investors need not enter the spot market; their forward contracts allow them to switch back from foreign to domestic currency. But speculators must sell foreign currency in the spot market; they must acquire the domestic currency they promised to deliver when they made their forward contracts. Excess demand in the spot market gives way at this point to

excess supply, and the foreign central bank loses the reserves it gained earlier.

The story told in Table 16-1 can be carried farther. Suppose that the foreign interest rate continues to exceed the domestic interest rate at the end of the cycle shown in the table. A new cycle will begin immediately. Investors will buy foreign currency spot and sell it forward, keeping the forward discount at OR' in Figure 16-5. Speculators will buy foreign currency forward. There will be excess demand in the spot market at the start of the new cycle. (It will indeed offset the excess supply that emerged at the close of the old one.) At the end of the new cycle, investors will move back into domestic currency, having sold foreign currency forward, and speculators must buy domestic currency to honor their forward contracts. Suppose instead that the foreign interest rate drops back to equality with the domestic rate at the end of the first cycle. The cycle will not be repeated. The supply curve in Figure 16-5 will shift back from $F'S'$ to FS, and the forward discount will go to zero.

Effects of a Change in Expectations

What happens when expectations change? Suppose that speculators begin to believe that the foreign currency will be revalued. As $\hat{\pi}$ becomes positive, the specu-

TABLE 16-1 Transactions in Spot and Forward Markets Resulting from an Increase in the Foreign Interest Rate

Time	Spot Market	Forward Market
When foreign interest rate rises	Investors buy foreign currency to buy foreign bonds	Investors sell foreign currency to cover positions
	Speculators do not enter spot market	Speculators buy foreign currency to open positions
When investments and forward contracts mature	Investors do not enter spot market	Investors deliver foreign currency sold forward for domestic currency
	Speculators sell foreign currency for domestic currency owed under forward contracts	Speculators deliver domestic currency bought spot for foreign currency bought forward

lators' demand curve shifts from *FD* to *F'D'* in Figure 16-6. The new value of $\hat{\pi}$ is given by *OR**, which is the forward premium at which speculators cannot make a profit and will not buy or sell foreign currency forward. The market-clearing value of δ goes to *OR'*, a premium smaller than *OR**, and speculators can expect to make a profit. Accordingly, they buy *OC'* foreign currency forward and investors sell it, because there is a covered interest differential that leads investors to buy foreign bonds. (Interest rates are equal here, and δ is positive.)

Although the forward rate goes to a premium here and went to a discount in the previous diagram, the two cases lead to similar transactions. Returning to Table 16-1, the increase in $\hat{\pi}$ leads to forward purchases by speculators, drives the foreign currency to a forward premium, and induces investors to buy foreign bonds. Therefore, investors buy foreign currency spot and sell it forward. Later, investors use their forward contracts to switch back to domestic currency, but speculators must buy domestic currency in the spot market to honor their forward contracts. If the spot exchange rate is not revalued, the foreign central bank will gain reserves at the start of the process and lose them at the end.

Using the Forward Rate to Predict the Spot Rate

If speculators were risk neutral, the *FD* curve would be horizontal in Figures 16-5 and 16-6, and the market value of δ could

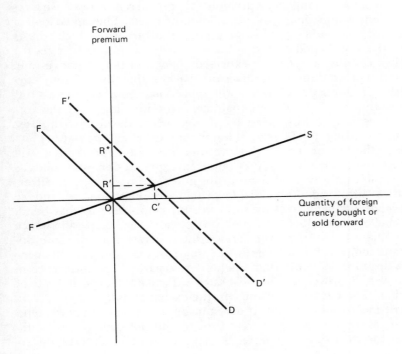

FIGURE 16-6 Effects of a Change in Expectations on the Forward Market
When interest rates are equal initially and $\hat{\pi}$ is zero, the *FS* and *FD* curves intersect at zero. When speculators start to believe that the foreign currency will appreciate, they begin to buy it forward; when $\hat{\pi}$ rises from zero to *OR**, the speculators' demand curve shifts from *FD* to *F'D'*. The foreign currency goes to a premium on the forward market, and the premium creates a covered interest differential favoring investment in the foreign bond. The market-clearing premium is *OR'*, at which speculators want to buy *OC'* foreign currency forward and investors want to sell that quantity forward.

not differ from $\hat{\pi}$, the expected change in the spot rate. Therefore, δ could be used to represent $\hat{\pi}$ in research on a number of important issues, including the formation of expectations.

This approach cannot be tested directly, as we have no independent measure of $\hat{\pi}$. But we can construct and test a *joint* hypothesis about the behavior of speculators. Suppose that speculators are risk neutral *and* that they do not make systematic errors when forecasting the future (i.e., they conform to the rational expectations hypothesis). On the first supposition, δ will represent the market's view about $\hat{\pi}$. On the second supposition, $\hat{\pi}$ will not differ systematically from $\dot{\pi}$, the actual percentage change in the spot rate. Therefore, the joint hypothesis can be tested by estimating this equation:

$$\dot{\pi}_{t+1} = a + b\delta_t$$

where $\dot{\pi}_{t+1}$ is the actual percentage change in the spot rate between time t and time $t + 1$, and δ_t is the forward premium at time t. If $a = 0$ and $b = 1$, the joint hypothesis stands up. If those two conditions are not met, it must be rejected (but we cannot know whether to reject the first or second supposition, or the two together).

Many economists have estimated this sort of equation. Some have obtained values for a and b that satisfy the test of the joint hypothesis, but most have obtained values for a that differ significantly from zero and values for b that differ significantly from 1. That is what happens in Table 16-2, where four values of a are close to zero but four values of b have the wrong sign (and the Canadian equation, which has the right sign for b has a negative value of a). In most studies, moreover, δ_t proves to be a poor predictor of $\dot{\pi}_{t+1}$. The equation does not "explain" much of the variation of the actual exchange rate. More research must be done on attitudes toward risk and

TABLE 16-2 Forecasting Equations for U.S. Dollar Exchange Rates

Currency	a	b
Pound sterling	0.0086	−0.2881
Deutsche mark	0.0214	−0.7815
Swiss franc	0.0481	−2.2145
Canadian dollar	−0.0076	0.8285
Japanese yen	0.0311	−2.8316

Source: Robert E. Cumby and Maurice Obstfeld, "International Interest Rate and Price Level Linkages Under Flexible Exchange Rates," in J. F. O. Bilson and R. C. Marston, eds., *Exchange Rate Theory and Practice* (Chicago: University of Chicago Press, 1984), Table 3.4. The calculations are based on weekly data for 1976–1981.

on the formation of expectations before we can know why.

SUMMARY

Investors must take account of future changes in exchange rates when comparing returns on foreign-currency assets with returns on domestic assets. They must look at the open interest differential, which adjusts the ordinary difference in interest rates for the expected change in the exchange rate. If investors believe that the foreign currency will appreciate, the open interest differential can favor investment in the foreign bond even when the foreign interest rate is lower than the domestic rate.

If investors are risk neutral, they will tend to treat foreign and domestic bonds as perfect substitutes. An open interest differential favoring the foreign bond will induce investors to shift completely to that bond. As they do so, however, they will reduce the foreign interest rate and raise the domestic rate, so capital movements will maintain open interest parity. The difference in interest rates will equal the expected rate of change in the exchange rate.

If investors are risk averse, they will tend to treat foreign and domestic bonds as imperfect substitutes. An open interest differential favoring the foreign bond will induce investors to buy that bond but not shift completely to it. They will hold diversified portfolios. An increase in the foreign interest rate will still produce a capital flow, but its size will be limited by the intensity of risk aversion, and it cannot maintain open interest parity.

Since expectations influence capital movements, they must also influence the behavior of a flexible exchange rate. An increase in the foreign interest rate will cause the foreign currency to appreciate. A change in expectations can do so, too. If investors begin to believe that other participants in the foreign-exchange market will increase their demand for the foreign currency, the open interest differential will favor foreign investment and investors will demand more foreign currency. The foreign currency will appreciate immediately when it is expected to appreciate in the future. When expectations are borne out by events, speculators make money and speculation is stabilizing. When expectations are contradicted, speculators lose money and speculation is destabilizing. But stabilizing speculation will not necessarily dominate foreign-exchange markets, even when stabilizing speculators prosper.

The forward foreign-exchange market is used by traders and investors to hedge against exchange-rate risk. A forward contract is a promise to exchange one currency for another at an agreed future date. The forward exchange rate is built into the contract. The forward rate can be at a premium or discount, compared with the spot rate, depending on supply and demand conditions in the forward market. The premium is used to compute the covered interest differential, which adjusts the ordinary interest-rate difference for the cost of hedging in the forward market.

When the covered interest differential is positive, investors buy foreign bonds and sell the foreign-currency proceeds forward. This is covered interest arbitrage, which tends to maintain covered interest parity. Speculators use the forward market to place bets on their expectations about future exchange rates. When they expect a currency to appreciate by an amount larger than the forward premium, they buy that currency forward.

An increase in the foreign interest rate leads investors to buy foreign currency spot and sell it forward. The currency will appreciate immediately and go to a discount on the forward market. Speculators will buy it forward to take advantage of the discount. When forward contracts mature, investors will deliver foreign currency to speculators in exchange for domestic currency. But speculators must sell foreign currency on the spot market to obtain the domestic currency they must deliver, causing the foreign currency to depreciate. A change in expectations can have similar effects. This time, however, speculators take the lead, and the foreign currency goes to a premium rather than a discount.

If speculators were risk neutral, the forward rate would be an efficient predictor of the future spot rate. This hypothesis can be tested jointly with another, that speculators form rational expectations and do not make systematic forecasting errors. The evidence tends to reject the joint hypothesis.

RECOMMENDED READINGS

For a thorough treatment of hedging, investing, and speculating under exchange-rate uncertainty, with well-chosen examples, see Ronald I. McKinnon, *Money in International Exchange* (New York: Oxford University Press, 1979), chs. 4, 5, and 7. The same subjects are examined more rigorously, with attention to stability, profitability, and related issues, in Egon

Sohmen, *Flexible Exchange Rates* (Chicago: University of Chicago Press, 1969), chs. iii–iv.

The analysis of the forward market in this chapter is based on S. C. Tsiang, "The Theory of Forward Exchange and Effects of Government Intervention on the Forward Exchange Market," *International Monetary Fund Staff Papers*, 7 (April 1959). See also J. Marcus Fleming and Robert A. Mundell, "Official Intervention on the Forward Market," *International Monetary Fund Staff Papers*, 11 (March 1964); reprinted in J. M. Fleming, *Essays in International Economics* (Cambridge, Mass.: Harvard University Press, 1971), ch. 10.

To understand thoroughly how exchange rates are affected by expectations, we must ask how investors form those expectations. This was the subject of a path-breaking paper by Rudiger Dornbusch, "Expectations and Exchange Rate Dynamics," *Journal of Political Economy*, 84 (August 1976).

Many other papers deal with this subject, but most of them use analytical methods more advanced than those in this book. Two papers illustrate the general approach using rather simple models: Rudiger Dornbusch, "Monetary Policy Under Exchange-Rate Flexibility," in J. R. Artus, et al., *Managed Exchange-Rate Flexibility* (Boston: Federal Reserve Bank of Boston, 1978), and Maurice Obstfeld, "Capital Mobility and Devaluation in an Optimizing Model with Rational Expectations," *American Economic Review*, 71 (May 1981).

For the influence of information on expectations and thus the exchange rate, see Jacob A. Frenkel, "Flexible Exchange Rates, Prices, and the Role of 'News': Lessons from the 1970s," *Journal of Political Economy*, 89 (June 1981).

On the rationality of expectations, see Jeffrey Frankel and Kenneth Froot, "Using Survey Data to Test Some Standard Propositions Regarding Exchange Rate Expectations," *American Economic Review*, 77 (March 1987), and "The Dollar as an Irrational Speculative Bubble: A Tale of Fundamentalists and Chartists," *The Marcus Wallenberg Papers on International Finance* (Washington, D.C.: International Law Institute, 1986).

The assertion that destabilizing speculators are bound to suffer losses has been used to appraise the effects of official intervention in the foreign-exchange market; see Helmut Mayer and H. Taguchi, *Official Intervention in the Exchange Markets: Stabilizing or Destabilizing?* (Basle: Bank for International Settlements, 1983).

On the use of the forward rate to forecast the spot rate and the "efficiency" of foreign-exchange markets, see Richard M. Levich, "Empirical Studies of Exchange Rates: Price Behavior, Rate Determination and Market Efficiency," in R. W. Jones and P. B. Kenen, eds., *Handbook of International Economics* (Amsterdam: North-Holland, 1985), ch. 19.

CHAPTER

17

STOCKS,
FLOWS,
AND MONETARY
EQUILIBRIUM

TWO VIEWS OF THE BALANCE
OF PAYMENTS

In Chapter 12, we went through balance-of-payments accounts from the top down. We started with transactions in goods and services and investment-income flows, paused to calculate the current-account balance, and went on to the capital account. The surplus or deficit in the balance of payments appeared at the end as the change in official reserves. It reflected official purchases or sales of foreign currency designed to keep the exchange rate from changing.

Therefore, we came to think of surpluses and deficits as measures of disequilibrium in the flow market for foreign exchange. More important, we saw them as reflections of events in many other markets—domestic purchases in markets for foreign goods, services, and assets, and for-

eign purchases in markets for domestic goods, services, and assets. In subsequent chapters, we looked at ways of dealing with surpluses and deficits by the use of policies affecting those events and markets. In Chapters 13 and 14, we studied ways of altering demands for goods and services—policies affecting incomes, prices, and exchange rates. In Chapters 15 and 16, we studied ways of altering demands for assets—policies affecting interest rates and exchange-rate expectations.

There is another way to look at the balance of payments. It is very old but has been revived. Instead of focusing on flows in the foreign-exchange market and those which lie behind them in markets for goods, services, and assets, it focuses directly on their monetary counterparts, the change in the stock of domestic money resulting from a balance-of-payments surplus or deficit.

This is the *monetary approach* to balance-of-payments theory, and it provides a monetary approach to exchange-rate theory. The monetary approach is built on a simple proposition:

A surplus in the balance of payments necessarily testifies to an excess demand for money at home and an excess supply abroad. A deficit testifies to an excess supply of money at home and an excess demand abroad.

Accordingly, the monetary approach stresses forces affecting the demand for money, rather than forces affecting the demands for goods, services, and assets, and puts particular emphasis on monetary policy, the main force affecting the supply of money.

ORIGINS AND ISSUES

It is easy to prove the basic proposition of the monetary approach. We will do so shortly. It is less easy to accept the strong conclusions sometimes drawn from it. Advocates of the monetary approach have adopted assumptions about prices, incomes, and other variables that allow them to develop simple models in which money is the *only* thing that matters for balance-of-payments behavior. We will build such a model to show how this conclusion is obtained and how the balance-of-payments model can be converted into an exchange-rate model.

Because the simple monetary model is based on restrictive assumptions, its predictions are not always borne out by experience. That is why it is hard to accept the policy recommendations extracted from it. Nevertheless, there are three reasons for looking at the model carefully. First, it is the direct descendant of the oldest balance-of-payments model, a model even older than the Ricardian model of comparative advantage. Second, it has inspired a large body of research on the implications of monetary policy for the behavior of a flexible exchange rate, and some economists continue to regard it as the most appropriate framework for policy analysis. Finally, the simplicity of the monetary model allows us to see clearly the importance of relationship between stocks and flows of assets. One such relationship cropped up in Chapter 15, where *IS* and *LM* curves were used to show how the stock of money is affected by balance-of-payments flows. Others will crop up in Chapter 18, which develops an elaborate model with many stocks and flows.

David Hume and the Specie-Flow Doctrine

The monetary approach to the balance of payments can be traced back to the middle of the eighteenth century. Writing in 1752, David Hume combined international money flows with the quantity theory of money, connecting the price level to the money supply, to produce a clear statement of the *specie-flow doctrine*, the earliest version of the monetary approach. He began with examples remarkably similar to those used in the modern literature, but his language was more eloquent:

Suppose four-fifths of all the money in Great Britain to be annihilated in one night, and the nation reduced to the same condition with regard to specie [money], as in the reigns of the Harrys and Edwards, what would be the consequence? Must not the price of all labour and commodities sink in proportion, and everything be sold as cheap as they were in those ages? What nation could then dispute with us in any foreign market, or pretend to navigate or to sell manufactures at the same price, which to us would afford sufficient profit? In how little time, therefore, must this bring back the money which we had lost, and raise us to the level of all the neighbouring nations? Where, after we have arrived, we immediately lose the advantage of the cheapness of labour and commodities; and the farther flowing in of money is stopped by our fulness and repletion.

Again, suppose that all the money in Great Britain were multiplied fivefold in a night, must not the contrary effect follow? Must not all labour and commodities rise to such an exorbitant height, that no neighbouring nations could afford to buy from us; while their commodities, on the other hand, became comparatively so cheap, that, in spite of all the laws which could be formed, they would run in upon us, and our money flow out; till we fall to a level with foreigners, and lose that great superiority of riches [money] which had laid us under such disadvantages?[1]

In a manner typical of classical economists, Hume went on to invoke natural law to prove that there must be a unique distribution of money among countries. Governments cannot alter it by mercantilist policies—by limiting imports and promoting exports to bring about a surplus in the balance of payments:

Now, it is evident, that the same causes, which would correct these exorbitant inequalities, were they to happen miraculously, must prevent their happening in the common course of nature, and must for ever, in all neighbouring nations, preserve money nearly proportionable to the arts and industry [income] of each nation. All water, wherever it communicates, remains always at a level. Ask naturalists the reason; they tell you, that, were it to be raised in any one place, the superior gravity of that part . . . must depress it, till it meets a counterpoise. . . .

Can one imagine, that it had ever been possible, by any laws, or even by any art or industry, to have kept all the money in Spain, which the galleons have brought from the Indies? Or that all commodities could be sold in France for a tenth of the price which they would yield on the other side of the Pyrenees, without finding their way thither [to Spain], and draining from that immense treasure? What other reason, indeed, is there, why all nations, at present, gain in their trade with Spain and Portugal; but because it is impossible to heap up money, more than any fluid, beyond its proper level.

---

[1] David Hume, "Of the Balance of Trade," in *Essays, Moral, Political and Literary*, 1752 (1777 edition).

Price effects play an important role in Hume's analysis. It can, indeed, be shown that his argument breaks down when the Marshall–Lerner–Robinson (MLR) condition is not satisfied. An increase in the quantity of money, whether it is "miraculous" or comes to a country in galleons, raises the price level. Higher prices, in turn, induce a switch in expenditure from home to foreign goods, and this is what causes the trade deficit, the outflow of money, and the return to monetary equilibrium. In some modern versions of the argument, by contrast, the increase in the quantity of money leads directly to an increase in imports, because it raises expenditure (absorption); the trade deficit develops immediately, without any observable increase in the price level.

An Echo of the Specie-Flow Doctrine

The main point made by Hume, that monetary equilibrium is preserved automatically by market forces, can be demonstrated without adopting the monetary approach to the balance of payments or invoking the quantity theory of money. The point was made in Chapter 15, which examined the effects of monetary policy under a pegged exchange rate.

Look back at Figure 15-4, which used *IS* and *LM* curves to trace the effects of an increase in the money supply produced by an open-market purchase of domestic bonds. In the absence of capital mobility, the increase in the money supply reduced the domestic interest rate and raised domestic expenditure, causing an increase in imports and a balance-of-payments deficit. With the passage of time, the deficit reduced reserves and thereby reduced the money supply. Eventually, the economy returned to its initial situation. The introduction of capital mobility speeded up the process. With perfect capital mobility, indeed, the whole increase in the money supply spilled out of the economy immediately. The open-market purchase of domestic bonds was offset at once by a capital outflow, as investors bought foreign bonds to replace domestic bonds sold to the central bank. The central bank lost reserves equal in amount to its additional bond holdings. The money supply did not change, even temporarily, and monetary policy lost any influence on the domestic economy.

These conclusions were reached by looking at events in the goods and bond markets rather than events in the money market. Furthermore, they held in a modern economy, where money is created by open-market operations, not brought in by galleons. In what follows, however, we will adopt the monetary approach and look at the money market.

DERIVING THE BASIC PROPOSITION

Although David Hume used a monetary model in the eighteenth century, proof of the basic proposition that justifies its use was not worked out until the nineteenth century. It is a special case of a general law named after Léon Walras, the French economist who built the first formal model of general equilibrium, in which all markets are interdependent. An algebraic demonstration of Walras' law is given in Note 17-1. This is what it says:

> **An economy cannot have excess demands in all its markets. If there are excess demands in some markets, there must be excess supplies in other markets.**

In an economy with markets for goods, markets for securities, and a market for money, Walras' law asserts that

Excess demand for goods

  + excess demand for securities

    + excess demand for money = 0

If there are positive excess demands for goods and securities, there must be a negative excess demand for money, and a negative excess demand is an excess supply.[2]

To turn this abstract statement into the basic proposition of the monetary approach, consider the economy just described, with markets for goods, securities, and money. When it has a deficit on current account, the economy is importing more goods than it is supplying to the outside world, and we can say that it is meeting an excess demand for goods by drawing goods from other countries. When it has a deficit on capital account, it is importing more securities than it is supplying, and we can say that it is meeting an excess demand for securities by drawing securities from other countries. But when it has a deficit in its balance of payments, it has excess demands for goods and securities taken together. Therefore, it must have an excess supply of money. Rewriting the previous equation,

Excess demand for goods

  + excess demand for securities

    = excess supply of money

Accordingly, the loss of reserves resulting from a balance-of-payments deficit can be viewed as the way in which the economy "exports" money to remove excess supply from its money market. The causes and cure of a balance-of-payments deficit can be studied by examining events in the goods and securities markets, or by examining events in the money market.

---

[2] There is, of course, no "market" for money in a closed economy, and money does not have a price of its own. In an open economy, however, we can think of the foreign-exchange market as the market for money and the exchange rate as its price. A difference between demand and supply will show up in the foreign-exchange market, affecting the exchange rate (the price of money) or reserves (the quantity of money).

Note 17-1

Consider an economy that has households, firms, banks, and a government. Households hold money, bonds, and claims on firms (shares) and have debts to banks. This is their balance sheet,

$$W^h = L^h + B^h + \pi F^h + E^h - H^h$$

where W^h is household wealth (net worth); L^h, B^h, and F^h are households' holdings of money, government bonds, and foreign bonds; E^h is the value of their claims on firms; and H^h is their debt to banks. (Foreign bonds are denominated in foreign currency and are thus multiplied by the exchange rate, π.)

Firms hold money, bonds, and capital (factories, etc.) and have debts to banks,

$$W^f = L^f + B^f + \pi F^f + K - H^f$$

where W^f is their net worth; L^f, B^f, and F^f are their holdings of money and bonds; K is their capital stock; and H^f is their debt to banks.

Banks hold cash reserves with the central bank, government and foreign bonds, and claims on households and firms,

$$L = L^c + B^b + \pi F^b + H^h + H^f$$

where L is the money supply (bank deposits), L^c is the cash reserve held with the central bank, and B^b and F^b are banks' bond holdings. The central bank holds government bonds and foreign-exchange reserves:

$$L^c = B^c + \pi R$$

Changes in B^c (bond holdings) reflect open-market operations. Changes in R (reserves) reflect intervention in the foreign-exchange market.

Assume that foreigners do not hold domestic money, bonds, or claims on firms, while households, firms, and banks do not hold claims on foreigners other than foreign bonds. Households will then own all firms ($E^h = W^f$), households and firms will be the only holders of money, and so on. Adding up the four balance-sheet equations, canceling common terms, and rearranging,

$$K + \pi R + \pi F^d - W^h + B^d + L^d - L = 0$$

where L^d is the total demand for money ($L^d = L^h + L^f$), while B^d and F^d are the total demands for bonds ($B^d = B^h + B^f + B^b + B^c$, and $F^d = F^h + F^f + F^b$).

Let B represent the supply of government bonds. Adding and substracting it from the left side of the previous equation:

$$(K + B + \pi R + \pi F^d - W^h) \\ + (B^d - B) + (L^d - L) = 0$$

Finally, take rates of change through time but fix the exchange rate:

$$(\dot{K} + \dot{B} + \pi\dot{R} + \pi\dot{F}^d - \dot{W}^h) + (\dot{B}^d - \dot{B}) \\ + (\dot{L}^d - \dot{L}) = 0$$

where $\dot{K}$ is the rate of change of the capital stock, and so on.

But the change in the capital stock is investment ($\dot{K} = I$), and the change in the supply of government bonds in the government's budget deficit ($\dot{B} = G - T$). Furthermore, the definition of the balance of payments says that $\pi\dot{R} = (X - M) - \pi\dot{F}^d$, because a country gains reserves when its current-account surplus exceeds its capital outflow (the increase in its holding of foreign bonds). Finally, the change in wealth is saving, which is defined in the familiar way ($\dot{W}^h = S = Y - C - T$). Therefore,

$$\dot{K} + \dot{B} + \pi\dot{R} + \pi\dot{F}^d - \dot{W}^h$$
$$= (C + I + G + X) - (Y + M)$$

But $C + I + G + X$ is aggregate demand in the goods market, and $Y + M$ is aggregate supply, so the excess demand for goods is

$$D(Y) = (C + I + G + X) - (Y + M)$$

Similarly, the excess flow demands for bonds and money are

$$D(B) = \dot{B}^d - \dot{B} \quad \text{and} \quad D(L) = \dot{L}^d - \dot{L}$$

Therefore, the previous version of the balance-sheet equation can be written as

$$D(Y) + D(B) + D(L) = 0$$

This is Walras' law. It says that the sum of excess demands must be zero. If some are positive, others must be negative (i.e., excess supplies).

A SIMPLE MONETARY MODEL

A simple model of the money market can be used to illustrate the monetary approach and its implications. We begin with factors affecting the demand for money, turn next to factors affecting the supply, and then introduce three assumptions that lead to the strong conclusions drawn from the model.

The Demand for Money

The demand for money may be taken to depend on the price level, real income, and the interest rate,

$$\frac{L^d}{P} = L(r, y) \tag{1}$$

where L^d is the quantity of money demanded, P is a price index, r is the domestic interest rate, and y is real income (output).[3] Multiply both sides of the equation by the price level:

$$L^d = L(r, y)P \tag{1a}$$

The demand for money rises with an increase in the price level and in real income

because households and firms require larger cash balances to handle larger flows of payments. The demand for money falls with an increase in the interest rate because bonds and other interest-bearing assets become more attractive when interest rates are high, and holders of money try to get along with smaller cash balances to build up their holdings of interest-bearing assets.

The Supply of Money

The supply of money consists of currency and bank deposits. Currency is supplied by the government, represented by the central bank. Its balance sheet looks like this:

CENTRAL BANK

Assets	Liabilities
Government securities	Currency outstanding
Foreign-exchange reserves	Cash reserves of commercial banks

Bank deposits appear on the balance sheets of commercial banks, which look like this:

COMMERCIAL BANKS

Assets	Liabilities
Cash reserves at central bank	Deposits
Government securities	
Loans to public, etc.	

---

[3] A different formulation is used in Chapter 18, where the demand for money is made to depend on wealth instead of income and is affected by the foreign interest rate as well as the domestic rate.

When these balance sheets are consolidated, cash reserves drop out, and the balance sheet for the whole banking system is:

BANKING SYSTEM

Assets	Liabilities
Domestic credit:	Money supply:
Government securities	Currency outstanding
Loans to public, etc.	Deposits
Foreign-exchange reserves	

Writing it as an equation,

Money supply = domestic credit
                + foreign-exchange reserves

Using L^s for the money supply, H for domestic credit, and R for foreign-exchange reserves,

$$L^s = H + \pi R \qquad (2)$$

As foreign-exchange reserves are measured in foreign currency, they are multiplied by the exchange rate, π, to convert them into domestic currency.[4]

Three Assumptions

Three assumptions are used to draw strong conclusions from the simple monetary model we are building:

1. There are no rigidities in domestic factor markets. The money wage rate is flexible enough to keep the real wage at its full-employment level. Therefore, real output stays at its full-employment level, and so does real income.[5]

2. There are no barriers to capital movements, and asset holders are risk neutral. There-

fore, open interest parity obtains. From equation (3) in Chapter 16,

$$r = r^* + \hat{\pi} \qquad (3)$$

where r is the domestic interest rate, r^* is the foreign interest rate, and $\hat{\pi}$ is the expected rate of change of the spot exchange rate. Hereafter, however, we assume that asset holders have *stationary expectations* ($\hat{\pi} = 0$).

3. The prices of domestic and foreign goods are linked by a strict relationship known as *purchasing-power parity* (PPP),

$$p = \bar{v} \cdot \pi p^* \qquad (4)$$

where p is the price of the domestic good in domestic currency, p^* is the price of the foreign good in foreign currency (and πp^* its price in domestic currency), and $\bar{v}$ is a constant.

The third assumption plays an important role in many balance-of-payments and exchange-rate models, and we study it closely later in this chapter, examining conditions under which $\bar{v}$ will be constant and recent evidence concerning its stability. Here we merely need to note what the assumption says about the prices index P affecting the demand for money. Let that index be a weighted average of p and πp^*, the prices of domestic and foreign goods measured in domestic currency:

$$P = \alpha p + (1 - \alpha)\pi p^* \qquad (5)$$

where α is the weight assigned to the domestic good and $1 - \alpha$ is the weight assigned to the foreign good. Using equation (4) to replace p in equation (5),

---

[4] An increase in π, however, does not automatically raise L^s, although equation (2) seems to say so. The central bank obtains a capital gain on its foreign-exchange reserves but does not issue money to balance its books. It tucks the gain away in its capital account, an item omitted from the central bank's balance sheet and from equation (2).

[5] To see how flexible factor prices maintain full employment, return to Figure 10-5. The demand for labor in the cloth industry is given by the E_C curve, and the demand in the wine industry is given by the E_W' curve. Let the prices of cloth and wine be fixed by

world markets (the third assumption made later). If the money wage is rigid and too high, there will be unemployment. Suppose that it is set at a level that puts the real wage at $\overline{OV}$ in terms of cloth, given the fixed price of cloth. The wine industry will demand OL_1' labor, the cloth industry will demand $\overline{L}L_1$, and L_1L_1' labor will be unemployed. If the money wage is flexible, by contrast, it will start to fall as soon as unemployment appears. When it reaches a level that reduces the real wage to OV^*, the wine industry will demand OL_1^* labor, the cloth industry will demand $\overline{L}L_1^*$, and there will be no unemployment.

$$P = \alpha(\overline{v} \cdot \pi p^*) + (1 - \alpha)\pi p^*$$
$$= [1 - \alpha(1 - \overline{v})]\pi p^* = k \cdot \pi p^* \quad (5a)$$

where $k = 1 - \alpha(1 - \overline{v})$ so k is a constant because α and v are constants. Furthermore, π is constant when the exchange rate is pegged. Therefore, the price index P depends entirely on p^*, the foreign-currency price of the foreign good. It is not affected by anything that happens in the domestic economy.

When we make all three assumptions, assume in addition that r^* and p^* are constant, and peg the exchange rate, we fix y, r, and P. Therefore, we fix the demand for money.

The Money Market and Balance of Payments

There are two ways to link money-market conditions with the balance of payments—by looking at the requirements of long-run equilibrium in the money market, or looking at the short-run effects of disequilibrium. We start with the requirements of long-run equilibrium.

In long-run equilibrium, the demand for money must equal the supply. When the demand is constant, the supply must be constant. Accordingly, any increase in the money supply must reverse itself eventually, and this is accomplished by a balance-of-payments deficit. In long-run equilibrium,

$$L^d = L^s = H + \pi R \quad (6)$$

Set the (pegged) exchange rate equal to 1 for convenience, use $\overline{L}^d$ to denote the constant demand for money that obtains when r, y, and P are constant, and rearrange equation (6):

$$R = \overline{L}^d - H \quad (6a)$$

This relationship is shown by the line LL in Figure 17-1. The demand for money is OL

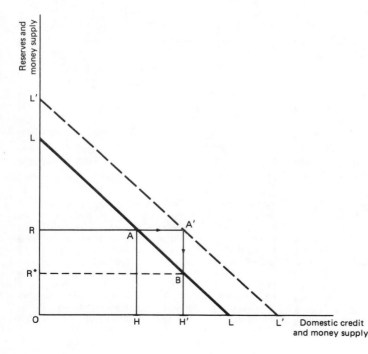

FIGURE 17-1 Long-Run Equilibrium in the Money Market

The demand for money is constant at OL. The supply is equal initially to the demand. The quantity of domestic credit is OH, and the stock of reserves is OR. When the quantity of domestic credit rises to OH', the supply of money rises to OL', and the economy moves first from A to A'. But the supply of money exceeds the demand by LL', and the economy must run a balance-of-payments deficit to reduce the money supply by reducing reserves. When reserves have fallen to OR^*, the supply of money returns to OL, and the economy moves to B. The money market is back in long-run equilibrium.

initially, and it equals the supply. If the quantity of domestic credit is OH initially, the stock of reserves is given by A and must be OR (equal to HL). Suppose that the banking system creates HH' additional domestic credit. If reserves do not adjust instantaneously, the economy must move temporarily to point A' on the new line $L'L'$. The money supply increases to OL' (the increase is LL', which equals HH'). The economy cannot stay at A', however, because there is an excess supply of money; the demand for money is still OL. Therefore, the economy must move eventually to B, which implies that the stock of reserves must fall to OR^*. The economy must run a balance-of-payments deficit that adds up over time to RR^*.

Under the assumptions adopted here regarding income, the interest rate, and price level, domestic credit creation produces a balance-of-payments deficit. It is indeed the only event that can do so. Similarly, credit contraction is the only event that can eliminate a balance-of-payments deficit and halt a loss of reserves. The balance of payments becomes a monetary phenomenon.

With perfect capital mobility, the assumption that gave us equation (3), the stock of reserves can change instantaneously. We saw this in Chapter 15, when looking at monetary policy under a pegged exchange rate. With perfect capital mobility, then, an economy can move directly from A to B in Figure 17-1. The loss of reserves RR^* can take place as soon as credit creation occurs. Under any other circumstance, the stock of reserves must change gradually, and the economy must go from A to B by way of A', following the arrows. To examine this process closely, we investigate the short-run effects of monetary disequilibrium.

Consider a simple economy in which money is the only asset, there is no capital formation, and the government's budget is always balanced. From equation (6) of Chapter 12,

$$X - M = S - I + T - G = S \qquad (7)$$

because $I = 0$ when there is no capital formation and $T = G$ when the budget is balanced. When money is the only asset, moreover, there can be no bonds, and we can make two more statements. First, there can be no capital movements, and a current-account surplus has to produce a balance-of-payments surplus,

$$\pi\dot{R} = X - M \qquad (8)$$

where $\dot{R}$ is the rate of increase in reserves and thus measures the surplus in the balance of payments. Second, households will not save unless they want to hold more money,

$$S = \lambda(\overline{L}^d - L^s) \qquad (9)$$

where λ represents the speed of adjustment, the rate at which households save in order to close a gap between the stock of money they want to hold (the demand for money) and the stock they actually hold (the supply of money).

Putting these three equations together and setting the exchange rate at 1 for convenience,

$$\dot{R} = S = \lambda(\overline{L}^d - L^s) \qquad (9a)$$

When there is an excess demand for money ($\overline{L}^d > L^s$), households save by reducing expenditure (absorption), and the current account moves into surplus; an inflow of reserves raises the quantity of money and gradually eliminates the excess demand. When there is an excess supply of money ($\overline{L}^d < L^s$), households *dis*save by raising expenditure, and the current account moves into deficit; an outflow of reserves reduces the quantity of money and gradually eliminates the excess supply.

This adjustment process is illustrated in Figure 17-2. The upper panel reproduces Figure 17-1. The demand for money is constant at OL and equal initially to the

FIGURE 17-2 Adjustment in the Money Market
The demand for money is *OL* and is constant. The supply of money is equal initially to the demand but rises to *OL'* because of an increase in the quantity of domestic credit from *OH* to *OH'*. The line *SS* describes the adjustment process. When the supply of money exceeds the demand by *LL'*, there is dissaving at the rate *OT'*, and reserves fall at the same rate, because dissaving is fully reflected in a balance-of-payments deficit. The stock of reserves falls to *OR'*, reducing the money supply to *OL"*. Dissaving is reduced to the rate *OT"*, which slows down the adjustment process. But the process cannot end until the money supply falls to *OL*, where dissaving is zero.

supply. The money market is in long-run equilibrium. When the quantity of credit rises from *OH* to *OH'*, the quantity of money rises to *OL'* and there is excess supply. The line *SS* in the lower panel represents the relationship shown by equation (9a). When there is no excess demand or supply in the money market, there is no saving, and reserves are constant. That is the case initially. When credit creation takes place, raising the quantity of money to *OL'*, there is excess supply. Households begin to dissave at the rate *OT'*, and reserves begin to fall at that same rate, reducing the money supply. When reserves have fallen to *OR'*, for example, the money sup-

ply has fallen to *OL"*, reducing the excess supply of money from *LL'* to *LL"*. Dissaving slows down from *OT'* to *OT"*, which diminishes the rate at which reserves are falling. But the adjustment process cannot stop until reserves have fallen to *OR**, cutting the money supply to *OL* and eliminating the excess supply completely.

Stocks, Flows, and Dynamics in the Monetary Model

The adjustment process can be summarized by a simple diagram connecting the stock and flow of reserves. Using equation (2), rewrite equation (9a):

$$\dot{R} = \lambda[\overline{L}^d - (H + R)]$$
$$= \lambda(\overline{L}^d - H) - \lambda R \qquad (9b)$$

This relationship defines the *DD* curve in Figure 17-3. Its position is given by the first term of equation (9b), which depends on the difference between the demand for money and quantity of domestic credit. An increase in the demand for money shifts it up; an increase in the quantity of domestic credit shifts it down. The slope of the curve is given by the second term of the equation; it says that there is an *inverse* relationship between R and $\dot{R}$, the stock of reserves and flow of reserves (the balance of payments).

The *DD* curve in Figure 17-3 is drawn to reflect the initial situation in Figure 17-2. When the demand for money was *OL*, the quantity of credit was *OH*, and the stock of reserves was *OR*; furthermore, there was no saving or dissaving, and reserves were constant. In Figure 17-3, there is no surplus or deficit in the balance of payments when the stock of reserves is *OR*, which means that the stock will stay at *OR*. When the quantity of credit rose to *OH'* in Figure 17-2, there was dissaving, and reserves began to fall. In Figure 17-3, the *DD* curve shifts downward to *D'D'*, producing a deficit *OT'* in the balance of payments. Thereafter, the economy moves along *D'D'*, following the arrows, and the balance-of-payments deficit declines. It is not eliminated, however, until the stock of reserves falls to *OR**.

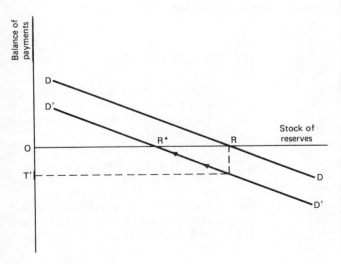

FIGURE 17-3 Credit Creation, the Balance of Payments, and Reserves The *DD* curve describes the relationship between the stock and flow of reserves (the balance of payments), given the demand for money and quantity of domestic credit. In the initial situation shown by Figure 17-2, the demand for money was *OL*, the quantity of credit was *OH*, the stock of reserves was *OR*, and there was no saving or dissaving. That situation is represented here by the *DD* curve. When reserves are *OR*, there is no balance-of-payments surplus or deficit, and reserves stay at *OR*. The increase in the quantity of credit to *OH'* shown in Figure 17-2 is represented here by shifting the stock-flow relationship downward to *D'D'*. When reserves are *OR*, the increase in the quantity of credit causes a deficit *OT'* in the balance of payments, and reserves start to fall. The economy travels along *D'D'*, following the arrows, until reserves have dropped to *OR**. The deficit is eliminated, and reserves stay at *OR**.

Dynamics of Devaluation

The *DD* curve in Figure 17-3 can be used to show how an exchange-rate change affects the balance of payments in a monetary model. Return to equation (1a), defining the demand for money, and use equation (5a) to replace the price index:

$$L^d = L(r, y)P = [L(r, y)k \cdot p^*]\pi \quad (1b)$$

A devaluation of the domestic currency, raising π, increases the price level. Therefore, it increases the demand for money. In Figure 17-4, the *DD* curve shifts upward to $D'D'$, producing a balance-of-payments surplus and inflow of reserves. But the surplus does not last forever. By raising the stock of reserves, it drives the economy along the $D'D'$ curve, which means that the surplus gets smaller and disappears eventually. The gradual increase in reserves adds to the money supply, reducing the excess demand for money produced by the higher price level. When reserves reach OR^*, the surplus vanishes. The effects of a devaluation are temporary, although they may last a long time.

What has happened to the MLR condition? It does not seem to play a role in Figure 17-4, and some proponents of the monetary approach say it is irrelevant.

They are wrong. The PPP assumption used to derive the monetary model is, in fact, a statement about the MLR condition. It amounts to saying that the real exchange rate is not affected by the volume of trade, so a country can increase its exports without reducing their relative price. In other words, the foreign demand for the country's exports is infinitely elastic, and the MLR condition is satisfied. When households save to build up their holdings of money, the goods they do not consume are sold to foreigners; the excess supply of domestic goods turns automatically into a trade surplus, and households are able to satisfy their demand for money.

A MONETARY MODEL OF EXCHANGE-RATE BEHAVIOR

The exchange rate is the price of one money in terms of another. That is a definition. But it becomes a strong prediction under the assumptions used in monetary models. The behavior of a flexible exchange rate can be explained by movements in money supplies. Those movements, moreover, depend primarily on national monetary policies, because there are no reserve movements to neutralize national policies.

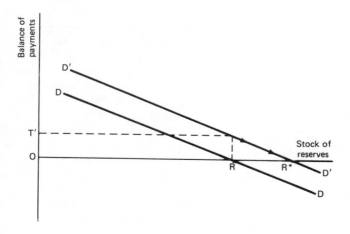

FIGURE 17-4 Devaluation in the Monetary Model
A devaluation raises the price level, increasing the demand for money. Therefore, it shifts the *DD* curve upward to $D'D'$, producing a surplus OT' in the balance of payments. But the surplus raises the stock of reserves, increasing the money supply, and the economy follows the arrows along $D'D'$. The surplus gets smaller as reserves get larger, and it vanishes when the stock of reserves reaches OR^*.

Money Stocks and the Exchange Rate

When the exchange rate is pegged, an economy can satisfy an excess demand for money by running a balance-of-payments surplus. It can export excess supplies of goods and bonds to import additional money. Conversely, it can get rid of an excess supply of money by running a balance-of-payments deficit.

When the exchange rate is flexible, an economy cannot adjust its money supply by running a surplus or deficit. Excess demand or supply in the money market must be eliminated by adjusting the demand for money rather than the supply. Under the assumptions of the monetary model, however, there is only one way to adjust the demand for money, raising or reducing the price level. And there is only one way to alter the price level, raising or reducing the exchange rate. Therefore, the exchange rate is the price that clears the money market.

These points can be made formally by rearranging equations used earlier to illustrate balance-of-payments adjustment. Returning to equation (9a), replace $\overline{L}^d$ with the expression in equation (1b):

$$\dot{R} = \lambda[L(r, y)(k \cdot p^*)\pi - L^s] \qquad (9c)$$

As there are no reserve flows when exchange rates are flexible, set $\dot{R} = 0$, and solve for the money supply:

$$L^s = L(r, y)k \cdot \pi p^* \qquad (9d)$$

Under the assumptions of the monetary model, however, r, y, and p^* are constant, which means that the exchange rate is the only variable that can adjust to maintain monetary equilibrium. Represent this conclusion by solving equation (9d) for the exchange rate:

$$\pi = \frac{L^s}{L(r, y)k \cdot p^*} \qquad (10)$$

The exchange rate depends on the money supply, L^s, on r, y, and p^*, and on the constant k (which depends on the constants α and $\overline{v}$).

Now write the foreign counterpart of equation (9d),

$$L^{*s} = L^*(r^*, y^*)k^* \cdot p^* \qquad (11)$$

where L^{*s} is the supply of foreign money expressed in foreign currency, r^* is the foreign interest rate, y^* is foreign real income, and k^* is the counterpart of k (defined by the weight α^* in the foreign price index and the constant $\overline{v}$ in the *PPP* equation). Solving for p^*,

$$p^* = \frac{L^{*s}}{L^*(r^*, y^*)k^*} \qquad (12)$$

and replacing p^* in equation (10),

$$\pi = \left[\frac{L^*(r^*, y^*)k^*}{L(r, y)k}\right]\left(\frac{L^s}{L^{*s}}\right) = \theta\left(\frac{L^s}{L^{*s}}\right) \qquad (13)$$

where θ is the ratio of $L^*(r^*, y^*)k^*$ to $L(r, y)k$. Clearly, θ is constant when interest rates and incomes are constant.

Equation (13) is the fundamental statement of the monetary approach to exchange-rate theory. It is illustrated by the line *OL* in Figure 17-5, which has a slope equal to θ. When the ratio of money supplies is *OB*, the exchange rate is *OR*. An increase in the domestic money supply that raises the ratio to *OB'* drives the exchange rate to *OR'*. The domestic currency depreciates when domestic money becomes more plentiful relative to foreign money.

Testing the Monetary Model

Attempts have been made to test the hypothesis illustrated by Figure 17-5. It works fairly well for periods in which one country's money supply is rising rapidly compared to those of other countries. It does not work well otherwise. It is based on strong assumptions about incomes and interest rates, as well as the PPP assumption,

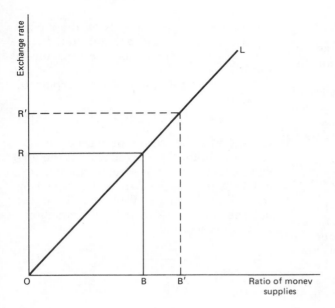

FIGURE 17-5   Exchange Rates and Money Supplies
The *OL* curve makes the fundamental statement of the monetary approach to exchange-rate theory. The value of the domestic currency depends on the supply of domestic money compared with the supply of foreign money. When the ratio of domestic to foreign money is *OB*, the exchange rate is *OR*. When the supply of domestic money rises, raising the ratio to *OB'*, the exchange rate rises to *OR'*. The domestic currency depreciates.

and those assumptions are not borne out by experience. Real incomes are not constant. Interest rates do not always conform to open interest parity, the condition imposed by equation (3). Therefore, most tests of the monetary approach to exchange-rate theory are based on less restrictive assumptions about incomes and interest rates.

One such formulation is derived in Note 17-2 and can be written

$$N(\pi) = N(L^s) - N(L^{*s})$$
$$+ n[N(y^*) - N(y)] + b\delta \qquad (14)$$

where $N(\pi)$ is the *logarithm* of the exchange rate, $N(L^s)$ and $N(L^{*s})$ are the logarithms of the money supplies, $N(y^*)$ and $N(y)$ are the logarithms of real incomes, b is a constant, and δ is the forward premium on the foreign currency defined in Chapter 16.

What does this equation say? It starts by saying the same thing as equation (13). The domestic currency depreciates when the domestic money supply rises more rapidly

than the foreign money supply. But it makes more statements. The domestic currency appreciates when domestic income rises, because an increase in y raises the demand for domestic money. The domestic currency depreciates when foreign income rises, because an increase in y^* raises the demand for foreign money. Finally, the equation says that the domestic currency depreciates whenever investors expect it to depreciate. That is the meaning of the last term, which uses the forward premium to represent investors' expectations. (Remember that a forward premium on the foreign currency is equivalent to a forward discount on the domestic currency. When δ is positive, investors expect the domestic currency to depreciate and start to sell it, and their sales cause it to depreciate immediately.)

Equations of this sort have been estimated for many periods and currencies. Here is an estimate for the early 1970s,

Note 17-2

Let the domestic demand function for money take this special form

$$L(r, y) = Ay^n e^{-br}$$

where A, n, and b are constants and e is the base of the system of natural logarithms. Let the foreign demand function be identical. Finally, let domestic and foreign consumers have identical tastes, so that $\alpha = \alpha^*$, and $k = k^*$. Under these assumptions, θ in equation (13) becomes

$$\theta = \frac{Ay^{*n} e^{-br^*}}{Ay^n e^{-br}} = \left(\frac{y^*}{y}\right)^n e^{b(r-r^*)}$$

According to equation (3), however, the interest rate difference must equal $\hat{\pi}$, the

expected rate of change of the exchange rate. Furthermore, $\hat{\pi}$ must equal δ, the forward premium on the foreign currency, when investors are risk neutral, and they *are* risk neutral in the monetary model. Therefore,

$$\theta = \left(\frac{y^*}{y}\right)^n e^{b\delta}$$

Substituting this expression into equation (13) and taking logarithms, we obtain equation (14). Its assumptions about demand functions are more restrictive than those of equation (13). Its assumptions about real incomes and interest rates are less restrictive.

pertaining to the exchange rate between the Deutsche mark and pound sterling:[6]

$$N(\pi) = 4.454 + 0.418N(L^s) - 0.915N(L^{*s}) - 0.171N(y^*) - 0.208N(y) + 0.0015\delta$$

This test is not very successful. The coefficients for the two money supplies have the expected signs; an increase in the German money supply, L^s, causes the Deutsche mark to depreciate vis-à-vis the pound; an increase in the British money supply, L^{*s}, causes the Deutsche mark to appreciate. But the coefficient for the German money supply is much smaller than 1, the value predicted by equation (14); in fact, it is not significantly different from zero. The coefficient for British income, y^*, is negative, whereas equation (14) says that it should be positive. And though the

coefficient for δ has the expected positive sign, it is very small. The author of this particular study concludes that his equation does not validate the monetary model represented by equation (14). Other authors come to similar conclusions.

PURCHASING-POWER PARITY

Although equation (14) relaxes one assumption adopted earlier in this chapter, allowing y and y^* to change, it relies on two other assumptions. The use of the forward premium, δ, to represent investors' expectations is based on the assumption that investors are risk neutral. Furthermore, the derivation of equation (14) depends strongly on the assumption that domestic and foreign prices are tightly linked by purchasing-power parity.

The purchasing-power parity doctrine is quite old. Its modern version is ascribed to a Swedish economist, Gustav Cassel, who

[6] John F. O. Bilson, "Rational Expectations and the Exchange Rate," in J. A. Frenkel and H. G. Johnson, eds., *The Economics of Exchange Rates* (Reading, Mass.: Addison-Wesley, 1978), p. 88.

was trying to define equilibrium exchange rates after World War I. According to Cassel, the exchange rate between two currencies is in equilibrium only when those currencies can buy the same bundles of goods and services:

The purchasing power parities represent the true equilibrium of the exchanges, and it is of great practical value to know those parities. It is in fact to them we have to refer when we wish to get an idea of the real value of currencies whose exchanges are subject to arbitrary and sometimes wild fluctuations.[7]

Note that Cassel was concerned with the use of PPP to define or choose exchange rates. Other economists treat it differently. They use it for predicting exchange-rate behavior rather than for appraising that behavior.

In this chapter, for example, PPP was introduced by equation (4). It was used to restrict the behavior of the price index P, which was used in turn to determine the demand for money. Therefore, PPP was employed to explain the behavior of the supply of money under a pegged exchange rate and thus the behavior of the balance of payments; thereafter, it was employed to explain the behavior of the demand for money under a floating exchange rate and thus the behavior of the exchange rate itself.

The monetary approach depends on the validity of the PPP doctrine, but the doctrine does not depend on the validity of the monetary approach. It is invoked frequently by economists who have reservations about the monetary approach, which is another reason for looking at it carefully.

Two propositions are employed to jus-

tify the expectation that exchange rates will conform to PPP. The first is the *law of one price*. The second has to do with the *neutrality of money*.

The Law of One Price and PPP

When used by itself, the law of one price is a statement about markets for a single product. It says that the price of a product must be the same in all markets, after allowing for transport costs and tariffs. This assertion is sensible enough, and we have been using it all along.

When used to support the PPP doctrine, however, the law of one price is extended *across* products. It is made to say that the price *level* in one country will always equal the price level in another. This extension is not strictly valid. There are two objections to it.

First, the products whose prices define the price level may not be identical from country to country. Even those products that seem to be similar are frequently different, which means that their prices will be different too. This point is illustrated by Table 17-1, which shows price movements for similar products in Germany and the United States. If the law of one price applied within each product group, the two countries' prices would move together. In fact, they move quite differently, which says that the products in each group may not be identical in Germany and the United States.

Second, the products that define price levels may be weighted differently from country to country, and differences in weights can drive a wedge between price levels even when the law of one price holds for each product individually. This point is illustrated by Note 17-3, which shows that a change in relative prices can change the observed relationship between national price levels when national price indexes use different weights.

---

[7] Gustav Cassel, *The World's Monetary Problems* (London: Constable, 1921), p. 28; quoted in Jacob A. Frenkel, "Purchasing Power Parity: Doctrinal Perspective and Evidence from the 1920s," *Journal of International Economics*, 8 (May 1978), p. 171.

TABLE 17-1 Changes in German and U.S. Prices for Selected Product Groups, 1968 to 1975

Product Group	Percentage Change in Ratio of German to U. S. Price
Apparel	64.3
Industrial chemicals	7.2
Agricultural chemicals	16.1
Plastic materials	13.4
Paper products	19.8
Metalworking machinery	69.2
Electrical industrial equipment	59.7
Home electronic equipment	77.5
Glass products	27.5

Source: Peter Isard, "How Far Can We Push the 'Law of One Price'?" *American Economic Review,* 67 (December 1977), Table 1. German prices are converted into dollars for comparison with U.S. prices.

In brief, the law of one price properly applied does not validate PPP. The law breaks when it is stretched.

The Neutrality of Money and PPP

What do we mean by the neutrality of money, and what does it do for the PPP doctrine?

Suppose that the quantity of money doubles overnight but all prices and incomes double, too, along with all assets and debts. No one will be better or worse off. No one will have more purchasing power. Therefore, there will be no changes in behavior and no change in any *real* magnitude. That is what is meant by the neutrality of money. It says that economic actors cannot be fooled by a purely numerical exercise.

Now transfer this example to an open economy. Let nominal (money) magnitudes

---

Note 17-3

The domestic price index, P, was defined by equation (5a):

$$P = [1 - \alpha(1 - \overline{v})]\pi p*$$

The foreign price index, $P*$, can be defined in the same way:

$$P* = [1 - \alpha*(1 - \overline{v})]p*$$

Multiplying $P*$ by π to convert it into its domestic-currency equivalent and dividing it into P,

$$\frac{P}{\pi P*} = \frac{1 - \alpha(1 - \overline{v})}{1 - \alpha*(1 - \overline{v})}$$

If the weights α and $\alpha*$ are the same, the ratio of price indexes cannot change. (This would be the case if P and $P*$ were indexes of consumer prices and the countries' consumers purchased identical "baskets" of goods.) If the weights are different, a change in $\overline{v}$ will drive a wedge between the price indexes. But $\overline{v} = \pi p*/p$, which is the relative price of the foreign good (the real exchange rate). Therefore, a change in relative prices will upset PPP when price levels are measured by indexes that use different weights.

double in one country but stay the same in the rest of the world. If the exchange rate does not change, domestic purchasing power will double in terms of foreign goods, even though it does not change in terms of domestic goods. If the exchange rate also doubles, however, domestic purchasing power will not change in terms of foreign or domestic goods. When money is neutral, PPP holds.

This illustration shows clearly the limited applicability of PPP. When a doubling of all prices is associated with a doubling of all other nominal magnitudes, a doubling of the exchange rate will neutralize it. If all other nominal magnitude do not change, however, the doubling of prices will have real effects on the domestic economy, and a doubling of the exchange rate cannot neutralize it. There is another problem. The doubling of money and prices must take place without lags and must be accompanied by an immediate doubling of all assets and debts. These things do not happen. Therefore, a careful economist will say that money is neutral in the long run, which means that PPP can hold only in the long run. In other words, PPP can be used to define the long-run response of the exchange rate to a purely monetary shock but not to describe actual exchange-rate behavior.

Some Evidence

Most economists are careful, but many look for short cuts. Therefore, PPP is frequently used as a rule of thumb, even by those who know that it has serious limitations. Recent evidence, however, calls this practice into question. It says that PPP can mislead us badly.

Let us solve equation (4) for the exchange rate and put the solution into logarithmic form:

$$N(\pi) = N(1/\overline{v}) + [N(p) - N(p^*)] \quad (3a)$$

TABLE 17-2   PPP Equations for U.S. Dollar Exchange Rates in the 1920s and 1970s

Currency	a	b
1921–1925		
French franc	−1.183	1.091
Pound sterling	−1.118	0.897
1973–1979		
French franc	−1.521	0.184
Pound sterling	0.712	0.165
Deutsche mark	−0.900	1.786

Source: Jacob A. Frenkel, "The Collapse of Purchasing Power Parities in the 1970s," *European Economic Review,* 16 (May 1981), Tables 1 and 2. The equations use wholesale prices for the United States and the other country involved in each comparison.

The validity of the PPP doctrine can thus be tested by making statistical estimates of this equation,

$$N(\pi) = a + b[N(p) - N(p^*)]$$

where a represents $N(1/\overline{v})$ and b should be approximately equal to 1 when the PPP doctrine holds.

Five such estimates are shown in Table 17-2, two for the 1920s and three for the 1970s. The estimates of b for the 1920s conform rather well to the PPP doctrine. Those for the 1970s do not; two are quite low and the third is quite high.

The author of these estimates used to assume PPP in most of his own theoretical work. He built models similar to those in this chapter. His empirical research, however, has led him to conclude that purchasing-power parity collapsed in the 1970s.

SUMMARY

The monetary approach to the balance of payments can be traced back to David Hume, who argued that surpluses and deficits are self-correcting, because of their effects on the money supply. The modern version is an application of Walras' law, which says that excess demands and supplies must sum to zero. Applied to an open economy, it says that a country with a balance-of-payments deficit can be regarded as having excess demands in its goods and bond markets taken together, and must therefore have excess supply in its money market. It "exports" its excess supply of money to satisfy its excess demands for goods and bonds.

Monetary models of the balance of payments are usually based on three assumptions. (1) There are no rigidities in factor markets, so output (income) stays at its full-employment level. (2) There is perfect capital mobility, so the domestic interest rate is tied tightly to the foreign rate. (3) Domestic and foreign prices are held together by purchasing-power parity, so the domestic price level is fixed when the exchange rate is pegged.

Under these assumptions, the demand for money is constant, and changes in the supply of money are reflected directly in the balance of payments. An increase in the quantity of domestic credit spills out as a balance-of-payments deficit. But a deficit reduces the money supply and is therefore self-correcting. Some monetary models focus on the requirements of long-run equilibrium in the money market. They show that there must be an inverse relationship between the quantity of domestic credit and stock of reserves. Other models focus on adjustment to short-run disequilibria. They show that an increase in the quantity of credit stimulates expenditure, producing excess demand in the goods market, a current-account deficit, and a loss of reserves.

Monetary models of the balance of payments have been adapted to explain the behavior of a flexible exchange rate. When there is no intervention in the foreign-exchange market, reserves cannot change, and the supply of money is determined by the quantity of domestic credit. The demand for money depends on the exchange rate, because the exchange rate affects the price level. An increase in the quantity of credit adds to the money supply and causes the domestic currency to depreciate. But tests of this hypothesis do not support it adequately.

Monetary models depend too heavily on restrictive assumptions. The purchasing-power parity doctrine plays a central role, and there are strong reasons for doubting its validity. The PPP doctrine cannot be derived from the law of one price, which holds only across markets for a single good. It can be derived from the supposition that money is neutral, but this means that it applies only to the long run and only with regard to monetary shocks. PPP should not be used to predict actual exchange-rate behavior, even as a crude rule of thumb.

RECOMMENDED READINGS

The best brief introduction to the monetary approach is provided in Jacob A. Frenkel and Harry G. Johnson, "The Monetary Approach to the Balance of Payments: Essential Concepts and Historical Origins," in J. A. Frenkel and H. G. Johnson, eds., *The Monetary Approach to the Balance of Payments* (Toronto: University of Toronto Press, 1976), ch. 1. The simple monetary model used in this chapter is adapted from Rudiger Dornbusch, "Devaluation, Hoarding, and Relative Prices," *Journal of Political Economy*, 81 (July 1973).

For a comparison of the monetary approach with others, see Harry G. Johnson, "Elasticity, Absorption, Keynesian Multiplier, Keynesian Policy, and Monetary Approaches to Devaluation Theory: A Simple Geometric Exposition," *American Economic Review*, 66 (June 1976); for a critical survey of the monetary approach, see Marina v. N. Whitman, "Global Monetarism and the Monetary Approach to the Balance of Payments," in *Reflections of Interdependence* (Pittsburgh: University of Pittsburgh Press, 1979), ch. 4.

On the monetary approach to exchange-rate theory, see Rudiger Dornbusch, "The Theory of Flexible Exchange Rate Regimes and Macroeconomic Policy," and John F. O. Bilson, "Rational Expectations and the Exchange Rate," in J. A. Frenkel and H. G. Johnson, eds., *The Economics of Exchange Rates* (Reading, Mass.: Addison-Wesley, 1978), chs. 2 and 5.

The evolution of recent thinking about PPP can be traced by comparing two papers by Jacob A. Frenkel; look first at "Purchasing Power Parity: Doctrinal Perspective and Evidence from the 1920s," *Journal of International Economics*, 8 (May 1978), and then at "The Collapse of Purchasing Power Parities During the 1970s," *European Economic Review*, 16 (May 1981).

Most economists have strong doubts about the validity of PPP, but some continue to follow Cassel and use it to define equilibrium exchange rates; see Ronald I. McKinnon, "Monetary and Exchange Rate Policies for International Financial Stability, *Journal of Economic Perspectives*, 1 (Winter 1988).

18

ASSET MARKETS, EXCHANGE RATES, AND ECONOMIC POLICY

INTRODUCTION

The monetary model in Chapter 17 drew attention to important propositions. It reminded us that markets are interdependent; an excess demand for goods and bonds must be matched by an excess supply of money. It stressed the role of the exchange-rate regime in determining how an open economy maintains monetary equilibrium. It showed why we must distinguish clearly between the short- and long-run effects of policy changes. This distinction arose in Chapter 14, when an increase in the money supply raised income in the short run but could not do so permanently with a pegged exchange rate. It arose again in Chapter 17, when the monetary model was used to study a devaluation. The devaluation led at once to a balance-of-payments surplus, but the surplus was not permanent. By raising reserves and the money supply, it caused an increase in absorption which reduced the surplus.

But the framework of the monetary model is too restrictive. Factor prices are perfectly flexible and output is thus constant at its full-employment level. This assumption keeps real income constant. Domestic and foreign prices are tied together by purchasing-power parity. Investors are risk neutral, so open interest parity obtains when there are no obstacles to capital movements. In brief, the monetary model directs our attention to the money market by drastically simplifying behavior in labor, product, and bond markets.

This chapter shows what can happen when these assumptions are relaxed. It presents a model richer than the monetary model, because output does not always stay at its full-employment level, the price level does not depend exclusively on the exchange rate, and the domestic interest rate is not tied to the foreign rate by open interest parity. The model will be used to trace the effects of various disturbances and policy changes.

A PORTFOLIO-BALANCE MODEL

The new model synthesizes much of our earlier work. It borrows its treatment of wage rates, employment, and output from the simple Ricardian model in Chapter 3. It borrows its treatment of income and price effects from Chapters 13 and 14. It borrows its treatment of capital flows from Chapter 16, where risk-averse investors held domestic and foreign bonds, and it takes its name from this last characteristic. Because investors hold diversified portfolios, the model itself is described as a *portfolio-balance model.*

The new model follows the monetary model in distinguishing sharply between the short run and long run. The short run is defined here as a period too short for flows to have any influence on stocks. The long run is defined as a period so long that the economy can reach a *stationary state,* where all stocks are constant because the flows affecting them have ended. The same definitions were used implicitly in Chapter 17. In Figure 17-4, for example, the short run was a period too short for the balance-of-payments surplus OT' to drive reserves away from OR, their initial level. The long run was a period long enough for the balance-of-payments surplus to raise reserves to OR^*, at which they were stationary because the balance-of-payments surplus had disappeared.

But this chapter stresses a different stock-flow relationship. It is the link between the stock of wealth and saving. The economy reaches a stationary state when wealth becomes constant. This happens when there is no saving or dissaving.

Although this model synthesizes much of our earlier work, it is still too simple to be realistic. There is no capital formation (investment). The government balances its budget at all times. Interest payments are ignored in the definitions of income, the budget, and the current-account balance. The demand for money depends on interest rates and wealth but not on income. Expectations are stationary. And the economy under study is too small to influence incomes, prices, and interest rates in the outside world.

Prices and Production

Consider an economy that specializes completely in a single good and has Ricardian characteristics. Labor requirements are fixed, so that employment, N, depends on output, Q,

$$N = a \cdot Q \tag{1}$$

where a is the fixed labor requirement per unit of output. The price of the domestic good depends on the labor requirement and the wage rate,

$$p_1 = a \cdot w \tag{2}$$

where p_1 is the price of the good and w is the wage rate. In a one-product economy, moreover, national income is the value of the product,

$$Y = p_1 \cdot Q \tag{3}$$

where Y is national income measured in domestic currency.

These equations can be given two interpretations: When the wage rate is fixed, equation (2) fixes the price of the domestic good, and an increase in national income raises output and employment. When employment is fixed, equation (1) fixes output, and an increase in national income raises the price of the domestic good and the wage rate.

These two interpretations are illustrated in Figure 18-1. The curve HH describes the relationship between the wage rate and em-

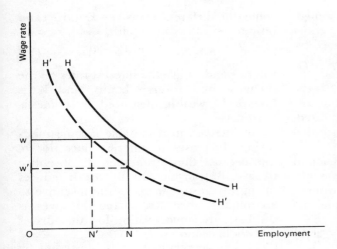

Wage rate

Employment

FIGURE 18-1 The Wage Rate and Employment
The *HH* curve describes the relationship between the wage rate and employment at a particular level of national income. When the wage rate is *Ow*, employment is *ON*. The effects of a change in national income depend on the behavior of the wage rate. Suppose that income falls, displacing *HH* to *H'H'*. If the wage rate is fixed, employment falls to *ON'*. If the wage rate is flexible, employment stays at *ON*, and the wage rate falls to *Ow'*.

ployment at a particular income level.[1] If the wage rate is *Ow*, employment will be *ON*. Let this be the full-employment level. Next, let national income fall, displacing *HH* to *H'H'*. If the wage rate is fixed at *Ow*, employment must fall to *ON'*. If employment is fixed at *ON*, the wage rate must fall to *Ow'*.

In the rest of this chapter, then, we can concentrate on the behavior of national income measured in domestic currency. When it rises in response to a disturbance or policy change, we can interpret the increase in either of two ways. We can assume that the wage rate is rigid, in which case output rises and the price of the domestic good does not change. Alternatively, we can assume that the wage rate is flexible, in which case the price of the domestic good rises and output does not change. These two possibilities can be combined in a single equation connecting the change in

the price of the domestic good with the change in national income:

$$\frac{dp_1}{p_1} = u\left(\frac{dY}{Y}\right) \qquad (4)$$

When the wage rate is rigid, $u = 0$ and p_1 does not change. When the wage rate is flexible, $u = 1$, and the change in p_1 is proportional to the change in Y.

Consumption, Saving, and the Current Account

Labor is the only factor of production in this model, and households supply labor. Therefore, households earn the whole national income. They use it for consumption, tax payments, and saving,

$$Y = C + T + S \qquad (5)$$

where *C*, *T*, and *S* are defined in the usual way and measured in domestic currency. Households divide their consumption between the domestic good and an imported good,

$$C = p_1 c_1 + p_2 c_2 \qquad (6)$$

where p_1 and p_2 are the prices of those goods measured in domestic currency,

---

[1] From equations (1) and (3), $N = a(Y/p_1)$. Using equation (2) to replace p_1, we obtain $N = Y/w$. Thus, the *HH* curve is a *rectangular hyperbola*; all rectangles inscribed beneath it have areas equal to *wN*, which is equal to *Y*. A decrease in national income is represented by an inward shift, such as the shift from *HH* to *H'H'*. The areas of rectangles beneath *H'H'* are equal to the new, lower level of national income.

while c_1 and c_2 are the quantities consumed. The behavior of p_1 was described by equation (4). The behavior of p_2 is described by

$$p_2 = \pi p_2^* \qquad (7)$$

where π is the exchange rate and p_2^* is the price of the foreign good measured in foreign currency. Unless otherwise indicated, p_2^* is fixed because the economy studied here is too small to affect it.

Households are one source of demand for the domestic goods. There are two others. Foreigners buy c_1^*, and the government buys c_1^g. The total demand must equal the supply:

$$c_1 + c_1^* + c_1^g = Q \qquad (8)$$

Multiplying both sides of equation (8) by p_1 and using equation (3),

$$p_1 c_1 + p_1 c_1^* + p_1 c_1^g = Y \qquad (8a)$$

But $p_1 c_1^*$ is X, the value of exports, and $p_1 c_1^g$ is G, the value of government spending (the government does not buy the foreign good). Furthermore, equation (6) says that $p_1 c_1 = C - p_2 c_2$, and $p_2 c_2$ is M, the value of imports. Therefore, equation (8a) becomes

$$C + X + G = Y + M \qquad (8b)$$

which is the familiar national-income equation. (There is no investment in it because there is none in the model.)

Finally, use equation (5) to replace Y in equation (8b), and set $G = T$, because the government balances its budget:

$$X - M = S \qquad (9)$$

This equation is equally familiar. It says that a current-account surplus must be matched by saving and a current-account deficit by dissaving. It is especially important here because of the role assigned to saving.

Saving and Wealth

In earlier chapters, saving depended on income. Here, it depends on disposable in-

come (the difference between Y and T) and on interest rates and wealth,

$$S = S(Y - T, r, r^*, W) \qquad (10)$$

where r and r^* are the interest rates on the domestic and foreign bonds, and W is household wealth measured in domestic currency.

An increase in disposable income raises saving. Increases in interest rates do so, too, because they strengthen the incentive to save. But an increase in wealth reduces saving, because it weakens the incentive to accumulate more wealth, and this gives us the basic dynamic relationship that drives the whole economy.

This basic relationship is illustrated by Figure 18-2, which deals with the simplest case in which disposable income is constant during the adjustment process. (In most cases studied later, disposable income changes, permanently or temporarily, depending on the character of the disturbance and the exchange-rate regime.) Saving is measured on the vertical axis and disposable income on the horizontal axis. The SY curve shows what households want to save at each income level; its slope is the marginal propensity to save out of disposable income. The position of the SY curve depends on interest rates and wealth. Let disposable income be OY so that saving is OS. Equation (9) says that the economy must have a current-account surplus. But saving adds to wealth, causing the SY curve to shift downward gradually. There is less and less saving at each income level. Eventually, the curve must drop to $S'Y'$, and saving ceases altogether, even if income remains at OY. At this juncture, moreover, the current account must be balanced.

The relationship between saving and wealth in equation (10) resembles the relationship between the balance of payments and reserves in the monetary model and can be drawn in a similar manner. In Figure 18-3, saving is measured on the vertical

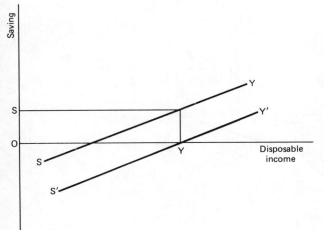

FIGURE 18-2 Saving and Income
The *SY* curve shows the relationship between saving and disposable income, given the interest rates and wealth, When disposable income is *OY*, saving is *OS*. But saving adds to wealth, and an increase in wealth reduces the incentive to save. The *SY* curve shifts downward gradually. When it falls to *S'Y'*, saving ceases, and wealth remains constant thereafter.

axis and wealth on the horizontal axis. The curve *SW* describes the relationship between them, given the interest rates and disposable income. Let wealth be *OW* to start so that there is no saving and the current account is balanced. The economy begins in a stationary state. Suppose that there is an increase in an interest rate or income. The *SW* curve is displaced to *S'W'*, households start to save *OS'* of their incomes, and the current account moves into surplus. As saving adds to wealth, however,

the economy travels along *S'W'*, following the arrows, until wealth rises to *OW'*, where saving ceases, the current account is balanced, and wealth is stabilized.

Equilibrium in the Goods Market

All the relationships described thus far can be combined in a single diagram to depict equilibrium in the goods market. In Figure 18-4, income is shown on the vertical axis and the exchange rate on the hori-

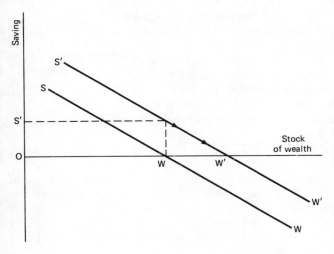

FIGURE 18-3 Saving and Wealth
The curve *SW* shows the relationship between saving and the stock of wealth, given the interest rates and disposable income. When wealth is *OW*, saving is zero. An increase in disposable income shifts the curve to *S'W'*, so saving is *OS'* when wealth is *OW*. The economy travels along *S'W'*, following the arrows, until wealth rises to *OW'* and saving goes to zero.

FIGURE 18-4 Equilibrium in the Goods Market
At points on the zz curve, the economy is in short-run equilibrium. The stock of wealth is the same at all points on the curve, but saving and the current-account balance vary from point to point. At points on the ZZ curve, the economy is in long-run equilibrium. The stock of wealth differs from point to point, but it is constant at each point, because the current account is balanced and saving is zero. The zz curve is upward sloping because a devaluation or depreciation of the domestic currency improves the current account and raises income. The ZZ curve is upward sloping and steeper than the zz curve because it shows the increase in income required to balance the current account at the new exchange rate. When the exchange rate is $O\pi_0$, the economy is at E_0, where zz and ZZ intersect; income is OY_0, the current account is balanced, and saving is zero. When the exchange rate is $O\pi_1$, the economy is at E_1 in the short run, where income is OY_1, the current account is in surplus, and saving is positive; it must go to E_1' in the long run, however, where income is OY_1', the current account is balanced again, and saving has gone back to zero.

zontal axis. The zz and ZZ curves identify goods-market equilibria.

The zz curve pertains to short-run equilibria. It shows how a change in the exchange rate affects national income before there has been time for wealth to change in response to the saving or dissaving that begins when the economy departs from its stationary state. By implication, the stock of wealth is the same at all points on the zz curve, but saving and the current-account balance vary from point to point. The zz curve is upward sloping whenever the MLR condition is satisfied; a devaluation or depreciation of the domestic currency raises national income by switching domestic and foreign demands to the domestic good. When the exchange rate is $O\pi_0$, national income is OY_0. When the exchange rate is $O\pi_1$, national income is OY_1.

The position of the zz curve depends on the level of foreign spending and on the foreign-currency price of the foreign good. An increase in either one of them shifts the curve upward by raising demand for the domestic good and thus raising national income at each exchange rate. Its position also depends on interest rates and wealth because they affect saving. An increase in an interest rate shifts zz downward; by enhancing the incentive to save, it reduces absorption (consumption) and thus reduces income. An increase in wealth shifts zz upward; by weakening the incentive to save, it raises absorption and thus raises income. All these propositions are proved algebraically in Note 18-1.

The ZZ curve pertains to long-run equilibria. It shows what must happen to national income, given the exchange rate, to keep the economy in a stationary state, where the current account is balanced, saving is zero, and wealth is constant. By implication, the stock of wealth is constant at each point on the ZZ curve but not the same from point to point; it must rise along with income to keep saving at zero. Whenever the MLR condition is satisfied, the ZZ curve is upward sloping, but we must interpret this statement differently than in the case of the zz curve.

Suppose that the economy is at E_0, where zz and ZZ intersect. Because E_0 lies on ZZ, the current account is balanced, there is no saving, and wealth is constant. Change the exchange rate from $O\pi_0$ to $O\pi_1$, but hold wealth constant temporarily.

The economy must move along zz to E_1, and income must rise from OY_0 to OY_1. But part of any increase in income is saved in the short run, which means that the current account is in surplus at E_1, the new short-run equilibrium point. The ZZ curve tells us what must happen in the long run when the exchange rate remains at $O\pi_1$. The economy must move to E_1', the new long-run equilibrium point, where income must rise to OY_1' in order to raise imports by enough to balance the current account. (Note again that wealth must rise with income as the economy moves along ZZ to E_1', because saving must fall back to zero. If wealth did not rise with income in the long run, the current account would go to zero but saving would increase, and that is impossible. Later we will represent this increase in wealth by shifting the zz curve upward to intersect ZZ at E_1'.)

The position of the ZZ curve depends on some of the same variables that determine the position of the zz curve. Once again, however, we must describe their influence in terms of their effects on the current-account balance and, therefore, the long-run change in income required to bring it back to zero. An increase in foreign spending or the foreign-currency price of the foreign good produces a current-account surplus. Therefore, it shifts the ZZ curve upward, showing the increase in income needed to eliminate the surplus. For details, see Note 18-1. The position of the ZZ curve, however, does not depend on interest rates or wealth. The current account is balanced all along the ZZ curve, so saving must be zero. Therefore, the position of the curve cannot be affected by changes in saving induced by changes in interest rates or wealth.

Summing up, the zz curve shows the short-run change in income produced by the expenditure-switching effects of an exchange-rate change. At points such as E_1, below the ZZ curve, there is saving and a

Note 18-1

To derive the zz and ZZ curves in Figure 18-4, we begin by rewriting equation (9) and defining demand functions for exports and imports,

$$S = p_1 c_1^* - p_2 c_2$$

$$c_1^* = f^*(p_1^*, p_2^*, C^*) \quad \text{and} \quad c_2 = f(p_1, p_2, C)$$

where p_1^* is the foreign-currency price of the domestic good, so $p_1 = \pi p_1^*$ and C^* is foreign consumption in foreign currency (all other variables are defined in the text).

Using the product rule given in Note 14-1, we can write

$$dS = p_1 c_1^*(\dot{p}_1 + \dot{c}_1^*) - p_2 c_2(\dot{p}_2 + \dot{c}_2)$$

where a dotted variable denotes a proportionate rate of change. But the economy begins in long-run equilibrium, so $S = 0$ initially, and $p_1 c_1^* = p_2 c_2$. Furthermore, $\dot{p}_1^* = \dot{p}_1 - \dot{\pi}$, and $\dot{p}_2 = \dot{p}_2^* + \dot{\pi}$. Therefore,

$$dS = p_1 c_1^*[\dot{p}_1 + \dot{c}_1^* - (\dot{p}_2^* + \dot{\pi}) - \dot{c}_2]$$

The changes in quantities, $\dot{c}_1^*$ and $\dot{c}_2$, can be written as

$$\dot{c}_1^* = -e_1^* \dot{p}_1^* + e_2^* \dot{p}_2^* + \left(\frac{1}{p_1^* c_1^*}\right) m_1^* \, dC^*$$

$$= -e_1^*(\dot{p}_1 - \dot{\pi}) + e_2^* \dot{p}_2^* + \left(\frac{\pi}{p_1 c_1^*}\right) m_1^* \, dC^*$$

$$\dot{c}_2 = -e_2 \dot{p}_2 + e_1 \dot{p}_1 + \left(\frac{1}{p_2 c_2}\right) m_2 \, dC$$

$$= -e_2(\dot{p}_2^* + \dot{\pi}) + e_1 \dot{p}_1 + \left(\frac{1}{p_1 c_1^*}\right) m_2 \, dC$$

Here, e_1^* is the own-price elasticity of foreign demand for the domestic good, e_2^* is the cross-price elasticity, and m_1^* is

the fraction of an increase in foreign consumption that is spent on the domestic good. Similarly, e_2 is the own-price elasticity of domestic demand for the foreign good, e_1 is the cross-price elasticity, and m_2 is the fraction of an increase in domestic consumption that is spent on the foreign good. Substituting the expressions for $\dot{c}_1^*$ and $\dot{c}_2$ into the equation for the change in saving and rearranging terms,

$$dS = p_1 c_1^*(e_\pi \dot{\pi} - e_{1t} \dot{p}_1 + e_{2t} \dot{p}_2^*)$$
$$+ \pi m_1^* \, dC^* - m_2 \, dC$$

where $e_\pi = e_1^* + e_2 - 1$, the MLR condition, while $e_{1t} = e_1^* + e_1 - 1$, and $e_{2t} = e_2^* + e_2 - 1$.

Three assumptions simplify this statement: (1) Uniform changes in nominal variables do not affect quantities; this assumption was introduced in Note 14-2, and it says that $e_2^* = e_1^* - e_c^*$, and $e_1 = e_2 - e_c$, where e_c^* and e_c are the consumption elasticities of foreign and domestic demands. (2) A change in total consumption induces an equiproportional change in the demand for each good; this assumption says that $e_c^* = e_c = 1$. (3) Goods are gross substitutes, meaning that an increase in the price of one good raises demand for the other; this assumption says that $e_2^* > 0$ and $e_1 > 0$. Under these assumptions, $e_{1t} = e_{2t} = e_t = e_2^* + e_1 > 0$. Furthermore, $e_\pi = 1 + e_t$, which says that the MLR condition is satisfied.

Finally, equation (4) says that $\dot{p}_1 = u(dY/Y)$, and equation (5) says that $dC = dY - dS$ when, as here, T and G are fixed. Using these expressions to replace $\dot{p}_1$ and dC in the previous equation, we obtain the *basic goods-market equation*,

$$(1 - m_2)\, dS = nYe_\pi\dot{\pi} - (m_2 + nue_t)\, dY$$
$$+ \pi m_1^* \, dC^* + nYe_t\dot{p}_2^*$$

where $n = (p_1c_1^*/Y)$, the share of exports in national income.

At all points on the ZZ curve, the current account is balanced, so saving is zero. Therefore, $dS = 0$ on the ZZ curve, and we can solve the basic goods-market equation for the change in Y which satisfies that condition,

$$dY = \left(\frac{nY}{N_L}\right)e_\pi\dot{\pi} + \left(\frac{1}{N_L}\right)(\pi m_1^* \, dC^* + nYe_t\dot{p}_2^*)$$

where $N_L = m_2 + nue_t$. This is the relationship given by the ZZ curve. The curve is upward sloping because $(nY/N_L)e_\pi > 0$ when the MLR condition is satisfied. It shifts upward with increases in C^* and p_2^*.

Saving is not always zero on the zz curve. When T and r^* are constant, however, equation (10) says that

$$dS = s_Y \, dY + s_r \, dr + s_W \, dW$$

Remember that an increase in wealth re-

duces saving $(s_W < 0)$. Substituting this expression into the basic goods-market equation and solving for the change in Y,

$$dY = \left(\frac{nY}{N_S}\right)e_\pi\dot{\pi} + \left(\frac{1}{N_S}\right)(\pi m_1^* \, dC^* + nYe_t\dot{p}_2^*)$$
$$- \left(\frac{1}{N_S}\right)(1 - m_2)(s_r \, dr + s_W \, dW)$$

where $N_S = s_Y + m_2(1 - s_Y) + nue_t$. This is the relationship given by the zz curve. The curve is upward sloping because $(nY/N_S)e_\pi > 0$ when the MLR condition is satisfied. But it is flatter than the ZZ curve, because $N_S - N_L = (1 - m_2)s_Y$, so $N_S > N_L$. The zz curve shifts upward with increases in C^* and p_2^*; it shifts downward with an increase in r, which reduces consumption by encouraging saving; it shifts upward with an increase in W, which raises consumption by discouraging saving.

When the wage rate is rigid $(u = 0)$, $N_S = s_Y + m_2(1 - s_Y)$, which corresponds to the expression $s + m$ in Chapter 13, because s_Y is the marginal propensity to save and $m_2(1 - s_Y)$ is the marginal propensity to import, each defined with respect to an increase in disposable income.

current-account surplus. At points such as E_2, above the ZZ curve, there is dissaving and a current-account deficit. The ZZ curve itself shows the long-run change in income required to balance the current account at each exchange rate, eliminate saving or dissaving, and bring the economy to a stationary state.

Wealth and Demands for Assets

Households hold three assets in this model: money, a domestic bond, and a for-

eign bond denominated in foreign currency. Formally,

$$W = L^h + B^h + \pi F^h \tag{11}$$

where L^h is the quantity of money held by households, B^h is the quantity of domestic bonds, and F^h is the quantity of foreign bonds.

The demands for the three assets depend on interest rates and wealth. We can write them this way:

$$L^h = L(r, r^*, W) \qquad (12)$$

$$B^h = B(r, r^*, W) \qquad (13)$$

$$\pi F^h = F(r, r^*, W) \qquad (14)$$

These equations look alike but are very different. An increase in the domestic interest rate raises the demand for the domestic bond but reduces the demands for money and the foreign bond. An increase in the foreign interest rate raises the demand for the foreign bond but reduces the demands for money and the domestic bond. An increase in wealth raises the demand for each asset but need not do so uniformly.

One of the three demand equations is redundant. When we know the level of wealth and the demands for two of the assets, we know the demand for the third. In this chapter, moreover, the foreign interest rate is fixed, which makes it most convenient to omit the demand equation for the foreign bond and concentrate on the characteristics of the markets for money and the domestic bond.

Households are the only holders of money (there are no firms), and the central bank is the only supplier of money (there are no commercial banks). The supply of money, L, is given by

$$L = B^c + \pi R \qquad (15)$$

where B^c is the quantity of domestic bonds held by the central bank and R is the quantity of foreign-exchange reserves measured in foreign currency. An increase in B^c represents an open-market purchase designed to raise the money supply. An increase in R represents intervention in the foreign-exchange market (a purchase of foreign currency) designed to prevent the domestic currency from appreciating. The demand for money must equal the supply, so

$$L(r, r^*, W) - (B^c + \pi R) = 0 \qquad (16)$$

There are two holders of the domestic bond: households and the central bank. The supply of bonds is fixed, because the

government balances its budget. Therefore, demand in the bond market will equal supply when

$$B(r, r^*, W) + B^c - B = 0 \qquad (17)$$

where B is the fixed supply.

Wealth and the Exchange Rate

We need one more relationship to complete this model. It is the relationship between wealth and the exchange rate. The stock of wealth is affected gradually by saving. It is affected immediately by a change in the exchange rate. Part of wealth is invested in the foreign bond, which is denominated in foreign currency. Therefore, a depreciation or devaluation of the domestic currency raises wealth instantaneously by conferring a capital gain on holders of the foreign bond. It raises the value of that bond in terms of domestic currency.

This relationship can be expressed algebraically, but a picture is more helpful. In Figure 18-5, the economy begins in long-run equilibrium. The stock of wealth is constant at OW_0. At time $t = t_1$, the domestic currency is devalued. Holders of the foreign bond obtain a capital gain, and wealth jumps abruptly. (The size of the jump increases with the size of the devaluation and with the fraction of wealth invested in the foreign bond.) If the devaluation produces a current-account surplus, wealth will grow gradually thereafter, under the influence of the saving that accompanies a current-account surplus. But the subsequent increase in wealth reduces saving, which slows down the growth of wealth itself. Eventually, the economy reaches a long-run equilibrium in which the stock of wealth remains at OW_1.[2]

---

[2] This last statement is not technically accurate. Wealth *approaches* OW_1 but does not actually reach it. In mathematical terms, long-run equilibrium is a state to which the economy converges *asymptotically*. It is a never-never land, because it does not exist in finite time.

FIGURE 18-5 Wealth and the
Exchange Rate
From time $t = 0$ to time $t = t_1$, the
economy is in long-run equilibrium.
Wealth is constant at OW_0. At time
$t = t_1$, the domestic currency is devalued. Holders of the foreign bond obtain
a capital gain, and wealth rises immediately. If the devaluation produces a current-account surplus, wealth will rise
gradually thereafter, due to the saving
that accompanies a current-account surplus. But the subsequent increase in
wealth reduces saving, slowing down
the increase in wealth itself. Wealth becomes constant eventually at OW_1, the
new long-run level.

Equilibrium in the Asset Markets

A single diagram can depict equilibrium
in the money and bond markets. In Figure
18-6, the interest rate is shown on the vertical axis and wealth is shown on the horizontal axis. The LL and BB curves identify
asset-market equilibria.

Points on the LL curve are those at
which the money market is in equilibrium,
given the supply of money. The curve is
upward sloping because an increase in
wealth raises the demand for money and
calls for an increase in the interest rate to
reduce demand and clear the money market. (There is excess supply in the money
market above LL and excess demand below
it.) The position of the curve depends on
the supply of money. An increase in supply
shifts the curve downward, because the demand for money must rise to absorb the
additional supply, so the interest rate must
fall at each level of wealth. By implication,
the LL curve shifts downward in response

to an open-market purchase or an increase
in foreign-exchange reserves.

Points on the BB curve are those at
which the bond market is in equilibrium,
given the supply of domestic bonds. The
curve is downward sloping because an increase in wealth raises the demand for
bonds and calls for a decrease in the interest rate to reduce demand and clear the
bond market. (There is excess demand in
the bond market above BB and excess supply below it.) The position of the curve depends on the supply of bonds available to
households. The total supply is constant
when, as here, the government balances its
budget, but an open-market purchase by
the central bank reduces the supply available to households. Accordingly, an open-
market purchase shifts the curve downward; the demand for bonds must fall to
match the decrease in supply, so the interest rate must fall at each level of wealth.

The properties of the LL and BB curves
are derived algebraically in Note 18-2,

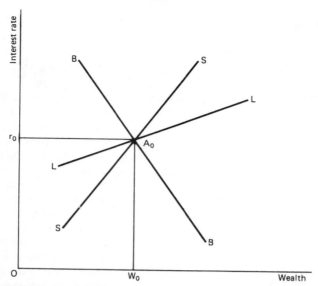

FIGURE 18-6   Equilibrium in the Asset Markets

At points on the *LL* curve, the money market is in equilibrium. The curve is upward sloping because an increase in wealth raises the demand for money and calls for an increase in the interest rate to maintain money-market equilibrium. At points on the *BB* curve the bond market is in equilibrium. The curve is downward sloping because an increase in wealth raises the demand for domestic bonds and calls for a decrease in the interest rate to maintain bond-market equilibrium. As the money and bond markets must be in equilibrium continuously and this can happen only at point A_0, the interest rate must be Or_0 and wealth must be OW_0. At points on the *SS* curve, saving is zero and the economy is in long-run equilibrium. This curve is upward sloping because an increase in wealth would induce dissaving and an increase in the interest rate would be needed to keep saving at zero. The *SS* curve shifts downward with an increase in disposable income; an increase in disposable income would induce saving, and a decrease in the interest rate or increase in wealth would be needed to keep saving at zero. As the *SS* curve passes through A_0, the economy is in long-run equilibrium when the interest rate is Or_0 and wealth is OW_0.

which also proves some propositions needed later in this chapter.

The money and bond markets must be in equilibrium at all times. Therefore, the interest rate and wealth are given by point A_0 in Figure 18-6, where *LL* intersects *BB*. This is the only point at which both markets can be in equilibrium simultaneously.

The domestic interest rate is Or_0, and wealth is OW_0. The ways that the markets reach equilibrium are described in the next section. They depend importantly on the exchange-rate regime.

The *SS* curve in Figure 18-6 describes a relationship that holds only in long-run equilibrium, when there is no saving. It is

Note 18-2

To derive the *LL* curve in Figure 18-6, use equation (16) to write

$$L_r\, dr + L_w\, dW - dB^c - \pi\, dR = 0$$

The effect of a change in r^* is omitted, as in Note 18-1, because r^* is constant in this chapter. (The effect of a change in π is also omitted because capital gains and losses on foreign-currency reserves are absorbed by the central bank and do not affect the money supply.) Solving for the change in r,

$$dr = -\left(\frac{L_w}{L_r}\right)dW + \left(\frac{1}{L_r}\right)(dB^c + \pi\, dR)$$

This is the relationship given by the *LL* curve. Remember that $L_r < 0$, because an increase in r reduces the demand for money. Therefore, the *LL* curve is upward sloping and shifts downward with increases in B^c and R.

To derive the *BB* curve, use equation (17) to write

$$B_r\, dr + B_w\, dW + dB^c = 0$$

The effect of a change in B is omitted, because B is constant when the government balances its budget. Solving for the change in r,

$$dr = -\left(\frac{B_w}{B_r}\right)dW - \left(\frac{1}{B_r}\right)dB^c$$

This is the relationship given by the *BB* curve. Remember that $B_r > 0$, because an increase in r raises the demand for the domestic bond. Therefore, the *BB* curve is downward sloping and shifts downward with an increase in B^c.

To derive the *SS* curve, set $S = 0$, hold T constant, and use equation (10) to write

$$s_Y\, dY + s_r\, dr + s_w\, dW = 0$$

Solving for the change in r,

$$dr = -\left(\frac{s_w}{s_r}\right)dW - \left(\frac{s_Y}{s_r}\right)dY$$

This is the relationship given by the *SS* curve. Remember that $s_w < 0$, because an increase in wealth reduces saving. Therefore, the *SS* curve is upward sloping, and an increase in disposable income shifts the curve downward.

In Figure 18-6, the *SS* curve is steeper than the *LL* curve. This is true when $(-s_w/s_r) > (-L_w/L_r)$ or $s_w L_r > s_r L_w$, which says that saving (absorption) is comparatively sensitive to changes in wealth, whereas the demand for money is comparatively sensitive to changes in the interest rate. This assumption is made in many macroeconomic models; when it is violated, a budget deficit reduces output because it "crowds out" private spending by raising interest rates.

The equations for the *BB* and *LL* curves can be solved for the short-run changes in W and R produced by an open-market purchase. Multiply both sides of both equations by $B_r L_r$ and put them together:

$$B_r L_w\, dW - B_r(dB^c + \pi\, dR)$$
$$= L_r B_w\, dW + L_r\, dB^c$$

Therefore,

$$(B_r L_w - L_r B_w)dW - B_r \pi\, dR = (B_r + L_r)dB^c$$

But $B_r L_w - L_r B_w > 0$ (because $L_r < 0$), and equations (11) through (14) tell us that $B_r + L_r + F_r = 0$, so $B_r + L_r =$

$-F_r > 0$ (because an increase in r reduces the demand for the foreign bond). Under a flexible exchange rate, R is constant so, an increase in B^e must raise W instantaneously. By implication, the domestic currency must depreciate to confer a capital gain on holders of the foreign bond. Under a pegged exchange rate, W cannot change right away, so an increase in B^e must reduce R instantaneously. (These results prove that the point A_1 in Figure 18-9 must lie below and to the right of the point A_0.)

Finally, use the equation connecting B_r, F_r, and L_r to rewrite the equation for the BB curve:

$$dr = \left(\frac{B_W}{L_r + F_r}\right)dW + \left(\frac{1}{L_r + F_r}\right)dB^e$$

Without any capital mobility, $F_r = 0$. The slope of the BB curve becomes B_W/L_r, and an open-market purchase shifts BB downward by as much as it shifts LL downward. With some capital mobility, $F_r < 0$. The BB curve gets flatter and shifts down less sharply. With perfect capital mobility, $F_r \to -\infty$. Foreign and domestic bonds become perfect substitutes, and r cannot change unless r^* changes, so the BB curve becomes horizontal and does not shift at all.

derived from equation (10) by setting $S = 0$. Points on the SS curve show combinations of the interest rate and wealth compatible with long-run equilibrium. The curve is upward sloping because an increase in wealth would induce dissaving and a higher interest rate would be needed to offset it. The position of the curve depends on the level of disposable income. An increase in disposable income would induce saving, and a lower interest rate or larger stock of wealth would be needed to offset it. Therefore, a permanent increase in disposable income shifts the SS curve downward, showing the reduction in the interest rate required to keep the economy in long-run equilibrium.

In Figure 18-6, the SS curve passes through point A_0. This says that the economy is in long-run equilibrium when the interest rate is Or_0 and wealth is OW_0. The corresponding level of disposable income can be obtained from the goods-market diagram introduced earlier. In Figure 18-4, the economy was in long-run equilibrium at E_0, where zz intersected ZZ. National income was OY_0, and disposable income can be obtained from national income by subtracting taxes (which are constant in this chapter).

USING THE PORTFOLIO-BALANCE MODEL

In the previous paragraph, we used the goods-market and asset-market diagrams together to locate the long-run levels of income, the interest rate, and wealth. We can use this same method to examine the effects of various disturbances and policy changes. The economy will be in long-run equilibrium at the start of each exercise. The disturbance or policy change will shift one or two curves immediately, driving the economy away from long-run equilibrium. We will look first for the new short-run equilibrium, examine its properties, and ascertain its implications for the subsequent path of the economy. This information will help us to locate the new long-run equilibrium. Each exercise must be conducted twice, however, because the behavior of the economy depends on the exchange-rate regime.

When the exchange rate is pegged, the stock of wealth can change only slowly, in response to saving or dissaving. In Figure 18-4, the exchange rate remains permanently at $O\pi_0$. In Figure 18-6, the stock of wealth remains temporarily at OW_0. But inflows and outflows of reserves affect the money supply, so the LL curve can move even when the central bank does not conduct open-market operations.

When the exchange rate is flexible, the stock of wealth can change immediately because of capital gains and losses on the foreign bond resulting from exchange-rate changes. In Figure 18-4, the exchange rate need not remain at $O\pi_0$. In Figure 18-6, the stock of wealth need not remain at OW_0, even temporarily. But there are no inflows or outflows of reserves, so the LL curve cannot move unless the central bank conducts open-market operations.

AN INCREASE IN FOREIGN EXPENDITURE

Let there be a permanent increase in foreign expenditure (consumption), raising the demand for the domestic good. In Figure 18-7, the zz curve shifts upward to $z'z'$, and the ZZ curve shifts upward to $Z'Z'$. If the exchange rate remains at $O\pi_0$, short-run equilibrium is displaced from E_0 to E_1, and income rises immediately from OY_0 to OY_1. Furthermore, E_1 lies below $Z'Z'$, which says that households start to save and the current account moves into surplus.[3]

Behavior Under a Pegged Exchange Rate

When the exchange rate is pegged, it must remain at $O\pi_0$ in Figure 18-7, which says that E_1 does indeed define the new short-run outcome, and income rises immediately to OY_1. This result is recorded in Table 18-1, which lists all the short- and long-run effects of the increase in foreign spending. But income does not stay at OY_1. It rises gradually through time, reflecting the increase in wealth produced by saving, until it reaches OY_1'. The proof is simple. When the long-run curve is $Z'Z'$ and the exchange rate is pegged at $O\pi_0$, long-run equilibrium must lie at E_1'. Therefore, the short-run curve must move gradually upward from $z'z'$ to $z''z''$, to intersect the long-run curve at E_1', and income must move with it.

TABLE 18-1 Effects of an Increase in Foreign Expenditure

Variable	CHANGE IN: Short Run	Long Run
Pegged exchange rate		
Income	+	+
Interest rate	0	−
Stock of wealth	0	+
Stock of reserves	0	+
Flexible exchange rate		
Income	+	0
Interest rate	0	0
Stock of wealth	0	0
Exchange rate	0	−

[3] Proof that E_1 lies below $Z'Z'$ is given in Note 18-1. As N_S is larger than N_L, the upward shift in zz is smaller than the upward shift in ZZ. The same point can be made by showing that E_2 lies horizontally to the left of E_0. Hold Y constant in Figure 18-7 and measure the change in π given by the equations for the zz and ZZ curves. The change given by the zz curve is $\dot\pi = -(1/nYe_\pi)\pi m_1^* dC^*$, which is identical to the change given by the equation for the ZZ curve. Note that the effects of an increase in foreign expenditure

closely resemble those of an increase in the price of the foreign good. An increase in C^* raises the foreign demand for the domestic good, and an increase in p_2^* switches foreign demand to the domestic good. (It switches domestic demand, too, but this merely reinforces the switch in foreign demand.) Therefore, the discussion in this section applies without much modification to an increase in the price of the foreign good.

FIGURE 18-7   Effects of an Increase in Foreign Expenditure on Goods-Market Equilibrium

The goods market begins in equilibrium at E_0, with income at OY_0 and the exchange rate at $O\pi_0$. An increase in foreign expenditure shifts the zz curve to $z'z'$ and the ZZ curve to $Z'Z'$. The exchange rate remains at $O\pi_0$ temporarily, even when it is flexible, but equilibrium is displaced immediately to E_1 and income rises to OY_1. As E_1 lies below $Z'Z'$, the adjustment process is driven by saving and a current-account surplus. Under a pegged exchange rate, the new long-run equilibrium must lie at E_1', so the short-run curve must move gradually to $z''z''$, and income must rise to OY_1'. The upward movement from $z'z'$ to $z''z''$ is produced by the decrease in the interest rate and increase in wealth shown in Figure 18-8. Under a flexible exchange rate, the new long-run equilibrium must lie at E_2, because the interest rate and wealth are constant in Figure 18-8 and the short-run curve must stay at $z'z'$. Income must fall back to OY_0. The domestic currency appreciates gradually from $O\pi_0$ to $O\pi_1$, and the expenditure-switching effect of the appreciation explains the reduction in income from OY_1 to OY_0. A flexible exchange rate insulates the economy from the income-raising effect of the increase in foreign expenditure, but full insulation is not achieved until the economy has returned to long-run equilibrium.

What causes this upward movement of the short-run curve? The increase in wealth and decrease in the interest rate shown in Figure 18-8, because they reduce the incentive to save and thus raise absorption. The economy begins at A_0, where the domestic interest rate is Or_0 and wealth is OW_0. It stays at that point temporarily, because the increase in foreign spending does not have any immediate effect on the positions of

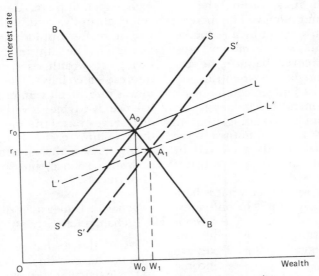

FIGURE 18-8 Effects of an Increase in Foreign Expenditure on Asset-Market Equilibrium

Asset markets begin in equilibrium at A_0, with the interest rate at Or_0 and wealth at OW_0. An increase in foreign expenditure does not affect the situation in the short run. Under a pegged exchange rate, however, saving raises wealth gradually and the interest rate falls. The economy travels along the BB curve to some such point as A_1, where the interest rate is Or_1 and wealth is OW_1. The corresponding movement of the LL curve to $L'L'$ testifies to an increase in reserves, which means that the balance of payments was in surplus during the adjustment process. The movement of the SS curve to $S'S'$ testifies to a permanent increase in disposable income, which goes with the increase in national income shown in Figure 18-7. Under a flexible exchange rate, the LL curve cannot move, and asset-market equilibrium must remain at A_0. There is a gradual appreciation of the domestic currency during the adjustment process, which imposes capital losses on holders of the foreign bond. The losses offset saving, keeping wealth constant at OW_0. As asset-market equilibrium stays at A_0, the SS curve cannot move, which says that there can be no permanent change in disposable income. This assertion is matched by the long-run result in Figure 18-7; the appreciation of the domestic currency takes national income back to its initial level.

the *BB* and *LL* curves; they depend on the supplies of bonds and money. With the passage of time, however, asset-market equilibrium is displaced to some such point as A_1, where the interest rate has fallen to Or_1 and wealth has risen to OW_1. As households save, wealth rises, raising the demands for bonds and money. The increase in demand for bonds is met by a reduction in the interest rate; the economy must move along the *BB* curve, because the supply of bonds cannot change when the government balances its budget continuously. The increase in demand for money is met by an increase in supply resulting from an increase in reserves. It is due in turn to the balance-of-payments surplus produced by the current-account surplus, and it drives the *LL* curve downward to $L'L'$.[4]

There is another way to see what is happening here. In Figure 18-7, income must rise permanently to OY'_1, because the economy must move gradually to E'_1 when the exchange rate is pegged at $O\pi_0$. Taxes are constant, however, so disposable income must rise by as much as national income. Accordingly, the *SS* curve must shift downward to $S'S'$ in Figure 18-8, which says that asset-market equilibrium must be displaced eventually to A_1, where $S'S'$ intersects *BB*. The movement of the money-market curve can be deduced from this long-run result, because that curve must pass through A_1 when the economy reaches long-run equilibrium. The downward movement of the money-market curve says in turn that there is a balance-of-payments surplus on the way to the new stationary state; the stock of reserves must rise gradually during the adjustment process.

Summing up for the pegged-rate case, an increase in foreign expenditure causes an immediate increase in national income, and the increase gets larger as time passes. The path of income looks like the path of wealth in Figure 18-5. An increase in foreign expenditure at time $t = t_1$ raises income abruptly, and income continues to rise thereafter until it reaches its new long-run level. The adjustment process involves saving, so wealth rises gradually, and the interest rate falls. The current account moves into surplus immediately, taking the balance of payments with it, and the inflow of reserves raises the money supply. When the economy reaches long-run equilibrium, saving ceases, the current account moves back into balance, and so does the balance of payments.

Behavior Under a Flexible Exchange Rate

When the exchange rate is flexible, it does not have to stay at $O\pi_0$ in Figure 18-7. In this particular instance, however, it does not change immediately. An increase in foreign spending does not alter the positions of the *BB* and *LL* curves, so asset-market equilibrium remains temporarily at A_0 in Figure 18-8. Therefore, wealth remains at OW_0, which tells us that the exchange rate does not change right away. The movement of national income to OY_1 in Figure 18-7 describes the short-run outcome with a flexible exchange rate as well as with a pegged exchange rate.[5]

When the exchange rate is flexible, however, the short-run goods-market curve

---

[4] The balance-of-payments surplus must be smaller than the current-account surplus, because the increase in wealth and decrease in the interest rate raise domestic demand for the foreign bond, producing a capital outflow as the economy moves to long-run equilibrium.

[5] Goods-market disturbances cannot affect the exchange rate immediately, because changes in national income do not affect the demand for money in this model. Therefore, the size of the short-run change in income is not affected by the exchange-rate regime. With asset-market disturbances, by contrast, a flexible exchange rate changes immediately. We will see this clearly when we study an open-market purchase.

cannot rise gradually to $z''z''$, as it did when the rate was pegged. It must remain at $z'z'$. Therefore, the new long-run equilibrium must lie at E_2, where $z'z'$ intersects $Z'Z'$. The domestic currency must appreciate gradually from $O\pi_0$ to $O\pi_1$, and income must fall from OY_1 to OY_0, the level at which it started.

What causes the domestic currency to appreciate? What keeps the short-run goods-market curve from rising to $z''z''$? When the exchange rate was pegged, the economy ran a balance-of-payments surplus at E_1. The central bank intervened in the foreign-exchange market to keep the exchange rate from changing. When the exchange rate is flexible, the central bank does not intervene, and the domestic currency must therefore appreciate. When there is no intervention, moreover, the money supply does not change. In Figure 18-8, then, the money-market curve must stay at LL, instead of falling to $L'L'$ as in the pegged-rate case, and asset-market equilibrium must remain at A_0. Wealth must be constant at OW_0, and the interest rate must be constant at Or_0. When they are constant, however, the short-run goods-market curve must stay at $z'z'$ in Figure 18-7, and the new long-run equilibrium must lie at E_2, where income is OY_0. The same result regarding income can be obtained directly from Figure 18-8. When asset-market equilibrium remains at A_0, the SS curve cannot shift. By implication, there can be no permanent change in disposable or national income. The short-run increase to OY_1 in Figure 18-7 must be reversed eventually.

There does appear to be something wrong here. When income is at OY_1 in Figure 18-7, households are saving, and wealth should be rising. How can wealth be constant in Figure 18-8? Two forces are at work, and they offset each other. Saving adds to wealth, just as in the pegged-rate

case. But the gradual appreciation of the domestic currency imposes capital losses on holders of the foreign bond. Those capital losses cancel the effects of saving and keep wealth from changing. This may seem to be a very special outcome, but it is fundamental to the logic of the model. A similar balancing of forces occurs in the process of adjustment to an open-market purchase.

Summing up for the flexible-rate case, the increase in foreign expenditure raises national income immediately by as much as in the pegged-rate case, but income falls thereafter. The adjustment process involves saving and a current-account surplus, and the domestic currency appreciates gradually. Wealth and the interest rate remain constant. When the economy reaches long-run equilibrium, income returns to its initial level.

Insulation Under a Flexible Exchange Rate

In Chapter 13, we saw that a flexible exchange rate can insulate the domestic economy against external shocks. That is what happened here. An increase in foreign expenditure raised national income in the short run, and the increase in income raised imports. But the increase in imports was not large enough to offset completely the increase in exports resulting from the increase in foreign expenditure. The current-account balance moved into surplus, and the domestic currency began to appreciate. The expenditure-switching effects of the appreciation drove the domestic economy back along the $z'z'$ curve in Figure 18-7 until income returned to OY_0.

Insulation can occur in other cases, including a switch in domestic demand between domestic and foreign goods. But the example given here warns us against counting on exchange-rate flexibility for *continuous* insulation. Insulation does not occur instantaneously, because income does not return to its initial level until the economy reaches long-run equilibrium. Furthermore, insulation occurs in respect of income (and employment) but not necessarily in respect of economic welfare. In the rigid-wage version of this model, p_1 does not change, and the economy is too small to influence p_1^*. Therefore, the appreciation shown in Figure 18-7 involves the real exchange rate as well as the nominal rate. There is a permanent improvement in the terms of trade, which raises welfare. A disturbance that led to a depreciation of the domestic currency would prevent a permanent reduction in income but would cause a deterioration in the terms of trade, which reduces welfare.

AN OPEN-MARKET PURCHASE

In the monetary model of the balance of payments, an increase in the money supply led to a gradual loss of reserves under a pegged exchange rate, and the loss of reserves reduced the money supply until it returned to its initial level. In the model studied here, an increase in the money supply leads to an *instantaneous* loss of reserves and a gradual loss thereafter. In long-run equilibrium, moreover, the money supply may not be back at its initial level. When the exchange rate is flexible, an increase in the money supply leads to an immediate depreciation of the domestic currency, but the exchange rate can go up or down thereafter. It need not depreciate steadily as it did in the monetary model.

An open-market purchase does not directly alter the positions of the zz and ZZ curves. By affecting asset-market variables, however, it affects the position of the zz curve indirectly. Accordingly, we start with the effects on asset markets, shown in Figure 18-9.

The economy begins at A_0, where BB, LL, and SS intersect. An open-market pur-

chase reduces the supply of domestic bonds available to the public, and a lower interest rate is needed to clear the bond market. The BB curve shifts downward to $B'B'$. But an open-market purchase raises the money supply, and a lower interest rate is thus needed to clear the money market. The LL curve shifts downward to $L'L'$. The two curves intersect at A_1, and Note 18-2 shows that A_1 lies below and to the right of A_0.

Behavior Under a Pegged Exchange Rate

When the exchange rate is pegged, wealth cannot change instantaneously, and A_1 cannot be an equilibrium point. Asset-market equilibrium must lie at A_1' in the left panel of the diagram, where wealth remains at OW_0 and the interest rate falls to Or_1.

How does the economy get to this point? When the central bank buys domestic bonds, driving the interest rate down, households want to hold more foreign bonds as well as more money. They keep some of the money created by the open-market purchase and use the rest to buy foreign currency in order to buy foreign bonds. The central bank must intervene in the foreign-exchange market to prevent the domestic currency from depreciating; it must use some of its reserves to meet the households' demand for foreign currency and thus take back some of the money created by its open-market purchase. The loss of reserves and reduction in the money supply are shown in Figure 18-9 by the shift in the money-market curve from $L'L'$ to $L_0'L_0'$, which intersects the new bond-market curve at A_1'. The bond market is cleared by the reduction in the interest rate to Or_1. The money market is cleared by the loss of reserves, which reduces the money supply from the level denoted by $L'L'$ to the level denoted by $L_0'L_0'$. These effects

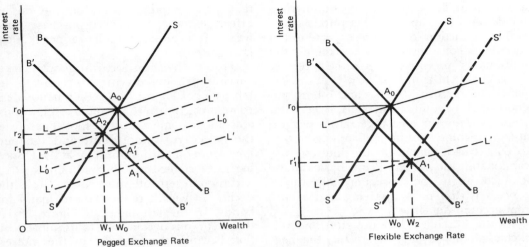

FIGURE 18-9 Effects of an Open-Market Purchase on Asset-Market Equilibrium

The asset markets begin in equilibrium at A_0, with the interest rate at Or_0 and wealth at OW_0. An open-market purchase shifts the BB curve to $B'B'$ and the LL curve to $L'L'$. Under a pegged exchange rate, wealth cannot change immediately, and asset-market equilibrium is displaced to A_1'. The interest rate falls to Or_1 and the money-market curve must shift back to $L_0'L_0'$, which says that there is an immediate loss of reserves. As an open-market purchase does not shift the ZZ curve in Figure 18-10, there can be no permanent change in national or disposable income, and the SS curve cannot shift. Hence, long-run equilibrium must be established at A_2, where $B'B'$ and SS intersect. Wealth falls gradually to OW_1, and the interest rate rises to Or_2. The money-market curve rises to $L''L''$, which says that there was a balance-of-payments deficit during the adjustment process. Under a flexible exchange rate, the money-market curve must stay at $L'L'$, and asset-market equilibrium is displaced to A_1. The interest rate falls to Or_1', by more than in the pegged-rate case, and wealth rises to OW_2, which means that there is an immediate depreciation of the domestic currency. Accordingly, income rises in Figure 18-10 by more than in the pegged-rate case. As the bond-market and money-market curves cannot shift again, long-run equilibrium must lie at A_1, and the SS curve must shift to $S'S'$. There is a permanent increase in disposable income, corresponding to the permanent increase in national income shown in Figure 18-10. If there is dissaving and a current-account deficit during the adjustment process, the domestic currency depreciates gradually to keep wealth at OW_2. If there is saving and a current-account surplus, the domestic currency appreciates gradually.

are listed in Table 18-2, which summarizes the results of an open-market purchase.

The reduction in the interest rate to Or_1 stimulates consumption by weakening the households' incentive to save. Therefore, the zz curve shifts upward to $z'z'$ in the left panel of Figure 18-10, and short-run goods-market equilibrium is displaced from E_0 to E_1 when the exchange rate is pegged at $O\pi_0$. Income rises immediately from OY_0 to OY_1. But a change in the interest rate cannot shift the ZZ curve, and E_1 lies above it. Accordingly, the subsequent adjustment process is driven by dissaving and a current-account deficit.

As the ZZ curve does not shift and the exchange rate is pegged at $O\pi_0$, the new long-run equilibrium must lie at E_0 in the left panel of Figure 18-10. This is the only point at which dissaving ceases and the current-account deficit disappears. By implication, the short-run goods-market curve must drop gradually back from $z'z'$ to zz, and income must return eventually to OY_0. This is the same long-run result that we obtained in Chapter 15. The income-raising effect of an open-market purchase must wear off eventually under a pegged exchange rate.

To see why the short-run goods-market curve must move downward, return to the left panel of Figure 18-9. When national income must return to its initial level, disposable income must do so, too. Therefore, the SS curve cannot shift, and the new long-run equilibrium must lie at A_2. Dissaving must reduce wealth gradually to OW_1, and the interest rate must rise to Or_2 as the decline in wealth reduces the demand for bonds. In the left panel of Figure 18-10, the zz curve is driven back to its initial position because the increase in the interest rate and decrease in wealth reduce absorption.

As the economy moves from A_1' to A_2 in the left panel of Figure 18-9, the money-market curve must move from $L_0'L_0'$ to $L''L''$. Reserves fall during the adjustment process, which says that the current-account deficit is accompanied by a balance-of-payments deficit. The decline in reserves, however, is not large enough to reduce the money supply to its initial level, as it did in the monetary model. Because $L''L''$ lies below LL, the money supply must be larger at A_2 than at A_0. The loss of reserves does not completely offset the open-market purchase.

Summing up for the pegged-rate case, an open-market purchase leads to an immediate increase in income, an immediate fall in the interest rate, and an immediate loss of reserves, because households add to their holdings of the foreign bond. Households start to dissave, the current account moves into deficit, and the balance of payments moves into deficit, too. There is a gradual decline in wealth and an additional loss of reserves. As in other models, monetary policy does not have any permanent effect on income under a pegged exchange

TABLE 18-2   Effects of an Open-Market Purchase

Variable	CHANGE IN:	
	Short Run	*Long Run*
Pegged exchange rate		
Income	+	0
Interest rate	−	−
Stock of wealth	0	−
Stock of reserves	−	−
Flexible exchange rate		
Income	+	+
Interest rate	−	−
Stock of wealth	+	+
Exchange rate	+	+

Note: These results pertain to the general case in which the domestic and foreign bond are imperfect substitutes. In the limiting case of perfect substitutability (perfect capital mobility), the interest rate does not change, and there is no short-run change in income under a pegged exchange rate.

FIGURE 18-10 Effects of an Open-Market Purchase on Goods-Market Equilibrium

The goods market begins in equilibrium at E_0, with national income at OY_0 and the exchange rate at $O\pi_0$. Under a pegged exchange rate, an open-market purchase shifts the zz curve to $z'z'$ because it reduces the interest rate. Equilibrium is displaced to E_1, and income rises to OY_1. There is dissaving and a current-account deficit. But long-run equilibrium must remain at E_0, because the ZZ curve cannot shift. Therefore, the short-run curve must move gradually downward from $z'z'$ to zz. This movement is produced by the increase in the interest rate and decrease in wealth shown in Figure 18-9. Income goes back to its initial level. Under a flexible exchange rate, the open-market purchase shifts the zz curve to $z''z''$, by more than in the pegged-rate case, because the interest rate falls farther and wealth rises immediately, reflecting the depreciation of the domestic currency. The larger shift in the curve is reinforced by the demand-switching effects of the depreciation. If the exchange rate goes from $O\pi_0$ to $O\pi_1$, equilibrium is displaced to E_1' and income rises to OY_1'. If the exchange rate goes to $O\pi_3$, equilibrium is displaced to E_1'' and income rises to OY_1''. In the first case, there is dissaving and a current-account deficit. In the second, there is saving and a current-account surplus. As the interest rate remains at Or_1' in Figure 18-9 and wealth remains at OW_2, the short-run goods-market curve stays at $z''z''$ and long-run equilibrium must lie at E_2. National income must go to OY_2, and the exchange rate must go to $O\pi_2$. If the exchange rate went to $O\pi_1$ in the short run, the domestic currency must continue to depreciate during the adjustment process; if it went to $O\pi_3$ in the short run, the domestic currency must appreciate during the adjustment process.

rate. The income-raising effect of the open-market purchase wears off gradually as the economy approaches long-run equilibrium.

Behavior Under a Flexible Exchange Rate

When the exchange rate is flexible, reserves cannot change. Therefore, the money-market curve must stay at $L'L'$ after the open-market purchase has shifted it from LL, and A_1 must represent short-run equilibrium in the right panel of Figure 18-9. But it *can* represent short-run equilibrium, because wealth can change instantaneously. As households attempt to buy foreign currency in order to buy foreign bonds, the domestic currency depreciates, conferring a capital gain on holders of that bond and raising wealth immediately to OW_2. The interest rate falls immediately to Or'_1, by more than in the pegged-rate case.[6]

Earlier chapters showed that monetary policy is more powerful under a flexible exchange rate, and that is true here, too. Look at the right panel of Figure 18-10. The short-run goods-market curve shifts from zz to $z''z''$, by more than in the pegged-rate case (when it shifted to $z'z'$), because there is a larger reduction in the interest rate and it is reinforced by an increase in wealth. Furthermore, the depreciation of the domestic currency from $O\pi_0$ to $O\pi_1$ switches domestic and foreign demands to the domestic good. Short-run equilibrium is displaced from E_0 to E'_1, and income rises all the way to OY'_1. As in the pegged-rate

[6] It is easy to show why the capital gain must be just large enough to raise wealth to OW_2. As $B'B'$ and $L'L'$ intersect at A_1, the money and bond markets clear when wealth is OW_2 and the interest rate is O_1. There is no excess demand for money or for the domestic bond. In that case, however, there can be no excess domestic demand for the foreign bond and no excess demand for foreign currency. Therefore, the depreciation of the domestic currency that raises wealth to OW_2 is just large enough to clear the foreign-exchange market.

case, however, the new equilibrium point lies above the ZZ curve; there is dissaving and a current-account deficit during the adjustment process.

When dealing with an increase in foreign expenditure, we found that income changed permanently under a pegged exchange rate and only temporarily under a flexible rate. Here, the outcomes are reversed. We have already shown that the change is temporary under a pegged rate. We will now show that it is permanent under a flexible rate.

When the exchange rate is flexible, there is no intervention in the foreign-exchange market. Therefore, the balance-of-payments deficit that emerged in the pegged-rate case is replaced by a gradual depreciation of the domestic currency. In the absence of intervention, moreover, the money-market curve remains at $L'L'$ in the right panel of Figure 18-9, and asset-market equilibrium remains at A_1. Wealth and the interest rate cannot change during the adjustment process. (There is, of course, dissaving, but its effect on wealth is offset by the depreciation of the domestic currency; holders of the foreign bond receive capital gains, and these keep wealth constant at OW_2.)

When wealth and the interest rate are constant, however, the short-run goods-market curve cannot move downward, as it did in the pegged-rate case. It must remain at $z''z''$ in the right panel of Figure 18-10, and the new long-run equilibrium must lie at E_2, where $z''z''$ intersects ZZ. The domestic currency must depreciate to $O\pi_2$, and income must rise gradually from OY'_1 to OY_2. Note finally that this outcome is fully consistent with the outcome in Figure 18-9. The permanent increase in income to OY_2 implies a permanent increase in disposable income, and that is what shifts the SS curve in Figure 18-9. It must shift to $S'S'$ when long-equilibrium remains at A_1.

Summing up for the flexible-rate case,

an open-market purchase leads to an immediate increase in income, an immediate depreciation of the domestic currency that raises wealth, and an immediate reduction in the interest rate. The increase in income is larger than in the pegged-rate case. In this particular example, the subsequent adjustment process is driven by dissaving and a current-account deficit. There is an additional depreciation of the domestic currency, which reinforces the income-raising effect of the open-market purchase. The path of the exchange rate looks like the path of wealth in Figure 18-5. An open-market purchase at time $t = t_1$ causes an immediate depreciation, and there is more depreciation on the way to the new long-run equilibrium.

Another Outcome

The language used in the previous paragraph hints at another possibility. Under a flexible exchange rate, there can be saving, a current-account surplus, and an appreciation of the domestic currency during the adjustment process.

Suppose that holdings of the foreign bond are very small initially so that a large depreciation of the domestic currency is

needed to raise wealth to OW_2 in the right panel of Figure 18-9. Let the exchange rate go all the way to $O\pi_3$ in the right panel of Figure 18-10, so short-run equilibrium is displaced to E''_1 and income rises to OY''_1. There will be saving and a current-account surplus during the adjustment process, because E''_1 lies below the ZZ curve. Therefore, the domestic currency will appreciate from $O\pi_3$ to $O\pi_2$ and income will fall from OY''_1 to OY_2. The path of the exchange rate is shown in Figure 18-11. The open-market purchase takes place at time $t = t_1$, and the domestic currency depreciates sharply. Accordingly, it must appreciate thereafter to reach $O\pi_2$, its long-run level.

This is a case in which the exchange rate "overshoots" its long-run level. There has been much discussion of "overshooting" in the recent literature, and many explanations for it. The explanation offered here, the small size of initial holdings of the foreign bond, may not be the most important. The phenomenon itself, however, is very important. Flexible exchange rates have been very volatile, and their volatility may be due to an inherent tendency for exchange rates to overshoot their long-run levels rather than approach them smoothly.

FIGURE 18-11   Overshooting in Response to an Open-Market Purchase
The economy is in long-run equilibrium from time $t = 0$ to time $t = t_1$ and the exchange rate is constant at $O\pi_0$. The central bank makes an open-market purchase at time $t = t_1$, and the domestic currency depreciates immediately. Here, it overshoots its long-term level, $O\pi_2$, and must therefore appreciate as the economy moves to long-run equilibrium.

Implications of Capital Mobility

Chapter 15 showed that capital mobility has important implications for the effectiveness of monetary policy. When the exchange rate is pegged, high capital mobility increases the speed with which income falls back to its initial level, and perfect capital mobility deprives monetary policy of *any* influence on income. When the exchange rate is flexible, high capital mobility enhances the effectiveness of monetary policy, and perfect capital mobility maximizes its effectiveness. The same things happen here.

The effects of capital mobility are analyzed in Figure 18-12 (using proofs supplied in Note 18-2). When there is no capital mobility whatsoever, the bond-market curve is very steep, and an open-market purchase shifts it downward by as much as the money-market curve. The bond-market curve is $\overline{BB}$ in Figure 18-12, steeper than curves in earlier diagrams, and an open-market purchase shifts it downward to $\overline{B'B'}$. The money-market curve is LL, and an open-market purchase shifts it downward to $L'L'$. The two curves intersect at A_1^0. When there is perfect capital mobility, the domestic interest rate is tied firmly to the foreign rate, as in the monetary model. The bond-market curve is $B*B*$, which is horizontal and does not shift at all. The interest rate stays at Or_0, the money-market curve shifts downward as it did before, and the intersection point is A_1^*.

Look first at the implications for monetary policy under a pegged exchange rate. As wealth cannot change immediately when the exchange rate is pegged, short-run equilibria must lie on the vertical line $A_0 A_1^0$. Without any capital mobility, A_1^0 is the equilibrium point. There is no backward shift of the money-market curve and no immediate loss of reserves. With perfect capital mobility, by contrast, A_0 is the equilibrium

point. There is no change in the interest rate or wealth. The money-market curve must snap back immediately to LL, and the instantaneous loss of reserves is exactly large enough to offset the open-market purchase. The money supply does not change. When the interest rate and wealth are constant, moreover, there can be no shift in the zz curve and no increase in income, even temporarily. Collecting these conclusions, an increase in capital mobility reduces the effectiveness of monetary policy under a pegged exchange rate. The short-run equilibrium points travel upward along $A_0 A_1^0$, the immediate loss of reserves gets larger, and the immediate increase in income gets smaller.

Look next at the implications of capital mobility under a flexible exchange rate and concentrate first on the short run.[7] As the money-market curve cannot move after it has shifted initially, short-run equilibria must lie on $L'L'$ in Figure 18-12, at a point between A_1^0 and A_1^*. Without any capital mobility, A_1^0 is the equilibrium point, and wealth is unchanged, which means that the exchange rate is unchanged. Furthermore, the shift in the zz curve is no larger than the shift in the pegged-rate case, because the change in the interest rate is the same. Therefore, the change in income is the same under flexible and pegged rates. With perfect capital mobility, by contrast, A_1^* is the equilibrium point. The interest rate is constant, but wealth rises to OW_1. The absence of an interest-rate effect reduces the size of the upward shift in the zz curve, but the wealth effect enlarges it, and it can be shown that the wealth effect dominates, raising income farther than in the pegged-

---

[7] There was no need to distinguish between short and long run in the pegged-rate case, because monetary policy does not have any permanent influence on income, regardless of the degree of capital mobility.

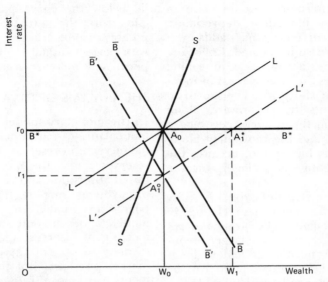

FIGURE 18-12 Influence of Capital Mobility on the Effectiveness of Monetary Policy

Without any capital mobility, the bond-market curve is $\overline{B}\overline{B}$, and an open-market purchase shifts it downward to $\overline{B}'\overline{B}'$, by as much as the downward shift of the money-market curve. With perfect capital mobility, the bond-market curve is B^*B^*, and it does not shift at all; the interest rate remains at Or_0. As wealth cannot change immediately under a pegged exchange rate, asset-market equilibria must lie on the line $A_0 A_1^0$. Hence, A_1^0 is the equilibrium point without capital mobility, and there is no immediate loss of reserves (no backward shift of $L'L'$). At the opposite extreme, A_0 is the equilibrium point with perfect mobility, and the loss of reserves offsets the whole open-market purchase ($L'L'$ shifts back to LL). As the money-market curve must remain at $L'L'$ under a flexible exchange rate, asset-market equilibria must lie on the line $A_1^0 A_1^*$. Hence, A_1^0 is the equilibrium point without any capital mobility, and there is no immediate change in wealth (no depreciation of the domestic currency). At the opposite extreme, A_1^* is the equilibrium point with perfect mobility and there is a large increase in wealth (a large depreciation). Furthermore, long-run equilibrium lies at A_1^0 without capital mobility and at A_1^* with perfect mobility, and SS curves must pass through those points. The curve passing through A_1 must lie below the curve passing through A_1^0, so the permanent increase in disposable income is larger with perfect capital mobility, and the permanent increase in national income must be larger, too.

rate case.[8] Furthermore, the increase in wealth implies an immediate depreciation of the domestic currency, which adds even more to the increase in income. Collecting these conclusions, an increase in capital mobility enhances the effectiveness of monetary policy in the short run. The short-run equilibrium points travel upward along $A_1^0 A_1^*$, the shift in the zz curve gets bigger in Figure 18-10, and the movement along the zz curve gets bigger too, because the exchange-rate change gets bigger. Income rises farther.

What about the effect of capital mobility on the size of the permanent change in income? It gets bigger. The larger the upward shift of the zz curve, the larger the increase in income needed to achieve long-run equilibrium. The same point can be made by looking again at Figure 18-12. When A_1^0 is the short-run equilibrium point, it is the long-run point, too, and a new SS curve must pass through it. When A_1^* is the equilibrium point, a new SS curve must pass through it instead, and it must

_____

[8] Rewrite the relevant portion of the equation for the zz curve given in Note 18-1:

$$dY = (nY/N_S)e_\pi \dot{\pi} - (1/N_S)(1 - m_2)(s_r \, dr + s_w \, dW)$$

The first term is the slope of the curve. The second tells us by how much it shifts. Without any capital mobility, the change in the interest rate is the vertical distance $r_0 r_1$ in Figure 18-12, and there is no change in wealth. The resulting shift in the zz curve can be written as $dY^0 = (1 - m_2)(s_r/N_S)r_0 r_1$. With perfect capital mobility, there is no change in the interest rate, and the change in wealth is the horizontal distance $W_0 W_1$. The resulting shift in the zz curve can be written as $dY^* = (1 - m_2)(-s_w/N_S)W_0 W_1$. But A_1^0 and A_1^* lie on the $L'L'$ curve, and the equation for that curve says that $dW = (-L_r/L_w)dr$. Therefore, $W_0 W_1 = (-L_r/L_w)r_0 r_1$, and $dY^* = (1 - m_2)s_w/N_S)(L_r/L_w)r_0 r_1$. Thus

$$dY^* - dY^0 = (1/N_S)(1 - m_2)[s_w(L_r/L_w) - s_r]r_0 r_1$$

$$= (1/L_w N_S)(1 - m_2)(s_w L_r - s_r L_w)r_0 r_1$$

In Note 18-2, however, we assumed that $s_w L_r > s_r L_w$. Therefore, $dY^* > dY^0$. The wealth effect dominates the interest-rate effect.

lie below the curve passing through A_1^0. Therefore, the permanent increase in disposable income is larger at A_1^*, the outcome with perfect capital mobility, and so is the permanent increase in national income.

THE ANALYSIS OF DEVALUATION

In the monetary model, a devaluation led to a balance-of-payments surplus and gradual increase in reserves. But the increase in reserves raised the money supply, which raised absorption and reduced the balance-of-payments surplus. The surplus disappeared eventually. In a portfolio-balance model, a devaluation causes an *immediate* increase in reserves, analogous to the immediate decrease caused by an open-market purchase. But the balance of payments can move into surplus or deficit which means that reserves can rise or fall during the adjustment process.

In Figure 18-13, a devaluation is represented by a permanent increase in the exchange rate from $O\pi_0$ to $O\pi_1$ in the left panel and an immediate increase in wealth from OW_0 to OW_1 in the right panel; the increase in wealth is due to the capital gain conferred on holders of the foreign bond. Any increase in wealth, however, leads households to demand more money and more domestic bonds. Therefore, they will use some of their capital gain to bid for those two assets; they will try to switch from foreign bonds to money and to domestic bonds. When they sell foreign bonds, moreover, they obtain foreign currency and sell it on the foreign-exchange market, and the central bank must intervene to keep the exchange rate pegged at $O\pi_1$. The central bank gains reserves, and the money supply rises, shifting LL downward to $L'L'$. Asset-market equilibrium is displaced from A_0 to A_1. The domestic interest rate falls from Or_0 to Or_1 to clear the bond market, and the money supply rises to clear the money market. These effects are listed in

FIGURE 18-13   Effects of a Devaluation

The economy begins in long-run equilibrium. The exchange rate is $O\pi_0$, national income is OY_0, the interest rate is Or_0, and wealth is OW_0. The domestic currency is devalued to $O\pi_1$. Looking first at the long-run effects, goods-market equilibrium must be established eventually at E_2, which means that the zz curve must move to $z''z''$ and national income must rise to OY_2. As disposable income must rise with national income, the SS curve moves downward from SS to $S'S'$, and long-run asset-market equilibrium must be established at A_2, where $S'S'$ intersects BB. Therefore, the money-market curve must move from LL to $L''L''$, and devaluation raises the stock of reserves. But there are two ways of reaching these long run outcomes. In this example, the devaluation raises wealth immediately to OW_1, reducing the interest rate to Or_1 and shifting the money-market curve to $L'L'$. There is an immediate increase in reserves, but it is smaller than the long-run increase ($L'L'$ lies above $L''L''$). The balance of payments must be in surplus during the adjustment process. Furthermore, the zz curve shifts to $z'z'$ in the short run, displacing goods-market equilibrium to E_1, which lies below the ZZ curve. There is saving and a current-account surplus during the adjustment process.

Table 18-3, along with other results of a devaluation.

The rise in wealth to OW_1 and fall in the interest rate to Or_1 stimulate absorption (consumption), and the zz curve shifts upward to $z'z'$. (The ZZ curve does not shift because there is no change in the level of income required to balance the current account.) Goods-market equilibrium is displaced from E_0 to E_1, and national income rises from OY_0 to OY_1. The increase in income is the joint result of the increase in absorption denoted by the shift of the zz curve and the demand-switching effect of

TABLE 18-3   Effects of a Devaluation

Variable	CHANGE IN:	
	Short Run	Long Run
Income	+	+
Interest rate	−	−
Stock of wealth	+	+
Stock of reserves	+	+

the devaluation denoted by the movement along the curve. In this particular example, the new goods-market equilibrium lies below the ZZ curve, so households start to save, and the current account goes into surplus.

In the long run, goods-market equilibrium must lie at E_2, because the exchange rate is pegged at $O\pi_1$. Therefore, the short-run curve must rise gradually to $z''z''$, and income must rise to OY_2. The shift in the curve is driven by rising wealth and a falling interest rate. Saving raises wealth to OW_2, and the interest rate falls to Or_2. Long-run asset-market equilibrium lies at A_2, below A_1, and the money-market curve must move gradually downward from $L'L'$ to $L''L''$. The money supply rises during the adjustment process, which tells us that reserves rise. The devaluation generates a balance-of-payments surplus. As in the monetary model, however, the surplus disappears when the economy reaches long-run equilibrium.

There is another possibility. The long-run outcomes are the same as those in Figure 18-13, but the short-run results are different. The long-run outcomes are the same because they are defined completely by the size of the devaluation. Long-run goods-market equilibrium must lie at E_2 when the exchange rate is $O\pi_1$. Income must rise eventually to OY_2, and there must therefore be a permanent increase in disposable income. Hence, the SS curve must shift to $S'S'$, which says that long-run asset-market equilibrium must lie at A_2. But the short-run results depend on the size of the increase in wealth produced by the devaluation.

Suppose that wealth rises immediately to a level higher than OW_2, because foreign bonds bulk large in households' portfolios, and they make large capital gains when the domestic currency is devalued. Asset-market equilibrium is displaced to a point on BB below A_2, so the interest rate falls below Or_2, and the money-market curve lies below $L''L''$. With a larger increase in wealth and larger decrease in the interest rate, there is a larger shift in the zz curve, and it lies above $z''z''$. Goods-market equilibrium is displaced to a point above E_2, and income rises to a level higher than OY_2. As the goods-market equilibrium point lies above the ZZ curve, there must be dissaving and a current-account deficit, which throw the adjustment process into reverse. Wealth must fall to reach OW_2, and the interest rate must rise to reach Or_2. The money-market curve must rise gradually to $L''L''$, which means that reserves must fall, and there must be a balance-of-payments deficit during the adjustment process. Finally, the goods-market curve must move gradually down to reach $z''z''$ and bring income down to OY_2.

To repeat, the long-run outcomes are the same in the two cases. The devaluation raises income and adds to the stock of reserves. But the paths are different. In the case described by Figure 18-13, income and other variables undershoot their long-run levels. In the other case, they overshoot them.

SUMMARY

The portfolio-balance model synthesizes much of our earlier work on the macroeconomics of an open economy. Supply conditions are Ricardian. Demand conditions reflect the income and price effects examined in Chapters 13 and 14. There are three assets—money, a government bond, and a foreign bond denominated in foreign currency. Investors are risk averse and hold all three assets.

The model separates short-run from long-run effects. Short-run effects are those that occur before flows have affected stocks. Long-run effects are those that pertain to the new stationary state, where all stocks are constant because the flows affecting them have ceased. The strategic stock-flow relationship in the model is the double link between saving and wealth. Saving adds to wealth, but an increase in wealth reduces saving. A change in the exchange rate affects wealth, too, because it confers a capital gain or loss on holders of the foreign bond.

An increase in foreign expenditure leads to a permanent increase in income when the exchange rate is pegged. There is a temporary increase when the rate is flexible, but the domestic currency appreciates gradually, reducing absorption and switching demand back to the foreign good. There is thus insulation from foreign disturbances, but it does not take place instantaneously.

An open-market purchase leads to a temporary increase in income when the exchange rate is pegged and to a permanent loss of reserves. With imperfect capital mobility, however, the loss is not large enough to offset completely the open-market purchase, and there is a permanent increase in the money supply. When the exchange rate is flexible, there is a permanent increase in income and a permanent depreciation of the domestic currency. The permanent depreciation can be larger or smaller than the depreciation that takes place instantaneously; the exchange rate can undershoot or overshoot its long-run level. As in other models, capital mobility diminishes the effectiveness of monetary policy under a pegged exchange rate, reducing the temporary increase in income. It enhances the effectiveness of monetary policy under a flexible exchange rate, raising the increase in income in the short run and the long run.

A devaluation of the domestic currency leads to a permanent increase in income and in the stock of reserves. But there are two ways of getting to this long-run result. When foreign bonds do not bulk large in investors' portfolios, wealth does not rise much on account of the capital gain conferred by the devaluation. Income and reserves rise immediately but by less than they must rise eventually, and the economy runs a balance-of-payments surplus during the adjustment process. When holdings of foreign bonds are large, wealth rises sharply. Income and reserves rise immediately by more than they must rise permanently, and the economy runs a balance-of-payments deficit during the adjustment process.

RECOMMENDED READINGS

The model in this chapter is adapted from the model in Polly R. Allen and Peter B. Kenen, *Asset Markets and Exchange Rates: Modeling an Open Economy* (New York: Cambridge University Press, 1983). But that model is more elaborate. It deals with changes in the supply of bonds resulting from budget deficits and surpluses, offers a more general treatment of goods markets, and introduces nonstationary expectations.

For an excellent survey of theoretical work on exchange-rate behavior that focuses on differences between monetary and portfolio-balance models, see Rudiger Dornbusch, "Exchange Rate Economics: Where Do We Stand?" *Brookings Papers on Economic Activity,* 1980 (1).

For a survey that stresses empirical work, see Maurice Obstfeld, "Floating Exchange Rates: Experience and Prospects," *Brookings Papers on Economic Activity,* 1985 (2).

19

THE POLITICAL ECONOMY OF INTERNATIONAL MONEY

INTRODUCTION

In Chapter 11, at the end of our survey of trade theory, we reviewed the history of trade policy and looked at current policy problems. This chapter plays an analogous role. It reviews the history of the international monetary system and looks at current problems. It pays particular attention to the role of the United States, because the U.S. dollar has been the main international currency for many decades and U.S. policies have affected the functioning of the monetary system.

The history of trade policy in Chapter 11 began with the early nineteenth century, when the United States embraced infant-industry protection and Great Britain moved toward free trade. Much can likewise be learned from the monetary history of the nineteenth century, when Great

Britain was the key-currency country but gold was important in theory and practice. Yet modern monetary institutions are very different from those of the nineteenth century, as is modern monetary theory, leaving less to learn from nineteenth-century history than from close inspection of recent experience. Therefore, this chapter concentrates on events since the Bretton Woods Conference of 1944, which designed the monetary system that came into being after World War II.

The chapter starts by reviewing events in the 1920s and 1930s that influenced the authors of the Bretton Woods agreement, then describes the agreement itself and the monetary system to which it gave rise. It goes on to review monetary relations under the Bretton Woods system, the breakdown of the system in the early 1970s, and the resulting shift from pegged to floating exchange rates. Thereafter, it examines the behavior of exchange rates in the 1970s and 1980s, the effects of the "oil shocks" of 1973 and 1979 and of major changes in national policies, and the problems of financing, adjustment, and debt arising from these and other events.

THE BRETTON WOODS SYSTEM

In Chapter 11, we noted that plans for postwar reconstruction were being made long before the end of World War II. American and British officials began to discuss them even before the attack on Pearl Harbor that brought the United States into the war, and they drafted an agreement on monetary matters that was ratified formally in 1944 by the International Monetary and Financial Conference held at Bretton Woods, New Hampshire. It established the International Monetary Fund (IMF) and the International Bank for Reconstruction and Development (IBRD), commonly known as the World Bank.[1]

Two aspects of earlier experience affected the design of the Bretton Woods system. Problems inherited from World War I, together with subsequent policy mistakes, contributed to a breakdown of monetary arrangements after the start of the depression in 1929. Furthermore, defects of the monetary system help to explain the

---

[1] In official usage, the term World Bank denotes a *pair* of institutions that make long-term loans to less-developed countries. The International Bank for Reconstruction and Development (IBRD) obtains its money by borrowing on international capital markets and lends it on market-related terms. The International Development Association (IDA) obtains its money from contributions by developed countries and lends it on concessional terms to the poorest of the less-developed countries. A third institution, the International Finance Corporation (IFC), is affiliated with the World Bank; it provides risk capital directly to private-sector projects in less-developed countries.

worldwide character of the depression and its severity.

Monetary Reconstruction in the 1920s

Some of the problems of the 1920s were mentioned in Chapter 11. International indebtedness grew rapidly during World War I and continued to grow thereafter, due partly to the Versailles Treaty, which imposed large reparation payments on Germany. There were big changes in current-account balances, resulting from changes in competitive positions and from wartime sales of income-producing assets. After the war, moreover, Germany and other Central European countries experienced terrible inflations. The story is told of the German housewife who needed a shopping basket to carry her money to market but could use a change purse to carry her groceries home. The inflations led to large exchange-rate changes, which fed back into prices and made the inflations worse, producing long-lasting doubts about the stability of floating exchange rates.

Governments stabilized their currencies eventually by linking the value of each currency to gold, but they did so sequentially, without much consultation, and they did not pay enough attention to the exchange-rate pattern that their decisions were producing. In 1925, for example, Great Britain reinstated the prewar link between the pound and gold, thus reinstating automatically the prewar exchange rate between the pound and dollar. This rate was unrealistic, because British prices were higher, compared to American prices, than before the war. Soon thereafter, France chose a new, low gold price for the franc, making the franc too cheap in terms of pounds and dollars. (The purchasing-power-parity doctrine discussed in Chapter 17 was developed by its author, Gustav Cassel, to deal with these situations. Although it has serious defects, its use might have led to more sensible exchange rates.)

This disorganized way of returning to pegged exchange rates is frequently blamed for the subsequent collapse of the monetary system. It reinforced changes in competitive positions that had already taken place, when it should have neutralized them. The attempt to restore the gold standard, however, was probably doomed from the start. Governments did not fully understand how it had worked before the war and could not therefore understand why it would not work in the postwar world.

The gold standard that came into being in the 1870s and lasted until World War I was different from the system described in textbooks of the day. Currencies were less closely linked to gold. In the United States, banks could issue paper money that was backed by government bonds instead of gold. In Britain, the Bank of England conducted open-market operations to ease or tighten credit. Governments did not obey the "rules of the game," which called on them to reinforce the money-supply effects of gold flows rather than offset (sterilize) those flows.

Furthermore, the process of balance-of-payments adjustment was more complicated than the specie-flow mechanism described by David Hume. Gold outflows did not cause prices to fall promptly. They led to higher short-term interest rates and to capital inflows. These could halt gold losses but could not correct deep-seated imbalances. When they did depress demand, moreover, they tended to cut incomes rather than prices; they brought into play the foreign-trade multiplier rather than the price effects predicted by textbook descriptions of the system.

The burden of adjustment was not always shared between surplus and deficit countries. It was often borne by countries at the fringes of the monetary system, in-

cluding the United States, because they were doubly dependent on credit flows from London. They were dependent directly on long-term flows to finance their current-account deficits, and these flows fell sharply whenever the Bank of England tightened credit to combat gold losses. They were dependent indirectly on short-term flows that were used to finance world trade in grain, cotton, wool, and other commodities. When credit conditions tightened in London, commodity dealers had to sell off inventories; their sales depressed prices and reduced the export earnings of the commodity-producing countries. Great Britain's trade balance improved, halting its gold losses, but some of the improvement was achieved by shifting the terms of trade in favor of Britain rather than changing the volume of trade.

If governments had understood the differences between prewar theory and practice, they might have been more sensitive to differences between old and new realities. But they did not fully grasp the extent to which World War I had altered those realities.

The international economy had become less flexible. We have already mentioned the piling up of debt, the building of new tariff walls, and the growing use of quotas. National economies had also lost some of their flexibility. Wage rates had become more rigid, due partly to the spread of unionization. Furthermore, many more governments could insulate their monetary systems from credit and gold flows, because they had established their own central banks, including the Federal Reserve System in the United States, and could thus flout the "rules of the game" by sterilizing gold flows.

There was weakness at the center of the system. Great Britain's competitive position had started to deteriorate long before World War I, but wartime inflation weakened it some more, and the restoration of the old gold parity in 1925 made it even harder for British industry to compete in world markets. Furthermore, New York and Paris had grown in importance as financial centers, so London could not dominate credit conditions as it had before the war.

Finally, there were changes in the role of gold itself. Governments and central banks had started to hold pounds and dollars as reserves, instead of gold, and some of them held most of their reserves in London. Even the Bank of France, a pillar of monetary orthodoxy, built up large holdings of pounds in the early 1920s.

Monetary Disintegration in the 1930s

The substitution of currencies for gold was seen at the time as a way to reduce the dependence of the monetary system on new gold supplies, but it proved to be a major flaw in the system. Great Britain had become a banker to foreign governments but was in a weak competitive position and had only small reserves of its own with which to "back" its obligations. Like any ordinary bank, Britain was exposed to a "run" by its depositors; unlike an ordinary bank, it did not have a "lender of last resort" to which it could turn for cash. The run finally came in 1931, ending the attempt to restore the gold standard.

During most of the 1920s, countries such as Germany ran current-account deficits and had to make large payments on their foreign debts. They were able to meet their obligations only by borrowing more money in New York and other financial centers and thus going farther into debt. Great Britain borrowed, too, but less directly; other countries built up their short-term claims on London. In 1928, however, the stock market boom in New York drained funds away from the bond market, reducing the capital outflow from the

United States, and the outflow ended in 1929, with the start of the depression. Germany and other countries halted payments on their debts, because they could not borrow more, and dealt a sharp blow to confidence in the monetary system. Furthermore, the Bank of France started to convert pounds into gold, depleting Britain's gold reserves. In 1931, Britain was forced to leave the gold standard, when a panic that began with the collapse of the Credit Anstalt, a major Austrian bank, spread across Europe to London and threatened to strip away the rest of Britain's reserves.

The system unraveled rapidly thereafter, as the depression deepened. Some small countries had left the gold standard in 1929 and 1930; other countries followed in 1931 and 1932. They let their exchange rates float, and many put direct controls on trade and payments in a further effort to insulate themselves from the spread of the depression. The United States devalued the dollar in 1934. It left the gold standard voluntarily in 1933 but chose a new gold price in 1934; the difference between the old price, ($20.67 per ounce) and the new price ($35.00 per ounce) amounted to a 70 percent devaluation of the dollar in terms of the currencies that were still linked to gold.

Countries that continued to peg their currencies to gold, such as France and Italy, tried to defend their exchange rates by erecting trade controls to reduce their imports but had also to pursue deflationary policies to keep from losing gold. They abandoned the effort in 1936, and their currencies depreciated. Thereafter, exchange rates settled down, and despite the large changes that had taken place, they were not very different from the rates that had prevailed in 1930, before Britain's departure from the gold standard. But the stabilization of exchange rates was not accompanied by any significant relaxation of controls on trade and payments.

Lessons Drawn from the Interwar Period

What lessons were learned from this sad history? A study written for the League of Nations in 1944, *International Currency Experience,* put them in terms that were widely accepted.

The setting of exchange rates, it concluded, must not be left to market forces, because floating exchange rates tend to be too volatile:

The twenty years between the wars have furnished ample evidence concerning the question of fluctuating *versus* stable exchanges. A system of completely free and flexible exchange rates is conceivable and may have certain attractions in theory. . . . Yet nothing would be more at variance with the lessons of the past.

Freely fluctuating exchanges involve three serious disadvantages. In the first place, they create an element of risk which tends to discourage international trade. The risk may be covered by "hedging" operations where a forward exchange market exists; but such insurance, if obtainable at all, is obtainable only at a price and therefore generally adds to the cost of trading. . . .

Secondly, as a means of adjusting the balance of payments, exchange fluctuations involve constant shifts of labour and other resources between production for the home market and production for export. Such shifts may be costly and disturbing; they tend to create frictional unemployment, and are obviously wasteful if the exchange-market conditions that call for them are temporary. . . .

Thirdly, experience has shown that fluctuating exchange rates cannot always be relied upon to promote adjustment. Any considerable or continuous movement of the exchange rate is liable to generate anticipations of a further movement in the same direction, thus giving rise to speculative capital transfers of a disequilibrating kind. . . .[2]

But the setting of exchange rates, the study said, must not be left entirely to individual governments:

An exchange rate by definition concerns more currencies than one. Yet exchange stabilization was carried out as an act of national sovereignty in one country after another with little or no regard for the resulting interrelationship of currency values in comparison with cost and price levels. This was so even where help was received from financial centers abroad. Stabilization of a currency was conceived in terms of gold rather than of other currencies. . . . From the very start, therefore, the system was subject to stresses and strains.[3]

Looking to the future, the study argued that exchange-rate decisions should be carefully coordinated.

Turning to experience in the 1930s, the study concluded that governments cannot be expected to sacrifice domestic economic stability merely to maintain exchange-rate stability:

Experience has shown that stability of exchange rates can no longer be achieved by domestic income adjustments if these involve depression and unemployment. Nor can it be achieved if such income adjustments involve a general inflation of prices which the country concerned is not prepared to endure. It is therefore only as a consequence of internal stability, above all in the major countries, that there can be any hope of securing a satisfactory degree of exchange stability as well.[4]

To achieve internal stability, moreover, major countries must harmonize their economic policies, especially monetary policies.

Even in the best of worlds, however, governments should not be expected to achieve complete stability and must therefore expect to experience balance-of-payments problems stemming from economic fluctuations at home and abroad. Furthermore, they should not have to count on short-term borrowing to finance balance-of-payments deficits. Flows of private capital can be perverse, the study

---

[2] League of Nations, *International Currency Experience,* 1944, pp. 210–211. The principal author was Ragnar Nurkse, whose work on the structure of the world economy was quoted in Chapter 11.

[3] Ibid., pp. 116–117.

[4] Ibid., p. 129.

argued, and can dry up completely just when they are needed. Therefore, official reserves should be large enough to meet normal needs, and they should be backed up by reliable supplies of reserve credit. These views were to influence strongly the design of the Bretton Woods system.

The Bretton Woods Agreement

One troublesome problem in the interwar period, the piling up of debt, was avoided in the 1940s. The United States gave outright aid to its allies during World War II; they did not have to borrow to pay for war materiel. Furthermore, wartime planners tried to distinguish carefully between the short-run needs of postwar reconstruction and long-run needs of monetary management. To help with reconstruction, the United States made a large loan to Britain and smaller loans to France, and it subscribed to the capital of the International Bank for Reconstruction and Development. When reconstruction proved to be more costly than anticipated, the United States started its own foreign-aid program. These and other highlights of monetary history under the Bretton Woods system are listed in Figure 19-1.

At the Bretton Woods Conference, governments tried to make sure that exchange rates would be chosen sensibly and altered only with good reason, that trade controls would not be used for balance-of-payments purposes, and that governments would be able to finance temporary balance-of-payments deficits so they would not have to change their exchange rates.

Under the Articles of Agreement of the International Monetary Fund, adopted at Bretton Woods, member governments were required to peg their currencies to gold or the U.S. dollar (which was, in turn, pegged to gold at $35 per ounce). The IMF had to approve those initial exchange rates and most changes made thereafter. To jus-tify a change in its exchange rate, a government had to demonstrate to the IMF that it faced a "fundamental disequilibrium" in its balance of payments.

The Articles of Agreement required governments to make their currencies *convertible* as soon as possible. They could continue to regulate capital movements; recall the view expressed in the League of Nations study that these had been destabilizing during the interwar period. They could also use tariffs and other trade controls for commercial-policy purposes. But they could not prevent residents of other countries from using or converting currencies acquired from current-account transactions. If a resident of Belgium acquired pounds by selling goods or services to Britain or from an investment-income payment, the Belgian was entitled to use the pounds for another current-account transaction, sell them to someone else who wanted to do so, or sell them to the Belgian central bank, which could then require the Bank of England to convert them into Belgian francs.

Britain made its currency fully convertible in 1947, but it had to retreat very quickly, because countries that had built up balances in London during the war rushed to cash them in for dollars and drained away much of the U.S. loan to Britain. Chastened by this experience, most governments moved slowly toward convertibility; European countries did not reach it until 1958, and many less-developed countries have never done so.

Finally, the Articles of Agreement of the IMF attempted to provide a reliable source of reserve credit. Under an early British plan drafted by John Maynard Keynes, the IMF would have functioned as a global central bank. It would have issued its own money, to be known as *bancor*. When a country ran a balance-of-payments deficit too large to be financed by drawing down reserves, its government would have borrowed bancor from the IMF and paid them over to countries with balance-of-payments surpluses. But this plan was too radical for the United States, which feared that it would wind up holding all the bancor. It proposed a different plan, adopted eventually at Bretton Woods. Instead of issuing its own currency, the IMF would hold a pool of national currencies that would be available to member governments needing to finance balance-of-payments deficits.

Each member of the IMF is assigned a *quota* that governs its subscription to the currency pool, its right to draw on the pool in case of need, and its voting power in the IMF. Suppose that two countries, Nord and

Sud, join the IMF. Nord is assigned a quota equivalent to $400 million. It has to pay the IMF a quarter of its quota, $100 million, in reserve assets, and the rest, $300 million, in Nordian francs.[5] Sud is assigned a quota equivalent to $200 million, and it must pay the IMF $50 million in reserve assets and $150 million in Sudian pesos. These payments appear at the top of Figure 19-2,

---

[5] In the early years of the IMF, reserve-asset payments were made in gold. These days, they are usually made in Special Drawing Rights (SDRs), which are defined and discussed in the next section of this chapter. (Furthermore, the IMF keeps its accounts in SDRs rather than the dollar equivalents used in this example.)

FIGURE 19-1   Monetary Chronology Under the Bretton Woods System

1944 Bretton Woods Conference agrees to establish International Monetary Fund (IMF) and World Bank
1945 United States terminates wartime aid to allies
1946 IMF comes into existence
     United States makes large loans to Britain and France
1947 President Truman proposes aid for Greece and Turkey
     France is first country to draw on IMF
     Britain restores and then suspends convertibility of pound
1948 Marshall Plan begins
     IMF decides that Marshall Plan recipients should not normally draw on IMF
1949 Britain and many other countries devalue their currencies
1950 European Payments Union (EPU) established
     Canada allows its currency to float
1956 Britain and France draw on IMF during Suez crisis
1958 European Economic Community (EEC) established
     Ten European countries restore currency convertibility and dissolve EPU
     United States begins to run large balance-of-payments deficits
1959 First increase in IMF quotas approved
1960 Gold price rises in London, and major governments stabilize it by selling gold
     President Eisenhower takes measures to reduce U.S. balance-of-payments deficit
1961 Germany and the Netherlands revalue their currencies
     United States starts to intervene on foreign-exchange markets and to build bilateral credit network
1962 IMF resources supplemented by General Arrangements to Borrow (GAB)
     Canada restores pegged exchange rate
1963 President Kennedy proposes interest equalization tax on American purchases of foreign securities
     Major governments begin first study of international monetary system

1964 Britain decides against devaluing the pound, draws on IMF, and obtains credits from other governments and Bank for International Settlements (BIS)

1965 President Johnson imposes "voluntary" restraints on foreign lending by American banks and corporations
Britain draws again on IMF and obtains additional credits

1967 Announcement of German agreement not to buy gold from the United States
IMF adopts plan for creating Special Drawing Rights (SDRs)
Britain devalues the pound

1968 United States moves from voluntary to mandatory capital controls
Management of gold price abandoned in favor of two-tiered market
France and Germany fail to agree on exchange-rate adjustments

1969 First Amendment to IMF Articles of Agreement comes into effect, authorizing SDR creation
France devalues the franc and Germany allows mark to float upward before adopting new peg

1970 First three-year allocation of SDRs begins
Canadian dollar allowed to float again
United States runs very large balance-of-payments deficit

1971 Germans propose joint float of European currencies; French favor devaluation of dollar instead
Austria and Switzerland revalue their currencies, and Germany and the Netherlands allow their currencies to float
President Nixon imposes wage-price freeze and 10 percent import tax and suspends convertibility between dollar and gold
Japan allows yen to float
At Smithsonian Institution in Washington, major governments agree to realign and peg exchange rates, devaluing dollar against most major currencies.

1972 European and Japanese governments intervene heavily to support the dollar
IMF establishes Committee on Reform of the International Monetary System (Committee of Twenty)
Britain allows pound to float

Source: Adapted from Robert Solomon, (New York: Harper & Row, 1982), *The International Monetary System 1945–1981*, pp. 383–398.

along with the *positions* of Nord and Sud, which depend on the IMF's holding of their currencies expressed as percentages of their quotas.

When the IMF's holdings of a member's currency are smaller than the member's quota, the member is said to have a *reserve position* equal to the difference. Thus, Nord starts with a reserve position equivalent to $100 million, and Sud starts with one equivalent to $50 million. Each has a reserve position equal initially to a quarter of its quota, the part of its subscription paid in reserve assets.

When the IMF's holdings of a member's currency are larger than the member's quota, the member is said to be using *Fund credit.* Under rules applied until recently, the IMF's holdings of a member's currency could not exceed 200 percent of its quota; therefore, the use of Fund credit was limited to 100 percent of the member's quota.[6] This cumulative ceiling was divided into

[6] In recent years, the IMF has created a number of special credit facilities which members can use at the same time that they draw on its general resources. Therefore, a member's access to Fund credit can exceed 100 percent of quota.

Quotas and Subscriptions

Nord's IMF quota is equivalent to $400 million. Sud's quota is equivalent to $200 million. Therefore, the IMF will hold these assets after Nord and Sud have made their subscriptions:

Asset	Millions of Dollars	Percentage of Member's Quota
Reserve assets	150	—
Nordian francs	300	75
Sudian pesos	150	75

Nord's *reserve position* is 25 percent of quota, equivalent to $100 million. Sud's *reserve position* is 25 percent of quota, equivalent to $50 million.

A Purchase by Sud

Sud purchases the equivalent of $150 million from the IMF, obtaining $50 million of reserve assets and $100 million of Nordian francs in exchange for Sudian pesos. The IMF will hold these assets after Sud's purchase:

Asset	Millions of Dollars	Percentage of Member's Quota
Reserve assets	100	—
Nordian francs	200	50
Sudian pesos	300	150

Nord's *reserve position* has risen to 50 percent of quota, or $200 million. Sud has used up its *reserve position* and also used $100 million of *Fund credit*; the IMF's holdings of pesos amount to 150 percent of Sud's quota, so the purchase has taken Sud through its second *credit tranche.*

A Repurchase by Sud

To repay Fund credit, Sud buys back pesos worth $100 million, using Nordian francs. The IMF will then hold these assets:

Asset	Millions of Dollars	Percentage of Member's Quota
Reserve assets	100	—
Nordian francs	300	75
Sudian pesos	200	100

Nord's *reserve position* has fallen back to 25 percent of quota, or $100 million. Sud has not rebuilt its *reserve position* (the IMF's holdings of pesos are equal to Sud's quota) but has repaid the *Fund credit* it used earlier.

FIGURE 19-2   Hypothetical Transactions with the International Monetary Fund four *credit tranches,* each equal to a quarter of a member's quota. Drawings in the first tranche are approved routinely; drawings in the higher tranches are not approved unless the member adopts policies designed to improve its balance of payments. This practice is known as *conditionality.*

To draw on IMF resources, a member purchases reserve assets and other members' currencies in exchange for the member's own national currency. The IMF decides what assets and currencies to provide, depending on the composition of its own resources. Suppose that Sud runs a balance-of-payments deficit and is allowed to purchase the equivalent of $150 million. The IMF provides $50 million of reserve assets and $100 million of Nordian francs. The effects appear in the middle of Figure 19-2. The IMF's holdings of Sudian pesos rise to 150 percent of Sud's quota. Therefore, Sud has used up its reserve position and has also used Fund credit. The IMF's holdings of Nordian francs fall to 50 percent of Nord's quota. Therefore, Nord's reserve position has risen to 50 percent of its quota.

In the normal course of events, Sud must repay fund credit by repurchasing some of its currency. Suppose that it uses Nordian francs worth $100 million to buy back Sudian pesos. The effects appear at the bottom of Figure 19-2. Sud has not rebuilt its reserve position; the IMF's holdings of Sudian pesos are exactly equal to Sud's quota. But Nord's reserve position has fallen back to 25 percent of quota.

There is another route to this result. Suppose that Nord's balance of payments moves into deficit as Sud's balance of payments improves, and Nord purchases the equivalent of $100 million. If the IMF chooses to provide Sudian pesos in exchange for Nordian francs, the outcome for Nord, Sud, and the IMF will be the same as in Figure 19-2. Nord's purchase of pesos will repay Sud's use of Fund credit.

This is how the IMF was expected to work. It was to be a revolving pool of currencies and reserve assets, whose composition would reflect temporary fluctuations in its members' balance-of-payments positions.

There have been six increases in IMF quotas. At the end of 1983, after the most recent increase, quotas totaled $94.5 billion and the U.S. quota was $18.8 billion, amounting to 19.9 percent of the global total. (Thus, U.S. voting power was large enough to veto certain classes of decisions, including decisions to amend the Articles of Agreement.)

MONETARY RELATIONS UNDER THE BRETTON WOODS SYSTEM

When looking back at monetary history since World War II, we are tempted to compare the instability of the 1970s with the apparent stability of the 1950s and 1960s, the years of the Bretton Woods system. Inflation and unemployment were high in the 1970s, world trade grew slowly, and there were large exchange-rate fluctuations. Inflation and unemployment were lower in most countries in the 1950s and 1960s, world trade grew rapidly, and exchange rates were fairly stable. But we tend to forget the balance-of-payments problems and exchange-rate crises of the 1950s and 1960s and the vigorous criticism of the Bretton Woods system.

An Overview

The United States and the U.S. dollar played important roles in the Bretton Woods system, but those roles changed sharply between 1945, when the system came into being, and 1971, when it started to disintegrate.

During the first postwar decade, the United States dominated the world economy, and debates about the monetary situation focused on the so-called *dollar shortage.*

The other industrial countries had suffered serious damage during the war and looked to the United States for capital goods needed to repair that damage, as well as for essential consumer goods they could not produce until it was repaired. Furthermore, the American economy was less open than it is today, and the United States could afford to be passive in internatonal monetary matters. It served as the *nth country* in the system, whose balance of payments and exchange rate reflected the policies of all other countries. When U.S. officials paid any attention to the international monetary situation, they viewed it in terms of other countries' problems.

In 1949, for example, Great Britain and many other countries devalued their currencies, making their economies more competitive relative to the American economy, but U.S. officials did not object. In fact, most historians agree that the British government was reluctant to devalue the pound but that U.S. officials advocated the devaluation because they were concerned about the outlook for Britain's balance of payments.

During that same decade, foreign governments and central banks started to accumulate dollars, just as they had accumulated pounds after World War I. The dollar began to serve as the main reserve currency. Like many other developments after Bretton Woods, this had not been planned. Washington did not deliberately seek a reserve-currency role for the dollar and did not give it much attention until the 1960s.

Postwar reconstruction was completed in the 1950s, and the situation changed. Although the American economy was still comparatively closed, it began to experience competition in foreign and domestic markets. Furthermore, American firms began to invest in Europe, causing a large capital outflow from the United States. Deficits appeared in the U.S. balance of payments, and there was talk about a *dollar glut* instead of a dollar shortage. The United States continued to act as the *nth* country but became increasingly uncomfortable about its role. It did not try to pursue an independent exchange-rate policy, but its views about other countries' problems began to reflect its concerns about the dollar.

In 1968, for example, France ran into a balance-of-payments problem that called for a devaluation of the French franc in terms of the Deutsche mark, but Paris and Bonn disagreed about the best way to achieve it. Each wanted the other to act. Paris wanted the mark revalued in terms of the dollar, which would have raised its value in terms of the franc; Bonn wanted the franc devalued in terms of the dollar, which would have had the same effect on its value in terms of the mark. Washington supported Paris, partly because a revaluation of the mark would have strengthened the competitive position of the United States relative to Germany, whereas a devaluation of the franc would have worsened it relative to France.

The United States abandoned its *nth*-country role in 1971, when its balance-of-payments deficit became very large. It set out to achieve a general realignment of exchange rate involving a significant devaluation of the dollar. The weakness of the U.S. balance of payments, however, did not reduce the dollar's role as a reserve currency. On the contrary, foreign official holdings of dollars grew faster. But most governments were dissatisfied with the situation and called for reform of the Bretton Woods system.

The Dollar Shortage

When Congress was asked to approve U.S. membership in the IMF and World Bank, it was promised that the American subscriptions to those institutions would be the last large contribution it would be asked to make to postwar reconstruction. This forecast proved to be too optimistic. As relations with the Soviet Union deteriorated, the economic problems of Western Europe were compounded by political problems culminating in the Berlin blockade of 1948 and the formation of the North Atlantic Treaty Organization (NATO) in 1949.

By 1947, it had become clear that the United States would have to make another major contribution. In a speech at Harvard, Secretary of State George Marshall proposed a new approach, which came to bear his name. If European governments would help each other, the United States would assist them:

The role of this country should consist of friendly aid in the drafting of a European program and in later support of such a program as far as it may be practical for us to do so. The program should be a joint one, agreed to by a number, if not all, European nations.

The Soviet Union was invited to participate in the new program in order to avoid a permanent division of Europe. But Moscow opposed joint economic planning, fearing that it would weaken Soviet control over Eastern Europe, and the governments of Western Europe went ahead on their own. They drafted a joint program and set up an organization to monitor it, and Congress approved the first U.S. contribution in 1948. During the first three years of the Marshall Plan, that contribution totaled almost $11 billion, equivalent to more than $50 billion at today's prices.

The Marshall Plan made three vital contributions to the reconstruction of the world economy. First, it allowed Europeans to purchase capital goods and raw materials, which they needed to start up their industries again. In other words, it relieved the dollar shortage directly. Second, it allowed them to dismantle controls on trade and payments they had kept in place to conserve scarce dollars. They started by establishing the European Payments Union (EPU), a credit network that helped them to trade among themselves without using dollars to settle all imbalances. In consequence, they liberalized intra-European trade faster than trade with the United States. When they began to export more to the United States, however, they relaxed restrictions on the use of dollar earnings. Third, the Marshall Plan helped European countries to acquire reserves—to buy a significant quantity of gold from the United States and build up dollar balances. At the beginning of 1958, when the European Economic Community (EEC) came into being, European governments were able to make their currencies convertible, and they abolished the EPU.

Nothing has been said thus far about the IMF, because its role was small at first. In fact, the IMF decided that countries receiving aid under the Marshall Plan should not purchase dollars from the IMF, a decision consistent with earlier attempts to distinguish clearly between the special needs of reconstruction and more ordinary needs for balance-of-payments financing. But something worrisome was also happening. Governments had started to alter their exchange rates without consulting the IMF. In 1949, the IMF was informed officially about the impending devaluation of the pound just before it was announced—and *told* that it would happen, not *asked* if it should happen. In 1950, Canada violated the Bretton Woods agreement by allowing the Canadian dollar to float but did not suffer any significant penalty.

The IMF became more active in 1956, not in overseeing exchange-rate policies but as a source of credit. War between Israel and Egypt, in which Britain and France were also involved, led to the closing of the Suez Canal. Trade in oil was disrupted, damaging the British and French economies, and foreign-exchange markets began to expect devaluations of the pound and franc. The British and French authorities had to intervene on the foreign exchange market to keep their currencies from depreciating, and both countries drew heavily on the IMF (as did Israel and Egypt).

These drawings were important for the precedents they set, as well as for their size. France was asked to adopt deflationary policies, because its problems were due largely to domestic inflation, not the Suez crisis, and the IMF was involved in discussions that led to a subsequent devaluation of the franc. Furthermore, the drawings were made under *stand-by arrangements* that have since become standard practice. France was given the right to draw a large sum from the IMF, more than it needed immediately, if it carried out the policies to which it was committed. Stand-by arrangements can combat speculation against a currency by showing that governments can mobilize enough reserves to intervene massively on foreign-exchange markets.

The Dollar Glut

In the early 1950s some economists believed that the dollar shortage could be permanent, that other countries might not "catch up" with the United States, even after repairing war damage, because the American economy was more innovative. (Their arguments were similar to one we hear today, that the United States and Europe will not catch up with Japan unless they imitate Japanese methods.) In 1958, however, the U.S. balance of payments deteriorated sharply. Dollar shortage gave way to dollar glut.

Most economists welcomed this development at first, as proof that Europe and Japan had recovered fully from World War II. They predicted that the U.S. balance of payments would improve after American firms had adapted to foreign competition.

The payments deficit did not go away, however, and made a sizable dent in the U.S. gold stock. Therefore, some economists began to believe that the dollar had become *overvalued* in terms of other currencies, partly because many currencies had been devalued during the previous decade and partly because of inflation in the United States.

Just before the U.S. election of 1960, speculation flared up in the London gold market, where most private gold trading takes place. It was fueled by rumors that the next American administration would devalue the dollar and thus raise the price of gold (because the value of the dollar was defined officially in terms of gold, not other countries' currencies). The United States sold gold in London in collaboration with other governments, and the price of gold declined. Even before his election, however, John Kennedy felt compelled to promise that he would not devalue the dollar.

The long-term outlook for the dollar was hard to evaluate. On the one hand, American goods were becoming more competitive. Recessions in 1957–1958 and 1960–1961 had reduced inflation in the United States, and exports were rising faster than imports. The balance-of-payments statistics in Table 19-1 show this pattern clearly; there were sizable current-account surpluses in the early 1960s. On the other hand, American firms were investing heavily in Europe, and other capital outflows were also growing. Believing that the current-account surplus would continue to grow and that capital outflows would taper off once U.S. firms had built up their facilities in Europe, the Kennedy administration declined to do anything drastic. It tried to reduce the dollar costs of stationing American troops in Europe, and it "tied" U.S. foreign aid to purchases of U.S. goods. It was reluctant to tighten monetary or fiscal policy and thus slow the growth of the domestic economy, because it had promised to reduce unemployment.

Taking an optimistic view about the long-term outlook, the Kennedy administration emphasized financing rather than adjustment and tried in particular to keep down gold losses. It sought to persuade foreign governments to hold dollar balances rather than gold, built up reciprocal credit lines with foreign central banks, and made small drawings on the IMF. To make sure that the IMF would have the currencies to handle a larger U.S. drawing, nine major countries joined with the United States in the General Arrangements to Borrow (GAB), promising to lend their currencies to the IMF if it needed them to handle a large drawing by one of the participants. The participants came to be known as the Group of Ten (G-10). In 1983, the GAB was made larger and more flexible; the participants will lend their currencies to the IMF if it needs them to handle a large drawing by *any* member.

Under the Bretton Woods system, the United States did not intervene regularly on foreign-exchange markets to stabilize the value of the dollar. That task was left to foreign central banks, which bought dollars with their own national currencies whenever the dollar began to depreciate. They had the right to buy gold with those dollars, but most of them declined to exercise it during the 1960s. France was the only important exception, because the French president, Charles de Gaulle, believed that the monetary system should be based on gold and that the reserve-currency role of the dollar conferred an "exorbitant privilege" on the United States—the ability to run a balance-of-payments deficit without losing reserves. He also wanted to reduce American influence in Europe by attacking the dominant role of the dollar.

When capital outflows did not taper off, the Kennedy administration imposed an "interest equalization tax" on American purchases of foreign securities, and the Johnson administration carried matters farther. In 1965, it asked American banks to limit their lending to foreigners voluntarily and asked American companies to limit their direct investments. In 1968, it shifted from voluntary to mandatory controls. By that time, however, the current account had weakened because of military outlays for the war in Vietnam and the effects of the war on the U.S. economy. The Johnson administration had tried to finance the war without raising taxes and allowed inflationary pressures to build up. The outlook for the dollar was getting worse.

Other countries' problems were also putting strains on the international monetary system, first those of Britain, then those of France.

Britain began to run balance-of-payments deficits in the early 1960s, and some members of the British government favored a devaluation. Washington objected, however, believing that a devaluation of the pound would touch off speculation against the dollar, another occasion on which U.S. views about other countries' policies were affected by concerns about their impact on the dollar. For this and other reasons, Britain continued to defend the existing exchange rate. It borrowed heavily from other governments and made three large drawings on the IMF. But Britain ran out of credit in 1967 and had run down its reserves, and the pound was finally devalued from $2.80 to $2.40.

In the spring of 1968, demonstrations and strikes by French students and workers led to large capital outflows from France. To end the strikes, moreover, the government raised wages, which damaged the competitive positive of French industry. When France and Germany could not agree on an exchange-rate realignment, France postponed action. In 1969, however, after the resignation of President de Gaulle, France devalued the franc without

TABLE 19-1 The U.S. Balance of Payments, 1961–1965 (annual averages in billions of dollars)

Item	1961–62	1963–64	1965–66	1967–68	1969–70
Exports of goods and services	30.9	36.5	42.8	49.8	61.6
Merchandise	20.4	23.9	27.9	32.1	39.4
Travel and transport	2.8	3.3	4.0	4.6	5.6
Investment income	5.3	6.5	7.5	8.7	11.3
Other	2.3	2.8	3.4	4.4	5.3
Imports of goods and services	−24.7	−28.1	−35.7	−45.2	−57.1
Merchandise	−15.4	−17.9	−23.5	−29.9	−37.8
Defense expenditure	−3.1	−2.9	−3.4	−4.5	−4.9
Travel and transport	−3.9	−4.5	−5.3	−6.2	−7.5
Investment income	−1.3	−1.7	−2.3	−3.1	−5.2
Other	−1.0	−1.1	−1.2	−1.5	−1.7
Unilateral transfers, except military, net	−2.6	−2.8	−2.9	−3.0	−3.1
Balance on current account	3.6	5.6	4.2	1.6	1.4
Increase (−) in U.S. assets abroad, net[a]	−5.9	−8.7	−7.4	−10.0	−11.1
U.S. government	−1.0	−1.7	−1.6	−2.3	−1.9
Direct investment	−2.7	−3.6	−5.2	−5.1	−6.8
Foreign securities	−0.9	−0.9	−0.7	−1.4	−1.3
Other	−1.3	−2.5	0.1	−1.1	−1.1
Increase (+) in foreign assets in U.S., net[a]	1.4	2.0	2.6	7.3	6.6
Direct investment	0.3	0.3	0.4	0.7	1.4
U.S. securities	0.3	—	—	2.7	2.7
Other	0.8	1.7	2.1	3.9	2.6
SDR allocations[b]	—	—	—	—	0.4
Balance on official settlements[c]	2.0	1.7	0.5	0.9	3.6
Increase (−) in U.S. reserve assets	1.1	0.3	0.9	−0.4	0.7
Increase (+) in U.S. reserve liabilities[d]	0.9	1.5	−0.4	1.3	2.9
Errors and ommissions	−1.1	−0.6	0.1	0.1	−0.9

consulting anyone, not even its partners in the EEC.

There *was* speculation against the dollar after the devaluation of the pound. It showed up in the gold market, as in 1960, and governments sold gold to keep its price from rising. They could not calm the market down, however, and sales were suspended early in 1968. Thereafter, there were two gold markets. Governments continued to deal with each other at $35 per ounce, the old official price, but would not sell gold on the London market, where the price would be determined by private supply and demand.

After the devaluation of the franc, there was more speculation, this time based on rumors that the mark would be revalued. The German authorities tried at first to keep the mark from appreciating by buying dollars in the foreign-exchange market, but they had to buy very large quantities.

1971–72	1973–74	1975–76	1977–78	1979–80	1981–82	1983–84	1985–86
73.2	128.4	163.7	202.2	314.4	363.0	347.6	366.1
46.4	84.5	110.9	131.4	204.3	224.2	210.9	220.2
6.8	9.8	12.6	16.0	22.5	28.2	27.6	30.2
13.7	24.7	27.3	37.2	68.3	85.0	81.6	88.3
6.3	9.0	12.8	17.6	19.3	25.7	27.6	27.5
-73.0	-118.3	-147.5	-211.8	-308.3	-355.7	-413.4	-479.5
-50.7	-87.1	-111.0	-163.8	-230.9	-256.4	-300.7	-353.4
-4.8	-4.8	-4.8	-6.6	-9.4	-11.7	-12.2	-12.3
-9.5	-13.0	-15.3	-19.2	-24.6	-28.7	-34.0	-40.6
-6.0	-10.9	-12.9	-17.9	-37.9	-53.6	-59.9	-65.1
-2.0	-2.5	-3.4	-4.3	-5.5	-5.4	-6.6	-8.1
-3.8	-5.5	-4.8	-4.8	-6.4	-8.2	-10.8	-15.5
-3.6	4.6	11.3	-14.4	-0.3	-0.9	-76.6	-128.9
-14.7	-28.1	-43.8	-48.1	-70.5	-11.0	-33.9	-61.9
-1.7	-1.1	-3.8	-4.2	-4.4	-5.4	-5.3	-2.4
-7.7	-10.2	-13.1	-14.0	-22.2	-3.6	-1.6	-22.7
-0.9	-1.3	-7.6	-4.5	-4.1	-6.8	-5.8	-5.4
-4.4	-15.5	-19.3	-25.4	-39.8	-94.9	-21.3	-31.5
3.4	18.6	16.8	24.4	46.2	84.2	89.9	156.1
0.6	3.8	3.5	5.8	12.8	19.5	18.7	22.0
3.4	2.4	4.6	3.7	7.2	11.5	26.2	75.2
-0.6	12.4	8.7	14.9	26.2	3.3	45.0	58.9
0.7	—	—	—	1.1	0.5	—	—
20.0	7.0	7.6	33.5	-4.0	-0.9	1.7	13.7
1.2	-0.7	-1.7	0.2	-4.6	-5.1	-2.2	-1.8
18.8	7.7	9.3	33.3	0.6	4.1	3.8	15.5
-5.8	-2.1	8.1	4.7	27.5	28.0	19.0	20.9

Source: U.S. Department of Commerce, *Survey of Current Business,* various issues.

Detail may not add to total because of rounding.

[a] Except reserve assets, shown below.

[b] An accounting entry to offset the increase (−) in U.S. reserve assets that occurs when the IMF allocates new special drawing rights to its member governments.

[c] A positive entry denotes a balance-of-payments deficit on the official-settlements definition.

[d] Foreign reserve assets held in the United States.

Therefore, they allowed the rate to float temporarily, the first major break in the pegged-rate system since 1950, when the Canadian dollar had been allowed to float. The dollar value of the mark rose by 10 percent during the next four weeks, after which the Germans began to intervene again, converting the appreciation into a revaluation by pegging the mark-dollar rate close to its new market level.

First Steps Toward Reform of the Monetary System

Economists began to criticize the Bretton Woods system in the 1950s. Some believed that exchange rates should float. Others did not go that far but warned that the political dynamics of the system were making rates too rigid. When a country's balance of payments moved into deficit, rumors of an impending devaluation began to circulate in the foreign-exchange market. If the government did not deny them, capital outflows built up, reserves fell, and the rumors became self-fulfilling; the government had to devalue. Once it had denied the rumors, however, it could not devalue voluntarily without admitting that its policies had failed and thus tarnishing its credibility.

These political dynamics made it hard for governments to talk about exchange-rate changes, even in the abstract. One official study listed the policy instruments that governments can use to deal with balance-of-payments problems. It did not even mention the exchange rate! Furthermore, most such studies emphasized financing rather than adjustment and devoted particular attention to reserve arrangements. Gold was the only reserve asset mentioned in the Bretton Woods agreement, and a change in its price was the only method mentioned for adjusting the supply of international reserves.[7] In the 15 years following World War II, however, gold stocks rose by little more than 1 percent per year, and the growth of dollar balances accounted for most of the increase in reserves.

In the interwar years, shifts in reserves from pounds to gold contributed to the crisis that forced Britain to leave the gold standard. Robert Triffin of Yale warned that the same sort of thing could happen again. In *Gold and the Dollar Crisis,* published in 1960, shortly before the first flurry of speculation in the London gold market, he posed what is now known as the Triffin dilemma. To supply reserves to the rest of the world, the United States had to run balance-of-payments deficits. As it did so, however, its own reserve position deteriorated, undermining international confidence in the dollar. The quantity of reserves could be increased only at the risk of reducing their quality.

Triffin recommended a new version of the proposal made by Britain during the negotiations that led to Bretton Woods. The IMF would issue its own currency when making credit available to members and would issue it in two other ways as well. Governments could buy it from the IMF in exchange for dollars and other reserve assets, and the IMF could conduct open-market operations, buying and selling securities, including World Bank bonds, to raise or reduce reserves. The IMF would begin to function as a global central bank.

This plan was too radical for most governments, however, and some had special reasons for opposing it. The United States wanted others to hold dollars and opposed the creation of any new asset that might compete with the dollar. France favored a larger role for gold and was reluctant to sacrifice sovereignty to any international institution. In 1965, however, the U.S. bal-

---

[7] Most governments opposed an increase in the price of gold, however, for a variety of reasons. First, it would confer large benefits on the Soviet Union and South Africa, the largest gold producers. Second, it would have complex effects on gold stocks and flows: it would raise the dollar value of existing gold stocks and the dollar value of gold output, but it would also increase the profitability of gold mining and thus raise the volume of output. No one could be sure that this would be the right combination of effects. Finally, an increase in the price of gold would favor countries holding large quantities of gold, compared to those holding large quantities of dollars. The United States was especially sensitive to this effect, because it was trying to persuade foreign governments to hold dollars rather than gold. The Bretton Woods agreement did provide for increases in IMF quotas, and these have taken place periodically, but they do not add to reserves, only to supplies of reserve credit.

ance of payments seemed to be on the mend, and Washington changed sides, urging the creation of a new reserve asset under IMF sponsorship. Governments turned from contemplation to negotiation, and they reached agreement in 1967. The IMF would be authorized to create Special Drawing Rights (SDRs) "to meet the long-term global need, as and when it arises, to supplement existing reserve assets."[8] The agreement took effect in 1969, and the first allocations of SDRs took place in 1970–1972. (A second round took place in 1979–1981.)

When SDRs are allocated, each government receives a quantity proportional to its quota in the IMF. Thereafter, it may use its SDRs to buy other members' currencies. If it cannot find a buyer for its SDRs, the IMF will "designate" one for it. SDRs are used most frequently, however, in transactions with the IMF itself. Members frequently receive SDRs when they draw on the Fund, and when there is an increase in IMF quotas, a quarter of the requisite subscription is normally paid in SDRs. The SDR was initially defined in terms of gold. It is defined today in terms of a "basket" of five currencies—dollars, pounds, marks, yen, and French francs.[9]

---

[8] Articles of Agreement of the International Monetary Fund, Article XVIII, Section 1 (a).

[9] The composition of the basket can be changed from time to time. This is how it was defined on August 31, 1987:

Currency	Number of Units	Dollar Value per Unit	Total Dollar Value
U.S. dollar	0.452	$1.0000	$0.452
Deutsche mark	0.527	0.5523	0.291
French franc	1.020	0.1653	0.169
Japanese yen	3.400	0.0070	0.236
U.K. pound	0.089	1.6331	0.145
Total	—	—	$1.293

Thus, 1 SDR was worth a little more than $1.29 in U.S. dollars.

The System in Crisis

When Triffin published *Gold and the Dollar Crisis,* the U.S. reserve position was still strong. Its gold holdings were larger than its liabilities to foreign official institutions. But the balance-of-payments deficits of the 1960s reduced its gold holdings, raised its liabilities, and weakened its reserve position. It had turned negative by 1970, when the balance-of-payments deficit widened sharply.

In the first three months of 1971, foreign governments and central banks had to buy more than $5 billion in the foreign-exchange market to prevent the dollar from depreciating; the balance-of-payments deficit was larger in those three months alone than in any previous year. There were new rumors that the Deutsche mark would be revalued, and speculation focused on the mark-dollar exchange rate. On a single day in May, the German central bank had to buy more than $1 billion. The next day, it had to buy another $1 billion during the first hour of trading. It suspended intervention, allowing the mark to float upward for the second time in two years.

In Chapter 13, we saw that a country with high unemployment and a balance-of-payments deficit should adopt an expenditure-switching policy. It should devalue rather than reduce absorption. That was the situation confronting the United States in 1971. In April, the trade balance slipped into deficit for the first time in this century, and the unemployment rate was close to 6 percent, a high level for those days.

American officials asked themselves how they could persuade other governments to revalue their currencies vis-à-vis the dollar. They did not want to devalue the dollar directly by raising the official price of gold, the only option open to them, because they did not want to break faith with foreign governments that had built up their dollar holdings, and because they were not sure that the technique would work. A higher dollar price for gold would not bring about a devaluation of the dollar if other governments continued to peg their currencies to the dollar in foreign-exchange markets.

Although the balance-of-payments deficit was huge in the first half of 1971, gold losses were small. Early in August, however, France bought some gold in order to repurchase francs from the IMF, and there were rumors of a large gold order by the Bank of England. The rumors were inaccurate but influential. On August 15, President Richard Nixon announced a dramatic policy change. To improve the domestic situation, he froze wages and prices temporarily and asked Congress to enact an investment tax credit to stimulate output and employment. To improve the international situation, he imposed an additional 10 percent tariff and instructed the secretary of the treasury to close the gold window—to suspend purchases and sales of gold.

These measures were designed to bring about a realignment of exchange rates. They imposed two penalties on any foreign government that refused to revalue its currency. Its exports would be penalized by the tariff, and it could no longer count on buying gold with dollars purchased in the foreign-exchange market to prevent its currency from appreciating. The Nixon administration was widely criticized for adopting "shock" tactics and breaking trade rules as well as monetary rules. The secretary of the treasury, John Connally, was criticized severely for being aggressively nationalistic. His blunt rhetoric, however, was partly designed for domestic consumption—to combat protectionist pressures in Congress.

In the days following the president's speech, several governments joined Germany by letting their currencies float, and that was what Washington wanted in the short run, along with an agreement by other countries to remove "unfair" trade barriers. But that was not what it wanted in the long run. It was not trying to substitute floating for pegged rates; it was merely trying to eliminate the U.S. balance-of-payments deficit by forcing large changes in exchange rates before they were pegged again.

After months of hard bargaining, a meeting at the Smithsonian Institution in Washington agreed on an exchange-rate realignment. Several governments revalued their currencies in terms of the dollar, and the United States devalued the dollar in terms of gold (the price of gold was raised from $35 to $38 per ounce). The United States, however, did not reopen the gold window. In other words, the new official price of gold was the one at which the United States would *not* buy or sell.

The governments also agreed to undertake a thorough review of the monetary system, including the roles of the dollar, gold, and the SDR, to explore ways of achieving "a suitable degree" of exchange-rate flexibility, and to liberalize trade policies. The commitment to review the monetary system led to the creation of the Committee of Twenty, whose work is discussed later in this chapter. The commitment to liberalize trade policies led to the Tokyo Round of trade negotiations.

When examining the effects of a devaluation in Chapter 14, we noted that short-run price elasticities may be too low to satisfy the Marshall–Lerner–Robinson condition. In that case, the current account will trace out a J-shaped curve in response to a devaluation, getting worse before getting better. That is what happened after the Smithsonian realignment, and the problem was compounded by domestic policies; the U.S. economy was expanding too fast. But many observers interpreted the situation differently, saying that the realignment had been too small to eliminate the U.S. balance-of-payments deficit and recommending another devaluation. In the middle of

1972, moreover, Britain ran into balance-of-payments problems and the pound was allowed to float, triggering another bout of speculation—a large capital flow from dollars into marks and yen. The Smithsonian Agreement was crumbling and taking the Bretton Woods system with it.

The end came early in 1973, with the events listed at the top of Figure 19-3. The U.S. government decided to devalue the dollar again. One by one, however, the other industrial countries let their currencies float. Switzerland had done so two weeks before the American decision, on account of a huge capital inflow; Japan followed right after the decision; and six members of the EEC, including France and Germany, did so jointly four weeks later.

FIGURE 19-3   Monetary Chronology Under Floating Exchange Rates

1973 Switzerland allows franc to float
United States announces 10 percent devaluation of the dollar
Japan allows yen to float
Six European countries allow their currencies to float jointly
Committee of Twenty issues outline for reform of monetary system
Oil "embargo" imposed with outbreak of Arab–Israeli war, oil prices rise, triggering first
large increase in OPEC oil prices
1974 France drops out of joint European float (snake)
United States ends controls on capital outflows and Germany relaxes controls on inflows
IMF establishes first oil facility
Committee of Twenty ends its work by proposing "evolutionary" reform of monetary
system
IMF shifts valuation of SDR from gold to "basket" of currencies
1975 France rejoins European snake
At Rambouillet summit meeting, major industrial countries agree to "legalize" floating
1976 At Kingston, Jamaica, IMF Interim Committee approves Second Amendment to IMF Articles
of Agreement, based on Rambouillet agreement
France drops out of European snake again
1977 Britain draws on IMF and obtains new credits from other governments to phase out
reserve-currency role of pound
Michael Blumenthal, U.S. secretary of the treasury, suggests that mark and yen might
appreciate against dollar
1978 Second Amendment to IMF Articles of Agreement enters into effect, "legalizing" the float
and reducing the role of gold
EEC countries agree to establish European Monetary System (EMS)
At Bonn summit meeting, Germany and Japan agree to stimulate their economies, and
United States agrees to deregulate oil prices
President Carter announces that United States will draw on IMF and intervene in defense
of dollar, and Federal Reserve tightens monetary policy
Unrest in Iran raises oil prices, triggering second large increase in OPEC prices
1979 IMF liberalizes access to resources
EMS comes into being
United States intervenes heavily to resist depreciation of the dollar
Paul Volcker, Federal Reserve chairman, announces sharp tightening of U.S. monetary policy and introduction of money-growth targets
1980 Germany and Japan borrow from OPEC countries to finance current-account deficits
United States intervenes to resist appreciation of dollar

1981 IMF adopts "enlarged access" policy, affirming 1979 liberalization, and borrows from
        Saudi Arabia to augment resources
      United States announces that it will no longer intervene to influence exchange rates
      Poland begins to experience severe debt problems
1982 Mexico asks commerical banks to reschedule its debts, gets "bridge loans" from United
        States and BIS, and applies for IMF drawing
      Brazil follows Mexico
1983 Debt problems spread as more than 25 countries seek to reschedule debts to banks ex-
        ceeding $65 billion
      IMF quotas raised by 50 percent to nearly $100 billion, and GAB enlarged and liberalized
      OPEC countries adopt output quotas as oil prices fall
1984 IMF begins to curtail "enlarged access" to resources
      Mexico and commercial banks agree on multiyear rescheduling involving almost $50 bil-
        lion of debt
      United States runs record budget and trade deficits and dollar appreciates sharply
1985 Dollar starts to depreciate
      In Plaza agreement, G-5 governments endorse and pledge to promote further depreciation
      United States resumes intervention
      James Baker, U.S. secretary of the treasury, calls for "adjustment with growth" by debtor
        countries and more lending by World Bank and commercial banks
1986 At Tokyo summit meeting, major industrial countries agree to "multilateral surveillance" of
        macroeconomic policies
      Commercial Banks pledge to lend Mexico $6 billion and lengthen previously rescheduled
        debt
      Central banks buy dollars to resist further depreciation
1987 Brazil suspends interest payments on debt
      In Louvre agreement, G-5 countries endorse and pledge to stabilize existing exchange rates
      Central banks intervene massively to support dollar
      Prices fall sharply on world stock markets and dollar starts to depreciate again

Source: Solomon, *The International Monetary System,* pp. 391–398, and International Monetary Fund, *IMF Survey* (various issues).

MONETARY RELATIONS UNDER FLOATING EXCHANGE RATES

Some central bankers say that they favored floating exchange rates before 1973 but could not convince governments to adopt them. In 1973, however, most said that the float should be temporary. In fact, the Committee of Twenty was instructed to design a system of "stable but adjustable" exchange rates, something like the Bretton Woods regime but with more flexibility in the pegs to improve balance-of-payments adjustment. But exchange rates never seemed quite ripe for pegging, and the temporary float continued. Eventually, the IMF Articles of Agreement were revised to "legalize" the float.

Trying to Put Humpty-Dumpty Together

The Committee of Twenty represented the whole membership of the IMF and, therefore, a wide range of interests and concerns. Nevertheless, its work was dominated by differences in view between the European and American participants. Both sides wanted to construct a more "symmetrical" system but used that term to stand for very different objectives.

The Americans wanted a more symmetrical adjustment process, in which surplus countries as well as deficit countries would work to eliminate imbalances. They also wanted to make sure that the United States would be free to alter its exchange rate without having to disrupt the monetary system, as in 1971. They suggested that an "objective indicator" be used to signal the need for balance-of-payments adjustment. When a country's reserves were lower than some critical level, it would be expected to tighten its domestic policies or devalue its currency. When its reserves were higher than some critical level, it would be expected to ease its policies or revalue its currency. Governments that failed to meet these expectations might be penalized in various ways.

The Europeans wanted a more symmetrical system of settlements, to prevent the United States from financing a balance-of-payments deficit by piling up dollar debt and thus postponing action to eliminate its deficit. Countries should run down reserves when they have payments deficits, and no country should accumulate another's currency as a reserve asset. They also asked the United States to redeem gradually the dollar balances that had already been built up. They suggested that those balances be handed over to the IMF in exchange for SDRs and that the United States should redeem them from the IMF at a rate dependent on its own balance-of-payments situation.

The Committee of Twenty might perhaps have reached agreement if the Americans and Europeans had put their plans together. The United States might have

agreed to reserve-asset settlement if the Europeans had agreed to use an objective indicator and thus participate more fully in correcting future balance-of-payments problems. But each side had reservations about the other's proposals. The Americans insisted that the dollar's role as a reserve currency had been a burden on the United States rather than a privilege, but they did not want to phase it out completely. They were especially reluctant to promise that the United States would redeem other countries' dollar holdings, which were about six times as large as U.S. reserves. The Europeans did not trust an objective indicator to trigger policy changes, because it might give false signals. (Ironically, they have since adopted an objective indicator in the European Monetary System, where movements in exchange rates rather than reserves have been used to trigger consultations concerning national policies.)

The work of the committee, however, was overtaken by events—the "oil shock" of 1973 and the problems it produced—and governments concluded that floating rates were here to stay. In November 1975, when the major industrial countries held their first economic summit meeting at Rambouillet, near Paris, they agreed to legitimize floating rates by amending the Articles of Agreement of the IMF. The Interim Committee of the IMF, its senior policymaking body, worked out the details in Kingston, Jamaica, and the Second Amendment to the Articles of Agreement came into force in 1978. It gave governments wide latitude in choosing exchange-rate arrangements but instructed the IMF to exercise "firm surveillance" over its members' exchange-rate policies. It did not rule out an eventual return to pegged exchange rates but set down preconditions which made that unlikely. Figure 19-4 reproduces key clauses from Article IV, which define the obligations of member

Article IV
Obligations Regarding Exchange Arrangements
Section 1.   *General obligations of members*

Recognizing that the essential purpose of the international monetary system is to provide a framework that facilitates the exchange of goods, services, and capital among countries, and that sustains sound economic growth, and that a principal objective is the continuing development of the orderly underlying conditions that are necessary for financial and economic stability, each member undertakes to collaborate with the Fund to assure orderly exchange arrangements and to promote a stable system of exchange rates . . .

Section 2.   *General exchange arrangements*

(a) Each member shall notify the Fund . . . of the exchange arrangements it intends to apply in fulfillment of its obligations under Section 1 of this Article, and shall notify the Fund promptly of any changes in its exchange arrangements.
(b) Under an international monetary system of the kind prevailing on January 1, 1976, exchange arrangements may include (i) the maintenance by a member of a value for its currency in terms of the special drawing right or another denominator, other than gold, selected by the member, or (ii) cooperative arrangements by which members maintain the value of their currencies in relation to the value of the currency or currencies of other members, or (iii) other exchange arrangements of a member's choice . . .

Section 3.   *Surveillance over exchange arrangements*

(a) The Fund shall oversee the international monetary system in order to ensure its effective operation, and shall oversee the compliance of each member with its obligations under Section 1 of this Article.
(b) In order to fulfill its functions under (a) above, the Fund shall exercise firm surveillance over the exchange rate policies of members, and shall adopt specific principles for the guidance of all members with respect to those policies. Each member shall provide the Fund with the information necessary for such surveillance, and, when requested by the Fund, shall consult with it on the member's exchange rate policies . . .

FIGURE 19-4   Extract from the Second Amendment to the IMF Articles of Agreement

governments and the responsibilities of the IMF.[10]

To carry out those responsibilities, the IMF adopted guidelines for exchange-rate management. Governments should inter-

[10] The reference there to "cooperative arrangements" was meant to cover the joint float of European currencies, which has since been superseded by the European Monetary System, described later in this chapter.

vene in foreign-exchange markets to counter "disorderly" conditions but should not attempt to maintain unrealistic rates. To spot such situations, the IMF looks out for sustained one-way movements in a country's reserves, large amounts of official borrowing or lending for balance-of-payments purposes, the introduction or intensification of direct controls on trade or capital movements, and the behavior of the exchange rate itself. But the IMF has no power to penalize governments that violate the guidelines.

The First Oil Shock

If a single event can take credit or blame for the decision to accept floating rates, it must be the increase in the price of oil that started in 1973. War broke out between Egypt and Israel in October, and Arab oil producers, such as Saudi Arabia, announced an "embargo" on sales to the Netherlands and United States, which maintained close relations with Israel. Prices rose sharply as oil companies bid for available supplies to serve their Dutch and American markets and build up their inventories. In December, the Organization of Oil Exporting Countries (OPEC), whose membership included Indonesia, Iran, Nigeria, and Venezuela, as well as Arab countries, looked at the high market prices and decided that the world could afford to pay them. They raised their contract prices, those at which they sell to large oil companies, from less than $3 per barrel to more than $9 per barrel.

The increase in oil prices had three large effects on the international economy. They show up clearly in Table 19-2, which describes internal developments in the seven "summit" countries (Canada, France, Germany, Italy, Japan, the United Kingdom, and the United States), and in Table 19-3, which describes the evolution of current-account balances.

First, it raised the prices of all goods that are made from oil, from gasoline to plastics, and the price increase spread quickly to other goods and services as wage rates rose to compensate for higher costs of living. Inflation rates were already high, and the increase in oil prices made them even higher. In Japan, for example, the inflation rate was close to 12 percent in 1973, twice what it had been in the previous decade, but rose to more than 24 percent in 1974.

Second, it reduced economic activity in the oil-importing industrial countries, acting much like an increase in taxes. Some of the oil-exporting countries, such as Saudi Arabia, could not spend their huge revenues immediately. As a result, they ran large trade surpluses which reduced aggregate demand in the oil-importing countries. Furthermore, some industrial countries adopted restrictive economic policies to combat the domestic price increases resulting from higher oil prices. For both reasons, their economies slipped into a deep recession. In the United States, for instance, gross national product had risen by 5.8 percent in 1973 but fell by 0.6 percent in 1974 and by another 1.2 percent in 1975. Unemployment climbed from an average of 4.9 percent in 1973 to an average of 8.5 percent in 1975.

Third, it drove the oil-importing countries into current-account deficits (which were, of course, the counterparts of the exporters' surpluses). In 1973, the industrial countries had run current-account surpluses totaling $20 billion. In 1974, they ran deficits totaling almost $11 billion. The less-developed countries were hit even harder. They usually run current-account deficits and cover them by borrowing and aid. In 1973, countries that were not major exporters of oil ran current-account deficits totaling about $11 billion. These widened to $37 billion in 1974, and grew to $46 billion in 1975, when the recession in industrial countries reduced the demand for the exports of the less-developed countries. The problems of those countries are summarized in Table 19-4, which shows that their exports rose rapidly in 1973 but fell in 1974 and 1975.

Countries that confront current-account deficits are usually expected to deflate or devalue. But that was not done. Deliberate cuts in aggregate demand would have reduced oil imports and, to that extent, reduced the current-account surpluses of the

TABLE 19-2   Economic Indicators for the Seven Economic Summit Countries, 1963–1987 (percentages)

Indicator	Average 1963–1972	1973	1974	1975	1976	1977
Change in real output[b]						
Seven summit countries	4.7	6.2	0.1	−0.7	5.3	4.4
United States	4.0	5.8	−0.6	−1.2	5.4	5.5
Germany	4.5	4.6	0.5	−1.6	5.6	2.8
Japan	10.5	8.8	−1.2	2.4	5.3	5.3
Inflation rate[c]						
Seven summit countries	3.7	7.5	13.2	11.0	7.9	7.9
United States	3.3	6.2	11.0	9.1	5.8	6.5
Germany	3.2	7.0	7.0	5.9	4.3	3.7
Japan	5.6	11.8	24.4	11.8	9.3	8.0
Unemployment rate[d]						
Seven summit countries	3.2	3.4	3.8	5.5	5.4	5.4
United States	4.7	4.9	5.6	8.5	7.7	7.0
Germany	0.9	1.1	2.3	4.1	4.0	3.9
Japan	1.2	1.2	1.4	1.9	2.0	2.0

Source: International Monetary Fund, *World Economic Outlook,* various issues.

[a] Estimated.

[b] Measured by change in gross national product or gross domestic product; the dollar value of each country's gross national product is used as its weight.

TABLE 19-3   Balances on Current Account, 1973–1987 (billions of U.S. dollars)

Country Group	1973	1974	1975	1976	1977	1978	1979
Industrial countries	20.3	−10.8	19.8	0.5	−2.2	31.9	−4.8
United States	9.1	7.6	21.2	7.5	−11.7	−12.3	2.5
Germany	7.0	13.0	7.6	7.7	8.5	13.4	−0.7
Japan	0.1	−4.5	−0.4	3.9	11.3	16.9	−7.9
Major oil exporters[b]	6.7	68.3	35.4	40.3	29.4	5.7	61.9
Other less-developed countries	−11.3	−37.0	−46.3	−32.6	−29.6	−41.9	−62.0
Total[c]	15.7	20.5	8.9	8.2	−2.4	−4.3	−4.9

Source: International Monetary Fund, *World Economic Outlook,* various issues; balances exclude official transfers.

[a] Estimated.

[b] Includes Algeria, Indonesia, Iran, Iraq, Kuwait, Libya, Nigeria, Oman, Qatar, Saudi Arabia, United Arab Emirates, and Venezuela.

頁

1978	1979	1980	1981	1982	1983	1984	1985	1986	1987[a]
4.5	3.4	1.1	1.6	−0.6	2.8	5.0	3.0	2.5	2.4
5.0	2.5	−0.2	1.9	−2.5	3.6	6.4	2.7	2.5	2.3
3.4	4.0	1.5	—	−1.0	1.8	3.0	2.5	2.4	1.9
5.1	5.3	4.3	3.7	3.1	3.2	5.1	4.7	2.5	2.7
6.9	9.3	12.0	9.9	7.0	4.4	4.4	3.8	1.9	2.6
7.6	11.3	13.5	10.4	6.1	3.2	4.3	3.6	1.9	3.4
2.7	4.1	5.4	6.3	5.3	3.3	2.4	2.2	−0.3	0.7
3.8	3.7	7.7	4.9	2.7	1.9	2.3	2.0	0.6	0.1
5.1	5.0	5.6	6.5	8.0	8.2	7.5	7.4	7.3	7.3
6.1	5.9	7.2	7.6	9.7	9.6	7.5	7.2	7.0	6.7
3.8	3.3	3.4	4.9	6.8	8.2	8.1	8.2	7.9	7.8
2.2	2.1	2.0	2.2	2.4	2.7	2.7	2.6	2.8	3.1

[c] Measured by change in index of consumer prices; the dollar value of each country's gross national product is used as its weight.

[d] Because countries use different definitions of unemployment, these rates are not strictly comparable across countries; each country's labor force is used as its weight.

1980	1981	1982	1983	1984	1985	1986	1987[a]
−40.7	0.9	0.5	−0.6	−37.6	−27.6	21.6	20.1
6.8	10.8	−3.6	−40.3	−98.0	−106.5	−128.8	−128.0
−9.1	0.8	10.2	10.1	13.4	19.5	43.7	47.0
−9.4	6.2	8.2	22.2	36.4	50.6	87.8	84.5
110.9	56.2	−4.8	−17.4	−4.3	6.4	−27.4	−14.4
−86.2	−111.9	−90.7	−56.3	−40.9	−43.9	−34.5	−41.6
−16.0	−54.8	−95.0	−74.3	−82.8	−65.1	−40.3	−35.9

[c] Reflects balances of countries not shown above (mainly the Soviet Union, countries in Eastern Europe, and China before 1977), as well as errors and asymmetries in the data; the increase in this number appears to be due to the growth of trade in services and of private transfers (payments appear to be reported more completely than the corresponding receipts).

TABLE 19-4   Economic Indicators for the Less-Developed Countries, Except Major
Oil Exporters, 1963–1987 (percentages)

Indicator	Average 1963–1972	1973	1974	1975	1976	1977
Change in real output[b]	6.0[c]	6.1	5.4	3.3	6.0	5.6
Inflation rate[d]	9.1[c]	21.9	28.5	27.6	27.3	27.7
Change in export volume	6.7	9.3	0.1	0.3	11.3	4.5
Change in terms of trade	0.3	5.3	−5.9	−8.5	5.9	6.3

OPEC countries. For the most part, however, they would have cut back imports of other goods and services, enlarging the deficits of other oil-importing countries. This sort of redistribution occurred in 1975, when the recession in the industrial countries eliminated their current-account deficits but increased those of the less-developed countries. There was a strong case for financing rather than adjustment, and that is what was done.

Some of the financing took place through the IMF. Many countries made large drawings in the ordinary way, but they also drew on special oil facilities established with money that the IMF borrowed from OPEC countries and a small number of industrial countries. As rapid adjustment was risky under the circumstances, the IMF did not impose strict policy conditions on most of the countries that used Fund credit. (It allowed them to draw on the oil facilities as well as the regular currency pool, so their drawings did not take them into the upper credit tranches, where strict conditionality is usually applied.)

Most of the financing, however, took place through a different channel. Unable to spend their large revenues quickly, OPEC countries were depositing huge sums with commercial banks. The banks were "recycling" the deposits by making large loans to governments and public-sector companies. At first, they lent mainly to developed countries such as Great Britain and Italy (which also drew on the IMF).

But they soon started lending to less-developed countries, and Table 19-5 shows how rapidly their lending grew. At the end of 1973, on the eve of the first oil shock, the less-developed countries owed $130 billion to all creditors together, and their debts to banks were about $17 billion. Three years later, their debts totaled $228 billion, and their debts to banks were $49 billion.

The Years of Dollar Weakness

In the first few months of floating, the dollar depreciated against most major currencies. Look at Figure 19-5, which shows the dollar-mark rate. The Smithsonian Agreement had pegged it at $0.31 per mark, where it stayed until the float began. By the middle of 1973, however, the mark was worth $0.41, and it stayed in that neighborhood until the first oil shock, when the dollar began to appreciate vis-à-vis the mark and yen. (Although the United States was the prime target of the Arab "embargo," it was believed to be less vulnerable to the increase in oil prices than countries such as Germany and Japan, which have no oil of their own, and the appreciation of the dollar reflected that belief.) Rates wobbled up and down thereafter, showing sharper short-term fluctuations than had been anticipated. In 1977, however, the dollar began to weaken.

The U.S. economy had recovered rather slowly from the recession of 1974–1975 but

1978	1979	1980	1981	1982	1983	1984	1985	1986	1987[a]
6.3	4.8	4.8	3.1	2.2	2.2	5.2	4.3	4.6	4.0
20.8	24.7	31.6	30.6	30.9	43.2	50.5	54.7	36.1	37.1
9.5	6.5	8.2	5.7	1.7	8.3	11.2	4.2	7.0	3.9
−4.0	−0.2	−3.9	−3.8	−2.3	—	1.4	−1.1	−3.2	−2.7

Source: International Monetary Fund, *World Economic Outlook,* various issues.

[a] Estimated.

[b] Measured by change in gross domestic product; the dollar value of each country's gross domestic product is used as its weight.

[c] Average for 1968–1972.

[d] Measured by change in index of consumer prices; the dollar value of each country's gross domestic product is used as its weight.

more rapidly than the German and Japanese economies. Most governments were fearful of inflation and reluctant to ease fiscal and monetary policies sufficiently to foster rapid recovery. In fact, Washington called on Bonn and Tokyo to join with it in speeding up recovery. The three countries, it said, were the "locomotives" that could pull the world economy back to prosperity. The United States could not do it alone. But Germany and Japan were slow to respond.

The more rapid recovery of the U.S. economy was raising imports faster than exports, and price effects were working in the same direction. The previous appreciation of the dollar had weakened the competitive position of the United States, and American prices were rising faster than German or Japanese prices. Therefore, the United States began to run a current account deficit in 1977. The dollar did not start to depreciate sharply, however, until the second half of the year, when capital inflows fell as foreign-exchange markets came to believe that Washington *wanted* the dollar to depreciate. At a press conference in Paris, the secretary of the treasury,

TABLE 19-5   Debts of Less-Developed Countries, Except Major Oil Exporters, 1973–1987[a] (billions of dollars)

Item	1973	1976	1979	1982	1985	1987[a]
Total debt outstanding	130.1	228.0	439.1	708.0	846.5	995.9
Short-term debt	18.4	33.2	75.0	147.1	127.2	129.0
Long-term debt	111.8	194.9	364.1	560.9	719.3	866.9
To official creditors	51.0	82.4	150.6	222.5	302.1	399.2
To commercial banks[b]	17.3	49.0	116.6	190.0	283.8	330.4
To other creditors[c]	43.5	63.5	96.9	147.6	133.4	137.3

Source: International Monetary Fund, *World Economic Outlook,* various issues.

[a] Estimated.

[b] Includes public and publicly guaranteed debt to banks and other financial institutions.

[c] Includes all unguaranteed debt.

FIGURE 19-5   Exchange Rate Between the U.S. Dollar and Deutsche Mark

This rate receives particular attention from governments and markets, along with the rate between the dollar and the yen. An increase denotes a depreciation of the dollar.

Source: International Monetary Fund, *International Financial Statistics* (various issues); market rates at end of quarter.

Michael Blumenthal, suggested that Germany and Japan might allow their currencies to appreciate more freely, not resist exchange-rate movements, because those countries had large current-account surpluses. He was not trying to "talk down" the dollar, but that is how markets interpreted his comments.

The dollar continued to weaken early in 1978, despite intervention by the U.S., German, and Japanese authorities and a modest tightening of U.S. monetary policy. In July, at the Bonn economic summit, the United States agreed to decontrol domestic oil prices and take stronger measures against inflation in return for promises by Germany and Japan to be better "locomotives" and stimulate their own economies. But financial markets did not have much faith in the economic policies of the Carter administration, and the measures it took to combat inflation did not restore confidence. The depreciation of the dollar was not arrested until November, when the Federal

Reserve tightened monetary policy more severely and the United States mobilized $30 billion of reserves by drawing on bilateral credit lines and the IMF and selling bonds denominated in Deutsche mark and Swiss franc. The U.S. authorities used those reserves to intervene on a larger scale than before, and markets were impressed. The dollar rose sharply.

The improvement was brief, however, because bad news kept on coming in. Inflation continued to accelerate in the United States, and unrest in Iran was raising oil prices. (By this time, moreover. higher oil prices were seen as injurious to the United States, because it had adjusted its internal oil prices more slowly than most other countries.) The new weakness of the dollar was not ended until a dramatic tightening of monetary policy in October 1979. The chairman of the Federal Reserve Board, Paul Volcker, flew back from an IMF meeting in Belgrade to announce an increase in the discount rate to 12 percent and a major modification in the conduct of monetary policy. It would no longer focus on interest-rate levels but would instead be guided by money-supply targets. American interest rates rose rapidly, and the dollar began to appreciate under the influence of a capital inflow.

Two More Attempts at Reform

The weakness of the dollar in 1977–1979 inspired two new attempts to improve the monetary system. One failed. The other succeeded.

When Robert Triffin proposed the conversion of the IMF into a global central bank, he suggested that governments should sell dollar balances to the IMF in exchange for its new currency. A similar suggestion was made during discussions in the Committee of Twenty, involving the conversion of dollar balances into SDRs. In 1978, the managing director of the IMF revived the idea, hoping to give the SDR a more important role, and the United States was interested for reasons of its own.

Soon after exchange rates started to float, governments and central banks began to diversify their currency reserves. They sold dollars in exchange for marks, yen, and other currencies. The German and Japanese governments tried to discourage diversification into their currencies; they did not want them to become reserve currencies. (Britain had already tried to liquidate the reserve role of sterling.) But they could not do much to halt the process. If a foreign government could not deposit marks with German banks, it could go to banks in London, Paris, or Zurich, which were glad to take them. The United States was also worried about diversification, believing that it was helping to weaken the dollar, and began to support the creation of a *substitution account* under IMF management, in which governments could deposit unwanted dollars in exchange for claims denominated in SDRs. Because the SDR is defined in terms of a basket of currencies, it is by itself diversified, and the availability of a substitution account might thus halt dollar sales by official holders.

At the IMF meeting in Belgrade, governments agreed in principle that the benefits and costs of any such account should be shared between the United States and the countries depositing dollars. When it came to deciding how that should be done, however, the agreement broke down. Potential depositors asked the United States to guarantee the SDR value of the dollars they would be depositing with the account. The United States declined, favoring instead the use of gold held by the IMF. By that time, moreover, the dollar was getting stronger, and governments were losing interest in the whole idea; they wanted to keep their dollars, not turn them in for SDRs. The plan was dropped.

The successful innovation was the creation of the European Monetary System (EMS) in 1979. For many years, Europeans had talked about forming a monetary union to complement their customs union. Six of them had taken a major step in 1973, when they allowed their currencies to float jointly against the dollar. The joint float was called the "snake" because it looked like one. Its girth was determined by the narrow margins within which exchange rates between participating currencies were allowed to fluctuate. The wigglings of the snake were caused by the joint float against the dollar. (Britain and Italy did not participate in the joint float, and France participated intermittently.)

France and Germany proposed a more formal arrangement in 1978, and it came into effect in 1979. It is modeled on the Bretton Woods system, but it has its own currency unit and uses an objective indicator to signal the need for balance-of-payments adjustment. The European Currency Unit (ECU) is defined in terms of a basket of currencies, much like the SDR. But the currencies are European; the dollar has been left out.[11]

Each EMS member agrees to fix the value of its currency in terms of the ECU, which produces a system of pegged exchange rates among the members' currencies. The pegged rates can be changed by devaluations or revaluations in relation to the ECU, and there have been a number of these realignments since 1979, some involving several currencies at once. Anticipations of exchange-rate realignments have produced speculative capital flows, as in the days of the Bretton Woods system, but these have been less disruptive, and

the European governments have resisted the temptation to defend exchange rates rigidly.

The success of the EMS has led some economists to reconsider their earlier doubts about pegged-rate systems—to ask if such a system could be established among a larger group of currencies, including the dollar and yen, as well as the mark, without inviting governments to make the mistakes that wrecked the Bretton Woods system. But the EMS has special features that would be hard to duplicate in a wider system. First, it is a creature of the European Community, which fosters political cohesion and a sense of collective responsibility for the success of the EMS and encourages its members to coordinate their monetary policies. Second, two important members, France and Italy, have used capital controls to limit speculation against their currencies. Third, exchange-rate realignments have been fairly small, partly because it has been possible to make them frequently, and small changes tend to provoke less speculation than large changes.[12] Finally, each member is entitled to borrow an unlimited quantity of the other members' currencies to finance intervention on the foreign-exchange market. It cannot be forced to devalue its currency because of a run on its reserves. It would be particularly difficult to reproduce this open-ended credit arrangement among a group of countries that included the United States, which was criticized in the 1960s for exploiting the special role of the dollar to finance its balance-of-payments deficits and has been criticized again in the 1980s for the same sort of offense.

---

[11] A European Monetary Fund was to give balance-of-payments credit to EMS countries and evolve eventually into a central bank for the European Community. It has not been established, however, and Britain has not even joined the exchange-rate arrangements of the EMS.

[12] There are two reasons: (1) Prospective profits are small when rate changes are small. (2) Actual rate changes are unpredictable when realignments are small, because the new and old bands containing the exchange rate can overlap, and a devaluation does not force the actual rate to change.

The Second Oil Shock
and the Onset of Debt Problems

The second oil shock started like the first, with political turmoil in the Middle East, and had similar effects on the world economy. Its long-run consequences, however, may turn out to be more serious.

The price of oil started to rise at the end of 1978, when the Iranian revolution disrupted that country's oil exports. Oil companies began again to scramble for supplies, and contract prices followed market prices, just as before. The average OPEC price rose from just under $13 per barrel in mid-1978 to almost $32 per barrel in mid-1980. The OPEC countries ran a huge current-account surplus, which reached $111 billion in 1980, and other countries ran huge current-account deficits. Inflation rates rose, but not as sharply as they did in the wake of the first oil shock, partly because many governments adopted sterner policies. The tightening of U.S. monetary policy in 1979 was the most dramatic instance. Those stern policies, however, produced a recession deeper and longer than in 1974–1975. In the United States, for example, the unemployment rate rose from an average 5.9 percent in 1979 to an average of 9.7 percent in 1982.

After the first oil shock, it took about five years for the OPEC surplus to disappear. After the second shock, it disappeared more rapidly. In fact, the OPEC countries were in current-account deficit by 1982, because of a sharp fall in their oil revenues. The worldwide recession had reduced the demand for OPEC oil and so had the high price of oil itself. Two price effects were working to reduce it. First, high prices were encouraging conservation. Second, they were encouraging production by countries outside OPEC, such as Mexico. But the less-developed countries continued to run large current-account deficits, and a new problem began to emerge.

Bank lending to the less-developed countries did not drop when the effects of the first oil shock wore off. Look back at Table 19-5, which shows that bank loans outstanding were more than twice as large at the end of 1979 than at the end of 1976. Some of the borrowing was used for capital formation, especially by public-sector companies; some was used to subsidize consumption. Looking at the matter from a balance-of-payments standpoint, some was used to cover current-account deficits and some to build up reserves. Lending got even larger in subsequent years, when current-account deficits were widened by higher oil prices. By the end of 1982, the total debts of less-developed countries, excluding those of OPEC countries, amounted to more than $708 billion.

The sheer size of the debt was not the main reason for concern, because no one expected it to be paid off quickly. (The United States was a large borrower in the nineteenth century and did not repay its debts completely until World War I.) Concerns arose because the debts were getting more burdensome.

Look at Table 19-6. When large borrowing began in 1973, the debts of less-developed countries, taken together, were not much bigger than their exports and amounted to about 20 percent of their gross domestic products. Furthermore, debt-service payments, including amortization payments, amounted to only 16 percent of the countries' current-account earnings. There were, of course, large differences among countries, with the figures for the countries of the Western Hemisphere exceeding those for others. From 1973 through 1979, most of the numbers got bigger, but not very rapidly. The borrowers' economies were growing along with their debts, and their export earnings were rising almost as rapidly as their debt-service payments. From 1979 to 1982, however, the numbers grew faster, partly because of

TABLE 19-6   Perspectives on the Debts of Less-Developed Countries, 1973–1987

Item	1973[a]	1979	1982	1985	1987[b]
Total external debt as a percentage of exports of goods and services					
Africa	71.5	107.1	153.8	181.0	227.7
Asia	92.9	75.7	88.4	100.0	100.0
Western Hemisphere	176.2	197.7	273.8	295.5	367.6
Total external debt as a percentage of gross domestic product					
Africa	19.4	30.6	37.5	44.9	54.4
Asia	19.7	16.7	22.1	27.2	31.7
Western Hemisphere	23.0	32.2	42.9	46.8	49.8
Debt service payments as a percentage of exports of goods and services					
Africa	8.8	15.3	22.1	28.7	27.0
Asia	9.6	9.4	11.9	12.9	11.2
Western Hemisphere	29.3	39.6	51.0	38.7	44.9
All countries[c]	15.9	14.1	19.5	20.5	20.7
Interest component	6.1	6.0	11.4	11.5	10.1
Amortization component[d]	9.8	8.1	9.1	9.0	10.6

Source: International Monetary Fund, *World Economic Outlook,* various issues.

[a]Excludes major oil exporters.

[b]Estimated.

[c]Includes countries in Europe and the Middle East now shown separately.

[d]Long-term debt only.

the further increase in debt, but largely because of a change in international conditions.

Interest rates rose to very high levels in international capital markets, because of a big increase in U.S. interest rates. Furthermore, the debtors' export earnings were reduced by the worldwide recession. Look back at Table 19-4, which shows that their exports grew by less than 2 percent in 1982 and that their terms of trade deteriorated for the fifth consecutive year. By 1982, debt-service payments were about 24 percent of exports, thanks mainly to the increase in the interest component. In fact, some countries had to pay more in interest on their old loans than they could raise by floating new loans, and that is an unsustainable situation.

The first major debt crisis took place in 1981, when Poland could not meet its obligations and asked its creditors to *reschedule* maturing debts—to turn them into longer-term obligations. The second crisis took place in 1982, when Mexico had to make a similar request, followed months later by Brazil, Argentina, and several other countries.

The problems of Poland led to deep concerns in Europe, because European banks held most of the claims on Poland. (Discussions in Washington concentrated on the political dimensions. Some members of the Reagan administration thought that Poland's creditors should refuse to reschedule its debts because the Polish government had imposed martial law and banned Solidarity, the independent trade union.) The problems of Mexico and Brazil led to deep concerns in the United States, because American banks were heavily involved. A small number of countries account for most of the banks' claims on less-developed countries, with Mexico and Brazil being the biggest debtors, and Table 19-7 shows that American banks have huge claims on the most heavily indebted countries. In 1982, indeed, the claims of the large American banks on the largest debtors were twice as big as the banks' own capital. The banks would have been insolvent if they had been compelled to write off their claims. In fact, they would have been in very serious trouble if either one of the two largest debtors had walked away from its obligations.

The Mexican crisis broke out in August 1982. The Mexican government suspended payments due to banks in 1983, pending an agreement to reschedule those payments, and started discussions with the IMF about the policies that Mexico would have to follow to qualify for a large drawing. These announcements halted all new lending to Mexico and threatened to undermine confidence in banks that had large claims on Mexico. Therefore, the U.S. government and the Bank for International Settlements (BIS) moved promptly to provide the Mexican government with short-term credit. In November, moreover, the managing director of the IMF asked the banks to make new loans to Mexico. On many previous occasions, IMF assistance had set a "seal of approval" on a country's policies and thus unlocked new lending by private institutions. This time, the IMF was asking banks to act in tandem with it.

The subsequent negotiations were com-

TABLE 19-7   Exposure of U.S. Banks to Debts of Less-Developed Countries, 1982 and 1986 (billions of dollars)

	ALL U.S. BANKS		NINE LARGE BANKS	
	1982	1986	1982	1986
Exposure in billions of dollars				
All less-developed countries	125	113	78	74
Fifteen major debtors[a]	90	87	54	57
Bank capital	66	111	27	44
Exposure as percentage of capital				
All less-developed countries	189	102	287	167
Fifteen major debtors[a]	136	79	201	129
Argentina	13	8	21	14
Brazil	31	21	46	36
Mexico	38	22	50	31
Venezuela	16	9	26	15

Source: Federal Financial Institutions Examination Council, *Quarterly Country Exposure Reports,* various issues; data for end of June.

[a]Argentina, Bolivia, Brazil, Chile, Colombia, Ecuador, Ivory Coast, Mexico, Morocco, Nigeria, Peru, Philippines, Uruguay, Venezuela, and Yugoslavia.

plicated, because hundreds of banks were involved and Mexico was in the midst of changing governments. In December, the IMF approved the "letter of intent" in which Mexico set forth the policies that it would follow to bring down inflation and reduce its balance-of-payments deficit. The IMF authorized a large three-year drawing. Several months later, the banks agreed to lend Mexico about $5 billion of new money, so that it could make its interest payments, and to stretch out the repayment of old debt due in 1983. By that time, however, many other countries had run into problems, including Brazil, Argentina, and some OPEC countries such as Nigeria, and each had to go through a similar process. Fortunately, governments agreed to speed up the next increase in IMF quotas, which was completed at the end of 1983 and gave the IMF enough money to satisfy the enormous demand for Fund credit.

It was widely thought at first that the debt crisis would end quickly. Interest rates would fall, and the world economy would recover from the global recession, raising the debtors' exports and their export prices. They would be able to meet their obligations without having to extract "involuntary" lending from the banks. By following domestic policies approved by the IMF, moreover, the debtors would stabilize their own economies, restore their creditworthiness, and attract voluntary lending. It made sense, then, for the debtors to go more deeply into debt, by drawing on the IMF and borrowing from commercial banks, to deal with the temporary crisis.

Most of the debtors *were* able to reduce their current-account deficits. (They had no choice, because they could not finance them.) But the domestic costs were very high. Growth rates and standards of living fell sharply, and unemployment rose. Furthermore, the largest debtors were unsuccessful in their efforts to control inflation. Their governments could no longer borrow freely from foreign banks and had to cover their large budget deficits by printing money. Time after time, the IMF was compelled to declare that the debtors had failed to meet the performance targets set out in their agreements with the Fund, and new policy packages had to be negotiated. In the process, the debtors grew increasingly hostile to the IMF, and some of them refused to have further dealings with it. This meant, in turn, that they could not negotiate with the commercial banks, which insisted that a government's policies have IMF approval before they would reschedule its debts or give it additional credit. To make matters worse, the world economy was growing rather slowly, and the debtors' export earnings were not rising as rapidly as expected.

Although events were challenging the economic forecasts on which the initial response to the crisis had been based, there did not seem to be any practical alternative. Special efforts were made to help the poorest debtors, especially in Africa, and the banks agreed to longer maturities and slightly lower interest rates when they made new agreements with the middle-income debtors. In 1984, for example, they agreed to a multiyear rescheduling of almost $50 billion in Mexican debt and stretched out some of it for more than 10 years. In 1986, they lengthened some of the same debt to 20 years and lent Mexico an additional $6 billion as part of a $12 billion package involving the IMF and the World Bank.

At the IMF meetings in 1985, the U.S. secretary of the treasury, James Baker, called for a change in emphasis. The debtors should continue to work closely with the IMF in an effort to achieve domestic stability but should also adopt economic reforms to foster "adjustment with growth" in the long run. The commercial banks should support those reforms by additional lending in collaboration with the World

Bank and other official institutions. But the Mexican agreement of 1986 was the only dramatic response. Elsewhere, the situation was becoming more worrisome. In 1986, Peru limited its interest payments to 10 percent of its export earnings. In 1987, Brazil suspended all of its interest payments until the commercial banks would agree to more favorable terms. Soon thereafter, most of the large American banks set aside additional reserves against the possibility that they might suffer losses on their foreign loans. It was commonly acknowledged that the debt problem would last for a long time.

The Years of Dollar Strength

The sharp increase in American interest rates, which was partly responsible for the debt crisis, also ushered in the years of the strong dollar. Look back at Figure 19-5, which shows that the dollar appreciated sharply in 1980 and continued to appreciate until 1985. But fiscal policy took over from monetary policy as the principal cause of the appreciation.

During his campaign for the presidency in 1980, Ronald Reagan promised to raise defense spending, reduce taxes, and balance the budget. He kept the first two promises but could not keep the third, and we may never know how he expected to keep it.

Some of his advisers subscribed to an extravagant version of "supply-side economics," which said that tax cuts would transform economic behavior; firms would invest more, labor would work harder, and economic activity would rise rapidly enough to bring in more tax revenue. Other advisers subscribed to the more orthodox view that the prospect of large budget deficits would force Congress to cut nondefense spending and thus achieve one of their long-run objectives, a reduction in the size of government. But both were

wrong. The economy did grow strongly but not strongly enough to offset the large tax cuts (and its growth can be explained by conventional economics—the workings of the national-income multiplier). Congress did reduce nondefense spending but it could not cut it far enough to balance the budget. The budget deficit grew from $16 billion in 1979, the last year of the Carter administration, to a peak of $204 billion in 1986.[13]

The Fleming–Mundell model in Chapter 15 helps to explain what the budget deficit did to the dollar. As the government borrowed to cover its deficit, it put upward pressure on domestic interest rates, attracting the very large capital inflows shown in Table 19-1. The resulting increase in the demand for dollars raised the price of the dollar, and the expenditure-switching effects of this appreciation, combined with the increase in imports produced by faster economic growth, drove the current account into deficit.

To understand the process fully, however, we must amend the Fleming–Mundell model to allow for the sluggish behavior of the current account; it did not start to deteriorate as soon as the dollar began to appreciate in 1980, and it did not start to improve as soon as the dollar began to depreciate in 1985. Therefore, market forces had to adjust the size of the actual capital inflow to match the slowly moving current-account balance. What market forces were at work?

Recall one main point made in Chapter 16. Capital movements are governed by the open interest differential, which allows for the influence of expectations as well as the difference between national interest rates. A capital inflow too large to match the

---

[13] These are calendar-year figures, not fiscal-year figures, and are based on the definitions used in the national-income accounts, not those used in budget documents.

current-account balance could thus be limited by an expectation that the dollar would depreciate. It would reduce the open interest differential. To generate that expectation, however, the dollar had to appreciate sharply in the short run, by more than it could be expected to appreciate in the long run, in order to foster the belief that it would begin to depreciate. The dollar had to overshoot, and that is what happened.

The Reagan administration welcomed the strong dollar at first, as a vote of confidence in U.S. policies. With the passage of time, however, the current account moved into deficit, averaging about $76 billion in 1983–1984 and rising to about $129 billion in 1985–1986, a number more than half as large as the total value of U.S. merchandise exports.[14] Large sectors of the American economy experienced unprecedented foreign competition at home and abroad, with the usual result. Industry and labor demanded an aggressive trade policy—more protection from import competition and retaliation against "unfair" practices pursued by other countries. Washington began to view the strong dollar as a liability.

What Goes Up Must Come Down

In the early 1980s, governments and central banks were heavily influenced by the monetary interpretation of exchange-rate behavior. Exchange rates were determined by monetary policies and expectations about future monetary policies, and intervention could not have any lasting impact, apart from its effect on the money supply. In 1985, however, those same governments began to manage exchange rates intensively. They sought first to bring the dollar down, then to prop it up. It is hard

to assess their success, however, because the dollar began to depreciate before they tried to bring it down, and it continued to depreciate after they started to prop it up.

The attempt to bring the dollar down was organized by the United States. Like the earlier effort in 1971, it was meant in part to blunt protectionist pressures. In September 1985, the finance ministers of the G-5 (France, Germany, Japan, Britain, and the United States) issued a communique known as the Plaza agreement, named after the New York hotel at which they met. They said that foreign-exchange markets had not fully reflected recent shifts in "economic fundamentals" and policy objectives, including the commitment of the United States to reduce its budget deficit. In light of those shifts, they said, "some further orderly appreciation of the main non-dollar currencies against the dollar is desirable." Then came the key sentence. "They stand ready to cooperate more closely to encourage this when to do so would be helpful." To make their meaning perfectly clear, they started immediately to intervene, selling dollars for marks and yen.

The dollar continued to depreciate in 1986, and governments themselves began to disagree about the fundamentals. The appreciation of the yen was cutting into profits and production in Japan. Tokyo wanted to stabilize exchange rates. But the corresponding depreciation of the dollar had not halted the growth of the U.S. current-account deficit. Washington wanted the dollar to fall farther.

In October 1986, however, the two governments agreed that the yen-dollar rate should be stabilized for the time being, and in February 1987, the G-5 met in Paris and issued another communique, known as the Louvre agreement. A portion of the text is reproduced in Figure 19-6, but other important parts of the agreement cannot be reproduced because they were not writ-

---

[14] These figures come from Table 19-1 and include official transfers; the smaller numbers in Table 19-3 exclude such transfers.

The Louvre Agreement

The Ministers and Governors were of the view that further progress had been made since the Tokyo Summit in their efforts to achieve sustainable, non-inflationary expansion. Their national economies are now in the fifth year of expansion, . . . although the level of unemployment remains unacceptably high in some countries. A high degree of price stability has been attained, and there have been substantial reductions in interest rates. Exchange rate adjustments have occurred which will contribute importantly in the period ahead to the restoration of a more sustainable pattern of current accounts.

Progress is being made in reducing budget deficits in deficit countries, and . . . important structural reforms are also being carried forward, including deregulation of business to increase efficiency and privatization of government enterprises to strengthen reliance on . . . market forces.

These positive developments notwithstanding, the Ministers and Governors recognized that the large trade and current account imbalances posed serious economic and political risks. They agreed that the reduction of the large unsustainable trade imbalances was a matter of high priority, and that the achievement of more balanced growth should play a central role in bringing about such a reduction. . . .

[They] agreed to intensify their economic policy coordination efforts in order to promote more balanced global growth and to reduce external imbalances. Surplus countries committed themselves to following policies designed to strengthen domestic demand and to reducing their external surpluses while maintaining price stability. Deficit countries committed themselves to following policies designed to encourage steady, low-inflation growth while reducing their domestic imbalances and external deficits. . . .

The Ministers and Governors agreed that the substantial exchange rate changes since the Plaza Agreement will increasingly contribute to reducing external imbalances and have now brought their currencies within ranges broadly consistent with underlying economic fundamentals, given the policy commitments summarized in this statement. Further substantial exchange rate shifts among their currencies could damage growth and adjustment prospects in their countries. In current circumstances, therefore, they agreed to cooperate closely to foster stability of exchange rates around current levels.

FIGURE 19-6   Extract from the Louvre Agreement of February 1987

ten down. It is therefore difficult to know who "broke" the Louvre agreement eight months later, when everyone was looking for someone to blame for the sharp drop in stock markets and the further fall in the value of the dollar.

Some say that the rest of the Louvre agreement was rather vague; the governments agreed in principle to take unspecified measures in order to keep exchange rates within an unspecified range for an unspecified time. Others say that it was tighter, involving a firm commitment to stabilize exchange rates within narrow bands, and this interpretation became increasingly popular because of the subsequent behavior of markets and governments.

Exchange rates were stable for several months following the Louvre agreement, despite frequent warnings by many economists that the dollar had not fallen far enough to correct the U.S. current-account deficit. But this stability was due in part to massive official intervention. Official purchases of dollars were far larger than at any other time since the collapse of the Bretton Woods system. Furthermore, central banks were working together to keep U.S. interest rates higher than German and Japanese rates.

These arrangements started to unravel, however, early in the autumn of 1987. The current-account deficit was not shrinking, expectations of inflation were reviving, and markets began to believe that central banks would start to raise interest rates. Furthermore, stock markets appeared to be faltering after rising steeply in the first half of the year. Matters came to a head in mid-October, when a small increase in one key German interest rate was criticized by Washington as a violation of the Louvre agreement (because it would require higher U.S. interest rates to maintain existing differentials). Prices fell on Wall Street at the end of that week, and the pessimism was contagious. When trading resumed on the following Monday, stock prices fell sharply all over the world, wiping out a whole year's profits.

Central banks responded boldly by reducing interest rates and promising that credit would be readily available to forestall a further fall in stock prices. But the dollar began to depreciate again as governments started to quarrel in public, and traders predicted that it would go on falling until the United States had demonstrated clearly that it would reduce its budget deficit. And this was only part of the policy problem. Governments and markets began to worry about a global recession, expecting consumers to cut back their spending because of their stock-market losses, and noting that U.S. budget cuts would work in the same direction. A strong case could thus be made for preventing an increase of interest rates in the United States, but low U.S. rates would weaken the dollar unless foreign interest rates were held down too.

Washington looked for another solution and called for more expansionary fiscal policies in Japan and Germany to offset a more restrictive U.S. fiscal policy and minimize the risk of a recession. But the German authorities resisted, for economic and political reasons, even after the U.S. Congress had agreed on measures to reduce the U.S. deficit. The makings of a policy bargain were there, but it was hard to put together.

Floating Exchange Rates in Theory and Practice

Under the Bretton Woods system, governments tended to postpone balance-of-payments adjustment until speculation in foreign-exchange markets forced them to act. We have encountered several such instances, including the British attempt to postpone devaluation until 1967, the disagreement between France and Germany that postponed the devaluation of the franc until 1969, and the decade-long attempt of the United States to finance its balance-of-payments deficits by exploiting the reserve-currency role of the dollar. When governments acted, moreover, they did not always choose appropriate policies. The political dynamics of the system discouraged use of the exchange rate. It became the remedy of last resort even in cases when it should have been the first. Governments interfered frequently with trade and capital movements.

Floating exchange rates were expected to solve these problems by dealing automatically with balance-of-payments deficits and surpluses. Governments would not be able to defer adjustment and would not be tempted to interfere with trade and capital movements. Furthermore, they would have more autonomy. First, they would have monetary autonomy, because they would not have to intervene in foreign-exchange markets and could therefore control their money supplies. Second, they would have policy autonomy, because exchange-rate changes would correct balance-of-payments problems, freeing monetary and fiscal policies for use in dealing with domestic problems. Finally, floating rates would insulate national economies from external shocks.

These promises were based implicitly on the expectation that governments would accept the economic consequences of exchange-rate changes, an expectation reflecting the belief that exchange rates would conform to purchasing-power parity (PPP). That belief has been confounded by experience.

If exchange rates obeyed PPP, they would change gradually, in response to differences in national inflation rates, and real exchage rates would be constant. The process of balance-of-payments adjustment could not affect employment, output, or the allocation of resources within and among countries. In Chapter 17, however, we saw that exchange rates have not followed PPP. There have been large changes in real exchange rates.

In countries where wage rates are linked closely to the cost of living, changes in nominal exchange rates have led quickly to changes in domestic prices, and real exchange rates have been rather rigid—too rigid for the exchange rate to be an effective expenditure-switching instrument. In most countries, however, wages and prices are sticky and have changed by less than nominal exchange rates. Therefore, changes in nominal rates have affected real rates. But nominal exchange rates have tended to overshoot their long-run equilibrium levels, causing real rates to do so, too. The depreciation of the dollar in 1977–1978 was excessive from this standpoint; so was the subsequent appreciation in 1980–1984.

Some economists attribute these exchange-rate swings to cyclical shifts in national policies and current-account bal-

ances. They ascribe the depreciation of the dollar in 1977–1978 to the expansion of the U.S. economy, which grew more rapidly than the German and Japanese economies, and the use of monetary policy to promote the U.S. expansion. They ascribe the subsequent appreciation of the dollar to the tightening of U.S. monetary policy and the emergence of large budget deficits.

Other economists do not deny the importance of these events but believe that wide swings in rates are built into the dynamics of exchange-rate determination. If a country begins in current-account deficit, its currency will start to depreciate. The depreciation will reduce the current-account deficit, but only with a lag (the J-curve effect), and the exchange rate will move too far before being arrested by the gradual improvement in the current account. The large movement in the rate will therefore produce a current-account surplus that causes the currency to appreciate, and the process will start again but in the opposite direction.

Whatever the causes of exchange-rate swings, governments are not indifferent to them, because of their real effects, which is one reason why floating exchange rates have not fulfilled the promises made on their behalf.

Some governments *have* removed controls on capital movements. In 1974, soon after the float began, the United States lifted its restrictions on outflows and Germany relaxed its restrictions on inflows. In 1979, Great Britain abolished its exchange controls. But floating rates bear some responsibility for the recent intensification of trade restrictions, because large swings in real rates have exposed important industries to foreign competition and strengthened protectionist pressures.

Governments *have* enjoyed more monetary autonomy, because they have not been compelled to intervene in foreign-exchange markets. But most of them have chosen to intervene extensively because they have not been willing to accept the domestic consequences of large exchange-rate changes. Secretary Blumenthal's statement in 1977 reflected American dissatisfaction with Japanese intervention designed to prevent the yen from appreciating. A year later, however, the United States intervened heavily to halt the depreciation of the dollar, and it intervened again in 1980 to slow down the subsequent appreciation. Furthermore, members of the EMS *must* intervene to defend the pegs connecting European currencies; they have thus given up the monetary independence they sought when they allowed their currencies to float. In 1987, moreover, all of the major governments attempted to stabilize exchange rates temporarily under the Louvre agreement.

Policy autonomy has been limited, too, partly because governments have not let floating exchange rates take care of their balance-of-payments problems, but also because floating rates cannot insulate economies from external shocks. One reason was given in Chapter 18. Complete insulation can occur only in long-run equilibrium, a state that economies never reach. Furthermore, it can occur only in respect of certain goods-market disturbances, not asset-market disturbances. In other words, high capital mobility gets in the way of insulation. A floating rate between the dollar and the mark, moreover, cannot insulate the American and German economies from events outside them, such as the oil shocks of the 1970s.

SUMMARY

The number of independent exchange rates is always smaller by 1 than the number of national currencies. Therefore, it is impossible in principle for all governments to pursue independent exchange-rate policies. The history recorded in this chapter can be summarized by looking at the ways in which governments have dealt with that problem.

At the end of World War I, the problem was ignored, not solved. Governments chose gold values for their currencies, and the resulting exchange rates led to large imbalances. Monetary arrangements broke down soon after the start of the depression, contributing to the economic damage done by the depression itself. The Bretton Woods Conference of 1944 tried to develop more orderly exchange-rate arrangements by establishing the International Monetary Fund, to oversee exchange-rate policies and give balance-of-payments credit to governments that maintained pegged exchange rates in the face of temporary deficits. The IMF was to deal with the nth-country problem by supervising national exchange-rate policies.

Matters worked out differently. The IMF could not control exchange-rate policies, although it came to be an important source of balance-of-payments credit. The nth-country problem was resolved by the willingness of the United States to let other countries adjust their exchange rates vis-à-vis the dollar. This solution worked well in the years of the dollar shortage. With the completion of postwar recovery, however, the United States began to run a balance-of-payments deficit, and the dollar shortage turned into a dollar glut. Believing that the deficit was temporary, the U.S. government opted mainly for financing rather than adjustment. It was able to postpone adjustment because of the reserve role of the dollar; the governments of surplus countries built up dollar balances instead of buying gold.

But the U.S. balance of payments worsened in the late 1960s, when inflationary pressures intensified in the United States. In 1971, the United States tried to initiate a general exchange-rate realignment—a political solution to the nth-country problem.

The realignment was achieved by the Smithsonian agreement but fell apart in 1973, when the United States tried to devalue the dollar unilaterally. One by one, other governments let their currencies float.

At first, the float was expected to be temporary, and an attempt was made to design a new monetary system in which exchange rates would be pegged but more readily adjustable than under the Bretton Woods system. The nth-country problem would be solved by using "objective indicators" to signal the need for balance-of-payments adjustment. But the effort failed in the wake of the first oil shock, and the Articles of Agreement of the IMF were amended to "legalize" floating.

If governments permitted exchange rates to float freely, such a regime would represent a market solution to the nth-country problem. There would be no need to reconcile national targets if governments did not have them. But governments have not allowed exchange rates to float freely, because exchange-rate fluctuations affect their economies in larger and different ways than those predicted by the early advocates of floating rates. In 1978, the members of the European Community established the European Monetary System to peg the exchange rates connecting their own currencies. The United States intervened heavily in 1978 to halt a depreciation of the dollar, and it tightened its monetary policy sharply in 1979 when the dollar began to depreciate again. Under the Plaza and Louvre agreements, moreover, it joined with other major countries in an effort to reverse an appreciation of the dollar, then to halt the subsequent depreciation.

Experience with floating rates is hard to evaluate, because the years of floating have been punctuated by large shocks, high inflation rates, and deep recessions that should not be blamed on the exchange-rate regime, and these disorders have produced new problems, including the debt problems of less-developed countries. It is likewise hard to evaluate the governments' efforts to limit exchange-rate fluctuations, because they have been sporadic and marked by disagreements among the participating governments about the very nature of their obligations.

RECOMMENDED READINGS

The best history of the monetary system, on which this chapter draws heavily, is in Robert Solomon, *The International Monetary System, 1945–1981* (New York: Harper & Row, 1982); for an excellent account organized analytically, with well-chosen passages from documents and commentary, see Gerald M. Meier, *Problems of a World Monetary Order* (New York: Oxford University Press, 1982).

On the attempt by the Committee of Twenty to rebuild the system, see John Williamson, "The Failure of World Monetary Reform: A Reassessment," in R. N. Cooper et al., eds., *The International Monetary System Under Flexible Exchange Rates* (Cambridge, Mass.: Ballinger, 1982); and Peter B. Kenen, "Convertibility and Consolidation: A Survey of Options for Reform," *American Economic Review,* 63 (May 1973), reprinted in P. B. Kenen, *Essays in International Economics* (Princeton, N.J.: Princeton University Press, 1980).

The role of the IMF is described in Margaret Garritsen de Vries, *Balance of Payments Adjustment, 1945 to 1986: The IMF Experience* (Washington, D.C.: International Monetary Fund, 1987); its policies are examined critically in John Williamson, *The Lending Policies of the International Monetary Fund,* Policy Analyses in International Economics, 1 (Washington, D.C.: Institute for International Economics, 1982).

Thoughtful assessments of experience with floating exchange rates are supplied in Morris Goldstein, *The Exchange Rate System: Lessons from the Past and Options for the Future* (Washington, D.C.: International Monetary Fund, 1984), and

Rachel McCulloch, *Unexpected Real Consequences of Floating Exchange Rates*, Essays in International Finance, 153 (Princeton, N.J.: International Finance Section, Princeton University, 1983).

An early and influential analysis of the problems posed by the U.S. budget and trade deficits was provided in Stephen Marris, *Deficits and the Dollar: The World Economy at Risk*, Policy Analyses in International Economics, 14 (Washington, D.C.: Institute for International Economics 1985); the main issues are set out very clearly in Paul Krugman, *Adjustment in the World Economy* (New York: Group of Thirty, 1987).

On the European Monetary System, see Jacques van Ypersele, "The European Monetary System: Past Experience and Future Prospects," in R. N. Cooper et al., eds., *The International Monetary System Under Flexible Exchange Rates* (Cambridge, Mass.: Ballinger, 1982); and Horst Ungerer et al., *The European Monetary System: Re-cent Developments* (Washington, D.C.: International Monetary Fund, 1986).

The roles of reserves and reserve assets in the monetary system are examined in several of the preceding works. Here are two more references: Stanley W. Black, "International Money and International Monetary Arrangements," in R. W. Jones and P. B. Kenen, eds., *Handbook of International Economics* (Amsterdam: North-Holland, 1985), ch. 22, and Andrew W. Crockett, "Control over International Reserves," *International Monetary Fund Staff Papers*, 25 (March 1978).

For contrasting views of the debt problem, see William R. Cline, *International Debt and the Stability of the World Economy*, Policy Analyses in International Economics, 4 (Washington, D.C.: Institute for International Economics, 1983), and Jeffrey Sachs, "Managing the LDC Debt Crisis," *Brookings Papers on Economic Activity*, 1986 (2).

20
MANAGING THE INTERNATIONAL ECONOMY

INTRODUCTION

Many international economic problems can be studied from two points of view, the cosmopolitan perspective of the world as a whole and the national perspective of a single country. In Chapter 10, for example, we saw that free trade is the best regime from a cosmopolitan perspective but not necessarily from a national perspective. A large country can increase its gains from trade by imposing an optimum tariff and can sometimes come out ahead even when other countries retaliate. In the process, however, it reduces the global gains from trade. Therefore, conflicts can arise between policy prescriptions derived from cosmopolitan and national approaches to a particular problem.

Most rules and arrangements that govern international economic relations represent attempts by the international commu-

nity to prevent individual governments from adopting national policy prescriptions at the expense of cosmopolitan prescriptions. The General Agreement on Tariffs and Trade (GATT) was established to prevent them from using tariffs to increase their gains from trade or for other narrowly national objectives. The International Monetary Fund (IMF) was designed to prevent them from engaging in competitive devaluations or using deflationary policies when they faced temporary balance-of-payments problems. Similar objectives are served by frequent policy consultations in the Organization for Economic Cooperation and Development (OECD) and other international gatherings, including the annual economic summits. These aim at encouraging the governments of major industrial countries to adopt *cooperative* solutions to their problems, especially in macroeconomic matters. Such solutions are frequently superior to those resulting from decentralized national decisions but are not always seen to be advantageous by individual governments.

The first chapter of this book was based mainly on the national perspective. It suggested that a nation can be viewed as a single economic unit participating in an international economy consisting of many such units. Much of our work on macroeconomic problems was also based on that perspective. In Chapters 15 and 18, for example, we showed how international capital mobility interacts with a country's choice between pegged and floating exchange rates to influence the ways in which monetary and fiscal policies affect the domestic economy. This final chapter, by contrast, is based mainly on the cosmopolitan perspective. It asks whether the rules and arrangements that govern international economic relations are adequate or need to be modified to cope with trends and problems in the world economy.

This chapter has another theme. A government is not always free to adopt the best policies, even when there are no conflicts between national and cosmopolitan benefits. It has to mobilize domestic political support, which takes time and can be especially difficult when the best policies differ sharply from those with which the government is closely identified. This obstacle frequently interferes with the international coordination of macroeconomic policies, because governments are reluctant to modify monetary or budgetary targets on which they have based their political reputations. In many cases, moreover, the government will be opposed by politically powerful groups whose interests do not coincide with the government's views about the national interest. In Chapter 6, we saw that factors specific to import-competing industries are injured by trade liberalization and can be expected to oppose it even when it is beneficial from the national perspective as well as the cosmopolitan.

THE ACTORS AND THEIR ROLES

The basic rules, arrangements, and institutions that govern international economic relations were put in place right after World War II. Some of them have been modified since. Chapter 11 examined the GATT codes on subsidies, government procurement, and other trade practices that have become prominent policy issues in recent years. Chapter 19 examined the Second Amendment to the Articles of Agreement of the IMF, which ratified the shift from pegged to floating exchange rates and made other changes in the monetary system. It has been argued, however, that present rules and arrangements are becoming obsolete and should be revised to reflect the changing structure of the world economy. Three structural changes are mentioned frequently:

1. The American economy is still the largest in the world, but its economic dominance has ended. Economic relations among the developed countries are no longer characterized by one-way dependence of Europe and Japan on economic performance in the United States. They reflect true two-way interdependence. In consequence, policy formation can no longer be described as a simple follow-the-leader process. It is, instead, a complex interactive process. Furthermore, the developed countries have become more similar in structure and openness.

2. The less-developed countries have become *less* alike in levels and growth rates of real income, economic structure, and importance for the world economy. We used to talk about the typical less-developed country as being a producer of raw materials, needing economic aid, and requiring preferential trade treatment. But we have become aware of large differences among them, and the differences themselves have become much sharper. Several countries in Asia and Latin America export manufactured

goods. Others have had less spectacular success but have grown rapidly. Many have been left behind, however, especially in sub-Saharan Africa. Large differences in income have emerged even among countries that export raw materials, because of movements in their terms of trade.

3. It still makes sense to think of countries as economic units but less than it did two decades ago, because of the growth of *transnational* actors. In Chapter 8, we looked briefly at the growth of multinational corporations. Banking has become multinational, too, in a process that has integrated national financial markets and was largely responsible for the surge of bank lending to less-developed countries. It was once thought that transnational actors would undermine national sovereignty. No country could impose a policy regime stricter than regimes elsewhere, because "footloose" firms and capital would emigrate rapidly. An exaggeration, perhaps, but true enough to pose hard problems. When businesses and banks are mobile enough to choose the most attractive policy regimes, governments must apply similar rules or delegate their rule-making powers to international institutions if they are to achieve their goals.

Convergence Among the Developed Countries

When the framework for present rules and arrangements was put in place at the end of World War II, the American economy was dominant in many ways. Its industries had not been damaged by the war, and it was thought to have a natural tendency to innovate, which would keep it at the forefront in technology and maintain its dominance. The dollar was the only international currency worthy of that designation, and the United States could serve as the *n*th country in the monetary system, because of its size, strength, and comparative immunity to external shocks.

Some say that postwar rules and arrangements were designed and imposed by the United States to suit and perpetuate its special role, that GATT rules and commitments to trade liberalization would perpetuate American dominance in world trade, while the Bretton Woods system would preserve the leading role of the dollar.[1] This interpretation ascribes too much foresight to American officials but does contain a grain of truth. The postwar system was well suited to the dominance of the United States, and its major flaws did not become apparent until American dominance had ended.

For as long as the United States was highly competitive in world markets but trade was relatively unimportant to the United States itself, American businessmen, unions, and farmers were more interested in opening up foreign markets than protecting domestic markets from import competition. There was strong support for trade liberalization. Other countries, moreover, could not readily refuse to join with the United States in the GATT tariff-cutting process. Access to American markets was too important for them to risk retaliation by the United States. On the monetary side, the growing role of the dollar as an international currency, combined with the large size of the American economy, encouraged the United States to let other countries solve their balance-of-payments problems by adjusting their exchange rates vis-à-vis the dollar—to have no exchange-rate policy of its own. Furthermore, it was easy for the United States to finance its

---

[1] Similar assertions are sometimes made about the international rules and arrangements of the nineteenth century, that they were put in place by Great Britain to protect its special role. On this view, the free-trade movement was designed to preserve Britain's leading position as a manufacturer by depriving potential competitors of infant-industry protection, while the gold standard was designed to preserve the dominance of London as an international financial center and extend the influence of the Bank of England over international credit conditions. (The analogy has been carried farther. British dominance, it is said, was backed by the Royal Navy, and American dominance was backed by the nuclear "umbrella" protecting America's allies.)

balance-of-payments deficits in the 1960s, because foreign governments and central banks could be persuaded to build up their dollar reserves.

But postwar reconstruction in Europe and Japan whittled away American dominance, and the catching-up process continued thereafter. Look at Table 20-1. In 1965–1980, the other industrial countries grew faster than the United States (Britain was the one exception). The Japanese economy grew at a remarkable rate. Furthermore, the American economy was becoming more open and, therefore, more vulnerable to import competition and protectionist pressures.

Table 20-1 makes two more points. The major industrial countries became more similar in structure and performance, and their performance has been less than satisfactory. Inflation rates were very high in 1979–1983, during and right after the second oil shock, and they differed markedly from country to country. They fell sharply thereafter, however, and so did the differences. But the struggle against inflation was costly. Growth rates in Japan and much of

Western Europe have been only half as high in the 1980s as they were in the previous 15 years, and too few jobs have been created. Unemployment rates rose sharply at the start of the 1980s, but some did not come down again. In fact, they rose farther in every major country except the United States.[2]

Divergence Among the Less-Developed Countries

The less-developed countries differ greatly in size and degree of development. They range in size from small city-states such as Hong Kong and Singapore to vast countries such as China, India, and Brazil. Yearly incomes are below $400 per person in much of Africa and in many Asian countries, including China with about 1 billion people, and Bangaladesh, India, and Indonesia, with 1 billion more. They are above $2,000 per person in some East

---

[2] Definitions of unemployment rates differ from country to country, and cross-country comparisons can be misleading. But the trend toward higher rates is unmistakable.

TABLE 20-1   Economic Indicators for the Seven Economic Summit Countries, 1965–1988, (percentages)

Country	REAL GROWTH[a]		INFLATION[b]		UNEMPLOYMENT		OPENNESS[c]	
	1965–1980	1980–1988[d]	1979–1983	1984–1988[d]	1979–1983	1984–1988[d]	1965	1985
Canada	4.8	2.6	9.7	4.0	9.1	9.9	19.5	28.0
France	4.3	1.5	11.8	4.1	7.5	10.6	12.1	23.7
Germany	3.4	1.6	4.9	1.5	5.3	7.9	19.0	33.0
Italy	3.8	1.6	17.1	7.1	8.2	10.8	13.4	26.8
Japan	6.3	3.5	4.2	1.6	2.3	2.8	10.3	14.5
United Kingdom	2.2	2.2	11.3	4.7	9.0	11.3	18.8	28.3
United States	2.9	2.6	8.9	3.3	8.0	7.0	4.7	8.5

Sources: International Monetary Fund, *World Economic Outlook* (various issues), and World Bank, *World Development Report*, 1987; figures on openness from Table 1–1, above.

[a]Growth rate of real gross national product or gross domestic product.

[b]Measured by change in consumer price index.

[c]Averages of exports and imports of goods and services as percentages of gross national product.

[d]Data for 1987 and 1988 are IMF estimates or projections.

Asian and Latin American countries, including Korea, Singapore, Argentina, and Mexico, and in some sparsely populated oil-exporting countries. But they are above $11,000 per person in most developed countries.

These large differences in income are reflected by large differences in other numbers indicative of human welfare. Look at the last three columns of Table 20-2, which show infant mortality, life expectancy, and high school enrollment. Life expectancy is below 55 years in most low-income countries but rises to 65 years in many middle-income countries.[3] (It exceeds 75 years in most of the developed countries.) High school enrollment is below 25 percent in most low-income countries but above 50 percent in some middle-income countries. (It averages 90 percent in the developed countries.)

There are likewise large differences in real growth rates, and these tell a distressing story. The gap between low-income and middle-income countries has been getting wider, because the middle-income countries have been growing faster. In many low-income countries, including most of Africa, real income per capita grew by about 1 percent per year from 1965 to 1985. In many middle-income countries, it exceeded 3 percent, and it was even higher in Brazil and Korea. These differences in growth rates were due in part to differences in growth rates of population, which tend to be higher in the low-income countries, but demography does not tell the whole story. Rates of growth of total output were different, too.

In recent years, moreover, there has been great diversity in economic performance. The slower economic growth of the developed countries affected less-developed countries in the early 1980s, but some were affected more harshly than others. The newly industrialized countries of East Asia, such as Korea, continued to grow rapidly, but three other groups lost ground: the countries of Sub-Saharan Africa, because of crop failures and sharp drops in their export prices; the heavily indebted countries, such as Brazil, because of domestic austerity; and the oil-exporting countries, because of falling oil prices. (Mexico and Nigeria were doubly unlucky, because they belong to both of the last two groups.) Inflation rates rose in some countries, especially in Latin America, but several countries suffered less inflation in the 1980s than in the 1960s and 1970s, including India, Indonesia, Korea, and Nigeria.

Slow growth in the 1980s affected industrial output in several countries; compare the growth rates of total and industrial output in Indonesia, the Philippines, Brazil, and Mexico. But some East Asian countries forged ahead, including Korea, and their exports of manufactured goods continued to grow, despite an intensification of protectionism in the developed countries.

The Growth of Transnational Actors

Transnational actors have many significant effects on the functioning of the international economy and on relations among national governments. For reasons set out in Chapter 8, they enhance the efficiency of the international economy and tend to reduce cross-country differences in national policies, especially in policies that impinge directly on profitability, such as corporate taxation. Their activities raise important problems, however, producing disputes between governments but also encouraging them to devise common rules or standards, most notably in matters relating to financial institutions and markets.

The growth of transnational activity can be illustrated by comparing some numbers

---

[3] In this and other instances, the Chinese figures are quite different and affect the figure for the low-income countries taken as a group.

TABLE 20-2 Economic and Social Indicators for the Less-Developed Countries, Main Country Groups and Largest Countries, 1985 (percentages unless otherwise indicated)

Country Group (and per capita income in U.S. dollars)	OUTPUT GROWTH			INFLATION RATE[a]		Ratio of Debt Service to Exports[b]	Infant Mortality per Thousand Births	Life Expectancy (years)	High School Enrollment[c]
	Per Capita 1965–1985	Total 1980–1985	Industry 1980–1985	1965–1980	1980–1985				
All countries (610)	3.0	3.3	3.5	16.8	44.2	19.7	71	61	38
Exporters of manufactures (520)	4.0	5.5	6.6	13.3	47.7	13.6	56	64	39
Highly indebted countries (1,410)	2.5	0.1	-0.9	26.6	89.0	27.8	66	62	47
Oil exporters (1,060)	3.1	1.0	0.2	15.3	28.9	25.6	88	58	37
Sub-Saharan Africa (400)	1.0	-0.7	-2.4	12.7	16.7	21.5	104	50	21
Low income (270)	2.9	7.3	9.3	4.5	7.5	7.9	72	60	32
Bangladesh (150)	0.4	3.6	4.7	14.9	11.5	16.7	123	51	19
India (270)	1.7	5.2	5.4	12.5	7.8	9.3	89	56	34
China (310)	4.8	9.8	11.1	na	2.4	na	35	69	37
Low middle income (820)	2.6	1.6	0.6	22.2	22.3	22.9	82	58	40
Indonesia (530)	4.8	3.5	1.0	34.3	10.7	19.9	96	55	39
Philippines (580)	2.3	-0.5	-2.8	11.8	19.3	15.9	48	63	68
Nigeria (800)	2.2	-3.4	-5.8	14.5	11.4	30.8	109	50	29
High middle income (1,850)	3.3	1.7	1.4	20.5	74.7	21.0	69	66	56
Brazil (1,640)	4.3	1.3	0.3	31.6	147.7	26.5	67	65	35
Mexico (2,080)	2.7	0.8	0.3	13.2	62.2	37.0	69	67	55
Korea (2,150)	6.6	7.9	9.7	18.7	6.0	15.2	72	69	91

Source: World Bank, *World Development Report*, 1987.

[a]Measured by change in consumer price index.

[b]Public debt only.

[c]Percentage of age group; figures for 1984.

already discussed with those for an earlier year. In Table 20-3, figures for 1985 shown initially in Table 8-2 are contrasted with those for 1977, a year for which we have nearly comparable numbers. The foreign affiliates of U.S. firms have not grown rapidly; in fact, they employed fewer workers in 1985 than in 1977 (the drop occurred mainly in manufacturing). But the U.S. affiliates of foreign firms grew hugely in size and number.

The internationalization of banking has been even more dramatic. Major banks have made foreign loans for more than a century, and some established foreign branches long before World War I. The structure that we know today, however, began to emerge clearly about 20 years ago. Foreign holders of U.S. dollars found it advantageous to deposit them with foreign banks, which were not bound by U.S. regulations limiting the interest rates they could pay. The dollar holders could earn more and could also achieve more anonymity, a feature attractive to those private holders who wanted to avoid detection by their own countries' governments, but also to certain official holders, such as the Soviet Union, worried about the availability of their dollar balances in the event of an international political crisis.

Banks that accepted these deposits had to lend out the dollars in order to earn in-

come, and the process led to the development of the *Eurodollar* market, now known as the *Eurocurrency* market, because national currencies other than the dollar are lent and borrowed, too. A Eurodollar deposit is defined as any dollar deposit held at a bank outside the United States, even an affiliate of a U.S. bank. A Eurodollar loan is defined symmetrically as a dollar loan made by a bank outside the United States.[4] Many Eurocurrency loans are made by one bank to another. Banks use them to adjust their cash positions and their net holdings of various currencies. The *interbank* component of the market can therefore be viewed as the international counterpart of the federal funds market in the United States, where American banks make short-term loans to one another, and it is connected to that market. It is also connected closely to the foreign-exchange market, because banks have two basic ways of managing their foreign-currency positions: (1) They can buy and sell currencies outright in the spot and forward foreign-exchange markets. (2) They can borrow and lend currencies in the interbank market. But many Eu-

[4] For this and other purposes, the International Banking Facilities (IBFs) of U.S. banks, described in Chapter 8, are treated as being outside the United States, although physically located in the country; their loans and deposits are treated as Eurodollar transactions.

TABLE 20-3 The Growth of Multinational Production

Item	1977	1985	Percentage Increase
Foreign affiliates of U.S. firms			
Assets (billions of dollars)	490	838	70.1
Sales (billions of dollars)	648	898	38.6
Employment (thousands of workers)	7,197	6,426	−10.3
U.S. affiliates of foreign firms			
Assets (billions of dollars)	134	736	449.2
Sales (billions of dollars)	183	630	244.3
Employment (thousands of workers)	1,129	2,854	152.8

Source: U.S. Department of Commerce, *Survey of Current Business*, August 1983, May and June 1987; data exclude banking affiliates.

rocurrency loans are made to nonbank borrowers, and much of the borrowing by less-developed countries that is now associated with the debt problem was channeled through the Eurocurrency market.

The market grew very rapidly after the first oil shock. The oil-exporting countries ran large current-account surpluses, built up cash balances, and placed them in the Eurocurrency market. The growth of the market is described by Table 20-4. In 1973, on the eve of the first oil shock, deposits totaled $315 billion. Nine years later, at the start of the debt crisis, they totaled $2,168 billion. By the end of 1986, they had climbed to $3,579 billion. Dollar deposits have accounted for somewhat more than 70 percent of the total, and their share has been fairly stable.

At first, foreign banks dominated the Eurocurrency market. But U.S. banks began to participate in the late 1960s, and many set up new foreign branches for the purpose. In 1968–1969, for example, U.S. banks started to compete aggressively for Eurocurrency deposits, which they lent to their head offices in the United States to meet domestic demands for credit, because the Federal Reserve System was pursuing a restrictive monetary policy. At about the same time, they began to use their foreign branches to find ways around the capital controls imposed by the United States. But they continued to expand their international activities after the controls were

lifted. In 1986, American banks accounted for about 17 percent of the deposit liabilities shown in Table 20-4. (Japanese banks accounted for the largest share, about 33 percent.)

Other forms of financial activity have become multinational. In 1981, international bond issues amounted to only $44 billion; in 1986, they totaled $220 billion. By the mid-1980s, moreover, most large Wall Street firms had acquired affiliates or partners in London and other financial centers, and foreign firms had acquired affiliates in New York. The stocks of major corporation were bought and sold in a dozen countries.

THE CASE FOR INTERNATIONAL COOPERATION

International cooperation is often criticized as threatening or sacrificing national sovereignty. That misses the point. The case for international cooperation starts when sovereignty has been impaired by international interdependence and governments acting on their own cannot act effectively. They cannot perform their basic functions unless they cooperate.

The Economic Functions of Governments

Most industrial countries and many less-developed countries rely mainly on market forces to allocate resources, distribute goods and services, and pay out incomes to

TABLE 20-4 Eurocurrency Deposits, 1973–1986 (end-of-year amounts in billions of dollars)

Item	1973	1979	1982	1986
Total deposit liabilities	315	1,233	2,168	3,579
Owed to banks	260	988	1,736	2,895
Owed to others	55	245	432	685
In U.S. dollars	233	887	1,741	2,553
In other currencies	82	346	427	1,026

Source: Morgan Guaranty Trust, *World Financial Markets*, various issues.

the factors of production. Yet governments play active roles in those economies. There are four basic reasons.

First, economies frequently display rigidities and other imperfections. Some of these reflect contractual arrangements that cannot be altered immediately, some reflect concentrations of market power, and some reflect other interventions by governments in pursuit of the objectives listed later. Constrained by rigidities and imperfections, markets may produce *suboptimal* outcomes, and governments intervene to improve these outcomes. In Chapter 10, for example, we saw that wage rigidity can cause unemployment. That particular illustration was meant to show why a wage subsidy is a better form of intervention than a tariff, but the underlying point is quite general. When markets are constrained by wage rigidity, they cannot always generate full employment, and there is a case for macroeconomic intervention—the use of monetary and fiscal policies to regulate aggregate demand.

Another illustration is relevant here, because it has an important international analogue. When markets are dominated by small numbers of firms, market outcomes may reflect interactive processes. Firms will not behave as competitive price-takers; each will make allowance for the others' actions. Such outcomes may be worse from the firms' own standpoint than fully competitive outcomes and are almost always worse from the consumers' standpoint.

Second, many economic activities have costs or benefits that are not fully reflected in market prices. These *externalities* distort resource allocation and the distribution of economic welfare. Air and water pollution are familiar examples. When firms pollute air or water supplies, they do not pay the full costs of making their products, which means that their customers do not pay them either. Some of the costs are borne by those who suffer the effects of the pollu-

tion. Environmental legislation seeks to deal with this problem by taxing activities that pollute air and water supplies or forcing firms engaged in those activities to bear the costs of reducing or preventing pollution. It tries to *internalize* the costs.

Third, certain goods are *public* in nature, in that markets cannot supply them in appropriate amounts. If households had to pay directly for fire and police protection, supplies of those services might be reduced. Each household would have an incentive to keep down its own costs by relying on neighbors to pay for the services. Households that refused to pay could be denied some services but could not be prevented from benefiting partially from some of the services purchased by their neighbors—protection against fire starting in a neighbor's house or protection provided by a cruising police car. National defense is another example and illustrates a second feature of many public goods. They are indivisible. No household can purchase its own supply of nuclear deterrence. Therefore, supplies of public goods must be determined by collective choice.

Two more public goods should be mentioned here, because they have important international counterparts. Organized society would break down if there were no laws or courts to enforce them, and economic life would be very hazardous without the definitions of property and contract provided by the legal system. Without money, moreover, economic activity would be based on barter, transactions costs would be very high, and complex forms of economic organization would be impossible. Legal and monetary arrangements are found in all societies, whether they be based on law or custom. They furnish the framework that households and firms need to formulate and execute long-term plans.

Fourth, governments redistribute income. They do it directly by tax-financed transfer payments, which go from rich to poor, young to old, and so on. They do it indirectly by distributing goods and services, including education and health care, in ways that do not always bear a close relationship to the distribution of tax burdens. Most activities of governments have important distributional effects, and governments do not always monitor them carefully. (That is why Chapter 1 suggested that trade and other policies that benefit some persons and injure others should not be said to increase welfare unless gainers actually compensate losers. It may not be enough to show that compensation is possible.) But many governmental activities and the structures of tax systems clearly reflect distributional concerns.

This list of reasons is incomplete, but no list, however long, would justify some government activities. Governments do not always intervene wisely and do not always use appropriate instruments. The costs of intervention are often understated, and the effects are not always understood fully. Too often, moreover, regulations pile up, as governments discover that their interventions are having unintended consequences and try to correct them by new interventions rather than backtracking. Too often, public policies reflect the requirements of political compromise rather than the welfare-optimizing processes that economists like to build into their models.

One more problem must be borne in mind. When firms and households decide for themselves how they will respond to an event, some are bound to make mistakes. By and large, however, those who make them are the ones who pay for them. When a government decides how the whole economy should respond to an event, it can also make mistakes. But all of its citizens are likely to pay for them. Therefore, a strong case can be made for decentralized decision making, whenever it is feasible, to keep down the risks and costs of systemic error.

The Benefits and Costs of Cooperation

Many tasks listed previously can be performed effectively by national governments. Even if there were a world government, we would not want it to preempt all the functions of national governments. In large countries such as the United States, many basic governmental functions are performed by state and local governments. They can be more responsive than the national government to local needs and preferences. We would therefore expect national governments to be more responsive than a world government to national needs and preferences. Furthermore, the case for decentralization applies globally. When based on a bad diagnosis or policy prescription, collective action on a global scale could be far more harmful than collective action on a national scale.

Nevertheless, national governments presiding over open economies cannot carry out some functions effectively. Small-group problems crop up in relations among governments and lead to suboptimal policy outcomes. Policy targets are not always independent, and certain policy instruments are shared. It is impossible, for instance, for all countries to have current-account surpluses simultaneously or for all to have appreciating currencies. Certain externalities are international; air pollution cannot be confined within a single country's borders. Other externalities appear initially to be national but become international when a single government tries to deal with them and transnational actors respond by moving to another country. Certain public goods are international, including the global counterparts of the legal framework and monetary system which each government provides at the national level. Finally, the international community is committed explicitly to reduce inequality across countries—to improve the international income distribution by transferring resources to less-developed countries.

In the absence of a global government, however, national governments must band together voluntarily. They must deal collectively with those problems that can be confronted only by joint action, by harmonizing national policies, by adopting common standards, or by looser forms of collaboration, including the exchange of information useful in designing national policies.

Cooperation should be recommended only when it is required—when governments acting individually cannot function effectively or when one country's actions threaten to nullify or interfere with other countries' actions. The case for cooperation should not be overstated, because cooperation is not costless. The reason is a sad fact of political life. Even when governments know that they will benefit from international cooperation, they may try to extract a price for acting sensibly. In GATT negotiations, for example, governments insist on regarding their own tariff cuts as "concessions" they must make in order to extract tariff cuts from others. Most of them know that the gains from freer trade derive from their own tariff cuts, but they are locked into a bargaining process by domestic political pressures and by traditional views about sovereignty. Furthermore, economic issues get tangled up with political issues, and disputes about trade and monetary matters complicate disputes about defense and diplomacy. The tendency to bargain leads, in turn, to delay and compromise, and the common policies adopted by this process are often late and weak.

There are, of course, exceptions to this generalization. Some forms of international cooperation occur routinely, and we take them for granted. Letters mailed in one country are delivered in another. Meteorological data are disseminated widely. Commercial airlines must conform to certain common safety standards. In some areas, moreover, cooperation has grown. Until recently, Switzerland refused to reveal any information about transactions with its banks but is now willing to supply it when there is reason to believe that secrecy would shield criminal activity. But cooperation is still sporadic and inadequate in many other areas.

Let us look at four policy problems that call for international cooperation to see why it is needed in each instance and the forms that it can take.

1. Recent trends in trade policy illustrate the need for cooperation in providing an important public good, a stable framework for planning by producers and investors. Here, governments must agree on comprehensive rules that they will impose on themselves, restricting their freedom to tax or subsidize trade flows and to use quantitative trade controls, and they must adhere strictly to those rules.

2. Recent attempts to manage exchange rates illustrate the need for cooperation in choosing and pursuing objectives involving a shared variable. Here, govenments must agree on their targets, the methods for achieving them, and an allocation of responsibilities. Hard questions also arise concerning the proper amount of publicity. Should governments announce their goals and thus risk a damaging loss of credibility if they fail to achieve them, or should they try to conserve credibility by being secretive?

3. The problem of exchange-rate management raises other questions about the need to coordinate national macroeconomic policies. But those questions would have to be faced even if exchange rates were allowed to float freely. The case for coordinating macroeconomic policies arises from the small-group problem, which can lead to suboptimal policy outcomes. This sort of coordination has been rare, however, and attempts to improve the process run up against many obstacles.

4. Trends in international banking and the handling of debt problems illustrate the consequences of externalities and the ways of dealing with unexpected crises. Here, cooperation can take many forms. Common standards are

needed in some cases, especially to regulate transnational actors. Improvisation may be best when dealing with crises, but it many call for very close cooperation, and long-term solutions may be needed to clear away the aftermath of a crisis.

When looking at these illustrations, let us try to appraise existing arrangements and then ask how deficiencies might be remedied.

TRADE POLICIES AND THE GATT

GATT has played two important roles in the recent history of trade policy. First, it has helped to liberalize trade flows by sponsoring a series of tariff-cutting conferences. Chapter 11 described the Kennedy and Tokyo rounds and discussed the issues facing the Uruguay round. Second, GATT has supplied a framework for the conduct of trade policies by prohibiting or limiting the use of certain trade controls and regulating other practices. Chapter 11 described some of the GATT codes adopted during the Tokyo round to regulate the use of export subsidies and antidumping duties and to reduce discrimination against foreign firms competing for government contracts.

The attempt to regulate national practices was, of course, essential to trade liberalization. If governments were free to subsidize exports and firms were free to engage in "predatory" dumping, demands for protection by the victims of those practices would reverse the process of liberalization. In other words, GATT rules and codes help to stabilize national trade policies and thus provide a framework for the expansion of world trade. GATT provides a public good similar in purpose and importance to the legal system in each national economy.

But Chapter 11 pointed to several developments that threaten the GATT system. Quantitative barriers have been imposed on many products, including textiles, automobiles, and steel. The United States and the European Community have been competing aggressively to increase their agricultural exports and have been using export subsidies for that purpose. Furthermore, the methods of the new protectionism have disturbing implications for the GATT system. The widespread use of "voluntary" export restrictions has made the trade-policy regime less transparent; it is hard to know who is doing what to whom and who is bearing the costs of protection. These methods also reflect a growing tendency to handle trade disputes on a bilateral basis, outside the multilateral GATT framework.

Some GATT codes may also be working to reduce the scope of the GATT system. Under the code on government procurement, for example, a participating government can continue to discriminate against foreign firms from nonparticipating countries. Nondiscrimination is praticed on a strictly conditional basis. That sort of reciprocity seems fair enough, but it tends to create mini-GATTs within the GATT, weakening the coverage of the most-favored-nation clause. This tendency will probably grow, moreover, as attention turns to the liberalization of trade in services, because that process will invite the writing of reciprocal agreements among small groups of countries.

Another trend is worrisome. We have seen that the less-developed countries are becoming more heterogenous—dissimilar in growth rates and market size and in their trade policies. Some are outward looking and have won large market shares for their manufactured exports. Others are still inward looking and rely primarily on promoting production for the home market. But even outward-looking countries continue to protect their domestic markets jealously, not only by tariffs and quotas, but also by domestic-content rules that force their firms to manufacture parts and components that they could import more cheaply. Some have even tightened their trade controls recently, in an effort to meet their debt-service obligations by reducing their imports. There is reason to fear that countries such as Brazil, which began to shift from inward-looking import substitution to outward-looking export expansion before the debt crisis, are shifting back again, and this can lead to slower growth in the long run. Finally, some less-developed countries subsidize their exports heavily, provoking the use of countervailing duties and quantitative restrictions by the developed countries.

The less-developed countries have complained justifiably about the trade policies of the developed countries and about the inadequate concessions they have received in GATT tariff bargaining. But their own trade policies make it harder to "sell" trade liberalization to voters in developed countries.

What can be done to strengthen the trading system? Many suggestions have been made, including proposals for regionalization—for closer cooperation among like-minded countries willing to engage in greater liberalization and obey tightly drawn rules. There has, indeed, been movement in this direction. In 1987, the United States and Canada agreed to eliminate gradually all barriers to trade between them—to establish a free trade area. But this strategy has a serious defect. From the inside, a regional scheme looks like a preferential arrangement. From the outside, it looks like a discriminatory arrangement. Therefore, regionalization could provoke retaliation and lead to a less liberal trading system, viewed from the global standpoint. Regional arrangements make sense in special circumstances—in Western Europe, for example, where creation of the European Community reflected an historic effort to unite ancient enemies. But the substitution of a regional approach for the GATT system could divide the world economy by producing rivalries between trade blocs.

The Uruguay Round of GATT negotiations is virtually certain to produce an agreement on trade in farm products, involving major modifications in domestic agricultural policies, and limiting if not prohibiting the use of export subsidies. It will probably devise a framework for subsequent negotiations on liberalizing trade in services. There will be additional tariff cuts, and the less-developed countries will probably do better than in previous GATT rounds. There will also be improvements in GATT procedures for settling trade-policy disputes, and a new GATT code is due to be completed. It is the one pertaining to "safeguard" procedures, which allow governments to protect domestic industries temporarily in the face of increased import competition. In the absence of such a code, defining the criteria for granting relief, limiting allowable levels of protection, and imposing strict time limits, governments will continue to act on their own and rely on quantitative trade restrictions.

But two tasks remain. First, the quotas and other quantitative barriers that have increasingly encumbered trade in automobiles, steel, and other manufactured products should be eliminated gradually. This might be done by replacing them with tariffs and thus bringing them within the GATT framework, then reducing the tariffs gradually and automatically, according to a schedule that gives affected industries adequate time to adjust but not enough time to procrastinate. Second, adjustment-assistance programs should be revived but modified. In the United States, for example, too much has been spent on supplemental unemployment compensation, compared with the amounts spent on job creation and retraining.

Three specific suggestions have been made for reforming adjustment assistance:

(1) Assistance should be given to groups of workers (and to firms and workers jointly) to help them create new jobs for themselves, rather than retraining workers individually. (2) Assistance should be combined with programs to revitalize communities heavily affected by job losses resulting from import competition. (3) Adjustment assistance should be financed by the revenues obtained from the temporary tariffs used to provide transitional protection—the tariffs imposed in keeping with the new GATT "safeguard" code.

EXCHANGE RATES, POLICY COORDINATION, AND THE IMF

The international monetary history reviewed in Chapter 19 raises a number of difficult questions. Is it wise and possible to manage exchange rates? Should governments coordinate their monetary and fiscal policies and, if so, for what purposes? What can the IMF contribute?

The Problem of Exchange-Rate Management

Floating rates have not fulfilled the promises once made for them, and some economists favor a return to pegged exchange rates. A few of them would have the world go to a new gold standard. Others want to reinstate gold-standard rules without giving gold a role. Central banks would be expected to engage in non-sterilized intervention and would thus subordinate their monetary policies to the maintenance of stable exchange rates.[5]

Plans like these, however, are unrealistic. They are meant to impose more "discipline" on governments, but governments resist that sort of discipline. Britain abandoned the gold standard in 1931. The United States did fatal damage to the Bretton Woods system in 1971 when it tried to realign exchange rates in order to resolve a serious conflict between external and internal balance. Discipline cannot be imposed merely by telling governments to maintain pegged exchange rates, not without creating an international institution strong enough to hold them to their obligations when it does not suit them to do so on their own, and we are very far from that sort of world.

The same point can be put much more generally. It is wrong to compare the existing exchange-rate regime, laboring under imperfect policies, with an idealized version of some other regime, where governments are well informed and well behaved. This is done too often, especially by those who have not studied international monetary history and do not know how earlier arrangements worked in practice. Such comparisons are bound to be misleading, by favoring reforms that cannot turn out well.

As a practical matter, moreover, the choice may not lie between freely floating rates and firmly pegged rates. The governments of the major industrial countries have ceased to favor freely floating rates, which led to the large movements in real rates discussed in Chapter 19, but they doubt their ability to defend pegged rates in a world of high capital mobility. Rumors of a realignment can touch off waves of speculation, causing huge amounts of

---

[5] Under one such plan, proposed by Ronald McKinnon of Stanford University, the major central banks would choose the appropriate growth rate for the global money stock, and each would then conduct its monetary policy to realize that growth rate. But each one would engage in nonsterilized intervention to peg its exchange rate. so that its national money stock would grow faster than the global stock when its currency was strong and more slowly than the global stock when its currency was weak. The system would work symmetrically, however, and the changes in the growth rates of the national money stocks would not affect the growth rate of the global money stock.

money to switch from currency to currency, and rumors can become self-fulfilling prophecies when central banks must intervene to stabilize existing rates and run down their reserves.

But what about the European Monetary System? It is a pegged-rate system and has been praised as a success by many who thought it would fail. There have been several realignments of EMS exchange rates, which have given the EMS an impressive flexibility, but they have not provoked speculative flows large enough to dominate the governments' decisions. The EMS has several features, though, that could not be replicated readily by a larger system that included the dollar, yen, and pound. Those features were listed in Chapter 19. Some of them deserve to be mentioned again.

First, the EMS is linked to the EC and draws on its members' loyalty to that larger institution. No government has withdrawn from the EMS, although influential voices urged France to leave and allow the franc to float in the early days of the Mitterrand government, which sought to stimulate domestic demand more forcefully than other European governments. And though it is hard to prove that the EMS has induced its members to coordinate their monetary and fiscal policies, there is encouraging evidence of close cooperation among the participating central banks, which have sought to manage capital movements by managing interest-rate differences.

Second, EMS members have agreed speedily on realignments, and the realignments have been fairly small. Speculators cannot make large profits from small realignments. Furthermore, the EMS has unusual credit arrangements that prevent its central banks from running out of reserves when they intervene to combat speculation. Each central bank can borrow unlimited amounts from the other central banks. As these are very short-term credit arrangements, a central bank is not likely to abuse

them by borrowing to finance a continuing payments deficit. But it can borrow freely to combat speculation.

Finally, the Deutsche mark is the only world-class currency in the EMS and has been the strongest European currency. These circumstances have limited the size and duration of speculative pressures. Suppose that the foreign-exchange market comes to expect a revaluation of the mark against the French franc. Frenchmen will sell francs for marks. But they are the only large holders of francs. Anyone else wanting to speculate against the franc must borrow francs to sell them. This limits the volume of speculation and tends to reverse it quickly (because Frenchmen will need their francs for domestic purposes, and others will want to pay back their debts). Now let us imagine that Britain joins the EMS, bringing in the pound, another world-class currency. Suppose that the foreign-exchange market comes to expect a revaluation of the mark against the pound. As there are many more footloose holders of sterling than francs, more money could move from London to Frankfurt than currently moves from Paris to Frankfurt. Furthermore, this would not be borrowed money, though that could move too, and it might not return to London quickly. The Bank of England could find it hard to repay reserves borrowed from other central banks.

Arrangements for the management of key exchange rates are thus likely to fall short of the very tight EMS arrangements. But should they be tighter than the rather loose arrangements set out by the Louvre agreement in 1987? Recall what Chapter 19 said about the Louvre agreement. On one interpretation of the unpublished portion, the governments merely agreed in principle to take unspecified measures to keep exchange rates in an unspecified range for an unspecified time; on another interpretation, they pledged themselves to stabilize exchange rates within a narrow range by intervening on the foreign-exchange market and by managing interest-rate differences. As time passed, however, the second interpetation became quite popular with market participants and with some officials, who described the Louvre agreement as a *target-zone* arrangement that could provide continuing exchange-rate stability.

A number of target-zone proposals have been made in recent years. They differ in the methods used for choosing the *central rates*, which provide the reference points for the target zones, and the ways in which the central rates would be realigned. They also differ in the sizes of the zones surrounding the central rates, the hardness of the boundaries defining the zones, and the methods to be used to prevent exchange rates from leaving the zones. Finally, they differ in the extent to which the plans themselves would be made public or would be known only to the governments concerned, as in the case of the Louvre agreement.

The best-known proposal was developed by John Williamson. Under his proposal, the central rates would be defined by the equilibrium values of the countries' real effective exchange rates (the real rates that would preserve internal and external balance over the long run). By implication, the central rates would be realigned automatically whenever econometric calculations showed that a country could not achieve internal and external balance at its existing central rate. The zones around the central rates would be fairly wide; the actual value of each country's real rate would be allowed to deviate from that country's central rate by as much as 10 percent. And the boundaries would be soft, not hard, since larger deviations could take place temporarily or in special circumstances. Finally, central banks would intervene to influence nominal exchange rates whenever movements in nominal rates threatened to drive real rates across the boundaries of the

zones, and they would coordinate their interest-rate policies to back up their intervention. Williamson's proposal would be made public, to stabilize the market's expectations about future exchange rates and discourage destabilizing speculation.

Experience under the Louvre agreement suggests that Williamson is right about the need for publicity. Governments run two risks when they are vague and secretive. First, they may find that they disagree among themselves about their obligations. Second, market participants will try to guess the governments' rules, will base their market conduct on *their* version of those rules, and will blame the governments for weakness or bad faith if they do not live up to the market's expectations. Both of these things happened in October 1987, when the Louvre agreement broke down. Governments may lose more credibility by refusing to commit themselves publicly than by falling short of well-publicized commitments.

Other features of Williamson's proposal may be less satisfactory. An attempt to set and realign the central rates by calculating long-run equilibrium rates may put too much faith in econometric methods and may not accomplish Williamson's purpose, keeping politics out of the process. If governments disliked the central rates produced by this technique, they would find econometricians to criticize the calculations. Furthermore, the wide, soft bands in Williamson's proposal may not stabilize exchange-rate expectations.

For these and other reasons, some advocates of target zones favor plans that look more like the EMS. The central rates would be nominal, not real, and they would be negotiated, not based on econometric calculations; the zones would be narrower and the boundaries would be harder. Plans of this sort, however, run up against the difficulty mentioned earlier. The EMS may be unique, because of its link with the EC, because participating central banks have access to large amounts of short-term reserve credit, and because the EMS might be very vulnerable if it included several world-class currencies.

It may not be possible for governments to find a satisfactory way of managing exchange rates. There may be no good resting place between freely floating rates, modified perhaps by episodic intervention of the sort that followed the Plaza agreement, and a much tighter system like the EMS, which calls for more cohesion and mutual trust than the major governments can be expected to display.

Macroeconomic Policy Coordination

Those who are skeptical about the feasibility of exchange-rate management remind us of another way to stabilize exchange rates. They point out that the large exchange-rate swings experienced in recent years can be blamed partly on policy mistakes. Exchange rates would be more stable if governments were well behaved.

But governments are bound to make mistakes, because they have imperfect information and imperfect models of the world economy, and they find it difficult to rectify their errors because of political commitments and constraints. Simple economic models once led us to believe that floating exchange rates would localize the consequences of such errors; they would insulate each country from its neighbors' policies. But that is not true. Exchange-rate arrangements can alter the *form* of economic interdependence but not its intensity. Furthermore, floating exchange rates tend to produce a peculiarly painful form of interdependence, because monetary and fiscal policies, as well as nonpolicy shocks, are made to impinge directly on the real economy. Changes in nominal exchange rates originate in asset markets but are turned into changes in real exchange rates, be-cause goods prices are not perfectly flexible.

Let us suppose, however, that governments were well behaved and did not make mistakes. Each country would still be affected by its neighbors' policies, and there would be a case for policy coordination, not merely to avoid large exchange-rate movements but also to optimize the *joint* effects of national policies.

If the world consisted entirely of small countries, there would be no such case for policy coordination. The foreign repercussions of one country's policies would be insignificant, and its government would not have to take international responsibility for them or allow for other governments' reactions. Exchange rates would still be "shared" because a depreciation of one currency would still imply appreciations of all others, but those appreciations would not seriously affect any other country's competitive position. National economies could still experience inflation or unemployment, and each country's situation would still depend critically on the behavior of the world economy and, therefore, the policies of all other countries. But it would be the average of all policies that mattered, not those of a small number of large countries, and it would not be particularly useful for any group of governments to coordinate their policies.

A similar situation would arise in another circumstance, a world in which one country was very large and all others were very small. The large country's policies would dominate, rather than the average of all countries' policies, and its government would be expected to take a cosmopolitan view when framing its policies. But it could not be forced or induced to do so, and there would be no room for policy coordination. The small countries would have to follow the leader, adapting their policies to those of the large country. This sort of situation prevailed for some years after World

War II, when the United States was the large country.

The U.S. economy is still very large, and the dollar continues to be the most important currency in international financial markets. Therefore, U.S. policies are more important than those of any other country for the evolution of the world economy. At the start of this chapter, however, we saw that the main industrial countries have become more alike in size and openness, and these structural changes have had two consequences. (1) Because the U.S. economy has become more open, the foreign repercussions of U.S. policies are significant today not only for their impact on other economies but also for their influence at home. (2) Because other economies have become larger compared to the U.S. economy, their policies affect the U.S. economy and the whole world economy more strongly than in earlier years. Under these circumstances, U.S. policymakers must pay attention to the international situation for national as well as cosmopolitan reasons. Furthermore, the governments of the major industrial countries must be viewed as a small group of economic actors whose decisions are truly interdependent and important jointly for the world economy. Suboptimal policy outcomes are likely to emerge in this sort of situation, and all countries can be hurt. In other words, the situation calls for policy coordination and for international supervision.

Why is small-group behavior likely to produce suboptimal policy outcomes? Suppose that there has been a worldwide recession. No single country may be able to recover on its own by expanding its money supply or taking other measures to stimulate demand. It runs the risk of getting ahead of the rest and facing a balance-of-payments deficit or seeing its currency depreciate if it has a floating exchange rate. An increase in domestic demand will raise its imports, and it can experience a capital outflow, too, if the increase in demand is engineered by monetary policy. The United States encountered these problems in 1977–1978, when it stimulated domestic demand more vigorously then other major countries. The dollar depreciated, the inflation rate rose, and monetary policy had to be tightened sharply in 1979. Incomplete recovery gave way to another recession.

Governments faced with these possibilities have an incentive to hang back and wait for other governments to act. Each will count on other countries' imports to raise its exports and thus bring about an export-led recovery. This incentive is particularly strong when exchange rates are floating, because a government that hangs back can hope to experience an appreciation of its currency. This will reduce the growth of the country's exports stemming from recovery elsewhere, weakening its own export-led recovery, but will also reduce the domestic prices of imported goods, diminishing the inflationary pressures that usually accompany economic expansion. In other words, laggards can hope to achieve a more favorable short-run trade-off between expansion and inflation than if they tried to generate a homemade recovery.

When governments fail to coordinate their policies, each may thus act timidly and disappoint the others' expectations. If one acts boldly, moreover, it may run into an external constraint, a balance-of-payments deficit or depreciating currency, and be forced to retreat. When governments act jointly, by contrast, they may be able to avoid unsatisfactory outcomes. If each government agrees to generate *some* homemade recovery, using appropriate policy instruments, each can hope to benefit from the others' efforts, and all can count more firmly on complete recovery.

One phrase in the previous sentence calls for more attention, the one about appropriate policy instruments. The need for policy coordination arises partly from the risk that national policies will be too timid when policies are formulated independently but outcomes are interdependent. It also arises from the need for each country to adopt an appropriate policy mix. In 1977–1978, the United States relied primarily on monetary policy to promote recovery, and the dollar depreciated. In 1982–1984, it relied primarily on fiscal policy, and the effects were described in Chapter 19. The budget deficit induced a capital inflow, and the dollar appreciated sharply. To complicate matters, several foreign governments were reducing their budget deficits. The policy mix in the United States was strongly skewed in one direction, with fiscal policy biased toward expansion and monetary policy relatively strict, and other countries were leaning in the opposite direction.

Governments talk frequently about the need for policy coordination, and economists have written extensively about it. Theoretical research has shown that policy coordination can be beneficial viewed from the participants' national perspectives; they can come closer to their policy objectives. It can also benefit the much larger number of small countries that do not participate directly in the process. There are exceptions, however, because governments can be tempted to adopt inflationary policies that they could not pursue individually because of exchange-rate or balance-of-payments constraints. In language used before, global mistakes can be worse than national mistakes. Coordination can also have perverse effects when it is conducted under uncertainty about the structure of the world economy or about the outlook for the future.

Quantitative research supports the case for policy coordination, although the measured gains are fairly small in some computations. Yet instances of policy coordination are very rare. Governments engage in frequent consultations, exchanging information about national policies and comparing economic forecasts, and these routine activities can lead to better policies by reducing uncertainty. They deserve more attention than they commonly receive. Governments also can collaborate effectively to preserve international arrangements and institutions. They worked together closely at the start of the debt crisis, when they sought to prevent a collapse of confidence in the international banking system, and at the time of the Plaza agreement, when they sought to produce a depreciation of the dollar and thus combat protectionist pressures in the United States. But it is hard to find cases in which they have agreed to modify their fiscal or monetary policies for the sake of better economic performance. Even in the case most frequently cited, the 1978 Bonn summit, the bargain did not involve mutual changes in macroeconomic policies; Germany and Japan altered their fiscal policies, but the United States altered its energy policies. There have been attempts to intensify coordination with the aid of the IMF, but large economic and political obstacles lie in the way.

The Role of the IMF

In its initial form, the IMF had functions analogous to those of the GATT. It was to provide a public good, monetary stability, by supervising governments' exchange-rate policies. Governments, in turn, could draw on the IMF to deal with temporary balance-of-payments deficits; they would not have to deflate or devalue. The designers of the IMF identified monetary stability with exchange-rate stability because of lessons drawn from experience. They had learned that an exchange rate is a shared variable, not to be managed by a single country pursuing its own national objectives. Furthermore, they identified exchange-rate fluctuations with other forms of economic instability—the hyperinflations of the 1920s and the global depression of the 1930s.

In its early years, the IMF did not attempt to influence its members' domestic policies unless they sought to use its financial resources, and some governments even opposed that practice. Discussions of domestic monetary and fiscal policies took place mainly in the OECD, which became the main agency for macroeconomic cooperation among the industrial countries. But the role of the IMF began to change with the move to floating exchange rates in the 1970s. Governments were still required to collaborate with the IMF in promoting "orderly exchange arrangements" and a "stable system of exchange rates,"[6] but stability would henceforth be achieved by pursuing appropriate domestic policies. The IMF was still to exercise "firm surveillance" over its members' exchange-rate policies but would have to review the whole range of domestic policies that affect exchange rates, especially monetary and fiscal policies. Accordingly, the IMF began to conduct regular consultations with each of its member governments. This procedure was inadequate, however, for a reason already mentioned. Because exchange rates are shared variables, they depend on interactions among national policies, not one country's policies taken by themselves.

The first attempt to rectify this defect was made in 1982, when the five governments whose currencies define the value of the SDR agreed to consult jointly with the managing director of the IMF concerning their exchange-rate policies. A more ambitious effort was inaugurated in 1986, when the seven summit countries began to review their objectives and forecasts collectively, using economic indicators prepared by the IMF and paying particular attention to the compatibility of national policies. The man-

aging director of the IMF participates in the process and can perhaps be expected to represent broader interests and concerns. It is not sufficient for the large industrial countries to follow compatible policies. They must pay attention to the quality of those policies, measured by their impact on the world economy.

Those most familiar with these practices, however, are not optimistic about their influence, not even on the compatibility of policies, let alone their quality. First, it is difficult in principle to define appropriate monetary and fiscal policies. Governments must agree implicitly about the workings of their economies and the ways in which policies affect them. They must also agree on the economic outlook. Furthermore, they must not disagree too sharply about priorities—the weights they should give to fighting inflation, reducing unemployment, stabilizing exchange rates, and so on. Agreements of this sort are not easy to obtain nationally and harder to obtain internationally. Second, political will is not always matched by political capability. Officials may agree on the need for governments to change their policies but cannot always carry out the necessary changes. They do not always win their bureaucratic and legislative battles. These internal problems are peculiarly difficult in the United States because of the separation of powers between the president and Congress and because a Republican president has sometimes to deal with a Democratic Congress, or vice versa. But they also arise in countries with parliamentary systems, especially when the government must rely on a political coalition.

EXTERNALITIES AND THE REGULATION OF TRANSNATIONAL ACTIVITY

When would we expect a government to seek help from others in regulating partic-

---

[6] These phrases come from Article IV of the IMF Articles of Agreement, shown in Figure 19-4.

ular economic activities? It must, of course, be able to convince them that its objectives are consistent with their own, but that is not enough. Even when aims are consistent, governments may want to pursue them independently rather than act jointly. Cooperation is costly, because bureaucracies must be made to work together and a common course of action may be hard to adapt to local conditions. Furthermore, cooperation is not always offered freely, because of the tendency to bargain, emphasized earlier, and because governments are jealous of their authority.

Governments are likely to act jointly only when they cannot expect to achieve their objectives by acting independently. Therefore, joint action is most likely when the problem facing a particular government is international in scope, because it involves private actors who lie beyond its jurisdiction, or threatens to become international as soon as a government tries to solve it, because it involves private actors mobile enough to leave its jurisdiction. Examples will clarify these generalizations.

Consider a case in which governments do not act together even when they have similar objectives, because they see the problem in national terms. The sale of pharmaceuticals in the United States is regulated by the Food and Drug Administration (FDA), which is concerned with safety and effectiveness. Some public-interest groups believe that the FDA should prevent American companies from exporting pharmaceuticals they are forbidden to sell at home. They also urge the U.S. government to reach beyond its borders and prevent the companies' foreign affiliates from making or selling those pharmaceuticals. Foreign governments, however, have not asked for such intervention and might not welcome it. The standards applied by the FDA may be quite appropriate, but other governments are not prepared to accept them automatically. They appear to believe that their own standards are right for them and that they have the means to enforce them within their borders.

Other instances involving consumer protection pose a clearer case for joint action or, at least, adherence to common standards. Airline safety is an example. A government cannot protect its citizens merely by imposing safety standards on domestic airlines and on foreign lines that use its airports. Its citizens are at risk whenever they travel on other foreign airlines (even when traveling on regulated carriers that share routes or facilities with unregulated carriers). Environmental pollution is another example. A government cannot protect its citizens' health merely by regulating industries within its borders; its air and water can be polluted by other countries' industries. Furthermore, damage to the oceans and atmosphere can have grave long-run consequences for all countries. But governments have not made much progress in dealing jointly with these externalities, because experts do not agree fully about the nature and gravity of the risks and the interests of governments are not identical. A small country that earns income from a fleet of supertankers may refuse to agree to strict international standards for building and running them, needed to minimize the risks of oil spills. Its government knows that ships fly its flag only because its standards are less strict than those of other countries; their owners might register them elsewhere if strict standards were applied. On a rational calculation, moreover, the country's own interest in the income from its fleet may exceed its interest in preventing oil spills.

Similar problems arise in the political domain. The United States has tried for many years to prevent the Soviet Union from purchasing strategic goods and technology. At times, it has even asserted jurisdiction over the foreign affiliates of U.S. firms and over foreign firms licensed by

U.S. firms to manufacture certain products. It cannot be successful, however, without cooperation by other governments, because the problem is international in scope. Foreign firms can sell goods to the Soviet Union when U.S. firms cannot. Cooperation has been forthcoming most of the time, but the United States and European governments have disagreed about particular goods and technologies. The United States has tended to define "strategic" broadly, to include almost all goods and technologies that would raise the efficiency of the Soviet economy. Other governments have tended to define it narrowly, to include only those goods and technologies that can be used directly or adapted easily by the Soviet armed forces. In language used earlier, governments disagree about the nature of the externalities involved—the noneconomic costs of various transactions.[7]

Regulating the Eurocurrency Markets

The Eurocurrency market developed because the United States tried to regulate its banking system more strictly and by different methods than other countries. But it continued to flourish after the United States removed the regulations that brought it into being. In the 1970s, moreover, central banks began to believe that they would have to regulate the market jointly.

The issue arose initially because of concerns about a macroeconomic problem.

Eurocurrency deposits are not subject to reserve requirements like those that limit the money supply in the United States. Therefore, some observers began to warn that deposit creation in the Eurocurrency market could undermine the central banks' control over the growth rates of their money supplies. If the Federal Reserve reduced the rate of monetary growth in the United States, but banks in the Eurocurrency market raised their lending in response, creating additional Eurodollar deposits, global dollar holdings could grow faster than the rate desired by the Federal Reserve.

These concerns led U.S. officials to suggest that central banks should agree to impose reserve requirements on Eurocurrency deposits. But that proposal ran into three objections that illustrate the obstacles to joint regulation.

First, many experts did not accept the underlying analysis. Although most banks are not obliged to hold cash reserves as "backing" for their Eurocurrency deposits, they hold reserves voluntarily to protect themselves against unexpected withdrawals. Furthermore, Eurocurrency deposits are not perfect substitutes for ordinary bank deposits. They are mostly time deposits; checks cannot be written against them. Therefore, deposit creation in the Eurocurrency market was not seen to threaten the effectiveness of national monetary policies.

Second, some central banks do not use reserve requirements to limit their domestic money supplies and did not want to impose them on a particular class of bank deposits. It was not clear, moreover, who should impose them on each bank. The U.S. authorities could not impose them on dollar deposits at German banks; the German authorities could not impose them on mark deposits at American banks. Jurisdictions are limited.

---

[7] Defense issues raise a larger problem. Members of the North Atlantic Treaty Organization (NATO) argue frequently about their military budgets. Each wants to consume the public good, collective security, at the lowest possible cost to itself. Attempts by NATO countries to agree on defense-spending targets can therefore be viewed as a primitive form of collective decision making at the international level, designed to provide a sufficient amount of the public good.

Third, the scheme would not work unless all countries agreed to participate, and some might refuse, for reasons like those of a country having a fleet of supertankers. If Singapore refused to impose reserve requirements on foreign-currency deposits at its banks, foreign banks would migrate to Singapore to do their Eurocurrency business there. Singapore might expect to gain more directly in income and tax revenues than it could lose indirectly on account of macroeconomic problems arising from excessive monetary growth in the world as a whole.

This proposal was not adopted. Within a few years, however, the central banks' attention shifted from macroeconomic problems to narrower but vital prudential problems—from concern about the quantity of Eurocurrency deposits to concern about the quality of Eurocurrency loans.

When a bank has made large loans that cannot be repaid, its depositors are likely to withdraw their funds. There will be a run on the bank that can force it close its doors. A run can also be started by rumors, and it can spread to other banks, especially those that have deposits at the first bank. Those banks can be forced to close, even though their own loans are sound, because their cash reserves are not big enough to meet large withdrawals. That is what happened in the 1930s, when banks in many countries, including the United States, had to shut their doors.

Because a country's payments system is an important public good and banks play a crucial role in that system, many measures have been taken to ward off runs that could close down the banking system. Central banks serve as lenders of last resort; they stand ready to make short-term loans to banks that are basically solvent but do not have enough cash to meet large withdrawals. Depositors have been insured against permanent losses resulting from

bank failures, the task of the Federal Deposit Insurance Corporation (FDIC) in the United States.[8] In every major country, moreover, governments examine the banks' books to discourage them from making unsound loans, limit their exposure to any single borrower, and force them to write off loans that have turned sour and build up balance-sheet reserves against those that might turn sour.

Who should do these things, however, when banks have affiliates in many countries and do business in many currencies? Who should be lender of last resort to the London affiliate of an American bank? Who should examine its books?

Central banks have worried about these questions for many years, and the debt problems of the less-developed countries have underscored their importance. We have seen that major U.S. banks have claims on Latin America almost as large as their capital, even after building up their loan-loss reserves. They would be close to insolvency if debtor countries were unable or unwilling to meet their obligations or to renegotiate them. Externalities complicate the problem. New lending by one bank can impair the quality of other banks' old loans; by increasing the borrower's debt burden, it can raise the probability that the borrower will be unable to meet its obligations. It is thus necessary for bank supervisors to know what their countries' banks have lent, what the banks' foreign affiliates have lent, and what other countries'

---

[8] The FDIC does not insure large deposits or deposit-like obligations, such as negotiable certificates of deposit (CDs). Furthermore, it protects depositors from losses but does not promise them immediate access to their money. Therefore, it tries to keep banks open rather than allowing them to fail and paying off insured deposits. In 1984, moreover, when the Continental Illinois Bank ran into trouble, the FDIC guaranteed all the bank's obligations, including large deposits by other banks.

banks have lent to their own banks' customers.

In 1975, bank supervisors from several countries agreed on a way to allocate responsibilities. The agreement was revised in 1983, after experience had exposed some ambiguities, and the new version was based on a simple principle. Each country's supervisors should examine the *consolidated* operations of that country's banks, even though this invades another country's jurisdiction. But modifications are made in certain instances. It is necessary to distinguish between branches and subsidiaries. Branches operate on behalf of their parents, and their operations can be consolidated with those of their parents. Subsidiaries are separately incorporated and frequently owned by parents from several countries, and supervision must be conducted jointly by the host and parent countries. It is also necessary to distinguish between problems of bank solvency and bank liquidity.

In 1987, the supervisors took a larger step. In the wake of domestic financial deregulation, banks in many countries faced more competition from other financial institutions and undertook new activities to compete more effectively. Supervisors worried about the riskiness of those activities and their own ability to regulate the banks in a world with widely different national rules. They began to move toward common standards. The process began with an agreement between the Federal Reserve System and the Bank of England to adopt the same definitions of bank capital and the same ways of measuring the riskiness of bank assets, in order to apply common standards of capital adequacy. Banks that failed to meet those standards would have to build up their capital or shift to less risky activities. Implementation was postponed, however, in an effort to extend the system. By the end of 1987, supervisors from all of the major countries had agreed

on the need for common standards and were developing definitions that they could apply together.

These arrangements do not deal with another issue. Who should be lender of last resort and provide liquidity when a bank's foreign affiliate runs into trouble? Central banks have not said much about this question. They claim to have thought it through but refuse to give their answer. They fear, understandably, that the publication of contingency plans could be counterproductive. On the one hand, banks and others might spot contingencies that are not covered, and this could produce a crisis of confidence. On the other hand, promises to deal with certain situations might encourage banks to take risks that lead to those very situations.[9] In some instances, moreover, central banks might find it easier or more effective to help a debtor than to help its creditors. That is what they did in 1982, when they made short-term loans to Mexico and Brazil. Central banks must plan carefully for contingencies but must also retain flexibility.

The Debt Problem Once Again

Central banks and governments showed their flexibility at the start of the debt crisis, but there has been increasing criticism of their subsequent behavior. Early optimism about solving the debt problem has given way to concern about the state of relations between debtors and creditors. The gravity of the situation was emphasized by Brazil's decision to suspend its interest payments in early 1987. Payments were resumed temporarily at the end of the year, but the future was uncertain.

---

[9] This is the problem of "moral hazard" encountered frequently in economics. An example illustrates it nicely. If you are fully insured against collisions, you may be less careful when you drive and more likely to scrape a fender in a parking lot. By insuring you against this outcome, the insurance company raises the probability of the outcome itself.

There is a market measure of that uncertainty. Banks and other institutions buy and sell the debts of less-developed countries, and the discounts on those debts have been getting bigger. In mid-1986, it was possible to buy $100 worth of Brazilian debt for about $76, a discount of 24 percent; a year later, the price had fallen to $55, a discount of 45 percent. Discounts on other countries' debts ran from 33 percent for Chile and the Philippines to 90 percent for Bolivia and Peru.

Banks have agreed to longer maturities and lower interest rates and have made new loans to help debtors meet their interest payments. Some debtors have reduced their obligations by taking advantage of the discounts quoted in the open market and buying back their own debt. Others have agreed to debt-equity swaps, which allow foreign investors to buy debt at a discount and redeem it for the debtor's domestic currency in order to make investments in the debtor country. But these and other innovations have not greatly reduced the magnitude of the debt problem, and debtor countries are starting to call for additional relief. Their appeal is backed by the threat that they will act unilaterally by suspending their interest payments indefinitely or repudiating their debts completely.

Advocates of organized debt relief believe that it would have less damaging effects than unilateral action. First, the governments of creditor countries would not be obliged to take punitive action against the debtor countries—to freeze the debtors' assets, keep out their exports, or halt new lending by the World Bank and other official institutions. Second, organized relief could be handled on an equitable basis, independently of the size or bargaining power of the debtor country, and the banks themselves would have wider options. Each bank could agree to participate at a predictable cost to itself or opt out and take its chances on future repayment.

Thus far, however, the governments of the creditor countries have rejected proposals for organized debt relief. They do not want to be accused of "bailing out" the banks at the taxpayers' expense or seeming to encourage irresponsible behavior by lenders or borrowers. Attitudes may change but are not likely to change quickly.

SUMMARY

Management of the international economy has been more difficult in recent years because the international community has become more complex and has faced hard problems.

The dominance of the United States has ended, and relations among the industrial countries have taken on the characteristics of small-group behavior. Their economies have become more open and more similar, and their policies are interdependent. No single government can underwrite prosperity or stability for the whole group, and decentralized decision making can produce suboptimal policy outcomes. By contrast, the less-developed countries have become more diverse in structure and policy. The oil-exporting countries prospered in the 1970s on account of large increases in the price of oil, but some such as Mexico and Nigeria had much difficulty in the early 1980s, when oil prices fell. Some countries have become exporters of manufactures, and the East Asian countries have been remarkably successful. But other countries have fallen behind, especially in Africa, and their problems have been compounded by deterioration in their terms of trade.

The activities of multinational actors, businesses and banks, have tightened the links among national economies, increasing the efficiency of the world economy. But they have created additional policy problems. Their mobility has made it harder for national governments to manage their domestic economies and made it more important for them to act jointly in dealing with certain policy problems. The problem of bank supervision came to the fore in the 1980s because of the debt crisis.

Protectionist pressures have grown stronger, and governments have relied on trade restrictions less transparent and more rigid than ordinary tariffs and harder to reduce by traditional GATT methods. The Uruguay Round is expected to produce an agreement to liberalize trade in agricultural products and modify domestic farm policies and to provide a framework for liberalizing trade in services. There is less hope for agreement, however, on dismantling the newer barriers to trade in manufactures. The less-developed countries can expect larger benefits than they obtained in earlier GATT rounds, which will help them to increase their exports and deal more effectively with their debt problems, but they can expect strong pressures to reduce their own trade barriers.

Although the major industrial countries have shown more interest in stable exchange rates, they have not been able to co-ordinate their monetary and fiscal policies, even in the face of very large imbalances resulting in part from U.S. budget deficits. They have been able to agree on new ways of approaching the problem, but it is too early to judge their effectiveness. Domestic political constraints interfere with policy coordination, and international institutions such as the IMF cannot have much influence on the process. The problem is made more difficult by disagreements about the workings of the world economy, disagreements about policy objectives, and uncertainty about the future.

There has been progress in handling global aspects of bank supervision but little progress in environmental management and other areas where joint regulation is required because of the importance of transnational actors and of international externalities. International cooperation is costly. It should not be undertaken unless it is necessary. But more cooperation is needed in many areas, including trade and macroeconomic management.

RECOMMENDED READINGS

Many of the issues raised in this chapter are examined in Richard N. Cooper, "Economic Interdependence and Coordination," in R. W. Jones and P. B. Kenen, eds., *Handbook of International Economics* (Amsterdam: North-Holland, 1985), ch. 23.

On trade relations and the GATT system, see Alan V. Deardorff and Robert M. Stern, "Current Issues in Trade Policy: An Overview," in R. M. Stern, ed., *U.S. Trade Policies in a Changing World Economy* (Cambridge, Mass.: MIT Press, 1987); on promoting domestic adjustment, see Gary Clyde Hufbauer and Howard F. Rosen, *Trade Policy for Troubled Industries*, Policy Analyses in International Economics, 15 (Washington, D.C.: Institute for International Economics, 1986).

For proposals to reform exchange-rate arrangements, see John Williamson, "Target Zones and the Management of the Dollar,"

Brookings Papers on Economic Activity, 1986 (1); Jacob A. Frenkel and Morris Goldstein, "A Guide to Target Zones," *International Monetary Fund Staff Papers*, 33 (December 1986); and Peter B. Kenen, *Managing Exchange Rates* (London: Royal Institute of International Affairs, 1988). More extensive reforms are proposed by Richard N. Cooper, "A Monetary System for the Future," *Foreign Affairs*, 63 (Fall 1984); and Ronald I. McKinnon, *An International Standard for Monetary Stabilization*, Policy Analyses in International Economics, 8 (Washington, D.C.: Institute for International Economics, 1984).

Recent analytical literature on policy coordination is reviewed in Stanley Fischer, "Macroeconomic Policy," in M. Feldstein, ed., *International Economic Cooperation* (Chicago: University of Chicago Press, 1988); current practices are reviewed in Andrew D. Crockett and Morris Goldstein, *Strengthening the International Monetary*

System: Exchange Rates, Surveillance, and Objective Indicators (Washington, D.C.: International Monetary Fund, 1987). The case for combining target zones with policy coordination is examined by John Williamson and Marcus H. Miller, *Targets and Indicators: A Blueprint for the International Coordination of Economic Policy,* Policy Analyses in International Economics, 22 (Washington, D.C.: Institute for International Economics, 1987).

On international banking and the Eurocurrency markets, see Ralph C. Bryant, *International Financial Intermediation* (Washington, D.C.: Brookings Institution, 1987); also Jack Gutten-

tag and Richard Herring, *The Lender-of-Last-Resort Function in an International Context,* Essays in International Finance 151 (Princeton, N.J.: International Finance Section, Princeton University, 1983).

Differing views on debt relief are found in the works by Cline and Sachs recommended at the end of Chapter 19. See also Rudiger Dornbusch, "Dealing with Debt in the 1980s," *Third World Quarterly,* 7 (July 1985); and Jeffrey Sachs and Harry Huizinga, "U.S. Commercial Banks and the Developing Country Debt Crisis: The Experience Since 1982," *Brooking Papers on Economic Activity,* 1987 (2).

INDEX